Antonio Rizzo

SCULPTOR AND ARCHITECT

Antonio Rizzo

SCULPTOR AND ARCHITECT

Anne Markham Schulz

PRINCETON UNIVERSITY PRESS, PRINCETON, NEW JERSEY

Copyright © 1983 by Princeton University Press
Published by Princeton University Press, 41 William St.,
Princeton, New Jersey
In the United Kingdom: Princeton University Press,
Guildford, Surrey

All Rights Reserved

Publication of this book was assisted by a grant from
the Publications Program of the National Endowment
for the Humanities

This book has been composed in Linotron Bembo

Clothbound editions of Princeton University Press books
are printed on acid-free paper, and binding materials are
chosen for strength and durability

Printed in the United States of America by Princeton
University Press, Princeton, New Jersey

LIBRARY OF CONGRESS CATALOGING
IN PUBLICATION DATA

Schulz, Anne Markham, 1938-
Antonio Rizzo: sculptor and architect.
Bibliography: p.
Includes index.
1. Rizzo, Antonio, fl. 1465-1498.   I. Title.
N6923.R54S3 1983   730'.92'4   82-9110
ISBN 0-691-04006-0   AACR2

FOR JEREMY

Contents

List of Illustrations

Preface

In HISTORIES of Renaissance art Antonio Rizzo is generally adjudged the major Venetian sculptor of the Quattrocento. Yet very little is known of him. Though his biography can be reconstructed from published documents with a certain degree of fullness, his art has long resisted definition: about his style there is no consensus. Whether as cause or consequence, approximately half of all the works that regularly figure as typical products of his hand are not by Rizzo, while nearly half of all the works that are demonstrably by him have not been linked with him before. On the basis of what evidence do we infer Rizzo's preeminence?

The history of Rizzo studies is not long. For nearly three centuries, from the beginning of the sixteenth to the end of the eighteenth Rizzo's name was virtually lost. A few scattered references in the eighteenth century—in Scipione Maffei's *Verona illustrata* and Giambattista Biancolini's supplement to Pier Zagata's chronicle of Verona, in Francesco Bartoli's guide to Rovigo, in Tommaso Temanza's lives of Venetian architects and sculptors, and in Enea Arnaldi's publication of the documents concerning the Palazzo della Ragione at Vicenza, in whose restoration Rizzo played a minor role—were harbingers of the rediscovery of Rizzo, but they do not tell us much about the artist. More valuable was the contribution of the erudite librarian of the Biblioteca Marciana, Jacopo Morelli, who, in a note to his 1800 edition of Marcantonio Michiel's *Notizie d'opere*, assembled almost all pertinent secondary sources, from Gregorio Correr to Bartoli. Abbot Giuseppe Cadorin vastly enriched our knowledge of Rizzo's work by several archival discoveries among the papers of the Venetian state. His discovery of documents in which Rizzo appears as *protomaestro* of the Ducal Palace enabled Cadorin to refute Francesco Sansovino's attribution of the Scala dei Giganti and the facades of the east wing of the Ducal Palace to one Antonio Bregno, an attribution that had prevailed for centuries. It was Cadorin who also drew attention to Marin Sanudo's account of Rizzo's embezzlement and flight. Giambattista Lorenzi's documentary history of the Ducal Palace, published in 1868, made clear for the first time to what extent Rizzo participated in the construction of the east wing of the Ducal Palace; as the fundamental source for any reconstruction of the vicissitudes of the Ducal Palace, Lorenzi's book has not been superseded. In 1893 Pietro Paoletti added new documents to the repertory of archival notices regarding Rizzo and, on the basis of Lorenzi's documents and the testimony of Sanudo and Domenico Malipiero, adumbrated a coherent history of the late-fifteenth-century rebuilding of the Ducal Palace. A few minor documents were found by Gustav Ludwig. More significant is the recent discovery of the payment for Rizzo's earliest works in the Basilica di S. Marco.

Although Rizzo has been well served by archivists' research, an understanding of his

art has not been much advanced by the work of critics. The article by Giovanni Mariacher in the second volume of *Arte veneta* is flawed by its adherence to traditional
attributions. The more ambitious study by Wiebke Pohlandt in the *Berliner Jahrbuch* of
1971 left Rizzo's oeuvre in a badly truncated state: though she wisely eliminated several
works that were not his, she found no authors for misattributed sculptures and presented no new works to take their place. To be sure, the paucity of inscribed or documented works and the absence of works attested to by early sources were formidable
impediments to an accurate enumeration of Rizzo's works. In addition, contemporary
works of other Venetian sculptors, easily confused with Rizzo's own, often possessed
no more certain attributions. It is no wonder, then, that many works formerly assigned
to Rizzo can be proved to have been executed by someone else or that many works
bearing the imprint of Rizzo's style have until now been assigned to other artists.

What made me hope that I might succeed in writing the story of Rizzo's art where
others had failed? Certainly I was not the first to scrutinize all the documents and secondary sources concerning Rizzo, nor the first to study at first hand the works generally
conceded to be his. What I do think was unique to my approach was that I set out to
write, not a biography of Rizzo, but rather a history of all Venetian Quattrocento sculpture. My acquaintance with Venetian sculpture was not far advanced before I realized
that the state, or rather lack, of knowledge made it quite impossible to know one sculptor without studying them all. Where very few objects went by their right dates or
authors, one risked omitting major works by focusing too narrowly. Indeed, even to
confine one's vision to Venice proved perilous. This work on Rizzo, then, is part of a
larger work on the sculpture of Venice and its dominions in the early Renaissance.
Decisions embodied in this book as to what is not by Rizzo are based on conclusions
reached in earlier studies as to what are works of Bartolomeo Bon, Niccolò di Giovanni
Fiorentino, and Pietro Lombardo; by the process of elimination, this book may help to
clarify our notions of Giovanni Buora, Antonio and Tullio Lombardo, Paolo Savin, and
others. Any reader at all familiar with the literature on Rizzo may wonder why there is
no discussion of the well-known Tombs of Ser Orsato Giustiniani, Vittore Capello, and
the Doges Marco and Agostino Barbarigo, reputed to be Rizzo's. I refer that reader to
my book and essay on Niccolò di Giovanni Fiorentino and Pietro Lombardo where
these monuments are treated in detail as works of theirs. Eliminating the erroneous
attributions to Rizzo lightened the task of describing the sculptor's oeuvre: I believe, in
fact, that many of my new attributions are obvious and might have been seen by anyone
not prejudiced by beliefs in the authenticity of extraneous works. What I hope emerges
from my definition of the artist's oeuvre is a cogent picture of Rizzo's style, his sources,
his development, his varying responses to the multifarious tasks imposed on him. The
pattern that emerges is not as neat as I would have liked: some works are inferior to
others, some are stylistically unlike others. Yet in every one of them I perceived some
element—a facial type, a way of treating drapery, a canon of proportions, a quality of
movement—that was typical of the artist. The range of quality and style in any artist's
production cannot be predetermined by his biographer: its limits depend upon the nature of the works that interlock. In Rizzo's case, interlocking works produce a range
which, however narrow in comparison with that of Nanni di Banco or Donatello, for
example, nevertheless seems wide in the context of Venetian Quattrocento sculpture.

Setting Rizzo's works in chronological order was occasionally facilitated by relevant documents. More often, secondary sources provided evidence of a circumstantial kind for dating Rizzo's works. Some of these secondary sources are well known to students of Venetian art, though not all had been applied before to Rizzo's sculpture. These included the diaries of Marin Sanudo and Domenico Malipiero and the history and the guide to Venice of Marc'Antonio Sabellico. Others had never before been examined for their potential contributions to the dating of Venetian monuments. These were uniformly travel books by pilgrims who, in the fifteenth century, regularly embarked for the Holy Land at Venice. Delayed by winds or tides or merely curious, they toured Venice and its islands, recording relics by the hundreds but also monuments and buildings. These pilgrim books providentially furnished new *termini* for Rizzo's *Adam* and *Eve*, his Tron Tomb, and the Scala dei Giganti. Those works by Rizzo for which neither documents nor secondary sources nor historical data provided evidence were dated on the basis of resemblances to more firmly dated works. Thus there emerged a pattern of development analogous to that of other north Italian artists of the time.

This book is illustrated by a complete corpus of photographs of the artist's work, of the highest quality I could procure. Most of the photographs were newly made at my behest and under my supervision by the expert photographers of the firm of Giacomelli at Venice; for Sig. Giacomelli's sympathy and kindness I am greatly indebted. Newly made photographs of the Scala dei Giganti were generously funded by the Gladys Krieble Delmas Foundation. They, as well as the photographs of the Tron Tomb and the *Annunciation* of the Madonna dell'Orto were made from scaffolding specially erected for the purpose.

I should like to thank collectively all those who assisted my research. Arch. Renato Padoan, formerly Soprintendente per i Beni Ambientali e Architettonici di Venezia, and Dott. Francesco Valcanover, Soprintendente ai Beni Artistici e Storici di Venezia, smoothed my way very often. I am grateful for the help at Venice of Dott.ssa Lucia Casanova of the Museo Civico Correr, Dott.ssa Angela Dillon of the Biblioteca Marciana, Geom. Giuseppe Fioretti of the Procuratoria di S. Marco, Arch. Umberto Franzoi, director of the Ducal Palace, Dott.ssa Sandra Moschini Marconi, director of the Ca' d'Oro, Dott.ssa Adriana Ruggeri of the Soprintendenza ai Beni Artistici e Storici di Venezia, and Padre Parrocco Domenico Carminati and sacristan Umberto Bognolo at S. Maria dei Frari. I also wish to acknowledge the kind permission of Duc Elie Decazes to study and publish the wellhead in the courtyard of his palace. At the Castello Sforzesco in Milan I was graciously assisted by Dott.ssa Maria Teresa Fiorio; at the Louvre, by Dr. Jean-René Gaborit; at the Kunsthistorishes Museum, Vienna, by Dr. Manfred Leithe-Jasper; at Vaduz, by Dr. Reinhold Baumstark, director of the Fürstlichen Sammlungen. Prof. George Stricivić indulgently translated for me material in Slovenian. Prof. Rudolf Winkes kindly answered numerous questions concerning Rizzo's antique sources. Chapter 3 has benefited from a critical reading by Prof. Debra Pincus, for which I am much obliged. Finally, I owe a debt of gratitude to Prof. Peter Meller for his knowledgeable advice on Rizzo's connections with the art of classical antiquity and numerous other matters, and to Drs. Peter Humfrey and Wendy Stedman Sheard for their contributions to the register of documents.

Providence, R.I.
July 1981

Antonio Rizzo

SCULPTOR AND ARCHITECT

Introduction

DOCUMENTS shed little light on the early history of Antonio Rizzo. His birth date is unknown. Since Rizzo had received a significant commission by 1465, we may suppose that he was born not later than 1440. His birthplace is recorded as Verona.[1] Rizzo's father, who died between 1484 and 1486, was Ser Giovanni;[2] he may be the "Maistro zuan rizo taiapria a verona," the dealer in Veronese marbles who supplied paving stones and *broccatello* for a tomb slab to the Venetian church of S. Maria della Carità in 1462.[3] A "Ioannes Ricius lapicida" from Milan paid taxes in Verona, in the *contrada* of S. Quirico, in 1456 and 1465.[4]

That Rizzo's sculptural debut took place in Verona we may surmise from the fact that the earliest extant notice of Rizzo—one which predates his known activity in Venice—consists of two epigrams and a distich written by the Venetian nobleman and beneficiary of the Basilica of S. Zeno at Verona, Gregorio Correr. The poems are undated but must precede Correr's death, presumably at the end of November 1464.[5] Gregorio Correr was born in ca. 1411. As a youth he was tutored by Vittorino da Feltre; he retained his humanistic interests throughout his clerical career. Named Apostolic Protonotary by Eugene IV, he obtained the benefice of S. Zeno in 1443 and took up residence in Verona in 1445. There he remained until his death. In August 1464, Correr was elected Patriarch of Venice but died before taking office. Under Correr, the Basilica of S. Zeno was reconstructed and the high altar was embellished with an altarpiece by the twenty-six-year-old Andrea Mantegna. In his epigrams and distich addressed to "Antonium Riccium Sculptorem," Correr patronized another young artist whose sculpture must have appeared as revolutionary in the context of Veronese art as did the painting of Mantegna.[6]

Although the quarrying of tufa and *broccatello* played an important role in the economic life of Verona, neither stone was suited to the high working of figurative sculpture. Therefore it is not surprising that the city lacked an indigenous school of master

[1] Colatius, (1475) 1486, n.p. [p. 41]; Paoletti, 1893, ii, p. 147.

[2] Lorenzi, 1868, p. 94, doc. 202; Paoletti, 1893, ii, p. 148, n. 11 (from the preceding page).

[3] Fogolari, *Arch. ven.*, 1924, pp. 109, 113.

[4] Mazzi, *Madonna Verona*, 1913, p. 31. See also App., p. 123.

[5] Correr's epitaph, recorded by Corner, *Eccl. Ven.*, 1749, xiii, p. 150, gives the former's death date as November 19, 1464. But Correr's testament, published by Puppi, 1972, pp. 73ff., doc. xvii, is dated

November 29, 1464. The mistake may be due to the fact that Correr died in Verona but was buried in Venice, in S. Giorgio in Alga.

[6] For Gregorio Correr, see Puppi, 1972, pp. 35ff. Correr's poems are listed as "Epigrammata II. & Distichon ad Antonium Riccium Sculptorem" by Degli Agostini, 1752, i, p. 132, no. xiv. The epigrams and distich, themselves, have never been traced; for their disappearance, see Pohlandt, *BJ*, 1971, p. 163, n. 5.

carvers. Stonemasons there certainly were, but sculptors, by and large, came from abroad. Where works by native craftsmen were not confined to the mundane tasks of stone-masonry they were mediocre in quality and *retardataire* in style. These traits define the only secure works by the native Bartolomeo Giolfino (ca. 1410–ca. 1486)—the fragments of an altar of 1433 with the twelve Apostles and SS. Nicholas and Anthony Abbot divided between the Pieve of S. Maria at Colognola al Piano (Verona) and the outdoor Altar of S. Niccolò at Colognola ai Colli, and the wooden polyptych of 1470 from the Oratory of S. Giovanni di Rodi of the Palazzo dei Querini at Presana, now in the Accademia, Venice.[7] Anonymous sculptures, such as the Monument of Spinetta Malaspina from S. Giovanni in Sacco, Verona, now in the Victoria and Albert Museum,[8] or the *Entombment* in S. Anastasia, Verona,[9] betray their provincial origin. The statue of *Christ the Redeemer* in the Veronese church of S. Fermo Maggiore reveals acquaintance with Michelozzo's *Risen Christ* from the Tomb of Bartolommeo Aragazzi in the Cathedral of Montepulciano, but its appropriation of Renaissance forms was only partial.[10] Perhaps Gregorio Panteo, commended in verses by his humanist son as "well known in the city / Which he beautifies by bringing forth live faces from marble / To carve whatever is pleasing in art or heaven"[11] was superior to the average artisan. Lombard by origin, he was recorded as a Veronese citizen in the *estimo* of 1443; he died in Verona between 1482 and 1487. For the Veronese church of S. Maria della Scala he carved the altar of Paolo Filippo Guantieri by January 22, 1445.[12] But the altar is lost and Panteo is not known to us through any extant works.

In any case, the most important Veronese sculpture of the first half of the fifteenth century was done by Florentines. Michele da Firenze, it seems, faced the Chapel of Andrea di Niccolò Pellegrini in S. Anastasia with seventeen terracotta reliefs of scenes from the life of Christ, five terracotta reliefs of saints, one donor portrait and two busts in terracotta; work was in progress in 1436.[13] Though marred now by inexpert resto-

[7] Fiocco, T-B, xiv, 1921, p. 70; Simeoni, 1909, pp. 460, 462; Ven., Gall. dell'Accademia. Catalogue by Moschini Marconi, 1955, pp. 189f., no. 212. For other attributions to Giolfino, see Simeoni, 1909, pp. 54, 114, 193, 487f.

[8] Pope-Hennessy, 1964, i, pp. 366ff., no. 392; Wolters, 1976, i, p. 97.

[9] Venturi, *Storia*, vi, 1908, p. 978; Cipolla, *L'arte*, 1915, pp. 297f.

[10] Wolters, 1976, i, pp. 270f., no. 222.

[11] Federici, i, 1818, p. 46.

[12] Brenzoni, *Arte e artisti*, 1959, i, pp. 95ff.; Brenzoni, 1972, pp. 226ff.

[13] The terracotta decoration of the Pellegrini Chapel consists of the following reliefs of scenes from the life of Christ: on the spectator's left, starting at the entrance and reading from top to bottom, (1) *Last Supper*, (2) *Entry into Jerusalem*, (3) *Baptism of Christ*, (4) *Adoration of the Magi*, (5) *Nativity and Annunciation to the Shepherds*, (6) *Christ's Agony in the Garden*, (7) *Christ's Descent from the Mount of Olives*, (8) *Christ Washes the Disciples' Feet*. On the right: (9) *Crucifixion*, (10) *Christ before Pilate*, (11) *Carrying of the Cross*, (12) *Ecce Homo*, (13) *Flagellation*, (14) *Arrest of Christ*, (15) *Resurrection*, (16) *Entombment*, (17) *Descent from*

the Cross. Between reliefs 5 and 6 are *SS. Leonard, Michael,* and *John the Baptist.* Between reliefs 14 and 15 are an unidentified *Saint, St. Dominic,* and the kneeling donor. Two busts in roundels are located beneath *Christ before Pilate.* Fragments of the altarpiece are preserved in the Museo del Castelvecchio, Verona.

The decoration of the chapel was ordered by Andrea di Niccolò Pellegrini in a testament of March 9, 1429. By the end of 1430 Pellegrini was dead. (Pellegrini, *Studi storici veronesi,* 1949-50, pp. 210ff.) Work on the chapel's decoration was not yet finished on July 12, 1436. (Cipolla, *L'arte,* 1914, p. 406, n. 4.) The sculpture of the chapel is customarily attributed to Michele da Firenze who, in turn, is identified with Ghiberti's assistant on the north Baptistry doors, Michele di Niccolaio Dini detto dello Scalcagna, and with a Michele da Firenze, author of a lost ancona made for Niccolò d'Este in 1440. The attribution of the sculptural decoration of the Pellegrini Chapel to Michele da Firenze rests on a document of July 12, 1436, in which "Michele da Firenze" (living in the *contrada* of S. Marco, Verona) is mentioned as working at the chapel. Unfortunately, the document neglects to record what he was

ration, even in their pristine state the reliefs must have betrayed very modest talents, however zealously applied. More successful were Nanni di Bartolo and Pietro di Niccolò Lamberti, both of whom arrived in Verona by way of Venice, which had gained dominion over the city on the Adige in 1405. In 1426 Nanni made the Tomb of Niccolò Brenzoni (d. 1422) for S. Fermo Maggiore.[14] The figures for which Nanni himself was responsible—the three sleeping soldiers, the angel supporting the lid of the sarcophagus, the two *putti*, and the prophet *Isaiah* at the apex of the tomb—reveal a new comprehension of masculine anatomy and movement, which unfolds in a three-dimensional space. But drapery is still Gothic in its complex curvilinear patterns produced by an abundance of heavy folds. Lamberti's Tomb of Cortesia Serego in S. Anastasia, executed between 1424 and 1429,[15] was influential in its union of sarcophagus, baldachin, and equestrian portrait flanked by warriors holding apart the curtain. But the unarticulated anatomy of the horse and the squat and inorganic figures make no advance upon the fourteenth-century equestrian portraits of the Scaligers. From Donatello's shop came the stucco relief of the half-length *Madonna and Child* in Via della Fogge. The two stucco casts of music-making *Angels* which accompany the relief and derive from the High Altar of the Santo, support a dating of ca. 1450.[16] The original location of the relief, however, whether identical to its present one or not, is unknown.

To survey Veronese sculpture of the second and third quarters of the fifteenth century is to reveal its poverty. Not only do there seem to have been no sculptors of merit with whom Rizzo might have worked, but there were few sculptures worthy of study. Yet I think it fairly certain that Rizzo did learn his trade from a Veronese *lapicida* of indifferent parts. For when Rizzo encountered the art of the *avant-garde* and wished to imitate it, he could only copy external traits: his training had not prepared him to comprehend and assimilate its principles. In this respect his first response to the art of the Florentine Renaissance recalls that of the young Mantegna and Giovanni Bellini.

Where the statuary of Rizzo's first works, the three altars for the Basilica of S. Marco, is gravely flawed, the ornament of architectural members reveals a master carver (Figs. 3, 6, 9). Rizzo's preparation in this branch of the art of stonemasonry was evidently thorough. Perhaps Rizzo had been apprenticed to the Veronese specialist in the carving

doing there. Subsequent documents in the same series call Michele "pittore," but another document which seems to refer to the same person—an *estimo* of the Veronese *contrada* of S. Marco of 1433—names Michele da Firenze, "intaiatore." (Fainelli, *L'arte*, 1910, p. 219; Cipolla, *L'arte*, 1914, p. 406, n. 4.)

Far more problematic is the identification of Michele da Firenze, probable author of the Pellegrini reliefs, with Michele detto dello Scalcagna, assistant of Ghiberti (for whom see Vas/Mil, ii, [1568] 1878, p. 255, and Marchini in Atti, *Jacopo della Quercia*, 1977, p. 201). This identification was argued by Fiocco, *Dedalo*, xii, 1932, pp. 546ff., on the basis of motifs in the reliefs that he believed were copied from Ghiberti's first Baptistry doors and Arnolfo di Cambio's *Nativity* on the facade of Florence Cathedral. But, in fact, the Pellegrini reliefs are singularly free of quotations or stylistic influences from Ghiberti's or Arnolfo's works. With as little certainty

can the Michele da Firenze, employed in the Pellegrini Chapel, be identified with the Michele da Firenze, "fabricator optimus figuarum," paid on March 5, 1440, for an ancona (whether painted, carved, or modeled is not specified), executed for the church of S. Maria degli Angeli in the Castle of Belfiore at the behest of Niccolò d'Este. (Venturi, *Arch. stor. dell'arte*, 1894, pp. 53f.)

[14] Wolters, 1976, i, pp. 268f., no. 220; Brunetti, in Atti, *Jacopo della Quercia*, 1977, pp. 189ff.

[15] Wolters, 1976, i, pp. 96f., 254f., no. 192. It is to Cuppini in *Verona e il suo territorio*, iii, pt. 2, 1969, pp. 355ff., that we owe the correct interpretation of the documents relating to Antonio da Firenze, the obscure *lapicida* to whom the tomb is currently assigned, and the persuasive attribution of the tomb to Lamberti.

[16] Pope-Hennessy, 1964, i, pp. 84f., no. 69; Pope-Hennessy, *Apollo*, Mar. 1976, pp. 176f.

of architectural ornament, Pietro di Antonio da Porlezza. Born in 1394 on Lake Lugano, Pietro is documented in Verona between 1433 and 1484. By 1492 he was dead.[17] At S. Anastasia, Pietro was responsible for the pavement begun in 1462 and for the framework of the Altar of St. Vincent Ferrer, executed in 1484-85 in accordance with the testament of Gian Nicola Manzini.[18] To be sure, the vocabulary of the latter derives from the ornament of Pietro Lombardo. But the carving of the frame testifies to a skill and interest in the embellishment of architectural members that may have been transmitted to the youth.

However that may be, the only Veronese work whose influence can be traced in Rizzo's art is Mantegna's altarpiece for the High Altar of S. Zeno, from whose figure of the Baptist Rizzo borrowed the anatomy and pose (Figs. 36, 209). Already conceived by January 5, 1457, the altarpiece was nearly finished by June 29, 1459, and had been transported from Padua to Verona by January 26, 1460.[19] Perhaps acquaintance with the S. Zeno Altarpiece aroused in Rizzo a desire to visit Padua. Or perhaps a previous knowledge of Paduan art intensified Rizzo's appreciation of the S. Zeno Altarpiece. In any case, the roots of Rizzo's art are to be sought, not in his native city of Verona, but in nearby Padua.

Situated between Venice and Verona, Padua, like Verona, was politically subordinate to Venice. But by the middle of the fifteenth century it had become the artistic source from which the best Venetian artists drew. The preeminence of Padua was due to Donatello, who arrived in 1443 and remained for a decade. Between 1444 and 1449 he executed the bronze Crucifix for the Santo (Fig. 210). The Monument of the Gattamelata in the Piazza del Santo was cast in 1447 and installed in September 1453, while the High Altar of the Santo, with its seven nearly life-size statues and four pictorial reliefs, dates from 1446 to 1450. Donatello's influence was almost immediately apparent in the fresco cycle of the Ovetari Chapel in the Eremitani. The frescoes, which resulted from a testamentary bequest of Antonio Ovetari, were commissioned on May 16, 1448, and were probably finished by January 28, 1455. The cycle included the four *Evangelists* in medallions in the cross vault painted by Antonio Vivarini between 1448 and 1451; *God the Father* and *St. James* in the vault of the apse, and four *Fathers of the Church* in roundels below them, executed by Niccolò Pizzolo between 1448 and 1453; six scenes from the life of St. James on the left wall of the chapel, the *Assumption of the Virgin* in the apse, *SS. Peter, Paul* and *Christopher* in the apse vault, and the *Martyrdom of St. Christopher* at the bottom of the right chapel wall by Mantegna, probably painted between 1448 and 1455; four scenes from the life of St. Christopher painted by Bono da Ferrara, Ansuino da Forlì, and one or two other artists who have not been securely identified.

The influence of the drapery style of such figures as Donatello's *St. Justina* (Fig. 208) and the *Madonna* from the Santo's altar can be traced in Rizzo's work: in his attempt to repeat Donatello's equivocal and arbitrary patterns, Rizzo produced effects remarkably similar to those in the drapery of Mantegna's earliest figures (Fig. 205), and Niccolò

[17] Brenzoni, *Arte e artisti*, 1959, i, p. 120.
[18] Cipolla, *L'arte*, 1914, pp. 186ff.; ibid., 1915, pp. 303f. Simeoni, 1909, p. 54, claimed for Pietro's *officina* the decoration of the entrance to the Cappella del Crocifisso in S. Anastasia made in accordance with the testament of Francesco Pellegrini in 1458. These misstatements were rectified by Cipolla, *L'arte*, 1915, pp. 298ff., who proved that the decoration of the entrance had resulted from a codicil of 1484 to the 1475 testament of Francesco Pellegrini. An inscription in the chapel dates its redecoration to 1488. There is no documentary basis for the attribution of the work to Pietro da Porlezza.
[19] Puppi, 1972, pp. 21ff.

Pizzolo's *Fathers of the Church* (Fig. 206) in the Ovetari Chapel, and the drapery of the sketches and paintings of Marco Zoppo (Fig. 204), trained, like Pizzolo and Mantegna, in the Paduan studio of Squarcione. The foremost striding figure in Rizzo's *Conversion of St. Paul* probably derives from Mantegna's *St. James Led to Execution* (Figs. 17, 212).

We do not know the dates of Rizzo's Paduan sojourn. We may surmise that it occurred between 1450 and 1455 when the impact of Donatello's art was not yet superseded by that of the precocious Mantegna. Indeed, the drapery style of Mantegna's later frescoes of the Ovetari Chapel, which so strongly influenced the Venetian sculpture of Niccolò di Giovanni Fiorentino,[20] had no effect on Rizzo. Upon his return, Rizzo probably executed works of which no trace remains, but whose novel style in Verona must have captured the attention of Gregorio Correr. Perhaps on the strength of a recommendation from Correr, Rizzo was called to Venice: by 1465 Doge Cristoforo Moro had entrusted the young sculptor with the commission for three altars in the Basilica di S. Marco.

Documents of 1465, 1466, and 1467 record payments to a "Magistro Ricio de Verona" for columns, capitals, and bases, and other architectural members, as well as thirty-three blocks of stone furnished to the Certosa of Pavia for its large cloister.[21] In the earliest publication of the documents the recipient of these payments, whose first name is never given, was identified as Antonio Rizzo.[22] Therefore, it has long been customary to assign to Rizzo a period of activity in the mid-1460s at the Certosa.[23] Encouraged by these documents, Arslan credited Rizzo with the wooden models for thirteen terracotta statues, which decorate the spandrels of the arcades of the large cloister; these statues he dated to ca. 1465.[24] But the figures that Arslan ascribed to Rizzo bear no resemblance to his documented or certain works. Indeed, the "Magister Ricio de Verona" of the Certosa is far more likely to have been the "Maistro zuan rizo taiapria a verona," who purveyed Veronese marbles at the Carità in 1462[25] and may be Rizzo's father, than to have been Antonio himself. In sum, there is no justification for assigning to Rizzo a Lombard interlude in the mid-1460s. So much the less warrant is there for crediting Rizzo in 1432 with an architectural career in Rome in the service of the pope.[26]

On the other hand, there is evidence that Rizzo made a brief trip to Florence sometime before the execution of his first Venetian commission. The gesture of the early "*Mars*" (Fig. 36) comes from Donatello's so-called *Jeremiah*. The ornament on the pilaster shafts of the Altars of SS. James and Paul (Figs. 1, 2) is very similar to that of Desiderio da

[20] Schulz, *NdiGF*, 1978, p. 16.

[21] Magenta, 1897, p. 460, n. 1; Bernstein, 1972, app. H, pp. 197f., docs. 1-6.

[22] Caffi, *Arte e storia*, June 5, 1887, p. 106.

[23] Burckhardt/Bode/Fabriczy, [8]1901, ii, pt. 2, p. 496; Malaguzzi Valeri, 1904, pp. 35f.; Planiscig, 1921, p. 62; Mariacher, *Aten. ven.*, 1942, p. 240; Dell'Acqua, *Proporzioni*, 1950, p. 124; Pope-Hennessy, [1]1958, p. 94; Salmi in *Umanesimo europeo*, 1963, p. 392; Pohlandt, *BJ*, 1971, p. 199; Brenzoni, 1972, p. 250; McAndrew, 1980, p. 62. Rizzo's supposititious activity at the Certosa inspired Malaguzzi Valeri, 1904, p. 36, to find traces of Rizzo's hand in two statues on the north flank of the Duomo of Milan.

[24] Arslan, *GBA*, Sept. 1953, pp. 111ff.; Arslan in *Storia di Milano*, vii, 1956, pp. 704f. Arslan's attri-

bution was accepted by Paccagnini, *Boll. d'arte*, 1961, pp. 90, 93; Romanini, *Arte lom.*, Jan.–June 1964, p. 94, and, with reservations, by Pope-Hennessy, [1]1958, p. 94. It was rejected by Mariacher, 1966, n.p. [p. 3]; Bossaglia in Albertini Ottolenghi *et al.*, 1968, pp. 48, 49; Pohlandt, *BJ*, 1971, pp. 190f., and Bernstein, 1972, pp. 148f., who pointed out that the sculptures must postdate the completion of the vaults, still unfinished in March 1467, and perhaps executed only after 1469, following completion of the colonnades.

[25] Connell, 1976, p. 142.

[26] Maimeri, *Vita veronese*, 1960, nos. 1-2, p. 17. This claim was advanced on the basis of two payments to "Antonio Riccio de Venetiis, magister palatii in civitate Hostiae."

Settignano's Tabernacle of the Sacrament. To be sure, these motifs could have been transmitted through drawings, though no such drawings are preserved. But the technique of Rizzo's relief of the *Conversion of St. Paul* (Fig. 17) presupposes knowledge of Donatello's *schiacciato* relief, particularly his *Ascension of Christ* in London, which could have been gained only at first hand. Desiderio's tabernacle was installed on August 1, 1461.[27] Probably Rizzo's trip was made soon afterward.

Rizzo's arrival in Venice sometime before 1465 coincided with the close of Bartolomeo Bon's career.[28] Bon died probably not long after making his will on August 8, 1464. His final years were occupied with the design and partial execution of the Ca' del Duca, begun in 1457 for Andrea Cornaro but sold in 1461 to Duke Francesco Sforza. From the late 1450s and early 1460s date the lower part of the portal of SS. Giovanni e Paolo, some of the architectural details of the main portal of the Madonna dell'Orto, and the unfinished statues of the *Angel* and *Virgin Annunciate* in the Victoria and Albert Museum, possibly intended for the portal. There is record of Bon's employment at the Ducal Palace in 1463. Very likely he was *protomaestro* in charge of the construction of the Arco Foscari, for which he carved the statue of *Arithmetic*. From August 9, 1465, dates the death of his quondam partner, Pantaleone di Paolo.[29] Evidently a reputed sculptor, Pantaleone is known to us only from a fragment of his much earlier Tomb of Jacopo della Torre from the Eremitani, Padua.[30]

In 1465 Niccolò di Giovanni Fiorentino was Venice's foremost sculptor.[31] At the time of its execution at the end of the 1450s or the beginning of the 1460s, his Tomb of Doge Francesco Foscari (d. 1457) in S. Maria dei Frari was by far the largest tomb ever executed in Venice; it initiated a trend toward increasingly grandiose ducal tombs. Niccolò seems to have succeeded Bartolomeo Bon as *protomaestro* of the Ducal Palace, contributing to the Arco Foscari its crowning pyramid and spires and five or six statues carved by him and his assistants. These comprise the *Moro* and *Gorgon Warriors*, *Rhetoric* and *Music*, *St. Mark*, and possibly the figure of the kneeling *Doge Moro*. To Bon's portal at the Madonna dell'Orto Niccolò and his shop added the central figure of *St. Christopher* and the *Virgin Annunciate* (Figs. 237-239). Ca. 1466 Niccolò undertook the execution of the Tomb of Ser Orsato Giustiniani for the defunct's funerary chapel at S. Andrea della Certosa. Niccolò's Tomb of Vittore Capello at S. Elena dates from ca. 1467-68. His undated relief of *St. Jerome* is in the Venetian church of S. Maria del Giglio. By April 1468 Niccolò had settled in Trogir; thenceforth his artistic activity was centered in Dalmatia.

By contrast, the focus of Pietro Lombardo's activity was Venice: for all but the first five of Rizzo's working years Pietro competed successfully with Rizzo for the best Venetian commissions. It is not known precisely when Pietro came to Venice; his arrival surely predates the earliest record of his presence there in 1474.[32] Between 1470 and 1475 Pietro executed the sculptural decoration of the Cappella Maggiore of S. Giobbe; the Tomb Slab of Doge Moro (d. 1471) in front of the altar is inscribed with the month of September 1470.[33] The retaining wall of the choir stalls in S. Maria dei Frari was

[27] Moreni, i, 1816, p. 15, n. 1.
[28] Schulz, *TAPS*, 1978, pt. 3, pp. 74ff.
[29] Paoletti, 1893, i, p. 42.
[30] Wolters, 1976, i, pp. 112f., 266f., no. 217.
[31] Schulz, *NdiGF*, 1978.
[32] Moschetti, Ist. ven. SLA. *Atti*, 1927-28, pt. 2, p. 1514, doc. xxvi.
[33] Paoletti, 1893, ii, p. 190; Colatius, (1475) 1486, n.p. [p. 46]. For the date of the composition of Colaccio's work, see Morelli in [Michiel]/Morelli, 1800, p. 189, n. 100.

completed in 1475; the style of its reliefs and statues marks it as an early work by the sculptor and his shop. Two tombs attributed to Lombardo and assistants are generally dated to the 1470s. They are the Tombs of Doge Pasquale Malipiero (d. 1462) in SS. Giovanni e Paolo and Doge Niccolò Marcello (d. 1474), originally in S. Marina and now in SS. Giovanni e Paolo. Pietro's Tomb of Doge Pietro Mocenigo (d. 1476), in SS. Giovanni e Paolo, executed between February 1476 and March 4, 1481,[34] is coeval with Rizzo's Tomb of Doge Niccolò Tron. Between 1481 and 1489 the church of S. Maria dei Miracoli was constructed and adorned under Pietro's supervision.[35] Pietro's double Tomb of Doges Marco and Agostino Barbarigo was erected at S. Maria della Carità between 1486 and 1501.[36] With Giovanni Buora and Bartolomeo Duca, Pietro was employed between 1489 and 1490 on the construction of the Scuola di S. Marco.[37] Between 1495 and 1509 Pietro decorated the Giustiniani Chapel at S. Francesco della Vigna for members of the Badoer family.[38] Lombardo succeeded Rizzo as *protomaestro* of the Ducal Palace in 1498[39] and remained in that position until his death in 1515.

Other marble sculptors of lesser importance active at the end of the fifteenth century in Venice include Giovanni Buora, responsible for the Tombs of Jacopo Marcello in the Frari (1484), of Doctor Jacopo Suriano in S. Stefano (ca. 1488-93), and of Senator Agostino Onigo (1490-92) in S. Nicolò, Treviso; and for the free-standing statues from the choir screen of S. Stefano (late 1470s-ca. 1488), and the so-called *Madonna delle Biade* of 1481-82 in a loggia of the Ducal Palace.[40] In the lunette of the main portal of S. Maria dei Miracoli is a relief of the *Madonna and Child* by Gian Giorgio Lascari, called Pyrgoteles after the only carver permitted by Alexander the Great to engrave his image. Pyrgoteles appears again as a collaborator of Pietro Lombardo at the Cappella Giustiniani, where the relief of *Christ Carrying the Cross* can be ascribed to him.[41] Andrea del Verrocchio, it seems, provided models for the Altar of the Virgin at SS. Giovanni e Paolo between 1482 and 1486.[42]

In Venice, Rizzo resided throughout his life in the parish of S. Giovanni Nuovo.[43] In 1469 he occupied a house owned by the Benedictine nuns of the nearby convent of S. Zaccaria.[44] Prior to May 1474 when he was summarily dismissed, Rizzo's father-in-law, Giacomo Gibellino, was employed as steward to the convent of S. Zaccaria.[45] The earliest notice we possess of Rizzo's marriage to Maria Gibellino dates from 1477.[46] Perhaps they were already married in 1469 when Rizzo rented a house presumably superintended by his father-in-law. Giacomo Gibellino, himself, owned at least two houses in the parish of S. Giovanni Nuovo. In 1480 they were the subject of a suit that Rizzo lodged against Gibellino. In recompense for part of the expense incurred by Rizzo in improvements to the houses, Rizzo was awarded a share of a small house that Gibellino owned there in 1486.[47] By this time Gibellino had died.[48] In 1499, Gibellino's widow, Isabeta, was still living at S. Giovanni Nuovo.[49]

[34] Boni, *Arch. ven.*, xxxiii, 1887, p. 244.
[35] Ibid., pp. 244ff.
[36] Schulz in *Studies . . . Janson*, pp. 171ff.
[37] Paoletti, 1893, ii, pp. 102f., doc. 72.
[38] Schulz, *Antichità viva*, Mar.-Apr. 1977, pp. 27ff.
[39] Lorenzi, 1868, p. 122, doc. 251.
[40] Munman, *Arte ven.*, 1976, pp. 41ff.; Munman, *Arte ven.*, 1979, pp. 19ff.
[41] Schulz, *Antichità viva*, Mar.-Apr. 1977, pp. 38f.
[42] Schulz in *Von Simson Festschrift*, 1977, pp. 197ff.

[43] Paoletti, 1893, ii, pp. 147f., n. 11, 149, n. 4; Cecchetti, *Arch. ven.*, xxxiii, 1887, p. 423.
[44] Paoletti, 1893, ii, p. 147, n. 11.
[45] Ibid.
[46] Ibid.
[47] Ibid., p. 148, n. 11 (from the preceding page); Ludwig, 1911, pp. 13f.
[48] He is first mentioned as dead in a document of 1484: ibid., p. 14.
[49] Paoletti, 1893, ii, p. 148, n. 1.

In her testament of May 4, 1499, Isabeta designated as her residual heir her daughter, Maria. As one of her executors she named Rizzo's and Maria's son Simplicio,[50] who was a goldsmith and jeweler. In 1490 he was ceded the broker's patent at the Fondaco dei Tedeschi by his father. He died in Rome in 1522.[51] Another son, Gian Stefano, was living at the Certosa di Pavia in 1489.[52]

In 1477 Rizzo was inscribed among the members of the Scuola Grande di S. Marco, probably in gratitude for the staircase and pulpit that the sculptor had executed for the confraternity's chapter hall the year before.[53] Simplicio joined the confraternity in 1495 and in 1502 was elected a dean.[54]

Rizzo's first known commission in Venice consisted of the three altars dedicated to SS. James, Paul, and Clement in the Basilica di S. Marco (Figs. 1, 2, 10).[55] In every respect this was a notable commission: its patron was the reigning doge; the altars were to be situated in the crossing and east end of the ducal church. By June 1469 work on the altars was complete. By this time, it would seem, Rizzo had succeeded Niccolò di Giovanni as chief sculptor at the Arco Foscari. Statues for the Arco continued to be produced in Rizzo's shop until his attention was diverted to the rebuilding of the east wing of the Ducal Palace in 1484. By then only one figure—Charity–Amor Dei—attributable on the basis of its style to an assistant of Pietro Lombardo—was still outstanding. Among the earliest statues executed by Rizzo for the Arco Foscari is the so-called Mars (Figs. 34-37), which shows the influence of Donatello and Mantegna. Probably it was finished when, not later than 1470, Rizzo was included in a list of artists in a sonnet by Giovanni Testa Cillenio, a poet active at Ferrara ca. 1475, as "worthy of praise."[56]

Among those artists who gave lustre to the city of Venice, Rizzo was named in a disputation composed by Matteo Colaccio in 1475. According to Colaccio, Rizzo was illustrious in architecture as well as sculpture.[57] Curiously, there is no other evidence that Rizzo practiced as an architect at so early a date, or indeed, before his appointment in 1484 as architect, in charge of rebuilding the Ducal Palace. That position, however, automatically elevated Rizzo within the ranks of architects. For the first time in October 1486, in a Ducal Palace document, Rizzo is called architect.[58] His renown as protomaestro of the Ducal Palace brought a request in 1496 from the Council of 100 of Vicenza that he advise on repairing the loggias of the Palazzo della Ragione, which had recently collapsed.[59] Evidently, Rizzo was mechanically adept, for together with Zorzi di Amadeo da Lugano, he invented a new form of mill and its requisite machinery, as well as the means to construct it, for which they requested a patent on September 27, 1488.[60] But Rizzo never ceased to regard himself as a sculptor and consistently signed himself "scultor" or "taiapiera," even where the notary introduced him in official acts as "inzegniro" or "architectus."[61]

[50] Ibid.
[51] Ibid., p. 148; Paoletti, 1929, p. 16, n. 4.
[52] "Alberto Maffiolo," Rass. d'arte, 1902, pp. 14f.
[53] Paoletti, 1893, ii, p. 149, n. 4.
[54] Paoletti, 1929, p. 16, n. 4.
[55] See ch. 1, n. 1, and Schulz, NdiGF, 1978, pp. 64f., n. 21.
[56] Ricci, Arte e storia, Feb. 20, 1897, pp. 27f.: "Antonio Riccio è ben de laude degno."
[57] Colatius, (1475) 1486, n.p. [p. 41]: "Habet item statuarios . . . Antonium riccium ueronensem statua

& archytectura clarissimos." For the date of its composition, see above n. 33. However, just as the notice regarding Antonello da Messina's S. Cassiano Altarpiece was evidently added after 1475 (n.p. [p. 41]), so the reference to Rizzo's architecture may have been inserted between the disputation's composition in 1475 and its publication in 1486.
[58] Lorenzi, 1868, p. 100, doc. 214.
[59] Zorzi, iii, 1937, pp. 127ff., docs. I-IV.
[60] Ludwig, 1911, pp. 14f.; Paoletti, 1893, ii, p. 161.
[61] On June 25, 1495, Rizzo signed himself, "Jo an-

What sculpture by Rizzo could Colaccio have known in 1475? *Adam* and *Eve* (Figs. 38-43, 45-51), probably completed before Doge Moro died in 1471, as Sabellico implies,[62] could be seen at either side of the main opening of the Arco Foscari. The Altar of the Scuola dei Barbieri in S. Maria dei Servi, with its four statues of *SS. Andrew, Luke, Cosmas,* and *Damian*, now preserved in S. Sofia (Figs. 60-63), probably dates not long after the appropriation of the altar to the guild in 1468.[63] The antependium with the relief of the *Man of Sorrows*, now incorporated in the retable of the Altar of the Sacrament in the Basilica of Aquileia (Figs. 53-59), may have been made for the Chapel of the Corpus Christi erected between 1468 and 1475.[64] An escutcheon-bearing *Angel* immured in the exterior wall of a house in the Rio Terrà Barba Fruttarol (Fig. 52) and two *Angels* on the Arco Foscari (Figs. 32, 33) can be dated, on the basis of their style, to this time.

The influence of Antonio Pollaiuolo, apparent for the first time in Rizzo's *Adam* and *Eve*, warrants the hypothesis of a second trip to Florence circa 1470. Perhaps Rizzo also saw there the antique statue of *Venus pudica*,[65] which he used for *Eve*. Other evidence of travel comes from the Tron Tomb reliefs of *putti* (Figs. 117, 118) carved at the end of the 1470s, which derive from a classical relief that is now, and presumably was then, at Ravenna (Fig. 219). On the other hand, such reliefs were frequently transcribed in drawings: Rizzo may have known the antique relief only indirectly.

Between July and August 1474 and between June 1478 and January 1479, Rizzo participated in two defenses of Scutari, besieged by the Turks.[66] In 1453 the Turks had conquered Constantinople. A treaty signed the following year produced an uneasy peace, which lasted only until 1463: throughout the second half of the fifteenth century the Turks posed a graver threat to Venetian security than any other force. In 1470 the Turks took Negroponte by sea; by land the Turkish cavalry penetrated as far west as Dalmatia and Friuli. In 1474 the Turkish attack on Scutari was successfully repulsed, but a second siege four years later ended in the defeat of the Venetians. At Scutari, Rizzo's knowledge of stonemasonry was put to use in quarrying stone, used probably to construct defensive walls and for cannonballs. We are told that he performed his duty conscientiously and was wounded. In a treaty signed with the Turks on January 25, 1479, at the conclusion of the second siege of Scutari, Venice surrendered the Albanian city and some Aegean islands and agreed to pay 10,000 ducats yearly for the privilege of trading with the enemy. Not long afterward, the painter Gentile Bellini and the sculptor Bartolomeo Bellano were dispatched by a conciliatory Signoria to the court of Mahommet II at Constantinople. In February 1483, Rizzo was awarded a monthly pension in recognition of his faithful wartime service.

tonio rizo taiapiera foi presente a quanto di sopra-scritto." (Cecchetti, *Arch. ven.*, xxxiii, 1887, p. 423.) On September 22, 1495, Rizzo wrote, "Io Antonio Rizo scultor foi presente a quanto è di sopra scritto." (Ludwig, 1911, p. 15.) The recommendations for the repair of the porticoes of the Palazzo della Ragione at Vicenza, written up in the spring of 1496, open thus: "Provision de fortificare el Portego del Palazzo . . . per magistro Antonio Rizo inzegniro de la Illustrissima Signoria di Venezia," but conclude in Rizzo's own voice: "Questa scriptura di sopra scripta è quanto mi Antonio Rizo sculptor ho ordinato se faza et in fede de questa ho sotoscripto de

mia mane propria." (Zorzi, iii, 1937, pp. 127f., doc. I.) Again, on July 15, 1496, Rizzo, referred to in the minutes of the meeting of the Council of 100 as "Architectus," called himself "mi Antonio Rizo sculptor." (Ibid., p. 129, doc. III.)

[62] Sabellico, 1487, dec. 3, bk. 9, n.p.
[63] Vicentini, *S. Maria de' Servi*, 1920, p. 91.
[64] Vale in *La Basilica di Aquileia*, 1933, p. 66, nn. 2, 3, 4, p. 67, n. 2.
[65] Rambaldi da Imola, 1887, iii, p. 280. See below, ch. 2, p. 34.
[66] Cadorin, 1838, pp. 163f., n. 19.

Between 1476 and 1484 Rizzo's commissions were numerous. In 1476 the sculptor was entrusted with the erection of a staircase and pulpit for the chapter hall of the Scuola di S. Marco;[67] they were destroyed by fire in 1485. The Tomb of Doge Niccolò Tron in S. Maria dei Frari (Fig. 64) can be dated securely between 1476 and 1480. Below the relief of the *Miraculous Cure of St. Anianus* on the portal of the Scuola dei Calegheri (Figs. 123-125) is inscribed the month of September 1479. The Altar of the Traghetto della Maddalena, now in the Museo Civico Correr (Figs. 126-129), was made probably not long after December 1479; the *Annunciate Angel* on the main portal of the Madonna dell'Orto (Figs. 119-122) was carved before March 1483. Rizzo's share in the Tomb of Giovanni Emo (d. 1483), originally in S. Maria dei Servi (Figs. 138-146), probably was finished by August 1485 when Rizzo claimed that pressure of work at the Ducal Palace had forced him to close his shop and neglect all other work.[68] The style of other sculptures warrants their dating to this time. They are a statue of *John the Evangelist* in the Staatliche Museen, East Berlin (Fig. 135), an *Angel* in the Kunsthistorisches Museum, Vienna (Figs. 132, 133), two *Victories* formerly in Berlin (Figs. 130, 131), and five statues from the Arco Foscari (Figs. 134, 136, 137, 147, 148).

Before 1485 Rizzo was apostrophized in five poems by the Triestine humanist and poet Raffaele Zovenzoni (1431-85). One distich lauded Rizzo's *Eve*; another recorded a statue—evidently lost—of Hercules. The frequency with which Rizzo's name recurs in Zovenzoni's work suggests that the two men were acquainted. Zovenzoni studied at Ferrara under Guarino Veronese and taught at Capodistria and Trieste, whence he was exiled because of his political involvements. He lived in Venice between 1470 and the beginning of 1473 and again from April 1475 until his death, except for two brief periods at the end of 1475 and in December 1476. Zovenzoni's death, probably in March 1485, provides a *terminus ante quem* for the composition of his poems addressed to Rizzo: it is not possible to date them more precisely.[69]

Other testimony to Rizzo's intercourse with humanists comes from Pomponius Gauricus' *De sculptura* of 1504, in which Rizzo figures as the friend of Rafaello Regio and Niccolò Leonico Tomeo.[70] Regio (1436-1520) was professor of rhetoric at Padua between 1482 and 1486 and again, between 1503 and 1508. At Venice he published a commentary on the *Metamorphoses* of Ovid in 1492. He translated the works of St. Basilius and Plutarch from the Greek and wrote commentaries to Quintilian's *Institutiones* and the younger Pliny's letters.[71] Rizzo could have known Tomeo (1456-1531) at Venice too. Born there, the son of an Albanian who had taken refuge in Venice, Tomeo studied Greek in Florence at the school of Demetrio Calcondila. Becoming proficient in the language, Tomeo boldly undertook to explain the works of Aristotle on the basis

[67] Paoletti, fasc. I, 1894, pp. 15f.

[68] Lorenzi, 1868, p. 97, doc. 207.

[69] Ziliotto, 1950, pp. 45, 57. Rizzo figures in an elegy entitled *Epitaphium Cicilidis Virgunculae suae*: ". . . O facies qualem Pario de marmore Crispus / finxit, et huic similis Cynthia, dixit, erat." (Ibid., pp. 80f., no. 41.) The following distichs treat of Rizzo or his work. *Crispo Veronensi marmorario clarissimo*: "Marmore de Pario mortaria, Crispe, dedisti / haec mihi: disperam, ni tibi gratus ero." (Ibid., p. 91, no. 79.) *Crispo marmorario nobilissimo*: "Marmor erant homines inspecta Gorgone: mar-

mor / nos sumus inspecto marmore, Crispe, tuo." (Ibid., p. 105, no. 121.) *Antonio Crispo marmorario*: "Herculis effigiem mirans Antonius inquit: / Corpora do superis, dic tibi dent animam." (Ibid., p. 114, no. 151.) *Evae marmoreae laus*: "Si tua forma fuit quae marmore vivit in isto, / quoi mirum si vir paruit, Eva, tibi?" (Ibid., p. 116, no. 163.)

[70] Gauricus, (1504) 1969, pp. 15, 255: "Antonius crispus, qui cum uobis (Regio and Tomeo) fuit familiaritas."

[71] Tiraboschi, xvi, ²1823, pp. 1424-1429; Gauricus, (1504) 1969, p. 18.

of Greek texts. To that end he was called to Padua in 1497, where he remained until 1504 (or 1507). His writings include translations of works by Aristotle and Proclos as well as poems in Italian. Marcantonio Michiel described the works of art he assembled at Padua. They included the Joshua roll, several works of classical antiquity, and a painting by Jan van Eyck.[72]

Gauricus also reported an event in which Rizzo confessed himself surpassed by a younger artist's skill. An entablature carved with foliate ornament by Tullio Lombardo was borne in triumph through the streets of Treviso. Drawn thither by the fame of the work and by his rivalry with Tullio's father Pietro, Rizzo was astonished by the precision of its carving and avowed that never before had entablatures been made like sword hilts, as Tullio had done. What greater marvel could compare to that, concluded Gauricus, than that Tullio's sculpture should deceive the most expert artist?[73] Although the story seems too pat a rhetorical device for enhancing Tullio's stature,[74] it may conceal a grain of truth. For of all Venetian sculptors, only Tullio exercised any influence on Rizzo, and although short-lived, that influence was extraordinarily profound.

Fifteen or twenty years younger than Rizzo, Tullio made his debut toward 1475 alongside his younger brother Antonio in the sculpture of the presbytery of S. Giobbe: the hands of the two apprentices can be distinguished in the *Evangelists* of the pilasters of the triumphal arch.[75] Francesco Sansovino recorded the participation of Tullio and Antonio in the carving of Pietro Lombardo's Tomb of Doge Pietro Mocenigo, finished by 1481;[76] their respective contributions have never been defined. During the later 1480s Tullio executed most of the figurative carving in S. Maria dei Miracoli. The two reliefs of scenes from the life of St. Mark on the facade of the Scuola di S. Marco, which Sansovino correctly assigned to Tullio,[77] probably date from 1489-90. In 1493 Tullio's Tomb of Doge Andrea Vendramin was under construction in S. Maria dei Servi.[78] Between 1495 and 1509 both Tullio and Antonio collaborated with their father in the decoration of the Cappella Giustiniani in S. Francesco della Vigna.[79]

Tullio's was a style that adhered to the letter of antique sculpture. In this it recalls the art of other north Italians—Antico, Moderno, Andrea Riccio—who aimed to mirror the external aspect of antique art rather than assimilate its principles, like their Florentine and Roman peers. In Tullio's sculpture the figure is abstracted and idealized: the larger stereometric form invariably takes precedence over details of anatomy. Surfaces are smooth—evenly rounded in statuary, flat in low relief. Two-dimensional patterns are

[72] Tiraboschi, xviii, ²1824, pp. 560-563; Gauricus, (1504) 1969, p. 17.

[73] Ibid., p. 255: "Sed ne ego Tullium praeterierim illaudatum? Equidem ni uererer uisum iri amiciciae, non uerae laudi datum iudicium de illo meum, dicerem profecto scalptorum omnium quos ulla unquam uiderit aetas praestantissimum, neque indignis ornaretur honoribus, An quid non priora ingenia, priora et miracula rediere? Circumferebantur in pompae morem Taruisii epistyliorum coronae quas ille iunior uarii intercelarat foliorum ornamentis, Aderat Crispus partim aemulacione quam cum patre Tullii gerebat, partim et tantae nouitatis fama permotus. Cunctis igitur admirantibus, qui tanta ueritate fieri potuerit? nunquam prius e marmore co-ronas factas fassus est quam gladiolo id ita esse deprehenderit, Quod mirius miraculum huic comparari poterit? Prudentissimum artificem Tullii celatura deceptum."

[74] Although the circumstances differed, the competition between the painters, Zeuxis and Parrhasios, described by Pliny the Elder, *Historia naturalis*, xxxv, 65, also ended with the deception of an expert.

[75] Schulz, *Antichità viva*, Mar.–Apr. 1977, pp. 35f.

[76] Sans., 1581, p. 18v.

[77] Ibid., p. 102r.

[78] Sheard, *Yale Ital. Studies*, 1977, p. 256.

[79] Schulz, *Antichità viva*, Mar.–Apr. 1977, pp. 29ff.

consistently regular, closed, continuous—as even, in their way, as surfaces. Drapery produces linear, schematic patterns, which serve to generalize the underlying anatomical forms. Figures conform to one type: members of a single race are not differentiated by facial type, proportions, costume. The pervasiveness of Tullio's influence must have been partly due to the ease with which the style, if not the quality, of Tullio's sculpture could be imitated. From the end of the 1470s until the middle 1480s Tullio's example so transformed Rizzo's art that one of Rizzo's works—the figure of *Charity* from the Tron Tomb (Figs. 87-90)—has been attributed to Tullio.[80] In Rizzo's wake came almost all the sculptors of Tullio's generation: his brother Antonio reacting to the early influence of his father, then Pyrgoteles, Alessandro Leopardi, Paolo Savin. The authority of Tullio's work imposed on Venetian sculpture of the end of the Quattrocento and the beginning of the Cinquecento an ineluctable standard: like the Gothic International Style seventy years earlier, Tullio's classicistic style was applied so consistently that, with few exceptions, the products of different sculptors can hardly be distinguished.

In the generalization of form, in the perfect stereometry of heads and folds, in the uniformity of textures, and the closed, smoothly curving contours, the style of Antonello da Messina resembles that of Tullio Lombardo. It is no wonder then that Rizzo should have been attracted to Antonello's painting when under Tullio's spell. Antonello is documented in Venice between 1475 and 1476; by March 1476 he had almost finished the *Sacra conversazione* commissioned by Pietro Bon for an altar of S. Cassiano (Fig. 225).[81] Antonello's art, like that of Tullio, was first transmuted by Rizzo in figures for the Tron Tomb executed at the end of the 1470s. Under the influence of Antonello, the violent expressions and highly charged movement of Rizzo's early Pollaiuolesque figures gave way to vacuous expressions and relaxed states bordering on lassitude. Facial types were significantly altered in the direction of Antonello's rotund heads. Antonello's death in the second half of February 1479 apparently coincided with the first appearance of his influence in Rizzo's work. It is no wonder then that the painter's death should have so afflicted Rizzo that a century later Rizzo's grief was still remembered.[82]

Though very different in style to the works of Tullio and Antonello, Verrocchio's Monument of Bartolommeo Colleoni (d. 1475) (Fig. 226) also finds an echo in Rizzo's work. By a bequest of 100,000 ducats to be used by Venice in the war against the Turks, Colleoni had insured the erection there of a memorial to himself.[83] In July 1479 the Senate ordered the executors of Colleoni's legacy to commission a bronze equestrian statue of the captain.[84] It seems that a competition was announced. In July 1481 a model was being sent from Florence[85] and by May 1483 three of the competing models were on view.[86] The commission was awarded to Verrocchio. By his death in June 1488 new clay models of horse and rider had been made, but casting had not commenced.[87] This was eventually entrusted to Alessandro Leopardi, and on March 21, 1496, the equestrian portrait was unveiled.[88] From a model by Verrocchio for the portrait of Colleoni, Rizzo

[80] Pincus, *AB*, 1969, p. 253, n. 33.
[81] Beltrami, *Arch. stor. dell'arte*, 1894, p. 57, doc. II.
[82] Vas./Mil., ii, (1568) 1878, pp. 572f.: "Rincrebbe la morte d'Antonello a molti suoi amici: e particolarmente ad Andrea [*sic*] Riccio scultore, che in Vinezia nella corte del palazzo della Signoria lavorò di marmo le due statue, che si veggiono ignude, di Adamo e di Eva, che sono tenute belle."
[83] Belotti, ²1933, pp. 419, 443.
[84] Cicogna, ii, 1827, p. 298.
[85] Passavant, 1959, pp. 228f., doc. xxxii; Covi, *AB*, 1966, p. 98.
[86] Faber, i, (1483-84) 1843, pp. 95f.
[87] Paoletti, 1893, ii, p. 264, n. 8.
[88] Sanudo, *Diarii*, i, 1879, coll. 96f.

took the scowl and roiled surface of the face of his *Effigy of Giovanni Emo* (Figs. 143, 144). Among Rizzo's autograph works, the style of Emo's portrait is unique.

In 1497 Rizzo assisted the Lombard sculptor, Gian Cristoforo Romano, in obtaining emery and Carrara marble for the decoration of the Studiolo of Isabella d'Este at Mantua.[89] It is the only irrefragable case of Rizzo's involvement in the purchase and the sale of stone, beyond acquisitions of Istrian limestone for the Ducal Palace. Paradoxically, it proves that Rizzo was not commercially active in the trade of stone. For rather than provide the stone himself, Rizzo only helped to locate a supply—far easier to do for him, with his many contacts as *protomaestro* of the Ducal Palace, than for a foreigner. Indeed, those references, found repeatedly among the documents concerning Pietro Lombardo or Giovanni Buora, to the sale of dressed or unsquared stone for projects on which the stonecarvers were not professionally engaged, are entirely missing from Rizzo's biography.

On September 14, 1483, fire destroyed most of the Palazzo del Doge in the east wing of the Ducal Palace.[90] By the end of 1484 Rizzo had been placed in charge of its reconstruction.[91] The northern half of the east wing, with the ducal apartments on the third floor and the Senato and Collegio on the fourth floor, was completed between that date and Rizzo's flight from Venice in April 1498. The Scala dei Giganti, which gave access to the east wing, begun ca. 1490, was in use by 1497.[92] The extension of the east wing southward to the southwest corner of the palace, on the other hand, was hardly more than started; it would not be finished for another fifty years.

Between 1484 and 1498 Rizzo's activity centered in the Ducal Palace. As *protomaestro*, he was responsible for its design, for the procurement of material, and for supervision of the work. With his own hands he executed almost all the reliefs of the Scala dei Giganti (Figs. 173-184), delegating to assistants only four out of the eight *Victories* (Figs. 195, 196, 199, 202) and one of the lesenes. For the *rio* facade of the Ducal Palace he provided a relief of *putti* supporting the *stemma* of the reigning doge, Marco Barbarigo (Fig. 155), and for one of the ducal chambers, a relief of the *Madonna and Child* (Fig. 161). In 1485 Rizzo claimed that the burden of work at the Ducal Palace had forced him to abandon his shop and neglect his other commissions.[93] In fact, only three other works—a relief of the *Madonna and Child* now in Vaduz (Fig. 160), a *vera da pozzo* in the *cortile* of Palazzo Decazes (Fig. 194) and the *Angel* in the Ca' d'Oro, from a lost and unidentified monument (Figs. 185-189), can be assigned to the final period of Rizzo's career.

The style of the few late works of sculpture indicates a repudiation of Tullio's influence and a partial reversion to earlier artistic norms. The movement of the Ca' d'Oro *Angel* is most like that of *Adam*; the facial type of the Madonna in the relief of the Camera degli Scarlatti finds its nearest analogue in *Eve*. In what is probably his final work—the *Victory* with laurel branch and apple from the Scala dei Giganti (Fig. 198)—Rizzo introduced into relief the effects of atmospheric perspective by streamlining forms and muting contrasts of light and shade. This innovation was adopted by Pietro Lombardo in his relief of the *Madonna and Child with Doge Loredan* in the Camera degli

[89] See App., p. 138.
[90] Sanudo, *Vite dei dogi* in Lorenzi, 1868, pp. 92f., doc. 198.
[91] Paoletti, 1893, ii, p. 144.

[92] Sanudo, *Diarii*, i, 1879, coll. 821f. See below, ch. 5, p. 90.
[93] Lorenzi, 1868, p. 97, doc. 207.

Scarlatti of the Ducal Palace[94] and by Giambattista Bregno in his statues of *Angels* from S. Maria dei Servi.[95]

In 1496 two senators were empowered to review the disbursement of funds for construction of the Ducal Palace.[96] An extraordinary sum had been spent and the senate appears to have suspected malversation. Indeed, by falsifying accounts, Rizzo had embezzled over 10,000 ducats. Stonemasons who had worked with him were implicated. Warned of his impending discovery, Rizzo sold all his goods and property in April 1498 and fled to the Romagna.[97] In February 1499 Rizzo was present in Cesena.[98] From there, it seems, he traveled to Ferrara.[99] On May 4, 1499, the sculptor was still alive.[100] Nothing further is heard of him. Probably he did not survive his disgrace by long.

Rizzo's name is recorded by more contemporary authors than that of any other Venetian sculptor of the fifteenth century. In his official history of Venice, published in 1487, Marc'Antonio Sabellico declared that the statues of *Adam* and *Eve* were the work of "Antonio Rizzo, the best sculptor of our time."[101] Luca Pacioli listed Rizzo among the worthy architects and marble sculptors of Venice as one who had "adorned the Ducal Palace with all sorts of figures."[102] The story of the rebuilding of the east wing of the Ducal Palace under Rizzo's supervision, the artist's defalcation and his flight to the Romagna, was told by Marin Sanudo and Domenico Malipiero.[103] Yet for the next two and a half centuries all memory of Rizzo vanished. Rizzo's *Adam* and *Eve* were regularly ascribed to the Paduan sculptor of the early sixteenth century, Andrea Riccio.[104] It was Andrea Riccio whom Vasari anachronistically had mourn the death of Antonello da Messina.[105] Paolo Giovio seems to have conflated not only Antonio Rizzo and Andrea Riccio, but also the Quattrocento Lombard sculptor active at Rome, Andrea Bregno.[106] The confusion of Rizzo and Riccio was facilitated by the identity of surname: both mean curly-haired—one in Venetian dialect, the other in Italian—and both artists are generally called Crispus by Latin writers. But while this may explain the failure of Vasari, relatively uninterested in, and ill-informed about Venetian art, to distinguish the two sculptors, it does not explain the blunder of Francesco Sansovino, son of the sculptor and architect Jacopo and author of a guidebook to Venice that was not superseded until the nineteenth century. How is it that Sansovino failed to read the inscription on the base

[94] Schulz, *Antichità viva*, Mar.–Apr. 1977, pp. 37f.

[95] Schulz, *BJ*, 1980, pp. 196f.

[96] Lorenzi, 1868, pp. 115f., doc. 240.

[97] Sanudo, *Diarii*, i, 1879, coll. 927f.; Sanudo, *Vite dei dogi* in Lorenzi, 1868, p. 93, doc. 198; Malipiero, *Arch. stor. ital.*, 1844, pt. 2, p. 674.

[98] Grigioni, *L'arte*, 1910, p. 45.

[99] Ibid., p. 44.

[100] Paoletti, 1893, ii, p. 148, n. 1.

[101] Sabellico, 1487, dec. 3, bk. 9, n.p.: "Antonii Crispi statuarii nostra tempestate optimi."

[102] Pacioli, 1494, Dedication to Guidobaldo, duke of Urbino, n.p.: "E in vinegia. del degno de marmi sculptore e architetto. Antonio rizzo. nello excelso ducal palazzo. de tutte sorte figure adorno. ala giornata el rendan chiaro."

[103] Sanudo, *Diarii*, i, 1879, coll. 927f.; Sanudo, *Vite dei dogi*, in Lorenzi, 1868, p. 93, doc. 198; Malipiero, *Arch. stor. ital.*, 1844, pt. 2, pp. 673f.

[104] Vas./Ricci, (1550) 1927, ii, p. 95; Vas./Mil., ii, (1568) 1878, pp. 572f.; Giovio, 1784, p. 233, "Ricci, Andrea," quoting an unpublished manuscript by Paolo Giovio (1484-1552); Guisconi [Sans.], 1556, n.p. [p. 6]; Sans., 1581, pp. 119rf.; Scardeone, 1560, p. 375.

[105] See above, n. 82.

[106] In a poem dedicated to "Ricci, Andrea," the author of *Adam* is said to have been born at Como—the diocese to which the birthplace of Bregno, as recorded in his epitaph in S. Maria sopra Minerva in Rome, belonged: "Un Riccio nel contato all'età nostra / Nacque di Como, che fu buon scultore, / Et l'opre di costui Venetia mostra; / Fece un Adamo, ch'è di tal valore, / Che di bellezza cogli antichi

of *Eve* and was so unfamiliar with the master's work that he gave the documented east wing of the Ducal Palace and the standing effigy of Tron to a mythical Antonio Bregno, fabricated seemingly for the occasion?[107] Can Rizzo's embezzlement of government funds and escape from punishment by flight have incurred the penalty of the deliberate suppression of his name? It would seem to have been so.

giostra.'' (Giovio, 1784, p. 233.) For Giovio's conflation of the three sculptors, see Schulz, *NdiGF*, 1978, p. 53.

[107] Sans., 1581, pp. 119v, 120r, 66r. For Sansovino's invention of Antonio Bregno, see Schulz, *NdiGF*, 1978, pp. 52f.

The Altars of S. Marco and Other Early Works

ANTONIO RIZZO's first documented works are the three altars erected at the behest of Doge Cristoforo Moro (1462-71) in the Venetian Basilica di S. Marco (Figs. 1, 2, 10). All are inscribed with the doge's name and titles. The year 1465, on the relief of the Altar of St. Clement, presumably records the completion of that work. All three altars were finished by June 28, 1469, when Rizzo acknowledged receipt of 35 ducats as the remainder due him for work on them.[1] The date of the commission is not preserved. It is unlikely that Moro's munificent donation to the ducal chapel antedates his accession to the ducal throne.

The dedication of the Altars of SS. Paul and James reflects the celebration, observed at S. Marco from its foundation, of the Apostles in addition to St. Mark. The church possessed the relics of SS. Paul and James, among those of the other Apostles.[2] A fourteenth-century missal of S. Marco included masses for the feast days of SS. James and Paul, as well as for the feast of the Conversion of St. Paul.[3]

The Altars of SS. Paul and James are located in the north and south transepts, respectively, at the eastern crossing of nave and transept; both face west. That of St. Paul may have replaced one erected on the same site over a hundred years earlier.[4] That of St. James occupies the site of the miraculous discovery of St. Mark's body in 1094.[5]

The two altars form a pair in appearance as well as location. Antependia, balustrades, and dossals are structurally identical; the reliefs of the lunettes correspond; the stances of the *Apostles* are inverted. Differences between the two altars reside chiefly in the treatment of altar frontal and ornamental details. In both, the Renaissance tabernacle serves as structural framework for the altar: the Altars of SS. Paul and James are among the earliest examples of its use in the context of an altar.[6] Given its classic formulation,

---

[1] ASV, Cancelleria inferiore, Busta 212 (Notaio Tomaso de Tomasi), c. 8v: "1469 Mensis Junij die 28 indictione secunda, Rivoalti. Ser Antonius Rizo lapicida de confinio Sancti Johannis Novi cum heredibus et successoribus etc. suis rogavit securitatem illustrissimo et excellentissimo principi et domino domino Christoforo Mauro inclito duci Venetiarum et successoribus suis de ducatis XXXV auri pro resto et completa solutione omnium laboreriorum per ipsum factorum circha tria altaria in ecclesia S. Marci et de omnibus et singulis quae quomodocumque agere secum habuit ab initio usque in presentem diem. Nunc autem etc.

Testes venerabilis presbiter Paulus Benedicto S. M. Iubanico plebanus et cancellarius et Johannes Bernardus de Calleotis gastaldio."

[2] Demus, 1960, pp. 7f.

[3] Tramontin in Tramontin et al., 1965, pp. 279f.

[4] Sans., 1581, p. 36r; Gradenigo, (1748-74) 1942, p. 132, Mar. 13, 1766.

[5] Stringa, *Vita di S. Marco*, 1610, p. 57r.

[6] J. Braun, 1924, ii, p. 369, cited only one earlier example of the tabernacle-retable—the retable in the sacristy of S. Maria in Monserrato, Rome, inscribed with the year 1463. Ghiberti's frame for Fra Angelico's Linaiuoli Triptych, Museo di S. Marco, Flor-

probably by Brunelleschi in the early 1420s, the tabernacle had been employed frequently in Florence in tombs and as frames for niches and tabernacles of the sacrament by the third quarter of the century. Its adoption for an altar was foreshadowed by Masaccio's fresco of the *Trinity*. In Venice, the earliest conjunction of pilasters supporting entablature and semicircular lunette is found in the Cenotaph of Federico Cornaro in S. Maria dei Frari, probably carved in the mid-1450s.[7] There, as in the Altars of S. Marco, pilasters are adorned with tendrils that approximate the shape of candelabra.[8] The ornament of Rizzo's altars, however, is closest to that of the wooden frame of Giovanni Bellini's Altarpiece of St. Vincent Ferrer in SS. Giovanni e Paolo (Figs. 3, 16, 203), to the shafts of the main pilaster order in the lower tier and the shafts of the pilasters of the upper tier, to the upper capitals and the spandrels below.[9] The dating of the Altar of St. Vincent Ferrer, work on which was underway on January 6, 1464,[10] does not permit the determination of precedence. Very likely, one or the other or both ultimately derived from the Tabernacle of the Sacrament carved by Desiderio da Settignano and immured in S. Lorenzo, Florence, in 1461.[11] The balustrades that narrowly flank the S. Marco altars, advancing to the foremost plane of the respective tables whose height they match (Figs. 1, 2), are typically Venetian.[12] In the antependium of the Altar of St. James (Fig. 1), the suspended bunches of fruit and paterae look classical but have no antique prototype.[13]

The verticality of the tabernacles' proportions (Figs. 1, 2) can be paralleled in other Italian works of the 1460s: Desiderio da Settignano, for instance, invariably elongated compositions borrowed from Bernardo Rossellino. The verticality of Rizzo's tabernacles is due less to the elongation of the pilasters than to the heightening of the entablatures—cornices especially—and to the advance of every element in the vertical sequence of the tabernacle's outer frame. Pilasters at either side project so much that they are exactly square in plan; shallow niches fail to counterbalance the assertiveness of piers. Indeed, the niches do not suffice to contain the statues in their entirety.

Characteristic of Rizzo's architecture are its sharp edges—the inevitable result of the juncture of flat surfaces at an angle of ninety degrees. Edges are predominantly straight. Capitals are cubic and ornament rarely turns a corner. Individual fields, like the shafts of pilasters or the frieze of the projecting portion of the base, are definitively framed by fillets. Surfaces are planar: niches are flattened; columns are eschewed; relief is low, and flutes are shallow. Ornament is dispersed with equal density over almost every surface of the altarpiece: even the inner lateral faces of the pilasters are carved. Rizzo's ornament is typically linear and open, composed of attenuated tendrils executed on a scale, and with a precision, appropriate to objets d'art (Figs. 3, 6, 9). The absence of any dominating element which, as unequivocal focus, might control and unite the diverse elements of the altar, is a frequent failing of Rizzo's works. The minor order is as closely allied with the major order as with the figure it is intended to enclose. Large free-

ence, employs the format of a tabernacle, but the vocabulary of its components is not yet fully Renaissance.

[7] Schulz, *NdiGF*, 1978, p. 6.
[8] Pincus, 1974, pp. 176f.
[9] Keydel, 1969, p. 99.
[10] Fogolari, *Dedalo*, xii, 1932, pp. 388f.
[11] Moreni, i, 1816, p. 15, n. 1.

[12] J. Braun, 1924, ii, p. 661. Other examples are in SS. Giovanni e Paolo, S. Maria Formosa, and S. Canciano.
[13] Paoletti, 1893, ii, p. 160, perceived a resemblance to the bunches of fruit on the approximately contemporary Tomb of Antonio Roselli by Pietro Lombardo in the Santo, Padua.

standing *putti* at the top of the altars compete with the saints rendered in slightly smaller scale. Dwarfed by the large and strongly projecting order, *SS. Paul* and *James* seem hardly of sufficient moment to have occasioned so monumental a frame.

Minor improvements in the Altar of St. Paul suggest that it is the later of the two. Its frieze was heightened at the expense of its architrave, limited now to two fasciae. Below the entablature, *rinceaux* were slightly enlarged in scale and reduced in number. In the Altar of St. James, the finicky bead-and-reel moldings that Rizzo inserted within the borders of the shafts of the large pilasters were replaced by plain strips in the Altar of St. Paul; it was in the lateral faces of the pilasters of the Altar of St. James that Rizzo seems to have lost patience (Fig. 9). More important still, *St. Paul* is larger than *St. James*. Inverted, *Paul*'s scallop shell provides a canopy.

A comparison of the two saints supports this relative dating. The figure of *St. James* (Fig. 3) is conditioned by the limitations of the form, massiveness, and axiality of the cubic block from which it comes. The figure is posed frontally. Its head is rigidly upright and limbs and torso hardly tilt. Contours are continuous, closed, and straight, and produce a rectangular silhouette. Drapery and limbs adhere to the body; concavities barely penetrate the surface. Even hand and book are parallel to the frontal plane. The forward face of the figure, preserved intact, is articulated by folds as linear, attenuated, and open, as minute and uniform in scale, and as evenly distributed over the entire surface, as the pattern of tendrils on the shafts of the pilasters.

By contrast, the pose of *St. Paul* (Fig. 6) involves a moderate torsion in which the orientation of leg and head are narrowly opposed. The unequal distribution of weight, apparent already in the figure of *St. James*, correctly results in a tilting of *St. Paul*'s pelvis. Folds of drapery converge over the weight-bearing hip. It is here that Rizzo placed the book which *St. Paul* reads intently. The frontal plane is qualified now by the projection of lower arms, hands and book, and knee. Hollows between folds are more deeply excavated. The contours of the figure are more varied, more broken—they do not follow so loyally the articulation of the niche. Axes of shoulders, head, the features of the face, are independent of architectural lines.

Proportions, too, have changed. *St. Paul*'s head has become smaller, his shoulders and torso broader, his limbs longer, his feet larger. Drapery marks the major divisions of the body and reveals more completely the contours of underlying forms. Where the taut folds of *St. James*'s drapery complement the rigidity of his stance, the swing of *St. Paul*'s folds echoes his suppler ponderation.

Were it not that traits from the heads of the two saints recur equally in later works by Rizzo, one would be tempted to attribute each to different sculptors. The transfixed stare and slackly opened mouth of *St. James* (Fig. 4), suggestive of a waking dream, give way in the head of *St. Paul* (Fig. 5), to an intelligent concentration on an object outside the self. In the head of *St. James* features are much larger in scale and precisely outlined by sharply incised grooves or narrow, raised borders. The symmetry of *St. James*'s face contrasts with the skewing of *St. Paul*'s nose and the leftward shift of the central axis of his mouth as compensation for the turn of the figure's head. The locks of the beards follow similar paths, but the strands of *St. Paul*'s beard are differentiated plastically.

Common to both figures (Figs. 3, 6) is a highly mannered treatment of folds: in neither is the pattern conditioned by the imagined cut or fabric of the garment. Folds are composed of narrow, tubular ridges, which, pinched here, bulging there, frequently change their three-dimensional form. Paths are arbitrarily irregular—now curved, now straight, now long, now short: as though immune to the effects of gravity, ridges writhe and squirm, shifting direction constantly. Folds are approximately uniform in size and degree of projection and uniformly corrugate the figure. Against the complications of the drapery, faces are reduced to insignificance.

Drapery such as this cannot be paralleled in the work of any marble sculptor of the time. It is found only in bronze sculpture where preliminary modeling in wax favored the elaboration of folds. Similar passages of drapery occur in the *Virtues* of the Baptismal Font in S. Giovanni, Siena, by Giovanni Turini and Goro di Neroccio (Fig. 207). The drapery style of these *Virtues* was inspired by Donatello's *Virtues* for the font. In their attempt to imitate the new style, which replaced Ghiberti's mellifluous rhythms with turbulent, rutted surfaces, Donatello's Sienese followers invented drapery as full of quirks and kinks as Rizzo's.

It is most unlikely that Rizzo knew the works of Giovanni di Turino or Goro di Neroccio. Donatello's works, however, must have been familiar. The statues of the High Altar of the Santo at Padua, particularly that of *St. Justina* cast by May 27, 1448 (Fig. 208), possess drapery whose folds betray a similar redundancy and derangement. Early paintings in the Ovetari Chapel—Andrea Mantegna's *SS. Peter* and *Paul* in the vault of the apse, begun by September 27, 1449 (Fig. 205), and Niccolò Pizzolo's *St. Gregory*, completed by 1453 (Fig. 206)—are indebted for their drapery style to *St. Justina* and its companions. Not unexpectedly, the drapery of these frescoed figures resembles the drapery of Rizzo's *Paul* and *James* as nearly as the difference of medium allows. So too does the drapery of figures by Marco Zoppo in a sketch of ca. 1465-75 (Fig. 204) and the polyptych of S. Clemente del Collegio di Spagna at Bologna. Like Mantegna and Pizzolo, Zoppo was a pupil of Francesco Squarcione at Padua; present in Squarcione's shop between ca. 1453 and 1455, he had ample opportunity to know the Paduan works of Donatello. Thus the source of the drapery style of Rizzo's *SS. James* and *Paul* can be localized in Padua between the end of the 1440s and the early 1450s. By 1455 the style had been superseded: Mantegna's later frescoes in the Ovetari Chapel introduced a type of drapery in which a sheer and clinging cloth explicitly diagrams the anatomy and volume of the figure. Although this style of drapery was extremely influential in Venetian sculpture of the late 1450s and 1460s, Rizzo's style was not affected by it.

Also in its abnormally large head and short legs and torso, *St. James* resembles the standing *Saints* of the High Altar of the Santo. Chest and shoulders of all are very narrow. In the case of Donatello's figures, this contraction probably was necessitated by the compact grouping of the figures on the altar. Their placement also must account for the adherence of arms to bodies. Though not subject to the same constraint of siting, Rizzo adopted the cramped gestures of Donatello's figures with the same adverse consequence—that arms appear too short.

Do the similarities between the earliest works of Rizzo and the Paduan sculpture of Donatello warrant the supposition that Rizzo was trained by Donatello? I think not. Very little sculpture was executed in stone in Donatello's Paduan shop, yet there is no evidence that Rizzo ever worked in any other medium. Under Donatello, Rizzo's obsessive execution of architectural detail would have been emphatically discouraged. Elementary errors in the portrayal of the mechanics of a contrapposto pose and the radical and sudden change in Rizzo's canon of proportions suggest, rather, the random experimentation of an artist who lacks an authoritative guide. The timidity with which Rizzo approached the block of stone from which he carved *St. James* and the rapidity with which he overcame his diffidence show that Rizzo had had little experience in figurative carving when he broached the commission for Doge Moro. What he subsequently learned he probably taught himself.

By contrast, the decorative detail of the Altars of SS. Paul and James is a paragon of craftsmanship. Indeed, the orthodox combination of classical members and ornament places the altars at the forefront of contemporary Venetian architecture. It would seem, therefore, that Rizzo was well trained in carving architectural detail. There is no reason to suppose that this training did not take place in Verona, where Rizzo was born and where his father presumably dealt in stone (though it is likely that the technique acquired there was supplemented by theoretical knowledge gained at Padua and Florence). Not enough is known of Veronese sculpture in the 1440s and 1450s to permit the identification of Rizzo's teacher. Only Pietro di Antonio da Porlezza, documented at Verona from 1433,[14] is known for the carving of architectural ornament: between 1484 and 1485 Pietro executed the framework of the Altar of St. Vincent Ferrer in S. Anastasia.[15] Apart from the pavement of S. Anastasia, begun in 1462,[16] it is the only certain work by him extant. The style of its ornament does not resemble Rizzo's, but its quality is what we might expect of Rizzo's teacher. Be that as it may, a training largely confined to the carving of architectural details would explain Rizzo's belated mastery of sculpture.

Below the statue of St. Paul is a relief of the saint's conversion, as recounted in Acts 9:3-9 (Fig. 17). On his way to Damascus, Saul was blinded by a light from heaven. The voice of Christ, inaudible to his companions, was heard to say, "Saul, Saul, why persecutest thou me?" Saul fell to the ground. Three days later, his sight restored, the saint was baptized as Paul into the Christian church.

Unusual in the context of Venetian relief is the particularity of the account of the saint's conversion. Narratives are not common in Venetian relief of the early Renaissance; where they do occur a few figures generally fill the field. In the *Conversion of St. Paul*, on the other hand, the scale of the main figure is sufficiently reduced to permit the introduction of an extensive and detailed landscape. The rendering of costume is equally circumstantial and archaeologically correct: the attachment of the saint's cloak to his cuirass conforms to Roman dress and the horse's harness lacks saddle and stirrups. St. Paul is accompanied by two figures that are not immediately relevant to the story but amplify its resonance. In embedding the dramatic action within its material and human context, Rizzo surely was inspired by Florentine art, where Ghiberti and Donatello had made relief as flexible a medium for storytelling as the novella. Yet so far from exploiting the dramatic potential of the story, Rizzo's composition hardly makes the narrative intelligible. Neither soldier expresses surprise or awe. The direction of the saint's glance is diametrically opposed to the location of Christ's hand. The horse rears but St. Paul maintains as firm a seat as if the horse stood still.

The scene of the saint's conversion is executed in the extremely low relief called

---

[14] Brenzoni in *Arte e artisti*, 1959, i, p. 120.   [16] Cipolla, *L'arte*, 1914, pp. 186ff.

[15] Cipolla, *L'arte*, 1915, pp. 303f.

schiacciato, which Donatello had introduced about half a century before in *St. George and the Dragon* at Or San Michele. Rizzo's relief represents the earliest example of its use at Venice. The aim of this technique was to simulate painting by eliminating the normal contrast between figures and objects carved in more or less relief, and the flat, solid background against which they were set. No longer an impenetrable barrier, the background creates an illusion of depth by means of landscape forms and clouds lightly etched on it. The relative position of objects in space is registered by a gradual decrease in scale and height of relief, distinctness of delineation, and degree of detail. The walled town in the rearmost plane is so faintly sketched upon the background that it seems obscured by leagues of intervening haze. The *schiacciato* relief and atmospheric perspective, the dissolution of the ground by means of clouds, the low point of sight revealed by the descending orthogonal of the wall in the distance, and the overlapping of the horizon, suggest acquaintance with Donatello's relief of the *Ascension of Christ and the Delivery of the Keys* in the Victoria and Albert Museum, London. But the anomalous projection of foreground forms at either side of the relief is Rizzo's own mistake. The canted right edge of the relief destroys the illusion of limitless recession by providing an exact measure of the real depth of the relief.

In other respects, too, Rizzo's relief is archaic. Along the bottom, the barren, creviced ground presents a uniform vertical edge, as in Byzantine painting and its derivatives, thus dividing the fictive space from the real space of the spectator. The scale of trees and hills is too small; leaves and fruit are too large. The olive trees diminish in inverse perspective, growing smaller as they advance. Paul's horse, represented parallel to the relief ground, occupies the foremost plane of the relief.[17] Thus it negates the illusion of depth fostered by the setting.

Errors in the foreshortening of the farther leg and foot of the foremost striding soldier and the upper torso and shoulders of St. Paul prove that Rizzo's ambition to depict twisting movement exceeded his ability. The void made by the lowered arm and torso of St. Paul, the responsive silhouettes of the two soldiers, and the continuous contours of the horse produce elegant patterns at the expense of the illusion of recession. The meticulous portrayal of armor, saddle cloth, the horse's mane, the leaves of the olive tree, betrays the predilections of the professional carver of ornament. The *rinceaux* embroidered on the saddle cloth imitate the pattern on the pilaster shaft directly to the right of the relief.

The canon of the striding soldiers reflects the lithe ideal of Mantegna's Ovetari frescoes. As in the figures from *St. James Led to Execution* (Fig. 212), the heads of Rizzo's figures are very small. Extremely muscular backs produce bowed contours. Legs are very long and tapered; feet are small. In both, buttocks are represented as though the figures wore no clothes. The figure seen from the rear recalls, in pose and view, the soldier at the front of the picture space in the center of Mantegna's fresco; the resemblance is greater still to an earlier version of the figure in the preparatory drawing in the Gathorne-Hardy collection. For the breadth of St. Paul's shoulders and the muscularity of his torso Rizzo was also indebted to Mantegna. The head of the soldier to the rear, with its exaggerated twist and tilt, its prominent bony structure and square jaw,

[17] Its pose and view can be paralleled in several drawings by Jacopo Bellini: Goloubew, ii, 1908, pls. xxxviii, xlvii, lxiii, xc.

may derive from the figure in the fresco of St. James with which Mantegna paid homage to Donatello's statue of *St. George*.[18]

The design of St. Paul's fluttering cloak represents an alternative to the pattern of folds described by the garments of his free-standing counterpart, one that recurs throughout Rizzo's career. It consists of lanes of approximately equal-sized triangles serially over-lapped. This configuration reproduces a regular twisting of the cloth, back and forth. The final fold in each sequence curves outward at the border; the cloth is tucked under at each corner. Folds are pressed flat: not even the twisting of the cloth increases the volume.

The Altar of St. Clement is no longer in its original state (Fig. 10). The large votive relief with Doge Andrea Gritti (1523-38), by a sculptor not yet identified, comes from the Chapel of St. Nicholas in the Ducal Palace;[19] it was transferred to its present site at the beginning of the nineteenth century.[20] Rizzo's altar probably consisted of the three crowning units—the free-standing statues of *SS. Mark* and *Bernardino* and the relief of the *Madonna and Child*—as seventeenth- and eighteenth-century guides describe it.[21] As patron saint of Venice, St. Mark was also patron of the ducal basilica, while St. Bernardino was particularly venerated by Doge Moro. Moro had known the saint personally. In 1451, a year after Bernardino's canonization, Moro had had construction started, at his own expense, of a chapel at S. Giobbe dedicated to the saint. In 1470 St. Bernardino was inscribed among the protectors of Venice at the instigation of the doge.[22] Cristoforo Moro's *Promissione*, or covenant of office, was illuminated in 1463 by Leonardo Bellini with the *Madonna and Child Enthroned* between St. Mark on her right and St. Bernardino on her left.[23]

Stylistically, the statues of *SS. Mark* and *Bernardino* (Figs. 20-21) stand midway between the figures of *SS. James* and *Paul* (Figs. 3, 6). *SS. Mark* and *Bernardino* possess the large head and short body of *St. James*, but *Mark*'s larger feet correspond to *Paul*'s. While the poses of *Mark* and *Bernardino* are closer to the rigid stance of *St. James* than to the easy ponderation of *St. Paul*, the tentative thrust of *Mark*'s weight-bearing hip and the turn of both heads foretoken the animation of *St. Paul*. The cloaks of *SS. Mark* and *James* are draped over the left shoulder and arm like Roman togas, and the pattern of *Mark*'s folds derives from *James*, but folds are made to seem more salient by being undercut, as in the mantle of *St. Paul*. Free-standing hands, less even contours, and the deviation from strict frontality in the posing of the heads presage the figure's subsequent liberation from the limitations of the block.

In the central relief the Virgin stands behind a ledge, supporting the Christ Child, seated there on a cushion (Fig. 22). With his right extended arm he makes a gesture of salutation as though to greet the imaginary supplicant at whom the Virgin looks. Instead of a cloud-filled sky denoting heaven, the anomalous background consists of a coffered vault, curved at the edges, flattened in the center, employed as though it were a wall.

---

[18] Dunkelman, *AB*, 1980, p. 233.

[19] F. Saccardo in Ongania ed., *Basilica*, vi, 1888, pt. 3 [1893], p. 275.

[20] Maier, pt. 1, ²1795, p. 158; Moschini, 1815, i, pt. 1, pp. 310f.

[21] E.g. Meschinello, ii, 1753, p. 97: "L'Altare è di marmo fino, ed ha per pala una pia Immagine di Maria con il Figlio in braccio scolpita in basso rilievo, con S. Pietro e S. Clemente alli lati." The

mistaken names of the *Saints* are probably to be explained by the dedications to SS. Clement and Peter of the chapel in which the altar stood and of the chapel with which it was paired, at the east end of the church.

[22] Cicogna, vi, pt. 1, 1853, p. 530.

[23] London, British Museum, Add. MS. 15816. For the illumination, see Moretti, *Paragone*, 1958, no. 99, p. 58.

The coffers are not rendered in perspective: although the curvature of the transverse divisions between the coffers indicates a low point of sight, transverse lines are parallel throughout. The effect produced is that of a Gothic diapered background.

As in *mezzo rilievo*, the plasticity of forms is partially abridged: the Madonna's contours, for the most part, are contiguous to the ground and the surfaces of forms are slightly flattened. Occasionally the undercutting of silhouettes indicates spatial intervals between two planes. Heads are rounded most despite the fact that they do not occupy the foremost plane of the relief.

The pattern of folds, in which ridges cover the figure with a tangled skein of lines, is similar to that of *St. Paul*. The physiognomy and figure type of the Christ Child and the clinging, transparent garment, with its broad sash, recur in the *putti* from the top of the Altar of St. Paul (Figs. 14-16). The circular shape and pronounced tear duct of the Christ Child's widely opened eyes resemble the eyes of the Christ Child in Squarcione's *Madonna and Child* in Berlin.

At the Altar of St. James, the ends of the balustrade's two arms are crowned by small candelabra-bearing *Angels*. Though its surface is more worn, the *Angel* on the right (Figs. 24, 26, 27) is superior, not only to its mate (Figs. 23, 25, 28), but to every other figure on the altars. Probably it was carved last. In the right-hand *Angel*, perfect balance is maintained despite the body's rotation around a central vertical axis. The principle of rotation does not yet inform the planar movement of the left-hand *Angel*. Here Rizzo vainly sought the same effect by bending the central axis of the figure. The result is merely an unsteady pose in which the pit of the neck is not aligned with the heel of the weight-bearing foot, and the oblique axes of hips and shoulders do not diverge. The bowing of the lowered hand of the left *Angel* enfeebles its gesture in order to enhance its silhouette. One might suppose the figure to have been intended for this lateral view (Fig. 23), in which, moreover, the pattern of fluttering folds receives its fullest exposition and imbalances of pose are neutralized by foreshortening, were it not for the fact that the spectator then faces neither a straight edge of the *Angel*'s rectangular base nor a straight edge of the balustrade (it is curious that these straight edges do not align) and that the *Angel*'s most visible shoulder and upper arm are not entirely finished. It was not long before Rizzo realized that the siting of the *Angels*, in which only the inner rear quadrants are hidden, demanded attention to the design of sides as well as front. Therefore, the *Angel* on the right offers several satisfactory views, although one—that in which the torso is seen frontally, the face in three-quarter view—remains preeminent. Emblematic of the isolated station of the figure at the center of the observer's orbit is the right *Angel*'s circular base.

On the balustrade of the Altar of St. Paul are two candelabra-bearing *Angels*, dated on the basis of style to the late Trecento (Fig. 2),[24] but installed on the altar only in 1885.[25] Their original destination is unknown: apparently it was not the Masegnesque tabernacle next to the Chapel of St. Peter, from which they were taken when moved to the balustrade. Perhaps Rizzo used them, or others very similar, as finials for the balustrade of St. Paul. There is no record of candelabra-bearing *Angels* by Rizzo on the Altar of St. Paul, and his own *Angels* on the Altar of St. James match them very nearly in size, pose, and expression.[26]

[24] Wolters, 1976, i, p. 219, no. 140.
[25] P. Saccardo, *Arch. ven.*, xxxi, 1886, p. 502.

[26] On the balustrade of the Altar of St. Paul the left *Angel* measures 43.5 cm. high; the right *Angel*,

A few works can be associated with the documented altars of S. Marco. One of these—a relief of the *Madonna and Child* in a *tondo*—was in a private collection in Amsterdam in 1930 when it was published by Planiscig as a work of the Master of the S. Trovaso altar frontal (Fig. 29).[27] Its location cannot be traced. Photographs show its surface to be badly worn. The Madonna stands behind a ledge. The Child, steadied by his mother, stands on the ledge. With his right hand he blesses a hypothetical worshipper whom the Madonna greets. The relief is of moderate height. The surfaces of forms are flattened; boundaries are only occasionally undercut and no portion of the relief appears to be free-standing. Only the innermost moldings of the frame are overlapped. The Madonna and her counterpart in the Altar of St. Clement are dressed identically: note especially the draping of the double veils. In both, the sheer gowns reveal small, high, hemispherical breasts placed far apart. The ridges made by the folds of the Madonna's cloak are typical of Rizzo. The Virgin's hands in both reliefs are excessively large and betray the same inorganic attachment at the wrist. The faceting of the upper and lateral surfaces of widely separated fingers produces blocklike forms. The exaggerated contrapposto of the Christ Child and the slight torsion of his upper body suggest that the Amsterdam *tondo* is slightly later than the Altar of St. Clement.

The composition of the Amsterdam *tondo* derives from a relief of the *Madonna and Child* in half-length before a niche by a member of Donatello's Paduan workshop (Fig. 220),[28] or, more likely, from a lost original by the master himself. Numerous replicas of the relief testify to the composition's popularity.[29] From the Donatellesque relief Rizzo took the turn and tilt of the Madonna's head and the gesture of both hands. The atypical features of the Amsterdam Christ may be due to Rizzo's model. The infant, identically placed, stands on a parapet; legs are similar but upper torso and arms were changed. The clothing of the Christ Child and the celestial background are also new. In Rizzo's prototype the Christ Child repeats the gesture of his mother. Though Rizzo did not use it here, he did adopt the infant's gesture of acceptance for his relief from the Altar of St. Clement (Fig. 22).

The Amsterdam *tondo* is the only fifteenth-century Venetian relief known to me in which the half-length Madonna occupies a circular field. Indeed, the *tondo* was rarely used in Venice for reliefs of any subject. Independent circular images had to be hung and were therefore poorly adapted to the adornment of an altar; it is likely that *tondi* generally were intended for private homes. The private possession of reliefs does not appear to have been widespread in Venice in the later fifteenth century. To judge from the number of extant painted *Madonnas* in half-length, on the other hand, the private

41.8 cm. high. On the Altar of St. James the left *Angel* measures 49.5 cm. high; the right *Angel*, 49.3 cm. high.

[27] Planiscig, *Dedalo*, x, 1929-30, p. 468.

[28] Pope-Hennessy, 1965, p. 22, no. 60.

[29] Exemplars in bronze are in Berlin-Dahlem, Staatliche Museen, inv. no. 3044; London, Wallace Collection; Washington, D.C., National Gallery of Art, Kress Collection, no. 60. Marble reliefs are in the Vatican, Museo Cristiano and Orbignano (Pistoia), S. Maria. Stucco versions are in London, Victoria and Albert Museum, inv. no. 7385-1861; Budapest, Szépművészeti Múzeum, inv. no. 2049 and formerly New York, Raoul Tolentino Collection. A painted and gilded terracotta relief is in Paris, Louvre, inv. no. 704. (The most recent summary of the literature is contained in Berlin-Dahlem, Stift. Preuss. Kulturbesitz, Staatl. Mus. Catalogue ed. Metz, 1966, pp. 89f., no. 501, and Budapest, Szépművészeti Múzeum. Catalogue by Balogh, 1975, i, pp. 59f., no. 51.) In addition, a drawing attributed to Pisanello of just the *Madonna and Child* is in Chantilly, Musée Condé, no. 4 (Fossi Todorow, 1966, pp. 123f., no. 171v). I am grateful to Prof. Meller for identifying the source of the Amsterdam relief.

possession of devotional paintings was not uncommon. Yet they are never *tondi* either. By contrast, Florentine paintings and reliefs of the *Madonna and Child* were often circular in format. A number of such reliefs are attributed to the hand or school of Donatello; a Madonna in a *tondo* appears in the background of Donatello's *Miracle of the Speaking Babe* from the High Altar of the Santo. The inclusion of a *tondo* with the half-length Madonna in the lunettes of tombs, customary from the Tomb of Leonardo Bruni on, gave the composition currency in Florence.

Three figures of the Arco Foscari, the monumental gateway at the exit of the court-yard of the Ducal Palace, can be assigned to this early period of Rizzo's career. Neither the dating nor the authorship of the Arco Foscari or its decoration is documented (Fig. 31); the attribution of the twenty extant fifteenth-century statues that crown the pin-nacles, made difficult by their inaccessibility and poor condition, has rarely been at-tempted. Yet a close analysis of the statuary and architectural details, combined with a reading of the coats of arms, permits an adumbration of the Arco's history. Construc-tion of the Arco Foscari was probably initiated under Bartolomeo Bon during the prin-cipate of Doge Francesco Foscari (1423-57). Under Bon, the gateway rose in the east through the acanthus frieze of the second story; the statue of *Arithmetic*, I believe, is his.[30] When he died, probably in the second half of 1464, he was apparently succeeded by the master of the Foscari Tomb, whom I recently identified with Niccolò di Gio-vanni Fiorentino. Under Niccolò, the architecture of the east face of the Arco Foscari was completed (Fig. 30) and five more figures—*St. Mark*, the *Gorgon Warrior*, the *Moro Warrior*, *Music*, and *Rhetoric*—were added. The statue of *Doge Moro Kneeling before the Lion of St. Mark*, which originally rested on the platform above the opening to the eastern balcony, may also have been carved by Niccolò.[31] The precise duration of Nic-colò's tenure at the Ducal Palace, possibly as *protomaestro*, is not known. By the end of 1467 negotiations were underway for the construction and decoration of the Chapel of Beato Bishop Giovanni Orsini of Trogir in the Cathedral of that city—a project that was to occupy the remainder of Niccolò's life—and by the spring of 1468 Niccolò was definitively settled in Dalmatia. In the mid-1460s Rizzo might have assisted Niccolò Fiorentino at the Arco Foscari, but it is more likely that Rizzo was engaged only after Niccolò's departure. The earliest of the statues that Rizzo contributed to the Arco are stylistically akin to figures from the Altars of S. Marco and could well coincide with Niccolò's resignation, not later than spring 1468. Five later figures which seem to have been executed in Rizzo's shop in the first half of the 1480s suggest that Rizzo remained in charge of the Arco Foscari until the fire in the east wing of the Ducal Palace in September 1483 deflected work from it. By that time, the architectural facing of the second story on the south, with the arms of either Doge Pietro Mocenigo (1474-76) or Doge Giovanni Mocenigo (1478-85) (Fig. 31), was probably complete. In 1494 Luca Pacioli remarked the presence of many figures on the Arco Foscari.[32] Not more than two of the present number can have been missing. The *Caritas–Amor Dei* on the central pinnacle of the south face appears to have been furnished by the shop of Pietro Lom-bardo, who succeeded Rizzo as *protomaestro* of the Ducal Palace on May 16, 1498. *Pru-dence*, at the extreme right of the east face, is a work of 1725 by Antonio Corradini.

---

[30] Schulz, *TAPS*, 1978, pt. 3, pp. 51ff.
[31] Schulz, *NdiGF*, 1978, pp. 18ff.

[32] Pacioli, 1494, Dedication, n.p. See Intro., n. 102.

The statue of *Doge Pietro* or *Giovanni Mocenigo Kneeling before the Lion of St. Mark* above the southern balcony, undoubtedly executed in Rizzo's shop if not by Rizzo himself, like the statue of *Doge Moro*, probably was destroyed in 1797 after the fall of the Republic: no trace of it remains.

The statues of the Arco Foscari have lost almost all their original surface. Yet we can still discern the master's hand in the *Angel* on the pinnacle of the south face immediately to the right of the clock tower (Fig. 33). Despite its youth, its face is very similar to *St. James*'s (Fig. 4). The foreheads of both are broad and low and so flattened as to seem slightly concave. The long, low, straight brows, which enframe the entire upper contour of the eye, produce sharp ridges whose lower slopes are slightly undercut. A fold of flesh overlaps the outer half of the upper lid. The accentuated curvature of the lids of wide-opened eyes and the large, distinct, prow-shaped tear duct are identical in both. In both, the rather flat eyeball contradicts the bulging lower lid, composed of a narrow, sharply defined rim and a large pouch beneath. In both, low but prominent cheekbones seem slung, like festoons, across the figures' cheeks. The noses of both are relatively short and straight. Lips, sharply defined by the undercutting of their borders, have a similar morphology.

Its frontality and rigid pose also link the statue to *St. James*. In both, the knees of the free legs turn in although the feet point out. The *Angel*'s hand conforms with the hands of the two Madonnas (Figs. 22, 29). The long garment, which enwraps the figure's feet, recurs in *St. Mark* from the Altar of St. Clement (Fig. 20). When new, the prominent ridges of the *Angel*'s skirt must have resembled the folds of *St. Paul*'s cloak (Fig. 6).

Slightly later than this *Angel* is a companion on the east face at the extreme left of the base of the main pyramid (Fig. 32). The figure is animated by the uneven division of weight between the legs, by the slight rotation from retracted foot to turned head, and by the momentary expression and focused glance. The unhappy expedient of supporting the figure's toes on shelves which protrude from the top of the base, used in the first *Angel* (Fig. 33), has been rejected. The breadth of shoulders, hips, and short neck, and the description of large, rounded, anatomical forms beneath adhering drapery, recall *St. Paul* (Fig. 6). The figure's dress, with its V-shaped neckline, is that of the left candelabra-bearing *Angel* from the Altar of St. James (Fig. 25). The pattern of folds over the knee and lower part of the weight-bearing leg is virtually the same as there. The *Angel*'s eyes and the hand that clutches at a fold, with its dislocated wrist and blocky fingers regularly spaced, are analogous to those of the Madonna from the Altar of St. Clement (Fig. 22).

A third figure that Rizzo contributed to the Arco Foscari in the late 1460s originally stood in the lower story of the structure, probably in the single niche that embellished the south face of the gateway before the demolition of the Scala Foscara necessitated the construction of a second niche to the left (Fig. 31). It is the so-called *Mars*, now removed to the interior of the Ducal Palace (Figs. 34-37, 44). Unlike the statues of the crowning of the Arco, it is made of white marble, not Istrian stone, which, more costly but less resistant, required a more sheltered situation. Though the *Warrior* cannot really be identified, its traditional name serves to distinguish it from the three *Warriors* that mount guard on the spires of the Arco Foscari, and we shall therefore retain it.

"*Mars*' " long hair and helmet with raised visor and the horse-head-shaped shield may come from Niccolò di Giovanni's *Moro Warrior*. Mantegna's S. Zeno Altarpiece, finished in 1459, on the other hand, supplied "*Mars'*" pose. From Mantegna's John the Baptist (Fig. 209) Rizzo took the awkward disposition of feet and legs and the excessive thrust of the weight-bearing hip. The anatomy of the statue's legs, their bony structure and musculature, graphically articulated by seams or grooves, finds its exact analogy in the legs of the painted Baptist. In both, the contours of calves and shins are pathologically bowed; knees are extremely bony and the thighs of free and engaged legs are flexed equally. Rizzo's assiduous description of the bony structure and musculature of "*Mars'*" torso makes no concession to the existence of a leather cuirass. Very likely "*Mars'*" anatomy was inspired by Donatello's *Crucified Christ* in the Santo at Padua (Fig. 210). So explicit a definition of the torso's anatomy is appropriate to a pose, like Christ's, which subjects the body to extraordinary tension. But "*Mars'*" is shown in a state of relaxation.[33] The gesture of "*Mars'*" left hand, which has no raison d'être in the context of the pose, derives from Donatello's so-called *Jeremiah* for the Campanile, a statue that Rizzo could have known at Florence.

Among Rizzo's works, *St. Paul* (Fig. 6) is most like "*Mars.*" Both are characterized by excessively broad shoulders spanned by an abnormally wide neck. Like "*Mars,*" *St. Paul* borrowed from Mantegna's Baptist the exaggerated thrust of the weight-bearing hip, the marked retraction of opposite hip and thigh, and the steep incline of the axis of the hips; unlike Mantegna's figure, the axis of the shoulders of Rizzo's statues hardly diverges from the axis of their hips. The folds made by the heavy, yet adherent, cloak of "*Mars*" are identical in style to those of *St. Paul* and the S. Clemente Madonna (Fig. 22), and resemble, more closely than any other work by Rizzo, the drapery of Mantegna's *St. Peter* (Fig. 205) and Pizzolo's *St. Gregory* (Fig. 206). Common to the heads of *St. James* and "*Mars*" (Figs. 4, 37) is the course of the low and flattened brows. In both, the brows are undercut by a narrow groove and the flap of flesh to which that groove belongs overlaps the outer part of the upper lid. The morphology of upper lips is similar and the lower lips of both are edged as though by cords. Incisions, by means of which the lips' texture was distinguished from that of the surrounding flesh, is found frequently in Rizzo's work, but, as far as I am aware, not in the work of any other Quattrocento sculptor.

"*Mars*" presents a more accurate account of Roman armor than any preceding work of Venetian sculpture; in this Rizzo proved himself Mantegna's heir. "*Mars'*" shield bears the head of the Medusa. In contrast to Niccolò di Giovanni's barefoot *Warrior*, "*Mars*" wears Roman sandals. Rizzo substituted pteryges with *putti*'s heads for the foliate ornament beneath the cuirass of Niccolò's figure and replaced the cloth skirt with proper, tassled strips. But the strips are made of chain mail, as they were in contemporary armor[34]—not leather, as in Roman armor. Nor is the fluted border of "*Mars'*" cuirass antique in origin.[35]

As in the *Conversion of St. Paul*, theme and interpretation are discrepant. "*Mars*" is unarmed and supports his shield with his right hand:[36] whatever he was meant to guard

---

[33] A copy of Mantegna's St. Christopher from the fresco of his martyrdom in the Ovetari Chapel reveals that Donatello's *Christ* had a similar effect on Mantegna's early anatomical drawing.

[34] See the effigy of Vittore Capello (d. 1467) from his tomb over the portal of S. Elena, Venice.

[35] For ancient cuirasses, see Vermeule, *Berytus*,

1959, pp. 1-82 and Vermeule, *Berytus*, 1964, pp. 95-110.

[36] In connection with this feature, Pohlandt, *BJ*, 1971, pp. 175ff., quoted a remark of Sans., 1581, p. 116v, regarding the statue of *S. Teodoro* on a column in the Piazzetta. For Sansovino, the shield held by *S. Teodoro* in the hand customarily used for attack

can have no need of protection now. His melancholy cast of countenance (Figs. 37, 44) jars with the conventional confidence of warrior or guardian. Within the history of the warrior's depiction, the face of "*Mars*" is unique; indeed, there is not another face in Rizzo's oeuvre that resembles it in type. The absence of idealization is unprecedented— not even Rizzo's portraits are as faithful. There is nothing martial or heroic in "*Mars*'" physiognomy; common standards of beauty do not obtain. As remarkable as the lack of idealization is the absence of deliberate expression. The features of the face are still and those devices—subtle alterations in the inclination of the lids or the protrusion of the brows—which had mimicked pathos since Hellenistic times, were eschewed. Yet the face of "*Mars*" eloquently expresses anxiety, fatigue, depression.[37] Not imposed by the sculptor from without, these saturnine traits must have been intrinsic to the features which the sculptor reproduced. Whose features were they? "*Mars*'" visage is that of a man between thirty and forty years old—the age Rizzo would have been when "*Mars*" was carved. Eyes focused, not at a distant object as in Donatello's militant *St. George*, but at something near at hand, are a hallmark of self-portraits. Such candid revelation of personality is rarely found outside autobiography and self-portraiture. In the morose lineaments of "*Mars*," I strongly suspect, Rizzo has left us a portrait of himself.

The statue of "*Mars*" is seriously flawed. Shoulders are too broad in relation to the narrow torso. The torso, particularly its lower half, is too long and is skewed to the left. The knee of the free leg is oddly placed. The profusion of bumps does not provide an accurate transcription of rib cage or stomach, but, rather, betrays that reluctance to leave any surface bare, evident in the drapery of *SS. Paul* and *James* (Figs. 3, 6) and the decoration of their tabernacles (Figs. 1, 2). The surface of the statue is so full of incident that no one part stands out as paramount. The excessive thrust of the pelvis was justifiable in Mantegna's *Baptist* (Fig. 209), where jutting hip provided support for arm and book. But in Rizzo's figure the movement of upper and lower body are unrelated: "*Mars*'" protruding hip defines a low center of gravity, as in a state of relaxation, while his arched back and raised thorax denote the elevation of the body's weight—a necessary prelude to movement. The gesture of the left hand has no reason; the expression of the face conflicts with the jaunty pose. Shield and visor, which could not be slipped down over the curls on the figure's forehead, are too small.

Yet despite its many defects, I do not think "*Mars*" is the work of an assistant. First, a master would not have delegated a statue such as "*Mars*." The use of marble and the setting of a niche confer upon the figure a status shared only by *Adam* and *Eve* at the Arco Foscari. Unlike the statues at the top of the structure, barely visible from the ground below, "*Mars*" was within easy view of a visitor to the Ducal Palace courtyard. The small scale on which the surface is carved and the extraordinary amount of detail contrast with the generalized treatment of the two *Angels* intended for pinnacles (Figs. 32, 33) and show, not only that Rizzo was aware of the greater visibility of the work, but that he overestimated the vision of his spectators. Second, "*Mars*'" flaws are not ones common to assistants, for there is nothing mechanical in the carving of its surface. Technical restrictions imposed by the material are now entirely overcome. The mass of

---

symbolized Venice's unwillingness to play the aggressor, but her readiness to defend herself when necessary. It is doubtful that this meaning was intended, either by the author of *S. Teodoro* or by Rizzo in "*Mars*."

[37] Noted also by Sheard, 1971, pp. 207f., and Pohlandt, *BJ*, 1971, pp. 179, 187.

the stone is perforated and internal contours are deeply undercut when elements are not actually free-standing. The front face of the original block can no longer be discerned, for forms inhabit every plane of depth. The constraints of the narrow, preexistent niche, and the plan and dimensions of the console which supports the statue's base, were boldly surmounted: the foot of *"Mars'"* free leg overhangs the base, while his shield, brought forward, overlaps the niche. Rather, like Mantegna's *St. Sebastian* in Vienna, *"Mars"* reveals an artist who sought to match, if not exceed, the achievements of the most advanced contemporary artists without a training adequate to his goals. In the depiction of the *Warrior*'s armor Rizzo was governed by a higher standard of archaeological accuracy than any that had obtained in Venetian sculpture up till then. In his description of anatomy, Rizzo emulated Donatello. In the figure's contrapposto Rizzo dramatized the disequilibria that endow the pose with the appearance of potential movement in the midst of actual repose. Rizzo's self-portrait in the *Warrior*'s disguise, if such it be, must have been intended as the culminating tour de force. In sum, the lapses in taste to which *"Mars"* testifies are surely due, not to the participation of an assistant, but to the extravagant bravura with which the debutant hoped, in the most prestigious commission he had received thus far, to impress his potential rivals and patrons.

CHAPTER TWO

Adam and *Eve* and
Related Works

Adam AND *Eve* (Figs. 39, 48) are Rizzo's masterpieces. That the artist himself perceived them as a test of competence passed successfully is suggested by the inscription of his name, ANTONIO · RIZO, on the base of *Eve*: it is the only instance in which the artist signed his name to sculpture. The figures are now installed in the Sala del Magistrato al Criminal in the Ducal Palace. Originally they occupied the niches in the lower story of the east face of the Arco Foscari—*Adam* on the left, *Eve* on the right. The spandrels of the arch that the statues flank bear the arms of Doge Francesco Foscari, who died in 1457. By then the niches undoubtedly were up, but the statues were not installed until later. How much later is a question that has not been resolved. Between 1485 and 1487 proofs of the statues' existence follow thick upon one another. An undated distich in praise of what is presumably our *Eve* must have been written by 1485, the probable death date of its author, Raffaele Zovenzoni.[1] In 1486 the statues were seen by Georges Lengherand.[2] In 1487 Marc'Antonio Sabellico published his *Res Venetae*, which contains specific mention of Rizzo's figures. But Sabellico's text implies that *Adam* and *Eve* had existed for some time. At the conclusion of his chronicle of Doge Cristoforo Moro's reign (1462-71), Sabellico wrote, "the interior part of the doge's vestibule, begun during the principate of Pasquale Malipiero [*sic*], was carried up to the summit under [Doge Moro]; where there are to be seen near the top a statue of him [Moro] of Parian marble and below that, two other statues of our first parents, the work of Anthony Rizzo, the best sculptor of our time."[3] Sabellico does not state that *Adam* and *Eve* were finished during the principate of Moro; on the other hand, he says nothing to contradict such an inference, which a reader might be led to make by the juxtaposition of the clauses. Nevertheless, we should hesitate to accept Sabellico's equivocal testimony in favor of an early date for *Adam* and *Eve* were it not that all stylistic indices point to a date in the early 1470s.

Though abstracted from their narrative context, *Adam* and *Eve* illustrate a specific place and moment in the story of Genesis—the fall from a state of grace. The upper surface of *Adam*'s base simulates a stony ground and the tree stump behind him rises from a mound of earth dotted with tiny plants. *Adam* and *Eve* have become conscious of their nudity, as their fig and grape leaves show. *Eve* covers herself with a conventional gesture of modesty and shamefully lowers her eyes. In her restored right hand she holds a

---

[1] Ziliotto, 1950, p. 57. For the distich, see above, Intro., n. 69, *Evae marmoreae laus*.

[2] Lengherand, (1485-86) 1861, p. 35.

[3] Sabellico, 1487, dec. 3, bk. 9, n.p. See below, cat. no. 9.

fruit. *Adam*'s head is turned and tilted and he gazes upward, presumably toward the voice of God. With a pathos worthy of a mourning John the Evangelist beneath the cross,[4] *Adam* places one hand upon his chest. In his other hand he displays the evidence of his crime—a pomegranate from which he has begun to peel the skin. God has just said to Adam, "Hast thou eaten of the tree, whereof I commanded thee that thou shouldest not eat?" and Adam replies, "The woman whom thou gavest to be with me, she gave me of the tree and I did eat."[5]

The choice of *Adam* and *Eve* to decorate the inner face of the gateway to the Ducal Palace is unusual,[6] but not unjustifiable. Statues of *Adam* and *Eve* not uncommonly flank the entrance portal of churches. In such a context they refer to man's corrupt state from which the Church is empowered to redeem him through the medium of Christ's sacrifice. Thus they remind the worshipper, about to enter the church, of his need for salvation accomplished through performance of the church's sacraments. In the setting of a governmental building, the meaning of the Fall was bound to differ slightly. St. Augustine and other early Christian Fathers maintained that no man dominated another in the state of grace. But in his fallen state, man was prey to an aggressive desire to master his fellows. To curb this evil, temporal government was needed: thus temporal government was a divinely appointed remedy for sin.[7] The Ducal Palace, whose inner entrance the figures flanked, was the administrative center of Venetian government and justice as well as the doge's residence; the doge, whose statue stood above outer and inner entrances, was the chief representative of temporal power in the Venetian state. The figurative decoration of the lowest story of the Arco Foscari thus established the premise for the existence of temporal government and the building that lodged it, just as *Adam* and *Eve*, on the portals of cathedrals, announced the raison d'être of the Church in both its physical and spiritual sense.

A third layer of meaning enriches Rizzo's portrayal of the Fall: *Adam* and *Eve* are vehicles for the opposition of active and passive modes. Although *Eve* seems about to move—the right leg is bent and the right foot is only partially supported—the greater portion of the body's weight has so completely sunk into abdomen and thighs that instantaneous movement would be inhibited. *Eve*'s pose is closed and contours are compressed into an oval. Her head is tilted downward slightly and her eyelids are lowered, as she withdraws into herself. By contrast, *Adam* epitomizes focused energy: every mus-

---

[4] Hubala in Egg *et al.*, [1]1965, p. 681, believed *Adam* to have been based on a figure of John the Evangelist from a Medieval *Crucifixion*, but cited no specific prototype. *Adam*'s gesture, as well as his pose and opened mouth, recur in the Apostle on the far right in Andrea Mantegna's undated *Death of the Virgin*, Prado, Madrid.

[5] Genesis 3: 11-12.

[6] In 1470 the use of statues of *Adam* and *Eve* to flank the entrance to a communal building was unprecedented in Italy. Indeed, statuary of any kind was almost never used to embellish the portals of governmental palaces. See Paul, 1963, pp. 117f.

[7] Carlyle/Carlyle, [3]1930, i, pp. 125-131. The Fall of Adam and Eve is also depicted in relief at the southwest corner of the Ducal Palace. Sinding-Larsen, *Acta ad archaeologiam*, 1974, pp. 168ff., inter-

preted the scene as an exemplum of "the principle of and the enforcement of law and justice in human society." In contrast to St. Augustine, St. Thomas, like Aristotle, believed that man was, by nature, a social and political animal, and that whether or not he had fallen, "man would have sought a society based on law." The inclusion of the Archangel Michael above the relief of *Adam and Eve* permits Sinding-Larsen to read the scene as the first instance of the just administration of lawful punishment. (A more effective way of embodying this idea would have been to portray the expulsion from the Garden of Paradise.) In any event, the absence of the avenging angel or any other sign of punishment from Rizzo's group and the concentration on Adam and Eve's acknowledgement of guilt makes an Augustinian interpretation of Rizzo's figures more plausible.

cle is tensed, every sinew strains with the effort of the figure's movement. *Adam*'s upward glance causes his back to arch. Caught in the midst of stepping forward, he raises one hand to his breast and turns his head as he addresses God. His open pose permits the creation of a more broken, less concentrated silhouette than *Eve*'s. Perhaps by this opposition Rizzo intended to allude to God's adjuration to Eve after the Fall, "thy desire shall be to thy husband, and he shall rule over thee"?[8]

As has often been observed, the pose of *Eve* derives from a classical statue of *Venus pudica*,[9] of a type identical to the *Medici Venus* in the Uffizi Gallery (Figs. 48, 213) in all respects except the position of the head, which, in the antique prototype, apparently faced front. The existence of such a statue in the Renaissance can be inferred from the numerous reflections of it in sculpture and drawing. In addition to Rizzo's *Eve*, these include Giovanni Pisano's statue of *Temperance* from the pulpit in the Cathedral of Pisa, and drawings by Gentile da Fabriano, Pisanello, Jacopo Bellini, Amico Aspertini, and Francisco d'Ollanda, who saw the statue in the Roman collection of Cardinal Della Valle. The statue itself is lost.[10] Presumably it is identical with that *Venus pudica* seen by Benvenuto Rambaldi da Imola at the end of the fourteenth century in a private house in Florence.[11] Probably it is not the antique *Venus* owned by Gentile Bellini, for apparently Bellini's statue lacked part of its arms,[12] whereas our *Venus pudica* was whole. Unsuited to *Temperance*, the pose of *Venus pudica* was ideal for *Eve*: in its use in the context of the Fall, Rizzo was anticipated by Jacopo Bellini.[13] From his antique prototype as reconstructed,[14] Rizzo took *Eve*'s stance, the position of her head, and the locks of hair falling on her chest. Though the right arm with which the *Venus pudica* concealed her breast fulfills a different purpose in the *Eve*, the position of the arm was hardly changed. With their left hands both figures hide their genitals.

But *Eve*'s facial type and hair, her proportions and anatomy, are thoroughly unclassical. In spite of her large face, her head is relatively small. Her neck is long. Though

[8] Genesis 3:16. Jan van Eyck's first parents from the Ghent Altarpiece show that Rizzo was not unique in bodying forth masculine activity and feminine passivity in contrasting figures of *Adam* and *Eve*. Indeed, the stage directions at the beginning of a twelfth-century drama of Adam and Eve contain the injunction: "Adam tamen proprius, vultu composito, Eva vero parum demissiori." (*Das Adamsspiel*, 1928, p. 1.)

[9] Waźbiński, 1967, pp. 34, 44, identified the source of Rizzo's *Eve* with the antique statue described by Ghiberti in his *Commentarii* (Ghiberti/Schlosser, 1912, i, p. 62). According to Ghiberti, the statue was discovered beneath the houses of the Brunelleschi in Florence, was taken to Padua by Lombardo della Seta (d. 1390), and was given by Della Seta's son to the Marquess of Ferrara (either Niccolò III or Lionello d'Este). (See Ghiberti/Schlosser, 1912, ii, pp. 188f., n. 2.) But the figure that Ghiberti described was draped at mid-thigh. Therefore, if it did represent Venus (which is not at all certain, since Ghiberti neither identifies it by name nor even mentions its sex), it must have belonged rather to the type of the *Venus of Capua* (for which see Bieber, 1977, pp. 43ff.)

than to the *Venus pudica*.

[10] Schmitt in Degenhart/Schmitt, *MJ*, 1960, pp. 101-106. For the known exemplars of the *Venus pudica*, see Felletti Maj, *Archeologia classica*, 1951, pp. 33-65.

[11] Rambaldi da Imola, 1887, iii, p. 280: "Ego autem vidi Florentiae in domo privata statuam Veneris de marmore mirabilem in eo habitu in quo olim pingebatur Venus. Erat enim mulier speciosissima nuda, tenens manum sinistram ad pudenda, dexteram vero ad mammillas, et dicebatur esse opus Polycleti, quod non credo."

[12] Bellini's statue of Venus formed the subject of a poem by Raffaele Zovenzoni, *In Venerem Gentilis Bellini*: "Qui Paphiam nudis Venerem vidisse papillis/optet in antiquo marmore Praxitelis,/Bellini pluteum Gentilis quaerat, ubi stans,/trunca licet membris, vivit imago suis." (Ziliotto, 1950, p. 109, no. 135.)

[13] London, British Museum, Jacopo Bellini, *Sketchbook*, fol. 42r: Goloubew, i, 1912, pl. II.

[14] Schmitt in Degenhart/Schmitt, *MJ*, 1960, pp. 103ff.

square, her shoulders are low and very small. The upper part of her chest is too narrow; her rib cage is too wide. Breasts consist of diminutive hemispheres; at the center a boss marks the nipple. Though placed very far apart, the breasts do not impinge upon the figure's contours. The distance from breast to navel and from navel to crotch is excessive; the area of the genitals, especially, is enlarged. The waist is barely indented; the hips are hardly any wider than the chest. The bulging thighs, lengthened at the expense of the figure's lower legs, contribute to the impression of weight. The feet, with their elongated toes, are very long and narrow.

The proportions of *Eve* have often been likened to those of *Eve* by Jan van Eyck as a means of stressing their fundamental Gothicism. To be sure, they are Gothic, but such proportions were not peculiar to northern art. Even Antonio Pollaiuolo, whose works were so often classical in subject and motif, employed a Gothic canon for female figures. The proportions and anatomy of Pollaiuolo's *Eve* from a drawing in the Uffizi Gallery (Fig. 214) are so similar to those of Rizzo's figure that we may posit Pollaiulo's female figures as a source for Rizzo's *Eve*. Characteristic of Pollaiuolo's female canon are small, square shoulders, high, small, hemispherical breasts placed far apart, tiny, circular nipples, a broad waist, and an elongated torso. Like that of Pollaiuolo's *Eve*, the highly articulated anatomy of Rizzo's figure registers the flaccid muscles of the upper arms, stomach, and abdomen, the bony structure of rib cage and clavicles. In both, contours are a succession of arcs of varying curvature and length, occasionally interrupted, as at the knees, by overlapping forms. That *Eve*'s proportions do not match the ideal of classical antiquity or our own should not blind us to the fact that they were thought perfect in the fifteenth century: "if thy form, Eve, were as it lives in this marble, what wonder that man has yielded to thee," wrote a contemporary humanist.[15]

In the statue of *Adam* (Figs. 39-43) Rizzo proved himself Pollaiuolo's most faithful follower. The proportions of the figure—the large head, the thick neck, the voluminous thorax, the long torso, the short legs—can be paralleled in Pollaiuolo's *Dancing Nudes* in the Villa Gallina at Arcetri (Fig. 216). In the description of the musculature, the protruding clavicles and straining tendons of the neck, *Adam* resembles Pollaiuolo's figures in the *Battle of the Ten Nudes* (Fig. 211). In both, joints are accentuated, for knuckles, knees, and ankles are made to protrude more sharply than they normally would do. *Adam*'s tightly flexed buttocks produce the same rounded and protuberant forms as in Pollaiuolo's bronze *Anteus* (Figs. 43, 215). Like that of *Anteus*, *Adam*'s sharply indented spinal cord divides his highly articulated back (Fig. 41). The tendons at the back of *Adam*'s bent knee, like those of *Hercules*, are recorded with the particularity of an anatomical diagram. From Pollaiuolo Rizzo learned to imbue the human body with movement—to arch the back, to bend the limbs, to animate the fingers. Pollaiuolo's figures habitually perform such violent acts that no part of the body is free of strain. Tensed muscles are more prominent than muscles in a state of relaxation; thus movement provided Pollaiuolo with an excuse for a complete transcription of the figure's musculature. *Adam*'s movement is less violent, but muscles are no less tense and therefore visible. The surface of the statue is as subject to constant indentation and projection, and its contours are as inflected, as those of Pollaiuolo's figures. *Adam*'s hair and physiognomy, characterized by a broad, square, bony jaw, a wide, blunt, protuberant chin,

---

[15] Zovenzoni, *Evae marmoreae laus*, in Ziliotto, 1950, p. 116, no. 163, quoted above, Intro., n. 69.

high, widely spaced cheekbones, and a flat, low forehead (Figs. 38, 45) derive from Pollaiuolo. In *Adam*, as in Pollaiuolo's figures, expression is vehement. *Adam*'s parted lips, which show the teeth, recur in the faces of Pollaiuolo's *Dancing Nudes* (Fig. 216).

Probably it was the influence of Antonio Pollaiuolo, whose work Rizzo might have come to know during a second trip to Florence ca. 1470, which accelerated Rizzo's maturation. Unlike that of "*Mars*" (Fig. 36), the pose of *Adam* (Fig. 39) now carries a specific message, one which corroborates the expression of the face. There is no part of the body that is not animated by the figure's movement, that does not shift its weight or turn or strain, and that, therefore, fails to contribute to the meaning of the whole. The pathos of the figure can be read in every part: if there survived only the hand and arm that proffer the pomegranate with such evident reluctance, we could reconstruct the whole. Yet the subordination of the pose to an expressionistic purpose produced no inorganic or clumsy movements, no distortions of anatomy or proportions. On the contrary, movements, by which *Adam* conveys the anguish with which he confesses wrongdoing, conform to the strictest rules of contrapposto. The accuracy of *Adam*'s anatomical structure was not surpassed in any sculpture of the fifteenth century.

Rizzo seems to have profited from his previous experience of fitting a figure to a niche of the Arco Foscari, for *Adam*, unlike "*Mars*," is adapted to a moderately distant view from below. Forms are fewer, larger, simpler. A comparison of the two faces (Figs. 37, 38, 44, 45) reveals in *Adam* the smoothing and faceting of the planes of cheeks and forehead. Indentations were either accentuated or eliminated altogether. The eyes are larger; the curvature of lids is more pronounced. Edges of forms are graphically defined by broad rims cut back sharply in the lids, by the incision of outlines in the brows, by the undercutting of the border of the lower lip, and by the exaggerated jutting of the jaw and chin. The face provides a focus: as the climax of the narrative, it makes explicit what the pose can only imply; as the culmination of the design, it orients the movement of limbs and body and concentrates their flamelike contours.

To a far greater extent than "*Mars*" (Fig. 36), *Adam* and *Eve* (Figs. 39, 48) were conceived as free-standing statues. Where "*Mars*'" limbs, drapery, and shield extend across the frontal plane, *Adam* and *Eve* are columnar: unlike "*Mars*," the blocks from which they were carved were as deep as they were wide. Instead of "*Mars*'" polygonal base with its broad front face, the bases of *Adam* and *Eve* are round. Only a very small portion at the rear of each statue is not completely finished. Yet, because the figures were destined for niches, the pose, gestures, expression, and attribute of each can be seen and comprehended from a single vantage point *en face*.

Various works can be associated with the statues of *Adam* and *Eve*. One of these is the relief of an escutcheon-bearing *Angel* in the Rio Terrà Barba Fruttarol (Fig. 52). Exposed on the facade of a house, it is in so deteriorated a state that its outlines are barely visible: a photograph made toward the turn of the century is a more reliable guide to its original appearance. The *Angel* stands, holding before him the top of a shield much too large ever to have served the purpose of defense. Neither setting nor ground is indicated. Indeed, the figure lacks one foot. This lack, as well as the extraordinarily long leg that the visible foot presupposes, may probably be explained by the replacement of the relief's bottom half when the house to which it was affixed changed ownership. The device of the upper half of the shield and the *Angel*'s hands seem also to have been recut. The existing coat of arms belonged to the nonpatrician Simbeni family, of which three members were Venetian notaries in the second half of the seventeenth and early eighteenth centuries.

The motif of a standing Angel with escutcheon is a very frequent one in Venetian sculpture. It is found on the front faces of Trecento sarcophagi.[16] On the facade of Venetian houses, generally immured above the portal, it is ubiquitous. As guardian of the house, the *Angel* fulfilled a function analogous to that of the *Lar familiaris* in ancient Rome.[17] Rizzo enlivened the standard composition by introducing into the *Angel*'s pose a slight degree of torsion and by turning and tilting the *Angel*'s head. Thus the symmetry characteristic of such heraldic compositions was qualified by differential foreshortening and by the lateral orientation of the *Angel*'s gaze. At the same time, the impression of a spatial ambience was created by a pose that seems to move through successive planes of depth.

Rizzo's authorship of the *Angel* is evident, above all, in its face. As in the face of *Adam* (Figs. 38, 52), eyes are shallowly embedded in their sockets. Set far apart, eyes are very large and opened wide, and the curvature of upper and lower lids and salient tear ducts is identical. In both, the glance is directed upward and to the left by the turn of the head and the elevation of iris and pupil, cut in half by the upper lid. The eyebrows, like those of *Eve* (Fig. 50), are composed of thin ridges that hardly project from the surface of the face. Their course—not quite a perfect arc—descends to the level of the outer corner of the eye. As in *Eve*, the receding chin is contained within the rounded contour of a double chin. The *Angel*'s left hand, with its wide arc from tip of thumb through index finger, must once have looked very like the left hand of *God the Father* in the Altar of St. Paul (Fig. 8). The strange coiffure, in which double corkscrew curls hang from either temple, was introduced by Rizzo in the heads of cherubim in the frieze of the Altar of St. James (Fig. 9). The vast superiority of the head of the escutcheon-bearing *Angel* warrants dating the work at some years' remove from the Altar of St. James.

More or less contemporary with the statues of *Adam* and *Eve* in the early 1470s is the relief of the *Man of Sorrows* from the Altar of the Sacrament in the Basilica at Aquileia (Figs. 53-59). The image of Christ as Man of Sorrows symbolized both Christ's sacrificial death and his bodily presence at the mass. Common to all representations of the Man of Sorrows is the conceptual nature of the theme. The scene, abstracted from any narrative or historical context, represents none of the stations of the cross. Christ is portrayed, as in the Crucifixion, nude but for a loin cloth, crowned with a wreath of thorns, wounded in chest and hands (Fig. 59). The sarcophagus refers both to his burial and to his resurrection. Christ is dead: his eyes are closed, his mouth drops open, his arms and hands are limp. But, upright in spite of the absence of sufficient means of support, he is, at the same time, portrayed as though alive. Presented hieratically, Christ is at the center of a symmetrical and isocephalic grouping, the focus of a central point of sight. He is not overlapped. Christ is shown in frontal view; arms are extended symmetrically to either side. His scale is very slightly larger than that of his companions. As a consequence, the tomb appears too shallow to accommodate his thighs. The Virgin Mary and St. John the Evangelist flank Christ as they flanked the cross. Em-

---

[16] Sarcophagus, Turin, Museo Civico, soon after 1300 (Wolters, 1976, ii, Fig. 16); Tomb of Pileo I da Prata (d. 1325), Prata di Pordenone, S. Giovanni dei

Cavalieri (ibid., ii, Fig. 52); Tomb of Lodovico della Torre, Aquileia, Basilica (ibid., ii, Fig. 356).

[17] Niero in Niero *et al.*, 1972, p. 268.

bracing Christ, the Virgin presses her face to his;[18] her pose is reminiscent of images in which the Madonna kisses her infant son. John turns away his face and bewails the death of Christ, thus distancing himself from the loving union of mother and son.[19] Angels, slightly reduced in scale, join the Virgin and St. John.[20] As bearers of attributes, rather than as participants, these relatively unmoved figures—mirror images of one another—frame the relief at either lateral extremity: a mute Greek chorus, they comment on the meaning of the scene through the medium of their inscriptions.[21]

Removed in time, the scene also is removed in place. The illusionistic technique of *schiacciato* relief, used in the *Conversion of St. Paul* (Fig. 17) to suggest infinite recession, is not used here. No more of a setting is indicated than ground, which nourishes a few sparse weeds. The ground does not appear to recede farther than that minimum required to accommodate figures disposed along the surface of the relief at the forefront of the pictured space: indeed, the ground meets the plain, impenetrable background of the relief at the sole of John's receding foot. Figures, whether standing or kneeling, fill almost the entire height of the relief: large empty areas, which normally suggest a circumambience of space, are wanting. The sarcophagus, depicted most unusually end on, would have excavated a recess in the imaginary space had its orthogonals not been overlapped so near their sources. The point of sight that they define—slightly above the middle of the relief—contradicts the very low horizon. A scroll overlaps the base and a part of the relief as though it belonged to the observer's space.

Evidence of Rizzo's hand is to be found in the description of Christ's anatomy—so similar to that of *Adam* in the figure's broad, square shoulders, voluminous chest, and flat high breasts with embossed nipples eccentrically placed (Figs. 39, 59). Christ's corkscrew locks are analogous to *Eve*'s (Figs. 47, 56) and a hallmark of Rizzo's sculpture. The Angel on the left of the *Man of Sorrows* is the twin of the right-hand candelabra-bearing *Angel* from the Altar of St. James (Figs. 26, 27, 59). In both, the slight bending of the knee and the identical disposition of the feet produce an unemphatic contrapposto. In contradiction to the repose implicit in the stance, the skirt flies back, producing an arrangement of similar folds, regularly spaced, whose roughly parallel courses pursue long uninterrupted curves: it is a pattern which, in Rizzo's oeuvre, is unique to these two works. The flourish at the hem of the chiton of the Aquileia Angel is identical to one at the hem of the candelabra-bearing *Angel* (Fig. 24). In both, the sash swags beneath the abdomen, restraining folds at the bottom of the peplum. A focused gaze and parted lips lend to both an expression of yearning.

The treatment of folds in the Virgin and St. John evolved from the fluttering cloak in the *Conversion of St. Paul* (Fig. 17); but the idiosyncratic forms that drapery takes in the Aquileia *Man of Sorrows* more generally characterize works by Rizzo of the later

[18] This motif can be traced as far back as an Italo-Byzantine panel painting in the Museo Horne, Florence—the earliest extant image to combine the Virgin Mary with the Man of Sorrows. See Schiller, ii, 1972, p. 211.

[19] The similarity of composition to that of Desiderio da Settignano's Tabernacle of S. Lorenzo, 1461, and Giovanni Bellini's Brera *Pietà* is probably fortuitous: the composition was widespread, having found its way into provincial Italian painting already by the Trecento. See Schiller, ii, 1972, fig. 733.

[20] Angels had first appeared in images of the Man of Sorrows in the lectern of Giovanni Pisano's pulpit at S. Andrea, Pistoia, 1301: ibid., p. 215. The grouping of Angels and Man of Sorrows with the Virgin and St. John is very similar to that of the antipendium of the Miroballo Monument by Jacopo della Pila and Tommaso Malvito in S. Giovanni a Carbonara, Naples.

[21] I have been unable to trace the source of the inscriptions.

1470s and early 1480s. Clothes are made of thin stuffs, soft and malleable and inclined to cling, like wool charged with static electricity. Where the cloth adheres, the surface is gently dented. By contrast, the surfaces of folds are smooth and nearly flat: volume is concentrated at edges, which are more or less rounded and sometimes undercut. At a turning, the volume of the fold is swelled by the pinching of the cloth. As though responding to the pressure which flattened them, folds spread unequally in all directions along a two-dimensional plane, effacing gradations in the volume of underlying forms and endowing the figure and its members with spurious boundaries. The paths described by the edges of folds recall string stretched taut too long which, having lost its elasticity, has begun to sag and droop. Borders are often rippled and shifts in the direction of a fold are invariably produced by curves.

A comparison of the two Angels suggests the participation of an assistant in the figure on the right. The organic basis of the contrapposto pose is undermined, in the right Angel, by the stiffened knee of the free leg and the feet, placed too closely together. The contours of feet, incorrectly foreshortened, are not affected by the joints of toes. The straight edges of major folds bear no relation to the contours of the legs, revealed so skillfully in the Angel on the left. The denting of surfaces where the cloth adheres becomes a mannerism in the hands of this assistant.

An assistant may have intervened also in the execution of the Virgin. The drawing of the Virgin's shoulder, and shrunken forearm reveal a deficient comprehension of anatomy. Here problems of foreshortening, solved successfully in the Evangelist, were shirked. It is not likely that the extra hand pressed against the Madonna's breast is Rizzo's blunder. The tendency to straighten edges of folds produces the same unfortunate results in the Virgin's hip and thigh as in the Angel on the right. Nevertheless, the stylistic consistency of the relief, in contradistinction to its quality, makes it likely that, at a final stage, Rizzo reworked those parts of the relief which he did not carve himself.

In assessing the quality of the relief the critic must allow for the lack of care, occasioned perhaps by haste, perhaps by the relative unimportance of the commission, expended in its execution. That the relief was worked rapidly and without regard to the niceties of design may be inferred from its paucity of detail and lack of finish. Even the smallest details were carved on a larger scale than in any work examined hitherto. Where elements are small, like locks of hair or weeds, they are standardized. The face of the sarcophagus is bare. Anatomical forms, like the face of the left-hand Angel (Fig. 53) or the contours of Christ (Fig. 59), are abstracted, not because Rizzo aspired to a higher ideality of form, but because the sculptor did not proceed to the intermediate stage of articulating elementary forms. Indeed, the Angel on the left is missing irises and pupils and Christ's crown lacks its thorns (Fig. 56). In the description of faces, liberal use was made of a point or the corner of a chisel for the incision of lines (Fig. 55); this provided a far more expedient means to the definition of the features than the circumstantial modulation of the surface would have done. No attempt was made to distinguish between textures. Nor was the relief polished: punch and chisel marks remain on the matt surface of the stone.

This lack of finish is not a unique failing of Rizzo's *Man of Sorrows*. Indeed, it seems characteristic of most schools of Quattrocento sculpture, aside from the Florentine, that a wide range of finish was tolerated. In Venetian sculpture one extreme is represented by the finest works of Rizzo and the sculpture of Tullio Lombardo, the other by Niccolò

Fiorentino's Tomb of Francesco Foscari and the sculpture of Pietro Lombardo, scored throughout by a claw chisel, whose traces Pietro never bothered to remove. Venetian artists and patrons often were satisfied by works that would not have passed muster in Florence, where standards had been set by the meticulous sculptures of Bernardo and Antonio Rossellino and Desiderio da Settignano. In part, Venetian artists and patrons were adjusting to necessity: Istrian stone from which so much of Venetian sculpture was carved does not take as high a finish as marble. Moreover, commissions that often consisted of vast numbers of quasi-identical figures, sometimes placed at great heights, did not lend themselves to careful execution. Nevertheless, such material explanations do not account for all the instances in which inferior or unfinished works issued from Venetian studios.

Except for the archivolt with palmettes and scrolls, and the cornice, which closes off the lunette, the reredos in which the relief of the *Man of Sorrows* (Figs. 57, 58) is incorporated does not appear to be an original work of the fifteenth century. Such perfect regularity in the ornamentation of pilaster shafts, where a single motif is repeated throughout and one pilaster of a pair is identical to the other, is never found in fifteenth-century architecture. The internal faces of the large pilasters are carved only up to the level of the capitals of the small order. The steep profile of the triangular pediment, crowned with a shell, is anomalous. The bronze *sportello* seems nineteenth century in style. The slabs surrounding the *sportello* were carved to fill spaces left over: no fifteenth-century altar possesses anything remotely similar. The double cornice of the base, which repeats itself but for a reversal of direction, is a solecism that the fifteenth century would have avoided: its existence here can be explained by the reuse—right side up on the top, upside down on the bottom—of pieces of a single entablature once intended for a different purpose. Probably the stippling of the base's frieze canceled an inappropriate inscription.

Indeed, it is unlikely that the *Man of Sorrows* originally belonged to a reredos at all. Its size and shape are those of an antependium. Its subject—the real body of Christ, which the host betokened—commonly figured on late Quattrocento antependia.[22] Probably when the relief was moved from altar to altarpiece, as we assume it was, the inscription in the scroll below the sarcophagus was erased. Since no documents or early descriptions of the relief remain, we can do no more than suggest a possible provenience. Between 1468 and 1475 a new chapel, dedicated to the Corpus Christi, was constructed at the Basilica of Aquileia. Its dedication and its architectural parts, enumerated in the documents, correspond to those of the ciborium that houses the dossal with Rizzo's *Man of Sorrows* (Fig. 58).[23] There is no record of construction of the chapel's

[22] Italian examples of the fifteenth century include: (1) Andrea Sansovino, Altar of the Sacrament, Florence, S. Spirito, probably soon after 1485; (2) Andrea della Robbia and others, Altarpiece of the Madonna della Misericordia, Arezzo, S. Maria delle Grazie, ca. 1500-1510; (3) Jacopo della Pila and Tommaso Malvito, Monument of the Miroballo family, Naples, S. Giovanni a Carbonara; (4) Tommaso Malvito and others, Recco Altar, Naples, S. Giovanni a Carbonara, 1504-5; (5) attributed to Tommaso Malvito, Altar of St. Jerome, Naples, S. Domenico Maggiore. In Desiderio da Settignano's

Tabernacle of the Sacrament, Florence, S. Lorenzo, 1461, and the Tabernacle of the Madonna dell'Ulivo by Benedetto, Giuliano, and Giovanni da Maiano, Prato, Duomo, 1480, the *Man of Sorrows* does not function liturgically as an antependium because these tabernacles did not contain altars. But compositionally, the reliefs, like altar frontals, served as bases to the tabernacles above.

[23] In March 1471 the Chapel of the Corpus Christi was endowed. Previously, in July of 1468, a "magister Antonius de Venetiis murarius sive lapicida" had been credited with 30 ducats for the delivery of

altar; for this reason we cannot be sure that an altar table did not already exist. On the other hand, the present altar table of the Altar of the Sacrament is clearly a pastiche. Thus, while the coincidence of the hypothetical date of the *Man of Sorrows* and the actual date of the Chapel of the Corpus Christi does not prove the relief's provenience, it does provide grounds for a plausible hypothesis.

A final group of works that can be dated to the first half of the 1470s is four statues in S. Sofia, Venice, of the *Apostle Andrew*, the *Evangelist Luke*, and the physicians, *SS. Cosmas* and *Damian* (Figs. 60-63). The statues come from the altar of the Scuola dei Barbieri which, from 1468 on, was located in the Venetian church of S. Maria dei Servi. An agreement of July 6, 1468, provided for the appropriation of an altar on the right side of the nave to be adorned with a painted altarpiece of the Virgin flanked by SS. Luke, Andrew, Cosmas, and Damian.[24] During the Napoleonic era, S. Maria dei Servi was suppressed and its monuments were dispersed. The four statues of *Saints* were first recorded in the nearby church of S. Sofia at the end of the nineteenth century.[25]

The identity of the figures in S. Sofia is proof of the statues' provenience. The Venetian barbers' guild, to whom the right to practice certain surgical procedures had been granted in 1311,[26] venerated SS. Cosmas and Damian as their patrons.[27] But SS. Luke and Andrew also held a special place in the devotions of the school. (It may be relevant that Luke was a physician himself, and was generally chosen patron by physicians and surgeons.) The transfer of the school to the Servi from its first meeting place in SS. Filippo e Giacomo occurred in 1465, on the feast of St. Luke (October 18).[28] On that day the school customarily met to elect its new *gastaldo*; on the feast of St. Andrew (November 30) the administration of the school was regularly transferred from the old, to the newly elected, official. On both feast days (as well as on that of SS. Cosmas and Damian: September 27) special masses were sung at the barbers' altar and the altar was arrayed with relics of SS. Luke and Andrew,[29] which were among the treasures of the

stone for the ciborium. The architectural details of the ciborium, as carved by Master Antonio, did not meet the approval of the master of the works and in April 1473 Antonio was fired. A year later Master Gasparino dei Matendelli da Lugano undertook to complete, by Lent of the following year, the work left unfinished by Antonio. This included the carving of two shells as well as the completion of a third, which had been left roughhewn; the completion of three architraves and two columns, one of which was already fluted; and the polishing of two capitals. (The documents were excerpted by Vale in *La Basilica di Aquileia*, 1933, p. 66, nn. 2, 3, 4, p. 67, n. 2.)

[24] Vicentini, *S. Maria dei Servi*, 1920, p. 91.

[25] Paoletti, 1893, ii, pp. 150, 160.

[26] Stefanutti, 1961, pp. 20, 77f.

[27] Tramontin in Tramontin *et al.*, 1965, p. 315.

[28] Cicogna, i, 1824, p. 97, nos. 213, 214; Levi, 1895, pp. 44f.

[29] See the initial agreement between the guild and the brotherhood of the Servi of July 19, 1462, concerning the appropriation of an altar. ASV, Mani morte, Convento di S. Maria dei Servi in Venezia, Busta 9, codice 2, 1 (parchment): "Questi

qui sotto sono li capitoli de tute le cosse che dimanda i barbieri per nome de la sua scuola et prima nuj adimandemo perpetualmente uno altar ne la giesia de madona sancta maria di Servj; el qual e a man senestra per mezo laltar del corpo de Christo e quel de San Nicolo, el qual suo altar al qual nuj possiamo fare cellebrare inperpetuo, e dire tute le nostre messe per le anime de tuti li nostri fradellj de la nostra scuola che sono passadi de questa vita e che passerano . . . Item dimandemo e voiemo havere imperpetuo uno luogo in el ditto luogo di Servi, zoe el suo reffictorio dove immaza in linstacte [si mangia nell'estate] da dover star quando faremo el nostro capitulo che sono doi volte alla no, el primo capitulo che nuj facemo sie el di de San Luca, e in quello di nuj facemo gastoldo nuovo, e el segondo capitulo che nui facemo sie el di de Sancto Andrea che el gastoldo vechio rende la scuola al gastoldo nuovo e in questi doi zorni de San Luca e da Sancto Andrea che nuj faciamo questi doi nostri capituli . . . Item dimandemo e voiemo che el di de San Luca che son el primo nostro capitulo quando nuj facemo gastaldo nuovo che in quello di de San Luca el sia cantado e cellebrado una bella messa al nostro altar la qual messa sia quella del spirito sancto, e sia aparado

Servi.[30] *SS. Luke* and *Andrew* (Figs. 60, 61) hold closed books; their long beards are emblematic of venerable age and of the wisdom embodied in their writings. Their age contrasts with the youth of *SS. Cosmas* and *Damian* (Figs. 63, 62), depicted in the active guise of physicians with mortar and medicine container, respectively, and with the palm fronds symbolic of their martyrdom. Sandals and mantles, draped like Roman togas, lend a Biblical authority to the patriachs. *Cosmas* and *Damian*, by contrast, are attired in contemporary fashion with cloak, *cappuccio*, shoes and, in the case of *Damian*, with doctor's scapular;[31] their hair is dressed in the contemporary mode. In facial type, *Cosmas* and *Damian* are virtually twins, as, indeed, they were believed to be. Perhaps it was for the sake of symmetry that *Luke* and *Andrew* were also made to look so much alike.

The Scuola dei Barbieri was neither wealthy nor prestigious. Its members could not afford to construct an independent meeting house; probably they did not have much money to decorate their altar. Rizzo's interest in the work is measured by his delegating the execution, and perhaps even the design, of all four statues to two or three assistants, one of whom, clearly, did not merit the assignment. *St. Andrew* is a pastiche of Rizzo's other works. From *St. Paul* (Figs. 6, 61) comes the figure's physiognomy and proportions, especially the breadth of chest and shoulders. However simplified, the drapery pattern betrays its source in the mantle of *St. James* (Fig. 3). Although the disposition of the left arm recalls the gesture with which Romans clasped their togas, the hand derives from *Adam*, from which even the scheme of veins was drawn (Fig. 39). The author of *St. Luke* adapted from *St. James* the facial type and draping of the cloak (Figs. 3, 60). *St. Luke*'s inferiority to *St. Andrew* proves the presence of a different, less capable, assistant.

SS. Cosmas and *Damian* (Figs. 63, 62) find their closest analogies in the *Man of Sorrows* from Aquileia (Fig. 59): perhaps the assistant who aided Rizzo in the execution of the relief also carved the physician saints. Facial types and hair are similar to those of the scroll-bearing Angels; the same dimpled chin occurs in *St. Damian* and the Angel on the right (Figs. 54, 62). The rippling of the surface in *St. Damian*'s thigh and between the folds of his cloak seems arbitrary and excessive, as it does in the Angel from the *Man of Sorrows* (Figs. 59, 62). The stiff-legged stance and the splaying of the feet characterize the poses of *St. Cosmas* and the Angel (Figs. 59, 63). The pattern of folds of *St. Cosmas*' cloak corresponds to the folds descending from the Virgin's arm.

Like the early *St. James* (Fig. 3), all four statues are monolithic in their retention of

---

prette diacono e subdiacono, e sia cantada cum organj azioche el spirito sancto ne spira tuti nuj, e conciedi e diane gratia che nuj possiamo ellegere, e fare uno gastoldo cum i suo compagnj, i qualli habiano a regere, e governar questa nostra benedeta scuolla, e tuti pregare lo eterno idio per le anime de tuti li nostri fradeli che serano passadi de questa vita, e per lo simile e voiemo che lo di de sancto Andrea al segondo nostro capitulo che el gastaldo vechio rende la scuola al gastaldo nuovo, el sia cantada una mesa cum organi prete diacono e subdiacono come e ditto el di de San Luca, a zioche el gastaldo nuovo abia gratia da lo eterno idio de podere regere, e governare questa nostra benedeta scuola, e per ben de le anime e di corpi . . . Item voiemo che i ditti frari

siano tegnudi imperpetuo in el di de San Luca, e in el di de Sancto Andrea alla nostra mesa de adornar el nostro altar cum alcune de le sue requilie [*sic*], e maxime cum quelle do reliquie de San Luca e de Sancto Andrea."

In a document of August 31, 1490, the Servites reaffirmed their obligation to sing masses at the altar of the *scuola* on the feast days of SS. Cosmas, Damian, Luke, and Andrew: ASV, ibid., cc. 9ff.

[30] Corner, 1758, p. 294.

[31] Corsini, 1912, passim. *St. Damian*'s scapular descends over his left arm to his wrist, but on the right it ends at the top of his arm and is tucked under. Thus his right flank and arm are freed.

the form, density, and axiality of the blocks from which they came. All are posed frontally; only the heads of *SS. Cosmas* and *Damian* deviate from a vertical axis or a fontal view. Concessions to the shifts in weight of a contrapposto pose are restricted to the slight projection of a knee or the dropping of a shoulder. Drapery and limbs adhere to the body. The limited projection and recession of forms and the absence of perforations guarantee the uniformity of the front face of the statues. Contours are closed and straight and endow the figures with blocklike shapes.

This period of Rizzo's activity closed with his participation in the defense of Scutari in Albania, besieged by the Turks between July 15 and August 28, 1474. Documents record that Rizzo performed conscientiously and that, either in this or in a subsequent siege of Scutari, he was wounded. In recognition of his faithful service he was later awarded a monthly pension to last for twenty years.[32] Undoubtedly this first experience of war affected Rizzo, but its influence cannot be perceived in any sudden change of style. Probably the most important result of Rizzo's military service was the enhancement of his reputation among the governors of Venice: perhaps it is as much to their appreciation of his patriotism as to his artistic merit that Rizzo owed the subsequent commission for the Tomb of Doge Niccolò Tron and his eventual appointment to the post of *protomaestro* of the Ducal Palace.

[32] Cadorin, 1838, pp. 163f., n. 19.

CHAPTER THREE

The Tron Tomb

ON JULY 21, 1476, Antonio Rizzo contracted with the Scuola di S. Marco to provide its chapter hall with a carved pulpit, supported by a bracket, and the exterior spiral staircase giving access to it, plus doors to and from the staircase, and a plain door leading to the attic. Work was to be completed by the next Christmas. Gentile Bellini, a member of the confraternity, had made a drawing of the pulpit and the door giving on to it, which Rizzo was to follow. The pulpit was to have five faces; its figures, carved in *mezzo rilievo*, were to be of white marble; behind the figures there was to be a background of black stone.[1] Unfortunately, Rizzo's most completely documented work does not survive: both pulpit and staircase perished in the *scuola*'s fire on March 31, 1485. The directives contained in the contract suggest that the reliefs were not pictorial narratives.[2] More likely, the reliefs consisted of single figures or small groups presented hieratically. In 1477 Rizzo was inscribed among the members of the Scuola di S. Marco, perhaps in gratitude for the successful completion of his task.[3]

The commission from the Scuola di S. Marco was probably executed concurrently with the initial campaign of work on what was to represent Rizzo's most extensive and prestigious private commission—the Tomb of Doge Niccolò Tron in S. Maria dei Frari (Fig. 64). The authorship of the tomb is not documented. In 1581 Francesco Sansovino attributed the standing *Doge* and "certain other figures" to Antonio Bregno.[4] His attribution was discredited in 1837 when Giuseppe Cadorin observed, on the one hand, that Sansovino also gave to Bregno the east wing of the Ducal Palace and the Scala dei Giganti, documented works of Rizzo, while on the other, that the existence of Antonio Bregno could not be independently confirmed.[5] Indeed, the similarity of the Tron Tomb *Prudence* and *Charity* to Rizzo's inscribed *Eve* (Figs. 48, 79, 89), observed by connoisseurs already in the nineteenth century,[6] gave substance to Cadorin's suspicion that Bregno was merely a pseudonym for Rizzo. Although the precise extent of Rizzo's contribution to the individual figures is still disputed, his responsibility for the conception and partial execution of the tomb has long been universally acknowledged.

[1] Paoletti, fasc. 1, 1894, pp. 15f.; Sohm, 1978, p. 62, n. 14, and p. 260, doc. 24.

[2] I am not convinced by the proposal of Tietze and Tietze-Conrat, 1944, p. 83, no. 289, that a design for one of the panels of the pulpit is contained in Giovanni Bellini's drawing of *St. Mark Healing St. Anianus*, Berlin-Dahlem, Staatliche Museen, no. 1357. To be sure, the disposition of Bellini's figures is excellently suited to a relief of medium height and the scene of the *Healing of St. Anianus* might well have figured on the pulpit. But Gentile, not Gio-

vanni, was specifically credited with having made the drawing of the pulpit. Furthermore, Rizzo's relief is not likely to have contained as detailed a background as that depicted in the drawing.

[3] Paoletti, 1893, ii, p. 149, n. 4.

[4] Sans., 1581, p. 66r.

[5] Cadorin, 1837, pp. 21f.; Cadorin, 1838, pp. 138f.

[6] Zanotto, i, 1842-53, II. "Cortile. Scalea dei Giganti opera di Antonio Riccio," p. 39, n. 69; Meyer, *JpK*, 1889, p. 197; Paoletti, 1893, ii, p. 143.

Niccolò di Luca Tron was born ca. 1399. As a merchant, resident at Rhodes for fifteen years, he amassed enormous wealth. After his return to Venice, he was made ambassador extraordinary to Pope Paul II and served for many years as Savio del Consiglio. In 1466 he became Procuratore di S. Marco de supra.[7] Following the death of Cristoforo Moro, Tron was elected sixty-eighth doge on November 23, 1471. During his principate, Cyprus became a Venetian protectorate. In its continuing prosecution of the war against the Turks, Venice, under Tron, allied itself with Ussan Hassan, sovereign of Persia. Tron's reign was notable for the reform of Venetian coinage, often counterfeited and debased. A copper bagattino, a silver half-lira, and a silver lira, equal in value to 20 soldi and called a trono, were newly minted. All of them bore on their obverse a bust-length profile portrait of the doge. The introduction of the ducal portrait bust on coins, however, was condemned as autocratic and prohibited immediately after the doge's death.[8] Tron died on July 28, 1473. His funeral took place three days later in S. Maria dei Frari, in the presence of the Venetian Signoria. The funeral oration was delivered by Ser Gianfrancesco Pasqualigo, who failed in the midst of his speech, much to his embarrassment.[9] Tron was survived by one son, Filippo.[10]

In his testament of August 2, 1466, made several years before becoming doge, Tron designated as his place of burial the tomb in S. Maria dei Frari in which his parents and other relatives had been buried.[11] We do not know in what part of the church the family tomb was situated. In any case, the doge was not buried there. Instead, on April 17, 1476, a new site within the church—one more honorific in itself, which, at the same time might accommodate "a conspicuous and magnificent monument"—was acquired for the doge's resting place. That site encompassed the entire left wall of the choir of the church, in imitation of, and in rivalry with, the Tomb of Doge Francesco Foscari on the right wall of the choir. The inscription on the tomb informs us that Filippo undertook construction of his father's tomb. This was standard practice in Venice, where the male heir or heirs customarily took upon themselves responsibility for the tomb of their legator, even when not so charged in the testament of the deceased. It was to Filippo that the General of the Franciscan Order, the Procurator of the Frari, and all the monks of the convent ceded the left wall of the Cappella Maggiore and to whom they granted the privilege of making a grave for himself and his heirs and successors *in perpetuum* in the pavement at the foot of the doge's tomb.[12] That grave is no longer

[7] Venice, Mus. Cor., MS Cicogna Cons. XI-E 2, Barbaro, vii, *voce*, Tron, p. 51v.

[8] Papadopoli, ii, 1907, p. 574, doc. xliv.

[9] Venice, Bibl. Marc., Cod. it., Cl. VII, 56 (= 8636), attributed to Erizzo, *Cronaca veneta*, 16th cen., n.p. [fol. 515r]: "adi xxxj del ditto Mese de Luio (1473), fù portado el suo corpo con grand'honor alla sepoltura, nella chiesia dei Frati Minori, et fatteli honoratissime essequie: L'oration funebre fù fatta per M. Zuanne Francesco Pasqualigo D. fu de Ser Alvise el qual mancò in mezo d'essa oration, ne la potè compir, che li fù una gran vergogna, essendo alla presentia della Signoria de Venezia che era venuta alla sopradette essequie." See also Sanudo, *RIs*, xxii, (1490-1530) 1733, col. 1198.

[10] For Tron's biography, see Da Mosto, 1966, pp. 227-231.

[11] ASV, Archivio Notarile, *Testamenti*, Busta 1214 (not. Antonio Marsilio), no. 1043: "Et prima lasso et hordino el mio chorpo sia sepelitto in frati Minori in la sepoltura fu sepolto messer mio padre e madre et altri nostri."

[12] ASV, Fondi ecclesiastici, S. Maria Gloriosa dei Frari, Chiesa e Convento, *Processi etc., T-Z*: ". . . Per Magnificum et Generosum Dominum Philippum Tronum, olim genitum, ipsius recollende memorie Serenissimi et Illustrissimi Principis Domini Nicolai Tron, perquisitum est, de habendo aliquem locum honorificum, in concludendo monumento conspicuo et magnifico, ubi cadaver ipsius Serenissimi Principis collacaretur: Petieritque instanter, Reverendissimum in Christo patrem, Dominum Magnificum Franciscum Sansondi, Generalem totius ordinis fratrum minorum, Dignissimum, Magnificum et Generosum Dominum Jacobum Maurocenum quondam Magnifici Domini Victoris de

marked; perhaps a tomb slab still exists beneath the new pavement of the church.[13]

The date of April 17, 1476, thus, provides a *terminus post quem* for the Tomb of Doge Niccolò Tron. It was finished by late spring 1480, when it was extolled as one of the two most beautiful tombs in all of Venice by the Milanese chancellor, Santo Brasca, detained in Venice between May 7 and June 5 on his way to the Holy Land.[14] Possibly the tomb was already completed by December 11, 1479, when the monks of the Frari accorded to members of the Alberto family the right of burial in front of the high altar "between the tombs of the two Princes."[15]

The Latin epitaph, written in Roman capitals, relates the major events of Tron's principate: the gaining of ascendancy in Cyprus, the alliance with Ussan Hassan, the banning and replacement of debased currency.[16] Apart from the words, OPTIMVS CIVIS OPTIMVS SENATOR, the epitaph contains no reference to Tron's life prior to his election to the principate of Venice. Thus the inscription legitimized the tomb, whose siting, scale, and wealth of sculptural embellishment heralded its occupant's preemi-

---

confinio Sancti Pauli, procuratorem ecclesie Beattissime Virginis Marie fratrum minorum de Venetiis, necnon omnes patres, magistros et fratres conventus predicti—: Quod placeat eis ipsi Magnifico et Generoso Domino Philippo Trono dare et concedere infrascriptum locum in ecclesia Beatissime Virginis Marie fratrum minorum de Venetiis . . . Qui sunt omnes patres, magistri et fratres discreti conventus predicti pro infrascriptis specialiter peragendis: Et omnes unanimes, voluntantes et concordes, nomine eorum discrepante, per se et successores suos, dederunt, tribuerunt et concesserunt, ac dant, tribuunt et concedunt ipsi Magnifico et Generoso Domino Philippo Trono olim ipsius recolende memorie Serenissimi et Illustrissimi Principis Domini Nicolai Troni olim incliti Venetiae Ducis, genito presenti. Et pro se et heredibus et successoribus suis, recipienti, stipulanti et acciptanti totum locum sinistrum introeundo in cappella maiori in ecclesia conventus eorum, ab summo usque ad deorsum, in totum et per totum, et tam per longitudinem quam latitudinem suis. Qui sit et esse debeat totus ad beneplacitum ipsius Magnifici Domini Philippi Troni, ubi pro libito olimtatis sue possit et valeat condere monumentum magnificum et nobile, pro cadavere ipsius Serenissimi et Illustrissimi Principis Domini Nicolai Troni collocandum. Cui Magnifico Domino Philippo Trono liceat ipsius monumentum condendi et adornandi prout ipsi videbitur et placuerit. Ac subtus eundem monumentum in terra condendi aliam sepulturam, que sit ac esse debeat ipsius Magnifici Domini Philippi Troni et eius heredum, successorum et descendentium in perpetuum tam marium quam feminarum in qua cadavera ipsius Magnifici Domini Philippi Troni, et eius heredum, successorum et ipsi Magnifico Domino Philippo collocari possint, semper et in perpetuum, absque aliquo obstaculo, controversia vel molestia ipsorum Reverendorum patrum, magistrorum et fratrum et eorum successorum ac cuiuscumque alterius persone de

mundo cuiusque cuiusque status, condictionis, gradus vel preheminentie existant. Ac quibus enim monumento et sepultura ulto unquam tempore sit nec esse possit aliqua persona tam ecclesiastica quam secularis [lacuna] uscumque status, gradus, condictionis vel preheminentie existant. Que habeat nec habere possit aliquam prerogatinam vel preheminentiam sed solum ipsi nobiles de cha Truno ut supra dictam et declaratum est. Qui autem Reverendissimus Dominus Generalis patres, magistri et fratres conventus, per se et successores eorum, sponte, libere et ex certa eorum animi scientia, et non requisiti, cum eorum successoribus se obtulterunt ac obligaverunt et obligant omni die in perpetuum celebrare ac celebrari facere unam missam in ecclesia ipsius conventus pro animabus ipsius, recolende memorie Serenissimi et Illustrissimi Principis Domini Nicolai Troni olim incliti Ducis Venetiarum, Magnifici et Generosi Domini Philippi Troni, eius geniti, et omnium aliorum de cha Truno."

[13] Filippo died on September 26, 1501, and was buried "in l'archa di so padre doxe," according to Sanudo, *Diarii*, iv, 1880, col. 144.

[14] Brasca, (1480) 1966, p. 48: "In questo San Francescho [*sic*: the church is Franciscan but was not dedicated to S. Francesco] vi sono le sepulture de li duci Francescho Foscari et Nicolao Trono de rimpecto l'una ad l'altra, che sono le due più belle sepulture de tuta Venetia."

[15] Pincus, *AB*, 1969, p. 247, n. 1.

[16] In translation the incription reads: "Niccolò Tron was the most eminent citizen, the most eminent senator, the most eminent prince of the aristocracy. By which most happy leader the most prosperous republic of Venice gained dominion over Cyprus. He joined with the king of the Parthians as a companion in arms against the Turks. With his living image he replaced debased coinage. To whose most innocent departed spirit his son Philip erected this deserved monument of divine work in everlasting eternity."

nence. Most exceptionally, the epitaph does not mention the doge's age at death or his death date.

The Tron Tomb is the first Venetian sepulcher to contain a double image of the defunct, portrayed once upright, once recumbent. The combination of recumbent and standing effigies is first found in French tombs toward the middle of the thirteenth century and in slightly later German tombs.[17] In these medieval tombs, the double image contrasted the secular and religious life of the deceased, or the state of life and death, or both. The first instance of a double image in Italian tombs is Arnolfo di Cambio's Monument of Pope Boniface VIII (d. 1303) in St. Peter's, finished in 1300; unfortunately, it is no longer possible to determine the pose of the live effigy or its relation to the tomb. In his Tomb of Henry VII (d. 1313) in the Camposanto, Pisa, executed in 1315, Tino da Camaino linked the recumbent effigy with a seated figure of the king. This formula was repeated in other tombs by Tino and his followers: in Italian tombs of the Trecento and early Quattrocento second effigies invariably are seated.

At the same time, there existed a few Italian examples of pedestrian effigies; but, unlike seated effigies, they were not paired with recumbent figures. Conspicuous examples include the statue of Enrico Scrovegni (d. 1336) in the Arena Chapel, Padua (if the figure did, indeed, designate a tomb or cenotaph) and the statue of Ranieri del Porrina (d. 1315) attributed to Gano da Siena in the Collegiata, Casole d'Elsa. In Venice, the earliest standing effigy belongs to the Tomb of Vettore Pisani (d. 1380) in SS. Giovanni e Paolo (originally in S. Antonio di Castello); it had no immediate successors. In the mid-1470s the motif suddenly came into favor. Pedestrian effigies were included in Pietro Lombardo's Tomb of Doge Pietro Mocenigo (d. 1476) in SS. Giovanni e Paolo; in Rizzo's Tomb of Giovanni Emo (d. 1483) in S. Maria dei Servi; in Giovanni Buora's Tomb of Jacopo Marcello (d. 1484) in the Frari; and in nearby Treviso, in the Tomb of Cristoforo Tolentino, formerly in S. Margherita, and in Buora's Tomb of Agostino Onigo (d. 1490) in S. Nicolò. At the beginning of the sixteenth century standing effigies achieved extraordinary popularity among Venetian sculptors. Examples include the Tombs of Melchiorre Trevisan (d. 1500) and Benedetto Pesaro (d. 1503) in S. Maria dei Frari; the Tomb of Dionigi Naldo da Brisighella (d. 1510) in SS. Giovanni e Paolo; the Tomb of Pellegrini Baselli Grilli (d. 1515) in S. Rocco, 1517; and the Tomb of Bartolino da Terni (d. 1518), S. Trinità, Crema, by Lorenzo Bregno.

Viewed either from the vantage of Italian tombs with double images of the deceased or from the vantage of Venetian tombs with standing effigies, the Tron Tomb is unique: it is the only tomb in which the deceased is represented once recumbent, once erect. This would seem a reversion to an older northern-European custom, but for the fact that in French and German medieval tombs with double effigies the standing figure is set above the recumbent one. Thus the image of the deceased in life was intended to allude to afterlife, to the fulfillment of the defunct's hope of resurrection. Where, in Venetian tombs, only the standing effigy appeared, resurrection was alluded to by the location of the effigy on the sarcophagus, in imitation of the risen Christ standing on his tomb.[18] Indeed, in the Tomb of Doge Pietro Mocenigo, the doge, upright on his sarcophagus, is paired on the central vertical axis with the resurrected Christ on his. The unusual location at the bottom of the tomb of the pedestrian effigy of Tron, on the

[17] For the history of this sepulchral tradition, see Bauch, 1976, pp. 161-185.

[18] See the Tombs of Pisani, Marcello, Emo, Onigo, Trevisan, Pesaro, and Bartolino da Terni.

other hand, makes it likely that the figure was intended to portray the doge before his death. Dressed in ducal habit, the statue is an accurate likeness of the doge as we know it from contemporary testimony (Figs. 65, 66).[19] Two stories higher, on axis with the standing figure, the recumbent effigy lies on the sarcophagus. After the interval of another story, and still on axis, there appears the *Resurrected Christ* standing on his sarcophagus. Christ's resurrection was a promise of resurrection to all believers. Between, and aligned with, the recumbent effigy and the *Resurrected Christ* is a personification of Hope, whose upward glance objectifies its meaning.[20] Thus by the simile of Christ's resurrection, and not by the literal representation of Tron in afterlife, did Rizzo allude to the ultimate resurrection of the doge.

Common to almost all Venetian tombs with standing effigies is the station of the deceased commemorated by the tomb: with the exception of the Tron and Onigo Tombs, all are dedicated to military leaders, and most Venetian pedestrian effigies are dressed in armor. The almost exclusive use of the standing effigy to celebrate outstanding soldiers seems a peculiarity of Venetian tombs. By contrast, northern-European tombs with standing effigies were dedicated indiscriminately to knights, rulers, clerics, even women. In Venice, on the other hand, the Tomb of Vettore Pisani seems to have established a precedent for memorials to military heroes. This was probably due less to aesthetic standards which his tomb established than to the prestige of its occupant: *Capitanio Generale* and renowned hero of the War of Chioggia, Pisani was widely acknowledged the savior of Venice. Two centuries later the association of pedestrian effigies with military heroes had become so common that Francesco Sansovino interpreted, ex post facto, the standing figure of Pisani as a glorification of martial virtue.[21]

The Tron Tomb is the first Venetian funerary monument in which large free-standing *Virtues* were introduced into niches excavated from the piers and background of the tomb. The prehistory of the motif is ramified: no single predecessor accounts for every aspect of the motif. From the beginning of the fifteenth century small *Virtues*, set in niches, frequently adorned the sarcophagi of Venetian tombs.[22] Slightly larger in scale are the niches with *Virtues* in the base of Pietro Lamberti's Tomb of Rafaello Fulgosio (d. 1427) in the Santo, Padua, executed between 1429 and 1431.[23] In the Tomb of Doge Tommaso Mocenigo (d. 1423) of 1423 by Lamberti and Giovanni di Martino da Fiesole in SS. Giovanni e Paolo, niches articulate the rear wall, as they do in the Tron Tomb. The figures within the niches are slightly larger still and are executed in the round; but they are *Saints*, not *Virtues*. Nearly life-size, free-standing *Virtues* appear at the top of the Mocenigo Tomb and at the head and feet of the effigy of Doge Francesco Foscari, but they are not in niches. Niches located one above the other in double-storied piers contain reliefs of *Saints* or *Virtues* in many Roman tombs of the third quarter of the fifteenth century.[24] In the Tomb of Pope Pius II (d. 1464) by Mino da Fiesole, originally in St. Peter's and now in S. Andrea della Valle, each lateral pier contains, above a base,

[19] Malipiero, *Arch. stor. ital.*, 1844, pt. 2, p. 661. See below, n. 39.

[20] First remarked by Pincus in *Studies . . . Janson*, 1981, p. 135.

[21] Sans., 1581, p. 8v: "hebbe (Pisani) a gloria della sua gran virtù, la statua pedestre."

[22] E.g., Tomb of Doge Antonio Venier (d. 1400), SS. Giovanni e Paolo; Tomb of Doge Tommaso

Mocenigo (d. 1423), by Pietro Lamberti and Giovanni di Martino da Fiesole, SS. Giovanni e Paolo, 1423; Tomb of Beato Pacifico by Nanni di Bartolo, S. Maria dei Frari.

[23] The source of this motif in the Fulgosio Tomb was Donatello and Michelozzo's Tomb of Baldassare Coscia (d. 1419) in the Baptistry, Florence.

[24] Pincus, *AB*, 1969, p. 252, n. 24.

three superimposed niches with *Virtues*.[25] Papal and ducal tombs are similar, not only in their common articulation of lateral piers, but also in their gargantuan size expressed in a multiplication of stories. Yet it is more likely that the tombs represent parallel developments than that one influenced the other.

The source of other motifs is more easily traced. Large-scale *Warriors* dressed in armor and supporting shields with the defunct's coat of arms (Figs. 91, 92) come from the Tomb of Francesco Foscari.[26] The Tron sarcophagus (Fig. 73) was copied from Niccolò di Giovanni Fiorentino's Tomb of Ser Orsato Giustiniani (d. 1464) formerly in S. Andrea della Certosa.[27] The panels with naked youths flanking tall vases filled with fruit and flowers (Figs. 117, 118) resemble the relief on the left of the lower story of Donatello's Cantoria, now in the Museo dell'Opera del Duomo, Florence. The source of Donatello's relief has been traced to a classical relief from the so-called *Throne of Ceres* in the Palazzo Arcivescovile in Ravenna (Fig. 219).[28] The earliest mentions of the antique relief do not antedate the eighteenth century,[29] but the existence of Donatello's work, identical in composition to the Roman relief, is sufficient proof that the "*Throne of Ceres*" was known in the fifteenth century. Very likely the antique relief, not Donatello's copy, was the source of Rizzo's loose interpretation.

The lunette of the tomb with the scene of *Christ's Resurrection* is crowned by a half-length blessing figure of *God the Father* (Fig. 64). On either side of the arch are statues of the *Annunciate Virgin* and *Angel*, as in the opposite Foscari Tomb. Thus the beginning and end of Christ's life were juxtaposed, and the hierarchy customary in Italian tombs, according to which the section of the tomb above the main entablature was reserved for scenes from sacred history or visions of heaven, was maintained. Below the main entablature mundane concerns intrude. The central tract is dedicated to the doge in his earthly epiphanies—in life and death; the effigies are linked by a verbal account of the doge's achievements. Around him are personifications which define the doge's intellectual and moral character: *Liberal Arts* flank the sarcophagus and effigy; *Virtues* are ranged above and accompany the standing *Doge* below. At outer edges two *Warriors* with Tron's escutcheon mount guard.

The Tron Tomb is unique among Venetian tombs in the number of personifications it contains. It is also unique in the negligence with which personifications were identified. Two figures have no attributes at all (Figs. 99, 104). Another possesses no more than a laurel wreath (Fig. 102)—an attribute found in too many contexts to serve as the sole means of identification. The uninscribed tablet of the middle figure on the right-hand pier could belong to either Arithmetic or Grammar (Fig. 96).[30] Charity appears three times—once as *Amor Dei* with flaming bowl (Fig. 89), once as *Amor proximi* with cloak heaped high with fruit (Fig. 103). The third personification of Charity holds a bowl (Fig. 100), but since fruit, flowers, or flame are absent, it is impossible to tell

[25] Meyer, *JpK*, 1889, p. 195.

[26] For the source of this motif, see Schulz, *NdiGF*, 1978, p. 13.

[27] Munman, *AB*, 1973, pp. 77, 79.

[28] Corwegh, 1909, p. 38. The connection between Rizzo's relief and the "*Throne of Ceres*" was independently observed by Pincus in *Studies . . . Janson*, 1981, pp. 147f., n. 26.

[29] Ricci, *Ausonia*, (1910) 1909, p. 253.

[30] Tervarent, ii, 1959, col. 367, *voce*, "tableau ou tablette." Identifying the tablet as the "tablet of the law," Pincus in *Studies . . . Janson*, 1981, pp. 143f., interpreted the figure as a personification of human order (in contradistinction to divine order symbolized by the lute-playing figure). But how can a tablet devoid of writing symbolize law? To me this seems its very antithesis.

under what species of Charity she occurs. By contrast, Faith and Temperance are missing altogether. An even more serious omission in a ducal tomb is Justice.[31] *Music* is
included as one of two Liberal Arts (Fig. 97), although there is no evidence that Tron
particularly practiced or patronized that art.[32] In contradistinction to these figures, a few
personifications observe the iconographic proprieties. They include *Hope* (Fig. 101),
Fortitude (Fig. 98), and *Prudence* (Fig. 79), if it originally held the snake it holds at
present.[33] The three figures that ornament the sarcophagus personify the attributes or
benefits of a well-run state.[34] On the right is *Security*, lounging negligently against a
column (Fig. 93); in the center, a sheaf of wheat distinguishes *Abundance*[35] or *Concord*[36]
(Fig. 94); at the left, with a palm frond, is *Peace* (Fig. 95). But in spite of the congruity
of these three figures, it is impossible to make of the Tron Tomb personifications an
articulate iconographic program. Evidently Rizzo introduced female personifications with
little reference to their ideological content, as he did when he took charge of the sculptural decoration of the Arco Foscari.[37] In justification we may observe that, by the time
of the Tron Tomb, the use of *Virtues* and *Liberal Arts* in architectural settings had become so conventional that a series of young draped women, by itself, probably sufficed
to convey the ideas of rectitude and culture.

At the time of its construction and until the end of the fifteenth century, the Tron
Tomb was, by far, the largest funerary monument in Venice (Fig. 64). As we have seen,
Filippo Tron was ceded the whole left wall of the choir, "from the top to the bottom
in its entirety as regards both its width and height." The archivolt of the tomb with its
central volutes reaches to the string-course at the height of the springing of the choir's
vault; the waist-length figure of *God the Father* breaks through the string-course to
emerge into the lunette of the choir. A frescoed dado extends the base of the tomb to
the bundles of colonettes at either end of the wall. The central rectangle of the tomb,
between the base and main entablature, is proportionate to the choir wall from floor to
string-course. That portion of the left wall of the choir which the architecture of the
tomb does not occupy is filled by a frescoed curtain, illusionistically suspended from
the string-course and pulled back as though to reveal the tomb.

Prior to the Tron Tomb all Venetian monuments that were neither free-standing
saints' shrines nor simple slabs were suspended on the wall high above the ground. In
the Tombs of Agnese (d. 1410) and Orsola (d. 1411) Venier in SS. Giovanni e Paolo
and Doge Francesco Foscari, elongated engaged columns linked monument and pave-

[31] In the Tomb of Doge Tommaso Mocenigo and
the Tomb of Doge Pasquale Malipiero (d. 1462) by
Pietro Lombardo, SS. Giovanni e Paolo, *Justice* is
singled out from the other *Virtues* by its location at
the apex of the tomb. (Cf. the position of *Justice* on
the Porta della Carta, Ducal Palace.) In the Tomb of
Doge Niccolò Marcello (d. 1474), by Pietro Lombardo, SS. Giovanni e Paolo, *Justice*, along with three
other *Virtues*, flanks the effigy. In the Tomb of Doge
Antonio Venier (d. 1400), SS. Giovanni e Paolo,
Justice appears among the seven *Theological* and *Cardinal Virtues* on the sarcophagus.
[32] The claim of Pincus in *Studies . . . Janson*, 1981,
pp. 143f., that this figure symbolizes divine har-
mony seems unsubstantiated to me.
[33] The figure's right hand is not original. For the

identification of *Prudence* as *Charity–Amor proximi*,
made on the basis of a hypothetical reconstruction
of its right hand, see Pincus, *AB*, 1969, pp. 247-256.
In refutation of Pincus's argument, see below, cat.
no. 16.
[34] Pincus in *Studies . . . Janson*, 1981, pp. 139ff.
[35] Ibid., pp. 141f.
[36] Tervarent, i, 1958, col. 199, *voce*, "gerbe de blé."
[37] The three draped female figures (Cat. no. 9),
which were added to the Arco Foscari under Rizzo,
bear no attributes at all. Their age, sex, and classicizing garments suggest that they were intended as
personifications, but it is impossible to guess what
they were meant to signify. See Schulz, *TAPS*, 1978,
pt. 3, p. 53.

ment. But the columns, attached not to the tomb but to the church wall, supported and enclosed only a fraction of the tomb. The Tron Tomb respects Venetian convention to the extent that its sarcophagus is ultimately borne by six consoles. But the sarcophagus is joined to, and surrounded by, a structure that rests upon the ground, like Roman and Florentine tombs. Like other Venetian tombs, the Tron Tomb is not excavated from the wall, but rather set against it: characteristically, it is the projection of the frame, rather than the recession of the background, which produces an enclosure.

Typical of Rizzo's architectural style is the flatness of the tomb. Most surfaces, including the rear walls of the three major niches, are flush with, or parallel to, the wall of the choir. Below the sarcophagus the plane of the central bay is aligned with the plane of the lateral piers. Projection and recession are minimal for small as well as large units. The niches of *Prudence* and *Charity* are extraordinarily shallow, while upper niches are segmental, rather than semicircular, in plan. The low relief of *putti* with vases hardly affects the planarity of the surface. Rizzo's compulsion to flatten forms is epitomized by his treatment of the double order of the central bay of the first story where the stepping of contiguous pilasters inexorably yields to the uniformity of an unbroken cornice.

Instead of a few large units scaled to the height of the entire tomb, a multitude of small units are scaled to the height of the nearly life-size statuary: the tomb contains so many stories that it might be mistaken for a facade.[38] The many units of which the design is composed are similar, when not identical, and uniformly blanket the entire surface. The same niche recurs eleven times and nine are filled by statues that can hardly be distinguished at a distance. The two scenes of *putti* are virtually identical. Upright rectangular panels function as plain slabs, reliefs, and epitaph. This mode of composition does not altogether inhibit the creation of a focus. Clearly, the sarcophagus with the effigy of the deceased, located at the center of the tomb, set against a ground of neutral slabs or moldings, and cantilevered forward, is the visual climax of the tomb. But the regular distribution of small, repetitive forms does cause the climax to seem a sudden and unexpected interruption rather than the culmination of concerted lines and patterns.

From the dense grid of verticals and horizontals curves are largely banished. The forms of which the Tron Tomb is composed are characteristically rectangular and closed. Edges are straight. As in the Altars of SS. James and Paul (Figs. 1, 2), capitals were omitted from the minor orders; therefore vertical profiles are rarely broken by the springing of volutes. The perpendicular juncture of every surface confers on edges the clarity of a ruled line. Moldings completely enclose every field, even the inner faces of the lateral piers. Contours of statues are closed, and limbs or attributes rarely cross the boundaries of niches. The tall and narrow proportions of the tomb and its components recall the verticality of the S. Marco Altars. Part of the tomb, like them, is richly ornamented: *rinceaux*, palmettes, and ribbons, carved in low relief, fill the first story and sarcophagus. The bareness of the rest exhibits that restraint which characterizes facades and funerary monuments at the beginning of the sixteenth century: its appearance in the 1470s is extraordinary.

Withal, the Tron Tomb embodies the vision of a sculptor, not an architect. Its design is conditioned by a colossal niche composed of rectangular piers and semicircular archivolt, but arch and niche are viewed, not as structures whose function is to support or

---

[38] E.g., the facade of S. Zaccaria.

contain, but as a backdrop against which to set relief and statuary. The niche is too shallow to contain entirely the sarcophagus, which projects beyond the plane of the lateral piers. The lateral piers, the monument's main supports, are divided, excavated, then anomalously ornamented with smaller pilasters. The extension of niches in a series linking piers and the interstice between them obscures the tectonic structure of the tomb. The width of archivolt and piers does not agree. Arches are stilted in the niches of the first story, segmental in the rest. As in Rizzo's later facades, each story is treated as an individual unit. To be sure, the breaking of the first three stories is continuous. But the height of every story changes in no apparent sequence and the A-B-C-B-A rhythm of the first three stories becomes A-B-B-B-B-B-A at the top. The basement of the tomb seems to extend beyond the edges of the tomb to the limits of the wall and therefore to belong equally to church and monument. An architect would surely have made a dado of the basement's height but changed its articulation.

Apart from its location on the ground—a feature that probably would have made its appearance in Venetian funerary monuments even without the precedent of the Tron Tomb—and its size, the Tron Tomb had little influence on the subsequent development of the ducal tomb. Already in his Tomb of Doge Niccolò Marcello (d. 1474) in SS. Giovanni e Paolo, Pietro Lombardo had utilized the tripartite articulation of the triumphal arch. The motif, developed in Pietro's Tomb of Doge Pietro Mocenigo, received its classic formulation in Tullio Lombardo's Tomb of Doge Andrea Vendramin. The triumphal arch offered an effective means of combining a single monumental order with life-size statuary. In addition, the centralized structure naturally produced a focus. These advantages, together with the idea of victory that its form conveyed, guaranteed to the triumphal arch an afterlife in the sepulchral sculpture of the High Renaissance. To the course of this development, the Tron Tomb was largely extraneous.

The bases of the statues on the tomb's first story (Figs. 66, 79, 89) are integral with the figures. Photographs made when *Prudence* was exhibited separately (Fig. 77) reveal that the vertical face of its base is unfinished. Evidently the base was to be inserted into the floor of the niche, as the figure and its companions are now installed. Concealment of the main device by means of which the stability of the statue was insured enhances the impression of reality: figures seem to stand naturally upon the niche's floor. Statues are life-size, free-standing, and executed in their entirety. The large niches, which leave much empty space around the figures, produce an ambience sufficient for a person, not the constricted setting of a statue. The marble of the *Doge*'s dress—that traditionally worn by him in public—was transmuted by its all over polychromy and gilding. In the figure of the *Doge*, where artistic aim coincided with the subject of a living man, these veristic devices were adjuncts to the exact reproduction of Tron's physiognomy (Fig. 65). Together they make the portrait of the doge as near a counterfeit of reality as any sculptor of the early Renaissance could extract from stone.

Yet Rizzo's impulse to create the illusion of a specific, living person contended with a contrary impulse that was no less potent—to seize the immutable and fundamental nature of the man. The *Doge*, represented frontally, is immobile (Fig. 66); his weight rests equally on both feet. As though more conscious of being seen than seeing, the *Doge* stares straight ahead with unfixed gaze. From the bust upward the figure is almost perfectly symmetrical. No momentary or transitory gesture, no expression or focusing of attention, detracts from the concept of the man in his essential and unchanging nature. The essential nature of the man is here, as in all medieval tombs, defined by his estate. His reticent demeanor, his size—larger, by a little, than that of any other figure in the tomb—and his ceremonial ducal garb, scrupulously copied, proclaim the elevated station of the doge.

Domenico Malipiero, a contemporary of Tron, tells us that the doge was of a serious nature. He was large; his face was ugly. His pronunciation was repugnant, for when he spoke he foamed at the lips. Malipiero thought the effigy very like its subject.[39] Yet Rizzo did not record Tron's physiognomy so faithfully that the sculptor succeeded in eliminating all traces of his style (Figs. 65, 68, 69). As in the head of *S. Bernardino* from the Altar of St. Clement (Fig. 19), brows arch high above the eyes. Folds of flesh beneath the brows encase the upper lids of both. The pronounced curvature of the lids of wide-opened eyes, the extended tear duct, and the creasing around the eyes, are similar in both. The long, horizontal furrows in *Tron*'s forehead and the wayward hairs of the brows that flame upward at the bridge of the nose, as though to consume the vertical folds of flesh that score the forehead, are also found in *St. Paul* (Fig. 5). *Tron* and *St. James* (Fig. 4) share the pouches beneath the lower lids, the low, knobby cheekbones, the deep furrows that seem to clasp the nostrils, and lips of analogous morphology and texture.

What change in Rizzo's style has been wrought by the passage of time? In the face of *Tron*, Rizzo realized the decorative potential inherent in the features, hair, and above all, the wrinkles of the face, manipulating them as though he were producing filigree. The arching of the brows is conditioned by the contour of the nose into which the brows descend. Brows, nose, and creases of the forehead together make a pattern that is independent of its representational significance. The curvature of the outer portion of the upper lid is parallel to that of the brow, while the entire contour of the lower lid is its mirror image. Wrinkles that constitute a series are invariably parallel. The S-shaped wrinkles around the nose echo the wrinkle at the inner corner of the right eye and the curling strands of the mustache at the corners of the mouth. The hairs of the brows are twisted in a cable pattern. The stone is worked more finely than in any of Rizzo's earlier sculptures: incisions register not only every lock of hair but every strand. Increased refinement of execution permitted the differentiation of textures with unparalleled virtuosity. The flesh of the lips is distinguished from that of the face, the hair of the beard from that of the brows. Locks of hair beneath the veil affect its surface and the background of the ornament of the *corno ducale* is minutely stippled.

The doge in life is contrasted with the doge in death (Fig. 67). The recumbent effigy lies on a cloth-covered bier, two cushions at his head, one at his feet. The *Doge*'s slightly parted lids denote eyes closed in death (Fig. 71); the *Doge*'s gesture signifies eternal rest. Attired in every other respect like the portrait of the *Doge* below (Fig. 66), the effigy lacks the *zoccoli* worn by Venetians for walking out-of-doors. Though the folds of the *Doge*'s cloak suit the figure's supine pose, the long, parallel folds of the *sottana* are modeled from a standing figure. The disposition of the feet also bespeaks a standing pose. In profile view (Fig. 73), however, upright feet furnish the figure with a vertical

---

[39] Malipiero, *Arch. stor. ital.*, 1844, pt. 2, p. 661: "L'è stà homo de gran natura, grosso, bruto de fazza, simile a la figura che è su la so sepoltura . . . l'è stà homo de gran animo; l'havea cattiva prononcia, de muodo che parlando el spiumava per i lavri." For other images of the doge, see Urbani de Gheltof, 1877, pp. 14f.

boundary equivalent to the boundary produced at the *Doge*'s head by the piling of the cushions. The central, longitudinal axis of the effigy runs between the parting of the cloak and the division of the feet. The crossing of the *Doge*'s hands marks the midpoint of the figure. The cloak is arranged symmetrically: even individual folds roughly correspond. For the sake of greater visibility, the figure's head and feet are turned very slightly forward. In addition, the figure is pulled forward to the edge of the bier and tilted slightly. Although not visible from below, the *Doge*'s proportions are strangely abbreviated: legs and feet are rendered in much smaller scale than is the upper half of the figure's body, while the width of the lower part of the figure also suffers radical reduction. The effigy is less finished on the farther, than on the nearer, side. Nevertheless, a great deal of care was expended on the execution of details that were hidden.

The pattern of folds made by the *Doge*'s cloak is analogous to the drapery of the Evangelist in the Aquileia *Man of Sorrows* (Figs. 59, 67). Folds fall in more than natural disarray: only a deliberate arrangement could have produced so intricate a pattern. Folds of varying sizes are dispersed over the entire surface covered by the cloak. With their supple contours, folds seem not to have assumed a fixed configuration. Series of short swags are linked by wide curves through several turns. On the outside of the figure (Fig. 72), folds, obliquely superposed, produce a pattern in which lines veer back and forth at uneven intervals. The limited plasticity of the mantle's folds and the adherence of the cloth belie the heavy velvet from which the garment actually was cut.

A comparison of the faces of live and dead effigies (Figs. 65, 68-71) justifies an attribution of the recumbent *Doge* to Rizzo. The morphology of the mouth and the wrinkled texture of the lips, the calligraphy of the locks of the beard, the wrinkles at the corner of the eye, the tremulous lines in the forehead, the flaring hairs of the brow, are identical in both. But the lesser degree of finish in the head of the recumbent *Doge* yields a work of lower quality. The even course of the brows lacks decorative pretensions and the vestigial hump of stone from which the mustache was carved produces the effect of a toupée.

The treatment of the *Doge*'s hands (Fig. 74) is idiosyncratic: similar hands are found in the Aquileia *Man of Sorrows* (Fig. 59) and in many later works. Each of the *Doge*'s hands was conceived as a closed unit from which parts were differentiated only secondarily. The individual fingers, including most of the thumb, were defined but not detached; the pinky is tucked under the fourth finger to a very slight extent. A long, shallow trough is created where the fingers join the hand. The surface of the fingers rises uniformly to the crest of flexed knuckles, then slopes downward without further break. Veins form a network of lozenges appliquéd to the otherwise smooth surface of the hand.

To the right of the *Pedestrian Effigy of Tron* stands *Prudence* (Figs. 76-80). The figure's resemblance to *Eve* (Fig. 48) provides conclusive evidence of Rizzo's authorship of the undocumented tomb. In her proportions, her long torso and short legs, in her distended abdomen and swelling thighs, *Prudence* is the twin of *Eve*. The excessively sloping and constricted shoulders contrast oddly with the breadth of chest. Small, high, hemispherical breasts are widely separated yet do not affect the figure's silhouette. *Prudence*'s hips are fuller than those of *Eve*, but waists are equally thick in both. Heads are small; necks are long. Thighs are lengthened at the expense of lower legs.

Prudence's pose seems to have been modeled on the stance of *Eve*. Though the body's weight is supported predominantly by one foot, axes of hips and shoulders are hardly inclined. The splayed feet are placed close together; most of the free foot is lifted from the ground. The major portion of the body's weight has sunk into the figure's hips and thighs: movement, clearly, is not imminent. Limbs remain close to the body conferring on the figure a closed silhouette. The head is turned and tilted downward. The hand exerts no pressure. All aspects of the pose combine to produce the most tentative of movements, as though Rizzo had meant to characterize the trait of prudence as conducive to indecisiveness and indolence.

Yet a good deal of what strikes us as weak and ineffectual in the pose is due, not to the artist's shrewd intent, but to the ineptitude of an assistant: evidently the statue was not brought to completion by the master. The back of the figure (Fig. 76) was delegated to an assistant: it is strange that Rizzo did not prefer to leave unfinished what could not be seen. The same assistant carved the lower part of the front of the statue including the flaccid, lumpy hand with its elongated fingers. Below the engaged knee, mantle and gown cling illogically to the leg. Where the taut convexities of *Eve*'s ankle, arch, and knuckles create the illusion of a bony structure, *Prudence*'s feet look like stockings stuffed with cotton wool.

The quirky folds on the figure's arm and projecting upper thigh are analogous to folds in the drapery of *St. Paul* (Fig. 6). The thin sash, which cinches the garment somewhat above the waist, has the same morphology in both. An antique draped female figure inspired the adherence of the sheer chiton to *Prudence*'s torso and thigh and the revelation of anatomy that this comports.[40] Folds are longer and thinner and less densely grouped than in *St. Paul*. Pliant folds, which part below the waist to meet at the crotch, diagram the abdomen's convexity.

The physiognomies of *Eve* and *Prudence* (Figs. 46, 47, 50, 81, 83, 85) are closely comparable. In both, the height of the bulging forehead is accentuated by the remarkable recession of the hair from the center of the crown. The fine ridges of eyebrows arch high above the eyes: in both, their course is nearly straight until they start a sharp descent toward the outer corner of the eye. Eyes are hardly recessed beneath the brows. On the flattened eyeball, pupil and iris are identically incised. At a certain distance beneath the eye the fleshy lower lid retreats to disclose the lower border of the socket. Full cheeks conceal the substructure of bone. The long, thin nose possesses small, flat, straight-edged nostrils, which barely project beyond the slope of the nose. The distance from nose to mouth is long. A tiny fold of flesh marks one corner of the mouth. The lower contour of the fuller, broader lower lip rises very slightly in the center. The small, receding, dimpled chin overlaps an incipient double chin.

Yet differences suggest that several years separate the execution of *Eve* and *Prudence*. In *Prudence*, face and features are elongated and attenuated; features are more widely separated. Even the small degree of modulation visible in *Eve* was eschewed in *Prudence*; forms are more nearly stereometric and therefore generalized. Edges are more precise, in part because they are now produced by facets, however small, and in part because

---

[40] Planiscig, 1921, p. 67, compared *Prudence*'s drapery with that of *Aphrodite* of the Fréjus type (*Venus Genetrix*, for which see Bieber, 1977, p. 46). Pope-Hennessy, 1958, p. 108, claimed the dependence of *Prudence* "from a statue of the type of Hera in the Capitoline Museum." I presume he meant the *Hera Borghese*, of which the best replica is in the Ny Carlsberg Glyptothek, Copenhagen (for which see Bieber, 1977, p. 48).

their course is made more regular, and deviations, more sudden and pronounced. The surface of the marble is more highly polished. The minutely incised curls that drape *Prudence*'s temples reproduce the locks of the *Doge*'s beard (Fig. 65).

Opposite *Prudence*, on the *Doge*'s left, stands *Charity* (Figs. 87-90). Her flaming bowl is a symbol of the love of God. In composition she is the complement of *Prudence* (Fig. 79). Both figures wear chitons, long-sleeved shirts, and mantles, wrapped around the legs and drawn together on inner hips. *Charity*'s ponderation mirrors that of *Prudence*. But where *Prudence* looks down, *Charity* arches her back and tilts her head so that her gaze is directed toward the upper reaches of the church—a metaphor for heaven—and thus toward the abode of God.

That Rizzo was responsible for *Charity* is proved by correspondences with *Eve* and *Prudence*. The proportions and anatomy of *Charity* and *Eve* (Figs. 89, 48) are virtually identical. Note the long neck and constricted shoulders. Breasts are small, high, and widely separated. In both *Charity* and *Eve*, tiny, embossed nipples mark the center of the hemispheres. *Charity*'s rib cage protrudes precisely as it does in *Eve*. The navel occupies the same position on the inclined surface of the abdomen. The exaggerated flexion of the wrist with cloak duplicates the elegant silhouette of *Eve*'s lowered arm and hand (Figs. 75, 89, 49, 51). Even the feet are morphologically similar.

The face of *Charity* (Figs. 82, 84) is comparable to that of *Eve* and *Prudence*. As in *Eve* (Figs. 47, 50), the peaked hairline recedes nearly to the crown of the figure's head, exposing a vast expanse of forehead. Short locks, which wave about the ears, follow similar courses, and twisted braids encircle the crowns of both. In *Prudence* (Figs. 81, 83), *Eve*, and *Charity*, bulging foreheads succeed high brows, produced by narrow ridges that pursue identical paths. *Charity*'s eyes are like those of *Prudence* but for the absence of irises and pupils. Upper lips are similarly contracted. As in the other figures, *Charity*'s short, receding chin is slightly dimpled and overlaps a nascent double chin.

But what a falling off is there! Features, made still more diminutive, occupy a disproportionately small area of the face while the expanse of flesh is correspondingly enlarged. Forehead, cheeks, and chin merge to create a single abstract form. Hardly a projection or indentation ripples the hemispherical surface of the face. Bony structure, whose gibbous forms ordinarily lend the face relief, played no role in the formation of this face. Its contour is regular and the amalgamation of locks of hair confers upon the face a geometric shape. Above the forehead, the hair was engraved, not carved, in order to preserve intact the stereometry of the cranial dome. The hair of the brows was barely indicated; textural differences were suppressed to favor the generalization of the surface. The edges of features were made regular and even. The silhouette of the nose was smoothed; the hollow in the center of the lower lip was filled. Upper and lower lids are symmetrical along a horizontal axis; eyes are nearly circular. As in antique statues, eyeballs lack irises and pupils. In contrast to the torpidity of *Prudence*, the face of *Charity* betrays that yearning which is the essence of love of God. But a sense of yearning is confined to opened mouth and upturned eyes—conventional signs of an emotion that the figure does not so much express as symbolize. How very differently did an intense emotion affect every limb and muscle of *Adam*'s body!

This radical change in the facial type of Rizzo's *Charity* is due, I think, to the influence of Antonello da Messina. Antonello is known to have worked in Venice between 1475 and 1476; he left behind a number of paintings, among which the S. Cassiano Altarpiece, executed for Pietro Bon by the early spring of 1476, was of fundamental importance for the subsequent development of Venetian painting. Like the head of *Charity* (Fig. 82), the heads of the Madonna and the Christ Child in the S. Cassiano Altarpiece (Fig. 225) are spherical: the surfaces of cheeks and foreheads are as even as if they had been turned on a lathe. Characteristic of Antonello's style are the elimination of anatomical detail and the geometric regularity of features. Textures are hardly distinguished: surfaces are as smooth and nondescript as vinyl. Heads of hair seem pressed from molds; neither hair nor veil modifies the geometric contour of the cranium. The inhibition of emotion in Rizzo's *Charity* can be traced to the mute inexpressiveness of Antonello's figures, which communicate neither by pose or gesture, nor by facial expression. Upturned eyes and opened mouth—those very means by which Rizzo expressed *Charity's* love—are all that disclose Sebastian's agony in Antonello's Dresden painting (Fig. 227).

Antonello's art has much in common with that of Tullio Lombardo whose influence also contributed fundamentally to the change in Rizzo's style. Tullio's style was modeled on antique Roman sculpture;[41] his art introduced a classicizing style, which dominated sculpture in northeast Italy until the advent of Jacopo Sansovino. Tullio's artistic personality is first discernible in the decorative sculpture of the choir of S. Giobbe, carved by Pietro Lombardo and his shop in the early 1470s.[42] According to Francesco Sansovino, Tullio assisted his father in the execution of the Tomb of Doge Pietro Mocenigo, finished by 1481, but his share in that work has never been defined. Because of the accidents of survival, Rizzo's *Charity*, completed by early 1480 at the latest, predates any of Tullio's sculptures with which it can be compared. *Charity* represents the first example of Tullio's influence: in the radical change in Rizzo's style which Tullio's art produced, *Charity* augured the course of Venetian sculpture through the first three decades of the sixteenth century.

Evidence of Tullio's influence can be seen in *Charity's* drapery (Figs. 88, 89), which differs from that of every one of Rizzo's figures examined hitherto. *Charity's* skirt has been lengthened so that its vertical folds gather about the figure's feet or rise above its arch. An identical configuration characterizes the drapery of all the *Virtues* from the sarcophagus of Tullio's Tomb of Doge Andrea Vendramin, in course of execution in 1493 (Figs. 223, 224). The neckline of *Charity's* chiton now is circular, like that of Tullio's *Justice* (Figs. 82, 224). The thin, flat, vertical strips, rendered in *schiacciato* relief, which describe the sheer and clinging fabric of *Charity's* dress, derive from Tullio: the same technique was used to the same end in the figure of Medusa from the Vendramin medallion of *Perseus*. The folds of *Charity's* mantle pursue the regular course of extended arcs typical of Tullio's drapery. Folds are frequently parallel to one another and evenly spaced. The folds of *Charity's* mantle are composed of even, narrow ridges, generally reenforced by an incision along one side. The quirks and kinks of *Prudence's* folds were relegated to a small area of *Charity's* projecting thigh. As in Tullio's figures, folds encircling the figure do not affect its straight, closed contour. The sudden downward swing of folds at the edge of *Charity's* projecting thigh recalls the changing directions of folds along the contour of the *Virtue* from the Vendramin sarcophagus (Fig. 223).

A comparison of the *Warrior* on the left of the Tron Tomb with Rizzo's *Adam* (Figs. 91, 39) reveals a change in style analogous to that of *Charity*. The *Warrior's* contrapposto

---

[41] For a definition of Tullio's style see Schulz, *Antichità viva*, Mar.–Apr. 1977, pp. 30ff.

[42] Ibid., pp. 35f.

produces the same differentiation of weight-bearing and free legs, the same slight divergence of the axes of hips and shoulders. But the *Warrior*, unlike *Adam*, is at ease. From below, both feet seem planted firmly on the ground. The body's weight has settled in hips and abdomen. Muscles are relaxed. As though oblivious of his role as guardian of the grave, the *Warrior*, with arm akimbo,[43] appears an uninterested bystander. As in the face of *Charity*, the surfaces of the body are smoother and more generalized than *Adam*'s. Clavicles are not described; the bones of the kneecap are not differentiated. Veins and tendons are concealed beneath the flesh. Less articulated contours, like the *Warrior*'s sloping shoulders, are rounded and unbroken. Across the upper torso, the paludamentum creates smooth passages, which traverse large tracts of the anatomy. Where folds arise from the surface of the adherent cloak, they are longer, smoother in outline, more nearly parallel, and more regularly spaced. The nervous tremor of Rizzo's folds is almost entirely gone. The folds of the sleeve of the tunic beneath the *Warrior*'s armor match those encircling the feet of *Charity* (Fig. 89). The repetitive carving of the ornamented greaves and cuirass betrays a certain lassitude. The articulation of leather straps is more summary than in "*Mars*" (Fig. 34) and the regular disposition of the straps makes no concession to the projection of the thigh.

The *Warrior*'s physiognomy (Fig. 86) belongs to Rizzo's female type: though less elongated, individual features are most similar to *Prudence*'s (Fig. 85). Comparison with "*Mars*" or *Adam* (Figs. 44, 45) reveals to what extent the features of the *Warrior*'s face have been contracted: large expanses of unmodulated cheek and brow produce vacuity—the effect of too few forms inhabiting too large an area—which characterized even more forcibly the face of *Charity* (Fig. 82). No traces of a skeletal structure are visible beneath contours as inflated and rotund as those of *Charity*. The stereometric form of cheeks, forehead, and chin are combined with features delineated graphically. Brows are formed by a projecting line. The eyes are bordered by rims composed of flat, raised strips with faceted sides. As in the mouth of the standing *Doge* (Fig. 65), the edges of the lips are raised—a sculptural equivalent to the thin black contour line common to late Quattrocento painting. Outlines of features, like the surfaces of the face, follow the simplest, most obvious course: the contour of the brow, for instance, no longer breaks over the outer corner of the eye. Textures are almost uniformly smooth. The flesh of the lips is not defined by incised lines and the regular hatching of the eyebrows conveys no sense of hair.

Like *Charity*, the left-hand *Warrior* betrays the influence of Antonello da Messina. Both the *Warrior* and *St. Sebastian* (Figs. 91, 227) are at rest; *St. Sebastian*'s weight has slumped into his hips and thighs; his muscles are relaxed. The same generalization of anatomical form, the same continuity of gently rounded contours, the same smooth, undefined textures, are apparent here. Both figures are emotionally remote—detached alike from the context of tomb or painting and from the observer, whom their fixed stares disregard.

Though we may deplore the stylistic reorientation of *Charity* and the *Warrior* as a

[43] Pohlandt, *BJ*, 1971, p. 191, n. 50, believed that the gesture was derived from Donatello's bronze *David* in the Bargello, which it does, in fact, resemble. But the gesture appears in many other works as well. For Erasmus it characterized the bearing of a soldier. Indeed, the gesture is found again in the pedestrian effigy of the Venetian commander, Jacopo Marcello, in S. Maria dei Frari and in both *Warriors* from the Tomb of the Doge Andrea Vendramin in SS. Giovanni e Paolo. See Brand, 1977, p. 212.

decline from the apogee of *Adam* and *Eve*, we should not therefore infer that figures which exemplify the new abstract and inexpressive mode were executed by assistants. The anatomical structure of the *Warrior*'s torso and his muscular arm and leg are those of *Adam* (Figs. 91, 39). The mechanics of the *Warrior*'s contrapposto are rendered faultlessly. The soldier's Roman armor is archaeologically correct. The figure's physiognomy finds numerous correspondences in Rizzo's oeuvre. The *Warrior*'s locks are identical in design and execution to *Adam*'s own (Figs. 86, 38).

The measure of Rizzo's achievement in the *Warrior* is given by its companion on the right, intended as a mirror image (Figs. 91, 92). The ponderation of the right-hand *Warrior* is impaired by numerous mistakes. The free hip is thrust out, not retracted, and the axes of hips and shoulders are parallel rather than divergent. As so often happened when a sculptor could not contrive to make his figure revolve upon its axis, the author of the *Warrior* on the right introduced a tilt, with the unfortunate result that the pit of the figure's neck falls beyond its weight-bearing heel and the *Warrior* appears unbalanced. The author of the *Warrior* on the right imitated the corrugated surface of the left *Warrior*'s torso but failed to understand the configuration of the rib cage. He adopted the position of the left *Warrior*'s bent arm but changed its gesture. As a consequence, elbow and upper arm are dislocated and the *Warrior*'s forearm is much too short. The folds of the paludamentum are flatter, straighter, more repetitive, than Rizzo's drapery at its most repetitive. The folds on the figure's forearm do not suggest recession beyond the visible boundary of the limb. Locks of hair are as uniform and repetitious as if extruded by a machine. In copying the left-hand *Warrior*'s physiognomy (Figs. 86, 111), the author of his companion made every form more definite, every contour more precise. Brows have two distinct boundaries; the hollows between the mouth and nose and below the lower lip have edges. Suffice it to note, as incontrovertible proof of an assistant's intervention, the frown-lines of the seventy-four-year-old *Tron* (Fig. 65) on the *Warrior*'s youthful brow.

Security and *Peace* at either end of the sarcophagus may safely be attributed to Rizzo. For *Security*'s pose and the draping of its mantle (Fig. 93), Rizzo was indebted to an antique figure type used frequently for statues of Aesculapius, less frequently for other draped male figures like Jupiter and Bacchus, and occasionally for female draped figures.[44] The same model probably served Antonio Lombardo for the statuette in the right-hand niche from his relief of the *Forge of Vulcan* in the Hermitage, Leningrad. Of all the statues of the Tron Tomb, the drapery of *Security* is closest to that of Tullio's figures. But its canon of proportions, its facial type and hair, are Rizzo's own. In *Peace* (Fig. 95), the pose and gestures, the downcast eyes and expressionless mouth, were drawn from *Eve* (Fig. 48). The mellifluous pattern of the figure's folds represents the most complete repudiation by Rizzo of his early style. The head is even more generalized than the head of *Charity* (Fig. 82): locks of hair are now amalgamated into a single mass, which merges with the face to form a perfect sphere.

Comparison with the two lateral *Personifications* of the sarcophagus makes evident the inferior quality of the central figure (Fig. 94). The figure's stance is unbalanced: in lieu of turning, the figure tilts. The series of horizontals produced by the various borders of

44 See Reinach, i, 1897, p. 188, no. 679, p. 287, no. 1147, p. 378, no. 1641B, p. 542, no. 2262, p. 553, no. 2312C, and ibid., ii, pt. 1, 1897, p. 34, no. 3.

dress and mantle is monotonous and divides adjacent portions of the body. A solecism like the gathering of the mantle's folds above the free leg suggests that Rizzo had no part in *Abundance/Concord*'s design.

The extent to which Rizzo participated in the execution of the other *Personifications* is moot (Figs. 96-104). I suspect that Rizzo supplied designs that he kept simple purposely, both because he meant to delegate the *Personifications'* execution and because he was impatient of their completion. Therefore figures are monolithic: limbs adhere to the body, and members or attributes are rarely free-standing. Projections and recessions are limited in number and extent; the statues' mass is never perforated. Drapery affects the linear design of figures but has little bearing on their three-dimensional form. Contours are predominantly smooth and straight. Yet, as is common in Rizzo's work, figures are less blocklike than they are columnar.

Rizzo imposed on all the figures a uniform quality and style. Figure and facial type, like age and sex, are constant. The frequent absence of attributes conduces to homogeneity. Poses deviate little from a standard contrapposto in which an unequal distribution of weight is generally manifested solely by the projection of a knee and turn of a free foot. When it does exist, expression is confined, as in *Charity*, to a focused glance and slightly parted lips. Heads are generalized; separate locks are rarely defined by plastic means. Little distinction was made between the fictive textures of cloth, flesh, and hair. Drapery alone gives variety to figures: indeed, the drapery of no two figures is alike. Patterns often are complex, hinting at the anatomy of underlying forms or lower layers of clothing in emulation of Hellenistic sculpture (Fig. 98).

I suspect that Rizzo did not leave the entire execution of every figure to assistants but intervened in the final stages of most. What Rizzo did, he did rapidly and summarily. In many places the rough surface of the figures betrays the use of the drill, claw chisel, and flat chisel. Indeed, the face of *Music* (Fig. 108) is no more than a sketch. That many of the figures are unfinished must be considered in an assessment of their quality and definition of their style. *Fortitude*'s face strikingly resembles that of *Charity* (Figs. 110, 82): that of *Music* employs the same schemata (Fig. 108). By contrast, the more highly finished face of *Charity–Amor proximi* (Fig. 103), based on Rizzo's *Prudence* (Fig. 81), reveals the presence of a scrupulous assistant. The tedious drapery pattern of the *Personification* with a tablet (Fig. 96) is relieved by a flurry of *schiacciato* folds at the bottom of the figure, which recalls the drapery at the feet of *Charity* (Fig. 89). The head of *Hope* (Fig. 109), less finished than, but otherwise identical in quality and style to, the head of the left-hand *Warrior* (Fig. 86), rests upon a body that bears no signs of Rizzo's hand (Fig. 101). By contrast, the folds in the cloak of even so inferior a figure as the *Personification* at the extreme left of five (Fig. 99) are comparable in design and execution to the folds in the paludamentum of the *Warrior* on the left (Fig. 91).

Rizzo's role in the execution of the figures crowning the tomb was also variable and partial. The preliminary blocking out of so simple a form as that of the *Virgin Annunciate* (Fig. 107) could have been entrusted to a mere apprentice, but the surface of the figure is probably the master's. To assign the work to Rizzo, however, is not to discount its failings: we must recognize that the sculptor bestowed upon this figure no more physical or mental effort than the minimum required to produce a finished work. From its want of plastic elaboration we might fancy it carved from a stone as unyielding as porphyry. The *Angel Gabriel* (Fig. 106) was also the product of collaboration. Probably the master carved the *Angel*'s face—similar to that of *Adam* (Fig. 38)—and established the course of several folds; the rest he left to an assistant. Begun by Rizzo, the *Risen Christ* (Fig. 105) was finished by an assistant. The stance is sure. The anatomy of the legs recalls that of the left-hand *Warrior* (Fig. 91). The taut tendons of the neck, the protruding sternum and clavicles, the flexed bicep, resemble *Adam*'s articulate anatomy (Fig. 39). But neither face, nor hands, nor drapery can be due to Rizzo. The lifeless surface of the figure's torso betrays the unskilled hand of an assistant.

The three faces of the sarcophagus are filled with four heads of Roman emperors (Fig. 73), none of which can be identified with certainty. The heads are presented as they appear on Roman coins—in profile view, truncated at the naked shoulders, a laurel wreath tied behind the head. But unlike Roman coins, the underside of the busts is shown, as if the busts were sculptures seen from below. The heads are carved in low relief on fields shallowly sunk into the face of the sarcophagus. In its modeling, the left-hand *Emperor* on the front face of the sarcophagus is superior to the other three. Oddly, its field is not centered within the wreath; rather, the medallion is shifted so far to the right that its right edge is concealed by the festoon. In a sharply lateral view, corresponding to a vantage opposite the center of the sarcophagus, the projecting wreath would naturally overlap the right edge of the left medallion. The medallion on the left is the only one in which this visual distortion is reproduced.

To their antique prototype the two reliefs of *putti* with vases owe the absence of an illusionistic space (Figs. 117, 118, 219). The projecting frame creates a boxlike space sufficient to contain relief of medium height. Figures stand on the inner face of the bottom of the frame which, not inclined, appears no deeper than it really is. But Rizzo's plain backgrounds and figures, which fill the height of the reliefs, attenuate even that frail spatial illusion produced by the sculptor's antique model. The relief of Rizzo's panel is lower than classical relief. Where the edges of forms in the so-called *Throne of Ceres* gradually recede, the edges of even the most plastic forms in Rizzo's panels are flat and sharply undercut: inward-slanting facets detach contours from the ground, creating the effect of spatial intervals by the line of shadow that follows silhouettes.

The panel on the left (Fig. 117) seems entirely autograph. The children are nearly the same age as the *putti* of the "*Throne of Ceres*"; by contrast, the actors in the right-hand relief (Fig. 118) are two or three years older. The less articulate contours of the children on the right are partly a result of their greater age and more mature physique, and partly a result of an assistant's hand, to which we may attribute also the awkward and repetitious tilt of the head of the right-hand figure, the absence of foreshortening in the vase, and the lack of overlapping among the fruits. But disparities of quality and style are not great: very likely the children in the right-hand panel were reworked by Rizzo.

The ornament of the architectural members shows as extreme a change in style as the figures do. Among the pilasters of the first story, one is unique: it is the first pilaster on the left (Fig. 112). The components of its *Pflanzenkandelaber* and capital are smaller in scale and carved in greater detail than the decoration of any of the other pilasters. Where the fleshy leaves, the bursting pods, the full-blown blossoms in the other pilasters depict vegetation at the height of summer, the spare forms of the pilaster on the left evoke the first unfolding of spring foliage. Ornament is composed of fine, linear forms, in which attenuated tendrils predominate over sprays of leaves or pods. The pattern thus produced is extremely open. Curving tendrils embrace a large proportion of the ground. In blossoms, each petal is separated from its neighbor and the edges of leaves are notched. Frequent configurations of radiating points encourage the interpenetration of space and substance. The diminutive vase and the absence of any other dense or massive form produce a pattern as light as it is open. This effect is enhanced by the planes and arrises of the very low relief.

The same style distinguishes the decoration of the spandrels of the niche containing *Prudence* (Fig. 115). In contrast to the spandrel of the niche with the effigy of *Tron* (Fig. 116), the scale of ornament is smaller, its carving more detailed. Tendrils are lengthened, while blossoms and leaves contract. Relief is lower and surfaces are flatter. A degree of spatial illusion in *Tron*'s spandrel, created by the gradation in height of the relief, over-lapping, and the foreshortening of sepals, contrasts with the flat extension of the pattern along a two-dimensional plane in the spandrel next to *Prudence*. The design of *Tron*'s spandrel is less abstract. Fronds possess a closer kinship to their counterparts in nature and the attachment of buds to stems is botanically plausible. Both designs consist of curves. But the leisurely rhythms and expansive pattern of the spandrel next to *Tron* contrast with the tension of the tightly coiled circles of the spandrel next to *Prudence*.

The first pilaster on the left and the spandrels of *Prudence*'s niche bear the earmarks of Rizzo's decorative style. Pilasters of similar design and style frame the Altars of SS. James and Paul (Figs. 3, 6, 9). The stretched coils of the spandrels of *Prudence*'s niche repeat a motif found in the large left-hand pilaster on the Altar of St. Paul (Fig. 6). In contradistinction, all the other pilasters (Figs. 112-114), like the spandrels of *Tron*'s niche, reproduce Pietro Lombardo's plastic ornament, its salient forms and rounded surfaces. Motifs are fewer and larger than Rizzo's, and more frequently repeat them-selves. Surfaces are very densely filled. Naturalistic forms typically show flora at its most mature.

Motifs, as well as style, can be matched in the vocabulary of Lombardo's ornament. These motifs include the triple acanthus leaf that functions as a vase from which the *Pflanzenkandelaber* rise (Figs. 113, 222), and the eagle, wings outspread, which stands at the summit of the shaft (Fig. 112). Masks, like the one in the capital of the second pilaster on the right (Fig. 112), are found throughout the interior of S. Maria dei Mi-racoli. Classicizing *rinceaux* that within their curves enclose rosettes, pods, and sprays of berries pecked by birds, were regularly used by Pietro for pilaster shafts, friezes, and soffits (Fig. 222). Indeed, the inner face of the pilaster immediately to the left of the standing *Doge* (Fig. 113) is similar enough to the pilasters of the Tomb of Doge Pasquale Malipiero (Fig. 221) to warrant the assumption of common authorship.

Thus the carving of most of the architectural ornament for the Tron Tomb seems to have been delegated by Rizzo to stonemasons previously employed by Pietro Lom-bardo. Can the assistants with whom Rizzo collaborated in the execution of the statuary of the upper stories have been Pietro's too? Certain stylistic peculiarities suggest just such a possibility. The massive bunches of tight curls, which frame the right-hand *Warrior*'s face (Fig. 111), cannot be matched among figures produced in Rizzo's shop but recur in the caryatid *Warrior* on the right, and the soldier in the first row on the left, of Lombardo's Tomb of Doge Pietro Mocenigo (Fig. 217). The stippled decoration of *Fortitude*'s armor (Fig. 110) recalls the armor of Doge Pietro Mocenigo. Stippled armor and jewels carved in relief, like *Fortitude*'s are worn by the *Virtues* in Pietro's Tomb of Doge Niccolò Marcello. The peplum of the central *Personification* of the Tron sarcophagus (Fig. 94) resembles those of the Angels in the lunette relief on the Tomb of Doge Pasquale Malipiero (Fig. 221). Perhaps we may construe as evidence of one assistant's employment under Rizzo the head of *Charity*, to the left of the Malipiero lunette (Fig. 218), copied from Rizzo's *Charity–Amor Dei* (Fig. 82).

In what sequence were the various parts of the Tron Tomb executed? It seems logical to suppose that those parts done most carefully were executed first. No doubt when Rizzo commenced work on the Tron Tomb he intended to create a monument worthy of its size and site and the station of the personage it honored. But it must have become apparent soon that to expend that effort required for the carving of the visage of the standing *Doge* or the first pilaster on the left on all the figures and architectural members of the tomb would have added untold years to the tomb's realization. Therefore Rizzo renounced most of the architectural ornament above the lowest story, simplifying and enlarging the moldings in the upper portion of the tomb. He simplified the design of *Personifications*, jettisoning the tomb's iconographic program. And he delegated to assistants the carving of remaining statuary and ornament. It is unlikely that Rizzo's own shop provided collaborators in sufficient number: despite the intervention of assistants in the Aquileia *Man of Sorrows* and the figures from the altar of the barbers' guild in S. Sofia, Rizzo's sculptural commissions were neither so extensive nor so many as to require more than three or four journeymen and apprentices. In contrast, Pietro Lombardo's shop was large. In the 1470s Pietro was liberally assisted in the decorative carving of the choir of S. Giobbe, the choir screen in the Frari, and three ducal tombs. Thus it is conceivable that Rizzo's assistants should have been drawn from Pietro's shop. In the matter of architectural ornament, Rizzo left these workers to their own devices: naturally they repeated schemata with which they were familiar. In the statues, Rizzo exercised more control, designing figures and establishing a common drapery style and facial type. In the final stage of work, Rizzo himself seems to have intervened. But figures were finished off in summary fashion in the evident belief that technical deficiencies would not be visible from the ground. Thus was the tomb completed expeditiously: from the date on which the site in the choir of the Frari was ceded to Filippo Tron to the day on which the finished tomb was seen by Santo Brasca, not more than four years had elapsed.

The architectural ornament of the Tron Tomb is easily divided into those parts executed by Rizzo or assistants trained under him and those parts carved by assistants of Pietro Lombardo. Among the former, in addition to the first pilaster on the left and the spandrels of the niche containing *Prudence*, is the sarcophagus of the doge (Fig. 73), whose moldings are similar in scale, style, and technique to those of the Scala dei Giganti (Figs. 191, 192). The earliest figures must include the two effigies of the doge (Figs. 66, 67). I suspect that *Prudence* (Fig. 79) also was carved during an initial campaign of work, in spite of an assistant's intervention, for the figure does not manifest the influence of Antonello da Messina or Tullio Lombardo, which produced so radical a change in Rizzo's style. The influence of Antonello and Tullio strongly affected all the other figures on the tomb—both those that Rizzo carved himself and those he delegated to assistants. The runnels made by the chiton's folds on the torso of *Charity–Amor Dei* (Fig. 88) suggest that Rizzo was uneasy imitating Tullio when he began the figure. Therefore we may hypothesize that *Charity* was the first of the statues carved in the new manner. Indeed, it is logical to suppose that Rizzo finished the statuary of the first and most visible story before proceeding to the rest. By contrast with *Charity–Amor Dei*, the drapery of *Security* and *Peace* at either end of the sarcophagus (Figs. 93, 95) is more boldly designed and more deftly executed. Along with the *Warrior* on the left (Fig. 91), *Security* and *Peace* probably represent a further stage in the assimilation of Tullio's and Antonello's art. Very likely, they were executed concurrently with the remaining *Personifications* and with the figures at the summit of the tomb.

It is possible that Rizzo's resolve to expedite the manufacture of the tomb was quickened by its interruption during the sculptor's participation in the second siege of Scutari in the latter half of 1478. We do not know whether it was in this or in the earlier siege that Rizzo was wounded: a period of recovery might have added greatly to the tomb's delay. It is also possible that Rizzo's military service conduced indirectly to his change in style. An absence of several months might have made Rizzo receptive to new stylistic currents and willing to essay a foreign style. On this admittedly weak foundation do I tentatively base my dating of the Tron Tomb, by proposing the execution of the two effigies, *Prudence*, the sarcophagus (minus its figures), and a few other architectural details, between the spring of 1476 and the spring of 1478, and the execution of the rest, between late winter 1479 and the winter of 1479/80.

CHAPTER FOUR

Works of Mid-Career

FROM the end of the 1470s until the mid-1480s Rizzo received more commissions for sculpture than at any other period during his career. Two prestigious commissions frame this time span—the Tron Tomb at the beginning, the Tomb of Giovanni Emo (killed in September 1483) at the end. During this period five statues for the Arco Foscari were supplied by Rizzo's shop, proving that in spite of other obligations, Rizzo remained in the employ of the Venetian government. Concurrent with these projects are several autograph works that are modest, both in purpose and in quality: like the statuary carved during the final campaign of work on the Tron Tomb and the statuary of the Emo Tomb, they betray a flagging of creative energy. This lapse is first apparent in works datable soon after the sculptor's return from the second siege of Scutari. If Rizzo was wounded then, its cause may have been partly physical. Until the mid-1480s a certain indifference characterizes all of Rizzo's sculpture; the assumption of foreign styles perhaps compensated for diminished powers of invention. But this state did not outlast the rebuilding of the Ducal Palace, which, challenging Rizzo's finest abilities, rekindled his ambition.

The *Annunciate Angel* from the main portal of the Madonna dell'Orto (Figs. 119-122) is frequently attributed to Rizzo. Its style, which stands midway between that of *Prudence* and *Charity*, warrants its dating to this period of Rizzo's career. Neither the author nor the date of the *Angel* is recorded. But documents regarding the construction of the portal furnish limits of 1460 to 1483 for the execution of the statue. Architecture and sculpture of the portal were commissioned from Bartolomeo Bon on June 21, 1460, by the Scuola di S. Maria e di S. Cristoforo, which had its seat at the Madonna dell'Orto. Work was largely paid for prior to Bartolomeo's death, probably in the second half of 1464.[1] I have hypothesized that two Annunciate figures in the Victoria and Albert Museum, London, were intended by Bon for the portal. But Bon did not live to complete them and they were not installed.[2] By contrast, none of the figures that do adorn the portal was executed by, or under, Bon. *St. Christopher* can be attributed to Niccolò di Giovanni Fiorentino and dated to the mid-1460s.[3] The *Virgin Annunciate* (Figs. 237-239), which derives its composition from Bon's *Virgin Annunciate* in London, also was carved in Niccolò's shop, in part by the master himself; it can be dated to 1467/68.[4] Thereafter, work seems to have been suspended for a time. In 1475 pieces of the portal were transported from Bon's workshop to the church. In 1481 the two marble columns that flank

[1] The documents concerning the portal of the Madonna dell'Orto were published by Gallo, Ist. ven. SLA. *Atti* (Cl. di scienze morali), 1961-62, pp. 203f., docs. 2, 3.

[2] Schulz, *TAPS*, 1978, pt. 3, pp. 57ff.
[3] Schulz, *NdiGF*, 1978, pp. 30ff., 36.
[4] See cat. no. 22.

the doorway were raised. In 1482 the portal's foliate ornament was carved. By March 1, 1483, the portal was fully installed.

Like *Prudence* (Figs. 78-80), the *Annunciate Angel* has an exceptionally long neck and a broad chest oddly combined with narrow, sloping shoulders. Both wear chitons over long-sleeved shirts, bound high above the waist by a narrow sash. Although the surface of the *Angel* is badly worn, it is possible to perceive, in the fine folds of the chiton and the tremulous folds of the shirt sleeves, configurations similar to those produced by *Prudence*'s drapery. As there, quirky folds gather most densely at the break between hip and thigh. The *Annunciate Angel*'s elongated face, long thin nose, brows produced by a thin ridge that arches high above the eye, fleshiness beneath the brows succeeded by a rounded hollow at the inner corner of the eye, truncated irises and pupils—the former incised, the latter partly drilled to produce a crescent-shaped indentation, recall *Prudence* (Figs. 81, 119). The contour of the sharply cut lower lids, the contracted mouth, the blunted dimpled chin and the incipient double chin are very similar in both. The *Angel*'s mantle is wrapped over the left shoulder like a toga, as in the statue of *St. James* (Fig. 3). The bottom of the cloak, where it descends from the *Angel*'s lowered arm, is rolled up like the border of the cloak of *St. Paul* in the altar of S. Marco (Fig. 6). But the folds below the figure's knees are analogous to those of *Charity*'s dress and mantle (Fig. 89). Folds are very long and flat; their diagonal paths seem to have evolved from arcs. Around the lower legs, drapery provides a columnar matrix, smooth in surface, regular in contour, from which bare feet, splayed to provide a stable base, partially emerge. Drawn upon this matrix are fine, thin folds, which fall in parallel strips to the ground. Thus a date for the *Annunciate Angel* at the end of the 1470s, when work on the portal again pressed forward after a hiatus of several years, seems most plausible.

A relief in the lunette of the portal of the Scuola dei Calegheri in Campo S. Tomà can also be assigned to Rizzo on the basis of its style (Fig. 124). An inscription informs us that the building which housed the shoemakers' guild was acquired in 1446.[5] A second inscription in the lintel of the portal gives the date of September 16, 1479.[6] We may assume that the latter date refers to the beginning of construction of the portal and that the lunette relief, which is the portal's only sculptured decoration, was made not long afterward.

The lunette relief shows the shoemaker, St. Anianus, seated before the gate of Alexandria. According to Jacopo da Voragine's *Golden Legend* (chapter lx, April 25), St. Mark's shoe broke as he was entering the city. He gave it to be repaired to Anianus. Working on the shoe, Anianus pierced his hand with an awl. St. Mark made mud with his saliva and rubbed it on the wound; Anianus was immediately cured. Converted by St. Mark, Anianus was baptized with all his house and eventually succeeded Mark as Alexandria's second bishop. He died a martyr's death. It was natural, therefore, that the Venetian shoemakers' guild should have chosen Anianus as its patron saint. As St. Mark's lieutenant and successor, the saint enjoyed a wider cult in Venice. In 1128 his body had

[5] The inscription, located on the left corner of the ground floor of the facade, reads: 1446 A DI 14 XB / FV COMPRADO / QVESTA SCOLLA / DEL ARTE / DI CALE-GERI. A second inscription at the right corner of the facade reads: MDLXXX / IN TEMPO DE MIS / MARCHO CAPO / GROSSO DAL / CHANPANIEL / GASTALDO ET / MISTRO ZVANE / DAL FRATEMASER / ET MISTRO GIV-LIO / DALA NOVIZA / SCHRIVAN ET / CHONPAGNI / FV RESTAVRATA. (This transcription was completed with the help of Venice, Mus. Cor., MS Cicogna 2017, Cicogna, *Inscrizioni*, i, p. 23v, nos. 209, 210; and Soràvia, ii, 1823, pp. 190f.)

[6] See below, cat. no. 19.

been brought from Alexandria to Venice and laid to rest in S. Maria della Carità: the suppositious day of his translation, December 2, was a Venetian feast day.[7] In the context of the life of St. Mark, the scene of St. Anianus's miraculous cure was frequently depicted in Venetian art.[8]

To some degree, Rizzo sought to create an authentic setting in his relief. Orange trees denote a warmer climate than Venice's. Battlemented walls with round-arched openings convey a distant time and place. Attentive to naturalistic detail, Rizzo placed the wound in Anianus's left hand, logically assuming that the right hand would have held the awl. Turban and beard characterize St. Anianus as Oriental. The figure, seated cross-legged on the ground, no doubt adopts the pose in which shoemakers customarily performed their work in ancient times.

The relief is covered with a thick layer of polychromy. Given the external location of the relief, we must assume the polychromy to be of recent date. We do not know whether the relief originally was painted. Most of the scene is carved in low relief. Elements of the setting and the farther arm of St. Mark hardly project at all. By contrast, the joined hands of the two saints, as the composition's focal point, are fully three-dimensional though not free-standing. Some contours, principally St. Mark's, are undercut; others are separated from the ground by an incision or narrow facet. The lunette is framed by an internal border, which is interrupted at the lower left corner.

As in the relief of the *Conversion of St. Paul* (Fig. 17), the protagonists of the *Miraculous Cure of St. Anianus* are disposed at the bottom of the composition and therefore at the forefront of the fictive space. Like St. Paul's steed, the figures are shown in profile; the action proceeds parallel to the plane of the relief. Very large in scale, the figures overlap large portions of the setting placed rather far behind them. Except for a connecting wall, the setting, too, runs parallel to the relief ground. The pictorial devices of overlapping, diminution in scale, and linear perspective were employed to create a sense of recession into space, but Rizzo ignored those rules by means of which recession could be made consistent and measurable. The orthogonals of the left half of the wall converge in a vanishing area—not a vanishing point—located in Mark's beard. The mostly parallel orthogonals seen through the opening in the wall do not converge at all. Nor do the orthogonals of the shoemaker's toolbox, inadvertently omitted from the perspective scheme. If the wall at the rear is made of the same stone as the walls in the front, then the courses of stone were reduced in size too much. Indeed, the divisions between courses in lateral and rear walls are not aligned and battlements rise at different levels. The battlement at the far right is missing its left face and the overlapped tower in the center seems to want its lower stories. The ground lacks any feature, like a foreshortened path or a *repoussoir* of rocks, that would mitigate its apparent verticality. These

[7] Tramontin in Tramontin *et al.*, 1965, p. 322.

[8] E.g. (1) mosaic, Cappella Zen, S. Marco; (2) left Cantoria, S. Marco; (3) one of ten enamels of the *Pala d'Oro*, S. Marco; (4) one of 14 scenes in the altar frontal of 1300, S. Marco; (5) relief by Tullio Lombardo, facade of the Scuola di S. Marco, probably 1489-90; (6) Cima da Conegliano, painting for a series of scenes from the life of St. Mark commissioned by the Confraternità dei Setaioli for their chapel in S. Maria dei Crociferi (now the Gesuiti), Berlin-Dahlem, Staatliche Museen; (7) Giovanni Bellini, drawing, Berlin-Dahlem, Staatliche Museen, no. 1357; (8) Giovanni Mansueti, painting for a series of scenes from the life of St. Mark for the Scuola di S. Marco, Venice, Accademia, probably early sixteenth cen.; (9) Giovanni Fazioli, painting, Venice, S. Tomà, eighteenth cen., which replaced the original altarpiece of the same subject by Jacopo Palma il Giovane.

may seem captious criticisms when applied to a relief which, perhaps, was originally painted. But the diminutive scale of the trees, like the trees in the *Conversion of St. Paul* (Fig. 17), represents as gross an error in the depiction of spatial relationships as those committed by painters of the fourteenth century.

Perhaps these mistakes should be blamed on an assistant whose share in the carving of the setting we may hypothetically locate between the right edge of the relief and the juncture of mismatched lateral and rear city walls. To an assistant, also, Rizzo entrusted the execution of the figure of St. Mark. Stunted proportions, stiff-legged movement, a tedious arrangement of folds contained within the silhouette of a single arc suggest that Rizzo hardly contributed even to the saint's design. But the damaged head of St. Mark is comparable in quality and style to the head of St. Anianus (Fig. 123). The brows of Mark and Anianus, like those of the *Pedestrian Effigy of Tron* (Fig. 68) and the *Emperor* on the left of the Tron sarcophagus, have the form and density of twisted cables. Their paths describe long arcs above deeply recessed eyes. Heavy lower lids with their multiple creases are identically formed in the *Emperor's* head. The radiating wrinkles at the corner of Anianus's eye are like those of the *Recumbent Effigy of Tron* (Fig. 70). The subdued meanders of elongated locks in Anianus's beard recur in the beards of the two *Effigies of Tron*. The tightly curled locks of St. Mark's beard, mustache, and hair recall *St. Mark* from the Altar of St. Clement (Fig. 18).

The figure of St. Anianus is masterly (Fig. 125). The shoemaker's humility is conveyed by his hunched back and stooping shoulders and the way in which he sits cross-legged on the ground; the saint's perseverence, by the way in which he grasps the awl; the martyr's faith, by the intently focused glance. The inclination of Anianus's head introduces creases in the nape and causes the tendon of the throat to stretch. By swiveling back the eyeball, Rizzo made manifest the upward direction of Anianus's glance. The overlapping of the farther shoulder by the throat, the foreshortened curve of the neckline of the tunic, and the foreshortening of the nearer shoulder and chest produce an impression of three-dimensional form. By contrast, the absence of foreshortening or, indeed, of any anatomical signpost, makes the disposition of the lower limbs impossible to apprehend. In compensation, the drapery pattern, on the legs especially, is of an elegance unparalleled in Rizzo's early work. With its several strata of intercalated folds, the drapery pattern resembles the right side of the mantle of the *Recumbent Effigy of Tron* (Figs. 67, 72). The cloth is loosely tucked beneath the legs of both and the corners of the garments make tapered points. Indentations like the bowl of a spoon, so numerous in the borders of the *Doge's* mantle, recur here in what seems like Anianus's farther knee. The technique of low relief favored the flattening of the drapery of St. Anianus and the smoothing of its surface; edges of folds that are rounded in the *Effigy of Tron* are defined by lines in the figure of the saint.

The relief of the *Miraculous Cure of St. Anianus* can be associated with an altar of which only parts survive in storerooms of the Museo Civico Correr and the Ca' Rezzonico at Venice. These parts comprise the left- and right-hand portions of an ancona and pieces of its disassembled frame. On the left, behind a kneeling Angel, stood John the Baptist and Mary Magdalene (Fig. 128). They were paired on the right with SS. Sebastian and Mark, and another kneeling Angel (Fig. 129). The center must have once contained an image of the Madonna and Child enthroned. The rectangular ancona probably was framed by the lower cornice and upper architrave and by the pilaster shafts and bases (but not the capitals—actually bases turned upside down) which were joined to the reliefs until the end of the last century (Fig. 126). Perhaps the lunette (Fig. 127), which is too high and narrow in relation to the ancona, once adorned a portal, to which its proportions are well suited. There is no reason to doubt that the altar was made for the facade of St. Eustachio (commonly known as S. Stae) from whose vicinity it comes: very likely it is one of two altars whose erection the Consiglio dei Dieci decreed on December 23, 1479.[9] These altars, flanking the main entrance of the church, as similar altars did at S. Maria Formosa, were meant to replace a portico where many "dishonest and dreadful acts were committed." Probably the altar remained *in situ* until the construction of the new facade of the church in 1710,[10] during which, it would seem, the relief was badly damaged. The altar was then acquired by the guild of gondoliers, who had it extensively restored.[11] They replaced its center with a relief of the *Madonna and Child*, which dates from the sixteenth century, and inserted beneath the new relief a slab inscribed with the date of 1569 and the names of the head, and two members, of a guild. Madonna and inscription, together, made a higher central field than that of the original altarpiece and it was therefore necessary to insert slabs beneath the wings, and capitals above the lesenes. Symbols of the guild of *gondolieri* were inscribed on the slabs and on the narrow strip at the base of the relief with the Madonna. It was probably at this time also that the altar was provided with its lunette, taken perhaps from a lateral portal of S. Stae. The reconstructed altar was then installed opposite S. Stae across the Grand Canal, at the Traghetto della Maddalena, where it was seen and reproduced by Johannes Grevembroch in 1754 (Fig. 127). In 1886 it was removed to the Museo Civico Correr.

The decree of the Consiglio dei Dieci provides a *terminus post quem* for the altar of December 23, 1479. There is no reason to suppose that work was long delayed. If the lunette relief did not originally belong to the altar, it need not have come from the same shop, or have been executed at the same time, as the altar. Its style suggests, however, that both altar and lunette were carved at approximately the same time by Antonio Rizzo.

Points of contact between the altar and Rizzo's works are many. The treatment of the waving locks of hair and beard of John the Baptist (Fig. 128) is similar to that of *St. James* from his altar in S. Marco (Fig. 4). The gesture with which the Baptist holds his cross resembles that with which *SS. Cosmas* and *Damian* hold their palms (Figs. 63, 62). The configuration of folds on the skirt of the Angel kneeling on the left is analogous to the drapery of St. Anianus (Fig. 125). The anatomy of St. Sebastian is virtually identical to that of *Adam* (Figs. 129, 39). Note in both the square shoulders, muscular arms, excessively pointed elbows, the taut tendons of the neck, protuberant Adam's apple, salient clavicles, and tendons attaching neck to shoulders, which bow the contour of the shoulders. The high breasts with embossed nipples laterally displaced have the same morphology in both. The turn and tilt of St. Sebastian's head, and the expression of his face, also recall *Adam*. Both in their form and their foreshortening, the eyes of

---

[9] Corner, *Supplementa*, 1749, pp. 192f.: "MCCCCLXXIX. Die XXIII. Decembris. Quod porticus Ecclesiae Sancti Hustachii, sub quo, sicut relatum est Capitibus hujus Consilii, committuntur multa inhonesta & enormia, diruatur, & fiant duo Capiteli ad fores ipsius Ecclesiae sicut ad Ecclesiam Sanctae Mariae Formosae factum fuit, & ita praecipiatur Plebano, & Procuratoribus ipsius Ecclesiae, ut faciant."

[10] Bassi, 1962, p. 216.

[11] See below, cat. no. 12.

St. Mark duplicate those of the Angel to the right of the *Man of Sorrows* in the Basilica at Aquileia (Fig. 54). The gesture with which Mark holds his book is found again in the hand of the Angel, holding the scroll, on the left of the same relief (Fig. 59). The gesture of Mark's other hand belongs to *Adam* (Fig. 39). Mark's hair, beard, and costume are those of *St. Mark* from the St. Clement Altar (Figs. 129, 18). The pattern of folds of the figure's cloak comes from the drapery of *St. James* (Fig. 3) or one of its derivatives, like the St. Clement *Mark* (Fig. 20). Similarities, thus, are more than adequate to establish Rizzo's authorship of this relief.

From the extant portions of the ancona we can surmise that its subject was a *Sacra conversazione*, that is, the pious community of saints and angels joined in veneration of the Christ Child.[12] The place of honor to the right of the Madonna is occupied by the precursor and the intimate companion of Christ; saints of lesser rank stand at her left. In contrast to the archaic isolation of individual saints on the separate panels of a polyptych, all the figures here, disposed in a semicircle, inhabit a single space. As the inner figures recede, their base lines rise in conformity with the inclination of the ground. Heads descend at approximately the angle of inclination of the floor, indicating a point of sight near the vertical center of the relief. (The descending hem of Sebastian's loincloth, on the other hand, denotes a lower point of sight.) Saints at the rear are diminished in scale, are overlapped by those at the sides, and are presented more nearly frontally. In contradistinction to the *mezzo rilievo* of the saints in front of them, the saints at the rear are carved in uniformly low relief; forms are graphically defined and contours adhere to the ground. A semicircular arrangement of figures within a unified space permitted easy communication among the actors. Indeed, all figures share a common focus: glances intersect at the center of the semicircle like spokes at a hub. The figures are united also in expression of fervid adoration. Neither Mary Magdalene nor St. Sebastian gives evidence of personal suffering: Mary Magdalene does not show the deprivations of her ascetic life; Sebastian does not bear the wounds of arrows, and the tree to which he is bound is barely visible. What is emphasized is not the historical and unique trial of each—an echo of Christ's agony by means of which saints and martyrs were distinguished from other mortals—but rather that adoration of a divine being in which saints and Christians shared in perpetual community.

A semicircular arrangement of figures invites a symmetrical composition to which concordant poses and views of opposite Saints and Angels also contribute. Beneath the covering of hair or cloth, the silhouettes of Sebastian and the Magdalene are mirror images. Mark and John close off the composition at either side by the continuity and verticality of outer contours. Each older, bearded saint is accompanied by a youthful saint. Yet the embodiment of the same poses by different physical types differently attired, and the slight alteration of gesture, qualify the bilateral correspondence. The saints are uniformly set against a neutral ground differentiated neither by design nor texture from the ground on which they stand. Like the setting of the Aquileia *Man of Sorrows* (Fig. 59), that ground recedes only a short distance from the foremost plane of the relief and standing figures occupy the entire height and breadth of the field. Thus, space is limited and there is nothing to distract our attention from the figures.

The reliefs from the Altar of the Traghetto della Maddalena suffered from the same

---

[12] For the iconography of the *Sacra conversazione*,   see Goffen, *AB*, 1979, pp. 198ff.

disregard as the Aquileia *Man of Sorrows*. Made of limestone, destined for an external and unprotected site, this altar is not likely to have excited the artist's zeal as the Tron Tomb must initially have done. That Rizzo expended little effort on its execution is manifested in numerous details. The canon of proportions is variable: the large heads of John and Mark, which make the figures seem slightly stunted, contrast with the diminutive heads of Sebastian and the Angel on the right. Anatomical detail is often wanting and the foreshortening of feet and the farther shoulders of Mark and John leaves much to be desired. Hems do not always reflect the structure of the folds that they terminate. Yet I do not think these faults are such as to warrant attribution to an assistant. For, in spite of inaccuracies in the transcription of visual reality, there are few aesthetic flaws: contours are fluent and elegant, patterns dense and continuously varied. No passages reveal that mechanical application of the chisel which signals an assistant's work.[13]

Even more egregious errors mar the carving of the lunette (Fig. 127). Yet it would be rash, I believe, to ascribe them to the intervention of an assistant. In the work of an inferior artisan, mistakes tend to be most numerous where the effort spent is greatest; but once Rizzo reached maturity, the expenditure of effort guaranteed perfection. It was, rather, haste and carelessness that produced unsatisfactory results. In the figure of God the Father, the generalized contours of skull and eyes, the undefined mouth, the excessive use of the point in the description of the eyes, the repetitious formulation of the locks, the absence of detail, betray a hurried execution. As a consequence, the faults—swollen jaws, skewed features, nonexistent neck and upper arms—are many. And yet, the identifying traits are Rizzo's: observe the faceted, slowly meandering locks of hair, the reverse curve of lower lids, the rather low and extremely knobby cheekbones. Similar features, including the shrunken neck, can be seen in the figure of God the Father from the lunette of the Altar of St. James (Fig. 7). If the blessing arm and hand were lowered, they would not be inferior in foreshortening or delineation of bony structure to that of God the Father from the Altar of St. James. The cuff of the figure's left sleeve yields to the force of gravity. Patterns made by the folds of the mantle are very similar to those of St. Mark in the Altar of the Traghetto della Maddalena (Fig. 129) and support the assumption of contemporaneity of lunette and ancona.

The similarity in design and scale between the Angels of the lunette and the Angels of the altar (Figs. 127-129) provide further evidence that the two reliefs were not intended for one work: such patent repetition in diverse sections of a single work would be most unusual in an Italian altar of the fifteenth century. In all four figures, the farther shoulder and upper arm were twisted forward, not because their author could do no better, but in order to create a fuller, more sinuous silhouette. As in the altar, the setting of the lunette consists of nothing more than a narrow strip of ground. The low viewpoint that such a narrow strip implies would have been justified by the height—presumably above the head of a potential spectator—at which the lunette probably once was placed.

Of about the same date as the Altar of the Traghetto della Maddalena are two reliefs of flying *Victories*, formerly in the Kaiser-Friedrich-Museum, Berlin, and missing since

---

[13] On the other hand, it is likely that an assistant did intervene in the carving of the framework, for the *Pflanzenkandelaber* of the pilasters are more closely allied to the schemata employed in the Lombardo shop than they are to Rizzo's types. They, too, are more crudely wrought than analogous shafts from the first story of the Tron Tomb.

World War II (Figs. 130, 131). Originally the *Victories* filled the corners of a triangular pediment. With both hands they supported an oval field, which probably contained a coat of arms. At one time *Victories* and blazon apparently crowned double doors, like those leading to two ramps of a staircase or a staircase and a corridor; the arched profiles of two doors—one larger than the other—can be inferred from arcs cut from the ground at the bottom of the reliefs. In pose and function, the figures are related to the *Victories* that frequently support the *tabula ansata* or *imago clipeata* on Roman sarcophagi. Like their classical prototypes, they are haloless and garbed in chitons; the chest of one of them is partly bared.[14]

The attribution of the *Victories* to Rizzo can be demonstrated by comparison with other works. The hair of the right-hand *Victory* is identical to that of the candelabra-bearing *Angel* on the left of the Altar of St. James (Fig. 28). The pattern made by the wing feathers of this *Victory* is analogous to that of the right candelabra-bearing *Angel* (Fig. 24). In the skirt of the left-hand *Victory*, the twisting swathe that ends in an arched wedge, recalls the fluttering cloak of St. Paul in the scene of his conversion (Fig. 17). Yet I do not think the *Victories* are as early as the Altars of S. Marco, for the shape and salience of the narrow, constantly swerving folds of the *Victories*' skirts resemble too closely the drapery of St. Mark in the Altar of the Traghetto della Maddalena (Fig. 129). In the forearm and leg of the right-hand *Victory* and in the arm of the *Angel* on the right of the altar, long low facets, which follow straight paths across the limb, define flat folds on one side only. The diminutive features of the *Victory* on the right are most akin to those of St. Sebastian. In the left-hand *Victory*, the upper arm, with its smooth surface, flat relief, and faceted contours, gently bowed for the bicep and pointed at the minuscule elbow, replicates the farther arm of St. Sebastian.

The *Angel* in the Kunsthistorisches Museum in Vienna (Figs. 132, 133) also belongs among the figures examined here: probably it does not postdate the Tron Tomb by much. The figure is usually identified as the *Annunciate Angel*—one of an Annunciation group of which the *Virgin* supposedly is missing. But comparison with *Angels* from contemporary Venetian Annunciations proves this a misnomer,[15] for in every one, the *Angel*, matched with the *Virgin* in proportions and size, is fully grown. Invariably *Gabriel*'s right hand is raised in blessing; his lowered left hand usually holds a lily. In groups of the Annunciation the two figures are turned toward one another to some degree. But our statue, meant to stand against a wall, was intended to be seen *en face*. This we can deduce from the vertical truncation of the bottom of the statue, visible in back, and from the statue's unfinished rear. Thus the figure's attention was focused on a hypothetical observer—not another figure. Although wingless and explicitly defined as male, the figure is undoubtedly an *Angel*, for his fluttering chiton betokens flight: the figure, it seems, has just alighted. Similar *Angels* are found in Venice in tombs or altars, flanking a statue of the *Risen Christ*, as in Pietro Lombardo's Tomb of Doge Pietro Mocenigo,

---

[14] For the difference between Victories and Angels, see Berefelt, 1968, pp. 22f., 34.

[15] Examples of fifteenth-century Venetian Annunciations carved in the round are: (1) gables, east facade, S. Marco; (2) Bartolomeo Bon and shop, London, Victoria and Albert Museum; (3) Niccolò di Giovanni Fiorentino, Foscari Tomb, S. Maria dei Frari; (4) main portal, Madonna dell'Orto; (5) Rizzo, Tron Tomb, S. Maria dei Frari; (6) shop of Pietro Lombardo, triumphal arch, S. Giobbe; (7) the beam above the High Altar of S. Stefano; (8) balustrade of the choir, S. Maria dei Miracoli; (9) Tullio Lombardo, Vendramin Tomb, SS. Giovanni e Paolo.

or the figure of a saint, as in the Altar of St. Luke, S. Giobbe. From its composition we may infer that, in a group of three, the *Angel* stood at the spectator's right.

The proportions of the *Angel* are much slenderer than those of the only *Angels* in Rizzo's oeuvre comparable to it in age—the *Angels* of the Aquileia *Man of Sorrows* (Fig. 59): in its proportions, the Vienna *Angel* recalls that process of elongation to which the features of *Prudence* were subjected. The *Angel's* pose confutes the prima facie evidence of folds: his irresolute movement, like that of *Prudence*, must be traced to *Eve* (Fig. 48). The gesture of his upraised hand—though not its meaning of adoration—is like *Adam's* (Fig. 39). The cupped hands with their sharply flexed wrists are typical of Rizzo: similar hands appear in the figures from the Aquileia *Man of Sorrows* (Fig. 59) and the *Recumbent Effigy of Tron* (Fig. 74).

Specific analogies with works by Rizzo suggest a date of ca. 1480. The pattern made by the folds of the skirt is very similar to that of the drapery of St. Anianus (Fig. 125). In both, folds are as flat, and their edges as sharp, as if they had been ironed down. Small folds are distributed with equal density over the surface of the figure. Folds are roughly triangular, though corners are made by hairpin turns. The *Angel's* waving locks, which give way to a dense and regular series of long corkscrew curls at the level of the ear, adopt the coiffure of the left-hand *Angel* in the lunette from the Altar of the Traghetto della Maddalena (Fig. 127). The *Angel's* face resembles most that of *Charity* (Fig. 82) and its analogues, like *Music* (Fig. 108). Inflated cheeks and double chin transform the head into a sphere. Small features are identically formed. The surface of the *Angel's* face, polished but not entirely smoothed, bears traces of the artist's method. As in *Music*, the carving of the cheeks proceeded transversally, not downward. In both, a narrow, flat chisel, rather than the claw chisel favored by Pietro Lombardo, was used in the final stages of carving.

An *Adoring Angel* from the Arco Foscari (Fig. 134) apparently was based on the Vienna *Angel*. Slender proportions, short torso, narrow shoulders, long neck, are similar in both. The *Angel's* topknot must once have resembled that of the Vienna *Angel*. In both figures, the same tentative pose belies tossed drapery. In both, the engaged leg inexplicably slants inward. Folds on this leg recall those in the sleeve of the right-hand *Angel* in the Altar of the Traghetto della Maddalena (Fig. 129). Flaws in the *Angel's* face and hands and the monotony of unvaried folds warrant an attribution of the Arco Foscari *Angel* to an assistant.

Two other statues, both draped, female figures, can be linked with *Personifications* from the later campaign of work on the Tomb of Niccolò Tron. The first of these (Fig. 137) is related to *Charity* (Fig. 89) in the disposition of feet and draping of lower legs and feet. In both, the mantle is pulled tight across the free leg; from the knee, long folds rise to the opposite hip. The figure's facial type was based on *Charity*, as was the morphology and gesture of its lowered hand; in its new context the gesture serves no purpose. In the design and execution of this figure Rizzo evidently gave his assistant little guidance. The companion to this figure by a second assistant (Fig. 136), looks like none of Rizzo's sculptures. Were it not for the part, which, receding swiftly, leaves exposed a vast expanse of rounded forehead, and the idiosyncratic, flexed wrist and arched hand, we might doubt the provenance of this work in Rizzo's shop. Its quality is inferior to anything seen hitherto.

From the end of this period dates the Tomb of Giovanni Emo. Originally installed in the Emo Chapel, dedicated to SS. John the Baptist and John the Evangelist, in S. Maria dei Servi, the tomb was disassembled after the suppression of the church in 1806.[16] From the tomb there survives only the statuary—the *Pedestrian Effigy of Emo* in the Museo Civico, Vicenza (Fig. 139), and the two shield-bearing *Pages* in the Louvre (Figs. 141, 142). Two drawings by Johannes Grevembroch preserve the original appearance of the tomb. One drawing records the effigy; particular attention was devoted to its polychromy.[17] A second drawing shows the tomb in its entirety (Fig. 138).[18] The sarcophagus, as drawn by Grevembroch, does not match the one with which the effigy is currently exhibited (Fig. 228). Probably the present sarcophagus comes from a different tomb.[19]

Giovanni di Giorgio Emo was born in 1425. As Venetian senator he participated in the elections of Doges Tron, Marcello, and Vendramin. On three significant occasions he occupied the office of ambassador. In 1474 Emo was sent to Matthias Corvinus of Hungary to persuade him to ally himself with Venice in the war against the Turks. In the following year Emo met with Sultan Mahommet II at Constantinople. In 1478 he was chosen to speak for Venice during the crisis that followed the Pazzi conspiracy at Florence. He served at Brescia as Venetian Capitanio and oversaw the reenforcement of Udine against the invasion of the Turks. Upon the death of Antonio Loredan in 1482, Emo was made Provveditore Generale in the war against Ferrara. Under Emo, the conquest of the Polesine was rapidly concluded with the taking of Lendinara and Badia. At the battle of Stellata in September 1483 Emo was hurt by his falling horse. He died on September 15, 1483.[20]

The chapel in which the tomb was built was appropriated to Giovanni Emo on January 1, 1482.[21] The epitaph, recorded in many sources, tells us that the tomb was erected after Emo's death by his five sons, Giorgio, Bertuccio, Leonardo, Pietro, and Gabriele.[22] The tomb was finished by 1493 when it was recorded by Marin Sanudo.[23]

Among Venetian Renaissance tombs, the format of the Emo Tomb is unique (Fig. 138). Its closest relative is the Tomb of Cardinal Niccolò Forteguerri (d. 1473), erected by Mino da Fiesole, probably between 1473 and 1480, in S. Cecilia in Trastevere, Rome (Fig. 229).[24] Both tombs rise from the pavement of the church. The Forteguerri Tomb, like that of Emo, is placed against, rather than excavated from, the wall. In both, a base containing the epitaph supports an aedicule framed at either side by free-standing col-

[16] A. Zorzi, 1972, ii, pp. 353, 356.

[17] Grevembroch, *Gli abiti*, i, p. 38. See Schulz, Washington, D.C., Nat. Gall. of Art. *Studies*, 1980, pp. 7ff., fig. 6.

[18] Grevembroch, *Mon. Ven.*, iii, 1759, p. 27. The caption below the illustration reads: "Statua pedestre nella Chiesa de' Servi di Venezia del Cavaliere Giovanni Emo, il quale dopo molte Ambascerie e Magistrature si morì trovandosi al governo della Guerra di Ferrara l'anno 1485."

[19] See below, cat. no. 17.

[20] For Emo's biography see Rumor, n.d. [1910?], pp. 63-68 and Venice, Mus. Cor., MS Cicogna 1536, Bergantini, "Memorie della famiglia Emo," pp. 290-303. The date of Emo's death was discovered by Corner, *Eccl. Ven.*, ii, 1749, p. 53, in a diary of the convent of the Venetian Servites.

[21] Vicentini, *S. Maria de' Servi*, 1920, pp. 49, 70f.

[22] In translation, the epitaph reads: "To Giovanni Emo, golden knight and most influential Senator, who at home and abroad, served on the greatest and highest magistratures and legations in Asia and Europe. Once the bridge at the Po was passed, he led the public standards to Ferrara. He perished, no less to the sorrow of his army than of his relatives. His most devoted sons erected [this tomb]." The epitaph was transcribed by Sansovino, Martinelli, Bergantini, Grevembroch, and Cicogna, among others. For Emo's sons, see Cicogna, i, 1824, p. 37, no. 3.

[23] Sanudo, (1493) 1980, p. 51: "Ai Servi è l'arca d'Andrea Vendramin doxe . . . *Item* quella di Zuan Emo, el morite Provedador in campo."

[24] Sciolla, 1970, pp. 91f., no. 42.

umns in front and pilasters behind. Above, an unbroken entablature carries an arched lunette. Brackets at either side of Mino's base may have once supported *putti*. The segmental lunette of the Emo Tomb terminated at either end by rosettes, the frieze embellished with *rinceaux*, and the fluting of the columns probably derive ultimately from Mantegna's S. Zeno Altarpiece. The exaggerated height of the Emo base and the unnecessary brackets are concessions to the Venetian tradition of pensile tombs. The quadripartition of the rear wall has been compared to the illusionistic door on the second story of the south face of the Arco Foscari (Fig. 31)[25] and the background of Donatello's *Cavalcanti Annunciation* in S. Croce, Florence,[26] both of which it resembles. The high drums, which provide pedestals for the columns, can be traced to an antique prototype known in the fifteenth century: a similar pedestal, embellished with beribboned festoons and a head suspended from a ribbon, as well as a Latin inscription, was drawn by Jacopo Bellini in his Paris sketchbook.[27]

In Desiderio da Settignano's Tomb of Carlo Marsuppini, S. Croce, Florence, of ca. 1460, free-standing figures of *putti* used as *reggistemma* make their first appearance in funerary sculpture. The motif was carried north by Pietro Lombardo, whose Paduan Tomb of Antonio Roselli of 1467 is flanked by *reggistemma*, grown now to the age of puberty. In age, function, and the absence of wings, the Emo *reggistemma* (Figs. 141, 142) imitate those of the Roselli Tomb. But, neither nude nor dressed like angels, the Emo *Pages* are uniquely clad in contemporary clothes: youths dressed like them throng the backgrounds of Carpaccio's paintings.[28] The initials I E on the *Pages'* doublets identify their dress as Emo's livery. Thus these youths are not anonymous or angelic creatures who merely serve as animate supports for Emo's arms. Rather, they are specific representatives of Emo's entourage and, as such, testify to his wealth and social status.

In the Emo Tomb the customary recumbent effigy was replaced by a pedestrian effigy raised on the sarcophagus (Fig. 138). As we have seen, this was the chosen mode for celebrating military heroes in Venetian funerary sculpture. Emo's post of Provveditore Generale in the war against Ferrara was noncombatant: as the highest ranking Venetian civilian, Emo advised the commander of the troops and reported on the commander's actions to the Collegio. Perhaps the image was thought fitting, nonetheless, because Emo had died in the field—a fact to which the epitaph specifically refers.

Emo is dressed in the vestments of office (Fig. 139)—a soft, high cap tilted downward slightly on the right and a high-collared cloak fastened on the right shoulder. A drawing by Grevembroch shows that the gown was red, the *berretta* black. The polychromy of the cloak simulated yellow and gold brocade.[29] Probably Emo is wearing the habiliment, known from later descriptions, of Provveditori Generali. But his hat is one com-

---

[25] Pincus, 1974, p. 196.

[26] Munman, 1968, pp. 195f.

[27] Fol. 44r: Goloubew, ii, 1908, pl. XLIII. Early sources locate the inscription in Este, Monselice, and Padua. See *Corp. inscr. lat.*, v, pt. 1, 1872, p. 248, no. 2553.

[28] The *Pages* are clad in supple buskins, particolored hose, a breastplate, and a skirt of chain mail. Over their armor they wear a pleated doublet ornamented with parallel zigzag stripes and the initials I E on the right breast. Doublets are tied at the waist with a sash. Slashed sleeves of a garment worn be-

neath the armor reveal an undershirt of thinner material. Above the elbows, puffed sleeves are adorned with broad pendant ribbons with aglets. In their costumes the Emo *Pages* seem to have influenced Giovanni Buora's *Pages* from the Tomb of Agostino Onigo in S. Nicolò, Treviso.

[29] Grevembroch, *Gli abiti*, i, p. 38. Emo is wearing the same habit in his portrait, attributed to Giovanni Bellini, in the National Gallery of Art, Washington. See Schulz, Washington, D.C., Nat. Gall. of Art. *Studies*, 1980, pp. 7ff.

monly worn by ambassadors—an office Emo held on three occasions.[30] His right arm wrapped in the cloak recalls Roman statues of *togati*, but may have been intended, rather, to show how the cloak was worn.

The winged lion of St. Mark in a medallion at the center of the sarcophagus (Fig. 138) is the emblem of Venice and may refer to Emo's exertions throughout his long career on behalf of the republic or to the specific command conferred upon him by the Senate as Provveditore Generale. The spurs, probably originally gilded, held by the right-hand *Page* (Fig. 141), represent the accoutrements to which Emo's appointment to the knightly order of the *Speron d'oro* entitled him. Emo's knighthood, mentioned in the epitaph, is alluded to for the third time by crossed keys and papal tiara near the center of the frieze.[31] Rayed mandorla and trotting horse or donkey, which accompany the insignia of the *Speron d'oro*, may have had a personal significance: I cannot ascribe to them any wider meaning.

In the style of its architecture (Fig. 138), the Emo Tomb differs fundamentally from Rizzo's structures—both those already analyzed (Figs. 1, 2, 64) and the east wing of the Ducal Palace (Figs. 152, 156). How unlike the uniform planes of Rizzo's architecture are the free-standing Composite columns with fluted shafts and circular carved bases, and the projecting base with brackets. Where the Tron Tomb and the Altars of S. Marco are completely enclosed by projecting piers, the interval between free-standing columns and rear wall of the Emo Tomb allows air to circulate and offers the possibility of oblique views. The effigy is not contained within a niche and the *Pages* are denied even the setting of a backdrop. The retraction of the base at either edge weakens the lateral borders of the tomb's foundation, while the siting of the *Pages* produces a composition with no borders at all. Where Rizzo habitually surrounded individual units, the Emo epitaph is unframed. In contrast to the straight edges of Rizzo's monuments, edges here are broken by brackets or statuary or doubled by the projection of the base. Contrast Tron's parallelipiped sarcophagus with the scalloped profile of Emo's sarcophagus, its edges interrupted by acanthus ornament applied to the corners of its frieze. The scale of the Emo Monument is determined by the size of the effigy: the standing figure does not seem reduced to insignificance either by the size and weight of the surrounding frame, as in the Altars of SS. James and Paul, or by the multiplication of stories, as in the Tron Tomb. The height of the monument is increased, not by an increase in the height of the aedicule or by the piling up of stories, but rather by the elevation of the base, which is perceived as only half belonging to the tomb. Unlike the S. Marco Altars,

[30] The most detailed description of the costumes of Venetian officials is that written by Cesare Vecellio, '1590. The habits of both ambassadors and "Generali di Venetia in tempo di guerra" described by Vecellio (pp. 84rff., 102vf.) possess features common to the habit of the effigy and portrait of Emo in the National Gallery, Washington, but neither corresponds entirely. According to Vecellio, both ambassadors and generals wore cloaks fastened with gold buttons on one shoulder: ambassadors' cloaks were fastened on the left; generals' cloaks were fastened on the right. Cloaks of generals were explicitly described as golden. Both the fastening and color of Emo's cloak speak in favor of a general's habit,
as does the absence of a gold necklace customarily worn by ambassadors. But Emo wears a hat that is very similar to the *berretta* assigned by Vecellio to ambassadors—not the hat of a Venetian general. It may be that the dress of various officials underwent minor modifications in the course of a century (although the generals' hat, described by Vecellio, was also worn by generals at the beginning of the sixteenth century: see the *Pedestrian Effigy of Benedetto Pesaro* [d. 1503] from his tomb in S. Maria dei Frari). Or perhaps Vecellio's rubric, "Generale," referred only to military commanders, while civilian Provveditori Generali wore a slightly different costume.

[31] Bascapè, 1972, p. 319.

ornament is confined to specific areas. It is not possible to judge the degree of the ornament's plasticity, but clearly it does not match the filigreelike ornament of Rizzo. Large areas of the surface remain bare. This, combined with the relative simplicity of design resulting from the use of a few large forms, produces a more compelling focus than Rizzo's monuments ever have. Indeed, the rich polychromy of the effigy must have enhanced the force of its attraction.

These differences of style suffice to throw into question Rizzo's authorship of the design. That Rizzo had no part in it is proved by the fact that motifs of the Emo Tomb do not appear in Rizzo's work: for analogies we must turn to the architecture of Pietro Lombardo and his sons. Columns in the round, whether linked with matching pilasters set at a slight distance behind them, as in the Tomb of Doge Andrea Vendramin (Fig. 231), or placed against the wall, as in the Corner Chapel in SS. Apostoli, frequently occur in the architecture of the Lombardo shop. In the Corner Chapel, the Tomb of Doge Niccolò Marcello, and the main portal of the Scuola di S. Marco, free-standing columns are elevated on tall drums. The drums by Tullio that support free-standing columns in the Bernabò Chapel, S. Giovanni Crisostomo, and the Cappella Zen, S. Marco, are ornamented, like those of the Emo Tomb, with rings from which ribbons, festoons, and heads attached to ribbons are suspended. The shape of the sarcophagus resembles that of the Tomb of Bishop Giovanni da Udine in the Duomo, Treviso, by Pietro Lombardo and his sons. The imbrication of the lower half of the Emo sarcophagus is found again on the Tomb of Bishop Giovanni, the Tomb of Dante in Ravenna, and twice in the Marcello Tomb. The plain lunette, composed of a segmental arch with a single dentil molding and patera ends, reappears at the top of the Tomb of Doge Pietro Mocenigo. *Rinceaux* adorning frieze and sarcophagus are a hallmark of the Lombardo shop. What could be more similar to the ornamentation of the Emo sarcophagus than the frieze above a doorway in S. Maria dei Miracoli or the frieze of the basement of the Vendramin Tomb (Fig. 230), where an acanthus leaf is bent around the corner as in the Emo Tomb?

I suspect that the Emo Tomb owes its design to Tullio Lombardo. With the Vendramin Tomb (Fig. 231), the Emo Tomb shares a free-standing Composite order which, separated by a considerable interval from the rear wall of the tomb, necessitated the projection of its center. The columnar architecture of the Vendramin Tomb produces a perforated structure in which space circulates freely, and inside and outside are scarcely distinguished. At the sides, where free-standing figures skirt the boundaries of the tomb, the space of tomb and ambient interpenetrate. (The octagonal pedestals at the ends of the Vendramin Tomb originally held the *Warriors*.) Consonant with the columnar architecture of the Vendramin Tomb, which subdivides without enclosing space, is the free disposition of its statuary: at the edges of the monument, on the sarcophagus, or at the top of the tomb where *Pages* stood, figures lack a special setting. Ornament is contained within limited areas: behind the effigy the wall is composed of simple slabs within projecting strips, which provide the statuary with a neutral backdrop. A single order determines the structure of the tomb. In contrast to the additive composition of Rizzo's Tron Tomb and Ducal Palace facades (Figs. 64, 152, 156), the components of Emo and Vendramin Tombs are integrated by the subordination of lateral elements to adjacent and more central ones. Both monuments are based on an A-B-A rhythm: sides are narrower and recessed behind the projecting center. The arrangement of figures produces an isosceles triangle.[32] In the Emo Tomb a second isosceles triangle with its apex also in the head of *Emo* is created by the graduated widening of sarcophagus and epitaph. These features distinguish a High Renaissance from a Quattrocento mode of composition. It is therefore not surprising that, despite Quattrocento prototypes, both Emo and Vendramin Tombs resemble ancient Roman structures—the Vendramin Tomb, Roman triumphal arches; the Emo Tomb, the aedicules with segmental lunettes in the Pantheon in Rome.[33]

But if Tullio, for some unknown reason, designed the Emo Tomb and oversaw the execution of its architecture, he did not conceive the figures. For where the figures of the Vendramin Tomb exist in an ideal realm, the figures of the Emo Tomb are anchored within a particular time and place. The guardians of the Emo Tomb represent the defunct's servants. By contrast, the guardians of the Vendramin Tomb are classical ephebes dressed in Roman armor who, unlike their predecessors in the Tron Tomb, do not anachronistically bear Vendramin's escutcheon. The *Pages* that stood at the top of the Vendramin Tomb are almost nude. *Adam* and *Eve*, which originally occupied the places of the *Warriors*, are representatives of another era, while the torch-bearing *Angels* behind the effigy exist eternally. As a second image of the doge, Tullio portrayed his subject in afterlife, in supplication before the heavenly throne of the Mother of God, not as he had last appeared before the Senate.

The situation of the effigy within an historical context, the definition of time and place, correspond to the use of devices that here, as in the *Pedestrian Effigy of Tron*, produces a deceptive imitation of reality. The unfinished base of the figure (Fig. 139), like that of *Tron*, apparently was inserted into the cover of the sarcophagus. The figure's dress was described exactly; its original polychromy concealed the nature of the stone. As the climax of the tomb, *Emo*'s face expressed the vehement emotion of a transient mood.

The scowl, which contorts *Emo*'s features (Figs. 143, 144), is unique in funerary portraiture. Its source lies, I believe, in the Equestrian Monument of Bartolommeo Colleoni by Andrea del Verrocchio (Fig. 226). The portrait of *Colleoni* was conditioned by physiognomic theory according to which the physical resemblance between men and particular animals mediated correspondences in character: the ferocity of the *condottiere* was evinced by his leonine features.[34] In the interests of accurate portraiture, Rizzo renounced the square face, hanging cheeks, heavy brow, and wide mouth—those features in which the similarity of men and lions were thought especially to reside—but he did adopt the deeply inset eyes, the beetling brows, the unflinching stare and knitted, furrowed brows. Like *Colleoni*'s, the contorted flesh of *Emo*'s forehead received a plastic definition: wrinkles are not mere incisions traced upon a flat surface, as they are in Rizzo's other heads, but are deep channels that have forced their way through mounds of flesh. The exaggerated modeling of pendulous jowls reflects the soft and malleable material of Rizzo's prototype—Verrocchio's clay model for the *Colleoni*.[35]

[32] See the engraving which shows the original state of the Vendramin Tomb in S. Maria dei Servi in Cicognara, ii, 1816, pl. xlii.

[33] Munman, 1968, p. 200.

[34] Meller in *Ren. and Man.*, 1963, ii, pp. 53ff.

[35] The monument of Bartolommeo Colleoni was not unveiled until March 21, 1496 (Sanudo, *Diarii*, i, 1879,

coll. 96f.). Therefore, it is not likely to have been the finished monument that provided inspiration for Rizzo's head of *Emo*. We must suppose, rather, that Rizzo was acquainted with Verrocchio's model or models. Unfortunately, Rizzo's reliance on a model by Verrocchio is of no assistance in dating the *Effigy of Emo*, for the competition for the equestrian mon-

In the head of *Emo* Rizzo's characteristic manner is disguised, not only by the influence of Verrocchio, but by the rapidity and carelessness of execution—a performance in keeping with the coarse limestone of the figure. The surface was not completely smoothed and the raw, chiseled facets, which mark the boundaries of projecting forms, like the jutting chin or folds of flesh, were not rounded off. Yet idiosyncratic features mark this as a work of Rizzo's. As in the head of the standing *Tron* (Figs. 65, 68), the eyebrows are formed of twisted cables; the course they follow is that of an elevated arch. The catenary curves of wrinkles in *Emo*'s lower lids recur in the head of *Tron*. The pursed lip and the folds of flesh loosely draped from the corners of the mouth recall the mouth of the *Warrior* on the left of the Tron Tomb (Fig. 86).

The inferior quality of the remainder of the *Emo* effigy (Figs. 139, 140) has long been recognized. In proportion to its head, the figure's body is much too tall. The legs, especially, are elongated. Shoulders are immense, but feet seem to belong to a figure half *Emo*'s size. Contrapposto affects only the position of the knee of the free leg; neither the axes of hips or shoulders, nor the position of the free foot, respond to the unequal distribution of the body's weight. The pattern of drapery presupposes no larger principles of design. Drapery adheres to the projecting leg as though the cloak were made of a sheer material and *Emo* were wearing nothing underneath. Its flaws justify an attribution of all but the head of the effigy to an assistant, who, evidently, had very scant acquaintance with Rizzo's work.

The *Pages* were so placed that shields with Emo's arms—two oblique (red) stripes on a neutral ground—furnished vertical boundaries to the tomb (Fig. 138). Figures, thus, turned toward the center of the tomb, although only the right-hand *Page*'s gaze would have been directed toward the effigy. Unfinished bases and Grevembroch's drawing reveal that here, too, figures were presented as though they stood immediately upon the cornice of the base. Neither figure is completely excavated from its matrix (Figs. 141, 142). To be sure, Rizzo's standing undraped figures never are, but unlike the left-hand *Warrior* of the Tron Tomb (Fig. 91) or *Adam* and *Eve* (Figs. 39, 48) or "*Mars*" (Fig. 36), there was no attempt to conceal or transform the inert mass of stone.

The style of the right-hand *Page* (Fig. 142) is virtually identical to that of the left-hand *Warrior* from the Tron Tomb (Fig. 91). The ponderation, the slight twist of the upper torso, the more pronounced turn of the head in the opposite direction, are shared by both. In both, the low center of gravity and the relaxed musculature denote complete repose, a state consistent with the reverie expressed by the faces. To the same degree as in the Tron *Warrior*, the smooth surfaces and gently rounded, unbroken contours of the Emo *Page* testify to the generalization of anatomical form. Despite their difference in age, the faces of the two are similar (Figs. 145, 86). Compare the paths of the long brows, the curvature of upper and lower lids, the delineation of truncated pupil and iris on the slightly bulbous eyeball, the definition of the lower border of the socket. Short noses are equally distant from upper lips; thicker lower lips, indented and slightly con-

ument, on the basis of which Verrocchio was awarded the commission, took place, at the latest, by May 1483. (Faber, i, [1483-84] 1843, pp. 95f.) The model with which Verrocchio won the competition was not the same as the clay models of horse and rider which the sculptor had completed by the time he died (Paoletti, 1893, ii, p. 264, n. 8) and which were

used in the casting of the monument, for the latter, we know, were larger in scale than the original model. Nevertheless, since the *condottiere* had died several years before the competition was announced, it is not likely that the physiognomy of *Colleoni* was greatly altered from one model to the other.

tracted in the center, are identical. Inflated cheeks and rounded chin produce in both a continuously rounded contour. This *Page* is one of the few figures by Rizzo to wear smooth bangs. Perhaps its coiffure was inspired by Antonello's *St. Sebastian* (Fig. 227). Like Antonello's figure, locks of hair contrive to produce a semicircular contour. The gesture with which the *Page* supports the shield is that of the Tron *Warrior*; the *Page*'s other hand duplicates the lowered hand of the Vienna *Angel* (Fig. 132).

In its deficient exposition of the mechanics of a contrapposto pose and its flawed description of anatomy, the left-hand *Page* (Fig. 141) betrays an assistant's hand. Facial features caricature those of the right-hand *Page* (Figs. 145, 146). More industrious than Rizzo, the assistant carved away the stone between the legs; unfortunately he removed too much of the inner leg as well.

Emo's odd proportions can be traced in two figures of the Arco Foscari; perhaps the same assistant was responsible for all three. They are the *Warrior* that supports the shield with Mocenigo arms—two roses on a divided field—on the left-hand pinnacle of the south face (Fig. 147) and the female draped figure immediately to the right of him (Fig. 148). All three figures are inordinately tall: the heads of all are disproportionate, though legs seem to have suffered most from the process of elongation and attenuation. Feet are diminutive. In the bodice of the female figure, tongue-shaped indentations resemble the depressions made in the folds along the side of *Emo*'s cloak (Fig. 140). The face of the *Warrior* was inspired either by the head of *Emo* or its source. Notable are the scowl produced by knitted brows, the fixed intensity of stare, the tightly sealed lips, the exaggerated modeling of the paunchy cheeks and jowl. How little does the *Warrior*'s face—the portrait of a fifty- or sixty-year-old man—suit his youthful body![36] Analogies with the effigy of *Emo* suggest a coincidence of date. If so, the shield supported by the *Warrior* must commemorate Giovanni Mocenigo, doge from May 1478 to November 1485, and not his brother, Pietro, doge from 1474 to 1476.

The chapel in S. Maria dei Servi, which was ceded to Giovanni Emo in 1482, and in which his tomb was built, was dedicated to SS. John the Baptist and John the Evangelist. Perhaps it is from the altar of this chapel that a half-life-size marble figure of the *Evangelist* comes (Fig. 135). The figure, identified as the Evangelist by the stem of a broken chalice in its right hand, is now in the Staatliche Museen, East Berlin. There is reason to think that originally it was paired with a figure of the Baptist, though no such figure can now be traced. Its composition indicates that the *Evangelist* was meant to be seen from the right, the face in front view, the body in three-quarter view. We might suppose that the sculptor had intended the figure to be installed at an angle were it not for the fact that the front face of the base is aligned with the front of the statue. More likely, then, the figure was installed parallel to the setting, but to the left of a potential spectator. What was on the right? While John the Evangelist was often portrayed as a very young man, our statue is the only instance I know in which he is represented as a child. Indeed, only one saint was not consistently pictured as adult. He is John the Baptist, who, in the fifteenth century, could be depicted at any age between infancy

---

[36] The *Warrior*'s dress is also very odd. His paludamentum is exceptionally long. A cuirass, on whose pteryges Mocenigo roses are carved, is combined with fifteenth-century plate armor, which covers the figure's arms. On his feet, the *Warrior* wears unclassical stockings, which reach nearly to his knees, and fifteenth-century *zoccoli*.

and adulthood, and often was depicted as a child. It may be that the *Evangelist*'s youth was due to a need for symmetry in a pairing with the *Baptist*, a pairing required in a chapel dedicated to the two St. Johns, as Emo's chapel was.

Support for this hypothesis derives from the statue's attribution to Rizzo and its dating to the period of the Emo Tomb. The languor of the *Evangelist*'s pose, gesture, and expression is a mood we have come to associate with Rizzo's works of the early 1480s. The face of *St. John* is most like that of the right-hand Emo *Page* (Fig. 145). Brows and lids have the same configuration. The noses of both are fairly short and pinched at the bridge. Lips are identical; in both, gently rising folds of flesh mark the corners of the mouths. The low, receding chin is dented at the bottom. A slight fullness beneath the chin and fleshy cheeks, which conceals all traces of a bony structure, lends to the face a smoothly rounded contour. Bangs cover the foreheads of both. Like Antonello's *St. Sebastian* (Fig. 227), the contour of the heads of *Evangelist* and *Page* is domical.

The draping of the *Evangelist*'s mantle freely follows a pattern used in classical antiquity for mantles worn by female figures, particularly for Ceres and Abundance. As in antique statues, the vertical folds of the tunic show beneath the mantle of the saint. The drapery of *St. John* and the Tron Tomb *Fortitude* (Fig. 98) undoubtedly possess a common source. The looping of the mantle's folds around the lateral boundary of the figure and the tongue-shaped depressions, which fill the interstices between swinging folds, recall the mantle of *Charity* from the Tron Tomb (Fig. 89). The perturbation of folds around the figure's feet resembles the pattern that results from the agitated folds at the bottom of the Tron *Arithmetic/Grammar* (Fig. 96).

Stylistically and qualitatively the statuary from Rizzo's final campaign of work on the Tomb of Doge Tron, the *Angel* from the portal of the Madonna dell'Orto, the *Page* from the Emo Tomb, and the East Berlin *Evangelist* form a coherent group: they represent one extreme in the range of Rizzo's style, characterized by an assimilation of the art of Tullio Lombardo and Antonello da Messina. Rizzo's works of this period, in which modes of dress and patterns of folds derived from antique prototypes, were more classicizing than they had been before or were to be again. No doubt the sculptor's interest in antique art was due to Tullio, for whom Roman sculpture constituted a unique standard of artistic excellence. Yet Rizzo did not compose exclusively in this ideal mode: like a refrain, the relief of *St. Anianus*, the Altar of the Traghetto della Maddalena, the *Victories*, the Vienna *Angel*, call forth echoes of earlier works. Rizzo seems to have reserved this native style for minor sculptures, commissioned by less important patrons for less conspicuous sites. Perhaps Rizzo sensed the falsity of his eclecticism, for his final works obey aesthetic principles enunciated by the Altars of S. Marco, *Adam* and *Eve*, *Prudence* and *Doge Tron*. At the apogee of his career, the Scala dei Giganti owed its merit to Rizzo's faithful cultivation of a vision and technique peculiarly his own.

CHAPTER FIVE

The Ducal Palace

IN THE fifteenth century the Ducal Palace consisted of three major entities. The south wing opposite the Bacino di S. Marco comprised the Palazzo Comunale; the west wing on the Piazzetta, the Palazzo di Giustizia. The Palazzo del Doge occupied the northern half of the east side of the Ducal Palace: from a point behind the apses of S. Marco, it extended south not far beyond the present Scala dei Giganti. In front of the Palazzo del Doge was a *cortile*; behind the Palazzo del Doge ran a canal called the Rio del Palazzo. Immediately to the south of the Palazzo del Doge was another *cortile*, which fronted the *rio*. Here stood an old structure with the Cappella di S. Nicolò and the Avogaria on the lower story, the Sala dei Pregadi above, and the Sala delle Arme. Beyond this, to the south was another small *cortile* or passage from which the stairs, which led to the loggias of the Palazzo Comunale and the Sala del Maggior Consiglio, ascended. Beyond this *cortiletto* rose the Torre Orientale at the southeast corner of the Ducal Palace.[1]

On September 14, 1483, fire broke out in the doge's private chapel in the Palazzo del Doge (not to be confused with the Cappella di S. Nicolò) and rapidly spread northward, ravaging the Ducal Apartments. Marin Sanudo's *Vite dei dogi* provides a contemporary account.

1483. On September 14 at 5 o'clock at night a fire broke out in this city in the Palazzo del Doge and began to burn in the chapel where the doge used to hear mass every day. It was caused by the sacristan, who left the wick of the candle lit after morning mass, thinking that he had extinguished it completely. The candle fell and caught fire and went on burning so that, at the said hour, fire broke out. There burned the Sala delle due Nape [Udienza] where the scene of Doge Cristoforo Moro going to Ancona on a crusade against the Turks was painted and where audiences were given in the presence of the Collegio. There burned the room nearby [Sala del Mappamondo] where the maps of the world and of Italy on two panels, recently made by Priest Antonio di Leonardo—a most excellent work by a supreme cosmographer—were kept and where the Savi gathered to consult. There burned the whole Palazzo del Doge except one part with a room called the Camera dei Dogi, where all the doges are painted with their *cartelli*, as in the Gran Consiglio. The Sala dei Pregadi [Sala del Senato] did not burn either, although the Ufficio dei Giudici del Proprio, which was below the palace [of the doge], did burn. The large bell with the hammer in the Campanile di S. Marco was rung because of the fire, and everyone ran to

[1] Sabellico, (1491-92) n.d., n.p. [p. 19v]: "reliquum latus [the east side] quod hodie ob nova[m] instauratio[n]e[m] e[st] pene dimidiatu[m] sub veteri structura vetustissima[m] nicolai edicula[m] habet: & tribu[n]al pro quo publici advocatores causas audiu[n]t: supra veteri i[n]stituto senatus habet: reliquum ubi vetus fuit pri[n]cipiu[m] sedes q[uae] medio ferrariensis belli te[m]pore deflagravit materia quidem nobili sed opere ad huc nobiliori ab uno ad fastigiu[m] est nuper instauratu[m]." (According to Mercati, 1939, ii, pp. 13f., the book was written in 1491-92.) See also Sanudo, *Diarii*, xl, 1894, col. 178, under November 1, 1525: "si ruina il palazo dove era la sala di Pregadi, la chiesola e la sala di le arme fino a terra." Cf. Bassi, *Critica d'arte*, May–June 1962, pp. 35f. and *Bassi* in Zorzi et al., 1971, p. 67. Bassi also included within the area of S. Nicolò, the Censori and the Quarantia Civil Vecchia.

help. The people from the Arsenal and others prevented the fire from spreading, so that only the residence of the doge burned. That night Doge Giovanni Mocenigo betook himself to the house of the captain of the prison in the courtyard of the palace. The palace was not opened soon enough because the doge feared being robbed. If it had been opened perhaps the fire might have been prevented from spreading so far, even if the Sala dei Pregadi was saved. A vast number of people had come to the Piazza S. Marco.

The following morning the doge went to live in Ca' Duodo, which is on the other side of the *rio* opposite the Palazzo del Doge, and a wooden bridge, covered and closed on the sides with windows, was built from the upper gallery of Ca' Duodo. By the bridge one could go from the Camera del Doge to the house where the doge was staying. The Collegio gathered in the afore-said Camera to hold audience. To Ser Alvise and Toma Duodo the Signoria paid 100 ducats a year as rent for their house.[2]

Today the east wing of the Ducal Palace is entire, joined to and integrated with south and west wings (Fig. 156). But it was not constructed at once or in one campaign of work. The first stage in the construction of the east wing naturally was devoted to replacing the wasted palace of the doge. That portion of the present east wing which resulted from this first campaign of work at the end of the fifteenth century is confined to its northern half, up to the area now occupied by the Scala d'Oro. This boundary is visible on the *cortile* facade of the east wing where, near its center, the height and artic-ulation of the uppermost story of the facade change slightly (Fig. 157). The loggia of the ground floor extended at least one and a half bays beyond this boundary to include at least six full bays to the south of the landing of the Scala dei Giganti. On the *rio* facade, the limit of fifteenth-century construction is indicated by the central axis of the central pier of the quadripartite opening of the ground floor.[3] In 1525 demolition of the structure that contained the Sala dei Pregadi and the Cappella di S. Nicolò commenced.[4] The southern half of the east wing, by means of which the Palazzo del Doge was linked with the Palazzo Comunale and the whole eastern perimeter of the large *cortile* received a uniform face, was built between 1533 and 1550 by Antonio Scarpagnino.

After the fire of 1483, opinion was divided on the extent of reconstruction that was opportune. Because of economic difficulties caused by the War of Ferrara (1482-84), the majority wished to do as little as possible, spending not more than 6,000 ducats in restoring the Palazzo del Doge to its original condition. Ser Nicolò Trevisan, Savio di Terraferma, on the other hand, proposed that a new Palazzo del Doge with a garden be constructed on the far side of the Rio del Palazzo where private houses then stood, that a building which would be restricted to the conduct of public affairs with rooms for the Signoria, the Collegio, and the Savii, be constructed on the near side of the *rio*, and that the two buildings be connected by a stone bridge. In the end moderation prevailed: it was decided to make the palace anew in three stories on the near side of the *rio*.[5]

[2] Lorenzi, 1868, pp. 92f., doc. 198, citing the un-published holograph of Sanudo's *Vite dei dogi* in the Bibl. Marc.

[3] Paoletti, 1893, ii, p. 154.

[4] Sanudo, *Diarii*, xl, 1894, col. 15, under October 2, 1525.

[5] Sanudo, *Vite dei dogi*, in Lorenzi, 1868, p. 93, doc. 198: "Et fu preso in pregadi adi . . . far fabricar il ditto palazo ducale in tre soleri qual sia bellissimo et li danari si toi aloficio dil sal: et altri di colegio voleano solamente refar il dito palazo come erra prima

con spexa solum di ducati 6000 ma ser Nicolo Tri-visan erra savio di terraferma erra dioppinion fusse comprato per la signoria le caxe dila dal rio e li fosse fato il palazo e habitation dil doxe et si andasse li per uno ponte marmoreo et questo diqua fusse fatto consar per le cosse publiche et non private dil doxe, ma non fo admessa taloppinion." Malipiero, *Arch. stor. ital.*, 1844, pt. 2, pp. 674: "La mazor parte sen-tiva de no spender più de 6,000 ducati in reparar el palazzo, per la stretezza de i tempi; ma dapuo' è stà ressolto de farlo tutto da nuovo. Nicolò Trivisan

Was the palace built anew from the foundations or were parts of the older structure incorporated in the new? Sanudo tells us that, after the fire, the Camera del Doge continued to be used for the Collegio's audiences and for access to the bridge that led to Ca' Duodo, but he does not specify how long the hall remained in use. An early sixteenth-century chronicle, on the other hand, informs us that demolition of what was left of the doge's habitation commenced immediately and proceeded to the foundations, that new piles were sunk and new foundations set.[6] Such a circumstantial account would inspire confidence were it not for the speed with which the palace was constructed. Moreover, numerous irregularities in the plan and elevation of the palace, irregularities incomprehensible in a Renaissance structure built from scratch, strongly suggest that the reconstructed palace, built on the site of the old one, made use of its foundations and those of its walls that were still sound.

On March 8, 1484, the Collegio entrusted the construction of the palace to the Provveditori al Sal, from whose funds work was to be financed.[7] By May 21, 1484, the Senate had determined that the palace should not expand beyond the *rio*. Architects with their models were summoned to appear at the end of the following week in order to testify to the most expedient means of rebuilding the palace.[8] It was probably not long after this that Antonio Rizzo was placed in charge of the reconstruction of the palace with an annual stipend of 100 ducats.[9] Although documents of 1484 do not explicitly call Rizzo *protomaestro*, he is referred to as though he were in charge.[10] The choice of Rizzo as supervisor of the works may have been influenced by the fact that he was already in the government's employ: a document of February 25, 1483, records Rizzo's acquisition of stone for what was probably the Arco Foscari.[11] As we have seen, many statues for the Arco Foscari had already been furnished by his shop. Perhaps too, Rizzo's valiant efforts in defense of Scutari, for which he had been awarded a pension on February 14, 1483,[12] played a role in his appointment.

Sabellico informs us that rebuilding of the Palazzo del Doge began in 1484.[13] By December 8, 1484, stone for the new palace was being quarried at Pola and Rovigno.[14] On January 31, 1485, it was decided that, of the 900 ducats destined each month for the repair of the Lido, 500 were to be diverted to the reconstruction of the palace.[15] In a petition to the Senate made in the summer of 1485, Rizzo averred that "since there was

voleva comprar tutte le case per mezo 'l palazzo, fin in cale delle Rosse, et de esse far el palazzo con giardin, e passar de là con un ponte de piera in sala de Colegio; e del luogho vechio, far sale e camere per la Signoria, per el Colegio, e per i Savii. Ma è stà deliberà de far la fabrica nuova in tre solari."

[6] Venice, Bibl. Marc., Cod. it., Cl. VII, 56 (= 8636), attributed to Erizzo, *Cronaca veneta*, n.p. [Principate of Giovanni Mocenigo, under September 14, 1483]: "et fù subito comenzado à deffar quello iera romaso della casa dove habitava el Principe, perfina le fondamente, et comenzò a palificar, et far fondamente molto grosse per tutto." The same passage occurs in Bibl. Marc., Cod. it., Cl. VII, 323 (= 8646), *Cronaca veneta*, p. 199r.

[7] Lorenzi, 1868, p. 92, doc. 198.

[8] Ibid., pp. 93f., doc. 199.

[9] Sanudo, *Vite dei dogi* in Lorenzi, 1868, p. 93, doc.

198; Malipiero, *Arch. stor. ital.*, 1844, pt. 2, p. 674.

[10] Paoletti, 1893, ii, p. 144; Lorenzi, 1868, p. 94, doc. 202.

[11] Paoletti, 1893, ii, p. 144. See App., pp. 126f.

[12] Cadorin, 1838, pp. 163f., n. 19. See App., p. 125.

[13] Sabellico, 1487, dec. 4, bk. 3, n.p.: "Pars illa Ducariae sedis quae medio tempore conflagrarat [sic] eodem anno quo in Gallia est debellatum coepta est a fundamentis restitui [sic]: Opus sane conspicuum diutissimeque duraturum: tota facies quae aquis incubat candido saxo & in adamantis speciem fastigiato superbe constructa: Est & a fronte qua forum spectat aureae aedis uestibulum non nihil peregrino lapide munitum."

[14] Paoletti, 1893, ii, p. 144.

[15] Lorenzi, 1868, p. 96, doc. 205.

demanded of him, the care of the construction of their palace to which he was devoting himself assiduously with his whole spirit and brain both night and day as was his wont, in order to do something pleasing to their lord and to meet the expectations that they had of him, he was compelled to abandon the shop which he was keeping and to neglect every other thing of his."[16] In response to his complaint that he was underpaid, Rizzo's salary was raised to 125 ducats per year.[17]

Ducal arms assist us in tracing the progress of construction. Work began at the northern end of the *rio* facade where the arms of Doge Giovanni Mocenigo (May 18, 1478, to November 4, 1485) adorn a lesene at the north corner of the basement. Under Doge Marco Barbarigo (November 19, 1485, to August 14, 1486) work was started on the *cortile* facade of the east wing, near the north end of the ground-floor arcade that bounds the present Cortiletto dei Senatori on the east: Marco Barbarigo's name appears on the capital of the third free-standing pier from the north corner in the east. But it was on the *rio* facade that work was concentrated. In his *Res Venetae*, Sabellico wrote: "Since the Republic was at peace at home and abroad, he [Doge Marco Barbarigo] turned his mind to the reconstruction of the Ducal Palace, work already begun; and with his care and diligence it came to pass, after the very few months that he was prince, that the whole massive structure of the quarters which face toward the east [the *rio* facade] was brought nearly to the top with superb work."[18] On March 12, 1486, Georges Lengherand contrasted the simplicity of the *rio* facade with the richness of the other external facades of the Ducal Palace.[19] Altered yet still recognizable, the *rio* facade of the Ducal Palace appears on the reverse of an engraved medal of Doge Marco Barbarigo.[20] In the mezzanine of the *rio* facade, above the portal with a single opening, two *putti* support a shield with arms of the Barbarigo family (Fig. 155). Barbarigo arms reappear between the first and second arches on the right of the quadripartite opening of the *rio* facade.

Doge Agostino Barbarigo's long reign (August 30, 1486, to September 20, 1501) encompassed almost all the work remaining on the reconstruction of the northern half of the Ducal Palace's east wing: under him the *cortile* facade of the Palazzo del Doge, as well as most of the internal decoration of the Appartamenti dei Dogi, was completed.

---

[16] Ibid., p. 97, doc. 207.

[17] Ibid., p. 114, doc. 239.

[18] Sabellico, 1487, dec. 4, bk. 3, n.p.: "Is republica domi forisque pacata: ad Ducarii refectionem opus iam antea inchoatum animum adiecit: Eiusque cura & diligentia est effectu[m]: ut paucissimis mensibus: quibus ille princeps fuit: Tota loci moles: quae ad ortum spectat: superbo opere ad summum ferme sit perducta."

[19] Lengherand, (1485-86) 1861, p. 35: "S'il est riche à ce costé, si est-il à tous autres costez, saulf à l'un qui regarde sur unne rue où la mer va au long d'icelle."

[20] Barbarigo, 1732, p. 67, no. xxxiii. The accompanying text, apparently based on Sabellico's *Res Venetae*, reads: "Republica domi forisque pacata, Marcus Princips ad publicam Ducis aedem instaurandam, exaedificandamque, quod Ioannes Mocenicus ante inceperat, animum sedulo adjecit. Is assidua cura, ac diligentia id effecit, ut brevissimo tempore, quo imperium obtinuit, omnis loci moles,

quae ad orientem solem spectat, ad exitum ferme, summa cum laude, perduceretur.

"Exstant etiamnum Insignia Barbadicae Familiae compluribus in locis, quae eo in opere eximiam illius Ducis magnificentiam perpetuo testentur."

The obverse is inscribed MARCVS BARBADICVS VENETORVM DVX. The reverse is inscribed DVCARIVM ESTRVCTVM.

The medal is not catalogued by Hill, 1930, and I have not succeeded in finding a specimen. Indeed, it is to be doubted whether this medal was actually coined during Marco Barbarigo's reign, or whether it was coined at all, for the image of the palace shows, in a position reversed with respect to the four-bay portal, the portal with double arcade that was constructed only after 1533 by Antonio Scarpagnino. Moreover, even the engravings seem to vary from exemplar to exemplar of this work. The copy consulted by me was that of the Bibliothèque Nationale, Paris.

Indeed, a large portion of the *cortile* facade was up by May 21, 1487. In his book published on that day Sabellico wrote: "after being declared doge . . . he [Agostino Barbarigo] followed in the footsteps of his brother [Marco] and he himself inaugurated his administration by the renewal of the Ducal Palace; which work on the facade where the entrance lies is in large part completed with magnificent and sumptuous display."[21] On October 12, 1486, a statute of the Venetian stonemasons' guild, according to which foreign master stonemasons, who were not citizens *de intus*, were denied the privileges of Venetian *maestri di bottega*, was relaxed in favor of Lombard masons for, according to Rizzo, they were necessary to the construction of the palace. Thus until such construction was completed, the Lombard masons were to be allowed to keep apprentices and buy and sell things appertaining to their craft. It was hoped this would encourage them to remain in Venice and would contribute to the speedy execution of the work.[22] In 1489 doors, window frames, and steps were being carved.[23] On October 10, 1491, Rizzo's salary was raised to 200 ducats.[24] In the same year the doge began to hold audiences in the new Ducal Apartments.[25] By March 19, 1492, his residence was habitable once again.[26] Apparently in August 1493 the Sala dei Pregadi or Senato on the top floor of the Palazzo del Doge was under construction. The *cortile* facade must have been entirely finished by this time, for Sanudo observed that it was lavishly gilded.[27]

Probably toward mid-1493 work on the palace was temporarily suspended for lack of funds. On September 11, 1493, the Council of Ten with its Giunta decided to meet the past and current wages of workmen with funds destined for the maintenance of the Lido.[28] On December 16, 1495, the same body voted to reduce the expenditure on the construction of the new palace to not more than 100 ducats per month. But the measure was not to go into effect immediately because a payment for marble for architraves in the new palace had just been authorized. From this document we learn that 13,868 ducats had been spent on the new palace in the previous three years.[29] A week later the Ten with its Giunta resolved to abolish the salaries and pensions of several people who were receiving stipends from the Ufficio del Sal.[30] Malipiero and Sanudo dated the slackening in construction of the Ducal Palace to 1496, blaming it on financial difficulties

[21] Sabellico, 1487, dec. 4, bk. 3, n.p.: "Post eius declarationem quum omnia ocio & luxu ut antea florerent fratris uestigia secutus & ipse a ducarii instauratione suam est administrationem auspicatus: quod opus a fronte qua uestibulum spectat magnifico & sumptuoso apparatu magna est ex parte confectum."

[22] Lorenzi, 1868, p. 100, doc. 214.

[23] Ibid., p. 104, doc. 225.

[24] Ibid., pp. 106f., doc. 230, p. 114, doc. 239.

[25] Venice, Mus. Cor., MS Cicogna 3533, Magno, *Annali veneti*, v, c. 134v: "nota del 1491 comenzado havia [the doge] a redurse a dar audientio in le sale nuove de quello de sopra."

[26] Malipiero, *Arch. stor. ital.*, 1844, pt. 2, p. 689: "A' 19 ditto [March], el Dose ha dà da disnar a cento poveri, e la note l'è andà a dormir in palazzo nuovo."

[27] Sanudo, (1493) 1980, pp. 33f.: "prima il palazzo dove habita lui [the doge], che è stato rinovato in 'sto tempo, et del 1492 compito, et il Dose ivi andato ad habitar; è sora canal—chiamato Rio de Palazzo—et fu fabricato in X anni però che il palazzo vecchio, in tempo de Zuan Mocenigo doxe, la notte si brusoe, et fo comenzato a rifar questo, che ha costato fin qui più di 100 000 ducati. Ha le faze tutte de piera viva lavorate, et intagliate con piere mandate a tuor per tutto 'l mondo; la faza da terra—dentro—è tutta indorata, et intagiata che è una bellezza a vederla, qui sono 4 camere indorate che *nunquam* vidi, né se ha visto le più belle da grandissimo tempo, et fattura, oltra l'oro, et spesa, salle eccellentissime; et l'Audientia publica, la salla de Pregadi—che al presente si lavora—che saranno degnissime." Sanudo dedicated his book to Agostino Barbarigo in August 1493.

[28] Lorenzi, 1868, p. 108, doc. 234.

[29] Ibid., p. 112, doc. 238.

[30] Ibid., pp. 113ff., doc. 239.

resulting from the wars that followed the invasion of Italy by the French under Charles VIII and the fall of Naples on February 22, 1495.[31]

As early as 1496 the Senate seems to have had some inkling of malversation in the administration of funds connected with the rebuilding of the palace: on March 22, 1496, the Senate provided that two representatives of its body be charged with reviewing all the money disbursed for construction of the palace and proceed against any malefactors that might be discovered.[32] Their investigations bore fruit two years later. Under the date of April 5, 1498, Sanudo committed to his diary the astounding news that

Francesco Foscari and Hironimo Capelo, appointed to examine the accounts of the Signoria, had found Master Antonio Rizo stonecutter, the master dedicated to the construction of the palace for the past thirteen years with a salary of 200 ducats per year, to have taken over 10,000 ducats by putting down that more had been spent in the construction of the palace of the doge, in which, up to now, it was discovered that 97,000 ducats had been spent, which is incredible, and a good part of this money had been stolen and not spent. In these days, Antonio, seeing that he had been found out, sold all his goods and his property and went toward Ancona and Foligno. He was called before the Council of Ten. It was believed that Master Simon Faxan, stonecutter, and others who worked with him stole a great deal.[33]

On May 16 Pietro Lombardo replaced Rizzo as *protomaestro* of the Ducal Palace at the reduced salary of 120 ducats annually.[34]

Both Sanudo and Malipiero state that when Rizzo's embezzlement was published and the sculptor fled, not half the work on the palace had been accomplished.[35] This seems to contradict all other testimony, including that of Sanudo himself, to the rapidity and extent of reconstruction. Now, at Barbarigo's death in 1501, the ground-floor loggia of the *cortile* facade extended at least one and a half bays beyond the rest of the east wing, for the sixth bay to the south of the Scala dei Giganti is bounded by a pier with Barbarigo arms. This indicates that the *cortile* facade of the east wing was meant to be extended to the south. In fact, in 1491-92 Sabellico clearly implied that the new construction in the east was meant to reach the southeast corner of the Ducal Palace.[36] Therefore, the decision to extend the east wing beyond the Appartamenti dei Dogi must have been made long before the flight of Rizzo.[37] Thus, when Sanudo and Malipiero wrote in 1498 that the palace was only half done, undoubtedly they meant that, although the northern half of the east wing was finished, or nearly so, the southern half was hardly begun. Probably construction of it had ceased in 1496 when both Malipiero

[31] Malipiero, *Arch. stor. ital.*, 1844, pt. 2, p. 699: "È stà dà principio sto mese de Zugno a far le fondamente del Relogio in piazza de S. Marco sora la Marzaria; . . . e benchè la fabrica del palazzo sia alquanto suspesa per la guerra de Napoli, niente de manco, azzochè no para che la Terra sia del tutto senza danari," and Sanudo, *Diarii*, i, 1879, coll. 205f: "A dì 10 zugno [1496], fo dato principio a butar zoso le caxe a l'intrar di marzaria in la piaza di San Marco sopra il volto, per far le fondamente di uno horologio . . . Et è da saper che la fabrica dil palazo, per queste guerre era alquanto suspesa; pur si andava fabricando."

[32] Lorenzi, 1868, p. 116, doc. 240.

[33] Sanudo, *Diarii*, i, 1879, coll. 927f.

[34] Lorenzi, 1868, pp. 121f., docs. 250, 251.

[35] Sanudo, *Vite dei dogi,* quoted in Lorenzi, 1868, p. 93, doc. 198: "ma da poi nelanno 1498 si trovo esser sta speso inlafabricha del ditto palazzo che si faceva enon erra fato lamita ducati 80 milia." Malipiero, *Arch. stor. ital.*, 1844, pt. 2, p. 674: "Questo Antonio Rizzo, del novantaotto, havea speso ottantamile ducati, e no era fatto la mità della fabrica."

[36] Sabellico, (1491-92), n.d., n.p. [p. 19v], quoted above, n. 1.

[37] Franzoi, 1973, p. 33, also believed this to have been the case, but did not explain his reasons.

and Sanudo commented that "work on the palace was suspended to a considerable degree."[38]

The portrait, initials, or arms of Doge Agostino Barbarigo are found repeatedly on all floors of the *cortile* facade of the Palazzo del Doge. In the ground-floor loggia Barbarigo's portrait and the initials A B are carved on the northwest face of the capital of the first free-standing pier at the northeast corner (Fig. 193). From the shape of the pier we may deduce that the ground-floor loggia was meant to continue along the north side of the *cortile* of the palace, around the present Cortiletto dei Senatori. But there is no evidence that any of the north side actually was built before the reign of Leonardo Loredan. Barbarigo's arms appear in the lunette above the tenth pier of the east loggia (Fig. 157), as well as in the capital of the thirteenth pier counting from the north, that is, the sixth bay beyond the Scala dei Giganti. On the *piano nobile* Barbarigo's arms adorn the south opening at the top of the landing of the Scala dei Giganti and the soffits of its two lateral arches. Barbarigo's arms recur five times on the third floor. On the fourth floor, arms appear once; the initials A B D[ux] are repeated twice. Inside the Appartamenti dei Dogi, each of the five fireplaces is marked with Barbarigo arms, initials, and, in one case, a portrait of the doge. In the Sala delle Mappe (Udienza) the reveals of windows at both ends of the room and the pilasters at the intersection of the Sala delle Mappe and the Sala dei Filosofi bear emblems of Barbarigo. In the Sala degli Scudieri Barbarigo's arms, name, or initials are found on the portal leading to the Sala delle Mappe and on the reveals of three of the four windows overlooking the *rio*. Inside the Ducal Apartments references to Barbarigo's successor, Doge Leonardo Loredan (October 2, 1501, to June 21, 1521), are confined to the outer lateral faces of the two balconies overlooking the *rio* on the third and fourth floors and to Pietro Lombardo's relief of the *Madonna Enthroned with Saints* in the Camera degli Scarlatti.

Under Pietro Lombardo, reconstruction of the new Palazzo del Doge was concluded. On June 21, 1503, the Provveditori al Sal were ordered to furnish Pietro with 4,000 pounds of lead in order to repair the roofs of the old and new palaces.[39] Almost all the decorative carving in the Appartamenti dei Dogi was executed by Rizzo and his shop, but the frieze of the portal that leads from the Sala degli Scudieri to the Sala delle Mappe is Lombardesque. A document records Antonio and Tullio Lombardo's execution of one marble fireplace hood and an addition to the corner of a second hood in the alcove of the Sala dell'Udienza piccola and the Sala itself, respectively (probably the two rooms on the *cortile* side of the Ducal Apartments to the north of the Udienza). The work had been done some years before December 28, 1505.[40] In fact, all five fireplaces of the doge's apartment are uniform in style and can be attributed to the second generation of Lombardos. By January 8, 1505, some, if not all, of the carved wooden ceiling of the Anticamera della Udienza (Camera degli Scarlatti) had been made by Maestro Biagio and his brother, Pietro da Faenza. By March 20, 1506, the ceiling was finished but not entirely installed. Biagio and Pietro had also executed the frieze below the ceiling of the Udienza.[41]

The external staircase, which leads from the courtyard to the loggia of the east wing's *piano nobile*, is known as the Scala dei Giganti from the colossal statues added many

[38] Malipiero, *Arch. stor. ital.*, 1844, pt. 2, p. 699; Sanudo, *Diarii*, i, 1879, coll. 205f., for which, see above, n. 31.

[39] Lorenzi, 1868, p. 127, doc. 261.
[40] Ibid., p. 138, doc. 283.
[41] Ibid., pp. 129f., doc. 266, pp. 132f., doc. 272.

decades after its completion (Figs. 165, 166). Work on the Scala dei Giganti seems to have been synchronized with that on the *cortile* facade and the ducal apartments: completion of the staircase postdates the completion of the fabric of the Appartamenti dei Dogi by only five years. The plan of the staircase must have been fixed by 1486/87, for the bay system of the second-story arcade makes allowance for the three round-arched bays at the top of the *scala* whose compound width does not equal the width of any whole number of bays with ogive arches (Fig. 158). There survives only one document that refers unequivocally to the construction of the staircase. Dated October 9, 1491, it is an order from the Signoria to the Provveditori al Sal "to reach an agreement with Master Antonio Rizzo concerning the continuation of the construction of their palace, for the figures as well as for the staircase and other necessary things that he knows how to do."[42] Unfortunately, this document does not tell us whether the staircase was more than merely planned. It is likely, however, that work had already commenced. Probably the marble for which Ser Zuan da Carrara was credited by the Ufficio del Sal with the immense sum of 1,220 ducats on December 17, 1490,[43] was destined for the Scala dei Giganti, since this was the only part of the Ducal Palace then under construction in which Carrara marble was used extensively. The staircase was in the course of installation between May 21 and June 4, 1494, when an awed visitor to the Ducal Palace wrote, "a new flight of steps is being built there—a stupendous and costly work—by which to ascend to the said palace from the side of the Church of St. Mark."[44] By late winter or early spring of 1497 the Scala dei Giganti had received some of its carved facing but was not yet finished. In the chronicle of his pilgrimage, Arnold von Harff recalled that "Doge Agostino Barbarigo, who is now having the palace covered with marble and gilt . . . was also building a whole marble staircase with beautiful carving, which at this time was not half complete, the half having cost 10,000 ducats."[45]

It is possible to establish a *terminus ante quem* for the completion of the Scala dei Giganti. Numerous allusions to Agostino Barbarigo appear in the reliefs embellishing the flight of steps and in the front faces of the *avancorpi*, but there are none to his

[42] Ibid., p. 106, doc. 229.

[43] Paoletti, 1893, ii, p. 152.

[44] Casola, (1494) 1907, p. 126. Casola, (1494) 1855, p. 6: "e se li fa di nuovo una scala per ascendere dicto palacio dal lato de la Giesia de sancto Marco, cosa stupenda e de grande spexa."

From a passage in which Casola recorded the conclusion of the Corpus Domini procession on May 29, McAndrew, 1980, p. 99, deduced that "finished or not, it [the Scala dei Giganti] was then usable." The passage reads: "E riposto che fu el sacramento del corpo de Christo, fu accompagnato el Duce da ogni homo in palazzo, e conciosi in cima de la scala fin che fu montato tutti li gentilhuomini con li peregrini, e poi salutando tutta la brigata andossene intra el palazzo in la sua abitatione, et uniusquisque reversus est in domum suam aut hospitium, perchè era hora de pranzo." (Casola [1494], 1855, p. 19.) It seems to me unlikely, however, that an unfinished staircase would have been used in a public procession: I prefer to think either that the staircase referred to was one erected to permit temporary ac-

cess to the Ducal Apartments during the building of the Scala dei Giganti or that Casola mistakenly implied that the doge gained direct access to his habitation from the staircase and that the staircase used was the one which led to the Sala del Maggior Consiglio.

[45] Harff, (1496-99) 1946, pp. 54f. In the original German, the passage reads: "Item hart beneuen sijnt Marx kirch suydenwart dae steyt des hertzogen pallais dat gar schoin is ind all daigs koestlicher gebouwet wirt van desem hertzouch Augustin Barbarigo, as he zo deser tzijt sijn rechte pallais leys buyssen ganss becleyden mit marmelensteynen ind dat oeuergulden. dar zo leys he eyn gantze steynen marmeltrappe maichen mit coestlichem werck gcsneden, die zo deser tzijt noch neyt halff reydt en wais. dan noch hayt hie helschet gekost x dusent ducaten." (Harff, [1496-99] 1860, p. 44.) For the dates of Harff's two sojourns in Venice between at least February 2 and 5, 1497, and soon after April 3, 1497, see Harff, (1496-99) 1946, p. xxxiii.

successor, Leonardo Loredan. It is often asserted, on the testimony of Sanudo's diary, that Leonardo Loredan, elected doge on October 2, 1501, was not sworn in on the Scala dei Giganti, and that the staircase was not used for this purpose until the coronation of Loredan's successor, Antonio Grimani, in 1521. This, however, is to misinterpret Sanudo, who does not say that Loredan was not sworn in on the Scala dei Giganti or that he was sworn in elsewhere, but rather merely fails to designate the precise location of the ceremony.[46] In fact, it probably did take place on the Scala dei Giganti. The earliest unequivocal reference to the use of the *scala* dates from November 22, 1497, when Sanudo reported the doge's reception of the Duke of Pomaria: "And having finished the office, [the Duke of Pomaria] with many of the gentlemen who were accompanying him, went to an audience with the Signoria. Received by the prince with great ceremony, he stayed for a long time, and then the prince accompanied him down to the staircase of stone."[47] Therefore, we must conclude that the final installation of the Scala dei Giganti was accomplished between early February and late November 1497.

During the principate of Doge Francesco Venier (1554-56) the tripartite arcade at the top of the staircase's landing (Fig. 158) was modified. A lion of St. Mark was placed in the frieze above the central arch and four lesenes with trophies in high relief were added above the piers. To mark these changes, Venier's arms, each supported by two *putti*, were carved from two preexistent roundels. The over-life-size statues of *Mars* and *Neptune* were executed by Jacopo Sansovino between 1554 and 1567.

The Appartamenti dei Dogi (Fig. 149) preserved the plan, common in Venetian palaces in the thirteenth century, of a central T-shaped hall, the stem of which was aligned with the longitudinal axis of the building; smaller rooms opened off the stem of the hall on either side.[48] In medieval examples the stem of the T spans the entire depth of the palace. Thus the head of the hall arrives at the building's main facade, permitting the illumination of the hall through windows densely grouped in the facade. In the Ducal Apartments, on the other hand, the head of the hall lies buried inside the fabric, at right angles to the *rio* and *cortile* facades. Light was obtained through openings clustered at either end of the crossbar of the T. In addition, two rooms were situated beyond the crossbar of the T-shaped hall. This anomalous arrangement is best explained by hypothesizing the incorporation within the fifteenth-century building of the earlier palace of the doge. Its plan can be read from the plan of Rizzo's structure. Presumably, the facade of the medieval Palazzo del Doge was formed by the crossbar of the T. If so, the palace would have been turned 90 degrees with respect to the present structure. Ori-

---

[46] Sanudo, *Diarii*, iv, 1880, col. 134: "et poi fo (Loredan) conduto per piaza, sul pulpito, *de more*, butando danari; et montoe in palazo a hore 16½, dove li fo posta la bareta ducal per el menor consier, qual fu . . . , et dicto *accipe coronam ducatus Venetiarum*." In the case of the coronation of Doge Antonio Grimani, Sanudo, ibid., xxx, 1891, col. 482, does explicitly situate the ceremony on the Scala dei Giganti.

[47] Ibid., i, 1879, coll. 821f.: "Et poi compito l'oficio, andoe [the Duke of Pomaria] con molti zentilhomini che li feva compagnia a l'audentia da la Signoria. Et recevuto dal principe con gran festa, stete

assai, et poi el principe lo acompagnò di sotto fino a la scala di piera." See also ibid., iii, 1880, col. 1170, under December 15, 1500: "Vene il reverendissimo cardinal regiense, legato apostolico . . . Et prima intrò in chiesa . . . Et poi el principe col colegio li andò contra fino a la schalla, et andati di sopra a l'audentia, dove fo tirato la chariega." See also ibid., iv, 1880, col. 680, under January 30, 1503: "Esso signor [the Duke of Urbino] ringratiò la Signoria *etc.*; et cussì andò suso per la scala granda di piera, e tutti si ralegrava a vederlo."

[48] Bassi in Zorzi *et al.*, 1971, p. 66.

ented toward the south, instead of toward the west, originally it would have fronted the *cortile* with the Cappella di S. Nicolò.

The *rio* facade is not parallel to the *cortile* facade or, indeed, to any north-south face of the Ducal Palace. As a result, the entire east wing is slightly trapezoidal in plan. In the Ducal Apartments, the axis of the stem of the T-shaped hall is parallel to the *rio* facade. Therefore, it was possible to create rectangular rooms on the *rio* side by skewing east-west walls. On the opposite side east-west walls are aligned with the major east-west axis of the palace, but rooms are distinctly trapezoidal.

Private rooms were separated from public rooms by the T-shaped hall. The rooms along the *rio* side constituted the private apartment of the doge and his family; the rooms along the *cortile* and to the south of the T-shaped hall were used for public functions. The different uses of the rooms were partly reflected in their ceilings: in contrast to the beamed ceilings and lunette vault of the doge's private chambers, the three public rooms on the *cortile* side were decked with carved wooden ceilings, sumptuously polychromed and gilded.[49] The crossbar of the T-shaped hall, now called the Sala dello Scudo, formed the major reception area where audiences were held in the presence of the doge and the Collegio. An internal stone staircase with a landing led from the floor below directly to the Udienza.[50]

The sumptuous interior decoration of the Appartamenti dei Dogi excited the admiration of Pietro Casola. In May 1494 he wrote:

The hall where the Doge and his Councillors hold audience constantly is not very large, but it is magnificently decorated, with its gilded ceiling and its painted and storied walls. . . .

With regard to the magnificence and decoration of the habitation of the aforesaid Doge—as I have seen many other princely palaces in this our time both in Italy and abroad, beginning at Rome—I venture to say that it is the most beautiful in Italy. It is so rich in carved work and everything gilded, that it is a marvel. One of the pages of the aforesaid Doge showed me everything, beginning with the bed in which he sleeps, and proceeding even to the kitchen, and in my opinion nothing could be added. The decorations are not movable, but fixed. There is no lack of marble and porphyry and woodwork subtly carved, and all is of such a nature that one is never weary of looking.[51]

On the floor above the Ducal Apartments were the chambers which accommodated meetings of the Senate and the Collegio (Fig. 150). The Collegio used the long, narrow room now called the Sala delle Quattro Porte (8 in the plan). The Senate occupied the largest room (5 in the plan). The two smaller rooms were used as anterooms to the

---

[49] It may have been to these ceilings that Sanudo was referring when he wrote of the four gilded rooms on the landward side of the Appartamenti dei Dogi. See above, n. 27.

[50] Sanudo, *Diarii*, i, 1879, col. 821: "A dì 20 [November 1497] . . . per farli ogni dimostration di careze, le vene [the doge] contra fino sul pato di la scala di l'audientia." Ibid., iii, 1880, coll. 928f., under October 18, 1500: "El principe li andò contra fino a la schala di sopra di l'audentia."

[51] Casola, (1494) 1907, p. 127. Casola, (1494) 1855, p. 7: "La sala dove de continuo sede el Duca a la audientia con li sui consiglieri non è troppo grande, me è ornata e magnifica, con lo celo adorato, le pa-

rieti dipinte e istoriate; . . . Quanto sii magnifica e ornata l'habitatione del prefato Duce; per haverne vedute de molte precipue in questa nostra età in Italia e di fora, comenzeando a Roma, ardisco de dire che sia la più bella de Italia, così richa de opera de intagli, e ogni cosa posto ad auro è piena de admiratione. Per uno suo donzello del prefato Duce me fu monstrata tutta incomenzando al lecto dove dorme, e procedendo fino alla cucina. Al mio judicio credo non se li possa adjungere; non sono ornamenti de tollere e de remettere ma stanno perseveranti; li non mancano in marmori e porfidi e in lignami subtili intagli; e de tal natura che non pono satiare l'homo de vedere."

Collegio and Senato. Although the rooms were larger than those on lower stories, their walls rested on bearing walls of the rooms below. On May 11, 1574, fourth-floor rooms were devastated by fire.[52] Their elaborate decorations date from the late sixteenth century.[53]

Very likely the irregularities of the facade designs (Figs. 152, 156) were due to preexistent elevations: Rizzo probably was forced to adapt the height of stories and the size, shape, and location of windows to the structure that had previously stood upon the site. The variation in the height of rooms on a single floor reenforces the likelihood that Rizzo was bound by the elevation of a structure that had grown by accretion over many centuries. If so, then Rizzo's idiosyncratic method of additively linking small, discrete units in endless series was better suited to the disadvantageous conditions under which he worked than a synthetic method would have been. It is doubtful whether any design could have produced unity. Rizzo's compositions, at least, had the advantage of focusing attention upon the smallest units so that the lack of integration was not so keenly felt. So much the more opportune was this method of composition on the *rio* side of the Ducal Palace where the whole facade could not be seen at once except in drastically foreshortened views.[54] The *cortile* of the Ducal Palace offered more favorable views and there, in fact, Rizzo took more care to integrate his composition.

The *rio* facade (Figs. 151-154) is identical in style to the architecture of the Tron Tomb (Fig. 64).[55] The facade consists of a dense grid of horizontals and verticals in which the dominant horizontals provided by the entablature of each story are carried through the entire length of the facade. No members span more than one story and only at the ends are there members which span an entire single story. Minor horizontals are broken only by the opening of doors and windows. Each story is divided into numerous horizontal units which, piled on top of one another, ultimately produce a sense of verticality.

Each story received a different treatment. To be sure, as long as openings were not vertically aligned—a fault for which Rizzo probably was not to blame—stories could not be identical. As long as predetermined openings did not occur at regular intervals, the articulation of individual stories could not be uniform. But it was only toward the top of the facade that Rizzo began to perceive these as remediable evils. Throughout the entire height of the face, the width of bays was determined by the variable distance between openings. Thus, narrow surfaces made one bay, wider surfaces were divided down the center, though a smaller unit might well have offered a module applicable to both. While the articulation of the upper stories corresponds to some extent, the first two stories bear little relation, either to each other or to the two upper stories. Even the entablature of the *piano nobile* was designed as a separate unit. Here oculi were distributed at equal intervals, as a consequence of which they are not aligned with the bay system of the story to which the entablature belongs. By contrast, the oculi of the fourth story are placed at unequal intervals, but the entablature is unified with the remainder of the story.

[52] Lorenzi, 1868, pp. 382f., doc. 785.

[53] Zorzi, *Arte ven.*, 1953, pp. 123-151.

[54] Jacopo de' Barberi's plan of Venice of 1500 shows the side of the narrow Rio del Palazzo opposite the Ducal Palace entirely filled with buildings.

[55] Bassi in Zorzi *et al.*, 1971, p. 68, compared the elevation of the *rio* facade with two drawings in the Latin translation of Filarete's treatise made by Antonio Bonfini d'Ascoli for Matthias Corvinus of Hungary in 1484: Venice, Bibl. Marc., Cod. lat., Cl. VIII, 2 (= 2796), Averulinus (Filarete), *Architecturae*, pp. 146r, 157r. I do not think the similarities are close enough to be significant.

The *rio* facade is composed of innumerable small, closed, rectangular fields, which uniformly blanket the surface of the building. Each field is completely framed. Even the individual stones of the rusticated basement are furnished with broad borders. Frames provide straight edges that only the projection of volutes occasionally interrupts. Within individual stories there is variation of dimension but not of motif. Lunettes are segmental throughout. Each story possesses a single order of uniform pilasters whose height was determined by the height of the springing of the windows' arches: there is no larger order to support the main entablature at the top of the facade which, resting sometimes on lesenes that rise from imposts or capitals, sometimes on a second entablature, is inadequately supported. As a consequence of this mode of composition, there is no central focus. Rizzo may have felt it unnecessary to stress a portion of the facade that was not visible in frontal view. But he did not emphasize the accessible north corner either, where nothing more than a heightened lesene in the first three stories, a doubling of pilasters in the fourth, and a stepping of the entablature in all mark the end of the long facade.

The flatness of the *rio* facade is notable: only the smallest components of the facade—moldings, festoons, the individual stones of the rusticated basement—possess relief. The facade was not stepped. Pilasters were used in preference to columns; there are no niches; entablatures were rarely broken, and then only minimally. Large unarticulated slabs of Istrian stone are emblematic of the facade's planarity. Typical of Rizzo are the pilasters' elongated proportions and the minute scale of the ornament of capitals.

The rustication of the basement (Fig. 151) is without precedent or parallel in Venice. Stones are shaped like pyramids with blunted tips; convex and concave pyramids alternate.[56] Also unusual is the grouping of free-standing column and flanking pilasters in the quadripartite opening of the third story (Fig. 154), for column and pilasters are not contiguous. The separation of pilasters and column made a plastic motif two-dimensional: instead of appearing to overlap recessed pilasters, the column is merely framed, first by a dark narrow border, then by wider, light pilasters. The exaggerated entasis of the column is conspicuous against the empty ground; the precise degree of swelling can be measured by the vertical edges of the pilasters. Carved ornament was applied to the thickest portion of the shaft, increasing and accentuating the entasis. The introduction of lesenes above the pilasters to provide support for the main entablature was taken over by Mauro Codussi in the facade of Palazzo Zorzi at S. Severo.

Cortile and *rio* facades are distinguished chiefly by degree of decoration: where the *rio* facade is relatively bare, virtually every surface of the *cortile* facade (Figs. 156-159) is filled with carving or inset *tondi* of porphyry and *verde antico*. The architrave of the third story is inlaid with niello. Sanudo described the *cortile* facade as entirely gilded.[57] Probably gilding was applied to all relief—festoons, capitals, *rinceaux*, ribbons, moldings—which stood out against the ground of Istrian stone.

The arcade of the *piano nobile* creates a compositional link with the *cortile* facades on south and west. The Gothic elevation of arches and the plan of piers with four applied columns derive from the earlier arcades; even capitals are late Gothic in style. But Rizzo elaborated upon the original design by inserting roundels of different colored stones

[56] See Ruskin, iii, 1853 (pt. 3, App. 5), pp. 210f.
[57] Sanudo, (1493) 1980, pp. 33f., for which, see above, n. 27. See also Gentile Bellini, *St. Mark's Day*

Procession in St. Mark's Square, Venice, Accademia, 1496.

between the arches. In Rizzo's day the second-floor arches of the *cortile* facades in south and west sat on plain brick walls. Instead of following this model, Rizzo repeated the second-floor arcade below. The bays of ground-floor and *piano nobile* arcades are aligned, but arch and pier of ground-floor arcade are Renaissance in style. Because, even with elevated piers, round arches produced lower openings, Rizzo put the oculi above, rather than between, the arches. The moldings of the archivolts and oculi imitate the simple plastic moldings of the Gothic arcades, but Rizzo characteristically transformed the plan of the piers into octagons whose faces resemble pilasters.[58] The articulation of the two upper stories was taken over from the upper stories of the *rio* facade. The cluster of five openings in the Udienza creates a focus slightly to the right of what would have been the center of Rizzo's original facade. But the windows of the Udienza are not aligned with the tripartite opening above the landing of the Scala dei Giganti.

The ornament of the *cortile* facade is denser and more plastic than the ornament we have hitherto associated with Rizzo. It is not to be supposed that Rizzo executed any of the ornament himself; very likely he delegated even its design. As we have seen, in 1486 Rizzo was assisted by several Lombard stonemasons,[59] and in fact, the style of the ornament of the *cortile* facade is closer to that of the exterior windows of Como Cathedral or the portal of S. Maria dei Miracoli at Brescia than it is to anything in Venice. Documents record the names of several stonemasons: in 1486 and 1495 Master Zuan di Primo da Spalato;[60] in 1486 a certain Giorgio, who may be the stonecutter Giorgio Gruato, mentioned in 1489 in connection with the execution of doors, window frames, and steps;[61] in 1486 a Master Domenico who was sawing porphyry and was replaced by Master Giacomo da Brescia in 1493;[62] in 1488 a Master Quintin, stonecutter;[63] in 1495 Alvise di Domenico, Master Bertuzzi, stonecutter, and Master Michiel Naranza, stonecutter;[64] and finally the Master Simon Faxan, stonecutter, who in 1498 was found to have stolen a great deal of money.[65] Other stonemasons, some of whom may be identical with those cited above, are recorded in unpublished documents. They are Michiele Bertucci, Alvise Bianco, Alvise di Pantaleone, and Stefano *tagliapietra*.[66] In 1581 Francesco Sansovino recalled that the grotesques in the vaults at the top of the stairs had been carved by Domenico and Bernardino Mantovani.[67] None of these craftsmen can be identified.

The relief located over a ground-floor portal of the *rio* facade, which shows two torch-bearing *putti* supporting a shield with Barbarigo arms surmounted by a ducal hat (Fig. 155), can be dated quite precisely to 1485-86.[68] Figures and blazon were carved in

---

[58] See McAndrew, 1980, p. 88.

[59] Lorenzi, 1868, p. 100, doc. 214. On October 25, 1491, the native members of the Venetian stonemason's guild complained to the Provveditori al Comun that they, who numbered only about 40, were outvoted in elections for the various offices of their guild by foreign members—126 stonemasons from Milan and other parts of Lombardy. The Lombards, they added, employed about 50 Lombard apprentices, but refused to teach Venetian youths. (Sagredo, 1856, pp. 283f., no. IIII.) Undoubtedly, a good many of these Lombards were employed in the construction of the Ducal Palace.

[60] Rambaldi, *Aten. ven.*, 1910, pt. 2, p. 102, n.; Lorenzi, 1868, pp. 113ff., doc. 239.

[61] Lorenzi, 1868, p. 99, doc. 211, p. 104, doc. 225.

[62] Ibid., p. 100, doc. 213; Rambaldi, *Aten. ven.*, 1910, pt. 2, pp. 101ff., n. 2.

[63] Lorenzi, 1868, p. 102, doc. 220.

[64] Ibid., pp. 113ff., doc. 239.

[65] Sanudo, *Diarii*, i, 1879, col. 928.

[66] Cadorin, 1838, p. 135.

[67] Sans., 1581, p. 120r.

[68] In age, costume, and function, the *putti* match the *Pages* that flank the *Pedestrian Effigy of Jacopo Marcello* in his tomb by Giovanni Buora in S. Maria dei Frari. The tomb was erected immediately after Marcello's death on May 19, 1484. See Brand, 1977, pp. 198f.

low relief. They fill a field whose shape and dimensions were fixed by architectural requisites—the width of the portal and the height of the attic above the ground-floor windows: in fact, the sculptural matter is not sufficient to fill the field. As in the Altar of the Traghetto della Maddalena (Figs. 128, 129), the figures occupy a setting denoted merely by a shallow floor whose slope implies recession; as there, a strip running along the bottom defines the front face of the stage. The *putti*'s drapery resembles most that of the Angels in the Altar of the Traghetto della Maddalena. Facial type and hair recall the *Pages* from the Emo Tomb (Figs. 145, 146). Indeed, the head of the left-hand *putto* and the head of the left-hand *Page* seem taken from a single model. In anatomy and foreshortening the *putti* of the Ducal Palace are inferior to the *putti* in relief to the left of the epitaph of Tron (Fig. 117); yet the figures are not as rigid as the left-hand Emo *Page* (Fig. 141). Flaws probably were due to Rizzo's want of interest in a relief intended for the back door of the doge's palace.

Comparison with the *Putti with Arms of the Barbarigo Family* allows us to date a relief of the *Madonna and Child* in the collection of the Prince of Liechtenstein at Vaduz (Fig. 160) to the mid-1480s. Though never before attributed to Rizzo, his hand is evident. The same configuration of folds overlaps the waist in the Madonna and the *putto* on the left (Fig. 155). The gown of the Madonna, like the *putto*'s dress, seems made of a sheer material because folds, indicated primarily by the finest of incisions, lack almost all plasticity. In both, this flattening affects the entire torso; by contrast, undraped areas are given more relief and are occasionally foreshortened. In the Madonna's mantle long, tortuous, cord-like folds recall the cloaks of the St. Clement Madonna (Fig. 22) and the Madonna from the *tondo* formerly in Amsterdam (Fig. 29). But the flatter folds of the later work are less distinctive. The facial type of the Madonna also has changed. As in the Tron Tomb *Charity* (Fig. 82), contracted features sit on the surface of a hemispherical face, whose smoothly rounded contours and unarticulated surface conceal all traces of a bony structure. The narrow ridges of the brows pursue the course of *Charity*'s brows; nostrils are equally diminutive and flat; the opening between slightly parted lips hardly extends beyond the line of nostrils; the lips, which vanish long before the corners of the mouth, have the same morphology in both. In both, the receding chin, blunt yet dimpled, is contained within the wider contour of a double chin.

The Madonna is shown seated behind a low ledge. No seat is indicated and the ledge implausibly truncates the figure's legs. Mother and Child are seen against a sky filled with distant clouds, like the backdrop of the relief from Amsterdam (Fig. 29); perhaps the borders at right and left denoted jambs of a window behind the figures. At an unknown date the top of the relief was cut down; we may surmise that originally the relief was just high enough to contain the Madonna's entire halo and a border one centimeter wide, and that the upper corners ended in right angles. The naked Christ Child is seated on his mother's thigh. His head is turned and tilted upward as he meets her lowered gaze. Thus the attention of both figures, concentrated upon each other, is contained within the fictive space of the relief. The Virgin raises her hand in a sign of welcome already used in slightly different form in the reliefs in Amsterdam and S. Marco (Figs. 29, 22). It was surely a later restorer who mistakenly supposed that the object of the Child's gesture was missing and supplied a cross. In fact, the infant's extended arms signify a desire to be embraced. Thus gesture and expression betray the Child's yearning for his Mother; to it she responds with dignified restraint.

More difficult to judge because of its coarse polychromy is a relief in the Camera degli Scarlatti (Fig. 161), a public chamber in the Ducal Apartments. It too depicts the Madonna and Child against a cloud-filled sky, accompanied now by two Angels and two heads of Seraphim. The marble relief is enclosed within a limestone frame bearing the inscribed date of 1529 and the arms and initials of nobles who can be identified tentatively as Michele di Marco Gritti, Giudice del Procuratore in 1529, Dottor Girolamo di Quintin Tagliapietra, a former official of the Camera dei prestiti, and Angelo di Marco Miani. Presumably it was they who supplied the frame. The relief itself dates from the end of the fifteenth century; perhaps it was made to commemorate the doge's return to the Ducal Palace in 1492.

In the treatment of the hair and veil, fastened by a button at the breast, the Virgin resembles her counterpart in the Liechtenstein relief (Fig. 160). The faces of both are equally rotund: unmodulated cheeks and brow preserve intact the inflated surface of a hemisphere, which eyes, hardly embedded within their sockets, do nothing to disturb. In other respects, however, the Madonna's face most resembles that of *Eve* (Fig. 50). Note in both the high forehead, which bulges at the temples before beginning its retreat to a receding part. Eyebrows, whose contours spring directly from the nose, arch high above the eyes. Fleshy pads beneath the brows are parted by grooves from the lowered lids encasing bulbous eyeballs. Contours of upper and lower lids, with slightly tipped tear ducts, are identical in both. In both, the slopes of the nose seem slightly concave and the sharply defined caret is similarly formed. The rather flat lower lip is contracted and indented in the center. Its edge protrudes as though outlined by a cord. The short, blunt chin is indented in the center of its lower edge and is succeeded by a nascent double chin. Beneath the fleshy necks, similarly creased, the same anatomical structure is just barely visible. The right hand of the Venetian Madonna, like the left hand of the Virgin in Liechtenstein (Fig. 160), possesses extraordinarily elongated fingers. The contours of the fingers are straight and the last knuckle of every finger is indented. Typically, the division between thumb and forefinger was prolonged nearly to the border of the hand. The splayed fingers of the Madonna's left hand recall the gesture of the Madonna in the St. Clement Altar (Fig. 22). Face and hair of the two Angels in the relief of the Camera degli Scarlatti are analogous to those of the *putti* in the relief with arms of the Barbarigo family (Fig. 155). The straight folds that traverse the Madonna's shoulder and upper arm are similar to those of the sleeve of the right-hand Angel in the Altar of the Traghetto della Maddalena (Fig. 129).

The relief of the *Madonna and Child* in the Camera degli Scarlatti is flatter than any of Rizzo's reliefs examined yet. In the relief in Liechtenstein (Fig. 160), as in the earlier Altar of the Traghetto della Maddalena (Figs. 128, 129), a few specific elements were carved in high relief while the undercut contours of overlapping planes implied spatial intervals. In the later relief even the most plastic forms do not exceed the limits of low relief and the elimination of most undercutting causes overlapping planes to telescope. As in all Rizzo's Madonna reliefs (Figs. 22, 29, 160), torsos and limbs are turned into the plane. Where foreshortening would have been unavoidable, as in a receding forearm, the member is conveniently overlapped. In less sharply receding members, like the farther shoulder of the Madonna and the ear and skull of the Christ Child in the reliefs in the Ducal Palace and Vaduz (Figs. 161, 160), and the right shoulder and right foot of the Christ Child in the former relief, the absence of foreshortening results in anatomical distortions.

In the relief of the Camera degli Scarlatti the earlier description of anatomy is sacrificed to a dense and uniform patterning of the surface: in this respect the relief represents the end of a gradual development. In the St. Clement Madonna (Fig. 22) the constriction of the waist was accentuated by a tie, and breasts were indicated, not only by their protuberance, but also by the divergence and confluence of folds. In the relief in Liechtenstein (Fig. 160), breasts were not defined. Though the position of the waist was indicated, its contraction was not. Yet the gradual widening of folds below the waist alludes to the abdomen's convexity, and the projecting legs rise from the surface of the relief. By the Madonna from the Ducal Palace (Fig. 161) neither the topography of the relief, nor the configuration of folds bears any relation to anatomical form. To be sure, a fold marks the division between chest and shoulder, but neither breasts, nor waist, nor abdomen affects the disposition of folds. Indeed, straight folds crossing the Madonna's shoulder or the Christ Child's thigh intentionally deny volume to the limb in question. The receding ledge at the foremost plane of the relief and the Virgin's upright torso are elided by a single plane of drapery, which falls plumb from the shoulders of the Virgin like a curtain hanging from a rod. No distinction by means of size, shape, or plasticity of individual folds is made between the fabrics of the Virgin's gown, cloak, or veil.

Two *schiacciato* reliefs by Rizzo decorate the Ducal Apartments. One adorns the base of an imaginary candelabra on the reveal of a window in the Sala degli Scuderi (Fig. 162);[69] the other embellishes a shield on the reveal of a window at the west end of the Sala delle Mappe (Fig. 163). Both portray a battle between two men, one of whom is mounted, the other on foot. The ideality of the scenes is expressed by the nudity of the participants; horses lack saddles and bridles. The reliefs are extremely worn and are better examined in photographs than *in situ*. The contours of the fallen man in the shield have been recut.

In both reliefs Rizzo reverted to the Pollaiuolesque style of his youth. The contest at its fiercest, the moment of intensest strain, which anticipates success, was chosen over victory and relaxation. The flexion of every muscle of horses and men, conveniently unclothed, testifies to extreme exertion; poses, in which every limb is bent and joints produce acute angles, are visual correlatives of the physical tension. The footsoldier in the relief of the candelabra resembles, to a striking degree, the departing soldier in the relief of the *Conversion of St. Paul* (Fig. 17). In both, buttocks are tensed, and the musculature of the arched back is accentuated by the retraction of the spinal cord. The stride of both is very wide and legs are disproportionately long. In composition too the reliefs are so alike that we must conclude Rizzo used his early work; but in plagiarizing, he corrected it. The torsion in the rider is expertly rendered now by means of foreshortening of the torso. The horse is sufficiently upright to be balanced momentarily. Trees, overlapped by the borders of the relief, are better scaled to figures and set a standard by which to judge the distance of similar objects in smaller scale. Though drawn more

[69] Paoletti, 1893, ii, p. 156, attributed this relief to "one of the most delicate and masterful chisels at work on the Scala dei Giganti." There is no other mention in the art historical literature of this relief or the one in the Sala delle Mappe.

economically, the landscape recedes much farther, and the low horizon, like the background of Pollaiuolo's panels with the feats of Hercules, permits the silhouetting of the figures against a distant landscape and the neutral sky.

A monumental staircase giving access to the east wing of the Ducal Palace from the *cortile* does not seem to have been comprehended in the project adopted in the spring of 1484 for rebuilding the Palazzo del Doge.[70] Indeed, its construction seems to have been motivated less by an architectural necessity than by a ceremonial one. On November 11, 1485, during the interregnum after Doge Giovanni Mocenigo's death on November 4, 1485, the Maggior Consiglio passed almost unanimously a motion that included in the ritual of the Doge's investiture his swearing in and coronation at the top of a ramp of stairs:

The principal insignia of our most serene doge is the ducal hat, which the doge wears on his head. Therefore, to give it form, he should receive it publicly and solemnly rather than in a hidden manner from the hands of private persons as was done up to now, without any other ceremony, but rather to the denigration of the ducal dignity: on account of which it was moved that when the future prince and his successors will be elected, and they will accept the banner of St. Mark at the altar and the doge will be brought through the piazza into the palace, he will ascend those stairs for the acceptance of the oath of fealty, then immediately after the aforesaid swearing, the veil will be placed on the head of the doge by the junior councilor and the ducal hat will be placed by the senior councilor saying these words: *Accipe coronam Ducatus Venetiarum.*[71]

The *corno ducale* was placed on the doge's head in a public ceremony for the first time eight days later, during the investiture of Doge Marco Barbarigo on November 19. Pietro Giustiniani located the ducal coronation beneath the arcades of the *piano nobile* of the Ducal Palace.[72] More likely, it was at the top of the great external staircase leading to the Sala del Maggior Consiglio, where formerly the doge had sworn the Promissione

[70] Neither Sanudo nor Malipiero mentions it in his discussion of the various plans advanced for the reconstruction of the Palazzo del Doge. See above, n. 5.

[71] Lorenzi, 1868, pp. 97f., doc. 208. According to Pietro Giustiniani (for which, see below, n. 72), this new law was drafted by a committee of five *correttori*—Zaccaria Barbaro, Federigo Cornaro, Marco Barbarigo, Pietro Priuli, and Tomaso Trevisan. For the ceremony of the investiture of the doge prior to the decision of 1485, see Romanin, [3]1973, iv, p. 395, doc. x: "Exit Ecclesiam cum frequentia populi per hostium magnus et venit ad palatium cum filiis et in superioi parte scalarum maior consiliarius presentibus ceteris super promissione recipit juramentum de promissione servanda. Et postmodum multitudine populi cum gaudio procedente ducitur ad podium palatii supra curiam ad secundum vel tercium arcum. Ibique verba dicit populo de electione sua et justitia servanda et quod omnes intendit equaliter regere et procurare ubertatem et statum et honorem dominii et quod quilibet agat bona opera quia erit ipsis benignus et gratiosus. Et finito verbo inde ducitur ad cathedram que est in sala unde ascenditur in palatium consilij. Et ibi sedet. Et postmodum surgit et dicit similia verba populo. Et inde ducitur ad aliam salam et cathedram ubi morantur domini de nocte licet aliquando prius vadat ad salam dominorum de nocte et postmodum revertitur ad illam unde ascenditur in palatium. Et postmodum ducitur et redit ad hospitia palatii et ibi quiescit."

[72] Giustiniani, 1560, bk. 9, p. 338: "M. Barbadicus omnibus fermè suffragijs in demortui locum Princeps à Patribus creatur: Et vacante ob Mocenici Principis mortem Ducatu, a quinque viris correctoribus, Zach. Barbaro, equite, & procuratore, Fed. Cornelio, M. Barbadico, Petro Priolo, & Thoma Triuisano, lata lex est. quam supremum Patritiorum concilium iussit, vt post hac a seniore consiliario Ducalis Insula gemmis ornata noui Principis capiti ad superiorem Palatij arcum publice imponeretur: Hac verborum, praefatione. Accipe coronam Ducatus Venetiarum: quum antea priuatorum manibus Principes veteri instituto intra domesticos Ducarij parietes eam assumere consueuissent: Et in Barbadico Principe, id primo seruatum est."

Ducale, that Marco Barbarigo received the *corno ducale*.[73] The first coronation known with certainty to have taken place on the Scala dei Giganti was that of Antonio Grimani in 1521, but the staircase probably was also used for the investiture of his predecessor, Leonardo Loredan, in 1501. Thereafter and throughout the republic's long history, it served as the site of the coronation of the doge. In addition, its landing was the setting of ceremonial welcomes and leave-takings by the doge: receiving a visitor at the steps on his arrival or accompanying him to its landing on his departure was a means by which the doge, and through him the Venetian government, made their esteem known publicly.[74] Processions in which the doge did not participate also made use of the Scala dei Giganti.[75] The stairs may have served as a platform for public announcements.[76] But since, for a long time, the *scala* furnished the only access to the *piano nobile* of the northeast wing of the Ducal Palace, its use cannot have been restricted to solemn occasions: it was a public staircase accessible to all who had business in the Palazzo del Doge.

In form and siting the Scala dei Giganti perfectly fulfilled conditions set by its primary function as a setting for the doge's coronation. Placed directly opposite the newly completed Arco Foscari and perpendicular to the east wing, the staircase prolonged the axis of the ducal procession from the Piazza S. Marco in the west, through the Porta della Carta, to the eastern limit of the Ducal Palace.[77] Free-standing, the staircase was visible from right and left. Its upper landing, wider than the ramp, provided an ample stage for the ceremony of coronation and oath taking and permitted the direct participation of many high officials. The tripartite opening at the rear of the landing—its bays increased in scale with respect to the rest of the arcade, its arches changed from pointed to round, its surfaces enriched with ornament—formed a monumental backdrop to the august proceedings.

In private and communal palaces in Venice and the Veneto it was customary to ascend to the *piano nobile* via an exterior, uncovered staircase. Just such a staircase had been decreed for the Sala del Maggior Consiglio in 1340.[78] But these staircases were almost never entirely free-standing. Rather, they were attached to a wall of the building to which they gave access in order to minimize the space required. Sometimes that wall was the facade containing the portal to which the staircase led; sometimes it was the curtain wall of a *cortile* that ran at right angles to the facade; sometimes the staircase clung to both.[79] But the narrow, single-branch, external staircase that projected perpen-

---

[73] See above, n. 71. A contemporary chronicle records the coronation of Doge Marco Barbarigo at the top of a flight of stairs: "more solito conduto fu nel duchal palazo et insta lordene decreto in la sua electione in sopra la scala del dito palazo aceptato per i consiglierj et capi di 40 jurado la sua promissione per el nobel homo zuanne daLeze menor conseglier posto fu la veta et per el nobel homo piero memo major conseglier posto fu la bareta duchal sopra il capo." (Venice, Mus. Cor., MS Cicogna 3533, Magno, *Annali veneti*, v, c. 2r. The same information is contained in Venice, Bibl. Marc., Cod. it., Cl. VII, 56 [= 8636], attributed to Erizzo, *Cronaca veneta*, n.p. [fol. 564r].) There is no evidence to support the suggestion of Muraro in *Essays . . . Panofsky*, 1960, i, p. 363, followed by Hubala in Egg

et al., ¹1965, pp. 640f. and Sheard, 1971, p. 22, that a provisional wooden staircase was erected for Barbarigo's coronation by Antonio Rizzo.

[74] Sanudo, *Diarii*, i, 1879, coll. 821f.; ibid., iii, 1880, col. 1170.

[75] Ibid., ii, 1879, coll. 637f.; ibid., iv, 1880, col. 680.

[76] Ibid., iii, 1880, col. 131.

[77] Sans., 1581, p. 119r, observed that, from a coin of vantage at the Campanile of S. Marco, the staircase was framed in its entirety by the opening of the Porta della Carta.

[78] Lorenzi, 1868, pp. 27f., doc. 80. The staircase was not built until 1415: ibid., p. 56, doc. 145.

[79] Chiminelli, *Aten. ven.*, 1912, pt. 1, pp. 209-253.

dicularly from the structure to which it gave access and was free-standing on both sides
was not totally unknown. There are a few medieval examples in Italy and elsewhere in
which such staircases lead to the great hall of the second story of public palaces; their
source was probably the German *Pfalz*.[80] In Venice, a medieval example survives in the
Ca' da Mosto, whose free-standing, frontal staircase debouches into the Corte del Leon
Bianco.[81]

Although not often built, such staircases were often represented in paintings, drawings, and reliefs: a favorite locus was the *Presentation of the Virgin in the Temple*. Free-
standing, frontal staircases provided settings in Jacopo Bellini's *Presentation of the Virgin*
from the predella of his altarpiece in S. Alessandro, Brescia, and Donatello's relief of
the *Healing of the Irascible Son* from the High Altar of the Santo, Padua, to cite just two
examples close in time and place to the Scala dei Giganti. A drawing of the *Presentation
of the Virgin* of ca. 1455 in Jacopo Bellini's British Museum *Sketchbook* (Fig. 232) contains
a staircase so similar in form, scale, and siting to the Scala dei Giganti (Fig. 166) that a
common source for both in an earlier staircase on the site of the Scala dei Giganti is
frequently inferred. Both Rizzo's and Bellini's staircases are situated in a courtyard. Both
possess rectangular uncovered landings considerably wider than the flight of steps; in
both, the lateral extensions of the landing are supported on arcades at right angles to
one another. The steps are bounded by open balustrades. Beneath the steps there is an
internal chamber with a window. In both, a bench runs along the wall beneath the
steps. At the top of the landing in Bellini's drawing is a tripartite opening similar, if
not identical, to that at the top of the Scala dei Giganti, composed of one round-arched
doorway and two smaller, round-arched windows.[82] The similarity of Bellini's and
Rizzo's staircases does speak in favor of some relation between the two, but whether
that is a common source in an external staircase which led to the earlier Palazzo del
Doge or in a staircase built or represented somewhere else, or whether the Scala dei
Giganti depends directly on Bellini's drawing, I cannot say. There is no record of an
earlier staircase on the site of the Scala dei Giganti. To be sure, it would have been
necessary to ascend to the Ducal Apartments somehow, and in all likelihood that ascent
was made via an exterior uncovered staircase. But I do not think a similar staircase in a
drawing by Bellini is, by itself, sufficient proof of an earlier staircase located on the site
of the present one, which looked just like the Scala dei Giganti.

The exigencies of the site conditioned Rizzo's design for the Scala dei Giganti: irregularities and unusual solutions in its plan and elevation[83] were necessitated by Rizzo's

---

[80] R. Ludwig, 1939, pp. 15f. Medieval Italian examples include the staircase of 1267 of the Palazzo
Papale at Viterbo and the staircase of the fourteenth-
century Palazzo dei Consoli at Gubbio. The free-
standing frontal staircase of the Palazzo Comunale
at Cortona probably dates from the beginning of the
sixteenth century. Ludwig distinguished this medieval type from the free-standing, frontal staircase,
which derives ultimately from the steps leading to
the porticoes of Roman temples and survives in the
steps in front of medieval church facades. This latter
type is characterized by its breadth and shortness,
sufficient only to surmount the podium on which
the church or temple stood. Ludwig, 1939, pp. 22f.,

believed the Scala dei Giganti to have derived from
the medieval type rather than from the antique staircase attached to the Roman temple front.

[81] Scattolin, 1961, pp. 18, [32], fig. 14.

[82] For the differences between the Scala dei Giganti and Bellini's staircase, see Pohlandt, *BJ*, 1971,
p. 192.

[83] These were first noted by Zanotto, i, 1842-53,
II. "Cortile. Scalea dei Giganti opera di Antonio
Riccio," pp. 7f.; and Rambaldi, *Aten. ven.*, 1910, pt.
2, pp. 91ff., and most recently, expounded with ex-
emplary thoroughness and precision by Franzoi, *Ven.,
Mus. Civ. ven. Boll.*, 1965, no. 4, pp. 17ff.

desire to integrate the staircase with the east wing of the Ducal Palace and with the Arco Foscari. The bottom step of the staircase is almost exactly as wide as the opening of the Arco Foscari and the center of the step is aligned with the central longitudinal axis of the Androne Foscari (Fig. 167). At the top of the staircase, the tripartite opening above the landing is incorporated within the bay system of the *piano nobile* arcade (Fig. 156): the location of the opening, therefore, was fixed by the width of the three bays that preceded it on the north. Aligned with different structures, the top and bottom of the staircase are not aligned with one another: the tripartite opening lies farther to the north than the bottom of the ramp (Fig. 168). Thus the center of the ramp does not coincide with the center of the landing. As a result, the landing extends farther to the left of the ramp than it does to the right. The measure of displacement of nonaligned axes of ramp and landing is given by the vertical strip of colored marble at the juncture of ramp and landing, by means of which the left half of the landing was widened by 35 centimeters (Fig. 166). The landing is parallel to the arcades of the east wing of the Ducal Palace, but the ramp is not perpendicular to the landing (Figs. 167, 168). Had it been, the divergence of nonaligned axes would have been greater than it is. Conversely, had the axis of the ramp been even more oblique, the center of the top of the ramp could have been made to coincide with the center of the landing. Rather than adopt one solution exclusively, Rizzo used them both, hoping—and not in vain—that two slight deviations would be less noticeable than one larger one. To be sure, Rizzo could have avoided the problem entirely by extending the tripartite opening to the south so that the center of the enlarged opening and landing coincided with the center of the Arco Foscari. Why did Rizzo not adopt so obvious a solution? Undoubtedly because a fraction of a bay would then have been left over at the southern limit of construction. As it was, the width of the landing also proved troublesome on the *pianterreno* (Fig. 172). The width of the landing and tripartite opening is not quite equal to four bays of the Gothic arcade. In order to retain the bay system of the *pianterreno* beneath the landing while introducing four bays in a space equal to approximately three and three-quarters bays, Rizzo reduced the width of the two central bays very slightly (2.53 m. versus 2.68 m.) and eliminated the support between them. These two bays, minus central support, correspond to the width of the ramp.

Other devices were adopted as a response to the predetermined height of the staircase and the exiguous space separating east wing from the Arco Foscari. Between the supports of the tripartite opening, the last four steps of the Scala dei Giganti were excavated from the depth of the facade (Figs. 168, 158). Utilizing as well the thickness of the parapet, Rizzo cut two steps at the top of the second flight from the upper landing. These expedients, which shortened the staircase, were supplemented by the retraction of the balustrade to the third step (Fig. 166), a device which made the staircase seem shorter than it really was without affecting its actual length. By means of rounded corners and continuous moldings, the last three steps were integrated with the benches, which return to the *avancorpi*. Thus lower steps appeared to recede rather than project.

The elevation of the *avancorpi* matches the arcade of the *pianterreno* (Figs. 156, 164, 170). Therefore, the *avancorpi* seem to belong to the arcade, not to the flight of steps. Yet the close relationship between the arcade and *avancorpi* was necessarily compromised. *Avancorpi* are marble; arcades are limestone. *Avancorpi* are more lavishly decorated; carved archivolts and soffits in the *avancorpi*, for example, contrast with plain arches elsewhere. Other devices deliberately link *avancorpi* and stairs (Fig. 166). The bead-and-reel molding of the balustrades and walls recurs in the shafts of the pilasters and the fields at the corners of the landing. The anthemion friezes in the entablature of the walls and the archivolts of the *avancorpi* are very similar. The rounded corners of the *avancorpi* reflect the plan of the benches and the last three steps. Nonetheless, the juncture of *avancorpi* and ramp seems fortuitous. Though moldings abut, they are not aligned or consistent. Particularly disturbing is the discrepancy in the height and articulation of bases and benches.

The tripartite opening above the upper landing (Fig. 170) reflects the elevation of the *avancorpi* rather than the elevation of the *piano nobile* arcade. Semicircular arches rest on piers of irregular Greek-cross plan (Fig. 168), whose faces are defined as pilasters. The bead-and-reel molding on the lateral faces of the piers was borrowed from the shafts of the pilasters of the *avancorpi* (Fig. 166). The moldings at the base of the pilasters of the piers match those at the base of the pilasters of the *avancorpi*. The same necking was used in both orders and in both, imposts include a bead-and-reel molding. The central bay of the tripartite opening is slightly wider and higher than the two flanking bays (Fig. 170). Its width was limited by the height of its arch, confined beneath the second-story entablature. As a consequence, the central opening could not embrace the entire width of the ramp.

Exterior and interior of the balustrades of the ramp are not identical (Fig. 166), for where the balustrade descends on the inside to the terminating pier, it is intercepted on the outside by the entablature. Therefore, on the interior, the last section, and a small part of the penultimate section, of the balustrade are blind. Thus the oblique descent of the interior wall of the balustrade follows and reiterates the descending profile of the steps. Where steps are largely hidden, the articulation of the wall reasserts the tectonic structure of the *cortile* facade of the Ducal Palace. The only drawback to this ingenious solution manifests itself on the interior where the balustrade abuts the pier at the bottom of the ramp, for the balustrade and the pier are not horizontally aligned.

The design of the walls of the ramp (Figs. 165, 166, 169) reveals Rizzo's architectural style at its most idiosyncratic. Typical is the planarity of the structure and the flatness of its individual parts. Except for the bench, no motif of any three-dimensionality exists. Walls are articulated by lesenes, which hardly project and therefore do not necessitate breaking the entablature. The reliefs of the lesenes are carved in *schiacciato* relief; the ornament of the frieze, in low relief. Between the lesenes are flat panels of *marmo africano*. Even the balusters, rectangular in plan, preserve the plane of the wall. A grid of horizontals and verticals defines the composition of the walls. The faces of the ramp are divided into diverse horizontal layers by the bench, entablature, and lintel above the windows. A multitude of small geometrical compartments, rather than a few large units scaled to the size of the entire staircase, are distributed uniformly over the surface. Of the same *marmo africano*, each compartment is as nearly equal to the others in size and shape as possible. Each is completely and identically framed. Indeed, even treads and risers are supplied with borders. Except for the bench, every part of the surface is embellished. To be sure, carving is confined to specific fields, but variegated stones and complex moldings fill the interstices between them. On the exterior, balusters are carved, and every riser has niello incrustation. Carved and smooth surfaces, a variety of materials comprising *marmo africano*, white marble, black niello, and the gilding of reliefs,[84] produced a multiplicity of texture, pattern, and color.

The ornament, carved with extraordinary precision on a minute scale, is of a refinement more commonly found in works of goldsmithery than in architecture. A corollary of the obsessive handling of detail was the constant change in the design of the lesenes and the niello incrustation of the risers: no pattern was repeated. At first sight this feature seems at variance with the repetitiveness we have defined as a constituent of Rizzo's architectural style. This seeming contradiction, however, is not irreconcilable. The motifs of lesenes and risers are miniature: lesenes and risers must be studied from such close vantages that only one is in focus at any time. By contrast, repetitive designs affect the larger whole. This we may posit as a principle of Rizzo's art: that where motifs are to be read sequentially they vary; conversely, where the design is to be read at once from a distant vantage point, and individual forms are necessarily perceived in conjunction with one another, patterns regularly recur.

Much has been written about the meaning of the ornament of the lesenes. Zanotto[85] and Pasini[86] interpreted at length the decorations, to which no more specific meaning attached than allusions—possibly unintentional—to the glories of ancient Rome as an antique parallel to Venice; to try to refute their readings would be otiose. The style of the ornament as well as many of its motifs—Roman cuirasses, helmets, shields, vases, cornucopias, candelabra, *rinceaux* and ribbons, *putti*, a Janus head, inscriptions in Roman majuscules—derive from ancient Roman sculpture. The initials S.P.Q.R.—Senatus Populusque Romanus—make specific reference to Rome. Signs of Venice include four images of the winged lion of St. Mark, one figure of *Justice* with sword and balance (?) (Fig. 173) and another with an olive branch, and two saints identified, when the reliefs were more legible than they are today, as the Venetian patrons, Mark and Theodore.[87] Several abbreviations include the name of the city. Agostino Barbarigo's initials appear twice, his arms once; once he is designated the patron of the work. There is no reason to suppose that these allusions to the doge, and those on the *avancorpi*, constitute a glorification of Barbarigo, as has recently been averred.[88] Ducal arms were commonly affixed to governmental buildings as records of the reign during which the fabric was erected. If the references to Barbarigo on the Scala dei Giganti had been specifically laudatory, no doubt such displays would have been prohibited in future upon the doge's death, just as the ducal bust was banished from Venetian coins after the death of Tron. To be sure, the costliness and magnificence of the Scala dei Giganti, like the extravagant *cortile* facade of the wing that housed the Ducal Apartments, both expressed and enhanced the grandeur of the ducal office. But throughout the history of the republic, it was the abiding care of the Venetian aristocracy to limit the power of the doge by keeping doge and ducal office separate.

Similarities between the decoration of the lesenes of the Scala dei Giganti and Tullio Lombardo's Tomb of Doge Andrea Vendramin have been remarked:[89] it is not possible

[84] Rambaldi, *Aten. ven.*, 1910, pt. 2, p. 96.

[85] Zanotto, i, 1842-53, II. "Cortile. Scalea dei Giganti opera di Antonio Riccio," pp. 8ff.

[86] Venice, Mus. Cor., MS P.D. C307, no. xvi, Pasini, *Cenni*, 1843, n.p. [pp. 10ff.].

[87] Ibid., n.p. [p. 19].

[88] Muraro in *Essays . . . Panofsky*, 1960, i, pp. 354ff., 359ff.

[89] Munman, 1968, pp. 238ff.

to assign priority to either one.[90] Common to both are vases flanked by *putti* or satyrs; in both, figures stand on vases as on pedestals. Fantastic helmets of similar design appear in both. Dragons perch on Rizzo's helmets as on Tullio's. A helmet in the form of a boar's head is worn by Tullio's scowling *Warrior*. These helmets, unknown in Venetian sculpture before the Scala dei Giganti or Vendramin Tomb, might have been introduced by Andrea del Verrocchio: in his bronze reliefs of *Alexander* and *Darius*, which Lorenzo de' Medici sent to Matthias Corvinus, helmets were crested with a dragon and dolphin, respectively.[91] But still nearer prototypes are contained in Marco Zoppo's sketchbook of ca. 1465-75 in the British Museum (Figs. 233, 234). There we find busts truncated and draped like Rizzo's profile portrait of a *Youth with Fantastic Helmet* (Fig. 178). Three folios show helmets, like Rizzo's, straddled by nude, winged *putti*. Large spirals may mark the position of the ear—in one case, providing a footrest for the *putto*. In another drawing, the visor, like Rizzo's, is composed of the upper part of an elephant's head and trunk. In both, the helmet is tied under the chin. The musical activity of a *putto* blowing on a pipe, on a helmet in another of Rizzo's reliefs (Fig. 175), may also owe its inspiration to Marco Zoppo.[92]

Many of the lesenes (Figs. 179, 180, 181) recall the style of the pilaster decoration of the Altar of St. James (Fig. 3) or the shaft of the first pilaster on the left of the Tron Tomb (Fig. 112). Intricate knots, the double meanders of ribbons, and the termination of ribbons in double points, find precise parallels in the antependium from the Altar of St. James (Figs. 1, 179, 183). Motifs are strung together loosely in vertical sequence; the ribbons from which they hang produce central vertical axes like the stems of *rinceaux* or *cándelabra* in the earlier pilasters. Designs that ornament the balustrades are oriented to the horizontal steps, not the diagonal axis of the ramp. To the extent possible, designs were made symmetrical. Motifs are characteristically long and thin: no susceptible element escaped elongation and attenuation. Therefore ribbons, vines, the neck of a bird, the hilt of a sword, register as little more than lines. Objects are pliable and light and therefore capable of being bent and waved: indeed, nothing that can curl or twist is spared from doing so. Curves become reverse curves; turns become spirals. Forms are not densely concentrated and rarely overlap; rather, they are distributed over the surface of the lesene so that a large proportion of the background remains visible. Forms are open; even at the center the ground intrudes. Closed contours alternate with contours broken by inverted or everted points. Curved points give shape to perforations of all

[90] The Vendramin Tomb was under construction in 1493. See Sheard, *Yale Ital. Studies*, 1977, p. 222.

[91] Vas./Mil., iii, (1568) 1878, p. 361. The suggestion of Verrocchio's influence was made by Munman, 1968, pp. 240f., and Pohlandt, *BJ*, 1971, pp. 194f.

[92] Other examples of bust-length profile figures in fantastic helmets include a drawing attributed to Zoppo in the British Museum: London, BM, Catalogue by Popham/Pouncey, 1950, p. 165, no. 265, two engravings, probably Ferrarese, dated ca. 1470-80: Hind, pt. 1, i, 1938, p. 261, nos. 32, 33, and an anonymous engraving: Levenson in Washington, Nat. Gall. of Art. *Early Italian Engravings*, 1973, p. 40,

no. 9. For Zoppo's British Museum sketchbook, see Dodgson, 1923, and London, BM, Catalogue by Popham/Pouncey, 1950, pp. 162f., no. 260. Armstrong, 1976, pp. 258ff., esp. 259ff., believed Zoppo's drawings to have been inspired by Verrocchio's reliefs. More likely, however, it was Donatello's capricious ornamentation of armor, as in the equestrian monument of the *Gattamelata*, that provided a source for both. Indeed, very similar fantastic helmets are worn by Roman soldiers in Donatello's relief of the *Crucifixion* from the north pulpit in S. Lorenzo. (The filiation of Zoppo's sketches and Rizzo's *Youth with a Fantastic Helmet* was kindly pointed out to me by Prof. Peter Meller.)

kinds (Fig. 179), to flames, leaves, shields, wings, the spouts of pitchers, masks, visors and neckpieces, the fluttering ends of ribbons, locks of hair.

Different in style from these lesenes, but as high in quality, are the reliefs with arms and trophies (Figs. 182, 183). Here overlapping forms densely fill the surface so that almost nothing of the relief ground is visible. A central vertical axis is largely concealed by the multitude of forms and is sometimes missing altogether. Patterns are generally asymmetrical and the orientation of forms, various. Nevertheless, I believe that these reliefs, too, are Rizzo's. Ribbons and weapons are elongated and attenuated. Overlapping serves not to conceal, but to identify receding planes: the superimposition of objects whose mass is contracted or whose form is open permits glimpses of as many as six successive layers (Figs. 174, 182, 183). Fluttering ribbons, intertwined to form complicated patterns, follow the same convoluted paths.

With the exception of the last lesene on the exterior at the top of the right balustrade, probably carved by an assistant, and the two internal lesenes at the top of the stairs, part of the campaign of restoration in 1728,[93] I attribute all of the lesenes to Rizzo. Each relief represents a wholly new invention; even individual motifs were rarely duplicated. Some reliefs are less complex than others but none is simple. Each is wrought with as much attention to detail as every other. Qualitative differences between reliefs reside, not in their equally ingenious compositions, but in the contours of individual forms: where some contours are imbued with the energy of a coiled spring, others, more generalized and less descriptive, are lax (Fig. 184). These mechanical outlines, I suspect, are due to the restorers of the eighteenth century who, finding many of Rizzo's reliefs badly worn, recut blurred contours;[94] they rarely attempted to recut the fine, internal details of Rizzo's forms.

The technical achievement of these reliefs deserves unbounded praise. On inhospitably long and narrow fields, Rizzo created designs of inexhaustible variety: in the intricacy of patterns as in individual curled forms, Rizzo anticipated the designs and vocabulary of Mannerist ornament. Knots are so accurately delineated that it is possible to trace their course and, in imagination, to unravel them. Swathes of drapery wave in one direction and are simultaneously twisted in another. But Rizzo was not content with the mere charting of convolutions—to show a ribbon or banner now from the front, now from the back; in addition, he threaded through their turns a band or twisted drape or spear (Fig. 176). Indeed, he loved to pass one object through another so that, at rapid intervals, a single object overlaps and is overlapped in turn (Fig. 174). Unique to Rizzo's reliefs in the history of ornament is the complexity of their spatial organization. By means of foreshortening, the volume of cuirasses, shields, heads, and figures is simulated (Fig. 183). Contours regularly take into account the continuation of the volume beyond the visual boundary of the form. Overlapping and minuscule reductions in the height of the relief, which rises no more than a centimeter at its highest, explicate the relative disposition of every object in a three-dimensional space. The undercutting of contours makes visible the otherwise invisible spatial intervals between succeeding planes. The texture and embellishment of every element manifests the care ordinarily bestowed on an autonomous work of art. And yet no single motif is seen in isolation from the rest.

---

[93] Rambaldi, *Aten. ven.*, 1910, pt. 2, pp. 223f., 227.   [94] Ibid., pp. 223ff.

The influence of the Scala dei Giganti was felt almost immediately. The lavish decoration of Mauro Codussi's staircase in the Scuola Grande di S. Giovanni Evangelista, for whose construction land was leased on August 14, 1498, reflects the sumptuous display of the ducal staircase. All flat surfaces on the upper landing of Mauro's staircase were encrusted with veined marbles; the front faces of pilasters were carved with pendent trophies; the base of the dome and the borders of spandrels at the entrance to the chapter hall were embellished with niello. Particularly indicative of foreign influence in Codussi's work is the atypical profusion of moldings such as bead and bead-and-reel, carved on a minute scale and applied, not only to the long entablature above the ramps, but also to the frames of *breccia* panels and sunken fields on pilaster shafts.

The so-called *Allegorical Figure* in the Ca' d'Oro (Figs. 185-189), I believe, reflects the experience Rizzo gained in carving the lesenes of the Scala dei Giganti. The provenience of the statue is not known. The persistence of the tradition that links the figure with the Tomb of Ser Orsato Giustiniani, formerly in the convent of S. Andrea della Certosa—a tomb from which we know it did not come[95]—gives basis to the supposition that the *Allegorical Figure* stood originally in the demolished church of S. Andrea.[96] Perhaps the figure is identical with the statuette called *Faith*, which Cicogna recorded in 1827 in the possession of an ex-Carthusian monk.[97] If so, Cicogna mistook the figure's attributes, which are not those of Faith. It has been suggested that they denote a Liberal Art:[98] crowns and scepters are attributes, for instance, of Rhetoric, Philosophy, Theology.[99] But this is most unlikely. In the first place, our figure is considerably younger than most personifications of Virtues or Liberal Arts. In the second place, the attributes do not define our figure's nature, for though she is the bearer of her attributes, she is not their owner. If the crown were hers she would be wearing it; if the scepter betokened her dominion it would be cradled in her arm. If not to her, then to whom do the attributes belong? In a painting from the school of Avignon (Fig. 236) a nimbed and winged Angel holds a crown with the very gesture of our figure. In her left hand the painted Angel holds a scourge, the instrument of Christ's flagellation. Thus the Angel presents contrasting symbols of Christ's humiliation and triumph. It is also to Christ that the crown and scepter of the *Allegorical Figure* must belong. Both are attributes of Christ Victorious. As such, they appear in the central panel of Jan van Eyck's Ghent Altarpiece; as such, they are borne by Christ himself in innumerable Venetian paintings of *Christ Enthroned Crowning the Virgin Mary*.[100] As allusions to crown and scepter, reed and crown of thorns are traditional attributes of Christ in scenes of his mocking. Iden-

[95] Schulz, *NdiGF*, 1978, pp. 23ff.

[96] Ven., Procuratie Nuove. *Arte a Ven.*, by Mariacher, 1971, p. 142, no. 67.

[97] Cicogna, ii, 1827, p. 57.

[98] Mariacher, *Arte ven.*, 1950, p. 105, tentatively identified the figure as *Rhetoric*. The truncated object at the right of the figure's base cannot be identified.

[99] Tervarent, i, 1958, coll. 125ff., *voce*, couronne; ibid., ii, 1959, coll. 336ff., *voce*, sceptre.

[100] E.g. (1) Paolo Veneziano, Washington, D.C., National Gallery of Art, 1324; (2) Paolo Veneziano, Venice, Accademia; (3) Paolo and Giovanni Veneziano, New York, Frick Collection, 1358; (4-5) Catarino, two paintings, Venice, Accademia; (6) Stefano di S. Agnese, Venice, Accademia; (7) Jacobello del Fiore, Venice, Accademia, 1438; (8) Antonio Vivarini, Wiesbaden, Neues Museum; (9) Antonio and Bartolomeo Vivarini, Turin, Museo Civico; (10) Antonio and Bartolomeo Vivarini, Osimo, Palazzo Municipale; (11) Bartolomeo Vivarini, New Orleans, La., Isaac Delgado Museum of Art; (12) Carlo Crivelli, Milan, Brera, 1493; (13) Vittore Crivelli, S. Elpidio a Mare, Palazzo Comunale; (14) Cima da Conegliano, Rome, private collection; (15) Cima da Conegliano, Bologna, Pinacoteca; (16) Cima da Conegliano, Venice, SS. Giovanni e Paolo.

tified as Christ's handmaiden, our figure thus proves herself to be an Angel and not the personification of a Liberal Art.

Although no mate to the *Angel* has even been discovered, she probably was paired with another *Angel* holding symbols of Christ's Passion. At the rear of the statue, behind the scepter, a small portion of the figure is unfinished. If this unfinished part were meant to be out of view—as we must assume it was—the figure would have occupied the left side of the monument from which it came. It must have been balanced, then, by a figure on the right. In the center, we may hypothesize an image of *Christ as Man of Sorrows* to which symbols of both defeat and triumph would have been appropriate. Such a group is more likely to have adorned an altar than a sarcophagus, whence the *Angel* is thought to come.[101] A half-length *Man of Sorrows* frequently crowns the center of Venetian polyptychs,[102] and similar free-standing statuettes of *Angels* flank the upper story of the Altar of the Virgin in SS. Giovanni e Paolo.[103]

Although the *Angel with Attributes of Christ* is only adolescent, she already possesses *Eve*'s proportions (Figs. 187, 48). Common to both figures are the square but diminutive shoulders, the hemispherical breasts located high on the chest and very far apart, the prominent nipples, the long torso, the thick waist, the protuberant belly and full thighs. In her movement, the *Angel* is closer to *Adam* (Fig. 39) than she is to any other of Rizzo's works. In both, Rizzo exaggerated the unequal distribution of weight: the free foot, largely raised from the ground, supports almost none of the body's weight. The axis of the hips descends sharply, but the axis of the shoulders is barely tilted. Above the free leg, the arm is bent and tensed; the other arm is lowered. Contrapposto is combined with a slight revolution in space in which the planes of torso and legs are narrowly opposed. Free-standing arms produce open poses. The turn and tilt of the head together with a clearly oriented gaze create the effect of focused attention. But these features are not unique to *Adam*, and the *Angel* and would not justify the attribution of the latter to Rizzo were it not for the extraordinary physical energy, which in both informs a fundamentally static pose. In part, this results from the momentary poise of the free foot and from the focused gaze. But to an even greater extent it is due to the flexion of individual muscles. Through the *Angel*'s clothes it is possible to discern the tension of her left thigh, the knitting of her knee, the tightening of her calf (Figs. 187, 188). Muscles of abdomen and stomach are flexed as the *Angel*'s center of gravity rises into her upper torso. The figure's torso lengthens with the elevation of her chest; her stomach is contracted as her thorax expands. The long, bony fingers of the hand that holds the crown and the sharply bent knuckles resemble the hand that *Adam* raises to his breast.

[101] Mariacher, *Arte ven.*, 1950, pp. 106f.; Ven., Procuratie Nuove, *Arte a Ven.*, by Mariacher, 1971, p. 142, no. 67.

[102] E.g. (1) Antonio Vivarini, Poreč, Basilica Eufrasiana, 1440; (2) Antonio Vivarini, Milan, Brera; (3) Antonio and Bartolomeo Vivarini, Bologna, Pinacoteca, 1450; (4) Antonio Vivarini, Rome, Pinacoteca Vaticana, 1464; (5) Antonio and Bartolomeo Vivarini, *Coronation of the Virgin,* Osimo, Palazzo Municipale; (6) Bartolomeo Vivarini and shop, Polyptych of Conversano, Venice, Accademia, 1475;

(7) Bartolomeo Vivarini and shop, Morano Calabro, S. Bernardino; (8) Mantegna, Milan, Brera; (9) Giovanni Bellini, *Coronation of the Virgin,* Pesaro, Museo Civico; (10) Carlo Crivelli, Massa Fermana, S. Silvestro, 1463; (11) Carlo Crivelli, Ascoli Piceno, Duomo, 1473; (12) Vittore Crivelli, *Coronation of the Virgin,* S. Elpidio a Mare, Palazzo Comunale.

[103] Schulz in *Von Simson Festschrift*, 1977, pp. 197ff. The *Angels* were probably a slightly later addition. They flank a relief of *God the Father* in half-length.

The continuous revolution of the figure, which embraces approximately 120 degrees, together with the round base, produce many views of nearly equal interest, as in the statues of *Adam* and *Eve*. Except from the rear, there is no vantage point from which the figure looks ungainly. As in the figures of *Adam* and *Eve*, however, there is one view in which the figure seems most satisfactory (Fig. 186)—a view from the left in which the face appears in profile while the free leg is seen *en face*. At this point the strut between hip and wrist disappears. Perhaps it was this view of the figure that first met the gaze of a spectator entering the precincts in which the figure stood.

Despite similarities to *Adam* and *Eve* sufficient to identify the author of the *Angel*, the style of the three works is not so close as to warrant dating to the same stage of Rizzo's career. The features of the *Angel*'s face are more idealized than those of *Eve* (Figs. 189, 50) and the hair is treated differently. Although the arrangement of folds over the knee of the engaged leg recalls the early *Angel* from the Arco Foscari (Figs. 187, 32), there is no drapery analogous in style to that of the *Angel with Attributes of Christ* in the early work or, indeed, in any work of Rizzo's. The carving technique of the individual folds, however, is that which Rizzo developed for the lesenes of the Scala dei Giganti: probably the *Angel* was made while work on the staircase was under way. The tops of folds are often flat or slightly concave; edges are faceted or undercut; the junctures of folds and ground are frequently marked by an incision. The surface of the figure is uneven: though projections are never radical, the matrix of stone is constantly invaded by short, quick forays. The free foot is largely free-standing. Narrow channels are deeply dug and individual curls are drilled, often from underneath. Frequent excavation of the surface produces a sharp and rapid alternation of light and shade, not dissimilar in its effect from the bead-and-reel or dentil moldings of the Scala dei Giganti. As in the ornament of the lesenes, smooth outlines alternate with serrated outlines produced by the jagged edges of brittle folds or uniquely tousled locks. A free-standing hand, splayed fingers, and the crown perched precariously on fingertips, produce a network of forms as open as any combination of ribbons, trophies, and spears.

A *vera da pozzo* in the *cortile* of the palace of Duc Elie Decazes (Calle Rota, 875 Dorsoduro) (Fig. 194) can be associated with the Scala dei Giganti. Nothing of the palace's early history is known that might help in the attribution or dating of the wellhead,[104] and the shield, which replaces a spray of leaves on the side of the *vera* facing the Grand Canal, is empty. On the basis of its style, the palace has been dated to the end of the fifteenth, or the beginning of the sixteenth, century.[105] The wellhead, evidently, is contemporary with the palace.

The customary form of Venetian wellheads of the fourteenth and fifteenth centuries—square at the top, round at the bottom—was derived from capitals.[106] Here, on the contrary, a cylindrical drum supports an octagonal rim—a common variation of the basic type, which Rizzo did not invent. Yet the decoration of the cylinder, which copies a Corinthian capital, reflects the wellheads' origin. Volutes serve as supports for the slightly projecting points of the octagon, acanthus leaves spread over the surface, and

[104] The earliest proprietors of the palace have not been discovered. The palace was acquired by the Contarini dal Zaffo in the second half of the sixteenth century. The palace then passed, in succession, to the Ruzzini, Manzoni, Angaran, and Mon- tecuccoli families, and finally to the Duc Polignac-Decazes. (Bassi, 1976, p. 94.)

[105] Ibid., pp. 94ff., with bibliography; Puppi/Puppi, 1977, pp. 236ff., no. 5.

[106] Arslan, 1970, pp. 326f.

the bottom of the wellhead is rimmed by necking. The band of the octagon, on the other hand, is treated like a frieze. Rizzo's wellhead apparently served as model for the sixteenth century *vera da pozzo* in Palazzo Mocenigo at S. Samuele.[107]

Motifs nearly identical to those that ornament the octagonal band can be found in the voussoirs of the *avancorpi* and in the friezes of the lateral walls of the Scala dei Giganti (Figs. 191, 192). To be sure, at the end of the fifteenth century in Venice anthemion friezes were not uncommon. But comparison with similar ones produced in Pietro Lombardo's shop (Fig. 235) allows us to isolate the unique features of Rizzo's rendering of the motif. The relief of Rizzo's frieze, both in the wellhead and in the Scala dei Giganti, is very low. The upper face of the relief is flatter than Pietro's; edges are often faceted instead of rounded and are accentuated by a chiseled line. Not only are forms less bulbous, but they also are less full. In comparison with the massy forms of Pietro's frieze, those of Rizzo's frieze are spare: leaves are thinner and more stalk is visible. Forms are distributed more loosely over the surface so that more of the background is visible. Curves have more spring. Beneath the frieze of the *vera da pozzo* is a thick protuberant necking like the one beneath the capitals of the *avancorpi* of the Scala dei Giganti (Fig. 164) and the ground-floor loggia of the east wing of the Ducal Palace. Acanthus leaves similar to those of the drum can be found among the capitals of the loggia of the *piano terra*. Similarly elongated volutes occur in the capital of the first pilaster on the left of the Tron Tomb (Fig. 112).

The major sculptural decorations of the Scala dei Giganti are the reliefs of *Victories* in the *avancorpi* (Figs. 195–202). In the classicism of their theme they complement the reliefs of the lesenes. The figures bear a variety of attributes—a flaming vase, torches, a garland or branches of laurel, an apple, a ducal hat wreathed with laurel, and a tablet inscribed with the words ASTREA DVCE. The laurel, like the *Victories* themselves, denotes triumph in war. The inscription signifies justice rendered by the doge. The apple borne aloft by a *Victory* (Fig. 198) is probably the golden apple which Eris, goddess of discord and war, threw down at the marriage of Peleus and Thetis. Inscribed "to the fairest," it was claimed by Hera, Athena, and Aphrodite. Paris awarded the apple to Aphrodite, who promised him the fairest woman for his bride. This was Helen, wife of Menelaus: her abduction led to the Trojan War. In her other hand, the *Victory* holds a laurel branch. Thus were symbols of discord and victory opposed.

The presence of the flaming vase and lighted torch (Figs. 195, 199, 200) cannot be justified so easily. In Francesco Colonna's *Hypnerotomachia Poliphili*, the vase from which a flame emerges betokens love; as a symbol of *Amor Dei* the flaming vase conveyed this meaning in the Tron Tomb. In addition, the flaming vase could mean intelligence, probity, or discord.[108] As a symbol of love, the lighted torch belonged to Venus or her companions, Cupid or Hymen. Symbolizing anger, it is also found as an attribute of Mars. It referred to peace only when, turned upside down, it was about to enkindle a pyre of arms.[109] Is its appearance here (and in the relief of *Putti with Arms of the Barbarigo Family* on the *rio* facade of the Ducal Palace [Fig. 155]) arbitrary: was it employed simply because, used often in antiquity, it accorded with the classicizing theme and style of the reliefs? Very likely, I should think, although its adoption may have been mediated by a

[107] Illustrated in Ongania, ed., 1889, ii, pl. 164.
[108] Tervarent, ii, 1959, coll. 396ff., *voce*, vase dont émane une flamme.
[109] Ibid., coll. 381f., *voce*, torche.

classical relief in which a figure, which looks exactly like a Victory, is portrayed flying upward with a lighted torch. This is the Hadrianic relief of the *Apotheosis of the Empress Sabina* in the Palazzo dei Conservatori, Rome. The relief comes from the Arco di Portogallo in the Corso in Rome, where it could be seen until, in 1662, the arch was demolished in order to permit the widening of the street.[110] The flying female figure that supports the deceased empress on her back is usually interpreted as Aeternitas, the personification of eternity;[111] the lighted torch it holds symbolizes the life of the resurrected empress among the eternal stars.[112] If, ignorant of the significance of life before and after death with which the lighted torch was generally endowed in Roman art, Rizzo had known the relief of the *Apotheosis of Sabina*, he might well have assumed the torch a fitting attribute of Victory. And, acquainted only with its supposititious connotation of triumph, he might well have thought it suited to the relief of *putti* with the Barbarigo *stemma*.

The poses of two *Victories* have antique prototypes. The pose of the *Victory* with laurel branch and apple (Fig. 198) was used frequently for warriors and dancing fauns in Roman sarcophagi. It occurs in a sarcophagus of *Achilles and Penthesilea* in the Belvedere of the Vatican; the sarcophagus was drawn by Giulio Romano. Another with the *Battle between Dionysus and the Indians* in the Museo Capitolino, Rome, also proves to have been known in the early sixteenth century.[113] A figure in the same pose, from a source no longer identifiable, was drawn ca. 1420-30, perhaps by a central-Italian sculptor.[114] The *Victory* with laurel branch and apple corresponds to the antique examples in its view, the turn of its head, and the disposition of its limbs. But Rizzo fundamentally transformed his model by altering its sex and costume and by adapting to flight a pose invariably used for striding. A maenad or other dancing figure seems to have inspired the pose of the *Victory* with tablet (Fig. 197), although no classical exemplars are known to have been accessible in the Renaissance.[115]

The poses of the *Victories* of the Scala dei Giganti accord with the shape of the field they inhabit: they are more upright than their counterparts in Roman art. All wear

[110] Simon in Helbig, ii, ⁴1966, p. 264, no. 1447.
[111] Ibid., pp. 569f., no. 1800. A strikingly similar idea seems to be expressed in the mid-fifteenth-century Tomb of Marchese Spinetta Malaspina from S. Giovanni in Sacco, Verona, now in the Victoria and Albert Museum. At the apex of the tomb is a flying *Victory*, which originally held two *cartellini*, one of which was inscribed ME COMITE AD COELVM FOELICITER INDE VOLABVNT.
[112] Gagé, *Reallexikon für Antike und Christentum*, vii, 1969, coll. 161f., 178f. Two coins, one commemorating the *consecratio* of Faustina the Elder, the other commemorating the *consecratio* of Faustina Junior, depict the same motif. (Mattingly, iii, 1930, p. 164, no. 1132, p. 349, no. 1699.)
[113] The following Roman sarcophagi contain possible prototypes: (1) *Achilles and Penthesilea*, Vatican, Belvedere: Robert, ii, 1890, pp. 113ff., no. 92; (2) *Achilles and Penthesilea*, Rome, Via Arco de' Banchi 8: ibid., p. 122, no. 99; (3) fragment of a sarcophagus with an *Amazonomachy*, Paris, Louvre: ibid., pp. 142ff., no. 134; (4) *Battle between Dionysus and the*

Indians, Rome, Museo Capitolino: Matz, iv, pt. 3, 1969, pp. 428ff., no. 238; (5) *Thiasos*, Sclafani, Sicily, Cathedral: ibid., iv, pt. 2, 1968, pp. 182f., no. 74; (6) *Dionysus and Ariadne*, Munich, Glypothek: ibid., pp. 202f., no. 85; (7) *Dionysus*, Moscow, Pushkin Museum: ibid., iv, pt. 1, 1968, pp. 153ff., no. 47; (8) Dionysiac sarcophagus, Rome, Museo Capitolino or Palazzo dei Conservatori: Reinach, iii, 1912, p. 209, no. 2. I am grateful to Prof. Peter Meller for pointing out to me the antique source of this *Victory*.
[114] Degenhardt/Schmitt, 1968, i, pp. 248f., no. 137.
[115] (1) Circular altar showing Pan making two Seasons dance, Rome, Lateran: Reinach, iii, 1912, p. 280, no. 1; (2) relief in bronze repoussé of a Bacchic dance and Ariadne in her chariot from the Tensa Capitoline, Rome, Palazzo dei Conservatori: ibid., i, 1909, p. 379, no. viii; (3) great dish from the Mildenhall Treasure, London, British Museum: Shelton in N.Y., Met. Mus. of Art. *Age of Spirituality*, cat. ed. Weitzmann, 1979, pp. 151f., no. 130.

chitons of sheer and abundant stuff, which tosses more rapidly than poses seem to warrant and, in so doing, enhances the figures' movement. All exemplify a type of relief in which the upper surface is both flattened and raised considerably above the background. The outer edges of the figures, as well as the contours of a few internal forms, are sharply undercut so that facets, slanting inward at an angle of 45 degrees, produce a ring of shadow around the figures. The effect of undercutting the contours is to make figures seem detached from the ground. This type of relief, invented by Desiderio da Settignano, was introduced to Venice by Pietro Lombardo, who used it throughout his long career.

The eight *Victories* are so various in style and composition that one might suppose all to have been carved by different sculptors. Therefore, it is no wonder that the names of so many well-known artists have been advanced as authors of these works. As long as the completion date of the Scala dei Giganti remained in doubt, there was some justification for proposing the authorship of Rizzo's successor as *protomaestro* of the Ducal Palace and for assuming that Tullio and Antonio, who are known to have aided their father in the decoration of the Appartamenti dei Dogi, were involved as well. But if the Scala dei Giganti was finished by 1497, then the Lombardo shop could not have participated in its carving. An alternative explanation for the *Victories'* stylistic diversity is Rizzo's delegation to assistants of the design and execution of all of them. While this seems a tenable assumption in the case of the inferior *Victories*, it is unlikely in the case of all. For the authors of half of the figures were unquestionably among the finest sculptors of their time. How then should they have been subordinates and have left behind no trace of other works? How should their names have vanished from archival documents and literary tributes? Surely an attribution of the best *Victories* to the master, who, capable of working in many different styles, introduced variety where repetition of theme might have resulted in monotony, is the more plausible solution.

The best *Victories* are four: the *Victory* with the inscribed tablet and the *Victory* with apple and laurel branch on the front, or west, face in the left-hand *avancorpo* (Figs. 197, 198); the *Victory* with flaming torch on the right of the front face of the right *avancorpo* (Fig. 200); and the *Victory* with *corno ducale* on the left side of the south face of the landing (Fig. 201). A fifth figure with laurel wreath on the right side of the south face (Fig. 202) seems to have been finished by Rizzo but blocked out and partly executed by an assistant who was responsible for its anatomical mistakes and unarticulated pose. I suspect that the hair of the *Victory* with tablet (Fig. 190) was recut in the eighteenth century and that the deformation of her forehead is due to imprudent restoration. Originally her face must have resembled very closely that of the *Angel with Attributes of Christ* (Fig. 189).

The *Victory* with *corno ducale* (Fig. 201) possesses most links with other works by Rizzo. The diminutive features, the square jaw, the protuberant, dimpled chin, the slightly parted lips, the tiny and widely spaced eyes, recall the physiognomy of St. Sebastian from the Altar of the Traghetto della Maddalena (Fig. 129). The broad band encircling the crown and tied in a bow just above the forehead recurs in a bust-length figure on a lesene of the Scala dei Giganti (Fig. 177). The exceptionally long peplum and the divergence of folds around the abdomen are found in the *Angel* of the Ca' d'Oro (Fig. 187). In both *Victory* and *Angel*, drapery adheres to the straight leg, revealing its contours with extraordinary thoroughness. Straight forking folds flash diagonally across the thigh and calf of both. The thick ridges of fluttering drapery around the foot of the *Victory* recall the drapery of the right-hand *Victory* formerly in Berlin (Fig. 131). The shape of individual folds at the bottom of the skirt matches folds in the mantle of the *Recumbent Effigy of Tron* (Fig. 67).

In the *Victory* with torch (Fig. 200), the straight, narrow folds of the bodice just above the waist, cleft at one end by a long incision, are analogous to the drapery that traverses the thigh of the infant Christ in the relief of the Camera degli Scarlatti (Fig. 161). In the *Victory* with tablet (Fig. 197), the configuration and flatness of folds on the calf of the forward leg resemble folds on the thigh of the Tron Tomb *Charity* (Fig. 89). The drapery that covers the knee and calf of the farther leg of the *Victory* with laurel wreath (Fig. 202) is remotely akin to the pattern of folds in the *Angel* of the Ca' d'Oro (Fig. 187) and an *Angel* from the Arco Foscari (Fig. 32).

The movements of the four figures attributable in their entirety to Rizzo (Figs. 197, 198, 200, 201) share certain features. Figures rotate about a central vertical axis, which joins the pit of the neck with the weight-bearing foot. In the *Victories* with ducal bonnet and tablet, rotation proceeds continuously in one direction; in the others, heads turn in a direction counter to the revolution of the body. In each, the legs are shown in profile—that view which most effectively produces the impression of forward motion. Indeed, as the flurried drapery makes clear, figures do not merely levitate but swiftly advance. Sometimes the directions of revolution and motion coincide; in the *Victories* with ducal bonnet and tablet, movement and motion are opposed. A description of revolution necessarily involves the overlapping and foreshortening of individual members. Thus the figures themselves realize a three-dimensional space.

In vesting the responsibility for creating the effect of space entirely in the figures, Rizzo accommodated to the fact that the figures are carved on fields that belong to an architectural structure. If Rizzo had filled the spandrels of the *avancorpi* with illusionistic settings, the form and function of the wall would no longer have been manifest and the wall would no longer have seemed an integral part of the ground-floor arcade. Therefore, settings were confined to small patches of clouds beneath the feet of the *Victories* and backgrounds remained bare and without distinctive texture. To be sure, Rizzo might have provided each of the figures with independent fields, smaller in scale than the spandrels and separately framed, whose pictorial treatment would have had no bearing on the signification of the wall. But the fields would have been small, and the figures, raised far above the eye-level of a visitor to the *cortile*, would hardly have been visible.

Rizzo chose that type of relief best suited to maintaining the integrity of the wall. Because the external contours of the figures are undercut, the figures seem detached from the background. However, just as Rizzo ultimately compromised the integrity of the wall by introducing cloudlets, so he compromised the consistency of his relief by carving certain minor elements in *schiacciato* relief. Hardly raised from the surface of the ground, the borders of these elements could not be undercut. Elements carved in *schiacciato* relief invariably occupy the most distant planes. They testify to a conflict between the sculptor's desire to indicate spatial recession by every means available and the architect's desire to preserve the architectural autonomy of the wall.

Less than perfect consistency is demonstrated also by the relation of some of the figures to the framing of the field. In the *Victories* with torch and *corno ducale* (Figs. 200, 201), peripheral portions of the figures are overlapped by the moldings of the field. Thus figures which seem to hover at some distance in front of the wall because their contours are undercut, are pressed back to the plane of the wall by the overlapping moldings. In the *Victories* with tablet and laurel branch and apple (Figs. 197, 198), on the other hand, substantial portions of the undercut relief overlap the frame. This compositional device reenforces the implications of the motion of the figures, portrayed in transit through an empty space. The perfect congruence of theme, technique, and composition suggests that these two *Victories* were executed last.

In the *Victory* with laurel branch and apple (Fig. 198) the *sfumato* effect of aerial perspective makes its first appearance in Venetian sculpture. As in contemporary paintings by Leonardo and later paintings by Giovanni Bellini and Giorgione, the traits of a distant object seen through hazy atmosphere were applied to an object in the foreground. The muted contrasts of light and shadow characteristic of aerial perspective result from the suppression in the *Victory* of all but the smallest changes in the level of the surface. The outline of the *Victory* was generalized; the shapes of her folds were streamlined.[116] Distinctions in the shape and size of folds almost disappear. But internal forms retain their definition and texture: internal lines rarely break and never entirely vanish, as they do, for instance, in Desiderio da Settignano's late reliefs. On the contrary, Rizzo's delineation of strands of hair and feathers is as obsessive as his treatment of the face of *Tron*. But lines are so finely etched that distance soon renders them invisible. Thus did Rizzo translate effects of painting into the alien medium of sculpture: the carving of the *Victory* with laurel branch and apple is the acme of Rizzo's technical achievement.

This *Victory* exemplifies the skill with which Rizzo formulated every element of his composition. The overlapping of the frame at top and bottom establishes the *Victory*'s complete autonomy. Yet the figure, centered within a constantly contracting and expanding field, responds to the curvature of its heavy frame. From armpit to knee and from knee to toe, the figure's silhouette respectively inverts and imitates the molding's divergent paths. Wing and laurel branch echo and balance the outline of the upraised arm. Midway between the two, the upright head, with its vertical silhouette, insures the ultimate stability of the image. Voids manifest as much forethought as solids; the crook of the farther arm and waist form a diamond; wing and arm divide symmetrically, while locks branch off symmetrically again in yet a third direction. Movement, which involves the flexion of almost every joint, coexists with contours composed of sustained arcs. *Sfumato* distances the figure from the realm of the observer and renders its existence intangible. Inhabiting a space which is neither ours nor that of its architectural setting, glimpsed as though from an immeasurable distance, the *Victory* is as ethereal a being as was ever bodied forth in stone.

I should like to think this *Victory* was Rizzo's artistic testament. Its quality is not surpassed by any work in Rizzo's oeuvre or by any sculpture produced in Venice in the early Renaissance. Its value is such that in a city dominated by a despot, its creator might have been forgiven the embezzlement of 10,000 ducats—Cellini was forgiven worse. But where the administration of government was spread among so great a number of the body politic, standards of conduct had to be upheld. So, facing imprisonment, Rizzo fled to the Romagna and there, in exile, aged and disgraced, he vanishes from sight.

---

[116] Cf. Leonardo da Vinci on aerial perspective: "In every figure placed at a great distance you lose first the knowledge of its most minute parts, and preserve to the last that of the larger parts, losing, however, the perception of all their extremities; and they become oval or spherical in shape, and their boundaries are indistinct." (MacCurdy ed., 1955, p. 1000.)

Conclusion

IN VENICE works of art were traditionally commissioned by three groups of patrons: the several governmental boards that oversaw the construction and embellishment of public buildings, religious and professional confraternities, and individuals or families. Among the first group were the salt commissioners. Since the thirteenth century, the Provveditori al Sal had administered the production, acquisition, and sale of salt—a state monopoly in Venice; in the second quarter of the fifteenth century supervision of the building and decoration of the Ducal Palace was added to their charge. When a new west wing for the Ducal Palace had been decreed in 1422, superintendence of its construction had been vested in the Procuratori di S. Marco de supra. Funds, to come from the proceeds of the sale of salt, were to be paid regularly by the Provveditori al Sal.[1] By 1425 this arrangement had proved impracticable; therefore, it was resolved to depute one or two other nobles to oversee the Provveditori's disbursement of funds.[2] We do not know precisely when surveillance of construction of the Ducal Palace was transferred from the Procurators of St. Mark's to the salt commissioners, but it must have occurred before 1438, when the Provveditori al Sal commissioned the Androne Foscari and the Porta della Carta.[3] The salt commissioners retained their jurisdiction over the fabric of the Ducal Palace until 1533, when a separate body of Provveditori sopra la fabricha del palazzo was specifically charged with this responsibility.[4] The Provveditori al Sal were patricians, members of the Maggior Consiglio. Their number ranged from three to six: under Doge Agostino Barbarigo membership was raised from four to six. Terms of office lasted sixteen months; no member might serve two consecutive terms. Ordinarily two commissioners oversaw the Ducal Palace and the buildings of the Rialto; occasionally one of the Provveditori was appointed to attend solely to construction of the palace.[5]

For most of his career Rizzo was employed by the Provveditori al Sal. He is first mentioned at work at the Ducal Palace—probably in connection with the Arco Foscari—only in 1483. The silence of Ducal Palace documents before that date may be due to the partial loss of the pre-1480 archive of the Ufficio del Sal.[6] In any case, Rizzo's first statues for the Arco Foscari, datable on the basis of style to the late 1460s, suggest that he was hired by the Provveditori al Sal upon the departure of Niccolò di Giovanni

---

[1] Lorenzi, 1868, pp. 58f., doc. 148.
[2] Ibid., p. 60, doc. 152.
[3] Ibid., pp. 66ff., docs. 158, 159.
[4] Ibid., p. 203, doc. 428.
[5] Ibid., p. 98, doc. 209, p. 129, doc. 265 and Sa-

nudo, (1493) 1980, pp. 107f. and 245f. For the Provveditori al Sal as overseers of the fabric of the Ducal Palace, see Rambaldi, *Aten. ven.*, 1910, pt. 2, pp. 98f., n. 1.
[6] Cadorin, 1838, p. 137.

Fiorentino in the early spring of 1468. It is likely that Rizzo succeeded Niccolò as chief architect and sculptor of the fabric. By this time the architectural design of the Arco had been fixed and most of the east facade had probably been erected. Though the south front was faced only later—a document of February 1483 probably refers to acquisition of stone for its completion[7]—its design introduced no innovations. During Rizzo's tenure at the Ducal Palace he and his shop added to the thirteen statues already carved for the Arco, seven figures for its summit and three for niches of its lower story. When Rizzo's attention was diverted from the Arco to the rebuilding of the Palazzo del Doge in 1484, only one figure apparently was lacking—the *Charity–Amor Dei*, which bears the imprint of the shop of Pietro Lombardo, Rizzo's successor as *protomaestro* of the Ducal Palace. The two earliest *Angels* and "*Mars*," carved at the end of the 1460s, and *Adam* and *Eve*, which probably date from the beginning of the 1470s, are all by Rizzo; the five later figures, datable to the early 1480s, are by assistants. The difference of a decade in the two groups of statuary and the acquisition of stone in 1483 suggest that work on the Arco Foscari was suspended from the early 1470s to the early 1480s.

The decoration of the Arco Foscari was nearly finished when the fire in the Palazzo del Doge compelled the transfer of activity to the east wing of the Ducal Palace. The Provveditori al Sal were specifically charged with its reconstruction by the Collegio, the highest executive council of the republic.[8] Plans were chosen by the Senate; very likely it was they who named the architect in chief. Rizzo seems to have been serving in that capacity by the end of 1484. He continued to do so until his flight from Venice in 1498. While employed on the rebuilding of the Ducal Palace, Rizzo accepted very little outside work. During the first years of construction he was too busy to take on other jobs: in a petition of August 1485, Rizzo claimed that he had abandoned his shop and was neglecting other things.[9] Probably the slackening of work in 1493 and 1496 provided respite, for it is from that period that the *Angel with Attributes of Christ* and the *vera da pozzo* of Palazzo Decazes seem to date.

As *protomaestro* of the Ducal Palace, Rizzo was responsible for all work of architecture and sculpture at the palace. He carved the reliefs of *Putti with Arms of the Barbarigo Family* and the *Madonna and Child* in the Camera degli Scarlatti; he designed and executed the Scala dei Giganti. There was only one commission for sculpture at the Ducal Palace that Rizzo did not receive. In 1496 the bronze doors of the Porta della Carta were commissioned by the Consiglio dei Dieci from Alessandro Leopardi.[10] The Monument of Bartolommeo Colleoni, successfully cast by Leopardi, had recently been unveiled and the government wished to show appreciation to its maker. Rizzo, by contrast, had no special competence in the medium of bronze. But the bronze doors, like the southern half of the east wing of the Ducal Palace, succumbed to the financial exigencies of the moment; unlike the east wing, they were never made.

Though both positions were subordinate to the salt commission, the office that Rizzo, and Pietro Lombardo after him, held as *proto della fabrica del palazzo* was distinct from that of *proto al Magistrato al Sal*. In July 1470 the latter office was filled by Zuan Davanzo, and then, until his death in December 1473, by the mason Domenico Bianco,

---

[7] Paoletti, 1893, ii, p. 144.
[8] The Pien Collegio was composed of the doge, the six ducal councilors, the three heads of the Council of Forty, the six Savii Grandi or del Consiglio, the five Savii di Terra Ferma, and the five Savii ai Ordini.
[9] Lorenzi, 1868, p. 97, doc. 207.
[10] Paoletti, 1893, ii, p. 267.

followed by Ser Niccolò Pain,[11] who, in turn, was succeeded on August 20, 1492, by Ser Bartolomeo Bon.[12] (Between August 22, 1496, and May 31, 1498, at least, Bon, admiral under Capitanio del Mar Melchiorre Trevisan, was temporarily replaced by Maestro Pietro Bon.[13]) Until he resigned in 1505, Bon's duties included the supervision of painters in the Sala del Maggior Consiglio and the maintenance of two pest hospitals,[14] public buildings that also came under the authority of the Provveditori al Sal. Likewise, Rizzo's office was distinct from the office occupied in 1470 by Antonio Zelega and later shared by the mason, Bartolomeo Gonella,[15] and the carpenter, Giorgio Spavento,[16] of *proto dei Procuratori di S. Marco de supra*, the board that oversaw the maintenance and decoration of the Basilica di S. Marco and church property in and around the piazza. To suppose, as has recently been done, that Rizzo executed the *Mori*, which strike the hours above the Torre dell'Orologio in Piazza S. Marco, because he was the major architect and sculptor in government employ between 1496 and 1499, when the tower was erected, is to mistake the jurisdiction of both the *proto del palazzo* and the Provveditori al Sal. In fact, construction of the Torre dell'Orologio was not supervised by the Provveditori al Sal, but by the Senate and Signoria, with the agreement of the Procuratori di S. Marco de supra.[17] But even had the Provveditori al Sal been in charge, it is unlikely that Rizzo would have been involved, for his duties were confined strictly to the Ducal Palace. In any case, the style of the *Mori* is that of Paolo Savin, to whom they have long been justly attributed.[18]

In 1476 Rizzo was commissioned to execute a staircase and a pulpit for the chapter room of the Scuola Grande di S. Marco. A year later Rizzo was inscribed among the members of the school. We may surmise that the confraternity would have engaged Rizzo to rebuild the *scuola* after the fire of 1485 had he not been fully occupied at the Ducal Palace. As it was, the commission was first entrusted to Pietro Lombardo in company with Giovanni Buora and Bartolomeo Duca; later it was transferred to Mauro Codussi. When, in 1490, a dispute arose between Lombardo, Buora, and Duca, and the members of the confraternity, Antonio Rizzo was elected one of two arbiters.[19]

Rizzo was not employed by any of the other *scuole grandi*. Both the Scuola della Carità and the Scuola della Misericordia had completed major works of construction or repair not long before Rizzo's debut and undertook no architectural projects in the succeeding years. During the period of Rizzo's activity only the Scuola di S. Giovanni Evangelista commissioned a new building: the atrium of the *scuola* is inscribed with the date of 1481.

[11] Cecchetti in Ongania, ed., *Basilica*, vii, 1886, pp. 213f., doc. 849; Paoletti, 1893, i, p. 44; Lorenzi, 1868, p. 104, doc. 224.

[12] Ibid., p. 107, doc. 232, p. 114, doc. 239.

[13] Ibid., p. 116, doc. 241, p. 118, doc. 243, p. 119, doc. 245.

[14] Ibid., p. 109, doc. 235, p. 114, doc. 239.

[15] Cecchetti in Ongania, ed., *Basilica*, vii, 1886, pp. 213f., doc. 849; Paoletti, 1893, ii, pp. 175, 120, doc. 123. On Gonella's death in 1505, Bartolomeo Bon resigned his position as *proto* to the Provveditori al Sal to become *proto dei Procuratori di S. Marco*: Paoletti, 1893, ii, p. 276.

[16] Lorenzi, 1868, p. 118, doc. 243.

[17] For the documents concerning the Torre dell'Orologio, see Erizzo, ²1866, pp. 23ff.

[18] A recent article by Cessi, *Medioevo e umanesimo*, 1979, ii, pp. 11-13, based on unacknowledged ideas of Prof. Michelangelo Muraro's, attributed the *Mori* to Antonio Rizzo. (Actually the idea was suggested as long ago as 1910 by Fabriczy in Burckhardt/Bode/Fabriczy, ¹⁰1910, ii, pt. 2, pp. 536lf.) Thus Cessi opposed Planiscig, 1921, pp. 287ff., who had compared the *Mori* to Savin's documented statue of *St. John the Baptist* in the Cappella Zen, S. Marco. Planiscig's attribution to Savin was accepted by Lorenzetti, ¹1926, p. 151; Venturi, *Storia*, x, pt. 1, 1935, p. 405; Hubala in Egg *et al.*, ¹1965, p. 628; and Ruhmer, *Arte ven.*, 1974, p. 59. Cessi offered no arguments that discredit Planiscig's conclusion.

[19] Paoletti, 1893, ii, p. 103, doc. 73.

Its design is usually attributed to Pietro Lombardo. From smaller confraternities Rizzo received modest commissions. Not long after 1468 he furnished four statues for the altar of the Scuola dei Barbieri at S. Maria dei Servi; for the Scuola di S. Cristoforo he carved the *Annunciate Angel* on the portal of the Madonna dell'Orto circa 1480; for the Scuola dei Calegheri, Rizzo made the relief above its portal dated 1479.

Doge Cristoforo Moro was the most eminent of Rizzo's patrons. For him Rizzo executed his first extant works—the three altars in the Basilica di S. Marco carved between circa 1465 and 1469. Can Moro have disapproved the result? Soon afterward, when the doge bethought the decoration of his funerary chapel in the presbytery of S. Giobbe with reliefs, statuary, and a tomb slab, he engaged, not Rizzo, but Pietro Lombardo, newly arrived in Venice. For another ducal family, Rizzo executed the Tron Tomb between 1476 and 1480. It was the only occasion on which Rizzo succeeded in wresting the commission for a ducal tomb from the Lombardos. Indeed, the Lombardos seem to have had a near monopoly of such commissions: during the period of Rizzo's activity, Pietro's shop produced the Tombs of Doges Malipiero, Marcello, Pietro Mocenigo, and the double Tomb of Marco and Agostino Barbarigo.[20] Tullio was commissioned to execute the Tomb of Doge Andrea Vendramin after Andrea del Verrocchio died, leaving for it no more than a design.[21] As late as 1522 the Tomb of Doge Giovanni Mocenigo, dead for more than a quarter of a century, was made by Tullio Lombardo.[22]

Tombs of private citizens were less desirable commissions. Except for the Trevisan Tomb of Bishop Giovanni da Udine, Pietro Lombardo made none. Rather, the greater number of private tombs at the end of the fifteenth century were delegated to the mediocre Giovanni Buora, who executed the Tombs of Jacopo Marcello, Jacopo Suriano, and the Trevisan, Agostino Onigo.[23] For the heirs of Giovanni Emo, Rizzo and his shop supplied a pedestrian effigy and two *Pages* for an aedicule apparently designed by Tullio. Beside the Moro, Tron, and Emo, and the original owners of Palazzo Decazes, Rizzo is not known to have worked for any noble Venetian family. When the Badoer conceived the decoration of their family chapel in S. Francesco della Vigna, they, too, gave Pietro Lombardo the commission.

Although there was no diminution in the volume of government or corporate patronage at the end of the fifteenth century, the proportion of private patronage increased. But the works commissioned by private patrons were almost invariably public ones. Tombs were commissioned most often. Altarpieces for family chapels also were ordered in considerable numbers but mural reliefs as chapel decoration were rare. Probably from diverse altars executed for the chapels of private patrons came Rizzo's *Angel* in Vienna and the *Angel with Attributes of Christ* in the Ca' d'Oro. His statue of *John the Evangelist* in East Berlin may have been made for the chapel of Giovanni Emo in S. Maria dei Servi. By contrast, the *vera da pozzo* of Palazzo Decazes, the *Victories* from the lunette of a portal, and the *Angel with Simbeni Arms* served secular functions. Though intended for private palaces, at least two of these were situated outdoors and thus, to some degree, were publicly accessible. In Rizzo's oeuvre only two works qualify as objects destined for publicly inaccessible, domestic interiors. They are the two reliefs of the *Madonna and Child*, in Vaduz and formerly in Amsterdam. Rizzo's activity is not

---

[20] Schulz in *Studies . . . Janson*, 1981, pp. 171-192.
[21] Sheard, *BJ*, 1978, pp. 133ff.

[22] Sheard, *Yale Ital. Studies*, 1977, pp. 249f., n. 34.
[23] Munman, *Arte ven.*, 1976, pp. 41ff.

unusual in this respect. Where in Florence the end of the Quattrocento saw wholesale production of objects for domestic consumption—portrait busts, small bronzes, private devotional reliefs, generally of the Madonna and Child, and busts of the infant Christ or John the Baptist—such works in Venice were exceptional.[24] It is a curious fact that, although the private palace existed as a significant genre of architecture in Venice centuries before it did in Florence, the interior decoration of the palace with sculptured and painted works of art became an object of concern in Venice much later than it did in Florence: throughout the fifteenth century, sculpture made for Venetian palaces almost always ornamented their exteriors. Conversely, Florence possessed nothing comparable to the Venetian genre of external, escutcheon-bearing *Angels* or free-standing *Warriors* set in niches on the facades of late Quattrocento palaces.[25] That the works of art commissioned by private patrons in Venice were intended to be seen by many people rather than enjoyed in the privacy of the patron's home testifies to the typically Venetian focus of both citizen and patrician class in the city's public life. In 1494 a pilgrim who stopped in Venice before departing for the Holy Land observed that "[Venetian gentlemen] are frugal and very modest in their manner of living at home; outside the house they are very liberal."[26]

Rizzo's activity centered in Venice. To be sure, an antependium was made for the Basilica of Aquileia, probably in the early 1470s. In 1491 Rizzo was invited to execute the statues that crown the Palazzo del Consiglio in his native city of Verona, but the pressure of work at the Ducal Palace forced him to decline. Between 1496 and 1498 Rizzo advised the Consiglio del 100 at Vicenza about the restoration of the porticoes of the Palazzo della Ragione. This necessitated occasional trips to Vicenza but no prolonged sojourns. No other works by Rizzo at, or for, cities outside Venice have been traced.[27] There is no evidence that Rizzo practiced as a sculptor in Cesena or Ferrara or elsewhere in the Marches or the Romagna after his flight from Venice.[28] By contrast, during the period of Rizzo's activity, Pietro Lombardo executed important works of sculpture for Padua, Ravenna, Treviso, and Bergamo.

With steady employment at the Ducal Palace, Rizzo appears the chosen sculptor and

[24] Even by the second quarter of the sixteenth century, Venetian palaces were not abundantly embellished with works of modern sculpture. Only Andrea di Odoni, who possessed numerous bronze statuettes, owned more than a few examples. More common were collections of antiquities. See Michiel/Frimmel, 1896, pp. 78ff.

[25] E.g., *Warriors* from the shop of Pietro Lombardo, Palazzo degli Ambasciatori on the Grand Canal; *Warriors* by Tullio Lombardo, facade, Scuola di S. Marco; *Warrior* by Giovanni Buora, Palazzo Civran near S. Maria del Carmine; *Warrior*, Palazzo Trevisan-Cappello, Rio del Palazzo.

[26] Casola, (1494) 1907, p. 143.

[27] Bartoli, 1793, p. 131, claimed as Rizzo's the winged *Lion of St. Mark*, which stood on the column designed by Michele Sanmichele in the Piazza Vittorio Emanuele II in Rovigo. This attribution is not confirmed by any other source or document. The *Lion* was destroyed in 1797; on the column is a replica carved by Natale Sanavio in 1881. (TCI, *Ve-*

neto, 1969, p. 437.)

[28] Gottschewski, *ZbK*, 1908, pp. 131f., attributed to Rizzo a wooden statue of *St. Sebastian* from Sangemini near Terni, now in the Pinacoteca, Perugia, and to an assistant of his, a wooden statue of *St. Sebastian* from S. Francesco, Stroncone, also near Terni. Morini, *Rass. d'arte*, 1911, pp. 70ff., ascribed to Rizzo or his shop three wooden sculptures: *Tobias and the Angel*, Museo, Cascia; the *Dead Christ*, S. Agostino, Cascia; *St. Sebastian*, Oratorio della Morte, Collegiata di S. Maria, Cascia. Gottschewski and Morini believed these works to have been executed after Rizzo's flight from Venice. These attributions are not persuasive and, apart from Brenzoni, 1972, pp. 250, 251, have not found their way into the literature on Rizzo. Planiscig, T-B, xxviii, 1934, p. 409, explicitly rejected them. For other, equally implausible, attributions of wooden sculptures to the hand, school, or direct influence of Rizzo, see Marquand, *Art in America*, 1917-18, pp. 53f., and Francovich, *Boll. d'arte*, 1928-29, pp. 481-488.

architect of the Venetian Signoria. Yet a comparison of the careers of Rizzo and Pietro Lombardo, Rizzo's rival as Gauricus informs us, discloses that Rizzo's commissions were neither as numerous nor as lucrative as Pietro's. The number, size, and complexity of Pietro's commissions obliged him to delegate the execution of the larger portion of his sculpture to assistants, among whom two talented sons bore important responsibilities. By contrast, Rizzo seems to have done most of his work himself. Though the hands of weak collaborators are sometimes visible in sculpture that issued from his shop, the sum of works ascribable to them is low. Probably Rizzo's assistants were not many.[29]

Indeed, Rizzo would not have benefited from an extensive shop. His aesthetic preference was for the small in scale. Monuments or facades are large in dimension but not in scale: an increase in size only produced an increase in the number of small components. Because Rizzo worked with small units, his designs tend to be repetitive. Yet the decorative detail was often extremely complex and continually varied—an even greater deterrent to entrusting work to others. It is with an obsessive attention to detail, defining form with the finesse of a goldsmith, that Rizzo would have always liked to work had circumstances allowed. At the Tomb of Niccolò Tron, Rizzo commenced with the figure of *Prudence* and the standing effigy in such a way that a lifetime would not have sufficed to finish the tomb as carefully as it was begun. The execution of minute detail, which demanded extraordinary technical virtuosity, could not be delegated to assistants, and only once, in four of the *Victories* of the Scala dei Giganti, was Rizzo sure enough of his collaborators to do so. Where figures were to be executed by assistants their designs were debased. *SS. Andrew* and *Luke* in S. Sofia or the *Personifications* from the Tron Tomb are so columnar and unmodulated in form, so simple and repetitive in design, and withal so standardized in appearance, as to seem mechanically produced.

Yet even the master himself did not always attain the standards he aspired to. In contrast to the wealth of detail and high finish of his best works, the Altar of the Traghetto della Maddalena or the lunette of the Scuola dei Calegheri show elementary errors of foreshortening and perspective. In the Aquileia *Man of Sorrows* textures were not distinguished; tool marks were not erased. Evidently there were times when Rizzo rebelled against the demands of his own perfectionism and sought the most expeditious means to the end of a finished work of art. By and large, this seems to have occurred when the work was of little moment or visually inaccessible. By contrast, Rizzo responded to his most notable commissions, like the Scala dei Giganti, the *Pedestrian Effigy of Tron*, and the three statues of the niches of the Arco Foscari, with a dedication and effort that was unparalleled in the work of any of his Venetian predecessors.

Sometimes Rizzo's nonchalance—the obverse of his perfectionism—affected execution of iconographic programs: twice Rizzo negligently failed to realize schemes whose iconography was already fixed and partly carried out. Rizzo himself established the hierarchy of the Tron Tomb, in which the Savior's life unfolds above an account of the mortal existence of the doge. But he neglected to give several of the figures, meant to personify aspects of Tron's character, identifying attributes. More flagrant still was Riz-

---

[29] It would seem that Rizzo abided by the rule adopted by the Venetian guild of stonemasons in 1407, according to which masters were forbidden from employing more than three apprentices at one time, exclusive of sons and brothers. (Sagredo, 1856, pp. 302f., no. XLVIII.) The Lombard stonecarvers who worked under Rizzo's supervision at the Ducal Palace were not his personal assistants, but rather, employees of the Provveditori al Sal.

zo's disregard of the preexistent program of the Arco Foscari. Except for its lowest row of pinnacles, the iconography of the Arco's crown derived from the cresting of the ducal basilica, with its statues of *St. Mark, Angels, Warriors,* and *Virtues:* thus east and west facades at the termination of parallel and adjacent, but inverted, axes were made to match in program, as they matched, to some extent, in architectural motifs.[30] At the summit of the Arco Foscari stood a statue of *St. Mark,* as there did atop the central gable of S. Marco's west facade. At an early stage the base of *St. Mark*'s pyramid was surrounded by six Gothic *Angels* in adoration. The subsidiary pyramid of the south face of the Arco Foscari apparently was destined for a *Virtue,* corner spires for guardian *Warriors.* At the lowest level, where seven pinnacles provided proper bases for the seven *Liberal Arts,* Bartolomeo Bon introduced a personification of *Arithmetic;* Niccolò di Giovanni Fiorentino followed suit with *Music* and *Rhetoric.* When Rizzo assumed charge of the Arco Foscari, four of the seven pinnacles on the lowest level, one corner spire, the subsidiary pyramid, and two pedestals at the rear of the central pyramid still lacked their statuary. The south pyramid was capped only after Rizzo's flight with a personification of *Charity–Amor Dei.* For the corner spire Rizzo supplied another *Warrior* and for the pedestals of the central pyramid, two *Angels.* But he transferred one Gothic *Angel* to a pinnacle of the lowest level and replaced him with an *Angel* whose youth and sex agree with that of his companions, but whose attitude does not betoken adoration. On the remaining pinnacles of the lowest level Rizzo set three female figures; they conform to the *Liberal Arts* in type, pose, and costume, but they possess no attributes.

All Rizzo's extant work is made of stone—Carrara marble or limestone from Istria or northern Italy. There is no evidence that Rizzo was skilled in the execution of bronze or wooden sculpture. In this respect, he resembles the majority of Venetian sculptors of the Quattrocento who, on the whole, were far less versatile than their Florentine peers. In Venice wooden sculpture was customarily executed by carvers from Germany, whence came the raw material. To be sure, Alessandro Leopardi, Vittorio Gambello, and Antonio Lombardo worked bronze as well as stone. But there is no Venetian to compare with Verrocchio or Pollaiuolo, expert in the fashioning of bronze, marble, silver, and terracotta sculpture, in painting, drawing, and engraving. If Rizzo knew only one material, however, he was familiar with all stages of its preparation. At Scutari he quarried stone; at the Ducal Palace he was responsible for its acquisition. Already in his earliest work Rizzo showed himself proficient in carving architectural details. The design of larger architectural units occasionally came within his purview. At Vicenza he advised on the statics of stone structures. His sculpture included both statuary and relief.

The care that Rizzo lavished on the ornamental relief of the Altars of S. Marco and the ability manifested in its execution suggest that he was trained in carving architectural detail. Perhaps it was under Pietro da Porlezza, who seems to have specialized in such work, that Rizzo was apprenticed at Verona. At an early age Rizzo felt the impact of Donatello's Paduan sculpture, of works which revolutionized the style of north Italian art. Like many of his contemporaries, Rizzo wished to imitate them. But lacking an education in the basic rudiments of a Renaissance style—in the correct articulation of the human body at rest or moving, in a rational disposition of drapery, in linear perspective—he could only approximate the external features of Donatello's art. It is re-

[30] Howard, 1980, p. 108.

markable to what extent the errors that mar his early works are common also to the juvenilia of Mantegna and Giovanni Bellini, similarly handicapped by a provincial training. In the early works of all three, anatomical mistakes are rife, poses are ungainly, proportions are inharmonious, drapery is composed of a welter of minute and sharply drawn folds that are unrelated to the structure of the body underneath. But for Rizzo, as for Mantegna and Bellini, this period of immaturity was quickly superseded by complete and perfect mastery.

Rizzo's mastery was first revealed in *Adam* and *Eve* carved for the Arco Foscari. Both reveal the profound influence of Antonio Pollaiuolo and testify to a trip to Florence in the early 1470s. In the explicit and accurate description of anatomy, in the movement which imbues every limb and muscle of the body, in the emphatic expression of features and gestures, *Adam* declares its kinship with works of the most advanced current of Florentine Quattrocento art—with Pollaiuolo's *Hercules*, Verrocchio's *Colleoni*, with Castagno's and Leonardo's *St. Jeromes*.

Rizzo's stylistic development did not follow a consistent evolutionary path. A comparison of early and late reliefs of the *Madonna and Child* reveal a flattening of the surface, a relative disregard of anatomical form, a greater redundancy in the pattern of minute, irregular folds in the later work. But Rizzo did not arrive at this style, which, indeed, was intrinsic even to his earliest works, through easily defined stages. On the contrary, from the end of the 1470s through the early 1480s, Rizzo's art, subjected to the influence of Tullio Lombardo and Antonello da Messina, underwent a metamorphosis. Movement was subdued, expressions made impassive. Anatomical forms were generalized and contours smoothed. Irregular folds yielded to long, parallel strips that hardly affected the evenness of stereometric surfaces. Rizzo's artistic transformation, however, was not total, for works coeval with the Tron Tomb *Charity* or East Berlin *St. John*, like the Altar of the Traghetto della Maddalena, remained true to the principles governing the sculptor's early works. In Rizzo's sudden and partial conversion, one senses a susceptibility to the influence of a new and highly fashionable style caused by a loss of confidence, rather than a conviction of the style's inherent superiority. That loss of confidence, apparently, was only temporary, for the alien classicistic strain in Rizzo's art did not outlast his nomination to the newly created and eminently prestigious post of *protomaestro della fabbrica del Palazzo Ducale*.

At the Ducal Palace Rizzo's tasks were more difficult than any he had encountered before—to fit a Renaissance structure to medieval foundations and walls, to integrate it with two other wings built in different epochs, to contrive within an awkward space a staircase that should serve at once for access to the Palazzo del Doge and a setting for the coronation of the doge, and, in addition, to procure supplies and lead an army of stonemasons. Though Rizzo could not resist the temptation to withhold a part of the vast sums that flowed through his hands, he was not guilty of artistic dishonesty and sought, again and again, to produce the finest work that lay within his capabilities. So great were they that Rizzo's sublimest work, the *Victory* with laurel branch and apple, was not surpassed by any other work of Venetian Quattrocento sculpture.

Digest of Documents
Concerning the Life and Works
of Antonio Rizzo

ANTONIO RIZZO came from Verona. (Colatius, [1475] 1486, n.p.; Paoletti, 1893, ii, p. 147 [document of August 26, 1491].) His date of birth is not recorded. Gregorio Correr, who died in late 1464, addressed two epigrams and a distich to "Antonium Riccium Sculptorem" (Degli Agostini, i, 1752, p. 132, no. xiv); by 1465 Rizzo had received and partly executed a prestigious sculptural commission (see below). These signs of repute, which presuppose a certain experience and attainment, make it unlikely that Rizzo was born after 1440.

Rizzo's father was Ser Giovanni. (Lorenzi, 1868, p. 94, doc. 202.) A Ser Iohannis Rizo of the Venetian parish of S. Giovanni Nuovo (the parish in which Antonio later lived) was documented on March 11, 1454. (Paoletti, 1893, ii, p. 147, n. 11.) This Ser Giovanni may be the sculptor's father. More likely, Rizzo's father is identical with the "Maistro zuan rizo taiapria a verona," a dealer in Veronese marble, mentioned in the accounts of S. Maria della Carità, Venice, in 1462. (Paoletti, 1929, p. 16, n. 1; Connell, 1976, p. 142.) March 1462, "m° rizo taiapria" was credited with 24 lire, 16 soldi to be paid by the prior Francesco of the Augustinian monastery at Verona, for slabs for the pavement in the chapels of the *barco* of the Carità. (Fogolari, *Arch. ven.*, 1924, p. 113.) November 5, 1462, Giovanni was debited for a lira's worth of spices. December 10, 1462, Giovanni was credited with 10 lire, 18 soldi for having supplied a slab of red stone for a tomb slab. (Ibid., p. 109.) A "Ioannes Ricius lapicida de Mediolano" paid taxes in Verona in the *contrada* of S. Quirico in 1456 and 1465. (Mazzi, *Madonna Verona*, 1913, p. 31. Mazzi, ibid., p. 36, also records a "Ricius lapicida de lacu Cumarum," living in the *contrada* of S. Marco, Verona, in 1443. Brenzoni in *Arte e artisti*, 1959, i, pp. 93, 120, and Brenzoni, 1972, p. 250, assumes that these are one and the same person. It is possible, since Lake Como was included in the diocese of Milan, but it is not certain.) Rizzo's father died between December 8, 1484, and April 1, 1486. (Lorenzi, 1868, p. 94, doc. 202; Paoletti, 1893, ii, p. 148, n. 11 [from the preceding page].)

Antonio was already married to Maria, daughter of Isabeta and Ser Giacomo Gibellino, in 1477. Maria was still alive on May 5, 1499. (Paoletti, 1893, ii, p. 147, n. 11, p. 148, n. 1.) Antonio's son Simplicio was a goldsmith and jeweler. In 1495 he joined the Scuola di S. Marco; in 1502 he was elected a dean. He died at Rome in 1522. (Paoletti, 1929, p. 16, n. 4.) Another son, Gian Stefano, witnessed a contract to Alberto Maffiolo da Carrara for the execution of a *lavabo* for the Certosa di Pavia on July 15, 1489. ("Alberto Maffiolo," *Rass. d'arte*, 1902, pp. 14f.)

Columns and Other Architectural Details for the Large Cloister of the Certosa at Pavia

1465 1465, Ricio was paid up to March 3. 8 lire, 4 soldi were transmitted to him by priest Ugo. (Bernstein, 1972, app. H, p. 197, doc. 2.) March 20, 1465, 105 lire were transmitted to "Magistro Ricio de Verona" by priest Celso of the order of S. Spirito as a deposit and payment for certain red columns at the price of 11 lire each. (Magenta, 1897, p. 460, n. 1; Bernstein, 1972, app. H, p. 197, doc. 1.) June 14, 1465, at Milan the goldsmith Zanino da Sesto received 121 lire, 10 soldi in Ricio's name. (Bernstein, 1972, app. H., p. 197, doc. 3.) December 14, 1465, 128 lire, 2 soldi were transmitted to Ricio by Fra Gabriele for colonettes, capitals, and bases, and for one dressed corner pier with its capital and base at a cost of 8 ducats. (Magenta, 1897, p. 460, n. 1;

1466 Bernstein, 1972, app. H, p. 197, doc. 4.) 1466, 20 lire were transmitted to Ricio by the smith, Maestro Ambrogio da Sesto, for columns previously de-

1467 livered. (Bernstein, 1972, app. H, p. 198, doc. 5.) 1467, 26 lire, 8 soldi were transmitted to Ricio by the prior at Venice (i.e., the prior of S. Andrea della Certosa) for thirty-three blocks of a flinty stone at a price of 16 soldi each. (Caffi, *Arte e storia*, June 5, 1887, p. 106; Bernstein, 1972, app. H, p. 198, doc. 6.) There is no reason to identify the Master Ricio named in these documents with the sculptor, Antonio Rizzo. In the Pavese documents Master Ricio's first name is never given and Rizzo was a very common surname. There is no independent evidence that Antonio Rizzo ever dealt in Veronese marbles. Attempts to trace the hand of Antonio Rizzo in the sculpture of the large cloister at the Certosa of Pavia have proved unsuccessful. Indeed, as Connell, 1976, p. 142, pointed out, the "Magistro Ricio de Verona" named in the documents of the Certosa is more likely to have been the "Maistro zuan rizo taiapria a verona" who supplied Veronese marbles to the Carità in 1462.

Altars of SS. James, Paul, and Clement, S. Marco, Venice

1465 1465 is inscribed on the Altar of St. Clement. June 28, 1469, Antonio Rizzo,
1469 living in the parish of S. Giovanni Nuovo, gave a receipt to Doge Cristoforo Moro for 35 gold ducats as the remainder owed for all work executed by him for the doge on the three altars of S. Marco. (ch. 1, n. 1.) The Altars of SS. James, Paul, and Clement are inscribed with Doge Moro's name.

1469 1469, Antonio Rizzo was residing in a house at S. Giovanni Nuovo belonging to the nuns of S. Zaccaria, to which they had added a mezzanine. (Paoletti, 1893, ii, p. 147, n. 11.)

Rizzo's Participation in the Two Defenses of Scutari (Albania),
Besieged by the Turks between July 15, 1474, and August 28,
1474, and June 22, 1478, and January 9, 1479

1478-79   January 14, 1483, two Franciscan monks from Scutari, Alvise q. Nicolo and
           Zuane q. Zorsi, swore that, during the second siege of Scutari, Antonio Rizzo
           stonecutter performed conscientiously in manning the batteries and mortars.
           Luca Bondomer, also of Scutari, testified that Antonio had quarried stone and
           done all he could in the defense of Scutari during the time of Alvise Quirini
1474   and Antonio Loredan (the first siege of Scutari). (Cadorin, 1837, pp. 47f., n.
1483   19; Cadorin, 1838, pp. 163f., n. 19.) February 14, 1483, in execution of the
           order of the Signoria and in consideration of the fact that Antonio comported
           himself faithfully at the siege of Scutari where he received many wounds,
           Messer Domenico Trevisan, Provveditore al Sal, awarded Antonio and his
           sons a pension of one ducat per month, paid monthly by the Ufficio del Sal.
           Payment of the pension was to be computed as having begun on January 17,
           1483, and was to continue for the next twenty years. (Ibid.)

Spiral Staircase and Pulpit of the *Sala Capitolare*, Scuola
di S. Marco, Venice

1476   July 2 and 7, 1476, having consulted the most expert engineers, the heads of
           the Scuola di S. Marco decided to construct, on the exterior of the wall over-
           looking the canal and in correspondence with the old pulpit in the interior of
           the chapter hall, a spiral staircase which should give access to the pulpit and
           continue up to the attic. For the adornment of the room there was also to be
           made a worthy and convenient pulpit, without which sermons could not be
           preached or orders read. July 21, 1476, a contract between Antonio Rizzo and
           the Guardian Grande and members of the sodality provided for the following
           works: a large, well-carved bracket of live stone, encircled by a cornice, for
           the base of the spiral staircase; a door of live stone giving onto the spiral
           staircase beneath the pulpit within the hall; a door of live stone leading from
           the spiral staircase to the pulpit, as it appeared in the drawing made by Gentile
           Bellini (painter and member of the sodality); a plain door giving access to the
           attic; and a pulpit of white marble with its large bracket constructed in ac-
           cordance with Bellini's drawing. The pulpit was to have five faces. Its figures,
           carved in *mezzo rilievo*, according to the best judgment of the Guardian Grande
           and the members of the confraternity, were to be of white marble. Behind
           the figures there was to be a background of black stone. Antonio was obliged
           to provide all the stone and marble that would be necessary for the work, as
           well as the rope and chain used in the spiral staircase. He promised to deliver
           the completed work by the end of the coming November, or by Christmas,
           at the latest. For the work Antonio was to receive 110 ducats. In addition, he
           received 15 ducats as a deposit. (Paoletti, fasc. 1, 1894, pp. 15f.) Rizzo's stair-
           case and pulpit were destroyed by fire on the night of March 31, 1485.

1477   1477, Antonio Rizzo, living in the parish of S. Giovanni Nuovo, was inscribed among the members of the Scuola di S. Marco. (Paoletti, 1893, ii, p.
149, n. 4.)

1477

1480

May 3, 1474 Rizzo's father-in-law, Giacomo Gibellino, was dismissed from
his post of steward of the convent of S. Zaccaria. In consequence of his dis-
missal and because of the payments that the nuns wished to condemn him to
make on account of his maladministration, Gibellino brought a lawsuit against
the convent, in which Rizzo acted as his guarantor. January 28, 1477, Antonio
Saraco, archbishop of Corinth and vicar general of the Benedictine Order,
assessed the expenses sustained by the convent in the suit and, for payment,
sent executory letters against the goods of Gibellino and against Rizzo. June
1, 1480, 40 ducats were given to Rizzo by the abbess of S. Zaccaria as reim-
bursement for the money Rizzo had given to his father-in-law, with the agreement that if the money could be gotten from Gibellino, it should be added to
the account of his expenses. June 7, 1480, the two parties to the suit were
absolved from payment by the sentence of an arbiter. (Ibid., pp. 147f., n. 11.)

1478   October 21, 1478, Antonio Rizzo was present in Venice. (Ibid.)

1480

1484

1486

November 24, 1480, sentence of three judges awarding Antonio in entirety
what he had sued for in recompense for improvements he had made to two
houses belonging to his father-in-law, Giacomo Gibellino, in the parish of S.
Giovanni Nuovo. (Ibid., p. 148, n. 11 [from the preceding page].) May 31,
1484, sentence of two judges awarding Antonio a small house in the parish of
S. Simone profeta in Bari with all its possessions and everything pertaining
to it, estimated at 60 ducats, in payment of a debt to Antonio. The house had
belonged to the late Ursia Ruggiero, from whom it had been inherited by her
brother, the late Giacomo Gibellino. (Ludwig, 1911, p. 14.) February 13,
1486, sentence of two judges giving Rizzo part of a modest house, which
belonged to the late Giacomo Gibellino, in the parish of S. Giovanni Nuovo,
in total payment of 160 ducats awarded Rizzo for his expenses of 49 lire di
grossi in a sentence of July 14, 1485, against the heirs of Giacomo Gibellino.
(Ibid., pp. 13f.) April 1, 1486, Antonio's claim of 120 ducats owed him by
right of the property in S. Giovanni Nuovo that had belonged to the late Ser
Giacomo Gibellino, and which had been assigned to the late Ser Jacopo Zo-
tareli for administration of the sentence, was annulled. May 18, 1486, Rizzo
presented a new claim for 40 ducats. (Paoletti, 1893, ii, p. 148, n. 11 [from
the preceding page].)

1486   June 17, 1486, Rizzo was living in the parish of S. Giovanni Nuovo. (Ibid.)

Ducal Palace, Venice

1483   February 25, 1483, Antonio Rizzo was employed at the Ducal Palace, probably on construction or decoration of the Arco Foscari. Letters of this date

asked the Podestà of Parenzo not to present obstacles, but rather to give every assistance to the boat sent to him so that Ser Antonio Rizzo might load stone for the portal of the palace. (Paoletti, 1893, ii, p. 144. The "portal of the palace" was reasonably interpreted by Paoletti as the Arco Foscari.)

On the evening of September 14, 1483, a fire in the Palazzo del Doge, in the northeast wing of the Ducal Palace, destroyed the Sala delle due Nape (Udienza), the Sala del Mappamondo, the office of the Giudici del Proprio on the ground floor, and the entire Appartamenti dei Dogi with the exception of the Camera dei Dogi. (Lorenzi, 1868, pp. 92f., doc. 198, citing the unpublished holograph of Marin Sanudo's *Vite dei dogi* in the Bibl. Marc.) March 8, 1484, the full Collegio entrusted the construction of the palace to the Provveditori al Sal, working in concert with Ser Hieronimo Michiel da S. Barnaba. As soon as possible they were to see that cleaning up began and proceeded expeditiously. (Ibid.) In his *Vite dei dogi*, Sanudo wrote that the Senate determined to rebuild the Ducal Palace in three stories with funds from the Ufficio del Sal. Certain members of the Collegio wished only to restore the palace to its original condition with an expenditure of 6,000 ducats. In opposition, Ser Nicolò Trevisan, Savio di Terraferma, proposed that the Signoria buy the houses on the far side of the canal and there construct the apartments of the doge, making them accessible from the near side of the canal by a marble bridge. Thus the palace on the near side of the canal should be strictly limited to the accommodation of public affairs. This proposal, however, did not pass. Antonio Rizzo was made supervisor of the reconstruction of the Ducal Palace at a salary of 100 ducats per year. (Ibid., p. 93, doc. 198.) Under the date of September 14, 1483, Malipiero wrote: "The house of Ca' Diedo opposite the palace was taken for the habitation of the doge, and with a wooden bridge one passes into the palace in that part of the ducal residence where the Signoria gathers. The majority did not want to spend more than 6,000 ducats in repairing the palace on account of the tightness of the times; but afterwards it was resolved to make it all anew. Nicolò Trevisan wished to buy all the houses opposite the palace up to the Calle delle Rosse and make of them a palace with a garden, and to pass from there into the Sala del Collegio by a stone bridge; and to make on the old site rooms and chambers for the Signoria, the Collegio, and the Savii. But it was decided to make the new building in three stories; and Antonio Rizzo, stonecutter, was made supervisor with 100 ducats per year." (Malipiero, *Arch. stor. ital.*, 1844, pt. 2, pp. 673f.) May 21, 1484, witnesses and engineers with their models were summoned by the doge (Giovanni Mocenigo) and his six ducal councilors to appear before the Collegio at the end of the following week in order that that body might learn from them the means and expenses necessary for rebuilding the Ducal Palace. The Senate would then deliberate upon the most opportune plan and appropriate expense. Expansion beyond the limits and boundaries of the old palace, that is, beyond the canal, was prohibited without the express permission of the Senate. (Lorenzi, 1868, pp. 93f., doc. 199.)

In his *Res Venetae* Sabellico wrote: "That part of the Ducal Palace which burned in the meantime, began to be rebuilt from the foundations in that year in which the war [of Ferrara] was brought to its conclusion [1484]." (Sabel-

1484

lico, 1487, dec. 4, bk. 3, n.p.) 1484, the Podestàs of Pola and Rovigno were urged to facilitate the loading of the boat sent in order that Rizzo might transport stone for the rebuilding of the palace. (Paoletti, 1893, ii, p. 144.) December 8, 1484, Ser Zuan di Simon and brothers from Rovigno consented to the transfer of 50 ducats from the sum due them for stone, then being delivered, for the new building of the palace, to Antonio Rizzo, to do with as he pleased.

1485   (Lorenzi, 1868, p. 94, doc. 202.) January 31, 1485, in order to hasten the completion of the ravaged palace, the six ducal councilors decided that, of the 900 ducats from the Ufficio del Sal which were destined each month to the restoration of the Lido and, for the most part, were not spent, 500 ducats should be used each month by the Ufficio del Sal for the rebuilding of the palace. Anyone violating this decision was to be brought before the Avogadori de Comun. The Provveditori al Sal were to keep separate accounts of all the expenses of the building. The 400 ducats left over were to remain for the repair of the Lido. (Ibid., p. 96, doc. 205.) July 12, 1485, letter from the Provveditori al Sal to the stonemasons, Maestro Bertuccio Rubini and Maestro Antonio di Ricio (not Rizzo) in Istria. Maestro Antonio was told to return to Venice as he was ordered in several letters from Antonio Rizzo. Maestro Bertuccio was told to send stone of the correct dimensions and not to impede the work of Ser Francesco Buxeto, who was coming to Istria and had been given the measurements of the stones that he was to send back. (Paoletti, 1893, ii, p. 149.)

August 18, 1485, in response to a supplication made by Antonio Rizzo, the Senate decided to award Rizzo the first broker's patent at the Fondaco di Farina to fall vacant after the other posts, already conceded by the Senate to people deserving of the Senate and the Venetian state, had been given out. Rizzo had made known that, since he was entrusted with the construction of the palace, to which he devoted himself assiduously with his whole spirit and brain both night and day, as was his wont, he was compelled to abandon the shop that he had been keeping and to neglect every other thing. Yet it was impossible for him to support his family on only his salary of 100 ducats per year. Wherefore he begged the Senate to provide him with an additional recompense so that he might labor attentively and vigilantly on the construction of the palace in order to finish it as everyone desired. (Lorenzi, 1868, p. 97, doc. 207.) 1485, Rizzo's salary was raised to 125 ducats per year. (Ibid., p. 114, doc. 239.)

November 26, 1485, the Collegio decided that there be elected a *provveditore* of the construction of the palace with a yearly salary of 300 ducats, of which he would receive half, to be paid from the funds of the Ufficio del Sal. The tenure of the *provveditore* was to last one year but he might be elected for one more year. He might not be elected to any other office, either within or outside the city, at the same time. First, he was to see that stone, wood, and other necessary things be conveyed quickly and to supervise and press the work forward in such a manner that it could be finished according to the demands and desires of the city. He was to recommend to the doge as well as to the Senate any provisions to help expedite the work so that decisions might be made more opportunely and to a greater extent on the basis of practice. All records of expenditures involved in the construction were to be reviewed and signed weekly by the *provveditore* and paid by the Provveditori al Sal. This decision was apparently overruled by a decision of the Senate according to which the solicitation of work on the palace was to remain the responsibility of the Provveditori al Sal. Each month one *provveditore*, chosen by lot or agreement, was to attend to the palace and to nothing else. Every week the Provveditori al Sal were to consult with their deputy and urge him to a speedy completion of the palace. (Ibid., p. 98, doc. 209.) Evidently it was to this event that Sanudo referred in his *Vite dei dogi* when he wrote: "Zuan da Leze, councilor, moved in the Senate that a noble be elected as supervisor with 200 ducats per year, but it was decided to give the charge to one of the Provveditori al Sal." (Ibid., p. 93, doc. 198. Sanudo, however, gives the impression that the event dates from 1498.)

In his *Res Venetae* Sabellico wrote: "Since the republic was at peace at home and abroad, he [Doge Marco Barbarigo] turned his mind to the reconstruction of the Ducal Palace, work already begun; and with his care and diligence it came to pass, that after the very few months that he was prince [November 19, 1485–August 14, 1486] the whole massive structure of the quarters that faces east was brought nearly to the top with superb work." (Sabellico, 1487, dec. 4, bk. 3, n.p.) January 14, 1486, the stonecutter, Maestro Zuan q. Primo da Spalato, was mentioned at work on the palace. (Rambaldi, *Aten. ven.*, 1910, pt. 2, p. 102, n.) February 25, 1486, in consideration of the scarcity of stonemasons available for dressing the stones used in construction of the palace, the Provveditori al Sal accepted the stonemason Giorgio as a master mason for the dressing of said stones. In order that Giorgio, pressed by many debts, might work freely, the *provveditori* issued him a safe conduct, which was to protect him from molestation by any of his creditors as long as Giorgio was engaged in construction of the Ducal Palace. (Lorenzi, 1868, p. 99, doc. 211.) July 5, 1486, aware that Maestro Domenico, engineer, was then engaged on construction of the palace, three Provveditori al Sal acceded to Domenico's request that the 14 ducats per year promised him by four councilors on October 28, 1485, for the rent of his house, be given him. (Ibid., p. 100, doc. 213.)

October 12, 1486, four of the six ducal councilors relaxed a statute of the Venetian stonemasons' guild passed in 1461 according to which foreign master stonemasons who were not citizens *de intus* were denied the privileges of Venetian *maestri di bottega*. Lombard master masons had complained that since, according to the rules of the guild, they could neither trade in any product or appurtenance of their craft, nor keep apprentices to work with them, they could not live from their art without taking refuge in other cities. Antonio Rizzo, called architect of the palace, had further testified that it was necessary for the construction of the palace that the Lombards remain. The four ducal councilors concluded that, until the construction of the palace was finished, the Lombard masons might keep apprentices and buy and sell things pertaining to their profession so that they might have reason for remaining in Venice and the palace might be completed more quickly. (Ibid., p. 100, doc. 214.)

In his *Res Venetae* Sabellico wrote: "After being declared doge [August 30,

1486

1486], when all things were flourishing as before in leisure and luxury, he [Agostino Barbarigo] followed in the footsteps of his brother [Marco] and inaugurated his administration by the renewal of the Ducal Palace; which work on the facade where the entrance lies is completed in large part [i.e., by May 21, 1487] with magnificent and sumptuous display." (Sabellico, 1487, dec. 4, bk. 3, n.p.) November 22, 1487, wishing to regulate the enormous expenditures continually made by the Ufficio del Sal for masonry, carpentry, and stonecarving for vaulted rooms, shops, and for the palace and prison, and to prevent the office from being criminally defrauded, the Provveditori al Sal decided that no agreement, contract, or voucher for the execution of any future work by any supervisor, *proto*, or anyone else, might be made unless the work to be done and the consequent expenses, both of material and labor, were first examined by three, or at least two, of the *provveditori*, along with the *proto* and anyone else who might be called upon. Once these matters had been examined, the voucher for the work was to be drawn up by the *proto* of the Ufficio del Sal and countersigned by the aforesaid (two or three) *provveditori*. The work was then to be assigned by auction or by some other means to the most serviceable master. Any infringement of the above regulation was to incur a fine of 100 ducats payable to the Ufficio del Sal. All contracts were to be recorded in a book specially designated for that purpose: only those contracts so recorded might be executed or paid. (Lorenzi, 1868, p. 101, doc. 217.)

April 1, 1488, the Provveditori al Sal determined that an order of distraint be made against Maestro Quintin, stonecutter at the palace, with the proviso that within a month he was to have declared he was not a debtor. Not having made that declaration at the end of that time, he would be sent back as debtor to the palace. (Ibid., p. 102, doc. 220.) February 6, 1489, in satisfaction of a debt to Rizzo, the Provveditori al Sal decided that Antonio was to collect 53 ducats, 20 grossi from Moro fruiterer and 32 ducats, 20 grossi from Zuan Rosso, retailer of foodstuffs, who were in debt to the Ufficio del Sal. Should Antonio fail to collect from them, the *provveditori* promised to repay him themselves. (Paoletti, 1893, ii, p. 162, n. 1.) February 13, 1489, Rizzo, called *proto del palazzo*, witnessed a contract for the construction of salt magazines at Chioggia. (Lorenzi, 1868, p. 104, doc. 224.) April 10, 1489, the Provveditori al Sal contracted with Giorgio Gruato stonecutter for the execution of doors of stone from the Brioni islands, window frames, and steps. (Ibid., doc. 225.) March 27, 1490, the Signoria ordered the Provveditori al Sal to suspend the order made by the Provveditori sopra la Camera degli Imprestiti concerning the money for the palace and prison and the payments due the Ufficio del Sal, until the Signoria heard the Provveditori al Sal on the subject of that money. In the meantime the Provveditori al Sal were to pay as usual those working on the prison and the construction of the palace. It was declared that those payments were not included in the order of the Provveditori sopra la Camera degli Imprestiti because they were necessary. (Ibid., pp. 105f., doc. 228.)

August 25, 1490, Rizzo, called "protomagister marmorarius noster famosissimus," was granted the broker's patent at the Fondaco dei Tedeschi in consideration of the work and skillful abilities and faithfulness so far demonstrated in the management, regulation, work, and building of the Ducal Palace. August 28, 1490, Antonio ceded his post to his son Simplicio. In the case of Simplicio's death, the broker's patent was to revert to Antonio and remain his for the duration of his life. (Paoletti, 1893, ii, p. 148.)

December 17, 1490, Ser Zuan Piero di Domenico da Carrara, citizen and inhabitant of Lucca, was credited with 1220 ducats by the Ufficio del Sal for marbles which had been delivered. (Ibid., p. 152.)

1491   Orators had been sent to Venice by the commune of Verona, in order to induce Antonio Rizzo to execute the statues that the commune wished to place above the Palazzo del Consiglio at Verona, then nearing completion. August 26/29, 1491, the orators wrote from Venice that they had spoken with Rizzo, who had replied that he could not leave Venice because he was involved in the construction of the palace. Nor would he be permitted to leave even if he substituted other workers. On the other hand, if Verona would make him some annual allowance he would repatriate willingly. The orators had asked Rizzo to write, if and when he should decide to come to Verona for the figures of the palace, which he agreed to do. But, they concluded, the commune should not expect him to come. (Ibid., p. 147; Brenzoni, Ist. ven. SLA. Atti, 1957-58, [Cl. di scienze morali], p. 306.)

October 9, 1491, the Signoria ordered the Provveditori al Sal to meet with Rizzo and to try to reach an agreement with him concerning his continuance as builder of their palace, for the figures as well as for the staircase and other necessary things that he knew how to do, in order that he might persevere with good spirit until the construction was completed. (Lorenzi, 1868, p. 106, doc. 229.) October 10, 1491, having seen the order of the Signoria, the Provveditori al Sal summoned Antonio. Rizzo reminded them that he had been appointed to supervise the construction of the palace, both to execute the figures as well as to do all other things necessary to its construction, and that he was supporting intolerable labors, with a salary of only 125 ducats. He could neither live nor lay any money by for his old age or for his family on his salary, for he had completely shut up and abandoned his shop (with which there was sufficient work to earn even three times his salary) in order to put to rest every suspicion. He therefore requested that he be provided with a suitable salary so that he should be able to serve in good spirit and faithfully as he had done up to then. Having seen how diligently Rizzo acted in regard to the said construction and his intolerable labors, as was evident from the works accomplished, and that he was personally necessary to the completion and beauty of such work, and so that he might persevere with good heart and spirit in the requirements of that work, the Provveditori al Sal unanimously awarded Antonio a yearly salary of 200 ducats to be paid by the Ufficio del Sal. (Ibid., pp. 106f., doc. 230, and p. 114, doc. 239.)

1492   1491, audience began to be held in the new upper rooms. (Venice, Mus. Cor., MS Cicogna 3533, Magno, Annali veneti, v, c. 134v.) March 19, 1492, the doge provided a banquet for one hundred paupers and that night went to

sleep in the new palace. (Malipiero, *Arch. stor. ital.*, 1844, pt. 2, p. 689.)
Between 1491 and 1492 Sabellico wrote: "The remaining wing [of the Ducal
Palace] which, because it is being built anew, is nearly half, has, beneath the
old fabric, the little and ancient church of S. Nicolo and the tribunal where
the public Avogadori listen to the cases; above, it has the Senate according to
the old usage. The rest, where there was the old seat of the doges, which
burned in the midst of the war with Ferrara, is now rebuilt from the bottom
to the top of truly noble material, but of still more noble work." (Sabellico,

1493   [1491-92] n.d., n.p. [p. 19v].) March 23, 1493, nails were acquired for the
construction of the palace. (Lorenzi, 1868, p. 108, doc. 233.) June 22, 1493,
in a letter addressed to Messer Antonio, Antonio Rizzo reported that Maestro
Giacomo da Brescia had been hired to replace Maestro Domenico engineer,
to saw porphyry for the palace. Where the late Maestro Domenico received
one ducat, in addition to free housing, for sawing 6½ feet, Maestro Giacomo
would saw 7 feet for the same recompense, as long as he should work for the
palace. (Rambaldi, *Aten. ven.*, 1910, pt. 2, pp. 101ff., n. 2.) In his *De origine,
situ et magistratibus urbis Venetae*, dedicated to Agostino Barbarigo in August
1493, Sanudo wrote: "There remains only to make some mention of the Ducal Palace where our most serene prince resides, which is at S. Marco, a most
beautiful and worthy work. First of all, the palace where he lives, which has
been renewed in the present time and finished since 1492 and the doge went
to dwell there. It is on the canal called the Rio de Palazzo. It was built in ten
years, since, one night during the reign of Doge Giovanni Mocenigo, the old
palace burned and rebuilding was begun which, up to now, has cost more
than 100,000 ducats. Its facades are of live stone, worked and carved, with
stones sent for from all over the world. The internal landward facade is entirely gilded and carved so that it is a beautiful thing to see. Here there are
four gilded rooms than which there have not been seen by me or anyone else
for a very long time ones more beautiful [on account of] the workmanship,
in addition to the gold and expense; most excellent halls, and the public Udienza,
the Sala dei Pregadi, which is now being built; they will be most worthy."
(Sanudo, [1493] 1980, pp. 33f.)

September 11, 1493, the construction of the palace and the new *fondaco* had
been suspended for lack of funds to pay the workmen. Therefore, notwith-
standing a motion passed by the council on August 21, 1493, the Council of
Ten with its Giunta decided to pay past and current wages from the funds
destined for the maintenance of the Lido, with the proviso that the transfer of
funds not prevent the repair of holes in the Lido. (Lorenzi, 1868, p. 108, doc.
234.)

1495   December 16, 1495, since 13,868 ducats had been spent on the new
palace in the past three years and the new palace had reached such a point that
a quarter of the previous monthly expenditure would more than suffice, the
Council of Ten with its Giunta decided to reduce the expenditure on the
construction of the new palace to not more than 100 ducats per month. The
council further ruled that this sum could not be exceeded without its permission and that the monthly expenditure of 100 ducats could be made only after

300 ducats had been deposited for the month. Any violators would be subject to a penalty. The money saved in this way and thus left over from the 300 ducats was to be consigned each month to the treasurer of the council. It was to remain there intact and bound under the penalties, bonds, and strictures fixed in the decision of the Monte Nuovo. A similar provision was made at the same time in regard to the old palace and prison, where expenditures were not to exceed 300 ducats per month. Three members of the council, however, decided that since the expenditure for marble for all kinds of architraves to finish the palace was just then made, the above regulation must be superseded temporarily in order not to impede completion by the new regulation. (Lorenzi, 1868, pp. 111f., doc. 238.) December 23, 1495, the Council of Ten with its Giunta decided to abolish the salaries and pensions of a number of people who received stipends from the Ufficio del Sal. Some years before, *provveditori* had been appointed to eliminate all superfluous expenses of the various offices of the Venetian government. Presumably in 1489, the *provveditori* had eliminated salaries and pensions paid out each year by the Ufficio del Sal, many of which had been known to be unnecessary or unimportant. But immediately thereafter many of the stipends were fully restored, while new pensions and salaries were awarded to others. Therefore, on December 23, 1495, the council approved the abolition of those salaries and pensions paid out by the Ufficio del Sal that had already been annulled by the special *provveditori*, and revoked those salaries and pensions that had been restored. They also abolished those salaries and pensions that had been conceded by mandate of the Senate or Collegio or by any other means, or that had been given anew by the Provveditori al Sal or by the Procuratori di S. Marco de citra. Violating this abolition would incur immediate privation of office. Moreover, any offender would be forced to make good out of his own property whatever sum he had wrongfully paid out. The council further resolved that no pension or salary for anything connected with the Ufficio del Sal could be instituted except by the approval of two-thirds of the council, under penalty of banishment from all councils. On the other hand, if anyone receiving a salary or pension was in such need or so meritorious that he deserved to be salaried or pensioned, then the heads of the Ten could testify to the merits of that person in the council. But any motion proposed in his favor would require a two-thirds majority of the council, with its Giunta, in order to pass. The council determined, further, that five persons inscribed in the rolls but not present should be fired, and that their pensions should cease. A salary, paid by the Ufficio del Sal every Saturday at different rates, had been given to them long before because their employment as masters of stonecarving at the new palace had been demonstrated, but they neither worked nor were needed. Included in the list of those employed by the Ufficio del Sal after the reduction of expenses in 1489 was Master Antonio Rizzo, *proto del Palazzo*, with a salary of 200 ducats per year for constructing the palace, according to a decision of October 10, 1491, by the Provveditori al Sal in response to an order of the Signoria. Note was taken that from 1485 to 1491 Rizzo had received 125 ducats per year. Four other stonemasons were also recorded. From the entry

relating to Alvise di Domenico, we learn that the Provveditori al Sal had had 60 ducats per month for the workmen attached to the Ufficio del Sal, of which there were seven. After the reduction of expenses only the four eldest workmen were retained. Alvise di Domenico was inscribed in the masters' roll at 13 soldi per day to keep accounts of the live stone that was being transported from Istria for the new palace and to take note of the masters of stonecarving at work at the palace, because he was solicitous and faithful to the affairs of S. Marco. Maestro Bertuzzi, stonecutter, was inscribed by the Provveditori al Sal at 18 soldi per day to solicit the masters and to go to Istria to quarry live stone for the palace. Maestro Zuan da Spalato stonecutter was inscribed, by order of the Signoria, at 24 soldi per working day as long as he worked at the construction of the new palace. Maestro Michiel Naranza stonecutter was inscribed at 17 soldi per working day to work on the new construction of the palace because he was in a very bad state, having lost the use of his feet in the service of the Signoria. (Ibid., pp. 113ff., doc. 239.) Malipiero and Sanudo

1496 dated the slackening in the rate of construction of the Ducal Palace to 1496. They blamed it on financial difficulties caused by the wars which followed the invasion of Italy by the French under Charles VIII and the fall of Naples to the French on February 22, 1495. (Malipiero, *Arch. stor. ital.*, 1844, pt. 2, p. 699; Sanudo, *Diarii*, i, 1879, coll. 205f.)

March 22, 1496, because enormous expenditures had been made by different ministers in the construction of the palace, of which, up to then, no accounts had been seen, the Senate determined that two gentlemen, to be elected from its body, be compelled under oath to review immediately all the money disbursed for, and things allotted in, the construction of the palace. Having inquired thoroughly into the matter, the two delegates might either proceed in sentence against any malefactors that they should discover in this way, or bring them before the councils, using the means and power that the Avogadori de Comun customarily employed when proceeding against delinquents. (Lorenzi, 1868, pp. 115f., doc. 240.) October 20, 1496, the heads of the Council of Ten instructed the Provveditori al Sal that they were to pay Maestro Antonio Rizzo the amount which he was owed from his salary up to the time of its modification by the Council of Ten (i.e., October 10, 1491, when Rizzo's salary was raised from 125 to 200 ducats). The *provveditori* were instructed to pay Rizzo at the rate of his salary prior to its modification and to give him, in everything, complete and due satisfaction. (Ibid., p. 119, doc. 244.) From documents of March 7, 1499, and July 19, 1499, we learn of the prior disagreement between Antonio Rizzo and three sworn appraisers appointed to estimate the value of Maestro Giorgio Spavento's restoration of the Sala del Maggior Consiglio and other works, on account of which disagreement Giorgio had never been paid by the Ufficio del Sal. (Ibid., p. 121, doc. 249, p. 123, doc. 252.)

1498 April 5, 1498, Sanudo wrote in his diary: "Francesco Foscari and Hironimo Capelo, appointed to examine the accounts of the Signoria, had found Maestro Antonio Rizzo stonecutter, the master dedicated to the construction of the palace for the past thirteen years with a salary of 200 ducats per year, to have taken over 10,000 ducats by putting down that more had been spent in the construction of the palace of the doge, in which, up to now, it was discovered that 97,000 ducats had been spent. . . . In these days, Antonio, seeing that he had been found out, sold all his goods and his property and went toward Ancona and Foligno. He was called before the Council of Ten. It was believed that Maestro Simon Faxan, stonecutter, and others who worked with him stole a great deal." (Sanudo, *Diarii*, i, 1879, coll. 927f.) Sanudo's *Vite dei dogi* contains the following account: "Antonio Rizo stonecutter was made supervisor with 100 ducats per year, but afterwards, in 1498, it was discovered that 80,000 ducats had been spent in the construction of the palace of which not a half had been done—80,000 ducats not spent, but, for the most part, stolen; wherefore Zuan da Leze, councilor, moved in the Senate that a noble be elected as supervisor with 200 ducats per year. But it was decided to give the charge to one of the Provveditori al Sal. And in the end it was discovered that Antonio Rizzo had stolen 12,000 ducats. He fled to Folgino and died there." (Lorenzi, 1868, p. 93, doc. 198.) Malipiero wrote: "Antonio Rizo was put in charge [of the rebuilding of the Ducal Palace] with 100 ducats per year. This Antonio Rizzo had spent 80,000 ducats by 1498 and not even a half of the building had been done; and it was discovered that he had falsified vouchers upon the Ufficio del Sal for 12,000 ducats; and he fled and went to the Romagna; and soon after, he died at Foligno; and everything of his that was found, was sold." (Malipiero, *Arch. stor. ital.*, 1844, pt. 2, p. 674.)

   May 16, 1498, Pietro Lombardo was placed in charge of construction of the Ducal Palace in Rizzo's stead. (Lorenzi, 1868, pp. 121f., docs. 250, 251.)

Petition for a Patent for the Production of Mills

1488	September 17, 1488, Antonio Rizo sculptor and Zorzi di Amadeo da Lugano petitioned the doge (Agostino Barbarigo) for a patent to construct mills, buildings, and mechanisms for which they had invented a new form and means of construction. They asked that the patent, which should extend to their heirs and descendants, last for seventy years, during which time no one else might be allowed to make or use the mills. The petition was granted by the Senate. (Ludwig, 1911, pp. 14f.; Paoletti, 1893, ii, p. 161.)
1489	November 10, 1489, Rizzo acted as guarantor for Ser Bernardin, salt merchant at the Rialto. (Paoletti, 1893, ii, p. 162, n. 1.)
1490	November 7, 1490, Rizzo and Mauro Codussi were chosen as arbiters to evaluate the work done on the frontispiece of the facade of the Scuola di S. Marco by Pietro Lombardo, Giovanni Buora, and Bartolomeo di Domenico Duca, in a dispute which had arisen between the members of the confraternity and the three stonemasons. (Ibid., p. 103, doc. 73.)
1493	February 22, 1493, Rizzo had designed two vaulted rooms in the Ufficio della Messettaria, one of which was provisionally offered for rent from March 1, 1493 to Messer Andrea Zanchani. (Ibid., p. 162, n. 1.)

1495   Early months of 1495, Rizzo and Pietro Lombardo were called upon to appraise Sebastiano da Milano's frame for the altarpiece of the high altar of S. Giovanni in Bragora. (Humfrey, 1977, app. 1, p. 402; Humfrey, *AB*, 1980, p. 355.)

June 25, 1495, Rizzo, living in the parish of S. Giovanni Nuovo, appeared as a witness in Venice. (Cecchetti, *Arch. ven.*, xxxiii, 1887, p. 423.) September 22, 1495, Rizzo witnessed the testament of Lucia Trevisano, widow of Ser Giorgio Bembo. (Ludwig, 1911, p. 15.)

Reconstruction of the External Loggias of the Palazzo della Ragione, Vicenza

1496   April 20, 1496, a part of the upper gallery surrounding the Palazzo della Ragione at Vicenza collapsed, just two years after the building had been completed. The Gothic palace, begun in 1449-50, had been encased in a double tier of loggias by Tommaso Formenton between 1481 and 1494. The upper portico possessed an arcade with pointed arches whose form and spacing corresponded to the ogival profiles of the windows of the principal *salone*. For every two bays of the upper gallery there was one bay in the ground-floor arcade. Its arches were semicircular. Immediately after its partial collapse, the building was buttressed to prevent it from falling down.

At some unspecified date Rizzo was summoned to Vicenza to advise on the repair of the structure. In later testimony he recalled having said to the deputies "that the galleries were badly constructed both beneath and above and the lower porticoes (were not made) with that durability which was proper to the city. And this because the columns on the bottom were made too wide and disproportionate, and that it was necessary to make the vaults narrower, with a different proportion from what had been made, and that if they wished to repair it, it was necessary to replace everything." The deputies had objected that the expense would be too great and asked Rizzo to see whether it was possible to repair it more cheaply. (Arnaldi, 1767, p. cxx, doc. E; Zorzi, iii, 1937, p. 129, doc. III.) Having apparently reduced the scope of his proposals, Rizzo committed his provisions to writing. Copper clamps were to be inserted in the cornice under the galleries and in all the vaults, particularly at their corners where one vault adjoined another. Copper chains were to be introduced at the corner of the portico above the summit of the vaults, in the arches above the capitals, and beneath the columns of the gallery, where they were to be leaded into the keystones of the vaults of the ground-floor portico. Because of the excessive width of the intercolumniations, Rizzo advised substituting for the round columns of the ground-floor portico, especially for those at the corners, square piers or pilasters. He reasoned that it would be possible to narrow the intervals between columns by increasing the width of the supports. But increasing the width of round columns (without increasing their height) would produce disproportionate members. Therefore piers were

preferable to columns. If, on the other hand, the deputies wanted round columns, the columns should be as thick as those then located at the corners,
and their capitals should be surmounted by square blocks in the form of beams.
Rizzo also suggested shortening the brackets of the vault so that half a foot
might be eliminated from the semicircular arches. Finally, he proposed re-
making the foundations at the corners of the building. The foundations there
should measure 10 feet on each face. At the bottom, beams of oak or larch as
thick as possible and 12 feet long were to be laid in two layers, one crossing
the other. Over that, slabs of stone, joined together with copper clamps, were
to be set. Above the foundations, the corner was to measure 2½ feet on each
face. Detail drawings of the foundation, the clamping of vaults to one another
at their corners, and the juncture of the buckle of a chain with a block of stone
accompanied the report. (Arnaldi, 1767, pp. cxviiif, doc. D; Zorzi, iii, 1937,
pp. 127f., doc. I.) Presumably this report was made somewhat before May
11, 1496, when Maestro Domenico, carpenter, was paid 2 ducats for having
made two wooden models of two columns of the portico of the palace. (Zorzi,
iii, 1937, p. 25, n. 3.)

Rizzo's proposals were criticized by the architect Alessio and others, who
claimed that the restoration Rizzo advised, in which the galleries were retained
as they were but the ground-floor portico was altered, would last several
years, but not forever. July 3, 1496, the Council of 100 empowered its deputies to consult with one, two, or more architects about means for restoring
the building, that would ensure the permanence of the fabric. The results of
those consultations were to be examined and deliberated by the council. (Ibid.,
pp. 128f., doc. II.)

July 7, 1496, Alvise Pace was sent to Venice to bring Rizzo back for further
consultation. (Ibid., p. 13, n. 2.) In accordance with the desire of the deputies
that restoration be permanent, Rizzo then made a written report of his new
proposals. That report was read in a second meeting of the Council of 100
held on July 15, 1496, at which Rizzo was present. In his second report Rizzo
stated that the galleries should be taken down, the stones kept apart and then
reinstalled, at which time all the vaults and other stones were to be clamped
in the necessary places. On the ground floor the columns or pilasters were to
be placed closer to one another and the columns of the ground-floor portico
and second-story gallery were to be aligned "so that every weight carries its
own weight." Should the council accept his proposals, Rizzo offered to make
a measured drawing that would show how the work was to be done. The
council approved Rizzo's new provisions, according to which the supports of
the ground-floor portico were to be made square and spaced as densely as the
columns of the upper gallery, and all the stones of the upper gallery were to
be taken down and then reinstalled. A model or drawing of this would be
given by Rizzo. The council further determined that work should not com-
mence without the presence of the architect and that the doge should be begged
to permit Rizzo to take charge of the construction for whatever length of time
might be conceded. This motion, they concluded could not be amended without the approval of three-quarters of the council. (Arnaldi, 1767, pp. cxixff.,

doc. E; Zorzi, iii, 1937, pp. 129f., doc. III.) The work of restoration began on August 4, 1496 with the dismantling of the upper loggia. (Ibid., pp. 27f.)

1498   March 22, 1498, there was passed in the Council of 100 a motion according to which the original loggias were to be retained and restored as Rizzo, Giorgio Spavento, and other experts had advised, because the work would be uniform and could be brought to a speedier conclusion. Work was to proceed in accordance with the proposals made by Spavento and was to be superintended by an architect chosen by eleven deputies who were to act as overseers of the work. (Arnaldi, 1767, pp. cxxiff., doc. F; Zorzi, iii, 1937, pp. 131f., doc. IV.) However, these provisions were not put into effect and work proceeded in a partial manner according to the preceding project. Part of the upper loggia was taken down. (Zorzi, iii, 1937, p. 14.) By August 1502 the ground-floor arcades had risen to the bottom of the second story on the northwest corner of the structure. In 1502 work was broken off and not resumed. In 1542 Giulio Romano furnished a new model for the building. Palladio's plan, in accordance with which the Palazzo della Ragione was finally rebuilt, was adopted in 1549. (Ibid., pp. 27ff., 144ff.)

1497   Between September 9, 1497, and October 23, 1497, Rizzo was involved in procuring emery and Carrara marble for the Studiolo of Isabella d'Este at Mantua. Isabella had commissioned a doorway and a window for the Studiolo from Gian Cristoforo Romano and had charged him with selecting at Venice the stone necessary for its decoration. Gian Cristoforo, in turn, applied to Rizzo, who located a source of emery and found for Isabella three thousand weights of Carrara marble at 3½ ducats per thousand weight. (Mantua, Archivio di Stato, Archivio Gonzaga, Busta 2992, Copialettere, Libro 7, c. 12, Libro 8, c. 65, Libro 9, cc. 1v, 4v; Busta 1436, cc. 145-146; Busta 1437. Two of the relevant documents were published by Luzio/Renier, 1890, pp. 137f. I am grateful to Drs. Clifford Brown and Wendy Sheard for permission to summarize the contents of these documents.)

1498   1498 having fled Venice, Rizzo stopped for a time at Cesena, then proceeded to Ferrara. This information is related by a late-fifteenth- and early-sixteenth-century chronicler from Cesena, Giuliano Fantaguzzi, who wrote under the year 1498: "Maestro Piero Rizo da Venezia, most worthy sculptor, in charge of the building of S. Marco for a long time and author of *Adam* and *Eve*, most beautiful figures, this year, having been imprisoned by Venice, fled and came to live here in Cesena and then went to Ferrara." (Grigioni, *L'arte*, 1910,
1499   p. 44.) February 4, 1499, Rizzo was present in Cesena where he witnessed a document. (Ibid., p. 45.)

May 4, 1499, apparently Rizzo was still alive. (Paoletti, 1893, ii, p. 148, n. 1.)

Catalogue

Entries are arranged alphabetically according to their present or former locations. In the individual entries the following topics are considered in sequence:

1. Location. Right and left refer to the spectator's right and left.
2. Description of monument when the monument is no longer extant.
3. Material and polychromy.
4. Condition, including elements missing or replaced.
5. Measurements. Dimensions are metric.

Height precedes width; width precedes depth.

6. Inscriptions.
7. Bibliography. Items are arranged in chronological order. Unpublished manuscripts have been included. Superscribed Arabic numerals preceding the date of publication indicate edition. Dates within parentheses indicate the date of composition or first publication.

A catalogue of authentic works is succeeded by a catalogue of rejected attributions.

AUTHENTIC WORKS

1. Amsterdam, Private Collection (formerly): *Madonna and Child*

Fig. 29

In 1930 the relief was privately owned in Amsterdam. I have not been able to trace it.

Marble.

Planiscig, *Dedalo*, x, 1929-30, p. 468.

In 1930 Planiscig attributed the relief to the so-called Master of S. Trovaso, the author of the antependium of the altar of the Cappella Clary in S. Trovaso, Venice.[1] The relief has elicited no other comment in the art-historical literature.

A copy of this relief is affixed to the wall of a house fronting the Rio di S. Marcuola at 2049 Cannaregio.[2] A second copy, within a rectangular field and lacking Angels and clouds, is immured in the courtyard of the Palazzo della Canonica at S. Marco.

[1] Planiscig, *Dedalo*, x, 1929-30, p. 468.
[2] Piamonte [1966], p. 161.

2. Aquileia, Basilica: *Man of Sorrows*

Figs. 53-59

The *Man of Sorrows* is incorporated into the reredos of the Altar of the Sacrament located immediately to the right of the presbytery at the east end of the basilica.

White marble. In the background are numerous traces of turquoise paint evidently applied over a gray ground. Gray paint is visible in Christ's crown of thorns and in the ground beneath the feet of the right-hand Angel.

The relief has not been brought to a high state of finish. The inscription in the scroll at the bottom of the relief has been obliterated. There are tiny chips in the index finger of Christ's right hand and in the scroll held by the left-hand Angel. Otherwise the relief is well preserved.

71.9 cm. x 118.1 cm.

TE CELEBRĀT POPVLI[,] TE / STĀTVR CVNCTA CRE-ATA is inscribed in the scroll held by the left-hand Angel. TV CAELI MV[N]DI QVE SA / LVS[,] TV VICTOR AVERNI is inscribed in the scroll held by the right-hand Angel. The scroll at the base of the relief originally contained a two-line inscription. It is no longer possible to make out more than a couple of letters and the remnant of a date.

Ferrante, 1852, p. 62; [Valussi], 1876, p. 20; Joppi, *Archeografo triestino*, 1895, p. 220; Nieman in Lanckoroński, 1906, p. 8; Swoboda in ibid., pp. 112, n. 8, 113; Planiscig, *Forum Iulii*, 1910, pp. 54f.; Planiscig, *Emporium*, 1911, p. 291; Folnesics/Planiscig, 1916, text, pp. 15, 28, pl. 16, fig. C; Planiscig, *Kunst und Kunsthandwerk*, 1916, p. 386; Costantini, n.d. [1916], pp. 61f.; Planiscig, 1921, p. 71; Planiscig, *VJ*, 1926, p. 102; Vale in *La Basilica di Aquileia*, 1933, pp. 66f., 71, 72; Morassi in ibid., p. 340; Scrinari, 1958, p. 66; Someda in *Arte e artisti*, 1959, i, pp. 329ff.; Donati, 1961, p. 33, n. 2; Brusin, [4]1961, p. 17; TCI, *Friúli*, 1963, p. 288; Tigler in Egg et al., [1]1965, pp. 41, 42; ibid., [2]1972, ii, pt. 2, pp. 41, 42.

The provenance of the *Man of Sorrows* has never been questioned: it is generally assumed that the relief was made for the position it now occupies in the reredos of the Altar of the Sacrament. But an examination of the motifs and execution of the reredos proves it a pastiche—perhaps of the early nineteenth century.[1] Indeed, it is unlikely that the *Man of Sorrows* was ever intended for a reredos at all: rather, its size and format match those of altar frontals where the theme of Christ as Man of Sorrows often figures.

If the *Man of Sorrows* was not originally intended for its present site, where does it come from? The relief is not documented or described in early sources; any proposal regarding its provenance, therefore, is purely hypothetical. It is with this proviso that I suggest, as the relief's origin, the Chapel of the Corpus Christi in the basilica at Aquileia, whose construction several documents record.[2] On March 10, 1471, Don Agapito della Pergola donated 50 ducats from whose income masses, to be said at the "new Chapel of the Corpus Christi," were to be endowed. Previously, on July 13, 1468, a Master Antonio da Venezia, mason or stonecarver, had been assigned 30 ducats for the delivery of stone for the "building around the tabernacle of Corpus Christi." Apparently, Master Antonio's work did not meet with unqualified approval and he was dismissed. On April 12, 1474, the dean of the chapter, Don Doimo, contracted with Master Gasparino dei Matendelli da Lugano for a price of 40 ducats for the execution and installation of work that Antonio had left unfinished. This comprised the completion of two stone shells ("cappae lapideas") that were not yet dressed, as well as a third that had been left roughhewn; the completion of two columns, one of which had been begun and was already fluted, while the other had not been dressed; the polishing of two capitals; the completion of three architraves. The work was to be finished by the coming Lent. The Chapel of the Corpus Christi is usually assumed to be the Altar of the Sacrament, which encloses the reredos with Rizzo's *Man of Sorrows*. The correspondence of the members enumerated in the documents with those of the Altar of the Sacrament, and the absence of any other structure in the Basilica of Aquileia with which the documents can be linked, lends credence to the identification.

Evidence that favors identifying the provenience of the *Man of Sorrows* with the Chapel of the Corpus Christi admittedly is scant. No document records the construction of an altar for this chapel. Therefore we do not know if a new one was made or not. On the other hand, the present altar table is not original. The relief's hypothetical date of 1470-75, arrived at independently on the basis of its style, supports the connection of the *Man of Sorrows* with the documented chapel. To the altar of a chapel dedicated to the body of Christ, the theme of Christ as *Man of Sorrows* would have been doubly apposite.

The attribution of the *Man of Sorrows* to Rizzo and the hypothetical connection of the relief with the Chapel of the Corpus Christi tempt us to identify the "magister Antonius de Venetiis murarius sive lapicida," initially responsible for constructing the chapel, as Antonio Rizzo.[3] But apart from the facts that known documents unfailingly record Rizzo's surname and that, strictly speaking, Rizzo did not come from Venice, nothing in the architecture of the tabernacle bears the slightest resemblance, either in motif or execution, to secure works by Rizzo. We may assume, therefore, that the fabrication of the architecture and sculpture was contracted separately in Venice.

Bernardino da Bissone, known to have been present in Aquileia in the early 1490s and supposed to have been employed, under Domenico dei Maffei, in the restoration of the basilica, is commonly credited with the relief of the *Man of Sorrows*. Traditional already by 1852,[4] the attribution to Bernardino survived a century's consideration of the work, despite obvious discrepancies of style between the relief and Bernardino's authenticated sculptures.[5] Indeed, in an effort to describe Bernardino's style in the *Man of Sorrows*, Planiscig repeatedly called on Rizzo, along with the Lombardos.[6] Not even Vale's publication of documents relating to the Chapel of the Corpus Christi, which were thought to provide a date for the Altar of the Sacrament and its supposedly authentic dossal approximately twenty years before Bernardino's arrival in Aquileia,[7] sufficed to eradicate the attribution. Someda was alone in using the new documents, as well as stylistic comparisons with Bernardino's documented works, in his successful rebuttal of the attribution. Identifying the Chapel of the Corpus Christi with the Altar of the Sacrament, Someda assumed that the first master of the chapel had also been charged with carving the relief, and therefore ascribed the *Man of Sorrows* to Antonio da Venezia. But Someda made no attempt to connect the relief with any other works and offered no hypotheses regarding Antonio's identity.[8] Perhaps for this reason, even the most recent and authoritative guidebooks retain the attribution of the *Man of Sorrows* to Bernardino da Bissone.[9]

[1] See above, ch. 2, p. 40.
[2] Vale in *La Basilica di Aquileia,* 1933, p. 66, nn.

2, 3, 4, p. 67, n. 2; Udine, Seminario Arcivescovile, Archivio Capitolare, *Acta Capituli Aquileiensis,* iii, c. 45.

[3] Vale, ibid., pp. 66f., believed that the nonfulfillment of Antonio's agreement, indicated by the existence of a subsequent contract with Gasparino dei Matendelli, was occasioned by Antonio's death. The documents, however, say nothing of Antonio's death and a systematic search of Vale's papers failed to uncover any other basis for this assertion. (Vale's papers are preserved in Udine, Arcivescovado, Biblioteca Arcivescovile, Sala Bartolini, MS Vale 522. I am grateful to Prof. De Biasio for having facilitated my search.) The absence of proof concerning Antonio's death removes any obstacle from identifying "magister Antonius de Venetiis murarius sive lapicida" with Antonio Rizzo.

[4] Ferrante, 1852, p. 62.

[5] [Valussi], 1876, p. 20; Swoboda in Lanckoroński, 1906, p. 112, n. 8, p. 113; Planiscig, *Forum Iulii,* 1910, pp. 54f.; Planiscig, *Emporium,* 1911, p. 291; Folnesics/Planiscig, 1916, pl. 16, fig. C; Planiscig, *Kunst und Kunsthandwerk,* 1916, p. 386; Planiscig, 1921, p. 71; Costantini, n.d. [1916], pp. 61f.; Planiscig, *VJ,* 1926, p. 102; Morassi in *La Basilica di Aquileia,* 1933, p. 340; Scrinari, 1958, p. 66; Tigler in Egg *et al.,* [1]1965, p. 42. Joppi, *Archeografo triestino,* 1895, p. 220, hesitantly suggested the authorship of Domenico dei Maffei.

[6] Folnesics/Planiscig, 1916, pl. 16, fig. C; Planiscig, *Kunst und Kunsthandwerk,* 1916, p. 386. Planiscig, 1921, p. 71, compared the Angels in the relief with the garland-bearing *Victory* of the Scala dei Giganti. Morassi in *La Basilica di Aquileia,* 1933, p. 340, explicitly rejected Planiscig's postulation of a stylistic affinity with the art of Rizzo. Like Costantini, n.d. [1916], p. 61, Morassi perceived similarities with the art of the Lombardos.

[7] Vale in *La Basilica di Aquileia,* 1933, pp. 66f. Vale inferred a *terminus ante quem* of 1471 for the *Man of Sorrows* from the endowment in that year of masses to be celebrated at the Altar of the Corpus Christi, despite the fact that masses could be, and often were, endowed before the altars at which they were to be said were built.

[8] Someda in *Arte e artisti,* 1959, i, pp. 329ff.

[9] TCI, *Friúli,* 1963, p. 288; Tigler in Egg *et al.,* [2]1972, ii, pt. 2, p. 42.

3. Berlin, Kaiser-Friedrich-Museum (formerly): *Victories*

Figs. 130, 131

The *Victories* were acquired in 1884 in Venice by the Kaiser-Friedrich-Museum (inv. nos. 220a, b). They were lost during World War II.

Istrian limestone.

Right *Victory*: 66 cm. x 108 cm.; left *Victory*: 66 cm. x 107 cm.

Berlin, Königl. Mus. Catalogue by Bode/Tschudi, 1888, pp. 54f., no. 174; Berlin, Königl. Mus. Catalogue by Schottmüller, [1]1913, p. 120, no. 292; Berlin, Staatl. Mus., Kaiser-Friedrich-Mus. Catalogue by Schottmüller, [2]1933, pp. 116f., no. 220.

The *Victories* were first catalogued by Bode and Tschudi as belonging to a Venetian sculptor of the end of the fifteenth century close in style to the master of the altar frontal in the Cappella Clary, S. Trovaso, Venice. To the author of the Berlin *Victories* Bode and Tschudi also assigned the relief of *Putti with Arms of the Barbarigo Family* on the *rio* facade of the Ducal Palace.[1] Noting analogies with the *Victories* of the *Scala dei Giganti*, which then passed as a joint work of Rizzo and the Lombardos, Schottmüller labeled the *Victories* in Berlin "manner of Antonio Rizzo?"[2] Convinced by Planiscig's attribution of the *Scala dei Giganti Victories* to Rizzo, Schottmüller unqualifiedly assigned the Berlin *Victories* to Rizzo in the second edition of her catalogue.[3]

[1] Berlin, Königl. Mus. Catalogue by Bode/Tschudi, 1888, pp. 54f., no. 174.
[2] Berlin, Königl. Mus. Catalogue by Schottmüller, [1]1913, p. 120, no. 292.
[3] Berlin, Staatl. Mus., Kaiser-Friedrich-Mus. Catalogue by Schottmüller, [2]1933, pp. 116f., no. 220.

4. East Berlin, Staatliche Museen: *St. John the Evangelist*

Fig. 135

St. John was acquired in Venice from the Pajaro Collection in 1841 by the Königliche Museen, Berlin (inv. no. 221). Since World War II the statue has belonged to the Staatliche Museen, East Berlin.

White Carrara marble. There are no traces of polychromy or gilding.

The figure is entirely finished. The *Evangelist*'s right hand has been reattached with mortar. The thumb and index finger are largely worn away and the bowl of the chalice, once held in the figure's right hand, is lost. Chips are missing from the toes of both feet and from the hem of the gown by the figure's right foot. The tip of the figure's nose is chipped slightly. The projecting surfaces of drapery, hair, and nose have been worn by rain.

84 cm. high.

[Wynne], 1787, pls. xxvii, xxviii; Berlin, Königl. Mus. Catalogue by Bode/Tschudi, 1888, p. 55, no. 175; Berlin, Königl. Mus. Catalogue by Schottmüller, [1]1913, p. 122, no. 298; Vienna, Ksthis. Mus. Catalogue by Planiscig, 1919, pp. 51f., no. 92; Planiscig, 1921, pp. 70f., 187; Schottmüller, *Kunstchronik und Kunstmarkt*, Feb. 3, 1922, p. 322; Valentiner, *Art in America*, 1925, p. 319; Berlin, Staatl. Mus., Kaiser-Friedrich-Mus. Catalogue by Schottmüller, [2]1933, p. 116, no. 221, pp. 118f., no. 218; Planiscig, T-B, xxviii, 1934, p. 409.

In 1786 *St. John the Evangelist* was installed on a socle in the garden of the Villa Altichiero near Padua by its owner, Angelo Quirini. On this site the statue was reproduced in two anonymous engravings for a book on Quirini's villa. In both engravings, *St. John* was depicted with chalice and halo.[1]

In the Berlin catalogue of 1888 the *Evangelist* figured as the work of a Venetian master of the second half of the fifteenth century.[2] Comparing it to the Tomb of Doge Pasquale Malipiero in SS. Giovanni e Paolo and the *Annunciate Angel* from the triumphal arch of S. Giobbe,

Schottmüller described the statue as having been carved in the manner of Pietro Lombardo.[3] Planiscig concurred,[4] although he later changed his mind. Noting analogies between *St. John* and *Prudence, Charity*, and the right-hand (?) shield-bearer from the Tron Tomb, and the *Pages* from the Emo Tomb, Planiscig attributed the *Evangelist* to Rizzo, albeit with some hesitation.[5] In her review of Planiscig's book, Schottmüller chose for special commendation Planiscig's new attribution of *St. John*.[6] Nevertheless, she retained the label, "manner of Pietro Lombardo," in the second edition of her catalogue.[7] Valentiner included *St. John* in a motley group of sculptures whose author he willfully identified as Pietro Lombardo.[8]

[1] [Wynne], 1787, pls. xxvii, xxviii. The socle was faced with an inscription dated 1786 and three Venetian Quattrocento reliefs of Angels subsequently acquired by the museum at Berlin (inv. no. 218).
[2] Berlin, Königl. Mus. Catalogue by Bode/Tschudi, 1888, p. 55, no. 175.
[3] Berlin, Königl. Mus. Catalogue by Schottmüller, ¹1913, p. 122, no. 298.
[4] Vienna, Ksthis. Mus. Catalogue by Planiscig, 1919, pp. 51f., no. 92.
[5] Planiscig, 1921, pp. 70f., 187. Planiscig, T-B, xxviii, 1934, p. 409, defined the figure as very close to Rizzo.
[6] Schottmüller, *Kunstchronik und Kunstmarkt*, Feb. 3, 1922, p. 322.
[7] Berlin, Staatl. Mus., Kaiser-Friedrich-Mus. Catalogue by Schottmüller, ²1933, p. 116, no. 221.
[8] Valentiner, *Art in America*, 1925, p. 319.

5. Vaduz, Collection of the Prince of Liechtenstein: *Madonna and Child*

Fig. 160

Acquired in Venice from the art dealer Guggenheim, the relief entered the collection of the Prince of Liechtenstein in 1882.[1] It is currently in storage in the prince's castle at Vaduz.

White marble. Traces of polychromy remain in the irises of the Madonna and in the border of the relief. There is no evidence of gilding.

The cross held by the Madonna is carved from a separate piece of marble and is attached with mortar. Most likely it is a later addition. Probably the relief was originally slightly higher than it is now and was rectangular. The corners of the ledge are badly chipped. The Virgin is missing the last joints of the last two fingers of her upraised hand. Other minor chips impair the surface of the fold that hangs from the Virgin's lowered hand, the top of her headdress, and the second and third fingers of her upraised hand. Otherwise, the relief is in good condition.

39.5 cm. x 33.5 cm.

Bode, text, 1892-1905, p. 46, n. 1; ibid., iv, 1895-96, pl. 164b; Vienna, Ksthis. Mus. Catalogue by Planiscig, 1919, pp. 52ff., no. 93; Planiscig, 1921, pp. 177ff., 198, 204; Bode, *Der Kunstwanderer*, May 15-31, 1922, p. 426; Schottmüller, *Rep. f. Kstw.*, 1924, p. 135; Planiscig, *Dedalo*, x, 1929-30, pp. 468f., 479; Planiscig, *Dedalo*, xi, 1930-31, p. 31; Tietze, *Vie d'Italia*, 1931, p. 402; Planiscig, T-B, xxvii, 1933, pp. 480f.; Bregenz, Künstlerhaus, Palais Thurn und Taxis. *Meisterwerke der Plastik*, ed. Sandner, 1967, p. 64, no. 99.

The caption beneath the illustration of the relief in Bode's work on Tuscan sculpture reads "unknown pupil of Donatello." But in the text, Bode described the relief as a reflection of the art of Antonio Rossellino.[2] Planiscig included the relief in a group of several late Quattrocento and early Cinquecento Venetian reliefs—for the most part, identical in theme but disparate in style—which he ascribed in 1919 to the Master of Altichiero[3] and in 1921 to Pyrgoteles.[4] The relief was dated to the 1480s.[5] Bode[6] and Schottmüller[7] were not convinced of the stylistic unity of the group, whether attributed to the Master of Altichiero or to Pyrgoteles. Indeed, Schottmüller was doubtful of the authenticity of our relief. By 1930 Planiscig had abandoned his attribution of the relief to Pyrgoteles, crediting instead the anonymous Venetian sculptor, active from ca. 1470, who carved the relief of S. Giovannino in S. Maria del Giglio.[8] Elsewhere Planiscig described the Liechtenstein relief as close in style to the sculpture of Pietro Lombardo.[9] Tietze illustrated it as the work of an unknown Venetian.[10] Planiscig's attribution of the relief to Pyrgoteles was adopted reservedly in the catalogue of the exhibition at Bregenz.[11]

¹ Letter of May 29, 1974 from Dr. Gustav Wilhelm.

² Bode, iv, 1895-96, pl. 164b; ibid., text, 1892-1905, p. 46, n. 1. Bode erroneously located the relief in the Museo Nazionale at Florence.

³ Vienna, Ksthis. Mus. Catalogue by Planiscig, 1919, pp. 52ff., no. 93. Planiscig named the master after the anonymous reliefs of the antependium in the Staatliche Museen, West Berlin (inv. no. 218) from the Villa Altichiero.

⁴ Planiscig, 1921, pp. 177ff.

⁵ Ibid., p. 204.

⁶ Bode, *Der Kunstwanderer*, May 15-31, 1922, p. 426.

⁷ Schottmüller, *Rep. f. Kstw.*, 1924, p. 135.

⁸ Planiscig, *Dedalo*, x, 1929-30, pp. 468f., 479; Planiscig, T-B, xxvii, 1933, pp. 480f.

⁹ Planiscig, *Dedalo*, xi, 1930-31, p. 31.

¹⁰ Tietze, *Vie d'Italia*, 1931, p. 402.

¹¹ Bregenz, Künstlerhaus, Palais Thurn und Taxis. *Meisterwerke der Plastik*, ed. Sandner, 1967, p. 64, no. 99.

6. Venice, Ducal Palace: *Madonna and Child*

Fig. 161

The relief is located over the northwest door of the Camera degli Scarlatti, in the Appartamenti dei Dogi of the Ducal Palace.

Marble. With the exception of the background, the entire relief is polychromed. The Madonna's dress and cloak are dark green; her veil and the garment of the Christ Child are white; the garment of the left-hand Angel and the sash of the Christ Child are olive brown; hair and eyes are brown; flesh is naturalistically colored; cheeks and lips are rose; wings, haloes, the button of the Madonna's veil, and the cuff of her dress are gilded.

A rectangular plug of marble is visible in the lower left corner below a chip in the molding of the relief. Several circular rusty holes centered within larger square holes, scattered over the surface of the relief, suggest that the relief was once shot at. The limestone frame (not illustrated) was added to the relief in 1529.

Relief minus its frame: 89 cm. x 68 cm.

· M · D · XXVIIII · is inscribed at the top of the frame. Initials surmounting coats of arms are inscribed in the brackets. From left to right, they are: · M · G · above Gritti arms; · HI · TA · above Tagliapietra arms; · A · M · above Miani arms. They may be the initials of Michele di Marco Gritti, Girolamo di Quintin Tagliapietra, and Angelo di Marco Miani, respectively.

Semrau, 1890, p. 82; Paoletti, 1893, ii, p. 266, n. 1; *Pal. Duc.*, 1912, p. 41; M. Ongaro, n.d. [ca. 1913], p. 72; Planiscig, 1921, pp. 202f.; Bode, *Der Kunstwanderer*, May 15-31, 1922, p. 426; Schottmüller, *Rep. f. Kstw.*, 1924, p. 135; Lorenzetti, ¹1926, p. 271; Planiscig, *Dedalo*, x, 1929-30, p. 469; Planiscig, T-B, xxvii, 1933, pp. 480f.; Serra, 1933, p. 21; Belvedere, 1960, p. 50; Bassi/Trincanato, 1964, p. 24; Hubala in Egg *et al.*, ¹1965, p. 650; Musolino in Tramontin *et al.*, 1965, p. 251; Franzoi, 1973, p. 50.

Although he did not hazard an attribution, Paoletti, unlike Semrau, recognized that the relief was earlier than the date incised in its frame.¹ Ongaro mentioned attributions to Alessandro Leopardi but neglected to cite his sources.² Planiscig associated the *Madonna and Child* with that heterogeneous group of Venetian reliefs with which he credited Pyrgoteles, but found its quality insufficient to justify an attribution to the master.³ Neither Bode,⁴ nor Schottmüller⁵ were persuaded of the stylistic unity of the group. Planiscig, himself, soon abandoned his reconstruction of Pyrgoteles's oeuvre.⁶ Lorenzetti labeled the relief "Paduan school, end of the 15th century."⁷ He was followed by Serra⁸ and Musolino.⁹ Belvedere,¹⁰ Bassi and Trincanato,¹¹ and Franzoi¹² accepted a Paduan provenance, but dated the *Madonna and Child* to 1529. Hubala identified its author as probably Venetian, under Paduan influence.¹³

¹ Paoletti, 1893, ii, p. 266, n. 1. Semrau, 1890, p. 82, merely dated the relief to 1529.

² M. Ongaro, n.d. [ca. 1913], p. 72. It was probably from the fact that Paoletti illustrated the relief in his chapter on Leopardi that Ongaro deduced an attribution which, in fact, Paoletti never made.

³ Planiscig, 1921, pp. 202f.

⁴ Bode, *Die Kunstwanderer*, May 15-31, 1922, p. 426.

⁵ Schottmüller, *Rep. f. Kstw.*, 1924, p. 135.

⁶ Planiscig, *Dedalo*, x, 1929-30, p. 469; Planiscig, T-B, xxvii, 1933, pp. 480f.

[7] Lorenzetti, ¹1926, p. 271.
[8] Serra, 1933, p. 21.
[9] Musolino in Tramontin et al., 1965, p. 251.
[10] Belvedere, 1960, p. 50.

[11] Bassi/Trincanato, 1964, p. 24.
[12] Franzoi, 1973, p. 50.
[13] Hubala in Egg et al., ¹1965, p. 650.

7. Venice, Ducal Palace: *Putti with Arms of the Barbarigo Family*

Fig. 155

The relief is located over a subsidiary portal toward the north end of the east facade of the Ducal Palace. It is visible only from the Rio del Palazzo.

Limestone.

A vertical crack divides the relief near its center. Otherwise the relief is well preserved. Two metal rings, apparently meant for torches, are attached to the background on either side of the shield.

Zanotto, i, 1842-53, I. "Piante ed esterno del Palazzo Ducale," p. 368; Berlin, Königl. Mus. Catalogue by Bode/Tschudi, 1888, p. 55, no. 174; Paoletti, 1893, ii, pp. 156f.; Burckhardt/Bode/Fabriczy, ⁷1898, ii, pt. 1, p. 122e; Venturi, *Storia*, vi, 1908, p. 1088; Moschetti, Padua, Mus. Civ. *Boll.*, 1914, p. 9; Venturi, *Storia*, x, pt. 1, 1935, p. 388; Mariacher, *Pal. Duc.*, 1950, p. 29; Pignatti, 1956, p. 36.

The relief has aroused little interest; nevertheless, there is some agreement in interpretation of its style. Bode and Tschudi attributed the relief to the master of the *Victories*, formerly in Berlin (cat. no. 3), whose style they found close to that of the altar frontal in the Cappella Clary, S. Trovaso.[1] Paoletti assigned the relief to the author of the *Victories* of the Scala dei Giganti, whom he identified as Antonio Rizzo.[2] Venturi also perceived resemblances between the *putti* and the *Victories* of the *scala* sufficient to justify the postulation of a single hand; but for him that hand was Antonio Lombardo's.[3] Mariacher credited Rizzo with the relief's design, if not its execution.[4] Moschetti assigned the relief to Pietro Lombardo.[5] Pignatti considered its author Paduan, perhaps close to Bartolomeo Bellano.[6]

[1] Berlin, Königl. Mus. Catalogue by Bode/Tschudi, 1888, p. 55, no. 174.
[2] Paoletti, 1893, ii, p. 157. Paoletti's influence is apparent in Burckhardt/Bode/Fabriczy, ⁷1898, ii, pt. I, p. 122e.
[3] Venturi, *Storia*, vi, 1908, p. 1088; ibid., x, pt. I, 1935, p. 388.
[4] Mariacher, *Pal. Duc.*, 1950, p. 29.
[5] Moschetti, Padua, Mus. Civ. *Boll.*, 1914, p. 9.
[6] Pignatti, 1956, p. 36.

8. Venice, Ducal Palace: Scala dei Giganti

Figs. 164-184, 190-192, 195-202

The staircase descends from the *piano nobile* of the east wing of the Ducal Palace to its courtyard opposite the Arco Foscari, dividing the Cortiletto dei Senatori on the north from the Cortile del Palazzo on the south. A room beneath the stairs once served as a prison.[1]

The steps are made of Istrian limestone from the quarries of Leme at Rovigno.[2] The lesenes are white marble, probably from Carrara.[3] The sides of the staircase are inlaid with panels of pink, gray, and white breccia marble, known as *marmo africano*.[4] The *avancorpi* are white marble. The openings of the lower part of the balustrade are blocked on the inside with slabs of gray slate. The niello designs of the risers employ a black paste of lead, silver, copper, and sulphur. In 1893 Paoletti saw traces of gilding in the arcade at the top of the stairs.[5] In 1910 traces of gilding were still visible in the reliefs of the lesenes.[6]

The *Lion of St. Mark* was placed in the frieze above the central arch at the top of the staircase during the principate of Doge Francesco Venier (1554-56). Destroyed in 1797, it was subsequently replaced with a replica by Luigi Borro.[7] From the same campaign under Doge Venier come the Venier coats of arms, carved from preexistent roundels, supported by *putti* in the frieze on either side of the lion, and the four vertical reliefs with trophies which enclose and divide the three bays at the top of the stairs.[8] The statues of *Mars* and *Neptune* on the upper landing of the Scala dei Giganti were commissioned from Sansovino on July 31, 1554.[9] Although not originally destined for Rizzo's staircase, the statues were installed there in January 1567. They give the staircase its name. The bases on which they stood were left unfinished.[10]

Between 1726 and 1728 the Scala dei Giganti was radically restored. The documents repeatedly assert that no liberties were to be taken in the reconstruction of the staircase. Between 1726 and 1727 new steps were carved by Angelo Rusteghello. Patterns for niello were incised in the risers by Bortolo Corbetto and three associates. From the summer of 1727 until the spring of 1728 the ornamental parts of the staircase were restored by Antonio Corradini, assisted by Rusteghello, Corbetto, Andrea Girardi, and their associates. The parapets and *avancorpi* were taken down. Cracked panels of *marmo africano* were replaced. New pieces of molding were inserted where needed. Each piece of the balustrade was repaired. Lesenes, whose reliefs were badly worn, were retouched or carved anew. (The latter comprise the two internal lesenes of the balustrade at the top of the second flight.) The rest of the lesenes were cleaned with small copper brushes, pumice, and caustic solutions. *Mars* and *Neptune* received new bases.[11]

In 1775 the three bays of the arcade at the top of the stairs were closed off with iron railings. In 1776 two enclosures made of grilles were erected at either side of the staircase. There they remained for approximately a hundred years.[12]

Length of entire staircase: 13.89 m.; width of entire staircase at level of ramp: 5.305 m.; width of interior of ramp: 4.02 m.; width of upper landing (including balustrades): 11.02 m.; depth of upper landing: 2.97 m.; height of upper landing (including parapet): 5.82 m.; width of left bay at top of staircase: 1.82 m.; width of central bay: 2.49 m.; width of right bay: 1.84 m.; length of lowest flight: 4.87 m.; length of second flight: 4.62 m.; depth of uppermost flight: 1.275 m.; width of lesenes: .105 m.[13]

Casola, (1494) 1907, p. 126; Harff, (1496-99) 1946, p. 55; Sans., 1581, pp. 119r, 120r; Moryson, i, (1594) 1907, p. 189; Coryate, 1611, pp. 196f.; Onofri, [1]1663, p. 228; Martinelli, [1]1684, p. 528; Pacifico, 1697, p. 528; Temanza, (1738-78) 1963, pp. 15f.; [Albrizzi], 1740, p. 30; Maier, i, [2]1795, pp. 193f.; Moschini, 1815, i, pt. 2, p. 407; Cicognara in Cicognara et al., i, [1]1815, n.p. [cc. 35v, 38rf, 52r, pl. 12]; Cicognara, ii, 1816, p. 151; Moschini, 1819, pp. 99f.; Moschini, ii, 1826, p. 12; Ticozzi, i, 1830, p. 216; Quadri, 1831, p. 6; *Collezione de' migliori ornamenti*, 1831, pls. I, III, V, XI, XVII, XIX, XX, XXV, XXX, XXXV, LXI, LXII, LXVII, XCI-XCIII, XCV-C; [Moro], 1835, pls. XV, XVI, XVIII, XIX; Cadorin, 1837, pp. 19-23; Cadorin, 1838, pp. 135-139; *Siti storici*, 1838, n.p., "Cortile del Palazzo Ducale"; Zanotto in Cicognara et al., i, [2]1838, p. 69, n. 17; E. Paoletti, ii, 1839, pp. 57, 60; Diedo/Zanotto, 1839, "Monumento al Doge Nicolò Trono," n.p.; Fontana, *Il vaglio*, Oct. 23, 1841, p. 343; Fontana, *Il vaglio*, May 21, 1842, pp. 162, 164; Zanotto, i, 1842-53, II. "Cortile. Scalea dei Giganti opera di Antonio Riccio," pp. 1-40; Mutinelli, 1842, pp. 35f.; Erizzo, *Gazz. di Ven.*, (Aug. 10, 1843) Aug. 16, 1843, pp. 739, 740; [Fontana], *Il gondoliere*, Sept. 2, 1843, pp. 277, 279; ibid., Sept. 6, 1843, pp. 281, 283; Givin, *La fenice*, n.d. [mid-Sept. 1843], pp. 94, 95; Erizzo, *Gazz. di Ven.*, (Sept. 20, 1843) Sept. 22, 1843, p. 866; [Fontana], *Il gondoliere*, Sept. 30, 1843, pp. 309, 311; Cadorin, *Il vaglio*, Sept. 30, 1843, pp. 506-508; [Fontana], *Il gondoliere*, Oct. 4, 1843, pp. 313f.; Cadorin, *Il vaglio*, Oct. 28, 1843, Supplement, pp. 1-15; "Critica," *Il gondoliere*, Oct. 28, 1843, pp. 341-343; [Fontana], *Il gondoliere*, Nov. 4, 1843, pp. 349f.; Venice, Mus. Cor., MS P. D. C307, no. xvi, Pasini, *Cenni*, Dec. 30, 1843; Zanotto in *Venezia e le sue lagune*, 1847, ii, pt. 2, p. 346; Carrer, Ven., Aten. ven. *Esercitazioni*, 1847, pp. 41f.; Selvatico, 1847, pp. 181f., 184; Selvatico/Lazari, 1852, pp. 54f.; Zanotto, *Nuovissima guida*, 1856, p. 125; Zanotto in Cicognara et al., i, [3]1858, "Aggiunta al Palazzo Ducale," p. 93; Bernasconi, 1859, pp. 12f., 16f.; Mothes, ii, 1860, pp. 60f.; Dall'Acqua Giusti, 1864, p. 35; Fulin/Molmenti, 1881, pp. 121f.; Gautier, 1881, p. 117; Toffoli, 1883, p. 11; Paoletti, 1893, ii, pp. 154, 155ff., 159, 197, 266; Merzario, 1893, ii, pp. 19ff.; Burckhardt/Bode/Fabriczy, [7]1898, ii, pt. 1, pp. 122e, 123c; Venturi, *Storia*, vi, 1908, pp. 1088, 1090f.; Michel, iv, pt. 1, 1909, p. 196; Ubertalli, 1910, p. xii; Rambaldi, *Aten. ven.*, 1910, pt. 2, pp. 87-121, 193-239; Musatti, *Arch. ven.*, 1912, pp. 203f.; Chiminelli, *Aten. ven.*, 1912, pt. 1, pp. 234-238; Bouchaud, 1913, pp. 160f.; M. Ongaro, n.d. [ca. 1913], pp. 17f.; Planiscig, *Kunst und Kunsthandwerk*, 1916, p. 386; Schubring, 1919, p. 248; Planiscig, 1921, p. 71; Valentiner, *Art in America*, 1925, p. 319; Planiscig, *VJ*, 1926, pp. 99, 102; Lorenzetti, ¹1926, p. 237; Ven., Ca' d'Oro. *Guida-catalogo*, by Fogolari *et al.*, 1929, pp. 79f.; Serra, 1933, p. 8; Morassi in *La Basilica di Aquileia*, 1933, p. 340, n. 5; Planiscig, T-B, xxviii, 1934, p. 409; Venturi, *Storia*, x, pt. 1, 1935, p. 387f.; R. Ludwig, 1939, pp. 22f.; Mariacher, *Arte ven.*, 1948, p. 82; ibid., 1950, pp. 105f.; Mariacher, *Pal. Duc.*, 1950, pp. 26f.; Muraro, *Scuola e vita*, Sept. 15, 1953, p. 4; Mariacher, *Arte ven.*, 1955, p. 47; Pope-Hennessy, ¹1958, pp. 349, 350; Mariacher in *Arte e artisti*, 1959, i, p. 204; Someda in ibid., i, pp. 328f.; Muraro in *Essays . . . Panofsky*, 1960, i, pp. 350-370; Bassi/Trincanato, 1960, p. 50; Donati, 1961, p. 33; Lorenzetti, ³1963, p. 242; Pignatti, 1964, pp. 10f.; Bassi, Vicenza, Cen. internaz. . . . Andrea Palladio. *Boll.*, 1964, pt. 2, pp. 183, 184ff.; Hubala in Egg *et al.*, ¹1965, pp. 640f.; Franzoi, Ven., Mus. Civ. ven. *Boll.*, 1965, no. 4, pp. 8-34; Wolters, Florence, Ksthis. Inst. *Mitt.*, 1965/66, pp. 290ff.; Mariacher, 1966, n.p. [p. 5]; Trincanato in Trincanato/Mariacher, 1966, n.p. [p. 4]; Munman, 1968, pp. 99, 238ff; Trincanato, 1969, p. 10; Pohlandt, *BJ*, 1971, pp. 191ff.; Bassi in Zorzi *et al.*, 1971, pp. 67f., 70, 72; Semenzato in ibid., pp. 207f.; Sheard, 1971, pp. 22, 26f., 188f., 338, n. 46, p. 422, n. 92; A. Zorzi, 1972, i, p. 44; Franzoi, 1973, pp. 34f.; Ruhmer, *Arte ven.*, 1974, p. 58; Pincus, 1974, pp. 19f., 249ff.; Connell, 1976, pp. 135f.; Wolters, 1976, i, pp. 122, 281, no. 240; McAndrew, 1980, pp. 89-101; Howard, 1980, pp. 110f.

The Scala dei Giganti belongs, and gives access, to that portion of the east wing of the Ducal Palace constructed during Antonio Rizzo's tenure as *protomaestro del palazzo*. In the evening of September 14, 1483, the Ducal Apartments in the east wing of the palace caught fire.[14] Several projects for the reconstruction of the palace had been made by about May 21, 1484.[15] Presumably not long afterward, and certainly by December 1484, Rizzo seems to have been placed in charge of rebuilding the

palace.[16] He retained that position until his flight from Venice in April 1498.[17] On May 16, 1489, Pietro Lombardo succeeded Rizzo as *protomaestro* of the Ducal Palace.[18]

The construction of a free-standing, monumental staircase with a spacious landing, placed on axis with the Androne Foscari and perpendicular to the structure to which it gave access, probably resulted from the decision of the Maggior Consiglio of November 11, 1485, to change the ritual of the doge's investiture to include his coronation at the top of a ramp of stairs.[19] The new ceremonial, decreed one week after the death of Doge Giovanni Mocenigo, was employed eight days later at the investiture of Marco Barbarigo on November 19, 1485.[20] The first coronation known with certainty to have taken place on the Scala dei Giganti was that of Doge Antonio Grimani on July 6, 1521,[21] although it was probably also used for that of Doge Leonardo Loredan on October 2, 1501.[22] Thereafter, every doge received the *corno ducale* on the Scala dei Giganti. The staircase also served as the site of the welcoming and leave-taking of foreign dignitaries by the doge,[23] and possibly as a platform for public announcements.[24]

The resemblance of the Scala dei Giganti in form, scale, and siting to the staircase represented by Jacopo Bellini, ca. 1455, in a drawing of the *Presentation of the Virgin* in his British Museum *Sketchbook* (Fig. 232)[25] induced Muraro and others to hypothesize the existence of an earlier staircase on the site of the Scala dei Giganti from which both the real and pictured staircases derived.[26] There is no literary, or other, evidence for the existence of such a staircase on this site. But we cannot state categorically that one never existed.

There survives only one document that refers unequivocally to the construction of the Scala dei Giganti. Dated October 9, 1491, it is a command from the Signoria to the Provveditori al Sal "to reach an agreement with Master Antonio Rizzo concerning the continuation of the construction of their palace, for the figures as well as for the staircase and other necessary things that he knows how to do."[27] While this document proves Rizzo responsible, in some measure, at least, for the Scala dei Giganti, it tells us no more in regard to the date of the staircase than that it was already planned by October 1491. In fact, the staircase must have been designed by 1486/87, because the bay system of the second-story arcade, evidently up by then, makes allowance for the three round-arched bays at the top of the *scala*.[28] The staircase is not likely to have been begun, however, until the reconstruction of the east wing of the Ducal Palace was fairly far advanced. We know from several sources that the reconstruction of the east wing proceeded with extraordinary rapidity: by May 1487 construction of the *cortile* facade had progressed sufficiently for work on the staircase to have begun.[29] The marbles for which the Lucchese, Ser Zuan Piero di Domenico da Carrara, was credited by the Ufficio del Sal with 1220 ducats on December 17, 1490,[30] very likely were destined for the Scala dei Giganti, since this was the only part of the Ducal Palace then under construction where Carrara marble was used extensively. Work on the *scala* had advanced to the stage of installation by the spring of 1494 when Canon Pietro Casola described the staircase "being built there (in the courtyard of the Ducal Palace) . . . by which to ascend to the said palace from the side of the Church of St. Mark" as "a stupendous and costly work."[31] In late winter or early spring of 1497 Arnold von Harff found the staircase "not half complete." Nevertheless, at least some of the carving, which he described as precious, must have been installed.[32] Completion was rapid for the staircase was in use by November 22, 1497, when, as a sign of extraordinary deference, the doge accompanied the duke of Pomaria from the *Udienza* down to the "scala di piera."[33] Allusions to Doge Agostino Barbarigo in the lesenes on either side of the flight of steps and in the *avancorpi*, together with an absence of allusions to his successor, Leonardo Loredan, confirm a dating of the Scala dei Giganti prior to Barbarigo's death on September 20, 1501.[34]

An engraving of the reverse of a medal with the Scala dei Giganti, supposedly made during the principate of Doge Agostino Barbarigo, was published in 1732.[35] A second engraving of the staircase is found in the same book decorating an initial.[36] The plan and elevation of the Scala dei Giganti were drawn by A. Mezzani and engraved by Musitelli for *Le fabbriche cospicue* of 1815. All irregularities of plan and siting were eliminated from the engravings.[37] Details of lesenes, friezes, and archivolts comprise twenty-two plates in a book of Venetian ornament. Only two are signed "Simonetti inc."[38] Thir-

teen other ornamental details were anonymously engraved for a book on ornament published in Venice a few years later.[39] Six plates in Zanotto's book on the Ducal Palace are devoted to engravings of the Scala dei Giganti. Drawn and engraved by M. Comirato and G. Zanetti, they show the plan, front, and side elevations, and several details of the ornamentation of the *scala*. The suppression of the *scala*'s irregularities of measurement and axis in the engravings of the plan and elevation here, too, endow the staircase with a false symmetry.[40] The accurate drawings of the plan, front, and side elevations, and transversal and longitudinal sections of the Scala dei Giganti, which accompany the article by Franzoi and are reproduced here (Figs. 167-172), were made by Silvano Boldrin.[41]

In his guide to Venice of 1581, Francesco Sansovino identified the architect and *protomaestro* of the east wing of the Ducal Palace as Antonio Bregno.[42] To him he assigned the Scala dei Giganti.[43] His attribution remained unchallenged[44] until, in 1837 Giuseppe Cadorin published documents which showed that Rizzo, *protomaestro del palazzo* during the principate of Agostino Barbarigo, had been responsible for the Scala dei Giganti. Indeed, failing to find Bregno's name in any document concerning the Ducal Palace or in any contemporary source, Cadorin concluded that he had never existed and that Bregno was merely another name for Rizzo.[45] Cadorin's discovery might be thought to have settled the attribution of the Scala dei Giganti. Instead it gave rise to an acrimonious polemic in which Gianjacopo Fontana,[46] writing anonymously, aggressively championed the cause of Bregno and, in opposition to reasoned accounts of Cadorin's documents by Erizzo,[47] Zanotto,[48] Givin,[49] and Cadorin, himself,[50] asserted that Bregno had worked as Rizzo's assistant at the Ducal Palace, in which capacity Bregno had executed the Scala dei Giganti. From this debate the partisans of Rizzo emerged victorious: by mid-century claims of Bregno's authorship had been abandoned.[51]

The only other name to have been opposed to Rizzo's and Bregno's as author of the Scala dei Giganti was that of Pietro Lombardo. In 1908 Venturi averred that the Scala dei Giganti was due principally to Pietro Lombardo, Rizzo's successor as *protomaestro* of the Ducal Palace, and to Pietro's shop. Venturi based this assertion primarily on the style of the *Victories* of the *avancorpi*, which he provisionally assigned to Antonio Lombardo, perceiving in them transmuted forms of Pietro's art. The ornamental carving of the staircase he ascribed to Pietro's shop.[52] In this, Venturi was, to some extent, preceded by Zanotto, who had listed Antonio and Tullio Lombardo among the many assistants working under Rizzo on the lesenes of the *scala*.[53] Schubring[54] and Valentiner[55] assigned the *Victories* to Pietro; Ubertalli, to Pietro and Antonio Lombardo as well as Rizzo.[56] In the *Victories*, Fogolari, Nebbia, and Moschini saw Pietro's influence, if not his hand.[57] Pignatti posited Pietro's participation in the plastic decoration of the staircase,[58] decoration with which Lorenzetti credited Pietro and his sons.[59] However, most critics have concurred with Rambaldi[60] and Planiscig,[61] who believed that very little remained to be done on the staircase when Pietro Lombardo was engaged to supervise construction of the Ducal Palace.

In 1893 Paoletti attributed to Rizzo all eight *Victories* of the *avancorpi*.[62] His attribution won acceptance by the majority of scholars.[63] Mariacher,[64] followed by Bassi and Trincanato,[65] favored an attribution of the *Victories* to a close collaborator of the master—one of the anonymous Lombard artisans recorded in the Ducal Palace documents. Pohlandt is unique in having observed differences of quality and style among the *Victories*, but she did not explicitly assign them to diverse assistants.[66]

In 1581 Sansovino wrote: "gli intagli a grottesche ne volti in cima alla scala, furono fatti da Domenico & Bernardino Mantouani."[67] Not only was Sansovino's unsubstantiated attribution accepted without question,[68] but it was expanded by Moschini and others to include all the nonfigurative carving of the staircase,[69] despite Zanotto's remonstrance that Sansovino had assigned to Domenico and Bernardino a precisely limited role.[70] In 1893 Merzario arbitrarily identified Bernardino da Mantova with Bernardino da Bissone.[71] The identification, approved by Planiscig,[72] recurs in accounts of the life of Bernardino da Bissone.[73] Where Merzario hesitantly identified Domenico with Domenico Solari,[74] Planiscig opted for Domenico dei Maffei, the superior of Bernardino da Bissone at Aquileia.[75] It is the latter identification that students of the Basilica of Aquileia generally adopt.[76] None of these identifications

is susceptible of proof: it is not possible to demonstrate the participation of any of these masters in the carving of the Scala dei Giganti. Indeed, no one has ever tried to do so.

The documents concerning the construction of the Ducal Palace during Rizzo's tenure as *protomaestro* name many artisans, none of whom is known as an independent artist.[77] Zanotto,[78] Bernasconi,[79] and Planiscig[80] cited these artisans in connection with the carving of the Scala dei Giganti, although the documents naming them do not refer specifically to the building of the staircase. Though their names have disappeared from recent discussions of the Scala dei Giganti, it is commonly held that Rizzo worked in concert with a number of assistants in the execution of its lesenes.[81]

The iconography of the lesenes was studied by Zanotto,[82] and Pasini,[83] who, in their misguided attempts to explain what are essentially conventional motifs, achieved little apart from deciphering some of the abbreviations. These are: S.P.Q.R.—Senatus Populusque Romanus; S.P.Q.V.—Senatus Populusque Venetus; S.C.—Senatus Consulto; A.B.D.V.—Augustinus Barbadico Dux Venetiarum; A.B.D.V.F.F.—Augustinus Barbadico Dux Venetiarum fieri fecit; S.V.D.Ecclesie—Senatus Venetus defensor Ecclesiae; OPRA V.—Opra Venetiarum.

On the basis of ceremonies conducted on the Scala dei Giganti, Muraro identified the staircase as a ducal throne.[84] As a metaphor the statement is evocative, but as a fact it is misleading. All we know of the use made of the Scala dei Giganti is that, in addition to providing normal access to the Ducal Apartments, it served as the focus of processions during the investiture of the doge and visits to the Ducal Palace by other personages of rank.[85] On the other hand, the doge's investiture customarily concluded with the ritual of his double enthronement, once in the "sala unde ascenditur in Palatium," and once "ubi ius dicunt officiales de nocte."[86]

Muraro further believed that the several allusions to Agostino Barbarigo, the representation of trophies, and the tripartite entrance to the portico, constituted glorification of Doge Barbarigo.[87] But if they had had such a meaning, similar displays surely would have been banned after Barbarigo's death. Rather, Barbarigo's name and arms appear on the Scala dei Giganti because the staircase was made during his principate. A glance at the Arco Foscari shows that it was customary to designate the reign during which a governmental monument was built by affixing the arms of the reigning doge. The references to victory that occur in the Scala dei Giganti must be applied, where accompanied by the ducal insignia, not to the person of Agostino Barbarigo, but to his office, and in other places, to the Venetian government, or more broadly still, to the Venetian state.

Hubala believed that the Scala dei Giganti was to be read in conjunction with the Arco Foscari, that the statuary of the Arco Foscari which the doge confronted during his coronation contained a message aimed specifically at him:

The blessing of St. Mark is directed toward the doge, the connection between worldly power and spiritual standards is placed before his eyes, he is exhorted to serve as ruler, to act virtuously, and to remain conscious of the limitations of earthly human nature. The opposition of the Scala dei Giganti and the Arco Foscari encompasses therefore the quintessence of Venetian state morality and is comparable to the opposition of the Porta della Carta and the Loggetta outside in the Piazzetta.[88]

Underlying this conclusion is the assumption, either that a staircase comparable in siting, appearance, and function to that of the Scala dei Giganti already existed when the Arco Foscari was begun (probably in the 1440s), or that the construction of such a staircase was intended. There is no support for either assumption. Furthermore, the statuary of the Arco Foscari does not conform to a consistent program: the arrangement of figures is not entirely logical and some personifications lack attributes. Third, since Mark was patron saint of Venice, his appearance as crowning figure of the Arco Foscari can be justified without reference to the doge. That the *Saint* faces the east wing of the Ducal Palace can be explained by the orientation of the Androne Foscari—an orientation determined long before the Scala dei Giganti was even thought of. Although the Androne Foscari is always spoken of as the main entrance to the Ducal Palace, it would be more accurate to call it an exit, for the *Evangelists* in the keystones of its vault are oriented so that they are legible only to someone leaving. Therefore the *androne*'s main facade is its east face and it is in conformity with this that *St. Mark* is sited.

[1] Rambaldi, *Aten. ven.*, 1910, pt. 2, pp. 95, 230.

[2] Ibid., p. 204.

[3] Ibid., p. 225, n. 1.

[4] Connell, 1976, pp. 135f.

[5] Paoletti, 1893, ii, p. 156.

[6] Rambaldi, *Aten. ven.*, 1910, pt. 2, p. 96.

[7] A. Zorzi, 1972, i, p. 44.

[8] Paoletti, 1893, ii, p. 155.

[9] Rambaldi, *Aten. ven.*, 1910, pt. 2, pp. 108ff.

[10] Ibid., pp. 115ff.

[11] Ibid., pp. 193ff.

[12] Ibid., pp. 230f.

[13] Measurements were taken from the original drawings by Geom. Silvano Boldrin.

[14] Lorenzi, 1868, pp. 92f., doc. 198, citing the unpublished holograph of Marin Sanudo's *Vite dei dogi* in Venice, Bibl. Marc.

[15] Ibid., pp. 93f., doc. 199.

[16] Sanudo, *Vite dei dogi* in Lorenzi, 1868, p. 93, doc. 198; ibid., p. 94, doc. 202; Malipiero, *Arch. stor. ital.*, 1844, pt. 2, p. 674.

[17] Sanudo, *Diarii*, i, 1879, coll. 927f.

[18] Lorenzi, 1868, p. 121, doc. 250, p. 122, doc. 251.

[19] Ibid., pp. 97f., doc. 208. For the earlier ceremonial, see Romanin, [3]1973, iv, p. 395, doc. x, quoted above in ch. 5, n. 71.

[20] Giustiniani, 1560, bk. 9, p. 338. Attention was first drawn to this passage by Pincus, 1974, pp. 250f.

[21] Sanudo, *Diarii*, xxx, 1891, col. 482.

[22] See above, ch. 5, p. 90.

[23] Sanudo, *Diarii*, i, 1879, coll. 821f.; ibid., iii, 1880, col. 1170.

[24] Ibid., iii, 1880, col. 131.

[25] For an analysis of the similarities and differences between the two staircases, see ch. 5, p. 100 and Pohlandt, *BJ*, 1971, p. 192.

[26] Muraro in *Essays . . . Panofsky*, 1960, i, p. 360, n. 43, citing Venice, Mus. Cor., MS P. D. C307, no. xvi, Pasini, *Cenni*, 1843; Hubala in Egg et al., [1]1965, p. 640; Trincanato in Trincanato/Mariacher, 1966, n.p. [p. 4]; Trincanato, 1969, p. 10; Bassi in Zorzi et al., 1971, pp. 67f.; Wolters, 1976, i, p. 122. Muraro thought the original staircase was made of wood, but the one drawn by Bellini seems to be made of stone.

[27] Lorenzi, 1868, p. 106, doc. 229. The document of April 10, 1489 (ibid., p. 104, doc. 225), which Pincus, 1974, p. 20, n. 23, applied to the dating of the staircase, does not concern the Scala dei Giganti. This can be inferred from the fact that the ends of the steps referred to in the document were to be morticed in the wall, while the ends of the steps of the Scala dei Giganti are flush with the walls of the balustrades.

[28] See above, ch. 5, p. 89.

[29] Sabellico, 1487, dec. 4, bk. 3, n.p., for which, see ch. 5, n. 21.

30 Paoletti, 1893, ii, p. 152.

31 Casola, (1494) 1907, p. 126.

32 Harff, (1496-99) 1946, p. 55, quoted above, ch. 5, n. 45.

33 Sanudo, *Diarii*, i, 1879, coll. 821f.

34 Muraro in *Essays . . . Panofsky*, 1960, i, p. 365, endorsed by Sheard, 1971, p. 188, mistakenly thought that the supposititious glorification of Barbarigo inherent in the appearance of the doge's arms and initials on the staircase would not have occurred after the decline in Barbarigo's political fortunes, which can be dated to 1494, and that the staircase, therefore, must have been finished by that date. Pasini, on the other hand, believed that construction of the Scala dei Giganti began soon after 1499 and that its installation coincided with the gradual dismantling of the principal wooden staircase in the courtyard of the Ducal Palace, whose final demolition was witnessed by Sanudo (*Diarii*, vii, 1882, col. 178) on Nov. 12, 1507. (Venice, Mus. Cor., MS P. D. C307, no. xvi, Pasini, *Cenni*, 1843, n.p. [pp. 9, 20], seconded by Muraro in *Essays . . . Panofsky*, 1960, i, p. 363, n. 58.)

35 Barbarigo, 1732, p. 22 of the exemplar in Paris, Bibliothèque Nationale. The medal is not catalogued by Hill, 1930, and I have not succeeded in finding a specimen.

36 Barbarigo, 1732, p. 73.

37 Cicognara et al., i, ¹1815, pl. 12 [c. 52r].

38 *Collezione de' migliori ornamenti*, 1831, pls. I, III, V, XI, XVII, XIX, XX, XXV, XXX, XXXV, LXI, LXII, LXVII, XCI-XCIII, XCV-C. Pls. XCI and XCII are signed.

39 [Moro], 1835, pl. XV, nos. 71, 74, pl. XVI, nos. 75-80, pl. XVIII, nos. 89, 90, 95, 96, pl. XIX, no. 97.

40 Zanotto, i, 1842-53, pls. XXVIII-XXXIII.

41 Franzoi, Ven., Mus. Civ. ven. *Boll.*, 1965, no. 4, pls. A-F.

42 Sans., 1581, p. 119v: "La faccia del Palazzo Ducale (percioche quello dauanti su la piazza è del publico per i magistrati, & quest'altro fu fatto per habitatione particolare del Principe) cominciata dal Doge Marco Barbarigo, & finita da Agostino suo fratello & successore, fu opera d'Antonio Bregno Architetto & Prothomastro del palazzo."

43 Ibid., p. 120r: "La predetta belliss. scala con la faccia dell'edifitio, fu comandata dal predetto Antonio Bregno."

44 Onofri, ¹1663, p. 228; Pacifico, 1697, p. 528; Moschini, 1815, i, pt. 2, p. 407; Cicognara in Cicognara et al., i, ¹1815, n.p. [cc. 35v, 38r]; Cicognara, ii, 1816, p. 151; Moschini, 1819, pp. 99f.; Ticozzi, i, 1830, p. 216; Quadri, 1831, p. 6; *Collezione di migliori ornamenti*, 1831, n.p. "Descrizioni," pl. I; *Siti storici*, 1838, n.p., "Cortile del Palazzo Ducale"; E. Paoletti, ii, 1839, p. 57.

45 Cadorin, 1837, pp. 19ff.; Cadorin, 1838, pp. 135ff. Cadorin's discovery was reported by Zanotto in Cicognara et al. i, ²1838, p. 69, n. 17, and

Diedo/Zanotto, 1839, "Monumento al Doge Nicolò Trono," n.p.

46 Fontana, *Il vaglio*, Oct. 23, 1841, p. 343, and May 21, 1842, pp. 162-164. [Fontana], *Il gondoliere*, Sept. 2, 1843, pp. 277-279, Sept. 6, 1843, pp. 281-283, Sept. 30, 1843, pp. 309-311, Oct. 4, 1843, pp. 313-314 and Nov. 4, 1843, pp. 349-350. On Fontana's side were Mutinelli, 1842, pp. 35f.; the anonymous author (Fontana himself?) of a review of Cadorin's *Pareri di xv architetti*, 1838, in *Il gondoliere*, Oct. 28, 1843, pp. 341-343, and Venice, Mus. Cor., MS P. D. C307, no. xvi, Pasini, *Cenni*, Dec. 30, 1843, n.p. [pp. 2ff.].

47 Erizzo, *Gazz. di Ven.*, Aug. 16, 1843, pp. 739-740 and Sept. 22, 1843, p. 866.

48 Zanotto in Cicognara et al., i, ²1838, p. 69, n. 17; Zanotto, i, 1842-53, II. "Cortile. Scalea dei Giganti opera di Antonio Riccio," pp. 35, n. 34, 37ff., n. 69.

49 Givin, *La fenice*, n.d. [mid-Sept. 1843], pp. 94f.

50 Cadorin, *Il vaglio*, Sept. 30, 1843, pp. 506-508, and Oct. 28, 1843, Supplement, pp. 1-15. For a fuller account of this polemic see Rambaldi, *Aten. ven.*, 1910, pt. 2, pp. 232ff.

51 But Bassi/Trincanato, 1960, p. 50, and Lorenzetti, ³1963, p. 242, continued to affirm that Rizzo undertook construction of the Scala dei Giganti under the supervision of the *proto del palazzo*, Antonio Bregno.

52 Venturi, *Storia*, vi, 1908, pp. 1088, 1090, copied by Bouchaud, 1913, pp. 160f. By 1935 (*Storia*, x, pt. 1, p. 387), all Venturi's hesitations concerning the attribution of the *Victories* to Antonio Lombardo had disappeared. Venturi, however, did acknowledge traces of Rizzo's influence in them.

53 Zanotto, i, 1842-53, II. "Cortile. Scalea dei Giganti opera di Antonio Riccio," p. 13; Zanotto, *Nuovissima guida*, 1856, p. 125. He was followed by Muraro in *Essays . . . Panofsky*, 1960, i, p. 362, n. 55, who provisionally assigned to the Lombardos some unspecified candelabras, as well as other things, and by Ruhmer, *Arte ven.*, 1974, p. 58, who entertained the possibility of Tullio's participation in the carving of the decorative reliefs, without coming to any definite conclusion.

54 Schubring, 1919, p. 248.

55 Valentiner, *Art in America*, 1925, p. 319.

56 Ubertalli, 1910, p. xii.

57 Ven., Ca' d'Oro. *Guida-catalogo*, by Fogolari et al., 1929, pp. 79f.

58 Pignatti, 1964, p. 11.

59 Lorenzetti, ³1963, p. 242.

60 Rambaldi, *Aten. ven.*, 1910, pt. 2, pp. 104ff. However, on p. 96, n. 1, Rambaldi wrote evasively that the possibility that the *Victories* had been executed in Pietro's shop could not be entirely excluded.

[61] Planiscig, *VJ*, 1926, p. 99; Planiscig, T-B, xxviii, 1934, p. 409.

[62] Paoletti, 1893, ii, pp. 157, 197, 266.

[63] Burckhardt/Bode/Fabriczy, ⁷1898, ii, pt. 1, pp. 122e, 123c, dating the figures to the end of Rizzo's career; Michel, iv, pt. 1, 1909, p. 196; Planiscig, *VJ*, 1926, p. 102, Rizzo's last work; Lorenzetti, ¹1926, p. 237; Ven., Ca' d'Oro. *Guida-catalogo*, by Fogolari *et al.*, 1929, p. 79; Planiscig, T-B, xxviii, 1934, p. 409.

[64] Mariacher, *Arte ven.*, 1948, p. 82; ibid., 1950, pp. 105f.; Mariacher, *Pal. Duc.*, 1950, p. 27; Mariacher, in *Arte e artisti*, 1959, i, p. 204.

[65] Bassi/Trincanato, 1960, p. 50.

[66] Pohlandt, *BJ*, 1971, p. 198. She credited the author of the sharply foreshortened head of a *putto* on one of the lesenes with the head of the *Victory* holding a laurel branch.

[67] Sans., 1581, p. 120r.

[68] Cadorin, 1838, p. 138.

[69] Moschini, 1815, i, pt. 2, p. 407; Moschini, 1819, pp. 99f.; Moschini, ii, 1826, p. 12; *Collezione de' migliori ornamenti*, 1831, n.p., "Descrizioni," pl. 1; *Siti storici*, 1838, n.p., "Cortile del Palazzo Ducale"; E. Paoletti, ii, 1839, p. 60; Selvatico/Lazari, 1852, p. 54; Zanotto, *Nuovissima guida*, 1856, p. 125; Toffoli, 1883, p. 11. Mothes, ii, 1860, p. 61, thought Domenico and Bernardino Mantovani were responsible for the *Victories* as well.

[70] Zanotto, i, 1842-53, II. "Cortile. Scalea dei Giganti opera di Antonio Riccio," p. 12.

[71] Merzario, 1893, ii, pp. 19, 21.

[72] Planiscig, *Kunst und Kunsthandwerk*, 1916, p. 386; Planiscig, 1921, p. 71.

[73] Morassi in *La Basilica di Aquileia,* 1933, p. 340, n. 5; Someda in *Arte e artisti*, 1959, i, pp. 328f. Cf. Donati, 1961, p. 33, who claimed that Bernardino

executed architectural details of the facades of the Ducal Palace. Sheard, 1971, p. 422, n. 92, acknowledged that the epithet "da Bissone" does not appear after Bernardino's name in any document connected with the Scala dei Giganti (or the Ducal Palace, we might add). Nevertheless, she thought it entirely possible that Bernardino had participated in the execution of the staircase.

[74] Merzario, 1893, ii, pp. 19, 21.

[75] Planiscig, *Kunst und Kunsthandwerk*, 1916, p. 386, but cf. Planiscig, 1921, p. 71: "probably Domenico Solari."

[76] Morassi in *La Basilica di Aquileia*, 1933, p. 340, n. 5; Someda in *Arte e artisti*, 1959, i, p. 329.

[77] See above, ch. 5, p. 94.

[78] Zanotto, i, 1842-53, II. "Cortile. Scalea dei Giganti opera di Antonio Riccio," pp. 12f.

[79] Bernasconi, 1859, p. 13.

[80] Planiscig, 1921, p. 71.

[81] Lorenzetti, ¹1926, p. 237; Mariacher, *Arte ven.*, 1948, p. 82; ibid., 1950, p. 106; Muraro in *Essays . . . Panofsky*, 1960, i, p. 362, n. 55; Mariacher, 1966, n.p. [p. 5]; Pohlandt, *BJ*, 1971, pp. 196f., 198; Semenzato in Zorzi *et al.*, 1971, pp. 207, 208.

[82] Zanotto, i, 1842-53, II. "Cortile. Scalea dei Giganti opera di Antonio Riccio," pp. 8ff.

[83] Venice, Mus. Cor., MS P. D. C307, no. xvi, Pasini, *Cenni*, 1843, n.p. [pp. 10ff].

[84] Muraro in *Essays . . . Panofsky*, 1960, i, pp. 351ff.

[85] Sanudo, *Diarii*, i, 1879, coll. 821f.; ibid., iii, 1880, col. 1170; ibid., iv, 1880, col. 680.

[86] ASV, *Libro di cerimoniale*, i, p. 4v.

[87] Muraro in *Essays . . . Panofsky*, 1960, i, pp. 354ff., 359ff.

[88] Hubala in Egg *et al.*, ¹1965, pp. 641ff., endorsed by Wolters, Florence, Ksthis. Inst. *Mitt.*, 1965/66, pp. 290ff.; Wolters, 1976, i, p. 281, no. 240.

9. Venice, Ducal Palace: Statuary of the Arco Foscari

Adam and *Eve*

Figs. 38-43, 45-51

Adam and *Eve* originally occupied the two niches on the second story of the east face of the Arco Foscari. Their place has been taken by bronze replicas. By 1926 *Eve* had been removed from the Arco to the interior of the Ducal Palace.[1] In 1951 both figures were installed in the Sala Grimani in the Appartamenti dei Dogi.[2] In 1964 the two statues were exhibited separately in the Sala del Magistrato al Criminal, and the Sala del Magistrato alle Leggi.[3] They are now shown together in the Sala del Magistrato al Criminal.[4]

White marble. Muraro found traces of priming which served as support for color.[5] The statues may once have been polychromed to imitate bronze, as Sheard suggests.[6]

The statue of *Adam* is almost entirely finished. Only the back of the hair, *Adam*'s left heel, and the rear of the base were left roughhewn. *Adam* has suffered most in the area of his face. His entire upper lip and the adjoining portion of flesh have broken off; their repair is unsatisfactory. *Adam's* nose is cracked. Restoration is particularly evident where the nostrils and septum join the face. The locks that cover the figure's forehead are also chipped. *Adam's* left elbow and forearm are badly cracked. His left thumb and a small piece of the pomegranate have been pieced. An area around the figure's right wrist, where the statue protruded from its niche, is badly worn. Above the wrist the stone is cracked. A crack divides the fig leaf from its vine.

The unfinished portions of *Eve* are largely confined to the center rear of the tree stump and a part of *Eve's* hair at the back. Two patches on *Eve's* right upper arm were not smoothed. The figure's right hand and a half of its right forearm are missing: her present arm and hand are due to the Venetian sculptor, Napoleone Martinuzzi.[7] The tip of *Eve's* nose has lost the outer layer of stone. A chip, missing from the lower lid of her right eye, has been partially mended. Locks of hair on the figure's right are pitted and chipped.

Adam: 216 cm. high. *Eve:* 214 cm. high.

ANTONIO · RIZO is inscribed on *Eve's* base.

Lengherand, (1485-86) 1861, p. 35; Sabellico, 1487, dec. 3, bk. 9, n.p.; Vas./Ricci, (1550) 1927, ii, p. 95; Guisconi [Sans.], 1556, n.p. [p. 6]; Scardeone, 1560, p. 375; Vas./Mil., ii, (1568) 1878, pp. 572f.; Sans., 1581, pp. 119rf.; Moryson, i, (1594) 1907, p. 189; Megiser, 1610, p. 120; Coryate, 1611, p. 193; Doglioni, 1662, p. 54; Onofri, [1]1663, p. 228; Martinelli, [1]1684, p. 528; Pacifico, 1697, p. 528; Rogissart/Havard, 1706, i, p. 62; [Albrizzi], 1740, p. 29; Temanza, 1778, p. 264; Giovio, 1784, p. 233, "Ricci, Andrea"; Zucchini, ii, 1784, p. 226; Maier, i, [1]1787, p. 174; Bartoli, 1793, p. 298; [Michiel]/Morelli, 1800, pp. 95f., n. 3; Moschini, 1815, i, pt. 2, p. 407; Cicognara in Cicognara *et al.*, i. [1]1815, n.p. [cc. 35v, 38v]; Cicognara, ii, 1816, p. 133; Moschini, 1819, p. 99; Zani, v, pt. 1, 1820, pp. 166ff., n. 256; *Siti storici*, 1838, n.p. "Cortile del Palazzo Ducale"; E. Paoletti, ii, 1839, p. 57; Zanotto, i, 1842-53, II. "Cortile. Adamo et Eva, statue di Antonio Riccio," pp. 1ff.; Selvatico, 1847, pp. 180f., 503; Zanotto in *Venezia e le sue lagune*, 1847, ii, pt. 2, p. 345; Selvatico/Lazari, 1852, p. 54; Burckhardt, [1]1855, pp. 620df.; Zanotto, *Nuovissima*

guida, 1856, p. 124; Bernasconi, 1859, pp. 10, 23f., 33, 58; Mothes, ii, 1860, p. 56; Gautier, 1881, p. 118; Fulin/Molmenti, 1881, p. 120; Perkins, 1883, pp. 212f.; Buckhardt/Zahn, [3]1874, p. 671b; Burckhardt/Bode, [5]1884, ii, pt. 2, p. 429e; Paoletti, 1893, i, p. 45, ii, pp. 141f.; Merzario, 1893, ii, p. 21; Burckhardt/Bode/Fabriczy, [7]1898, ii, pt. 1, pp. 121bf.; Guggenheim, 1898; Kirchner, 1903, pp. 110f.; Bode, i, 1907, p. 38; [Valentiner], N.Y., Met. Mus. of Art. *Bull.*, Dec. 1908, p. 230; Venturi, *Storia*, vi, 1908, pp. 1065f.; Michel, iv, pt. 1, 1909, p. 191; Paoletti, "Bregno, Antonio," T-B, iv, 1910, p. 568; Morini, *Rass. d'arte*, 1911, pp. 71f.; N.Y. Met. Mus. of Art. Catalogue by Breck, 1913, p. 66, no. 67; Bouchaud, 1913, pp. 111, 121ff.; M. Ongaro, n.d. [ca. 1913], p. 15; Schubring, 1919, pp. 243f.; Planiscig, 1921, pp. 57ff.; Bode, [6]1922, p. 150; Planiscig, *VJ*, 1926, pp. 98f.; Lorenzetti, [1]1926, pp. 85, 234f.; Fogolari, n.d. [ca. 1927], p. oppos. pl. 8; Francovich, *Boll. d'arte*, 1928-29, p. 486; Serra, 1933, pp. 8f.; Planiscig, T-B, xxviii, 1934, p. 409; Fiocco, *Enc. ital.*, xxix, 1936, p. 502; Planiscig, *VJ*, 1937, pp. 103f.; Detroit, Inst. of Arts. *Italian Sculptures*, 1938, by Valentiner, n.p., nos. 93-94; Mariacher, *Le arti*, 1940-41, p. 198; Mariacher, *Arte ven.*, 1948, pp. 76ff.; Mariacher, *Pal. Duc.*, 1950, p. 22; Cevc, *Likovni svet*, 1951, pp. 209ff.; Adelmann/Weise, 1954, p. 6; Pignatti, 1956, p. 30; Clark, 1956, pp. 110, 395; Esche, 1957, p. 25; Pope-Hennessy, [1]1958, pp. 108, 349f.; Ruhmer, 1959, pp. 40, 43; Bassi/Trincanato, 1960, p. 46; Muraro in *Essays . . . Panofsky*, 1960, i, pp. 359, 368; Bassi/Trincanato, 1964, p. 90; Romanini, *Arte lom.*, Jan.-June 1964, p. 98; Hubala in Egg *et al.*, [1]1965, pp. 680f.; Mariacher in Trincanato/Mariacher, 1966, n.p., figs. 20-21; Seymour, 1966, p. 199; Mariacher, 1966, n.p. [pp. 4f.]; Waźbiński, 1967, pp. 34, 44; Trincanato, 1969, p. 9; Pincus, *AB*, 1969, p. 249, n. 16; Pohlandt, *BJ*, 1971, pp. 165-175; Bassi in Zorzi *et al.*, 1971, p. 68; Semenzato in ibid., pp. 204f.; Sheard, 1971, pp. 171f., 221, 355f., n. 52; Ven., Procuratie Nuove. *Arte a Ven.*, by Mariacher, 1971, p. 139; Brenzoni, 1972, p. 250; Janson in *Propyläen Kstge.*, vii, 1972, p. 306, nos. 276a, b; Ljubljana, Narodna galerija. *Gotska plastika*, by Cevc, 1973, pp. 119f., nos. 77-78; Franzoi, 1973, p. 149; Pincus, 1974, pp. 190ff., 210-233, 253ff., 299-316, and passim; Connell, 1976, p. 136; Mariacher, *Aten. ven.*, 1976, p. 71; Munman, *AB*, 1979, pp. 637ff.

"Mars"

Figs. 34-37, 44

Until recently "*Mars*" occupied the right-hand niche below the balcony, on the south face of the Arco Foscari. Between 1960 and 1963 the statue was removed to the interior of the Ducal Palace, where it was installed in the corridor outside the apartments of the Quarantia Criminale. Its place was taken by a bronze replica.[8]

White marble. There is no evidence of polychromy or gilding.

Parts of the figure that were not visible when the statue was installed within its niche were not entirely finished. The pattern of chain mail is not incised along the figure's right flank. Between the figure's legs the inside of the cloak is not smoothed. At the rear of the figure, folds in the cloak are carved on a larger scale and in less detail than they are in front. Marks of a large point and claw chisel are visible in the fold that descends from the figure's right arm. In the rear, the bottom of the cloak and the figure's hair and helmet are no more than roughhewn.

"*Mars*' " right hand and the upper part of the shield he holds are not original. The overhang of the base, the central lappet with *putto*'s head, the projecting knee, and the border of the chiton are badly chipped. Here and there the surface is flaking, but losses are minor and, on the whole, the statue is well preserved.

218 cm. high.

Moschini, 1815, i, pt. 2, p. 406; Moschini, 1819, p. 99; E. Paoletti, ii, 1839, p. 58; Zanotto, i, 1842-53, II. "Cortile. Prospettive del medesimo," p. 7; Selvatico/Lazari, 1852, p. 54; Zanotto, *Nuovissima guida*, 1856, p. 124; Burckhardt/Bode, [4]1879, p. 400c; Della Rovere, n.d. [ca. 1880], p. 8; Fulin/Molmenti, 1881, p. 120; Toffoli, 1883, p. 12; Paoletti, 1893, ii, p. 142; Burckhardt/Bode/Fabriczy, [8]1901, p. 499e; Venturi, *Storia*, vi, 1908, p. 1066; Michel, iv, pt. 1, 1909, p. 191; Ubertalli, 1910, p. xi; *Pal. Duc.*, 1912, p. 10; Pozzi, *Revue numismatique*, 1914, p. 205; Schubring, 1919, p. 244; Planiscig, 1921, pp. 156f., 168f.; Bode, [6]1922, p. 150; Lorenzetti, [1]1926, p. 235; Fogolari, n.d. [ca. 1927], p. oppos. pl. 10; Fiocco, *Dedalo*, viii, 1927-28, p. 454; Serra, 1933, p. 9; Fiocco, *Enc. ital.*, xxix, 1936, p. 502; Mariacher, *Le arti*, 1940-41, p. 197; Mariacher, *Arte ven.*, 1948, p. 78;

Mariacher, *Pal. Duc.*, 1950, p. 22; Bassi/Trincanato, 1960, p. 46; Lorenzetti, [3]1963, p. 240; Hubala in Egg *et al.*, [1]1965, p. 650; Mariacher, 1966, n.p. [p. 5]; Munman 1968, pp. 87, 237; Mariacher, *Le muse*, x, 1968, p. 145; Pohlandt, *BJ*, 1971, pp. 175ff.; Sheard, 1971, pp. 2, 166, 201, 207f.; Semenzato in Zorzi *et al.*, 1971, pp. 204, 205; Franzoi, 1973, p. 28; Pincus, 1974, pp. 207f., n. 1, pp. 316-322; Connell, 1976, p. 136.

Mocenigo Warrior

Fig. 147

The statue occupies the middle-sized pinnacle to the left of the central pyramid on the south face of the Arco Foscari.

Istrian limestone.

The figure's left forearm and the upper part of the shield appear to have been pieced, but may simply have cracked. The left wrist is cracked through and a crack has developed in the skirt behind the shield. The right hand originally seems to have held aloft a sword whose blade is missing. Apart from the abraded fingers of the left hand, there are no major losses. However, almost nothing of the original surface is preserved.

Paoletti, 1893, i, p. 43, ii, p. 142; Mariacher, *Le arti*, 1940-41, pp. 197, 198; Mariacher, *Arte ven.*, 1948, p. 78; Mariacher, *Pal. Duc.*, 1950, p. 21; Semenzato in Zorzi *et al.*, 1971, p. 204; Pincus, 1974, pp. 324, 336f., 461; Munman, *AB*, 1979, p. 640.

Three Angels

Figs. 32, 33, 134

1. The *Angel*, whose left hand is raised to his chest and whose right grasps a fold which traverses his thigh, is located on the east face of the Arco Foscari, at the extreme left of the base of the main pyramid (Fig. 32). 2. The *Angel*, with hands crossed at his waist, stands on a low pinnacle of the south face of the Androne Foscari to the right of the clock tower (Fig. 33). 3. The *Angel*, with hands crossed on his chest in an attitude of adoration, occupies a corresponding pinnacle on the south face to the left of the clock tower at the juncture of the Androne Foscari

and the west wing of the Ducal Palace (Fig. 134). The last two *Angels* originally occupied the pedestals, now empty, at the rear of the largest pyramid. They faced the rear of the Porta della Carta. They were probably moved to the clock tower facade in 1615 when that facade was finished.[9]

Istrian limestone.

Where the original surface of the three figures is preserved the surface has turned black. Very little of this surface remains.

Paoletti, 1893, i, p. 44, ii, p. 142; Pincus, 1974, pp. 30, 323, 324, 329f., 333f., 461.

Three Personifications

Figs. 136, 137, 148

1. The figure, whose right hand intercepts folds on its chest and whose left rests on its hip, occupies the low pinnacle on the south face of the Arco Foscari at the juncture of Arco and Androne Foscari (Fig. 137). 2. The figure, whose left hand is raised to its breast and whose lowered right hand gathers folds of its cloak, occupies the low pinnacle on the south face immediately to the right of Fig. 137 (Fig. 148). 3. The figure, whose right hand is raised to its waist and whose left rests on its thigh, stands directly behind the first *Personification* on a pinnacle in the same series, at the juncture of the Arco Foscari and the Androne Foscari, on the side of the basilica. The figure faces the rear of the Porta della Carta (Fig. 136).

Istrian limestone.

The drapery that originally fell from the right arm of the third figure has broken off. Where the original surface of the three figures is preserved the stone has turned black. Very little of this surface remains.

Paoletti, 1893, i, p. 44, ii, p. 142; Mariacher, *Le arti*, 1940-41, pp. 197, 198; Mariacher, *Arte ven.*, 1948, p. 78; Romanini, *Arte lom.*, Jan.-June 1964, p. 102, n. 4; Pincus, 1974, pp. 30, 329f., 334, 337f., 461.

The history of the construction and embellishment of the Arco Foscari can be reconstructed on the basis of documents, the coats of arms that ornament it, and the masonry fabric itself, partially laid bare during a recent restoration.[10] The Arco Foscari comprises the eastern end of

a passageway, known as the Porticato della Carta or the Androne Foscari, which leads from the Piazza S. Marco to the courtyard of the Ducal Palace. The passageway runs between the external transept wall of S. Marco on the north and the meter-thick walls of a much older fabric belonging to the medieval Ducal Palace on the south. The Porta della Carta at the west end of the passageway was commissioned from Giovanni and Bartolomeo Bon on November 10, 1438, and was built between 1440 and 1443.[11] On January 28, 1438, Stefano Bon Cremonese was commissioned to build four vaulted bays of a corridor between the church and the preexistent palace walls;[12] according to Franzoi, these are the four central bays of the six-bay corridor. Above the corridor there was probably an open terrace.[13] Construction of the Arco Foscari, which incorporates the final bay of the corridor, began in the east: under Doge Francesco Foscari (1423-57), whose arms appear in the two spandrels of the ground-floor arch, the lower story of the east facade was built. Its second story, the central pyramid, and the eastern pinnacles were completed under Doge Cristoforo Moro (1462-71), whose arms ornament the spandrels of the second-floor arch, the base of the central pyramid, and the shield of the *Warrior* standing on the pinnacle at the northeast corner of the Arco.[14] Moro's kneeling figure originally appeared within the second-story arch, resting on the cornice over the entrance to the balcony. In his *Res Venetae* of 1487, Sabellico wrote that the "interior part of the doge's vestibule, begun during the principate of Pasquale Malipiero [1457-62] [sic] was carried up to the summit under [Doge Cristoforo Moro]."[15] The south face of the Arco Foscari was finished under Doge Pietro Mocenigo (1474-76), or Doge Giovanni Mocenigo (1478-85), or both. Mocenigo arms appear twice in the spandrel of the arch of the second story, and once in the shield of the *Warrior* standing on the pinnacle at the southwest corner. A statue of one or the other Mocenigo kneeling before the lion of St. Mark was originally located above the second-story lunette of the south face of the Arco Foscari. On February 1, 1472, the Senate ordered the Ufficio del Sal to reenforce the exterior of S. Marco by throwing an arch from the church to the "palatium novum."[16] The arch still exists at the western end of the terrace above the Androne Foscari; the arms of Doge Niccolò Tron (1471-73) originally filled both spandrels. Above the arch is a second buttressing arch whose segmental profile and cresting can be seen in Gentile Bellini's *St. Mark's Day Procession in St. Mark's Square* of 1496, Accademia, Venice. Opposite this arch, at the eastern end of the terrace, is a door that gives access to the room beyond the balcony of the Arco Foscari. Above the portal are Mocenigo arms. The arms and portal, however, must come from elsewhere, for the room to which the door gives access, and the rooms above it, were constructed only in the eighteenth century.[17] Work on the Arco Foscari was probably not quite done on February 25, 1483, when a document records that Antonio Rizzo was expecting delivery of stone from Parenzo for the "porta del palazo."[18]

The base of *Eve* is inscribed with Rizzo's name. Nevertheless, until 1800, when Jacopo Morelli bestowed on Rizzo a historical identity,[19] the statues of *Adam* and *Eve* were widely considered Andrea Riccio's.[20] Only Sabellico,[21] Temanza,[22] and Bartoli[23] assigned the works correctly. Since 1800, however, Rizzo's authorship of *Adam* and *Eve* has not been doubted: indeed, the figures invariably serve as touchstones for other attributions to the sculptor.

The dating of *Adam* and *Eve*, on the other hand, is hotly disputed. The original position of the statues favors an early dating: *Adam* and *Eve* occupied niches on the lower level of the east face of the Arco Foscari to which the arms of Doge Francesco Foscari (1423-57) are prominently affixed. But documentary evidence concerning Rizzo's employment at the Ducal Palace supports a later dating. Rizzo's name does not figure in palace records before February 1483, when he apparently was acquiring stone for its portal. On the evening of September 14, 1483, the Ducal Apartments in the east wing of the palace burned. Probably in the late spring, and certainly by December of 1484, Rizzo seems to have been named *protomaestro* in charge of its reconstruction. Rizzo held that post until 1498. But neither the location of the statues, nor the date of Rizzo's documented employment at the Ducal Palace, is decisive in the dating of *Adam* and *Eve*: since the figures could well have filled niches that had long stood empty, and since Rizzo was certainly employed at the Ducal Palace long before record of his activity there begins, both kinds of evidence are virtually irrelevant.

Relevant evidence for the dating of the statues, however, is supplied by the almost contemporary testimony of Marc'Antonio Sabellico, according to whom the two statues seem to have been executed under Doge Cristoforo Moro.[24] Pohlandt also brought to bear on the dating of the statues the undated distich addressed to Rizzo by the Triestine humanist, Raffaele Zovenzoni, which lauds a marble *Eve*—presumably the figure of the Arco Foscari.[25] But Pohlandt mistakenly sought to win from this a *terminus ante quem* of 1475.[26] In fact, the distich permits us to date the work no more precisely than before March 1485, the probable date of Zovenzoni's death.[27] Acknowledging advice from Munman, Pohlandt also claimed two statues of *Adam* and *Eve* carved by Janez Lipec around 1484 for the town hall at Ljubljana as evidence that Rizzo's figures were completed by that date.[28] To be sure, Lipec's figures and their placement do reflect those of Rizzo.[29] But the figures, themselves, are undated (in fact, the town hall was only finished later[30]): 1484 designates, not the date of the figures, but merely the period when Janez Lipec is supposed to have flourished.[31] Therefore, the year 1484 can be applied to two of Lipec's works only in a most hypothetical and approximate fashion. Rizzo's *Adam* and *Eve* were seen by Georges Lengherand on March 12, 1486.[32]

With regard to the dating of the figures, critics fall into several distinct groups. Until the beginning of this century, most assumed a dating during the *principate* of Doge Moro. These divided into those who placed the figures toward the beginning of Moro's reign, owing to the presence of both Foscari and Moro arms on the east face of the Arco Foscari,[33] and those who dated the statues toward the end of Moro's reign or simply designated 1471 as the latest possible date for the execution of the works.[34] In his many writings on Antonio Rizzo, Mariacher propounded a date of 1470-80 on the basis of what he perceived as the extraordinary resemblance of *Eve* to *Prudence* of the Tron Tomb, dated by him soon after 1476.[35] Mariacher succeeded in converting most Italian art historians.[36] In 1842-53 Zanotto reasoned that Rizzo would not have carved the figures until he had been named *protomaestro* of the Ducal Palace following the fire of 1483.[37] This position, too, is well represented.[38] Paoletti believed that the figures did not date much before the completion of the Arco Foscari during the *principate* of Giovanni Mocenigo.[39] Considerations of style led Pincus to agree. Designating *Eve* as the later of the two figures, she posited Sabellico's composition of *Res Venetae* during 1484-85 as a *terminus ante quem* for their execution.[40] Planiscig linked the document of October 9, 1491, expressing the hope that Rizzo might persevere "with the figures as well as the stairs" of the Ducal Palace, to the statues of *Adam* and *Eve*. This, he asserted, provided documentary confirmation of a dating arrived at independently on grounds of style.[41] Taking into account a great deal of evidence not previously used, Pohlandt judiciously returned the statues to the *principate* of Doge Cristoforo Moro.[42]

In 1907 Bode suggested that two bronze statuettes of *Adam*, one in the Kunsthistorisches Museum at Vienna (Inv. 5739), the other in the collection of the Comtesse de Béarn at Paris, might have been made by Rizzo as studies for his statue on the Arco Foscari.[43] This proposal was endorsed by Valentiner, who related to the two statuettes a third, of *Adam*, in the Metropolitan Museum, New York.[44] Breck was inclined to view all three as preparatory studies for the Palazzo Ducale *Adam*.[45] The identification of the Vienna *Adam* as a study for Rizzo's figure was not incorporated in either of the two catalogues of bronzes in the collection at Vienna.[46] Recent literature on Rizzo's *Adam* and *Eve* fails to mention the bronzes. Indeed, there is no evidence of any direct connection.

An engraving of *Adam* and *Eve* by G. Buttazzon appears in Zanotto's book on the Ducal Palace.[47]

Although no early sources testify to the location of the so-called "*Mars*," we may assume that it was intended, from the start, for a niche in the lower face of the Arco Foscari, for its size, material, and format conform to those of *Adam* and *Eve*. Since *Adam* and *Eve* could have been paired only on the east face of the Arco Foscari, "*Mars*" must have been located on the south, in the niche it occupied until recently at the right corner of the structure. (The mate to this niche was added only at the beginning of the seventeenth century when the south face of the Arco Foscari was completed after the demolition of the Scala Foscara in 1608.) A woodcut of 1590 published by Vecellio shows a figure in the right-hand niche. But the drawing of it is too general to permit identification with our, or any other, figure.[48] Moschini, the first critic to mention the statue, saw it in 1815 on the south face of the Arco, to one side of the statue of *Francesco Maria della Rovere* by Giovanni Bandini.[49]

Accompanied by a number of Roman statues on the south face of the Arco Foscari and Androne Foscari, "*Mars*" first entered the literature as a work of classical antiquity.[50] It was christened "*Mars*" and attributed to Antonio Rizzo for the first time in the guidebook by Selvatico and Lazari.[51] Although Zanotto assigned it to one of the Bon,[52] the attribution to Rizzo has prevailed up to the present day.[53] But Serra thought that "*Mars*" was more likely shopwork than autograph.[54] In 1921 Planiscig included the work among a large group of heterogeneous statues that he ascribed to the ill-defined Paduan sculptor Giovanni Minelli, and dated it to ca. 1500.[55] The attribution to Minelli was noted by Lorenzetti,[56] and accepted reservedly by Fogolari,[57] although both recognized its style as Rizzesque. Pincus agreed with Planiscig so far as to define its origin ca. 1500 in Padua.[58] Mariacher,[59] followed by Bassi and Trincanato,[60] recognized its inferior quality but nevertheless was inclined to attribute it to Rizzo. Hubala[61] and Mariacher[62] dated "*Mars*" to ca. 1480; Sheard believed it postdated the Tron Tomb.[63] From the similarity between "*Mars*" and the *Moro Warrior* on the northeast pinnacle of the Arco Foscari, Pohlandt concluded that the latter figure was derived from the former. This conclusion allowed Pohlandt to apply to "*Mars*" the *terminus ante quem* of the *Moro Warrior*, whose arms date its execution between 1462 and 1471.[64] Pohlandt's initial conclusion, however, is unwarranted: the figures are largely independent of one another and what few similarities exist could be accounted for as well by the precedence of the *Moro Warrior*. Long ago, Fogolari observed that the statue does not represent Mars,[65] but he offered no alternate identification and the label is generally retained, as it has been here, for the sake of convenience.

To Antonio Rizzo or his shop Paoletti gave the *Warrior* with the hatchment of the Mocenigo family.[66] In two articles of the 1940s Mariacher unqualifiedly assigned the *Warrior* to Rizzo. He dated it prior to 1483 and claimed to see the influence of Bellini in its head.[67] In his later guide to the Ducal Palace, however, Mariacher forebore from giving it an author.[68] Pincus, on the other hand, believed that the *Warrior*, along with several other pieces, had been executed at the beginning of the seventeenth century to replace a fifteenth-century figure.[69]

The three *Angels* and the three draped female figures are rarely treated individually in the art-historical literature. Comparing them to the statuary of the Tron Tomb, Paoletti assigned the six figures to the hand or shop of Antonio Rizzo.[70] Mariacher attributed to Rizzo the first and second draped female figures, and dated them to the principate of Pietro Mocenigo, from 1474 to 1476.[71] Romanini singled out the first *Personification*, which she believed carved by Rizzo before his supposititious trip to Lombardy.[72] Pincus disputed the originality of all six, assuming them to have been executed during the reconstruction of the clock-tower facade between 1602 and 1618.[73]

[1] Lorenzetti, [1]1926, p. 235.

[2] TCI, *Ven.*, 1951, p. 133; Muraro, 1953, p. 113.

[3] Bassi/Trincanato, 1964, p. 90.

[4] Franzoi, 1973, p. 149.

[5] Muraro, *Essays . . . Panofsky,* 1960, i, p. 359.

[6] Sheard, 1971, pp. 355f., n. 52. This may have occurred around the beginning of the seventeenth century when Rogissart and Havard, 1706, i, p. 62, misidentified their material as wood. Earlier writers—Vas./Ricci, (1550) 1927, ii, p. 95; and Vas./Mil., ii, (1568) 1878, pp. 572f.; Coryate, 1611, p. 193; and Onofri, [1]1663, p. 228—called them marble or alabaster.

[7] Pincus, *AB*, 1969, p. 249, n. 16.

[8] Bassi/Trincanato, 1960, p. 46; Lorenzetti, [3]1963, p. 240; Hubala in Egg *et al.*, [1]1965, pp. 648ff.

[9] Franzoi, *Ven., Mus. Civ. ven. Boll.*, 1977, p. 14.

[10] Ibid., pp. 9-26.

[11] Schulz, *TAPS*, 1978, pt. 3, p. 32.

[12] Lorenzi, 1868, pp. 66ff., doc. 158; Gallo, *R. di Ven.*, 1933, pp. 287, 293.

[13] Franzoi, *Ven., Mus. Civ. ven. Boll.*, 1977, p. 10.

[14] Moro's arms also appear above the entrance to the staircase located at the north end of the balcony, but they may have been taken from another site, for the staircase itself is made of pieces of the Scala dei Giganti discarded during its eighteenth-century restoration.

[15] Sabellico, 1487, dec. 3, bk. 9, n.p.

[16] Gallo, *R. di Ven.*, 1933, pp. 289ff.

[17] Franzoi, *Ven., Mus. Civ. ven. Boll.*, 1977, pp. 20f.

[18] Paoletti, 1893, ii, p. 144.

[19] [Michiel]/Morelli, 1800, pp. 95ff., n. 3.

[20] Vas./Ricci, ii, (1550) 1927, p. 95; Guisconi [Sans.], 1556, n.p. [p. 6]; Scardeone, 1560, p. 375; Vas./Mil., ii, (1568) 1878, pp. 572f.; Sans., 1581,

pp. 119rf.; Doglioni 1662, p. 54; Onofri, [1]1663, p. 228; Martinelli, [1]1684, p. 528; Pacifico, 1697, p. 528; Rogissart/Havard, 1707, i, p. 87; [Albrizzi], 1740, p. 29; Giovio, 1784, p. 233, "Ricci, Andrea"; Zucchini, ii, 1784, p. 226; Maier, i, [1]1787, p. 174.

[21] Sabellico, 1487, dec. 3, bk. 9, n.p.

[22] Temanza, 1778, p. 264.

[23] Bartoli, 1793, p. 298.

[24] Sabellico, 1487, dec. 3, bk. 9, n.p.: "Nec ea parte tantum ciuitas illius ducatu ornata sed & pars interior Ducarii uestibuli iam a Maripetri principatu incoata sub eo [Doge Moro] ad summum est deducta: ubi circa fastigium illius statua ex pario marmore uisitur: atque duae aliae primorum parentum illi subiectae opus Antonii Crispi statuarii nostra tempestate optimi": Attention was first drawn to this passage by Hubala, quoted by Pohlandt, *BJ*, 1971, p. 174, who, however, cited the wrong work by Sabellico.

As Pincus, 1974, pp. 315f., claims, this passage does not explicitly state that the statues were made under Doge Moro, but the context encourages this reading. Our construction is supported by the interpretation of Sabellico's successors. Cf. Venice, Bibl. Marc., Cod. it., Cl. VII, 56 (= 8636), attributed to Erizzo, *Cronaca veneta*, n.p., see 1471: "1471. Fù anche finido in tempo del sopradetto M. lo Dose [Cristoforo Moro], el palazzo da una banda et fulli messo nella summità la statua di esso Dose Moro de marmoro, et due altre statue bellissime d'Adam, et Eva nude de tutto tondo le quale furono scolpite da Andrea Rizzo Padoan, diligente scultor, le qual sono alquanto più basso della statua del Dose, et furono fatte poi metter in piedi in dui nicchi, che sono in fazza della scala grande descouerta, che và in palazzo." Under 1471 the author states that he took his record of the principate of Cristoforo Moro from a "cronica antica." Perhaps his source is that chronicle quoted without citation by Cicognara *et al.*, i, [1]1815, n.p. [c. 35v].

[25] See above, intro., p. 12.

[26] Pohlandt, *BJ*, 1971, p. 174, states that Zovenzoni is recorded as having lived in Venice between 1470 and 1475. In fact, he is known to have lived in Venice between 1470 and the beginning of 1473 and then, again, from April 1475 until his death, except for two brief interludes, one at Trent at the end of 1475 and the other at Treviso in December 1476. See Ziliotto, 1950, pp. 33, 42, 52, 53.

[27] Ziliotto, 1950, p. 57.

[28] Pohlandt, *BJ*, 1971, p. 174.

[29] Cevc, *Likovni svet*, 1951, pp. 209ff.

[30] Ibid., p. 211.

[31] All information concerning Janez Lipec, including the attribution to him of the statues of *Adam* and *Eve* from the town hall at Ljubljana, comes from Janez Gregor Dolničar, *Bibliotheca Labacensis publica Collegii Carolini Nobilium*, MS, Library of the Seminary, Ljubljana, for which see Cevc, *Likovni svet*, 1951, p. 202. The manuscript was written shortly before the author's death in 1715. Dolničar claims

that his information was taken from archival sources. The pertinent passage reads: "Joannes Lipez, quem nascentem Labacum excepit. Clarus sui aevi sculptor, floruit is circa annum salutis 1484, quo vetus curia Labacen, in publico foro structa, sculpsit is statuas Adami et Evae, quae hodiedum prostant, ad omnem artis peritiem, ut constat ex M. S. Regist. Ciuitatis." The statues, now in the Mestni muzej, Ljubljana, inv. nos. MM 2006, MM 2007, are catalogued in Ljubljana, Narodna galerija, *Gotska plastika*, by Cevc, 1973, pp. 119f., nos. 77-78.

[32] Lengherand, (1485-86) 1861, p. 35.

[33] [Michiel]/Morelli, 1800, p. 95, n. 3; Selvatico/Lazari, 1852, p. 54; Burckhardt/Zahn, [3]1874, p. 671b; Fulin/Molmenti, 1881, p. 120; Burckhardt/Bode, [5]1884, ii, pt. 2, p. 429e; Burckhardt/Bode/Fabriczy, [7]1898, ii, pt. 1, p. 121b; Guggenheim, 1898, p. 9; Paoletti, "Bregno, Antonio," T-B, iv, 1910, p. 568; Morini, *Rass. d'arte*, 1911, pp. 71f.; Bouchaud, 1913, p. 111; Bode, [6]1922, p. 150; Serra, 1933, p. 8; Brenzoni, 1972, p. 250.

[34] Cicognara in Cicognara *et al.*, i, [1]1815, n.p. [cc. 35v, 38v]; Burckhardt, [1]1855, pp. 620d.; Bernasconi, 1859, pp. 10, 33; Mothes, ii, 1860, p. 56; Gautier, 1881, p. 118; Perkins, 1883, p. 212, n. ‡; Kirchner, 1903, p. 110.

[35] Mariacher, *Arte ven.*, 1948, pp. 76ff.; Mariacher, *Pal. Duc.*, 1950, p. 22; Mariacher, 1966, n.p. [pp. 4, 5], with evident confusion in the count of decades; Mariacher in Ven., Procuratie Nuove. *Arte a Ven.*, 1971, p. 139. See also Mariacher, *Le arti*, 1940-41, p. 198.

[36] Pignatti, 1956, p. 30; Bassi/Trincanato, 1960, p. 46; Muraro in *Essays . . . Panofsky*, 1960, i, p. 368; Romanini, *Arte lom.*, Jan.-June 1964, p. 98; Trincanato, 1969, p. 9.

[37] Zanotto, i, 1842-53, II. "Cortile. Adamo ed Eva, statue di Antonio Riccio," p. 2.

[38] Venturi, *Storia*, vi, 1908, p. 1065; Bouchaud, 1913, p. 121, contradicting an assertion made on p. 111; Planiscig, 1921, pp. 62f., 66; Adelmann/Weise, 1954, p. 46, n. 5; Pope-Hennessy, [1]1958, pp. 108, 349f.; Seymour, 1966, p. 199.

[39] Paoletti, 1893, ii, p. 141. Janson in *Propyläen Kstge.*, vii, 1972, p. 306, nos. 276a, b, dated the figures ca. 1485.

[40] Pincus, 1974, pp. 315f., seconded by Munman, *AB*, 1979, p. 640, n. 11.

[41] Planiscig, *VJ*, 1926, pp. 98, 99; Planiscig, T-B, xxviii, 1934, p. 409. Detroit, Inst. of Arts, *Italian Sculptures*, 1938, by Valentiner, n.p., nos. 93-94; Adelmann/Weise, 1954, p. 46, n. 5; and Bassi in Zorzi *et al.*, 1971, p. 68, concurred in Planiscig's dating. The document of 1491 is published by Lorenzi, 1868, p. 106, doc. 229.

[42] Pohlandt, *BJ*, 1971, pp. 174, 179.

[43] Bode, i, 1907, p. 38.

[44] [Valentiner], N.Y., Met. Mus. of Art. *Bull.*, December 1908, p. 230.

[45] N.Y., Met. Mus. of Art. Catalogue by Breck, 1913, p. 66, no. 67.

[46] Vienna, Ksthis. Mus. Catalogue by Schlosser, 1910, pp. 1f. [Taf. III, 2]; Vienna, Ksthis. Mus. Catalogue by Planiscig, 1924, p. 10, no. 11.

[47] Zanotto, i, 1842-53, pl. XVIII.

[48] Vecellio, [1]1590, p. 101r.

[49] Moschini, 1815, i, pt. 2, p. 406.

[50] Ibid.; Moschini, 1819, p. 99; E. Paoletti, ii, 1839, p. 58.

[51] Selvatico/Lazari, 1852, p. 54.

[52] Zanotto, i, 1842-53, II. "Cortile. Prospettive del medesimo," p. 7.

[53] Zanotto, *Nuovissima guida*, 1856, p. 124; Burckhardt/Bode, [4]1879, p. 400c; Della Rovere, n.d. [ca. 1880], p. 8; Fulin/Molmenti, 1881, p. 120; Toffoli, 1883, p. 12; Paoletti, 1893, ii, p. 142; Burckhardt/Bode/Fabriczy, [8]1901, ii, pt. 2, p. 499e; Venturi, *Storia*, vi, 1908, p. 1066; Michel, iv, pt. 1, 1909, p. 191; Ubertalli, 1910, p. xi; *Pal. Duc.*, 1912, p. 10; Pozzo, *Revue numismatique*, 1914, p. 205; Schubring, 1919, p. 244; Bode, [6]1922, p. 150; Fiocco, *Dedalo*, viii, 1927-28, p. 454; Fiocco, *Enc. ital.*, xxix, 1936, p. 502; Mariacher, *Le arti*, 1940-41, p. 197; Hubala in Egg *et al.*, [1]1965, p. 650; Munman, 1968, pp. 87, 237; Pohlandt, *BJ*, 1971, pp. 175ff.; Sheard, 1971, pp. 2, 166, 207; Semenzato in Zorzi *et al.*, 1971, pp. 204, 205; Franzoi, 1973, p. 28.

[54] Serra, 1933, p. 9.

[55] Planiscig, 1921, pp. 156f., 168f. Before Planiscig, Toffoli, 1883, p. 12, had also dated the figure to 1500.

[56] Lorenzetti, [1]1926, p. 235.

[57] Fogolari, n.d. [ca. 1927], p. oppos. pl. 10.

[58] Pincus, 1974, pp. 207f., n. 1, p. 321f.

[59] Mariacher, *Pal. Duc.*, 1950, p. 22. Mariacher, *Arte ven.*, 1948, p. 78, and Mariacher, 1966, n.p. [p. 5], simply noted a close relationship to *Adam*.

[60] Bassi/Trincanato, 1960, p. 46.

[61] Hubala in Egg *et al.*, [1]1965, p. 650.

[62] Mariacher, *Le muse*, x, 1968, p. 145.

[63] Sheard, 1971, p. 207.

[64] Pohlandt, *BJ*, 1971, p. 179.

[65] Fogolari, n.d. [ca. 1927], p. oppos. pl. 10.

[66] Paoletti, 1893, i, p. 43, ii, p. 142.

[67] Mariacher, *Le arti*, 1940-41, pp. 197, 198, n. 14; Mariacher, *Arte ven.*, 1948, p. 78. Semenzato in Zorzi *et al.*, 1971, p. 204, seconded Mariacher's dating and attribution of the *Warrior* to Rizzo.

[68] Mariacher, *Pal. Duc.*, 1950, p. 21.

[69] Pincus, 1974, pp. 328f. Pincus's dating received the qualified assent of Munman, *AB*, 1979, p. 640.

[70] Paoletti, 1893, i, p. 44, ii, p. 142.

[71] Mariacher, *Le arti*, 1940-41, pp. 197, 198; Mariacher, *Arte ven.*, 1948, p. 78.

[72] Romanini, *Arte lom.*, Jan.-June 1964, p. 102, n. 4.

[73] Pincus, 1974, pp. 30, 328ff., 333f., 337f., 461.

10. Venice, Galleria Giorgio Franchetti alla Ca' d'Oro: *Angel with Attributes of Christ*

Figs. 185-189

The *Angel* is currently in storage at the Ca' d'Oro.

White marble with gray veins. There are no traces of polychromy or gilding.

At the bottom rear of the statue, on the left, a very small passage of the surface remains unfinished. The rest of the back of the skirt is only summarily worked. The *Angel* is badly worn and its surface is chipped all over. Borders, particularly, have suffered. More serious is the mutilation of the figure's left foot and the base beneath it. The figure is missing most of its left thumb and index finger. The middle finger of its right hand is chipped, as are curls, especially on the left. Into a broad hole in the middle of the *Angel*'s back there were once inserted two rods to hold the statue in place.

82.5 cm. high x 25 cm. wide.

Cicogna, ii, 1827, p. 57; Selvatico/Lazari, 1852, p. 210; Fulin/Molmenti, 1881, p. 141; Meyer, *JpK*, 1889, p. 194, n. 3; Paoletti, 1893, ii, p. 144; Burckhardt/Bode/Fabriczy, [7]1898, ii, pt. 1, p. 122d; Venturi, *Storia*, vi, 1908, pp. 1060f., n. 2, pp. 1089f.; Michel, iv, pt. 1, 1909, pp. 193, 194; Rambaldi, *Aten. ven.*, 1910, pt. 2, p. 107, n. 1; Paoletti, "Bregno, Antonio," T-B, iv, 1910, p. 569; Muñoz in Pollak/Muñoz, ii, 1911, p. 117; Chiminelli, *Aten. ven.*, 1912, pt. 1, pp. 237f.; Pozzi, *Revue numismatique*, 1914, p. 205; Planiscig, 1921, p. 63; Valentiner, *Art in America*, 1925, p. 319; Lorenzetti, [1]1926, pp. 85, 659; Planiscig, *VJ*, 1926, pp. 98f., 102; Ven., Ca' d'Oro. *Guida-catalogo*, by Fogolari *et al.*, 1929, pp. 79f.; Planiscig, T-B, xxviii, 1934, p. 409; Venturi, *Storia*, x, pt. 1, 1935, pp. 390f.; Fogolari, [2]1950, p. 9; Mariacher, *Arte ven.*, 1950, pp. 105ff.; Lorenzetti, [3]1963, p. 426; Hubala in Egg *et al.*, [1]1965, p. 984; Ven., Procuratie Nuove. *Arte a Ven.*, by Mariacher, 1971, p. 142, no. 67; A. Zorzi, 1972, ii, p. 396; Schulz, *NdiGF*, 1978, pp. 43f., n. 66.

Acquired by the Museo Archeologico, Venice, the *Angel with Attributes of Christ* was displayed in the Camera degli Stucchi of the Ducal Palace between 1852 and 1921.[1] For a short time it was exhibited in the Accademia di Belle Arti[2]

before its definitive transferral to the Ca' d'Oro where, by 1929, it was on view in the *portego*.[3] There it remained until placed in storage during the present restoration of the museum.[4]

In 1852 Selvatico and Lazari identified the provenance of the *Angel* as the destroyed Tomb of Ser Orsato Giustiniani from the demolished Venetian church of S. Andrea della Certosa.[5] Until 1926, when Planiscig conclusively refuted the connection of our figure with the Giustiniani Tomb by confirming the identity of three other, stylistically dissimilar *Virtues*, with lost statues from the tomb,[6] the *Angel* was generally believed to have come from the Giustiniani Tomb.[7] Dissent was voiced only by Planiscig[8] and Venturi, who tentatively suggested that the statue might once have occupied the place of Jacopo Sansovino's *Mars* or *Neptune* on the balustrade of the landing of the Scala dei Giganti.[9] This hypothesis won the approval of Fogolari, Nebbia and Moschini,[10] and Lorenzetti,[11] but was rejected by Rambaldi,[12] Chiminelli,[13] and Mariacher, who pointed out that the unfinished rear of the statue precluded such a siting.[14]

In spite of two immediate objections, I suspect, with Zorzi,[15] that our *Angel* is the statuette, called *Faith*, which Cicogna recorded in 1827 as having come from the Giustiniani Tomb and as having passed into the possession of Don Bruno Stiore of S. Pietro di Castello.[16] In favor of the identification of the figure owned by Don Stiore in 1827 and the figure that turned up in the Camera degli Stucchi in 1852 are the facts that the figure recorded by Cicogna was small, that the earliest notice of our figure—as well as most later ones—erroneously claimed its origin in the Giustiniani Tomb, and that our figure was thrice called *Faith*,[17] although neither of its attributes is symbolic of that virtue. If the figures are the same, then it is likely that the *Angel*, like the Giustiniani Tomb, comes from S. Andrea. Don Bruno Stiore was an ex-Carthusian monk who might have obtained the statue when the church was wantonly demolished after its suppression in 1810.[18]

As long as the *Angel* was believed to have come from the Giustiniani Tomb, attribution of the work shared the fate of the entire tomb and thus depended primarily upon considerations extraneous to the figure's style.[19] Among those who addressed themselves to the style of the figure, attribution of the *Angel* veered between Antonio Rizzo, Pietro Lombardo, and Antonio Lombardo. Proponents of the hand, shop, or manner of Pietro Lombardo comprised Venturi,[20] Valentiner,[21] and Fogolari, Nebbia, and Moschini.[22] Some years later Venturi tentatively advanced the authorship of Antonio Lombardo.[23] The attribution to Rizzo, his shop, or circle, was advocated by Lorenzetti,[24] Planiscig (recanting an earlier opinion),[25] Mariacher,[26] and Hubala.[27] Planiscig[28] and Mariacher[29] thought the *Angel*, similar to one or another of the *Victories* of the Scala dei Giganti, a late work. Indeed, perceiving the intervention of an assistant in the figure's face, Mariacher hypothesized that the figure had been left unfinished when Rizzo fled from Venice.

[1] Selvatico/Lazari, 1852, p. 210; Planiscig, 1921, p. 63.
[2] Planiscig, *VJ*, 1926, p. 98. Lorenzetti, [1]1926, p. 659, saw it in Sala XXIV.
[3] Ven., Ca' d'Oro. *Guida-catalogo*, by Fogolari *et al.*, 1929, p. 79.
[4] Hubala in Egg *et al.*, [1]1965, p. 984.
[5] Selvatico/Lazari, 1852, p. 210.
[6] Planiscig, *VJ*, 1926, pp. 94ff.
[7] Fulin/Molmenti, 1881, p. 141; Meyer, *JpK*, 1889, p. 194, n. 3; Paoletti, 1893, ii, p. 144; Burckhardt/Bode/Fabriczy, [7]1898, ii, pt. 1, p. 122d; Michel, iv, pt. 1, 1909, p. 193; Paoletti, "Bregno, Antonio," T-B, iv, 1910, p. 569; Muñoz in Pollak/Muñoz, ii, 1911, p. 117; Pozzi, *Revue numismatique*, 1914, p. 205; Lorenzetti, [1]1926, p. 659, and, anachronistically, A. Zorzi, 1972, ii, p. 396.

[8] Planiscig, 1921, p. 63.
[9] Venturi, *Storia*, vi, 1908, p. 1060, n. 2, pp. 1089f.
[10] Ven., Ca' d'Oro. *Guida-catalogo*, by Fogolari *et al.*, 1929, pp. 79f.
[11] Lorenzetti, [3]1963, p. 426, but cf. Lorenzetti, [1]1926, p. 659.
[12] Rambaldi, *Aten. ven.*, 1910, pt. 2, p. 107, n. 1.
[13] Chiminelli, *Aten. ven.*, 1912, pt. 1, pp. 237f.
[14] Mariacher, *Arte ven.*, 1950, pp. 106f.; Ven., Procuratie Nuove. *Arte a Ven.*, by Mariacher, 1971, p. 142, no. 67.
[15] A. Zorzi, 1972, ii, p. 396.
[16] Cicogna, ii, 1827, p. 57.
[17] Fulin/Molmenti, 1881, p. 141; Meyer, *JpK*, 1889, p. 194, n. 3; Paoletti, "Bregno, Antonio," T-B, iv, 1910, p. 569.
[18] Cicogna, ii, 1827, p. 52.
[19] For the attribution of the tomb, first to Antonio Dentone named by Francesco Sansovino, and later, to Rizzo, see cat. no. 23.
[20] Venturi, *Storia*, vi, 1908, pp. 1089f. However, in a footnote to his discussion of the Giustiniani Tomb, Venturi, ibid., pp. 1060f., n. 2, casually called it a late work of Rizzo's.
[21] Valentiner, *Art in America*, 1935, p. 319.
[22] Ven., Ca' d'Oro. *Guida-catalogo*, by Fogolari *et al.*, 1929, pp. 79f.; Fogolari, [2]1950, p. 9.
[23] Venturi, *Storia*, x, pt. 1, 1935, pp. 390f.
[24] Lorenzetti, [1]1926, p. 659.
[25] Planiscig, *VJ*, 1926, pp. 99, 102; Planiscig, T-B, xxviii, 1934, p. 409. By contrast, Planiscig, 1921, p. 63, was certain that the work was not by Rizzo, but proposed no alternative attribution.
[26] Mariacher, *Arte ven.*, 1950, pp. 105f.; Ven., Procuratie Nuove. *Arte a Ven.*, by Mariacher, 1971, p. 142, no. 67.
[27] Hubala in Egg *et al.*, [1]1965, p. 984.
[28] Planiscig, *VJ*, 1926, pp. 99, 102; Planiscig, T-B, xxviii, 1934, p. 409.
[29] Mariacher, *Arte ven.*, 1950, pp. 105f.

11. Venice, Madonna dell'Orto: *Annunciate Angel*

Figs. 119-122

The *Annunciation* adorns the exterior of the main portal of the Madonna dell'Orto. The *Angel* stands to the left of the portal's lunette, the *Virgin* to the right.

Istrian limestone.

The *Angel*'s right hand and the rear of his cloak are badly chipped. The statue has lost much of its original surface.

173.5 cm. high.

Moschini, 1815, ii, pt. 1, pp. 9f.; Moschini, 1819, p. 207; E. Paoletti, iii, 1840, p. 27; A. Zanetti, *Enc. ital.*, iv, 1841, p. 1339; Selvatico, 1847, p. 139; Zanotto in *Venezia e le sue lagune*, 1847, ii, pt. 2, p. 154; Zanotto, *Nuovissima guida*, 1856, p. 325; Mothes, i, 1859, p. 254; V. Zanetti, 1870, p. 52; Burckhardt/Bode, [5]1884, ii, pt. 2, p. 427b; Semrau, 1890, p. 269; Paoletti, 1893, i, p. 55, ii, p. 143; Venturi, *Sto-*

ria, vi, 1908, pp. 994, 1061; Bouchaud, 1913, p. 87; Schubring, 1919, p. 237; Venturi, *Storia*, viii, pt. 2, 1924, pp. 315f.; Lorenzetti, ¹1926, p. 395; Fiocco, *Enc. ital.*, xxix, 1936, p. 502; Bigaglia, 1937, p. 10; Mariacher, *Aten. ven.*, 1940, p. 156; Mariacher, *Le arti*, 1940-41, p. 196; Arslan, *GBA*, Sept. 1953, p. 107; Muraro, 1953, p. 252; Mariacher, *Arte ven.*, 1955, p. 41; Gallo, Ist. ven. SLA. *Atti* (Cl. di scienze morali), 1961-62, pp. 200f.; Romanini, *Arte lom.*, Jan.-June 1964, pp. 91, 102, n. 4; Mariacher, 1966, n.p. [pp. 3, 4, 6]; Ven., Procuratie Nuove. *Arte a Ven.*, by Mariacher, 1971, p. 139; Pohlandt, *BJ*, 1971, p. 204; Pincus, 1974, p. 138, n. 31; Connell, 1976, p. 19; Clarke/Rylands, eds., 1977, p. 11; Schulz, *NdiGF*, 1978, p. 48, n. 106.

In 1893 Paoletti published a record from the *catastici* of the Scuola di S. Cristoforo dei Mercanti of the commission for the portal of the Madonna dell'Orto.[1] The commission itself came to light only much later; it was published by Gallo in 1961-62 along with several payments for the portal.[2] Gallo's documents showed that the portal had been commissioned on June 21, 1460, by the Scuola di S. Maria e di S. Cristoforo from Bartolomeo Bon. The portal was to contain a figure of *St. Christopher* at the summit, a *Madonna* in the middle, and other carvings. The work was to be finished within fifteen months. For the work and installation, which was to be done at the sculptor's expense, Bartolomeo was to receive 250 ducats. Payments to Bartolomeo date from July 13, 1460, to October 12, 1461, by which time he had received 215 ducats. Payments to a master mason in July 1461 and between February and August 1462 are probably for walling in the frame.[3] Nevertheless, subsequent payments suggest that the portal was still far from complete when Bartolomeo died, probably in the second half of 1464. In 1475 a piece of the portal was transported from Bartolomeo's workshop to the church. The two marble columns, which had been brought to the site in 1466, were not raised until 1481. Foliage for the door was carved the following year. By March 1, 1483, the portal was finally installed.

The *Annunciation* does not figure in any early source. However, in his guide of 1581 Sansovino attributed to Bartolomeo Bon *St. Christopher* above the center of the portal.[4] On the basis of this attribution, the *Annunciation* also

was long regarded, with varying degrees of confidence, as Bon's.[5] Dissenters included Zanotto, who provisionally assigned the group to the late Trecento sculptor Giovanni de' Santi,[6] and V. Zanetti, who tentatively ascribed it to the anonymous Gothic author of the twelve *Apostles* atop the facade.[7] To Paoletti belongs the credit of having characterized the *Annunciation* as Renaissance. Commenting on the similarities between the *Angel* and Rizzo's *Prudence* from the Tron Tomb (erroneously called *Charity*), Paoletti explicitly assigned *Angel* and *Annunciate Virgin* to different, unnamed sculptors.[8] Until recently, he was the only critic to have distinguished between the styles of the two figures.[9] Venturi included *St. Christopher* as well in his attribution of the portal's statuary to that anonymous, archaizing companion of Antonio Rizzo he held responsible for *St. Helen* from the Capello Tomb, S. Elena, the figures of the *Annunciation* from the Foscari Tomb, S. Maria dei Frari, and the statues above the lunette of the portal of the Scuola di S. Marco.[10] Influenced by Paoletti's suggestion that an assistant of Bon might have completed *St. Christopher*,[11] Venturi later replaced Rizzo's companion with a pupil of Bon's in his attribution of the portal's statuary.[12] Although the *Annunciation* is regularly compared with works associated with the so-called Antonio Bregno (i.e., Niccolò di Giovanni Fiorentino), like the Capello and Giustiniani Tombs, or the *Annunciation* of the Foscari Tomb, no one has ever proposed assigning the group to Bregno. Instead, the *Annunciation* almost invariably figures as a work of Rizzo[13] or his school.[14] The explanation to this paradox is that the *Virgin* (Figs. 237-239) is by Niccolò and his shop,[15] while the *Angel* is by Rizzo. Pohlandt, on the other hand, rejected the attribution of the *Annunciation* to Rizzo. Though she perceived analogies with the "Bregno" oeuvre, she refrained from making any attribution.[16] Biased by the portal's documents, which he discovered, Gallo reasserted Bon's authorship of all three figures.[17]

From Paoletti's report of the date of the commission, Mariacher concluded that the portal had been completed ca. 1460. To that date he assigned the statues of the *Annunciation*.[18] His dating won acceptance by Arslan,[19] Romanini,[20] and Connell,[21] although documents published in between proved the portal still unfinished in 1482. Pincus, alone, dated the *Annunciation* to the late 1470s.[22]

[1] Paoletti, 1893, i, p. 55.

[2] Gallo, Ist. ven. SLA. *Atti* (Cl. di scienze morali), 1961-62, pp. 203f., docs. 2, 3. See also Schulz, *TAPS*, 1978, pt. 3, pp. 74f.

[3] Connell, 1976, p. 19.

[4] Sans., 1581, p. 59r.

[5] Moschini, 1815, ii, pt. 1, pp. 9f.; Moschini, 1819, p. 207; E. Paoletti, iii, 1840, p. 27; A. Zanetti, *Enc. ital.*, iv, 1841, p. 1339; Selvatico, 1847, p. 139; Mothes, i, 1859, p. 254; Burckhardt/Bode, [5]1884, ii, pt. 2, p. 427b; Schubring, 1919, p. 237.

[6] Zanotto, *Nuovissima guida*, 1856, p. 325.

[7] V. Zanetti, 1870, p. 52, followed by Bigaglia, 1937, p. 10.

[8] Paoletti, 1893, i, p. 55, ii, p. 143.

[9] Schulz, *NdiGF*, 1978, pp. 33, 48, n. 106.

[10] Venturi, *Storia,* vi, 1908, pp. 994, 1061, plagiarized by Bouchaud, 1913, p. 87.

[11] Paoletti, "Bono," T-B, iv, 1910, p. 316.

[12] Venturi, *Storia,* viii, pt. 2, 1924, pp. 315f.

[13] Fiocco, *Enc. ital.*, xxix, 1936, p. 502; Mariacher, *Le arti*, 1940-41, p. 196; Arslan, *GBA*, Sept. 1953, p. 107; Romanini, *Arte lom.*, Jan.–June 1964, p. 91; Mariacher, 1966, n.p. [pp. 3, 6]; Ven., Procuratie Nuove, *Arte a Ven.*, by Mariacher, 1971, p. 139; Connell, 1976, p. 19.

[14] Lorenzetti, [1]1926, p. 395; Muraro, 1953, p. 252.

[15] Cat. no. 22.

[16] Pohlandt, *BJ*, 1971, p. 204.

[17] Gallo, Ist. ven. SLA. *Atti* (Cl. di scienze morali), 1961-62, pp. 200f.

[18] Mariacher, *Aten. ven.*, 1940, p. 156; Mariacher, *Le arti*, 1940-41, p. 196; Mariacher, 1966, n.p. [p. 3].

[19] Arslan, *GBA*, Sept. 1953, p. 107.

[20] Romanini, *Arte lom.*, Jan.–June 1964, p. 102, n. 4.

[21] Connell, 1976, p. 19.

[22] Pincus, 1974, p. 138, n. 31.

12. Venice, Museo Civico Correr: Altar of the Traghetto della Maddalena

Figs. 126-129

The altar has been disassembled. The separate parts of its relief are deposited in the storerooms of the Museo Civico Correr. The framework, slabs with gondolas, and the inscription are distributed among three storerooms of the Ca' Rezzonico.

The figurative portions of the altar are Italian limestone. There are no traces of original polychromy of gilding. The pilasters and archivolt are Istrian limestone.

Portions of the original altar comprise the two wings with saints and angels, and most of the framework—architrave and cornice, and the pilaster shafts with their bases. The lunette with its archivolt is contemporary, but probably did not originally belong to the altar. The *Madonna and Child* is sixteenth century. The inscription dates from 1569. The capitals and slabs with gondolas probably date from the period of the altar's reconstruction in the early eighteenth century.

The surface of the lunette is very badly worn; most damaged areas are those that projected most. The perimeter is chipped in several places. The entire surface is covered by a film of dirty gray paint. In the left-hand wing of the ancona, the center of the Baptist's face is gashed from brow through upper lip; his nose is almost totally demolished. The index finger of his pointing hand is almost entirely lost. His cross is badly chipped. An elbow and two toes of the Magdalene are chipped. The profile of the Angel is mutilated. This wing, too, is covered by a film of dirty gray paint. In the right-hand wing, a large piece is missing from the background behind the head of St. Mark. St. Mark's nose is badly chipped and the surface of the stone in the area of his leg and foot is very worn. Half of St. Sebastian's lower lip has been destroyed and his toes are damaged. Again, the Angel's profile is mutilated. The peplum of her chiton is chipped. The surface of the relief is covered with a film of dirty gray paint.

Lunette: 69.5 cm. x 125 cm. x 2.2 cm.; left wing: 103 cm. x 55.6 cm. (exclusive of the Magdalene's elbow which measures 1.5 cm. in width) x 10.1 cm.; right wing: 102.5 cm. x 56 cm. x 9 cm.; *Madonna and Child*: 89.8 cm. x 48.9 cm.; left pilaster (with base): 102 cm. high; right pilaster (with base): 102.5 cm. high.

P̊MÅCO M is inscribed at the bottom of the left wing. The inscription seems to be incomplete: probably it continued in the center of the ancona. The mutilated inscription in the slab below the Madonna was transcribed by Gre-

vembroch. It read: IN TEMPO Ø CIPRIAN / DA
CENEDA GAST E / ANZOLO FANTINATO / ANDREA
PADOAN / COPAGNI / M · D · LXVIIII.[1]

Grevembroch, *Mon. Ven.*, ii, 1754, p. 24; F.,
Gazz. di Ven., Oct. 2, 1834, p. 1; Tassini, (1863)
[8]1970, p. 360; G. Saccardo, *La difesa*, June 2-3,
1886, n.p. [p. 2]; Venice, Bibl. Marc., Cod.
it., Cl. VII, 2289 (= 9125), Fapanni, "Altarini,"
Monumenti veneziani, ii, 1870-88, p. 44, no. 28,
n.p. [p. 80], no. 3; ibid., 2512 (=12217), Fapanni, *Inscrizioni*, 1874?-89, p. 52; Lazzarini,
Bull. di arti, Sept. 1894, p. 2; Rizzi, Ist. ven.
SLA. *Atti* (Cl. di scienze morali), 1972-73, p.
301; Mariacher, *Apollo*, Sept. 1975, pp. 180f.

In 1754 the altar was drawn by Johannes Grevembroch.[2] The altar was then immured on the
exterior of a building at the Traghetto della
Maddalena (Cannaregio 2178/2178A), where it
remained until it was transferred to the Museo
Civico Correr in 1886. In the caption beneath
his drawing, Grevembroch reported that the
altar had been taken by the *gondolieri* of the
Traghetto della Maddalena from a location near
or next to S. Eustachio (commonly known as
S. Stae) on the opposite bank of the Grand
Canal.[3] Saccardo plausibly connected the altar
with a decree of the Consiglio dei Dieci of December 23, 1479, according to which the portico of S. Stae, in which many "dishonest and
dreadful acts were committed," was to be
demolished and, in its place, two altars were to
be erected at the door of the church. Saccardo
reasonably surmised that the altar was moved
across the canal when S. Stae received a new
facade.[4] By 1710 the construction of the new
facade was underway, a competition for its design having been held the previous year.[5]

What did the original altar look like? The inscription, dated 1569, the sixteenth century
Madonna and Child, and the slabs with gondolas
cannot have formed part of the original altar.
If, as seems to be the case, the architrave is
original and uncut, and if the pilaster shafts are
original and stood on either side of the relief,
then the width of the altarpiece must have been
the same before, as it was after, its reconstruction. There is no reason to think that the lateral
wings have been cut on top or bottom. Indeed,
the height of the lateral slabs corresponds quite
closely to 3 Venetian feet (1 Venetian foot =
34.7 cm.). Thus the height of the original relief
was probably equal to the height of the wings,
minus the slabs with gondolas. The height of

the pilaster shafts with their bases equals the
height of the wings. Therefore, we may deduce that the pilasters were used without the
capitals (which, in fact, are merely bases turned
upside down) to frame the relief and support
the architrave. The original relief must have
presented the Madonna with the infant Christ,
for the latter was surely the object of the Angel's veneration and of the pointing finger of
John the Baptist. The Christ Child must have
been placed rather low, for the gazes of the
Angels and the Baptist intersect at a point
slightly below what would have been the midpoint of the central slab.

The lunette could not have formed part of
the original altarpiece. In width it would have
corresponded neither to the width of the entire
ancona nor to the width of any conceivable
central portion, even if that portion were wider
than my reconstruction indicates. Taller than
the lateral slabs, the lunette would have made
far too large a pediment. Indeed, the scale of
the Angels of the lunette slightly exceeds that
of the Angels of the ancona. What original
purpose then might the lunette have served? Its
dimensions make approximately 2 Venetian feet
high by 3.5 Venetian feet wide. Thus its height
is 7.75 cm. (or approximately .25 Venetian foot)
more than its radius. Now, where arches
crowning altars are either segmental or semicircular, lunettes crowning portals are customarily more than half as tall as they are wide.
(The main portal of the Madonna dell'Orto,
for example, has a lunette of identical shape and
proportions.) Very likely, therefore, the archivolt and relief—as wide as an ordinary door—
originally surmounted a subsidiary portal of S.
Stae.

At what point was the altar transformed? Its
reconstruction must have taken place when the
guild of gondoliers acquired the altar. The inscription below the Madonna names the officer
and members of a guild. The slabs flanking the
inscription, introduced to fill spaces left below
the wings of the original ancona when a new
Madonna and Child and inscription were inserted in the center, are incised with gondolas.
So is the footrest of the Madonna's throne. In
view of its mutilation, one may reasonably assume that the *gondolieri* acquired the altar shortly
after the old facade of S. Stae was demolished.
If so, then the reassemblage of the ancona, plus
the addition of the lunette of a portal as crowning pediment, would date from the early eight-

eenth century. A *terminus ante quem* is provided for the reconstruction of the altar by Grevembroch's drawing of 1754.

But the inscription is dated 1569, which accords with the style of the *Madonna and Child*. To be sure, the relief of the *Madonna and Child* is carved from a separate slab and therefore was not necessarily originally linked with the inscription. Nevertheless, the inscription and concordant sixteenth-century style of the *Madonna and Child* might lead us to conclude that in 1569, and not in 1710, the surviving portions of the fifteenth-century altar were acquired by the gondoliers, who then commissioned a *Madonna and Child* to replace a missing center and commemorated that fact by an inscription. That neither the *Madonna and Child* nor the inscription was expressly carved to supplement the fifteenth-century wings, is proved by the lack of correspondence in the base lines of central and lateral fields: clearly, the only portions to have been expressly carved for the reconstructed altarpiece were the lateral slabs with gondolas. If neither *Madonna and Child* nor inscription were specially carved for the reconstructed altarpiece, then its reconstruction need not have taken place in the mid-sixteenth century. Available evidence thus permits us to hypothesize that the extant portions of the fifteenth-century altar and fifteenth-century portal lunette were combined with the *Madonna and Child* from a sixteenth-century altarpiece and

an inscription of 1569 only in the eighteenth century.

The antiquarians of the nineteenth century concurred that the original altarpiece was Lombardesque.[6] Mariacher recently attributed the two lateral panels to a "master who was accustomed to soften the original Lombard harshness with Venetian rhythms; a style that was close to the work of Amadeo, or Mantegazza."[7] Rizzi misbelieved that the altar illustrated by Grevembroch was lost.[8]

[1] Grevembroch, *Mon. Ven.*, ii, 1754, p. 24.
[2] Ibid., p. 24.
[3] Ibid.: "1569. Fu merito de' Gondolieri al traghetto della Maddalena ivi collocare questa Immagine ornata da laterali Figure, trasportate dall'opposta situazione presso il Tempio di Santo Eustachio."
[4] G. Saccardo, *La difesa*, June 2-3, 1886, n.p. [p. 2]. For the decree, published by Corner, *Supplementa*, 1749, pp. 192f., see above, ch. 4, n. 9.
[5] Bassi, 1962, p. 216.
[6] F., *Gazz. di Ven.*, Oct. 2, 1834, p. 1; Tassini, (1863) [8]1970, p. 360; G. Saccardo, *La difesa*, June 2-3, 1886, n.p. [p. 2]; Venice, Bibl. Marc., Cod. it., Cl. VII, 2289 (= 9125), Fapanni, "Altarini," *Monumenti veneziani*, ii, 1870-88, p. 44, no. 28, n.p. [p. 80], no. 3.
[7] Mariacher, *Apollo*, Sept. 1975, pp. 180f.
[8] Rizzi, 1st. ven., SLA. *Atti* (Cl. di scienze morali), 1972-73, p. 301.

13. Venice, Palazzo Decazes: *Vera da Pozzo*

Fig. 194

The *vera da pozzo* is located in the *cortile* of the palace of Duc Elie Decazes (Calle Rota, 875 Dorsoduro).

Wellhead and base are made of Istrian limestone. There are no traces of polychromy or gilding.

The surface of the wellhead is badly worn. The top of the rim is chipped.

85.5 cm. high x 111 cm. in diameter.

Venice, Bibl. Marc., Cod. it., Cl. VII, 2288 (= 9124), Fapanni, "Sponde pregevoli dei pozzi,"

Monumenti veneziani, i, p. 19, no. 9; Ongania, ed., 1889, i, pl. 73.

Record of the wellhead survives from shortly before 1889 when Fapanni noted its location and commented on its fifteenth-century friezes.[1] The *vera da pozzo* was published in 1889 in Ongania's collection of Venetian wellheads, where it was identified as a work of the fifteenth century.[2]

[1] Venice, Bibl. Marc., Cod. it., Cl. VII, 2288 (= 9124), Fapanni, "Sponde pregevoli dei pozzi," *Monumenti veneziani*, i, p. 19, no. 9.
[2] Ongania, ed., 1889, i, pl. 73.

14. Venice, Rio Terrà Barba Fruttarol:
Angel with Simbeni Arms

Fig. 52

The relief is immured in the wall of a house fronting the Rio Terrà Barba Fruttarol (4714 Cannaregio). It has been there probably at least since 1893.[1]

White marble. No traces of polychromy or gilding.

The surface of the relief is extremely worn. The relief is carved from two slabs joined horizontally at the top of the column in the shield. The lower slab is probably a later replacement, added when the relief passed into the possession of a family whose arms were different from those of the relief's original patron. The joint between the two slabs is very conspicuous. The lower part of the shield is much too long; as a consequence, the angel's foot occurs much below the level where the proportions of the figure would lead us to expect it. One of the angel's feet was not carved at all. The carving of the lower part of the relief is clumsy in the extreme. Star and bird in the upper part of the shield, as well as the angel's hands, also seem recut.

83 cm. x 35.3 cm.

Paoletti, 1893, ii, p. 163, fig. 40, p. 296; Vucetich, n.d., i, Parrocchia di SS. Apostoli, no. 36; Comune di Ven., 1905, p. 92, Cannaregio, no. 456; Planiscig, *Pantheon*, Jan.–June 1929, p. 220; Planiscig, *Dedalo*, x, 1929-30, pp. 467f.

The relief was drawn by Antonio Vucetich at the end of the nineteenth century.[2] Although Paoletti published a photograph of our relief, he gave it only passing mention as a work of secondary importance.[3] The compiler of the 1905 list of sculptural fragments on the exterior of Venetian buildings was more perceptive of its quality, but could offer no attribution.[4] In 1929 Planiscig gave the relief to an anonymous sculptor in the circle of Antonio Rizzo, presumed author of the Berlin antependium with Angels from the Villa Altichiero, the *Madonna delle Biade* in the Ducal Palace, and the *Madonna and Child* in the Seminario Patriarcale, but not of the altar frontal of the Cappella Clary in S. Trovaso. Only a few months later, however, Planiscig assigned the relief to the so-called Master of S. Trovaso.[5]

The Simbeni family, to which the arms belong,[6] was not patrician. Acts and testaments notarized by three members of the family, Francesco, Giovanni Francesco, and Pietro, between 1648 and 1710, are preserved at the Archivio di Stato, Venice.

[1] Paoletti, 1893, ii, p. 163, fig. 40; Comune di Ven., 1905, p. 92, Cannaregio, no. 456.
[2] Vucetich, n.d., i, Parrocchia di SS. Apostoli, no. 36. In the margin another hand has written "Simbeni? Limbeni?"
[3] Paoletti, 1893, ii, p. 163, fig. 40, p. 296.
[4] Comune di Ven., 1905, p. 92, Cannaregio, no. 456, where it was called "scoltura bellissima della fine del sec. xv."
[5] Planiscig, *Pantheon*, Jan.–June 1929, p. 220. Planiscig, *Dedalo*, x, 1929-30, pp. 467f.
[6] Ven., Mus. Cor., Cassettiere, De Pellegrini, *Stemmario*, 1890, *voce*, Simbeni.

15. Venice, S. Marco: Altars of SS. James, Paul, and Clement

Altar of St. James

Figs. 1, 3-4, 7, 9, 11-13, 23-28

The altar is located at the northeast corner of the south transept of the basilica.

Except for the saint's bamboo staff, the entire altar is made of dark, yellowish marble. There is no evidence of polychromy or gilding.

The antependium of the Altar of St. James is composed of several diverse pieces of stone. The bases of the pilasters and the moldings that connect them constitute three separate pieces. A large slab furnished the central relief and shafts. The two capitals and upper strip of molding enframing the relief comprise a fifth piece. Small areas of the relief and left pilaster have been effaced by repeated immersions in saltwater. The right upper arm, right hand, and both ankles of the left-hand *putto* are severely cracked. The surfaces of the two candelabra-bearing *Angels* have been badly worn by frequent handling. Otherwise the altar is well preserved.

Altar: 3.737 m. x 1.785 m.; left *putto*: 52.3 cm. high; middle *putto*: 52.7 cm. high; right *putto*: 52.4 cm. high; lunette: 40 cm. x 95.5 cm.; *St. James*: 106.5 cm. high; left candelabra-bearing *Angel*: 49.5 cm. high; right candelabra-bearing *Angel*: 49.3 cm.; front of the altar table: 102 cm. x 156 cm.; relief of the altar table: 68.5 cm. x 113.5 cm.

DVCE INCLITISSIMO ET PIENTISIMO / DNOCRISTO-FORO · MAVRO · PRINCIPE is inscribed in the center of the base of the dossal.

Altar of St. Paul

Figs. 2, 5-6, 8, 14-17

The altar is located at the southeast corner of the north transept of the basilica.

Except for the wooden crossbar of the hilt and the blade of *St. Paul*'s sword, the entire altar is made of dark, yellowish marble. The crossbar of the sword's hilt is gilded; its blade is silvered. There is no other evidence of polychromy or gilding.

The sides of the altar consist of separate pieces of stone. The antependium was executed from variously shaped slabs whose highly visible seams form illogical divisions. The moldings that run beneath the pilasters and relief constitute a separate piece of stone. From a second piece, the shaft of the left-hand pilaster, the relief, and the left and lower strips of molding were fashioned. From a third piece comes the right-hand strip of molding and the right pilaster shaft. The upper strip of molding and the capitals of the pilasters were cut from the slab that forms the top of the altar. The right upper corner of the relief is chipped. Its surface is so badly effaced by immersions in saltwater that large areas are no longer visible.

The first and second toes of *St. Paul*'s right foot and the bottom of his cloak are chipped. The Baroque crossbar of *St. Paul*'s hilt indicates a later restoration. The tips of God's upraised fingers are chipped. The central *putto* lacks his right hand. The left hand of the left

putto is chipped. The feet of all three *putti* are only roughly worked. With these exceptions, the statuary of the altar is well preserved. The candelabra-bearing *Angels* were added to the altar in 1885.

Altar: 3.743 m. x 1.7 m.; left *putto*: 52.2 cm. high; middle *putto*: 55.4 cm. high; right *putto*: 55 cm. high; lunette: 39.5 cm. x 96 cm.; *St. Paul*: 111.5 cm. high; front of altar table: 103.8 cm. x 156 cm.; *Conversion of St. Paul*: 65.5 cm. x 111.7 cm.

DVCE INCHLETISSIMO ET PIENTISSIMO / DNOCRISTO-FOROMAVRO is inscribed in the center of the base of the dossal.

Altar of St. Clement

Figs. 10, 18-22

The altar is located in the basilica's right apsidal chapel dedicated to St. Clement.

The relief is carved from white marble. The yellowish marble of *St. Bernardino* is extremely mottled, as is the gray marble of *St. Mark*. Gilding is visible in the book of *St. Mark* and in the book and disc of *St. Bernardino*. In the relief, gilding is found in the Virgin's halo and the coffers of the background, and is applied consistently to the inscription and ornamental carving of the frame.

The noses of *SS. Bernardino* and *Mark* are chipped. A crack runs through the base and right foot of *St. Mark*; he has lost part of each of the last four fingers of his right hand. There are multiple cracks in his neck.

The large relief, which serves as base to the Quattrocento portions of the altar, portrays St. Nicholas, flanked by SS. James on the left and Andrew on the right, adored by Doge Andrea Gritti (1523-38). It comes from the altar of the Chapel of St. Nicholas in the Ducal Palace and was installed on the altar of St. Clement ca. 1810 when, after the fall of the Venetian republic, the palace chapel was secularized.

Relief with frame: 141.5 cm. x 85 cm.; relief without frame: 70.5 cm. x 54 cm.; *St. Mark*: 82.3 cm. high; *St. Bernardino*: 84 cm. high.

DVCE · SERENISSIMO · DÑO · CHRIST / OFORO MAVRO · M · CCCCLXV · is inscribed in the center of the base of the relief.

Sans., 1581, pp. 36r, 37v; Stringa, *Vita di S. Marco*, 1610, p. 57r; Stringa, *La Chiesa di S. Marco*, 1610, pp. 23v, 24r; Onofri, ¹1663, pp. 88, 93f., 96; Martinelli, ¹1684, pp. 11, 12f.; Pacifico, 1697, pp. 243, 248, 250; [Albrizzi], 1740, p. 15; Corner, *Eccl. Ven.*, 1749, x, pp. 136, 138; Meschinello, ii, 1753, pp. 39, 75, 97; iii, 1754, p. 44; Grevembroch, *Varie venete curiosità*, i, 1755, p. xiii, fig. 39; Gradenigo, (1748-74) 1942, pp. 107, 109, 132; Corner, 1758, p. 192; [Visentini], 1761, pp. 25, 33, 35; Zucchini, ii, 1784, pp. 58, 79f., 91; Maier, pt. 1, ²1795, pp. 158, 159, 160; Moschini, 1815, i, pt. 1, pp. 310f., 321f., 360f.; Cicognara in Cicognara *et al.*, i, ¹1815, n.p. [cc. 20r, 21r]; Moschini, 1819, pp. 85, 89, 91; [Labus] in *Chiese principali*, 1824, "S. Marco," p. 12; *Collezione de' migliori ornamenti*, 1831, pls. xiii, xvi; Piazza, 1835, p. 8, E. Paoletti, ii, 1839, pp. 36f.; Zanotto in *Venezia e le sue lagune*, 1847, ii, pt. 2, pp. 46, 59; Selvatico, 1847, p. 192; Selvatico/Lazari, 1852, pp. 24, 26, 37; Cicogna, vi, pt. 1, 1853, p. 580; Cappelletti, iii, 1853, pp. 326f.; Cappelletti, 1854, pp. 74f.; Zanotto, *Venezia prospettica*, 1856, "Intorno della Basilica di S. Marco," n.p.; Zanotto, *Nuovissima guida*, 1856, pp. 49, 55, 94; Bernasconi, 1859, pp. 29, 37, 38f., 59, 62; Mothes, ii, 1860, p. 69; Bernasconi, 1863, p. 24; Lübke, 1872, ii, p. 189; Guerzoni, Ven., Accademia. *Atti*, 1878, p. 16; Burckhardt/Bode, ⁴1879, p. 401d.; Fulin/Molmenti, 1881, pp. 79, 82f., 98; P. Saccardo, *Arch. ven.*, xxxi, 1886, p. 502; Cecchetti in Ongania, ed., *Basilica*, vii, 1886, p. 88, doc. 365, p. 205, doc. 797, p. 217, doc. 890; Pasini, 1888, pp. 128f., 150f., 161; Perosa in Ongania, ed., *Basilica*, vi, 1888, pt. 2 [1890], pp. 202, 208, 210; F. Saccardo in Ongania, ed., *Basilica*, vi, 1888, pt. 3 [1893], pp. 274, 275; Meyer, *JpK*, 1889, pp. 202, 203; P. Saccardo, 1890, p. 18; Paoletti, 1893, ii, pp. 160f., 197; Burckhardt/Bode/Fabriczy, ⁷1898, II, pt. 1, p. 124d; Bibb, *The American Architect*, July 15, 1899, p. 19; Malaguzzi Valeri, 1904, p. 177, n.1, pp. 193, 335; Marini, 1905, p. 103; Venturi, *Storia*, vi, 1908, pp. 464ff., 1091; Marangoni, n.d. [1910], p. 22; Bouchaud, 1913, p. 164; Moschetti, Padua, Mus. Civ. *Boll.*, 1914, p. 18; Berti, n.d. [1916], pl. 18; Schubring, 1919, p. 248; Planiscig, 1921, pp. 203f.; Planiscig, *ZbK*, 1921, pp. 143ff.; Bode, ⁶1922, p. 152; E. W. Braun, *Belvedere*, 1922, p. 44; J. Braun, 1924, ii, pp. 369, 661; Lorenzetti, ¹1926, pp. 190, 191, 196; Planiscig, 1927, p. 21f.; Callegari, *Dedalo*, ix, 1928-29, pp. 368, 372, 374; Moschetti, T-B, xxiii, 1929, p. 344; Fiocco, *R. di Ven.*, 1930, p. 264, fig. 4, p. 272; Fiocco, *R. d'arte*, 1930, p. 467; Venturi, *L'arte*, 1930, p. 191; Planiscig, T-B, xxvii, 1933, pp. 480f.; Venturi, *Storia*, x, pt. 1, 1935, pp. 388ff.; ibid., x, pt. 3, 1937, p. 17, n. 1; Mariacher/Pignatti, 1950, pp. 41f.; Muraro, 1953, pp. 68, 72; Musolino, 1955, pp. 88f.; Mariacher, *Arte ven.*, 1955, p. 44, n. 1; Robertson, *WJ*, 1960, p. 52, n. 23; Demus, 1960, p. 43; Pozzi/Ciapponi, *Lettere italiane*, 1962, p. 158; Pope-Hennessy, 1964, i, p. 351, no. 376; Hubala in Egg *et al.*, ¹1965, pp. 712, 713, 719; Mariacher, 1966, n.p. [p. 5]; Robertson, 1968, pp. 7f.; Keydel, 1969, pp. 81f., 99; Sheard, 1971, p. 195; Pincus, 1974, pp. 173ff.; Paris, Jacquemart-André. Catalogue by Gavoty, 1975, n.p., no. 116; Middeldorf, 1976, p. 57, K 1305; Wolters, 1976, i, p. 216, no. 137, p. 219, no. 140; Munman, *Arte ven.*, 1976, p. 61, n. 49; Schulz, *NdiGF*, 1978, p. 54; Middeldorf, *Apollo*, Apr. 1978, p. 318; McAndrew, 1980, p. 63.

The Altar of St. Paul may have replaced one dedicated to that saint, erected in 1334[1] and consecrated on March 13, 1339.[2] The Altar of St. James occupies the site in which the body of St. Mark miraculously discovered itself on June 25, 1094.[3] The inscription on each of the three altars designates their patron as Doge Cristoforo Moro (1462-71). Paoletti thought it not unlikely that the commission for the altars had resulted from the doge's gift on November 2, 1464, of a jeweled hanging from which money was to be obtained for the embellishment of S. Marco.[4] But the commission for the altars might also have originated in a previous donation to the church: the document which records the gift of Moro's hanging reports that, on the occasion of his election, Moro allocated to the church's embellishment money traditionally spent for jousts and feasts by newly elected doges.[5] The year of 1465 inscribed on the framework of the relief of the Altar of St. Clement probably refers to the relief's completion. An anonymous fifteenth-century chronicler reported the removal in 1469 of the two lamps marking the site where the body of St. Mark was discovered, from the columns behind the Altar of St. James, to the Altar of St. Leonard; Paoletti seems to have regarded this report as establishing the date of completion of the Altars of SS. James and Paul.[6] Paoletti's dating, as well as his attribution of the altars to

Antonio Rizzo, have been confirmed by a recently discovered document of June 28, 1469. In the document Rizzo acknowledged receipt of 35 gold ducats as the remainder owed him for all work executed by him for Doge Moro on the three altars of S. Marco.[7]

Documents record diverse restorations of the altars. On April 10, 1587, Master Bernardin, sculptor, was paid "for having fixed the figure that was thrown down from the Altar of St. Paul, for having made for it a hand and book."[8] The document does seem to refer to our altar, but, paradoxically, the undamaged hand and book of St. Paul are original. On July 15, 1604, proposals were made to affix halos to the figures of SS. Paul and James and to make the left-hand Angel on the Altar of St. James, which was broken.[9] This last presumably refers to a putto and not the left-hand candelabra-bearing Angel, which shows no sign of damage. Probably the putto was only repaired—the putto on the left is badly cracked in several places and the fractures of the ankles are crudely restored—for the style of the figure matches that of its mates. On November 16, 1788, money was allocated for reerecting a statue that had fallen from the Altar of St. Clement.[10] This was probably St. Mark, which bears considerable signs of damage. Between 1795 and 1815 the anonymous relief with Doge Gritti adoring St. Nicholas, which had originally served as the altarpiece of the Chapel of St. Nicholas in the Ducal Palace,[11] was installed on the Altar of St. Clement.[12] In 1885 the two candelabra-bearing Angels were removed from the niches of the Masegnesque tabernacle next to the Chapel of St. Peter and were installed on the balustrade of the Altar of St. Paul.[13] The relief and statues of the Altar of St. Clement were recently cleaned and their gilding renewed.

The Altar of St. James was drawn by Chevalier and engraved by Bernatti for Le fabbriche cospicue of 1815.[14] Unsigned engravings of a pilaster and a pilaster base from the Altar of St. James were included in a book of engravings of architectural ornament in 1831.[15]

In 1815 Cicognara attributed the Altars of SS. James and Paul to Pietro Lombardo.[16] Although the two altars were accepted as autograph only by Selvatico,[17] Zanotto,[18] Bode,[19] Marangoni,[20] Schubring,[21] and Callegari,[22] they have been viewed consistently as either products of Pietro's shop or reflections of his style.[23] Meyer claimed as probable works by the au-

thor of the Altar of St. James, the Virtues from the Lombardo shop's Tomb of Niccolò Marcello in SS. Giovanni e Paolo and the statues of Pages flanking the standing effigy in the Tomb of Jacopo Marcello in S. Maria dei Frari,[24] recently attributed to Giovanni Buora. Hubala assigned to Pietro Lombardo and his shop the statue of St. James. Venturi is alone in having given both altars once to Antonio Lombardo.[25]

On the basis of a document of January 12, 1561, according to which Danese Cattaneo was credited for the procurement of marble for two figures of SS. James and Paul, to be placed in the church of S. Marco,[26] F. Saccardo attributed the statues of saints in the Altars of SS. Paul and James to the pupil of Jacopo Sansovino and dated them to 1560.[27] Although Paoletti countered, on the one hand, that the statues from the altars exhibited an early Renaissance style, and on the other, that the pertinent document did not name the altars as the destination of the statues,[28] he did not dissuade Venturi from the erroneous attribution of SS. James and Paul to Cattaneo.[29] Lorenzetti thought the statue of St. Paul, later than the rest of the altar, perhaps was Cattaneo's,[30] while Moschetti merely assigned to a "strange hand" the two statues of altars otherwise attributed to Pietro Lombardo.[31] Muraro gave St. Paul to Cattaneo,[32] an attribution that Hubala considered "doubtful."[33] Sheard asserted that the figure of St. James had been "severely recut in the sixteenth or seventeenth century,"[34] while Pincus described both reredoses in their entirety as sixteenth-century pastiches of fifteenth-century motifs.[35]

Raffaele Cattaneo did not live to expound his attribution of the Altars of SS. James and Paul to Luca della Robbia.[36] Its influence may be perceived in F. Saccardo's attribution of the two altars (exclusive of the statues of SS. James and Paul) as well as the Altar of St. Clement to an unknown Florentine.[37] Otherwise, the attribution appears to have found no favor. Paoletti thought it possible that the design for the architecture of the two altars had been furnished by, or reflected the advice of, the Paduan sculptor Bartolomeo Bellano.[38]

In 1859 Bernasconi advanced the name of Antonio Rizzo as author of the Altars of SS. James and Paul. His attribution has proved to be correct, but, based principally on the comparison of the S. Marco Altars with secure works by Pietro Lombardo, like S. Maria dei Miracoli, which Bernasconi arbitrarily claimed for Rizzo, it inspired little confidence.[39] Observing that the ornament did not, in fact, resemble that of S. Maria dei Miracoli, Paoletti rejected the grounds for Bernasconi's attribution, but championed the authorship of Rizzo nonetheless, adducing stylistic comparisons that are valid still.[40] Yet Paoletti's demonstration was almost universally ignored[41] and it was not until the 1950s that critics began to consider possible links with the art of Antonio Rizzo.[42] In an unpublished dissertation of 1969 Keydel reported the discovery of the payment of 1469 to Rizzo,[43] but the information remained unknown to all but a handful of American students of Venetian Quattrocento sculpture.[44] The document was first published in 1978.[45]

In 1921 the relief of the *Conversion of St. Paul* was attributed by Planiscig to Agostino di Duccio.[46] The attribution was explicitly rejected by Fiocco, who gave it to Pietro Lombardo,[47] and by Venturi, who apparently believed that the relief was made many years after Agostino's death in 1481.[48]

Observing the similarity between the ornament of a pilaster of the Altar of St. James and the ornament of the Scala dei Giganti, the anonymous author of the explanatory captions to the plates in a book of engraved architectural ornament was disposed to attribute both to the same masters. These were the otherwise unknown Domenico and Bernardino da Mantova credited by Francesco Sansovino with the ornament in the vaults at the top of the staircase of the Ducal Palace.[49]

Eight years after the installation of the candelabra-bearing *Angels* on the balustrade of the Altar of St. Paul, Paoletti linked them with the earlier Trecento Altar of St. Paul recorded by Sansovino without explicitly proposing such a provenance.[50] No one has sought to claim them for the author of Moro's altar.[51] Hubala mistakenly invoked an alien provenance also for their companions on the balustrade of the Altar of St. James.[52] Middeldorf assigned to these a Lombard origin.[53]

Less conspicuous, the Altar of St. Clement has received far less attention than the twin altars in the crossing of the church. F. Saccardo gave the altar and, less confidently, the front piers of the balustrade to that unknown Florentine responsible for the Altars of SS. James and Paul.[54] Relief and statues were associated with Pietro Lombardo or his shop by Venturi,[55] Mariacher and Pignatti,[56] Robertson,[57] and

Hubala.[58] The relief was included among the motley group of Madonna reliefs out of which Planiscig fashioned an oeuvre for Gian Giorgio Lascari, called Pyrgoteles.[59] Only Braun,[60] Muraro,[61] and, with reservations, Hubala[62] concurred in the attribution. Apparently, even its originator soon abandoned it.[63] To Robertson, the relief seemed close in style to the sculpture of Antonio Rizzo.[64]

[1] Sans., 1581, p. 36r.

[2] Gradenigo, (1748-74) 1942, p. 132, March 13, 1766.

[3] Stringa, *Vita di S. Marco*, 1610, p. 57r.

[4] Paoletti, 1893, ii, p. 161.

[5] Cicogna, vi, pt. 1, 1853, p. 579.

[6] Paoletti, 1893, ii, p. 161, and Cecchetti in Ongania, ed., *Basilica*, vii, 1886, p. 210, doc. 815.

[7] See above, ch. 1, n. 1.

[8] Cecchetti in Ongania, ed., *Basilica*, vii, 1886, p. 217, doc. 890.

[9] Ibid., p. 88, doc. 365.

[10] Ibid., p. 205, doc. 797.

[11] F. Saccardo in Ongania, ed., *Basilica*, vi, 1888, pt. 3 [1893], p. 275. It was described there by Sans., 1581, p. 120r. The altarpiece apparently was standing on the altar when the first mass was celebrated in the new chapel on December 5, 1523: Sanudo, *Diarii*, xxxv, 1892, col. 254.

[12] Cf. the detailed descriptions of the altar by Maier, pt. 1, ²1795, p. 158, and Moschini, 1815, i, pt. 1, pp. 310f.

[13] P. Saccardo, *Arch. ven.*, xxxi, 1886, p. 502; P. Saccardo, 1890, p. 18.

[14] Cicognara et al., i, ¹1815, pl. on [c. 21r].

[15] *Collezione de' migliori ornamenti*, 1831, pls. xiii, xvi.

[16] Cicognara in Cicognara et al., i, ¹1815, n.p. [c. 20r].

[17] Selvatico, 1847, p. 192.

[18] Zanotto in *Venezia e le sue lagune*, 1847, ii, pt. 2, p. 59. In his *Nuovissima guida*, 1856, pp. 55, 94, however, Zanotto betrayed a certain hesitancy in his attribution of the altars to Pietro Lombardo.

[19] Burckhardt/Bode, ⁴1879, p. 401d; Bode, ⁶1922, p. 152.

[20] Marangoni, n.d. [1910], p. 22.

[21] Schubring, 1919, p. 248.

[22] Callegari, *Dedalo*, ix, 1928-29, pp. 372f.

[23] Piazza, 1835, p. 8; Selvatico / Lazari, 1852, pp. 26, 37; Mothes, ii, 1860, p. 69; Lübke, 1872, ii, p. 189; Guerzoni, Ven., Accademia. *Atti*, 1878, p. 16; Fulin/Molmenti, 1881, pp. 82f., 98; Pasini, 1888, pp. 128f., 150f.; Burckhardt/Bode/Fabriczy, ⁷1898, ii, pt. 1, p. 124d; Bibb, *The American Architect*, July 15, 1899, p. 19; Marini, 1905, p. 103; Lorenzetti, ¹1926, pp. 190, 196 (except for the figure of *St. Paul*); Mos-

chetti, T-B, xxiii, 1929, p. 344 (except for the figures of *SS. James* and *Paul*); Mariacher/Pignatti, 1950, pp. 41f.; Muraro, 1953, pp. 68, 72 (except for the figure of *St. Paul* and the relief of the *Conversion of St. Paul*); Robertson, *WJ*, 1960, p. 52, n. 23.

[24] Meyer, *JpK*, 1889, p. 202.

[25] Hubala in Egg *et al.*, ¹1965, p. 712. Venturi, *Storia*, x, pt. 1, 1935, pp. 388ff.

[26] Cecchetti in Ongania, ed., *Basilica*, vii, 1886, p. 216, doc. 877.

[27] F. Saccardo in Ongania, ed., *Basilica*, vi, 1888, pt. 3 [1893], p. 274.

[28] Paoletti, 1893, ii, p. 160.

[29] Venturi, *Storia*, vi, 1908, pp. 464ff.; ibid., x, pt. 3, 1937, p. 17, n. 1.

[30] Lorenzetti, ¹1926, p. 196.

[31] Moschetti, T-B, xxiii, 1929, p. 344.

[32] Muraro, 1953, p. 72.

[33] Hubala in Egg *et al.*, ¹1965, p. 719.

[34] Sheard, 1971, p. 424, n. 6.

[35] Pincus, 1974, p. 174, n. 4.

[36] The attribution was reported by Perosa in his supplement to Cattaneo's "Storia architettonica della basilica," written after Cattaneo's death on December 6, 1889: Perosa in Ongania, ed., *Basilica*, vi, 1888, pt. 2 [1890], pp. 202, 208.

[37] F. Saccardo in Ongania, ed., *Basilica*, vi, 1888, pt. 3 [1893], p. 274.

[38] Paoletti, 1893, ii, p. 161. Keydel, 1969, pp. 241f., n. 14, found the proposal "intriguing." Otherwise, it has produced no echo in the art-historical literature.

[39] Bernasconi, 1859, pp. 38ff.

[40] Paoletti, 1893, ii, pp. 160f.

[41] Only Berti, n.d. [1916], pl. 18, seems to have adopted Paoletti's attribution.

[42] Muraro, 1953, p. 72; Mariacher, 1966, n.p. [p. 5].

[43] Keydel, 1969, p. 82.

[44] Sheard, 1971, p. 424, n. 6; Pincus, 1974, p. 175, n. 4; Munman, *Arte ven.*, 1976, p. 61, n. 49.

[45] Schulz, *NdiGF*, 1978, pp. 64f., n. 21.

[46] Planiscig, *ZbK*, 1921, pp. 143ff.; Planiscig, 1927, pp. 21f.

[47] Fiocco, *R. di Ven.*, 1930, p. 264, fig. 4, p. 272; Fiocco, *R. d'arte*, 1930, p. 467.

[48] Venturi, *L'arte*, 1930, p. 191.

[49] *Collezioni de' migliori ornamenti*, 1831, n.p., "Descrizioni," pl. xiii; Sans., 1581, p. 120r.

[50] Paoletti, 1893, ii, p. 160.

[51] For the history of their dating and attribution, see Wolters, 1976, i, p. 219, no. 140.

[52] Hubala in Egg *et al.*, ¹1965, p. 719.

[53] Middeldorf, 1976, p. 57, K 1305.

[54] F. Saccardo in Ongania, ed., *Basilica*, vi, 1888, pt. 3 [1893], p. 274.

[55] To Venturi, *SS. Mark* and *Bernardino* recalled the style of Pietro Lombardo: *Storia*, vi, 1908, p. 1091, plagiarized by Bouchaud, 1913, p. 164.

[56] Mariacher and Pignatti, 1950, p. 42, assigned the relief of the altar to Lombardo's shop.

[57] To Robertson, *WJ*, 1960, p. 52, n. 23, the relief appeared Lombardesque.

[58] Hubala in Egg *et al.*, ¹1965, p. 713, assigned *St. Mark* to Pietro's shop.

[59] Planiscig, 1921, pp. 203f.

[60] E. W. Braun, *Belvedere*, 1922, p. 44.

[61] Muraro, 1953, p. 68.

[62] Hubala in Egg *et al.*, ¹1965, p. 713. Lorenzetti, ¹1926, p. 191, simply recorded the attribution.

[63] Planiscig, T-B, xxvii, 1933, pp. 480f.

[64] Robertson, 1968, pp. 7f.

16. Venice, S. Maria dei Frari: Tomb of Doge Niccolò Tron

Figs. 64-118

The tomb occupies the left wall of the choir of S. Maria dei Frari.

Of the statues, the three on the first story are made of marble; the rest are limestone. Plain areas of the tomb are encrusted with panels of veined marble. The rear walls of the first-story niches are plaster. The remainder of the tomb is carved from limestone.

There is much evidence of gilding and polychromy. The necklines, belts, and borders of the cloaks of both the large and small *Personifications* of the second, third, and fourth stories are consistently gilded. In some *Personifications*

the hem of the gown is also gilded. *Music*'s lute handle and the lining of *Hope*'s cloak are gilded. Gilding is visible on projecting elements in the niches of the *Personifications* and in their lower bases. The irises and pupils of the *Personifications*, *Gabriel* and the *Virgin*, and the *Resurrected Christ* are painted. The shoes of the recumbent effigy are red. Traces of gold in its cloak probably indicate the imitation of brocade. Gilding is also evident in the raised pattern of the cushions at the effigy's head and feet and in the lion's paws of the bier. Originally, all the clothing of the standing *Doge* was either gilded or polychromed. His gown and mantle imitated gold brocade with the Persian motif of the pine cone, common in fifteenth- and six-teenth-century Italian and Flemish stuffs.[1] The *Doge*'s belt was gilded; his shoes were red. The irises of both the *Doge* and *Prudence* were tinted black. The foliate relief of the second story, and the epitaph, were gilded. The shields borne by the two *Warriors* show crimson stripes.

The tomb is very well preserved. In the stand-ing effigy, the cloak is missing a small chip at the *Doge*'s right wrist. The original right hand and wrist of *Prudence* are lost. Two unfinished patches in her drapery show where the attrib-ute originally held in *Prudence*'s right hand was attached to her torso. The index finger of the statue's left hand is chipped. So, too, is the tip of *Charity*'s nose. Damage is visible in the left foot and base of *Music*, the base and lower por-tion of the gown of *Arithmetic/Grammar*, and the base of the fourth-story *Charity*. The re-cumbent effigy is perfectly preserved. But the inner half of the cushion beneath the *Doge*'s head is only roughhewn, while the inner half of the cushion beneath his feet lacks its raised pattern. The incised border of the ducal bonnet van-ishes toward the rear. The right big toe of *Se-curity* is chipped. The rear upper arm of the *Angel Gabriel* has been hacked off in order to make the statue fit within the narrow space provided by the top of the pier. The *Angel*'s blessing hand has not been entirely extricated from its matrix of stone. The frescoes sur-rounding the tomb were restored between 1902 and 1915.[2]

Prudence: 170.7 cm. high; standing *Doge*: 189.8 cm. high; *Charity*: 169 cm. high.

NICOLAVS · THRONVS · OPTIMVS / CIVIS OPTIMVS SENATOR OPTIMVS / ARISTOCRATIAE PRINCEPS FVIT · / QVO FELICISS DVCE FLORENTISS / VENETORV RES · P · CYPR · IMPERIO / ASCIVIT · CVM · REGE · PAR-THOR CONTRA · TVRCHVM · SOTIA · ARMA / CON-IVNXIT · FRAVDATAM · PECV / NIAM · VIVA · ILLIVS · EFFIGIE · RESIGN / AVIT · CVIVS · INNOCENTISSIMIS / MANIBVS · HANC · MERITĀ · DIVINI · / OPERIS · MOLEM · PHILIPPVS · FILIVS / PENNI · ETNITATE · POSVIT ·

Brasca, (1480) 1966, p. 48; Lengherand, (1485-86) 1861, p. 42; Sabellico, 1487, dec. 3, bk. 9, n.p.; Sabellico, (1491-92) n.d., n.p. [p. 12]; Sanudo, (1493) 1980, p. 51; Harff, (1496-99) 1946, p. 67; Sanudo, RIs, xxii, (1490-1530) 1733, col. 1198; Sans., 1581, pp. 66r, 67rf.; Hen-ninges, 1598, p. 1155; Superbi, 1629, ii, pp.

60f.; Onofri, [1]1663, p. 177; Martinelli, [1]1684, pp. 335f.; Pacifico, 1697, p. 375; Coronelli, n.d. [ca. 1710], "Depositi," n.p.; [Albrizzi], 1740, p. 209; Gradenigo, (1748-74) 1942, p. 237; [Giampiccoli], 1779, p. 79; Maier, i, [1]1787, p. 379; *Nuova cronata veneta compilata del 1795*, 1813, p. 81; Moschini, 1815, ii, pt. 1, p. 184; Cico-gnara, ii, 1816, pp. 151f.; Moschini, 1819, p. 272; Cicognara in Cicognara *et al.*, ii, [1]1820, n.p. [c. 74v]; Soràvia, ii, 1823, pp. 93ff.; Ze-nier, 1825, p. 5; Ticozzi, i, 1830, p. 216; Ca-dorin, 1837, p. 22; Cadorin, 1838, p. 138; Diedo/Zanotto, 1839, "Monumento al Doge Nicolò Trono," n.p.; E. Paoletti, iii, 1840, pp. 91f.; Zanotto, i, 1842-53, II. "Cortile. Scalea dei Giganti opera di Antonio Riccio," p. 38, n. 69; Selvatico, 1847, pp. 179f.; Zanotto in *Ve-nezia e le sue lagune*, 1847, ii, pt. 2, pp. 123ff.; Selvatico/Lazari, 1852, p. 179; Burckhardt, [1]1855, p. 622a; Zanotto, *Nuovissima guida*, 1856, p. 465; Bernasconi, 1859, p. 23; Mothes, ii, 1860, p. 55; Fulin/Molmenti, 1881, p. 291; Perkins, 1883, pp. 213, 358; Burckhardt/Bode, [5]1884, ii, pt. 2, p. 429b; Meyer, *JpK*, 1889, pp. 195ff.; Semrau, 1890, pp. 282f.; Merzario, 1893, ii, p. 25; Paoletti, 1893, ii, pp. 142ff., 157, 160, 247; Biscaro, 1897, pp. 41f.; Burck-hardt/Bode/Fabriczy, [7]1898, ii, pt. 1, p. 121a; Bibb, *The American Architect*, Nov. 4, 1899, p. 36; Pauli, [2]1900, pp. 69f.; Venturi, *Storia*, vi, 1908, pp. 1061ff.; Michel, iv, pt. 1, 1909, pp. 192f.; Morini, *Rass. d'arte*, 1911, p. 72; Bou-chaud, 1913, pp. 111-120; Schubring, 1919, pp. 242f.; Weisbach, 1919, p. 100; Scolari, *Venezia*, 1920, pp. 163, 168; Planiscig, 1921, pp. 64ff.; Bode, [6]1922, p. 150; Venturi, *Storia*, viii, pt. 2, 1924, pp. 505ff.; Lorenzetti, [1]1926, p. 555; Planiscig, *JpK*, 1926, pp. 96f., 98; Guyer, 1928, p. xix; Francovich, *Boll. d'arte*, 1928-29, pp. 486ff.; Fogolari, 1931, p. oppos. pl. 10; Plani-scig, T-B, xxviii, 1934, p. 409; Fiocco, *Enc. ital.*, xxix, 1936, p. 503; Planiscig, *VJ*, 1937, p. 100; Mariacher, Ist. ven SLA. *Atti* (Cl. di scienze morali), 1937-38, pt. 2, p. 585; Da Mosto, 1939, pp. 122ff.; Mariacher, *Arte ven.*, 1948, pp. 73ff.; Muraro, 1953, p. 281; Jacob, 1954, p. 182; Mariacher, *Arte ven.*, 1955, pp. 41f.; Pope-Hennessy, [1]1958, pp. 107f., 349; Sinding-Lar-sen, *Acta ad archaeologiam*, 1962, p. 164; Hubala in Egg *et al.*, [1]1965, pp. 824f.; Seymour, 1966, p. 199; Mariacher, 1966, n.p. [p. 4]; Munman, 1968, pp. 79-109, 114, 128, 335; Pincus, *AB*, 1969, pp. 247-256; Keydel, 1969, pp. 181f.; Deiseroth, 1970, pp. 186f,; Pohlandt, *BJ*, 1971, pp. 180ff.; Sheard, 1971, pp. 124, 125, 163f., 195f., 207, 236, 336, n. 31, p. 368, n. 54, p. 404, n. 51, p. 466, n. 27, p. 467, n. 32, pls. 233A, B; Ven., Procuratie Nuove. *Arte a Ven.*, by Mariacher, 1971, pp. 139ff., no. 66; Heynold-v. Graefe, *Weltkunst*, July 15, 1971, p. 893; Mandelli, *Critica d'arte*, 1972, no. 124, p. 42; Munman, *AB*, 1973, pp. 77-85; Pincus, 1974, pp. 196ff., 312f., 353f., n. 180, p. 397; Connell, 1976, p. 135; Wilk, 1977, p. 11; Sheard, *BJ*, 1978, p. 132; Munman, *AB*, 1979, p. 640; Munman, *Arte ven.*, 1979, p. 28, n. 28; Pincus, *Arte ven.*, 1979, pp. 29, 38, 39; McAndrew, 1980, pp. 63ff.; Trevisani in Treviso, S. Nicolò *et al.*, *Lotto a Treviso*, 1980, ed. Dillon, p. 68; Pincus in *Studies . . . Janson*, 1981, pp. 127-150.

Neither the authorship nor the date of the Tron Tomb is documented. Yet narrow limits for the date of the tomb's construction can be determined. In his testament of August 2, 1466, Niccolò Tron, not yet doge, ordered his burial in S. Maria dei Frari "in the tomb in which his father and mother and other members of his family were buried."[3] Instructions regarding burial were a customary feature of Venetian testaments and do not warrant the assumption, made by Pohlandt, that Tron entrusted the construction of his tomb to Rizzo before his death.[4] Indeed, since Tron's instructions are at variance with the tomb as built—the doge was not buried in the family grave but in a separate monument—we may be certain that he had no hand in it. The doge died on July 28, 1473. The epitaph of the Tron Tomb informs us that Filippo, the doge's son and heir, was responsible for erection of his father's tomb. Work on the tomb had not yet begun on April 17, 1476, when Filippo was ceded the left wall of the choir at the Frari for the tomb. At the same time Filippo was granted permission to make a tomb to be used *in perpetuum* for himself, his heirs, and his descendants, in the pavement at the foot of his father's monument.[5] The tomb was completed by late spring of 1480 when it was seen by Santo Brasca, detained in Venice between May 7 and June 5, on his way to the Holy Land.[6] Quite possibly the tomb was already finished by December 11, 1479, when the monks of the Frari accorded to members of the Alberto family the right of burial in front of the high altar "between the tombs of the two Princes."[7]

The present right hand of *Prudence*, which holds a snake, is restored. The restoration of the hand must postdate 1839, when the Tron Tomb was illustrated in *I monumenti sepolcrali*, for the hand of *Prudence*, as engraved, does not match the present hand.[8] In 1839 the hand was probably already missing. This we can deduce from the fact that the engraving does not show *Prudence*'s original gesture either: the position of the right forearm (which, unlike the hand, is original), was not reproduced in the engraving. That the designer of the engraving should have taken the liberty of changing the forearm to suit the hand he had invented for the figure makes it likely that the figure was then in a mutilated state.

In 1969 Pincus identified what she believed to be the original lost hand of *Prudence*, with a hand holding half a bowl which serves as an *acquasantiera* in the Scuola di S. Giorgio degli Schiavoni at Venice.[9] Since a bowl filled either with a flame or with fruits and flowers is an attribute of Charity, she reasoned that the original figure could not have been intended as a representation of Prudence. Since the figure's companion already holds the flaming bowl, emblem of that aspect of charity characterized by love of God, Pincus concluded that our figure must have stood originally for the aspect of charity defined by love of man—*Amor proximi*. This hypothesis received the qualified assent of Mariacher[10] and Heynold-v. Graefe,[11] but was rejected by Pohlandt.[12]

Indeed, two objections may be made to it. In the first place, the hand holding the bowl in the Scuola di S. Giorgio looks neither like the flaccid left hand of *Prudence*—the work of an assistant—nor like the plump hands, executed by Rizzo himself, with which *Charity-Amor Dei* holds her bowl and mantle. Nor does the bowl of the Scuola di S. Giorgio *acquasantiera* match the bowl that *Amor Dei* holds. Second, our figure was called *Prudence* already in 1823—certainly before the figure's hand was restored and possibly before the hand was lost.[13] In sum, I think it unlikely that the change of attribute and gesture, by means of which *Amor proximi* became *Prudence*, would have occurred in a period that had already learned the value of accurate restoration: surely, we are on safer ground if we assume, with Munman, that the original hand looked like the present one.[14]

The tomb was engraved by Vincenzo Coronelli at the beginning of the eighteenth century.[15] His reproduction bears very little resemblance to the actual tomb. Two measured engravings of the tomb, one showing the tomb as a whole, the other, a detail of the sarcophagus and effigy, were first published in Diedo and Zanotto's *I monumenti sepolcrali* of 1839. Drawn by P. Querena, the first illustration was engraved by Simonetti, the second by Zanetti.[16]

In 1581 Francesco Sansovino attributed to Antonio Bregno the statue of *Doge Tron* along with other unidentified figures from the tomb.[17] Bregno's name continued to be linked with the tomb until the middle of the nineteenth century. Occasionally, Sansovino's attribution to Bregno of the standing *Doge* and "diverse altre figure" was adopted unchanged.[18] Other writers gave to Bregno the tomb in its entirety,[19] all of its sculpture,[20] most of its statuary,[21] or only the figure of the *Doge*.[22] In the French edition of his Venetian guide, Moschini introduced the name of Paolo Bregno, the putative brother of Antonio who, he thought, had probably assisted Antonio in the execution of the tomb.[23] Moschini's double attribution of the tomb was adopted by Burckhardt.[24] But in 1837 Cadorin pointed out that the surname, Bregno, as used by Sansovino, was merely another name for Rizzo.[25] It followed that the statue of the *Doge* and the other figures of the Tron Tomb attributed to Bregno actually were Rizzo's.[26] The name of Bregno was soon replaced by that of Rizzo in the attribution of the tomb.[27] Although Bernasconi mentioned the tomb only once in his monograph on Rizzo in the course of reporting its attribution by Selvatico and Zanotto,[28] and Biscaro[29] gave the tomb to Pietro Lombardo, the Tron Tomb has long enjoyed a reputation as Rizzo's major work.

Nevertheless, even to the dilettante it was obvious that the entire tomb did not share the high quality of some of its parts. Perkins thought the tomb unworthy of Rizzo's reputation.[30] Cicognara,[31] Burckhardt,[32] Mothes,[33] and Zanotto[34] hypothesized the participation of other sculptors. Since the mid-nineteenth century, controversy has waged over the precise extent of Rizzo's personal responsibility: so far, only Rizzo's authorship of *Prudence* has escaped question.

It is only very recently that the attribution to Rizzo of the first-story *Charity* has been doubted: in the critical literature *Charity* and *Prudence* were traditionally linked by their common attribution to the master of the shop.[35] In 1969 Pincus attributed the obvious difference in style be-

tween the two to different authorship: *Charity* she gave to Tullio Lombardo.[36] Her attribution was accepted by Sheard,[37] and, with reservations, by Wilk,[38] but rejected by Pohlandt[39] and Munman.[40] Mariacher simply ignored Pincus's attribution.[41]

Before it was repudiated by Venturi in 1908,[42] the attribution of the standing *Doge* to Rizzo was not questioned,[43] except by Bode, and Bibb.[44] Although Venturi later changed his mind,[45] he succeeded in persuading Bouchaud,[46] Da Mosto,[47] Hubala,[48] Pincus,[49] McAndrew,[50] and Planiscig, though Planiscig, too, later recanted. The majority of critics have considered it the work of Rizzo;[51] no other author has ever been proposed.

The statues of *Virtues* and *Liberal Arts* occupying upper-story niches, as well as *Christ* and the *Annunciate Virgin* and *Angel*, are generally recognized as products of Rizzo's shop, rather than his hand. Paoletti is unique in having attributed to the master the *Annunciate Angel* and *Music*.[52] Occasionally the two *Warriors* occur among those works attributed indiscriminately to the shop;[53] occasionally they are claimed for Rizzo himself.[54] On the other hand, the left-hand *Warrior*'s evident superiority induced some scholars to assign the figures to different sculptors. Burckhardt attributed the left-hand *Warrior* to Lorenzo Bregno, whom he defined as the major force in the shop of Antonio and Paolo Bregno.[55] Paoletti,[56] Planiscig,[57] and Guyer[58] ascribed the left-hand *Warrior* to Rizzo. Mariacher suggested that an assistant of Rizzo's had intervened to a greater extent in the *Warrior* on the right than in his companion on the left.[59] Although he acknowledged the superiority of the figure on the left,[60] Munman was inclined to think that both *Warriors* had been designed and partly executed by Rizzo.[61] Pohlandt thought that the sculptor of the two *Pages* of the Tomb of Giovanni Emo, whom she could not identify, might have done the left-hand *Warrior*.[62] Sheard believed that Rizzo was assisted extensively in his execution of the left-hand *Warrior*; but its mate, in its entirety, she gave to an assistant, hypothetically identified with Tullio Lombardo.[63]

The recumbent effigy of the *Doge* was specifically ascribed to Rizzo by Paoletti,[64] Fabriczy,[65] and Munman.[66] Pohlandt could not decide whether the figure were a mere copy of the portrait of the standing *Doge* or an autograph work of Rizzo's.[67] The three *Personifica-*

tions ornamenting the sarcophagus were given to Rizzo by Fabriczy,[68] Venturi,[69] Bouchaud,[70] and, with reservations, by Munman.[71] Pohlandt assigned *Security* to the author of the left-hand *Warrior*.[72] Munman stands alone in having given to Rizzo the heads of emperors in medallions on the sarcophagus.[73]

The reliefs with *putti* were claimed for Rizzo by Meyer,[74] Planiscig,[75] and Pope-Hennessy.[76] Cicognara thought the reliefs, which he found similar in style to the antependium with angels in the Cappella Clary, S. Trovaso, were by a hand other than the master's (who, for him, was Antonio Bregno).[77] Munman believed the right-hand relief largely carved by Rizzo, while its pendant, he thought, was due to a member of the shop.[78] Pohlandt attributed the reliefs to the sculptor responsible for *Security* and the *Warrior* on the left.[79]

In 1908 Venturi denied Rizzo's responsibility for the architecture of the tomb.[80] No one besides Bouchaud, Venturi's plagiarist, has doubted Rizzo's authorship of the tomb's design.[81] Venturi himself eventually changed his mind.[82] Pohlandt,[83] following Zanotto,[84] observed that the foliate ornament of the first-story pilasters, which has nothing in common with the decoration of the *Scala dei Giganti*, closely resembles architectural ornament by Pietro Lombardo.

Pincus dedicated two studies to an interpretation of the tomb's iconography. In 1969 she sought to identify the figures of *Charity* and *Prudence* in the lowest story of the tomb as the contrasting Charity–Amor Dei and Charity–Amor Proximi, respectively.[85] I have given my reasons above for disbelieving the second of these two identifications and for preferring the appellation *Prudence*. In 1981 she interpreted various motifs as contributing to a portrayal of the doge "as the central figure in effecting the harmonious workings of the state."[86] The three *Personifications* of the sarcophagus were credibly read, from left to right, as Peace, Abundance, and Security. As a personification of divine order Pincus identified the figure with lute; her companion with the tablet signified to Pincus the order of the state. To this it may be objected that if these figures had been intended to convey a meaning beyond, or different from, that usually connoted by their attributes—a lute for music, an uninscribed tablet (not a book) for Arithmetic or Grammar—their author would surely have revealed that meaning by some more pointed means, like inscriptions. Indeed, Pincus knew no examples of an uninscribed rectangular tablet symbolizing civil law; nor do I. The four busts of emperors Pincus construed as personifications simultaneously of the four ages of man and the four humors. In refutation it may be observed that the four heads do not represent the same person, as Pincus claimed, and that there is virtually no distinction in age between the two she called "Youth" and "Prime." The alignment of the different heads with parts of Tron's effigy lying above them seems to me insufficient to warrant an interpretation of the busts as the four humors. Finally, in the reliefs with *putti* Pincus saw the "message of ongoing life." This, too, is hard to credit since an identical motif occurs in Donatello's Cantoria (and nowhere else in Renaissance art prior to the Tron Tomb, as far as I know), where it cannot have had any such funerary meaning. Indeed, the very different contexts in which the motif was used suggests that, in both cases, its function was purely decorative.

[1] Scolari, *Venezia*, 1920, p. 168.

[2] Ibid., pp. 168, 171.

[3] Venice, ASV, Archivio Notarile, *Testamenti*, Busta 1214 (not. Antonio Marsilio), no. 1043, for which, see above ch. 3, n. 11.

[4] Pohlandt, *BJ*, 1971, p. 190.

[5] ASV, Fondi ecclesiastici, S. Maria Gloriosa dei Frari, Chiesa e Conventi, *Processi, etc.*, *T-Z*, for which, see above ch. 3, n. 12.

[6] Brasca, (1480) 1966, p. 48, for which, see above ch. 3, n. 14.

[7] Pincus, *AB*, 1969, p. 247, n. 1. On the basis of this document, Pincus, seconded by Pohlandt, *BJ*, 1971, p. 190, assumed that "a substantial part, if not all, of the Tron tomb had been built" by 1479. Sheard, 1971, p. 404, n. 51, inferred from the document a *terminus ante quem* of 1479 for the architectural framework of the tomb, but was more cautious in *BJ*, 1978, p. 132, n. 36.

[8] Diedo/Zanotto, 1839, n.p., pl. 2. In all other respects the engraving of the tomb is very accurate.

[9] Pincus, *AB*, 1969, pp. 249ff.

[10] Ven., Procuratie Nuove, *Arte a Ven.*, by Mariacher, 1971, p. 141, no. 66.

[11] Heynold-v. Graefe, *Weltkunst*, July 15, 1971, p. 893.

[12] Pohlandt, *BJ*, 1971, pp. 189f.

[13] Soràvia, ii, 1823, p. 93. In his commentary on the engraving of the Tron Tomb, Zanotto in Diedo/Zanotto, 1839, "Monumento al Doge Nicolò Trono," n.p., also called the figure *Prudence*.

[14] Munman, 1968, p. 81.

[15] Coronelli, n.d. [ca. 1710], "Depositi," n.p.

[16] Diedo/Zanotto, 1839, n.p., pls. 2, 3.

[17] Sans., 1581, p. 66r: "La Statua di Nicolò Trono Doge 67. con diuerse altre figure, che vi sono fu lauorata da Antonio Bregno."

[18] Pacifico, 1697, p. 375; *Nuova cronaca veneta compilata del 1795*, 1813, p. 81; Moschini, 1815, ii, pt. 1, p. 184.

[19] Cicognara in Cicognara *et al.*, ii, [1]1820, n.p. [c.74v]; Ticozzi, i, 1830, p. 216.

[20] Zenier, 1825, p. 6.

[21] Cicognara, ii, 1816, pp. 151f.

[22] Soràvia, ii, 1823, p. 93; E. Paoletti, iii, 1840, pp. 91f.; Burckhardt, [1]1855, p. 622a.

[23] Moschini, 1819, p. 272. Thus Moschini applied to the Tron Tomb information from the questionable legend of Marco Sebastiano Giampiccoli's engraving of 1777 of the Tomb of Doge Francesco Foscari, S. Maria dei Frari, to which attention had been drawn three years earlier by Cicognara, ii, 1816, p. 153.

[24] Burckhardt, [1]1855, p. 622a.

[25] Cadorin, 1837, pp. 21f.

[26] This also applied to the Scala dei Giganti, *q.v.*

[27] Zanotto in Diedo/Zanotto, 1839, "Monumento al Doge Nicolò Trono," n.p.; Selvatico, 1847, p. 179; Selvatico/Lazari, 1852, p. 179; Zanotto, *Nuovissima guida*, 1856, p. 465; Fulin/Molmenti, 1881, p. 291. Burckhardt, [1]1855, p. 622a, however, retained the name of Bregno.

[28] Bernasconi, 1859, p. 23.

[29] Biscaro, 1897, pp. 41f.

[30] Perkins, 1883, pp. 213, 358. Nevertheless, he conceded that the tomb might have been designed by Rizzo.

[31] Cicognara, ii, 1816, p. 152.

[32] Burckhardt, [1]1855, p. 622a.

[33] Mothes, ii, 1860, p. 55.

[34] Zanotto in *Venezia e le sue lagune*, 1847, ii, pt. 2, pp. 123ff.

[35] Zanotto, i, 1842-53, II. "Cortile. Scalea dei Giganti opera di Antonio Riccio," p. 38, n. 69; Mothes, ii, 1860, p. 55; Burckhardt/Bode, [5]1884, ii, pt. 2, p. 429b; Meyer, *JpK*, 1889, p. 197; Paoletti, 1893, ii, p. 143, who interchanged *Charity* and *Prudence*, introducing a confusion that has plagued the literature on the Tron Tomb ever since; Burckhardt/Bode/Fabriczy, [7]1898, ii, pt. 1, p. 121a; Venturi, *Storia*, vi, 1908, p. 1061; Michel, iv, pt. 1, 1909, pp. 192f.; Morini, *Rass. d'arte*, 1911, p. 72; Bouchaud, 1913, pp. 118f.; Planiscig, 1921, pp. 66ff.; Bode, [6]1922, p. 150; Lorenzetti, [1]1926, p. 555; Planiscig, *VJ*, 1926, p. 96; Guyer, 1928, p. xix; Fogolari, 1931, p. oppos. pl. 10; Planiscig, T-B, xxviii, 1934, p. 409; Fiocco, *Enc. ital.*, xxix, 1936, p. 503; Da Mosto, 1939, pp. 124f.; Mariacher, *Arte ven.*, 1948, p. 74; Pope-Hennessy, [1]1958, p. 349; Hubala in Egg *et al.*, [1]1965, p. 824; Mariacher, 1966, n.p. [p. 4]; Munman, 1968, pp. 88ff.; Janson in *Propyläen Kstge.*, vii, 1972,, p. 306, nos. 276a, b.

[36] Pincus, *AB*, 1969, p. 253, n. 33; Pincus, *Arte ven.*, 1979, pp. 29, 38.

[37] Sheard, 1971, pp. 163f.

[38] Wilk, 1977, p. 11.

[39] Pohlandt, *BJ*, 1971, pp. 184ff., 190.

[40] Munman, *AB*, 1973, p. 79; Munman, *AB*, 1979, p. 640.

[41] Ven., Procuratie Nuove, *Arte a Ven.*, by Mariacher, 1971, pp. 139ff., no. 66.

[42] Venturi, *Storia*, vi, 1908, p. 1061.

[43] Zanotto, i, 1842-53, II. "Cortile. Scalea dei Giganti opera di Antonio Riccio," p. 38, n. 69; Zanotto, *Nuovissima guida*, 1856, p. 465; Mothes, ii, 1860, p. 55; Meyer, *JpK*, 1889, pp. 197f.; Paoletti, 1893, ii, pp. 142f.; Burckhardt/Bode/Fabriczy, [7]1898, ii, pt. 1, p. 121a.

[44] Burckhardt/Bode, [5]1884, ii, pt. 2, p. 429b; Bibb, *The American Architect*, Nov. 4, 1899, p. 36. But cf. ibid., July 15, 1899, p. 19.

[45] Venturi, *Storia*, viii, pt. 2, 1924, p. 505, n. 1.

[46] Bouchaud, 1913, p. 116.

[47] Da Mosto, 1939, p. 125.

[48] Hubala in Egg *et al.*, [1]1965, p. 824.

[49] Pincus, 1974, p. 397.

[50] McAndrew, 1980, p. 69, who conceded that "the master may have touched the head."

[51] Planiscig, 1921, pp. 68f.; Planiscig, *VJ*, 1926, pp. 96, 97, n. 4; Fiocco, *Enc. ital.*, xxix, 1936, p. 503; Mariacher, Ist. ven. SLA. *Atti* (Cl. di scienze morali), 1937-38, pt. 2, p. 585; Mariacher, *Arte ven.*, 1948, p. 74; Pope-Hennessy, [1]1958, p. 349; Mariacher, 1966, n.p. [p. 4]; Munman, 1968, pp. 90f.; Pohlandt, *BJ*, 1971, pp. 183f.; Ven., Procuratie Nuove, *Arte a Ven.*, by Mariacher, 1971, p. 139, no. 66.

[52] Paoletti, 1893, ii, p. 143.

[53] Burckhardt/Bode, [5]1884, ii, pt. 2, p. 429b; Lorenzetti, [1]1926, p. 555; Planiscig, T-B, xxviii, 1934, p. 409; Fiocco, *Enc. ital.*, xxix, 1936, p. 503; Da Mosto, 1939, p. 125.

[54] Meyer, *JpK*, 1889, p. 197; Venturi, *Storia*, vi, 1908, p. 1061; Bouchaud, 1913, p. 119; Fogolari, 1931, p. oppos. pl. 10; Pope-Hennessy, [1]1958, p. 349; Hubala in Egg *et al.*, [1]1965, p. 824.

[55] Burckhardt, [1]1855, p. 622a.

[56] Paoletti, 1893, ii, p. 143.

[57] Planiscig, 1921, p. 68.

[58] Guyer, 1928, p. xix.

[59] Mariacher, *Arte ven.*, 1948, p. 76.

[60] Munman, 1968, pp. 91f.

[61] Both *Pages* were labeled workshop pieces by Munman in *Arte ven.*, 1979, p. 28, n. 28.

[62] Pohlandt, *BJ*, 1971, pp. 190f., n. 50.

[63] Sheard, 1971, pls. 233A, B.

[64] Paoletti, 1893, ii, p. 143.

[65] Burckhardt/Bode/Fabriczy, [7]1898, ii, pt. 1, p. 121a.

[66] Munman, 1968, pp. 94ff., 335; Munman, *AB*, 1973, p. 81.

[67] Pohlandt, *BJ*, 1971, p. 191, n. 50.

[68] Burckhardt/Bode/Fabriczy, [7]1898, ii, pt. 1, p. 121a.

[69] Venturi, *Storia*, vi, 1908, p. 1061.

[70] Bouchaud, 1913, p. 119.

[71] Munman, 1968, p. 93. Munman, *AB*, 1973, p. 79, continued to attribute the design of all three *Personifications* to Rizzo, but was less persuaded that their execution—undertaken, he thought, by a single sculptor—was due to the master of the shop.

[72] Pohlandt, *BJ*, 1971, p. 191, n. 50.

[73] Munman, 1968, p. 94; Munman, *AB*, 1973, p. 81.

[74] Meyer, *JpK*, 1889, p. 197.

[75] Planiscig, 1921, p. 68.

[76] Pope-Hennessy, [1]1958, p. 349.

[77] Cicognara, ii, 1816, p. 152.

[78] Munman, 1968, pp. 92f.

[79] Pohlandt, *BJ*, 1971, p. 191, n. 50.

[80] Venturi, *Storia*, vi, 1908, p. 1064.

[81] Bouchaud, 1913, p. 120.

[82] Venturi, *Storia*, viii, pt. 2, 1924, pp. 505ff.

[83] Pohlandt, *BJ*, 1971, p. 198.

[84] Zanotto in *Venezia e le sue lagune*, 1847, ii, pt. 2, pp. 123f.

[85] Pincus, *AB*, 1969, pp. 247-256.

[86] Pincus in *Studies . . . Janson*, 1981, pp. 127-150.

17. Venice, S. Maria dei Servi (formerly): Tomb of Giovanni Emo

Figs. 138-146

Only the statuary of the tomb survives. The *Effigy of Giovanni Emo* is exhibited in a loggia of the courtyard of the Museo Civico, Vicenza (inv. no. E II 29a). The two *Pages* are in the Louvre, Paris (inv. nos. 1627, 1628).

The original appearance of the tomb is preserved in a watercolor drawing by Johannes Grevembroch.[1] It shows the tomb raised on a high double-tiered base, the broad center of which projects. At the top of the base, the epitaph entirely fills the frieze of the salient portion of the base. Above the epitaph ten acanthus volute brackets support the projecting floor. The aedicule, which rests on it, is aligned with the salient portion of the base. At either side a fluted free-standing Composite column rests on a high circular base whose front face is decorated with a severed head on a ribbon and two festoons hanging from a central ring. At the sides of the drum ribbons are intertwined. Behind the columns are pilasters, which apparently match the columns. Together, pilasters and columns support a flat ceiling embellished by a double row of coffers with rosettes. Above the columns is an entablature, its frieze ornamented with *rinceaux* flanking a central group of crossed keys with a papal tiara, a rayed *mandorla* and a running donkey (?). The lunette consists of a very low segmental arch with fluted archivolt terminating in paterae with rosettes. Recessed in the rear wall of the aedicule are four equal rectangles disposed in two tiers. At the top of the base, on either side of the aedicule, stand life-size, adolescent *Pages*.

The sarcophagus is raised on its own base consisting of a step and plain moldings. The area between the legs of the sarcophagus is filled; in the center is a winged head. The upper half of the sarcophagus, decorated with *rinceaux* flanking a central image of the half-length lion of St. Mark within a wreath, forms a parallelepiped. The lower half, covered with imbrication, curves inward toward the legs. Curved lion's-paw legs embrace the entire height of the lower part of the sarcophagus. The sarcophagus lacks a cover. The over-life-size statue of *Giovanni Emo* stands on the sarcophagus.

The statue of *Emo* is made of *pietra d'Idria*, a coarse limestone. The *Pages* are carved from Istrian limestone.

Grevembroch's illustration in *Monumenta Veneta* reveals gilding on the ornament of the bases of the columns, on alternate moldings and the ornament of the frieze of the entablature, on alternate moldings of the lunette, on the projecting portions of the capitals, on the wreath and lion of St. Mark, the foliate ornament, edges of the scales and legs of the sarcophagus, on the winged head beneath it, on alternate moldings, and the brackets of the base. *Emo's* gown and cloak were evidently painted in imitation of brocade. The effigy's hat was also polychromed. The *Pages'* hair, sashes, and borders of doublets and puffed sleeves, were polychromed.

In a second drawing by Grevembroch of the effigy alone, the figure wears a yellow cloak with a gold design, and a black *berretta*.[2] A white shirt is visible at cuffs and neck. The sleeve of *Emo's* gown is red.

A fissure, which penetrates the entire depth of the statue from the top of the right shoulder to the wrist, has severed *Emo*'s arm from his body. Probably the arm was originally pieced. Half of *Emo*'s left foot is broken off. The statue is flat and unfinished in back.

The *Pages* are well preserved. The matrix of stone remains between the leg and shield in both *Pages* and between the lower portion of the legs of the right-hand *Page*. It has been suggested that a helmet, which had disappeared by the time Grevembroch drew the tomb, may once have rested in the crook of the elbow of the right-hand *Page*.[3]

Munman estimated that the tomb originally measured approximately 9.2 m. x 5.2 m.[4] *Emo*: 217 cm. x 75 cm.; left *Page*: 128 cm. x 37 cm.; right *Page*: 124 cm. x 40 cm.

IOANNI HEMO EQVITI AVRATO SENATORI GRAVISS QVI DOMI FORISQ AMPLISS MAGISTRATIBVS SVMMISQVE IN ASIA / ET EVROPA LEGATIONIBVS FVNCTVS QVVM PADO PONTE SVPERATO PVBLICA SIGNA FERARIAM ADMOVISSET / NON MINORE EXERCITVS QVAM SVORVM LVCTV INTERIIT FILII PIENTISSIMI POSVERE.[5]

Sanudo, (1493) 1980, p. 51; Sans., 1581, p. 58r; Sans./Stringa, 1604, p. 145r; Superbi, 1629, ii, p. 73; Martinelli, [1]1684, p. 258; Pacifico, 1697, p. 334; [Albrizzi], 1740, p. 188; Corner, *Eccl. Ven.*, 1749, ii, p. 53; Grevembroch, *Gli abiti*, i, p. 38; Grevembroch, *Mon. Ven.*, iii, 1759, p. 27; Venice, Mus. Cor., MS Cicogna 1536, Bergantini, "Memorie della famiglia Emo," p. 290; [Giampiccoli], 1779, p. 60; Maier, pt. 1, [2]1795, p. 363; *Diario patrio per Venezia*, 1806, p. 37; Cicogna, i, 1824, pp. 36f., no. 3; Magrini, 1855, p. 61; Venice, Bibl. Marc., Cod. it., Cl. VII, 2511 (= 12216), Fapanni, *Vicende e mutazioni*, p. 155; [Visinoni], *Bull. di arti*, Aug. 1877, pp. 34-37; Fulin/Molmenti, 1881, p. 255; *Elenco . . . di Vicenza*, 1881, p. 36, "Sculture," no. 5; Meyer, *JpK*, 1889, p. 198; [Bianchini], 1892, p. 10; Paoletti, 1893, i, p. 22, n. 5, ii, pp. 149f., 203; Burckhardt/Bode/Fabriczy, [7]1898, ii, pt. 1, p. 122c; Vicenza, Mus. Civ. Minozzi, *Inventario*, 1902, p. 124, no. 64, p. 126, no. 86; Marquet de Vasselot, *Les arts*, July 1903, pp. 28, 30; Hermann in Egger/Hermann, *ZbK*, 1906, p. 95; Venturi, *Storia*, vi, 1908, pp. 1064f.; Michel, iv, pt. 1, 1909, p. 193; Ongaro, Vicenza, Mus. Civ. *Boll.*, Jan.–Mar. 1910, pp. 9f.; Rumor/Ongaro, ibid., pp. 20-25; Rumor, n.d. [1910?], pp. 47ff.; Bouchaud, 1913, p. 121;

Pozzi, *Revue numismatique*, 1914, p. 205; L. Venturi, *L'arte*, 1916, pp. 49f.; Michel in Paris, Louvre. Catalogue by Leprieur *et al.*, 1917, pp. 42f., nos. 24, 25; Marquand, *Art in America*, 1917-18, pp. 54, 60; Schubring, 1919, p. 243; Vienna, Ksthis. Mus. Catalogue by Planiscig, 1919, p. 52, no. 92; Bortolan/Rumor, 1919, p. 153; Vicentini, *S. Maria de' Servi*, 1920, pp. 70ff.; Vicentini, *Ideale risurrezione*, 1920, pp. 34ff.; Planiscig, 1921, pp. 69f.; Paris, Louvre. Catalogue, i, 1922, p. 92, nos. 750, 751; Bode, [6]1922, p. 150; Planiscig, *VJ*, 1926, p. 98; Lorenzetti, [1]1926, p. 85; Francovich, *Boll d'arte*, 1928-29, pp. 484, 488; Planiscig, T-B, xxviii, 1934, p. 409; Paris, Petit Palais. *Exposition de l'art italien*, cat., 1935, pp. 328f., nos. 1073, 1074; Serra, *Boll. d'arte*, 1935-36, pp. 89f.; Fiocco, *Enc. ital.*, xxix, 1936, p. 503; Fasolo, 1940, p. 45, no. 168; Mariacher, *Arte ven.*, 1948, pp. 78ff.; Vicenza, Mus. Civ. *Inventario E-II*, 1950, "Statuaria e pezzi vari," no. 29; Pope-Hennessy, [1]1958, p. 349; Vicenza, Mus. Civ. Catalogue by Barbieri, 1962, pp. 229ff.; Hubala in Egg *et al.*, [1]1965, p. 825; Mariacher, 1966, n.p. [p. 5]; Munman, 1968, pp. 192-201, 335; Deiseroth, 1970, p. 269, n. 551; Pohlandt, *BJ*, 1971, pp. 190f., n. 50; Ven., Procuratie Nuove. *Arte a Ven.*, by Mariacher, 1971, p. 139; Sheard, 1971, pp. 80, 95ff., 197; A. Zorzi, 1972, i, p. 135, ii, p. 353; Pincus, 1974, p. 195, n. 21, pp. 196f., 397; Connell, 1976, p. 135; Munman, *Arte ven.*, 1976, p. 44; Wolters, 1976, i, p. 125; Sheard, *Yale Ital. Studies*, 1977, p. 262, n. 13; Munman, *Arte ven.*, 1979, p. 28, n. 28; Schulz, Washington, D.C., Nat. Gall. of Art. *Studies*, 1980, pp. 7ff.; McAndrew, 1980, p. 81.

On January 1, 1482, the left apsidal chapel in the Venetian church of S. Maria dei Servi was ceded to Giovanni Emo and his heirs by the chapter of the Servi in exchange for an earlier family chapel dedicated to S. Matteo which, located beneath the *barco*, had been destroyed in the rebuilding of the church. The chapel's altar was to be dedicated to SS. John the Baptist and John the Evangelist. The new chapel would provide space for one or more sepulchers, which would be built there for Giovanni Emo and his descendants.[6] Presumably Emo's tomb was erected in this chapel. In his guide to Venice, Francesco Sansovino located the Emo Tomb in the Servi near the sacristy.[7] The sacristy was situated immediately to the left of the left apsidal chapel: a door in the center of the left chapel wall led to the sacristy.[8] Stringa's account of the siting of the tomb as near, but outside, the chapel is probably the result of a solecism.[9]

Giovanni Emo died on September 15, 1483.[10] The inscription on his tomb informs us that the monument was erected by Emo's sons. The tomb was completed by 1493 when it was listed by Marin Sanudo in his *Cronachetta*.[11] A more precise dating than the outer limits furnished by Emo's death and Sanudo's *Cronachetta* is not possible on the basis of external data.

The Emo Tomb remained at the Servi until the suppression of the church in 1806 and its gradual demolition.[12] In 1818 the effigy was acquired by the Vicentine count, Girolamo Egidio di Velo, for his Villa di Velo.[13] Upon his death in 1831, the statue was bequeathed to the Museo Civico, Vicenza.[14] In 1910 it was exhibited in a ground-floor room of the southern wing of the museum.[15] From the Servi, the *Pages* passed to the Villetta Scarabellin sul Terraggio, where they were purchased in 1873 by the Venetian antique dealer Carrer. Carrer sold them to a dealer from Marseilles, from whom they were acquired by M. Sommier Dal Sommier. Thence they entered the Paris collection of the Marquise Arconati-Visconti.[16] In 1914 she gave the *Pages* to the Louvre.[17]

The sarcophagus exhibited with the effigy in the Museo Civico, Vicenza, is generally thought to have come from the Emo Tomb.[18] Although it dates from the same epoch as the figure and, doubtless, is Venetian, it cannot have belonged to the Emo Tomb, for it disagrees with the sarcophagus of the Emo Tomb as reproduced by Grevembroch.[19] The birds and human heads of the sarcophagus in Vicenza are absent from the *rinceaux* of Emo's sarcophagus. The tomb chest in Vicenza can never have possessed lion's-paw legs; the Emo sarcophagus did not have a cover.

Since Meyer first attributed the tomb to Rizzo,[20] the monument or its extant parts generally have been recognized as his.[21] Sometimes Rizzo's shop was thought to have intervened.[22] The inferior quality of the pedestrian effigy led Ongaro to suggest that the tomb, designed by Rizzo, might have been executed by assistants.[23] Venturi, on the other hand, thought that Rizzo had carved the effigy for a tomb possibly designed by others.[24] Munman attributed to Rizzo the *Pages* and head of *Emo* but called the remainder of the standing figure

shop work.[25] Pincus believed the tomb had been designed by Rizzo and executed in his shop. To the master himself she ascribed, with a certain hesitation, only the portrait head of *Emo*.[26]

On occasion, the Lombardos or their school have been credited with the Emo *Pages*. Visinoni proposed assigning the *Pages* to Pietro, Antonio, and Tullio Lombardo.[27] Venturi suggested as their author the follower of Pietro Lombardo who participated in the carving of the Onigo Tomb in S. Nicolò, Treviso.[28] In 1917 Planiscig assigned the *Pages* to Pietro Lombardo,[29] though he came to regard them afterward as that portion of the tomb most assuredly by Rizzo.[30] Recently Munman identified all three figures as products of Rizzo's shop.[31]

---

[1] Grevembroch, *Mon. Ven.*, iii, 1759, p. 27.

[2] Grevembroch, *Gli abiti*, i, p. 38.

[3] Michel in Paris, Louvre. Catalogue by Leprieur et al., 1917, p. 43, no. 25.

[4] Munman, 1968, p. 193.

[5] Cicogna, i, 1824, p. 36, no. 3.

[6] Rumor, n.d. [1910?], pp. 47ff., n. 2; Vicentini, *S. Maria de' Servi*, 1920, pp. 49, 70f.

[7] Sans., 1581, p. 58r: "Et vicino alla sagrestia, si vede la statua pedestre di marmo sopra ricchissimo sepolcro per molto oro, di Giouanni Emo." See also Superbi, 1629, ii, p. 73.

[8] Vicentini, *S. Maria de' Servi*, 1920, pl. XVI oppos. p. 48.

[9] Sans./Stringa, 1604, p. 145r: "Et vicino alla Sagrestia si vede la cappella della famiglia Ema, & poco discosto il deposito con la statua pedestre di marmo, posta sopra un ricchissimo sepolcro messo ad oro di Giovanni Emo." Very likely Stringa's siting of the tomb, near, but outside, the chapel resulted from a grammatical error in which "poco discosto," meant to refer to the position of the tomb in relation to the sacristy, was mistakenly juxtaposed with the newly introduced phrase "cappella della famiglia Ema." Vicentini, *S. Maria de' Servi*, 1920, p. 72, n. 3, drew attention to Stringa's emendation of Sansovino's text.

[10] Corner, *Eccl. Ven.*, 1749, ii, p. 53.

[11] Sanudo, (1493) 1980, p. 51.

[12] A. Zorzi, 1972, ii, p. 356.

[13] Rumor, n.d. [1910?], p. 51.

[14] Vicenza, Mus. Civ. Catalogue by Barbieri, 1962, p. 232.

[15] Ongaro, Vicenza, Mus. Civ. *Boll.*, Jan.–Mar. 1910, pp. 9f.

[16] Rumor, n.d. [1910?], pp. 51f.

[17] Paris, Louvre. Catalogue i, 1922, p. 92, nos. 750, 751.

[18] Inv. no. E II 29b. The sarcophagus measures 71 cm. x 228 cm. x 73 cm. Only Munman, 1968, p.

192, and Pincus, 1974, p. 196, n. 22, doubted its provenience in the Emo Tomb.

[19] Grevembroch, *Mon. Ven.*, iii, 1759, p. 27.

[20] Meyer, *JpK*, 1889, p. 198.

[21] Paoletti, 1893, i, p. 22, n. 5, ii, pp. 149f.; Burckhardt/Bode/Fabriczy, [7]1898, ii, pt. 1, p. 122c (with reservations); Vicenza, Mus. Civ. Minozzi, *Inventario*, 1902, p. 126, no. 86; Bouchaud, 1913, p. 121; Pozzo, *Revue numismatique*, 1914, p. 205 (with reservations); L. Venturi, *L'arte*, 1916, p. 49; Marquand, *Art in America*, 1917-18, p. 54; Schubring, 1919, p. 243; Planiscig, 1921, pp. 69f. (with reservations concerning the statue of *Emo*); Paris, Louvre. Catalogue, i, 1922, p. 92, nos. 750, 751; Bode, [6]1922, p. 150; Lorenzetti, [1]1926, p. 85; Francovich, *Boll. d'arte*, 1928-29, p. 488; Planiscig, T-B, xxviii, 1934, p. 409; Serra, *Boll. d'arte*, 1935-36, pp. 89f. (with reservations); Fiocco, *Enc. ital.*, xxix, 1936, p. 503; Fasolo, 1940, pp. 44f., no. 168; Mariacher, *Arte ven.*, 1948, pp. 78ff.; Vicenza, Mus. Civ. *Inventario E-II*, 1950, "Statuaria e pezzi vari," no. 29; Pope-Hennessy, [1]1958, p. 349; Vicenza, Mus. Civ. Catalogue by Barbieri, 1962, p. 232; Deiseroth, 1970, p. 269, n. 551; Ven., Procuratie Nuove, *Arte a Ven.*, by Mariacher, 1971, p. 139; Sheard, 1971, pp. 80, 96; A. Zorzi, 1972, i, p. 135, ii, p. 353.

[22] Planiscig, *VJ*, 1926, p. 98; Mariacher, 1966, n.p. [p. 5].

[23] Ongaro in Rumor/Ongaro, Vicenza, Mus. Civ. *Boll.* Jan.–Mar. 1910, p. 25.

[24] Venturi, *Storia*, vi, 1908, pp. 1064f.

[25] Munman, 1968, pp. 196ff., 335.

[26] Pincus, 1974, p. 197, n. 22, p. 397.

[27] [Visinoni], *Bull. di arti*, Aug. 1877, p. 36.

[28] Venturi, *Storia*, vi, 1908, p. 1065. This hypothesis was rejected by Marquand, *Art in America*, 1917-18, p. 54.

[29] Vienna, Ksthis. Mus. Catalogue by Planiscig, 1919, p. 52, no. 92.

[30] Planiscig, 1921, pp. 69f.; Planiscig, *VJ*, 1926, p. 98.

[31] Munman, *Arte ven.*, 1979, p. 28, n. 28.

18. Venice, S. Sofia: *SS. Andrew, Luke, Cosmas, Damian*

Figs. 60-63

SS. Andrew and *Luke* flank the high altar of S. Sofia, *St. Andrew* on the right, *St. Luke* on the left. *SS. Cosmas* and *Damian* are located on the entrance wall, flanking the main portal of the church, *St. Cosmas* on the left, *St. Damian* on the right of a spectator facing the door.

Pietra di Aurisima. There is no evidence of polychromy or gilding.

The statues are flat and unfinished at the rear. The metal halos of *SS. Andrew* and *Luke* appear to be later additions. The left foot of *St. Cosmas*, the mortar, and the drapery that hangs from the figure's left arm, are chipped. *St. Andrew*'s left thumb and the hem of his drapery are chipped. Otherwise, the statues are well preserved.

St. Andrew: 114 cm. high. *St. Luke*: 112 cm. high. *St. Cosmas*: 110 cm. high. *St. Damian*: 116 cm. high.

S ANDREAS; S LVCAS; S COSMA; S DAMIAN are inscribed on the bases of the respective statues.

Paoletti, 1893, ii, pp. 150, 160; Vicentini, *S. Maria de' Servi*, 1920, p. 91; Vicentini, *Ideale risurrezione*, 1920, p. 55; Lorenzetti, [1]1926, p. 412; Mariacher, *Arte ven.*, 1948, pp. 79f.; Muraro, 1953, p. 254; Hubala in Egg *et al.*, [1]1965, p. 763; Mariacher, 1966, n. p. [p. 5]; A. Zorzi, 1972, ii, pp. 355, 359; Niero, 1972, pp. 75, 76f.

Paoletti suggested that the four statues had originally embellished the altar of the barbers' guild in the Venetian church of S. Maria dei Servi.[1] There is every reason to accept the provenance he gives. Apparently too poor, or possessing too few members to acquire a building of its own, the Scuola dei Barbieri met in the Servi under the protection of SS. Cosmas and Damian.[2] The earliest agreement between the guild of barbers and the Servites dates from July 19, 1462. In it, the guild was ceded an altar on the left side of the church between the Altars of the Corpus Christi and S. Niccolò and was granted permission to hold meetings in the convent's summer refectory on the feast days of SS. Luke and Andrew.[3] The transfer of the *scuola* from its first meeting place in the church of SS. Filippo e Giacomo to S. Maria dei Servi on October 18, 1465, was recorded in an inscription.[4] Another inscription commemorated the construction of the oratory of the barbers' guild in 1468.[5] A second agreement between the guild of barbers and the chapter of the Servi, made on July 6, 1468, to some extent modified the agreement of six years earlier. The guild was now ceded the second altar from the entrance against the right, or south, wall of the church—an altar that was then dedicated to St. Mark. The barbers' new altar was to be dedicated to SS. Cosmas and Damian or to whomever else the guild wished, and was to be adorned with a painted altarpiece portraying the Virgin in the center, and, at the sides, SS. Luke, Andrew, Cosmas, and Damian.[6] The altar was in existence when a new accord was made between the barbers and the Servites on August 30, 1490.[7]

After the suppression of the church and convent of S. Maria dei Servi by the Napoleonic decree of 1806, the church was gradually demolished as pieces were sold off for building material.[8] Many of the surviving works of art were dispersed among other Venetian churches. The church of S. Sofia, itself, was suppressed in 1810 and reopened to the cult only in 1836.[9] It may, or may not, be significant that Fontana's guide of 1836 makes no mention of the statues.[10] In any case, it was not until 1893 that the four statues were recorded there.[11] When Lorenzetti saw them in 1926 they were evidently arranged as they are today.[12]

Publication of the statues is due to Paoletti. He related the drapery of SS. Andrew and Luke to that of SS. James and Paul from their altars in S. Marco, which he attributed to Rizzo, and the style of all four statues to the statues of the Emo Tomb.[13] Those few who subsequently

took notice of the statues followed Paoletti's lead, finding the figures carved in Rizzo's style.[14] Only Muraro assigned the saints to the school of the Lombardos.[15]

[1] Paoletti, 1893, ii, p. 160.
[2] Onofri, ²1682, p. 163.
[3] Venice, ASV, Mani morte, Convento di S. Maria dei Servi in Venezia, Busta 9, codice 2, 1 (parchment), for which, see above ch. 2, n. 29.
[4] Cicogna, i, 1824, p. 97, nos. 213, 214; Levi, ³1895, pp. 44f.
[5] Cicogna, i, 1824, p. 97, no. 214. The oratory, dedicated to SS. Cosmas and Damian, was adjacent to the Servi's cloister. See also Vicentini, Cinque secoli, 1920, pp. 13f.
[6] Vicentini, S. Maria dei Servi, 1920, p. 91.
[7] Venice, ASV, Mani morte, Convento di S. Maria dei Servi in Venezia, Busta 9, codice 2, cc. 9ff: "Et prima, chel Altar solito de la ditta Schuolla di barbieri rimagnia in ditta giessia di madona sancta Maria di servi di venezia come se al presente et lese."
[8] A. Zorzi, 1972, ii, pp. 356f.
[9] Fontana, 1836, pp. 15, 71ff.; A. Zorzi, 1972, ii, p. 541.
[10] Fontana, 1836.
[11] Paoletti, 1893, ii, pp. 150, 160.
[12] Lorenzetti, ¹1926, p. 412.
[13] Paoletti, 1893, ii, pp. 150, 160.
[14] Lorenzetti, ¹1926, p. 412; Mariacher, Arte ven., 1948, pp. 79ff.; Hubala in Egg et al., ¹1965, p. 763; Mariacher, 1966, n.p. [p. 5]; A. Zorzi, 1972, ii, p. 355; Niero, 1972, pp. 75, 76.
[15] Muraro, 1953, p. 254.

19. Venice, Scuola dei Calegheri: Miraculous Cure of St. Anianus

Figs. 123-125

The relief occupies the lunette above the main portal of the former school of the shoemakers' guild in Campo S. Tomà (S. Polo 2857).

Limestone. The entire surface of the relief is polychromed.

The relief is very dirty. But apart from St. Mark's chipped nose, the relief is in very good condition.

109.5 cm. x 145.2 cm.

MCCCCLXXVIIII ADI XIIIIII SENTEBRIO NĒL
TĒPO DE M̄ POLO DE MAŚ LVCHA DE
GRIGVOL · ZVANE ·
is inscribed in the portal's architrave.

Grevembroch, Mon. Ven., iii, 1759, p. 28; Soràvia, ii, 1823, pp. 189ff.; Selvatico, 1847, p. 240; Selvatico/Lazari, 1852, p. 192; Zanotto, Nuovissima guida, 1856, p. 491; Mothes, ii, 1860, p. 80; Tassini, 1863, i, p. 108; Fulin/Molmenti, 1881, p. 307; Tassini, 1885, p. 94; Paoletti, 1893, ii, p. 226; Levi, ³1895, pp. 50ff.; Burckhardt/Bode/Fabriczy, ⁷1898, ii, pt. 1, p. 125h; Vucetich, n.d., ii, Parrocchia di S. Maria Gloriosa dei Frari, no. 4; Levi, 1900, i, n.p., Parrocchia di S. Maria dei Frari, no. 38; Comune di Ven., 1905, p. 123, S. Polo, no. 250; Venturi, Storia, vi, 1908, p. 1091; Bouchaud, 1913, p. 164; Schubring, 1919, p. 248; Venturi, Storia, viii, pt. 2, 1924, p. 521; Lorenzetti, ¹1926, p. 547; Moschetti, T-B, xxiii, 1929, p. 344;

Muraro, 1953, p. 276; Pope-Hennessy, [1]1958, p. 114; Donati, 1961, p. 23; Pope-Hennessy, 1964, i, p. 353, no. 379; A. Zorzi, 1972, ii, p. 547; Franzoi/Di Stefano, 1975, p. 51; Howard, 1980, p. 101.

The *Miraculous Cure of St. Anianus* was drawn by Johannes Grevembroch in 1759[1] and by Antonio Vucetich, at the end of the nineteenth century.[2]

Inscriptions located at either corner of the ground-floor facade of the school relate that the guild's residence was bought on December 14, 1446, and restored in 1580.[3] The portal is dated by inscription to September 16, 1479.[4]

Early critics of the relief called it Lombardesque.[5] Paoletti tentatively assigned it to a Lombard master.[6] In the seventh edition of *Der Cicerone*, Pietro Lombardo was specifically credited with the relief.[7] The attribution was adopted by Venturi[8] and Lorenzetti,[9] and has prevailed in almost all subsequent citations of the relief.[10] Muraro[11] and Howard[12] more cautiously assigned the relief to the circle of the Lombardos.

[1] Grevembroch, *Mon. Ven.*, iii, 1759, p. 28.
[2] Vucetich, n.d., ii, Parrocchia di S. Maria Gloriosa dei Frari, no. 4.
[3] See above, ch. 4, n. 5. See also Levi, [3]1895, p. 50.
[4] The date is frequently misread as 1478.
[5] Soràvia, ii, 1823, p. 190; Selvatico, 1847, p. 240; Selvatico/Lazari, 1852, p. 192; Zanotto, *Nuovissima guida*, 1856, p. 491; Tassini, 1863, i, p. 108; Fulin/Molmenti, 1881, p. 307; Levi, [3]1895, p. 50.
[6] Paoletti, 1893, ii, p. 226.
[7] Burckhardt/Bode/Fabriczy, [7]1898, ii, pt. 1, p. 125h.
[8] Venturi, *Storia*, viii, pt. 2, 1924, p. 521. In 1908 Venturi, *Storia*, vi, p. 1091, had described the lunette as in the "manner of Pietro Lombardo," suggesting certain reservations.
[9] Lorenzetti, [1]1926, p. 547.
[10] Bouchaud, 1913, p. 164; Schubring, 1919, p. 248 (illustrating, however, the relief of the same subject by Tullio Lombardo on the facade of the Scuola di S. Marco); Pope-Hennessy, [1]1958, p. 114; Pope-Hennessy, 1964, i, p. 353, no. 379; A. Zorzi, 1972, ii, p. 547; Franzoi/Di Stefano, 1975, p. 51.
[11] Muraro, 1953, p. 276.
[12] Howard, 1980, p. 101.

20. Vienna, Kunsthistorisches Museum: *Angel*

Figs. 132-133

The *Angel* is exhibited in Room xxx of the Kunsthistorisches Museum (inv. no. 7463).

White marble. There are no traces of polychromy or gilding.

At the rear the bottom of the statue is unfinished. A small hole in the crown of the head formerly served for the attachment of a halo. The statue is in excellent condition.

83 cm. high.

Hermann in Egger/Hermann, *ZbK*, 1906, p. 95; Vienna, Ksthis. Mus. Catalogue by Planiscig, 1919, pp. 51f., no. 92; Planiscig, 1921, pp. 77f.; Moschetti, T-B, xxiii, 1929, p. 344; Berlin, Staatl. Mus., Kaiser-Friedrich-Mus. Catalogue by Schottmüller, [2]1933, p. 116, no. 221; Vienna, Ksthis. Mus. Catalogue by Planiscig/Kris, 1935, p. 57, no. 42; Vienna, Ksthis. Mus. Catalogue by Mahl *et al.*, 1966, pp. 19f., no. 211.

The *Angel* comes from the collection of Marchese Tomaso degli Obizzi in the Castello di Cataio (Comune di Battaglia, near Padua). In his testament of 1803, Obizzi specified that, upon his death, his estate should pass to Ercole III d'Este, ex-duke of Modena (d. 1803), and upon Ercole's death, to Ercole's grandson, the youngest son of Ercole's daughter, Riccarda Maria Beatrix. Beatrix was married to Archduke Ferdinand von Österreich. Their youngest son was Archduke Maximilian von Österreich-Este (d. 1863). Since Ercole predeceased Obizzi, the collection passed to Archduke Maximilian when Obizzi died in 1805. From Maximilian, the collection was inherited by Archduke Franz V of Modena and from him, by Archduke Franz Ferdinand (d. 1914). In 1896 the latter had the major portion of the Este collection brought to Vienna and installed in the Palais Modena in the Beatrixgasse. The collection was open to the public between 1904 and 1908, when its transfer to the Neue Hofburg commenced. Its installation for exhibition there was completed only in 1916. In 1922 the Este collection was incorporated into the Kunsthistorisches Museum.[1]

Hermann attributed the *Angel* to the Venetian school of the end of the fifteenth century, citing resemblances to the Angels of the Tabernacle in the Castello Sforzesco, Milan, attributed to the Master of S. Trovaso, and to the left-hand *Page* of the Emo Tomb, whose facial type, he thought, betrayed a striking similarity to that of the Vienna *Angel*.[2] Planiscig ascribed the *Angel* to Pietro Lombardo and surmised that, along with a pendant statue of the *Annunciate Virgin*, the figure originally ornamented the gable of an altar.[3] The attribution to Pietro Lombardo was recorded by Moschetti.[4] It appears in the two most recent sculpture catalogues of the Kunsthistorisches Museum.[5] Mahl interpreted the resemblance of the *Angel* to Rizzo's Emo *Pages* as evidence of Rizzo's influence on Pietro Lombardo.

[1] Vienna, Ksthis. Mus. Catalogue by Planiscig, 1919, pp. vff. For Tomaso degli Obizzi, see Fantelli, *Padova e la sua provincia*, Nov.–Dec. 1977, pp. 12f.
[2] Hermann in Egger/Hermann, *ZbK*, 1906, p. 95.
[3] Vienna, Ksthis. Mus. Catalogue by Planiscig, 1919, pp. 51f., no. 92; Planiscig, 1921, pp. 77f.
[4] Moschetti, T-B, xxiii, 1929, p. 344.
[5] Vienna, Ksthis. Mus. Catalogue by Planiscig/Kris, 1935, p. 57, no. 42; Vienna, Ksthis. Mus. Catalogue by Mahl *et al.*, 1966, p. 19, no. 211.

REJECTED ATTRIBUTIONS

21. Milan, Castello Sforzesco, Museo d'Arte Antica: Tabernacle

Fig. 240

The tabernacle is exhibited in Sala XIII of the Museo d'Arte Antica (inv. no. 1086).

White marble. There are no signs of polychromy or gilding.

The *sportello* or central image of the tabernacle is missing. No holes for hinges exist within the frame. The opening for the *sportello* or image has been extended to the bottom of the relief as though to accommodate an object not originally intended for it. The lintel of the central frame is carved from a separate piece of stone. A joint is visible at the juncture of walls and ceiling of the setting. Where the joints cross the foremost moldings at either edge of the relief, the stone has been chipped as though to conceal the true nature of the joints. The outer frame of the relief is pitted and chipped. In spite of this, the Angels are extraordinarily well preserved. Small peripheral areas of drapery on the left and right show minute chips. The nose and fingers of the innermost Angel on the left are chipped. A crack in the nose of the foremost Angel on the left has been repaired. Otherwise the surface is pristine.

145 cm. x 166 cm.; each wing: 48 cm. wide.

[Mongeri], [1]1881, p. 25, no. 95; Sant'Ambrogio, *Arch. stor. lom.*, 1892, pp. 153f., 158f.; Paoletti, 1893, ii, p. 159; Fabriczy, *Rep. f. Kstw.*, 1894, pp. 250f.; Milan, Castello Sforzesco. *Guida sommaria*, 1900, p. 19; Sant'Ambrogio, *Lega lom.*, June 22-23, 1900, pp. 1-2; Modigliani, *L'arte*, 1900, p. 396; Meyer, ii, 1900, p. 188, n. 1; Burckhardt/Bode/Fabriczy, [8]1901, ii, pt. 2, p. 499b; Malaguzzi Valeri, 1904, pp. 91ff.; Migeon, *Les arts*, March 1905, pp. 13f.; Hermann in Egger/Hermann, *ZbK*, 1906, p. 95; Venturi, *Storia*, vi, 1908, pp. 466f., 1088; Planiscig, 1921, pp. 190, 198; Vigezzi, 1928, p. 100; Planiscig, *Pantheon*, Jan.–June 1929, p. 220; Vigezzi, 1934, pp. 31, 153f., no. 464; Mariacher, *Aten. ven.*, 1942, p. 240; Caspary, 1964, pp. 51f., 142f., n. 115; Precerutti Garberi, 1974, pp. 14f., 66, figs. 44-45, p. 76.

The tabernacle comes from the Milanese collection of Giuseppe Bossi whence it passed to the Accademia di Brera. There the tabernacle was displayed enframing a relief of the *Madonna and Child*, which did not belong to it.[1] In 1864 the tabernacle entered the Museo Archeologico Municipale at the Castello Sforzesco (no. 1121). By 1900 the *Madonna* was exhibited separately.[2] When two separate collections were formed for archeological, and other, works of art at the Castello Sforzesco, the tabernacle became part of the Civiche Raccolte d'Arte.[3]

First published in 1881, the tabernacle was assigned by Mongeri to the Tuscan school of the fifteenth century.[4] In 1892 Sant'Ambrogio traced the tabernacle and the relief of the *Ma-*

donna and Child which it framed to Giovanni Antonio Amadeo's original altar in the Duomo, Milan, erected by the Albanese captain Alessio Tarchetta, in 1480.[5] Meyer[6] and Malaguzzi Valeri[7] denied any relation between the tabernacle and the style or works of Amadeo. Vigezzi compromisingly described the tabernacle as late-fifteenth-century Lombard.[8] It is under this label that the work was recently reproduced[9] and is currently exhibited.

Meanwhile, Paoletti attributed the tabernacle to Rizzo. Among the many works ascribed to the sculptor, Paoletti designated as closest to the style of the tabernacle, the *Victories* of the Scala dei Giganti and the antependium from the Cappella Clary in the Venetian church of S. Trovaso, which no longer is considered his.[10] An attribution to the S. Trovaso Master was espoused by the author of the summary guide to the collections of the Castello Sforzesco.[11] Though he made no attribution, Meyer also thought the tabernacle most like the antependium of S. Trovaso.[12] Disavowing an earlier opinion,[13] Planiscig ascribed the tabernacle to the S. Trovaso Master.[14] To the author of the *Adoring Angel* from the Cappella del Rosario in SS. Giovanni e Paolo, Venice (now in the sacristy), the work was given by Fabriczy.[15] Hermann found the greatest affinity to the tabernacle in the *Angel* in Vienna, which he attributed to the Venetian school of the end of the fifteenth century.[16] Venturi assigned the relief to Pietro Lombardo.[17] In his perception of Florentine components in the style of the tabernacle, Caspary was influenced by Planiscig.[18]

In my opinion, the tabernacle is a nineteenth-century forgery. The perspective construction, in which the corners of the room coincide with the corners of the relief, is abnormally schematic. The invasion of the area of the ceiling by the frame of a hypothetical *sportello* is architecturally unjustified and aesthetically unpleasing. Nor do the moldings that define the boundaries of subsidiary rooms, attached as they are to the rear wall and ceiling, make any better structural sense. The tabernacle is a pastiche whose figural ingredients were taken from the Scala dei Giganti. The nearer leg of the foremost Angel on the left copies that of the *Victory* with apple and laurel branch (Fig. 198). The coiffure of the Angel at the far

right was also borrowed from this *Victory*. The head of the innermost Angel on the right comes from the torch-bearing *Victory* (Fig. 200); the head of the Angel at the extreme left, from the *Victory* with inscribed tablet (Fig. 197). A comparison of Angels and *Victories* reveals how mechanically, and with what equal emphasis throughout, details, such as hair, were rendered. Costumes are illogically complicated: how are we to understand the slashed sleeve of the angel at the rear of the left-hand group or the puff of drapery at his cuff? An extraordinary ringlet, longer than all the rest, outlines the front of this figure's shoulder like a seam. Equally suspicious is the pattern of damage in the tabernacle, which produced deep craters in the outer molding but left the figures virtually untouched.

[1] Paoletti, 1893, ii, p. 159, fig. 35.

[2] Sant'Ambrogio, *Lega lom.*, June 22-23, 1900, p. 1.

[3] Letter of Dec. 9, 1976, from Dott.ssa Maria Teresa Fiorio.

[4] [Mongeri], [1]1881, p. 25, no. 95.

[5] Sant'Ambrogio, *Arch. stor. lom.*, 1892, pp. 153f., 158f.; Sant'Ambrogio, *Lega lom.*, June 22-23, 1900, pp. 1f. Reporting Sant'Ambrogio's findings, Fabriczy, *Rep. f. Kstw.*, 1894, pp. 250f., does not seem to have been convinced of the tabernacle's provenance. The Tarchetta Altar was recomposed in 1834: some original pieces are preserved in the Castello Sforzesco.

[6] Meyer, ii, 1900, p. 188, n. 1.

[7] Malaguzzi Valeri, 1904, pp. 91ff.

[8] Vigezzi, 1934, pp. 153f., no. 464.

[9] Precerutti Garberi, 1974, pp. 14, 66, figs. 44-45.

[10] Paoletti, 1893, ii, p. 159.

[11] Milan, Castello Sforzesco. *Guida sommaria*, 1900, p. 19. Migeon, *Les arts*, March 1905, p. 13, mistakenly claimed the church of S. Trovaso as the tabernacle's place of origin.

[12] Meyer, ii, 1900, p. 188, n. 1.

[13] Planiscig, 1921, p. 190 simply called the work Venetian.

[14] Planiscig, *Pantheon*, Jan.-June 1929, p. 220.

[15] Burckhardt/Bode/Fabriczy, [8]1901, ii, pt. 2, p. 499b, c.

[16] Hermann in Egger/Hermann, *ZbK*, 1906, p. 95.

[17] Venturi, *Storia*, vi, 1908, pp. 466f., 1088.

[18] Caspary, 1964, pp. 51f. Cf. Planiscig, 1921, pp. 190, 198.

22. Venice, Madonna dell'Orto:
Annunciate Virgin

Figs. 237-239

The *Annunciation* adorns the exterior of the main portal of the Madonna dell'Orto. The *Virgin* stands to the right of the portal's lunette, balancing the *Angel* on the left.

Istrian limestone.

The surface is badly worn but there are no major losses. A broad crack runs through the figure's veil at the back of its head and along its left shoulder and upper arm.

180.5 cm. high.

For references see above, Venice, Madonna dell'Orto: *Annunciate Angel*, cat. no. 11, to which add Schulz, *TAPS*, 1978, pt. 3, p. 61; Schulz, *NdiGF*, 1978, p. 33.

The documentary history of the portal decoration is given in catalogue entry no. 11, concerning the *Annunciate Angel* from the Madonna dell'Orto. A summary of scholarly opinion regarding the attribution and dating of the *Virgin* is also found there.

That the *Angel* (Figs. 119-122) and *Annunciate Virgin* are by different authors can be inferred from numerous discrepancies in style. Unlike the *Angel*, the composition of the *Virgin* apparently was derived from that of the *Annunciate Virgin*, recently attributed to Bartolomeo Bon and an assistant, in the Victoria and Albert Museum, London, and hypothetically connected with an early scheme by Bon for the decoration of the portal.[1] The *Virgin's* slender proportions contrast with the broad hips and shoulders, the spherical breasts, and protruding abdomen of Rizzo's female type. Facial types and hair are dissimilar; in both design and execution the drapery of the two figures differs. The organic contrapposto of the *Angel* contrasts with the *Virgin's* stance, in which the unequal distribution of weight has no effect upon the axes of hips and shoulders; the position of the *Virgin's* twisted foot is physically impossible.

Photographs newly taken from a scaffold permit a more confident attribution of the *Annunciate Virgin* to the shop of Niccolò di Giovanni Fiorentino, author of *St. Christopher* at the center of the portal. I now believe that the *Virgin* was made according to Niccolò's design and with his participation. To Niccolò himself I would assign the *Virgin's* head and upper torso (to her waist), her entire inner arm, and her left hand. The similarity of the *Virgin's* drapery style to that of figures formerly associated with Antonio Bregno and recently assigned to Niccolò Fiorentino—in particular, to that of *Music* from the Arco Foscari—was observed some time ago.[2] The elongated proportions, the long neck, small head, and diminutive shoulders of the *Virgin*, now reveal themselves as those of *Music*. The fastening and draping of the cloak on the *Virgin's* shoulders resemble those of the *Annunciate Virgin* from the Foscari Tomb in S. Maria dei Frari. The face finds precise analogies for its shape, features, and hair, in the heads of *Justice* and *Prudence* from the Tomb of Doge Francesco Foscari. The *Virgin's* raised arm and hand can be compared with the corresponding limb of *St. Helen* from the Capello Tomb at S. Elena. The gesture of the *Virgin's* lowered hand repeats that of *Charity* from the Foscari Tomb. By contrast, the figure's lower two-thirds are due to an assistant, who seems to have exercised complete independence in the draping of the cloak.

Very likely the *Virgin* was made at approximately the same time as *St. Christopher*, for which I have proposed a date of 1465-67.[3] A *terminus post quem* is provided by the death, probably toward the end of 1464, of Bartolomeo Bon, under whom the portal was begun. In December 1467, Niccolò was present at Trogir to negotiate a contract for the Duomo's Orsini Chapel. In April 1468, he took up residence there in order to execute the work. Niccolò's delegation of a substantial portion of the *Virgin* and the assistant's apparent departure from Niccolò's instructions in the figure's lower half, suggest that the *Virgin* dates from the end of Niccolò's Venetian sojourn and that the statue may have been completed in his absence. I am inclined, therefore, to date the *Annunciate Virgin* to 1467/68.

[1] Schulz, *TAPS*, 1978, pt. 3, p. 61.
[2] Schulz, *NdiGF*, 1978, p. 33, 48, n.106.
[3] Ibid., pp. 32, 36.

23. Venice, S. Andrea della Certosa (formerly): Tomb of Ser Orsato Giustiniani

Of the tomb only five statuettes of *Virtues* survive. They are: *Temperance* and *Charity*, Kress Collection, Museum of Art, El Paso, Texas (inv. nos. K1917, K1918, respectively); *Hope*, Metropolitan Museum of Art, New York (inv. no. 56.15.1); *Fortitude* and an unidentified *Virtue*, Cassa di Risparmio di Padova e Rovigo, Padua.

A drawing of the tomb, made by Johannes Grevembroch in 1754,[1] permits its reconstruction. On a parallelepiped sarcophagus with imbricated cover, a low bier with lion's-paw feet supported the effigy of Giustiniani in the full-sleeved robe of a senator. Beneath the center of the bier was a winged heart. A sheathed sword rested on the cover of the sarcophagus. The face of the sarcophagus was divided into two compartments in each of which a beribboned garland surrounded a scallop shell medallion on which was superposed a profile portrait of a Roman emperor. Six projecting semicircular bases supported female statuettes personifying virtues.

At the left corner of the tomb stood *Hope*, her hands crossed on her chest, her head inclined, and her gaze directed upward. Opposite her stood *Charity*, her upraised bowl filled with fruit. In the center, a statuette of *Justice*, no longer extant, held the severed head of a man. The three remaining *Virtues* presumably were disposed along the side of the sarcophagus not reproduced by Grevembroch. *Temperance* holds a vase; *Fortitude* wears armor beneath her chiton and leans upon a column. The last *Virtue* possesses no attribute.

The *Virtues* are carved from white marble.

Hope is the best preserved of the figures: damage is limited to the chipping of the ridges of some folds. *Temperance*'s vase is broken. The figure's nose, the right corner of the right eye, the chin and the bottom of the right earlobe have been restored. The ridges of folds at the front of the figure are slightly chipped. The head of *Charity* is modern. The right arm is broken below the elbow; the area of the wrist has been restored. In the base are two holes meant for dowels.[2] The heads of *Fortitude* and the unidentified *Virtue* are modern. *Fortitude* is missing most of her left arm. The index finger of the figure's right hand is chipped. A portion of the skirt toward the rear of the statue has been cut away. The center of the base has been arbitrarily restored. The *Virtue* is missing her right hand and a part of her lower arm. The statue is cracked through at the level of the ankles; a large chip is missing from the ankle of the right foot. The base and the ridges of some folds are chipped.

ILLE PROCVRATOR VENETA / MODO MAXIMVS VRBE / ORSATVS IACET HIC IVSTI / NIANVS EQVES. / QVI TVRCOS BIMARI CLASSIS / PRAEFECTVS AB ISTHMO / DVM FVGAT O FATVM QVAN / TA TROPHEA RAPIS / DECESSIT ANN. X. MCCCCLX / IIII. V. IDVS QVINT. / MARINVS IVSTINI / ANVS PATRVO / DE SE BENEME / RITO EXTRVI / CVRAVIT[3]

Sabellico, (1491-92) n.d., n.p. [p. 48]; Sanudo, (1493) 1980, p. 52; Sanudo, *RIs*, xxii, (1490-1530) 1733, col. 1180; Contarini, n.d. [ca. 1542], bk. 4, n.p.; Venice, Bibl. Marc., Cod. it., Cl. VII, 791 (= 7589), *Cronaca Veniera*, p. 151; Sans., 1581, pp. 80rf.; Superbi, 1629, ii, p. 67; Coronelli, pt. 1, 1696, p. 45; Grevembroch, *Mon. Ven.*, i, 1754, p. 92; Cicognara, ii, 1816, p. 174; Cicogna, ii, 1827, pp. 55ff., no. 4; Ticozzi, i, 1830. p. 406; Cicogna, iv, 1834, p. 629; Moschini, 1842, p. 46; Selvatico, 1847, p. 228; Selvatico/Lazari, 1852, pp. 210, 272; Zanotto, *Nuovissima guida*, 1856, p. 557; Mothes, ii, 1860, p. 156; Fulin/Molmenti, 1881, pp. 141, 340, 435; Meyer, *JpK*, 1889, p. 194; Paoletti, 1893, ii, pp. 144, 226, 247; Burckhardt/Bode/Fabriczy, [7]1898, ii, pt. 1, pp. 122c, 122d; Venturi, *Storia*, vi, 1908, pp. 1058ff.; Michel, iv, pt. 1, 1909, pp. 193f.; Paoletti, "Bregno, Antonio," T-B, iv, 1910, p. 569; Muñoz in Pollak/Muñoz, ii, 1911, p. 117; Planiscig, 1921, p. 63; Vienna, Secession, Vereins der Museumsfreunde. *Meisterwerke*, 1924, p. 14, nos. 89-91; Amsterdam, Muller and Co. *Collections . . . Castiglioni*, Nov. 1925, p. 32, no. 110; Lorenzetti, [1]1926, pp. 85, 659; Planiscig, *VJ*, 1926, pp. 93-102; Ven., Ca' d'Oro. *Guida-catalogo*, by Fogolari *et al.*, 1929, pp. 79f.; Berlin, Ball and Graupe. *Die Sammlung Castiglioni*, by Falke, 1930, p. 44, no. 112; Piva, 1930, p. 131; Planiscig, T-B, xxviii, 1934, p. 409; N.Y., A. S. Drey Galleries. *Sculpture*, 1935, p. 14, no. 33; Fiocco, *Enc. ital.*, xxix,

1936, p. 502; Brooklyn, N.Y., Institute of Arts and Sciences, Museum. *European Art 1450-1500*, 1936, no. 52; Detroit, Inst. of Arts. *Italian Sculptures,* 1938, by Valentiner, nos. 93, 94; Ragghianti, *Critica d'arte,* 1938, p. 183; Middeldorf, *Pantheon,* July–Dec. 1938, p. 318; Mariacher, *Arte ven.,* 1948, pp. 69ff.; Mariacher, *BM,* 1950, p. 127; Mariacher, *Arte ven.,* 1950, p. 105; Mariacher, *R. d'arte,* 1951-52, pp. 185-189; "Additions," N.Y., Met. Mus. of Art. *Bull.,* Oct. 1956, p. 46; Phillips, N.Y., Met. Mus. of Art. *Bull.,* Feb. 1957, pp. 150f.; Pope-Hennessy, [1]1958, pp. 107, 349; El Paso, Texas, Museum of Art. *Kress Collection,* by Shapley, 1961, no. 21; Zangirolami, 1962, p. 209; Romanini, *Arte lom.,* Jan.–June 1964, pp. 92f.; Mariacher, 1966, n.p. [pp. 3f]; Mariacher, *Le muse,* x, 1968, p. 145; Munman, 1968, pp. 52f., 60-67, 102f.; Pincus, *AB,* 1969, pp. 251f.; McAndrew, *AB,* 1969, pp. 24f., n. 44; Pohlandt, *BJ,* 1971, p. 200; Ven., *Procuratie Nuove. Arte a Ven.,* by Mariacher, 1971, p. 139; Munman, *BM,* 1971, pp. 138, 141; A. Zorzi, 1972, i, p. 82, ii, pp. 394ff.; Munman, *AB,* 1973, pp. 77, 79, 81; Pincus, 1974, pp. 195f., n. 21, pp. 346ff.; Middeldorf, 1976, pp. 63f.; Connell, 1976, p. 134; Sheard, *Yale Ital. Studies,* 1977, pp. 266f., n. 23; Schulz, *NdiGF,* 1978, pp. 23-25, 28, 35f., 59f., 71; Munman, *AB,* 1979, p. 640.

Ser Orsato Giustiniani was elected Procurator of St. Mark's in 1459 and Capitano del Mar in 1463. Leader of the Venetian navy in the war against the Turks, he died at Modon on July 11, 1464. His funeral was celebrated in Venice on August 4, 1464. In his testament of June 15, 1462, Giustiniani had ordered his burial in S. Andrea della Certosa. Three hundred ducats, to be disbursed by Ser Giovanni da Brazza, steward to the Procurators of St. Mark's, were left for the completion of the tomb. Should that not suffice, Marino Giustiniani, son of Orsato's brother Pancrazio and Orsato's heir, was to contribute what was lacking. On or before April 22, 1466, the Procurators of St. Mark's agreed to give Giovanni da Brazza 300 ducats for making the tomb; on that day they gave Giovanni 200 ducats. On December 1, 1466, they gave him the remaining 100 ducats. If the tomb had already been begun by April 22, 1466 (or indeed, by June 15, 1462), it cannot have been very far advanced by the time the procurators made their payments. The inscription on the tomb stated that the tomb was constructed for his uncle by Marino Giustiniani. The free-standing marble tomb stood at the center of a richly ornamented funerary chapel erected, probably also by Marino, to house the tomb. The chapel was located in the old church dedicated to SS. Eufemia, Dorothy, Tecla, and Erasma in the minor cloister of the later fifteenth-century church of S. Andrea della Certosa. As a result of the Napoleonic suppression, S. Andrea was consigned to the army and then demolished. Its ornaments and furnishings were sold.[4]

The first of the Giustiniani figures to come to light was *Temperance,* acquired for the collection of Count Gregory Stroganoff in Rome from the Venetian antique dealer Zuber. Thence it passed to the collection of Camillo Castiglioni at Vienna, where it remained until 1930. In 1924 *Hope* and *Charity* were owned by Bruno Kern, Vienna. In 1952 *Charity* and *Temperance* were purchased from Paul Drey, New York, for the Kress Collection. *Hope* was acquired from the Blumka Gallery by the Metropolitan Museum in 1956.[5] In 1951 Mariacher discovered *Fortitude* and the unidentified *Virtue* in a private collection in Padua.[6]

In his guide of 1581 Sansovino attributed the tomb to Antonio Dentone.[7] Although nothing was—or is—known of this sculptor, his name prevailed until the end of the nineteenth century[8] when, on the basis of the similarity between the Giustiniani and Tron sarcophagi first observed by Meyer,[9] Paoletti proposed an attribution to Antonio Rizzo.[10] Paoletti's attribution and its immediate acceptance must be judged in light of the fact that, at the time, the only statue widely and erroneously regarded as belonging to the tomb was Antonio Rizzo's *Angel with the Attributes of Christ* in the Ca' d'Oro.[11] Yet subsequent knowledge of three of the original figures by connoisseurs like Planiscig did not lead to the rejection of Paoletti's attribution.[12] Indeed, Rizzo's authorship was generally accepted even by those, like Mariacher, who perceived analogies with figures from the Foscari Tomb, then universally assigned to Antonio Bregno.[13]

In a recent book I included the Giustiniani *Virtues* within a group of Venetian works comprising the Tomb of Francesco Foscari, S. Maria dei Frari, *St. Mark,* the *Moro* and *Gorgon Warriors* and *Music* and *Rhetoric* from the Arco Foscari, the Tomb of Vittore Capello, S. Elena, the statue of *St. Christopher*, Madonna dell'Orto, and the relief of *St. Jerome in the Desert*, S. Maria del Giglio, which seemed to me stylistically consistent. These I attributed to Niccolò di Giovanni Fiorentino, active as sculptor and architect in Dalmatia from 1468 until his death in 1505.

The *Giustiniani Virtues*, I argued, show the imprint of Niccolò's style to varying degrees. *Temperance*, comparable in stance, drapery, and coiffure to *Music* from the Arco Foscari, and in facial type to *Justice* from the Foscari Tomb and *St. Helen* from the Capello Tomb, is closest of all to Niccolò's other sculpture. The left *Angel* from a tabernacle in the Duomo, Šibenik, employs the same schemata of folds. *Hope*, by contrast, is farthest removed from Niccolò's other works. Despite differences in style, none of the Giustiniani *Virtues* is very good; possibly each was carved by a different assistant. Those that deviate most from Niccolò's style may have been completed after the master's departure for Trogir, presumably in April 1468.[14]

1 Grevembroch, *Mon. Ven.*, i, 1754, p. 92.
2 Middeldorf, 1976, p. 63.
3 Cicogna, ii, 1827, pp. 55, 58.
4 Schulz, *NdiGF*, 1978, p. 23.
5 Middeldorf, 1976, p. 63; Schulz, *NdiGF*, 1978, p. 43, n. 65.
6 Mariacher, *R. d'arte*, 1951-52, pp. 187ff.
7 Sans., 1581, p. 80r.
8 Grevembroch, *Mon. Ven.*, i, 1754, p. 92; Cicognara, ii, 1816, p. 174; Cicogna, ii, 1827, p. 57; Ticozzi, i, 1830, p. 406; Moschini, 1842, p. 46; Sel-

vatico, 1847, p. 228; Selvatico/Lazari, 1852, pp. 210, 272; Mothes, ii, 1860, p. 156; Fulin/Molmenti, 1881, pp. 340, 435; Meyer, *JpK*, 1889, p. 194.
9 Meyer, *JpK*, 1889, p. 194.
10 Paoletti, 1893, ii, pp. 144, 226.
11 See above, cat. no. 10.
12 Planiscig, *VJ*, 1926, pp. 96f.
13 N.Y., A.S. Drey Galleries. *Sculpture*, 1935, p. 14, no. 33; Fiocco, *Enc. ital.*, xxix, 1936, p. 502; Brooklyn, N.Y., Institute of Arts and Sciences, Museum. *European Art 1450-1500*, 1936, no. 52; Detroit, Inst. of Arts. *Italian Sculptures*, 1938, by Valentiner, nos. 93, 94; Ragghianti, *Critica d'arte*, 1938, p. 183; Middeldorf, *Pantheon*, July–Dec. 1938, p. 318; Mariacher, *Arte ven.*, 1948, pp. 69f.; Mariacher, *BM*, 1950, p. 127; Mariacher, *R. d'arte*, 1951-52, pp. 187f.; Pope-Hennessy, ¹1958, pp. 107, 349; El Paso, Texas, Museum of Art. *Kress Collection*, by Shapley, 1961, no. 21; Romanini, *Arte lom.*, Jan.–June 1964, pp. 92f.; Mariacher, 1966, n.p. [p. 4]; Munman, 1968, pp. 102f.; Pincus, *AB*, 1969, p. 251; Ven., Procuratie Nuove. *Arte a Ven.*, by Mariacher, 1971, p. 139; A. Zorzi, 1972, i, p. 82, ii, p. 394.

McAndrew, *AB*, 1969, pp. 24f., n. 44, attributed the tomb to Dentone and Rizzo. To Dentone he specifically gave the effigy of Giustiniani. Pohlandt, *BJ*, 1971, p. 200, rejected the attribution to Rizzo and cautiously advanced the name of Dentone. Middeldorf, 1976, p. 63, could not adjudicate between the claims of Rizzo, Bregno, and Dentone. Pincus, 1974, pp. 346ff., attributed the Giustiniani Tomb to a close associate of Rizzo, responsible also for the Cenotaph of Frederico Cornaro in the Cappella Cornaro, S. Maria dei Frari, and the *Moro Warrior* from the Arco Foscari. She believed, however, that only *Hope* was autograph. Munman, *AB*, 1979, p. 640, disagreed.
14 Schulz, *NdiGF*, 1978, pp. 25, 28, 35f., 59f., 71, and *passim*.

24. Venice, S. Elena: Tomb of Vittore Capello

The Capello Tomb surmounts and surrounds the main portal of S. Elena.

Except for the veined marble background, the architectural components of the tomb are made of Istrian limestone. Figures are probably marble.

The rear faces of both statues were left unfinished. The bottom rear corner of *St. Helen* was cut away in order to accommodate the platform beneath the supports of the sarcophagus, while an arc was excavated toward the rear of

Capello's base in order to accommodate *St. Helen*'s base. The saint's left hand and crown are missing. Her drapery, the index finger of her right hand, her face, and the projecting plates of armor on *Capello*'s knees and elbow have been chipped. In *Capello*'s left hand is the stump of an object that can no longer be identified.[1] The exposed portions of the kneeling figure have been badly worn by rain.

D · IM / VICTOR CAPPELLVS IMPERATOR MARITI / MVS MAXIMIS REBVS GESTIS III ET LX / ANNOS NATVS AB ANNO SALVTIS M̊CCCCLXVII / III IDVS

MARCIAS IN EVBOIA PERRIT HIS EIVS / OSSA IN
CAELO ANIMA

ANDREAS LODOVICVS / PAVLVS FILII PIENTIS-
SIMI // PARENTI OPTVMO / POSVERVNT is divided
between the plinths of the two columns.

Sanudo, (1493) 1980, p. 52; Sanudo, *RIs*, xxii,
(1490-1530) 1733, col. 1184; Sans., 1581, p. 78r;
Garzoni, [1]1585, p. 696; Superbi, 1629, ii, p. 57;
Coronelli, pt. 1, 1696, p. 46; Venice, Bibl.
Marc., Cod. it., Cl. VII, 1676 (= 9037), *S.
Elena*, foll. 119ff.; Grevembroch, *Mon. Ven.*,
iii, 1759, p. 41; Gradenigo, (1748-74) 1942, p.
133; Cicognara, ii, 1816, p. 174, pl. xxxix;
Moschini, 1819, p. 42; Cicognara in Cicognara
et al., ii, [1]1820, [cc. 74rf.]; Diedo in ibid., [cc.
154rff.]; Soràvia, i, 1822, p. 105; Cicogna,
Giornale, 1822, p. 307; Cicogna, iii, 1830, pp.
373ff., no. 8; Ticozzi, i, 1830, p. 406; Quadri,
1835, p. xviii, no. 23, p. 31, pl. xiv, no. 23;
E. Paoletti, 1837, pp. 200f., ii, 1839, p. 238, pl.
oppos. p. 240; Zanotto in Diedo/Zanotto, 1839,
n.p.; Diedo and Zanotto in Cicognara *et al.*, ii,
[2]1840, pp. 30, 155; Moschini, 1842, p. 55; Sagredo, *Annali universali*, July–Sept. 1843, p. 197;
Sagredo in *Venezia e le sue lagune*, 1847, i, pt.
2, p. 407; Zanotto in ibid., ii, pt. 2, pp. 101,
164; Selvatico, 1847, pp. 228f.; Selva-
tico/Lazari, 1852, pp. 124, 169, 272; Burckhardt, [1]1855, p. 628b; Zanotto, *Nuovissima guida*,
1856, pp. 294, 380, 666f.; Zanotto, *Venezia
prospettica*, 1856, n.p., "Tempio de' Santi
Giovanni e Paolo"; Mothes, ii, 1860, p. 156;
Fulin/Molmenti, 1881, pp. 226, 278, 292, 436;
A. P. Zorzi, *L'art*, 1883, pt. 4, p. 213; Boito,
1884, pp. 72ff.; Venice, Bibl. Marc. Cod. it.,
Cl. VII, 2283 (= 9121), Fapanni, *Chiese claustrali*, pp. 70rf.; Meyer, *JpK*, 1889, pp. 194f.;
Paoletti, 1893, ii, pp. 142, 144f.; Paoletti, *L'arte*,
1902, p. 125; Comune di Ven., 1905, p. 112,
S. Polo, no. 86; Venturi, *Storia*, vi, 1908, pp.
1061, 1064; Paoletti, "Bregno, Antonio," T-B,
iv, 1910, p. 569; Bouchaud, 1913, p. 110; Pozzi,
Revue numismatique, 1914, pp. 201-206; Berti,
n.d. [1916], p. 9; L. Venturi, *L'arte*, 1916, pp.
49f.; Schubring, 1919, p. 244; Planiscig, 1921,
pp. 36, 64; Molmenti/Mantovani, [2]1925, p. 35;
Lorenzetti, [1]1926, pp. 85, 543; Gallo, *R. di Ven.*,
1926, pp. 485, 520, doc. xli; Planiscig, *VJ*, 1926,
pp. 97f.; Fiocco, *Dedalo*, 1927-28, p. 454; Guyer,
1928, p. xix; Molmenti, ii, [7]1928, p. 354; Planiscig, T-B, xxviii, 1934, p. 409; A. Scarpa, 1935,
p. 55; Fiocco, *Enc. ital.*, xxix, 1936, p. 502;
Mariacher, *Le arti*, 1940-41, p. 196; Mariacher,

Arte ven., 1948, pp. 72f.; Mariacher, *BM*, 1950,
p. 127; Pope-Hennessy, [1]1958, p. 349; Muraro,
1953, p. 220; Muraro in *Essays . . . Panofsky*,
1960, i, p. 362; Zangirolami, 1962, pp. 213f.;
Romanini, *Arte lom.*, Jan.–June 1964, pp. 91ff.;
Zava Boccazzi, 1965, pp. 96, 342, n. 77; Hubala in Egg *et al.*, [1]1965, p. 861; Mariacher,
1966, n.p. [p. 4]; Munman, 1968, pp. 54ff., 67-
75, 99-103, 335; Mariacher, *Le muse*, x, 1968,
p. 145; McAndrew, *AB*, 1969, pp. 24f., n. 44;
Pincus, *AB*, 1969, p. 250; Ven., Procuratie
Nuove. *Arte a Ven.*, by Mariacher, 1971, p.
139; Pohlandt, *BJ*, 1971, pp. 200ff.; Munman,
BM, 1971, pp. 138-145; Brenzoni, 1972, p. 251;
A. Zorzi, 1972, i, pp. 135, 137, ii, p. 499; Wolters, *Pantheon*, 1974, p. 131; Pincus, 1974, p.
173, n. 3, p. 310, n. 106, pp. 311f.; Franzoi/Di
Stefano, 1975, pp. 20, 534f.; Connell, 1976, p.
135; Sheard, *Yale Ital. Studies*, 1977, pp. 264f.,
n. 19; Schulz, *NdiGF*, 1978, pp. 25-30, 36, 71,
72; McAndrew, 1980, pp. 72ff.

Commander of the Venetian navy in the war
against the Turks, Vittore Capello died at Negroponte on March 13, 1467. News of his death
had reached Venice by April 7, 1467. Capello's
body was returned to Venice, where it was apparently buried just inside the entrance to S.
Elena. Capello's tomb is not documented. The
inscriptions on the plinths record that the monument was erected by Capello's three sons, Alvise, Paolo, and Andrea. After the suppression
of S. Elena in 1807 the statues of *Capello* and
St. Helen were removed to SS. Giovanni e Paolo. The architectural surround (minus the
crowning vase, incorporated into the altar of
the oratory of the Seminario Patriarcale at S.
Maria della Salute, and the inscription of the
lintel, which remained behind) was installed on
the main portal of S. Aponal. At the beginning
of the present century architecture and sculpture were reunited at S. Aponal. The entire tomb
was reconstructed on its original site, probably
in 1943.[2]

The Capello Tomb is the earliest Venetian
example of a funerary monument incorporated
into the exterior portal of a church. The iconography of its figures cannot be matched in
any other tomb. Probably the grouping of *Capello* and *St. Helen* depends from the obverse
of Venetian ducats in which the doge kneels
before St. Mark; together, doge and saint hold
the *vexillum Sancti Marci*. The medallic image
signified the investiture of the doge by the patron saint of Venice. By analogy, the Capello

Tomb may be assumed to signify the investiture of Capello as Capitano del Mar by St. Helen in 1466.[3]

The Capello Tomb was drawn by Johannes Grevembroch in 1759.[4] An engraving of the tomb published by Cicognara in 1816 still shows the tomb *in situ*.[5] Similarly, figures and architecture are integrated in a measured engraving of the tomb's plan and elevation by Mezzani and Dala published in 1820. A second engraving by Mezzani and Musitelli illustrates some of the monument's architectural details.[6] Engravings published in 1835 and 1839 depict the figures and sarcophagus as they were installed at SS. Giovanni e Paolo.[7] The engraving by Querena and Musitelli, which appeared in 1839, portrays figures and architectural framework as installed at S. Elena; the engraving gives the plan as well as the elevation of the frame.[8]

In his guide of 1581 Sansovino ascribed the Capello Tomb to Antonio Dentone, reputed author of the Giustiniani Tomb.[9] The attribution to Dentone was not disputed until 1893 when an examination of the tomb's architecture induced Paoletti to assign it to Antonio Rizzo. Evident analogies between *St. Helen* and figures from the Foscari Tomb and Arco Foscari he tentatively explained by the possible collaboration of a second master.[10] Paoletti's hesitant suggestion of collaboration was affirmed by Venturi[11] and Munman,[12] both of whom attributed to an assistant the execution of the saint. Nevertheless, Paoletti's ascription of the tomb to Rizzo gained wide currency.[13] Alternative solutions focused on Antonio Bregno, favored at one time by Planiscig[14] and Fiocco,[15] and Antonio Dentone, whose name was recently reintroduced by Pohlandt.[16]

The date of the tomb is not documented: a dating shortly after Capello's death was generally accepted but could not be proven. Arguments for a later dating of ca. 1476 based on the architecture of the tomb, propounded by Mariacher,[17] were effectively refuted by Romanini.[18]

In a recent book I sought to demonstrate Niccolò di Giovanni Fiorentino's authorship of the Capello Tomb.[19] In her proportions, pose, and drapery, *St. Helen* was shown to resemble *Rhetoric* and *Music* from the Arco Foscari and *Prudence* from the Tomb of Doge Francesco Foscari in S. Maria dei Frari. The saint's face was compared with that of the statuette of *Temperance* from the Tomb of Ser Orsato

Giustiniani. Similarities between the portraits of Capello and Doge Foscari were adduced. All these works, as well as the *Gorgon* and *Moro Warriors* and *St. Mark* from the Arco Foscari, the statue of *St. Christopher* from the main portal of the Madonna dell'Orto, and the relief of *St. Jerome in the Desert* in S. Maria del Giglio, I argued, formed a consistent group that could be associated, through numerous stylistic and iconographic links, with the sculpture of Niccolò di Giovanni Fiorentino at Trogir and Šibenik.

The postulation of Niccolò Fiorentino's authorship of the Capello Tomb permitted a precise determination of its date.[20] On December 19, 1467, Niccolò was in Trogir to delegate authority in the making of an important contract. The contract was signed on January 4, 1468 in Niccolò's absence. Only on April 26, 1468 did he reappear in Dalmatia, where he seems to have been continuously active for the next five years. Presumably Niccolò's hasty departure from Trogir was occasioned by the necessity of completing the Capello Tomb before undertaking what was to prove the most extensive sculptural commission of his career.

---

[1] Schulz, *NdiGF*, 1978, pp. 26f.

[2] A. P. Zorzi, *L'art*, 1883, pt. 4, p. 213; Schulz, *NdiGF*, 1978, p. 25. Franzoi/Di Stefano, 1975, p. 535, gave the date of its return to its original site as 1929. This cannot be correct. See A. Scarpa, 1935, p. 55.

[3] Schulz, *NdiGF*, 1978, p. 26.

[4] Grevembroch, *Mon. Ven.*, iii, 1759, p. 41.

[5] Cicognara, ii, 1816, pl. xxxix.

[6] Cicognara *et al.*, ii, [1]1820, pls. on cc. 155, 156.

[7] Quadri, 1835, pl. xiv, no. 23; E. Paoletti, ii, 1839, pl. oppos. p. 240.

[8] Diedo/Zanotto, 1839, n.p.

[9] Sans., 1581, p. 78r. Sansovino's attribution was adopted by Garzoni, [1]1585, p. 696; Grevembroch, *Mon. Ven.*, iii, 1759, p. 41; Cicognara, ii, 1816, p. 174; Moschini, 1819, p. 42; Cicognara in Cicognara *et al.*, ii, [1]1820, [cc. 74rf.]; Diedo in ibid., [c. 154r]; Soràvia, i, 1822, p. 105; Cicogna, iii, 1830, p. 375; Ticozzi, i, 1830, p. 406; Quadri, 1835, p. xviii, no. 23; E. Paoletti, i, 1837, pp. 200f., ii, 1839, p. 238; Zanotto in Diedo/Zanotto, 1839, n.p.; Sagredo in *Venezia e le sue lagune*, 1847, i, pt. 2, p. 407; Zanotto in ibid., ii, pt. 2, p. 101; Selvatico, 1847, pp. 228f.; Selvatico/Lazari, 1852, pp. 124, 169, 272; Burckhardt, [1]1855, p. 628b; Zanotto, *Nuovissima guida*, 1856, pp. 294, 380, 666f.; Mothes, ii, 1860, p. 156; Fulin/Molmenti, 1881, pp. 226, 278, 292, 436; A. P. Zorzi, *L'art*, 1883, pt. 4, p. 213; Boito, 1884, p. 73;

Meyer, *JpK*, 1889, p. 194 and anachronistically, Zangirolami, 1962, pp. 213f.

[10] Paoletti, 1893, ii, pp. 142, 145.

[11] Venturi, *Storia*, vi, 1908, pp. 1061, 1064. Venturi's analysis was plagiarized by Bouchaud, 1913, p. 110. Cf. Muraro, 1953, p. 220.

[12] Munman, 1968, pp. 68ff., 102; Munman, *BM*, 1971, pp. 141f.

[13] Pozzi, *Revue numismatique*, 1914, p. 206; Berti, n.d. [1916], p. 9; L. Venturi, *L'arte*, 1916, pp. 49f.; Schubring, 1919, p. 244; Lorenzetti, [1]1926, pp. 85, 543; Gallo, *R. di Ven.*, 1926, p. 485 (with reservations); Mariacher, *Le arti*, 1940-41, p. 196; Mariacher, *Arte ven.*, 1948, pp. 72f.; Mariacher, *BM*, 1950, p. 127 (with the collaboration, and under the influence, of Bregno), and other places; Pope-Hennessy, [1]1958, p. 349; Muraro in *Essays . . . Panofsky*, 1960, i, p. 362; Romanini, *Arte lom.*, Jan.–June 1964, pp. 91ff.; Zava Boccazzi, 1965, p. 96; Hubala in Egg *et al.*, [1]1965, p. 861; Pincus, *AB*, 1969, p. 250; Brenzoni, 1972, p. 251; A. Zorzi, 1972, i, p. 135, ii, p.

499; Pincus, 1974, p. 311; Franzoi/Di Stefano, 1975, pp. 20, 535; McAndrew, 1980, p. 72.

[14] Planiscig, 1921, pp. 36, 64, followed by Guyer, 1928, p. xix. However, in *VJ*, 1926, pp. 97f., and T-B, xxviii, p. 409, Planiscig gave the tomb to Rizzo.

[15] Fiocco, *Dedalo*, viii, 1927-28, p. 454, but in *Enc. ital.*, xxix, 1936, p. 502, Fiocco espoused the orthodox attribution to Rizzo.

[16] Pohlandt, *BJ*, 1971, pp. 202ff. McAndrew, *AB*, 1969, p. 25, n. 44, believed that Rizzo and Dentone collaborated on the tomb.

[17] Mariacher, *Arte ven.*, 1948, pp. 72f.

[18] Romanini, *Arte lom.*, Jan.–June 1964, pp. 92f. A dating in the 1470s or early 1480s posited by Pincus, *AB*, 1969, p. 251, n. 21, was retracted in her later dissertation: Pincus, 1974, p. 173, n. 3, p. 310, n. 106.

[19] Schulz, *NdiGF*, 1978, pp. 27ff. and *passim*.

[20] Ibid., p. 72.

25. Venice, S. Maria della Carita (formerly): Tomb of Doges Marco and Agostino Barbarigo

From the demolished tomb there survive isolated pieces of the sculptural decoration: the statue of the kneeling *Doge Agostino Barbarigo* in the antesacristy of S. Maria della Salute, Venice; a relief of the *Resurrection of Christ* on the ground floor of the Scuola di S. Giovanni Evangelista, Venice; three bronze reliefs, two of which portray the *Assumption of the Virgin* and a third with the *Coronation of the Virgin*, now in storage at the Galleria Giorgio Franchetti alla Ca' d'Oro, Venice. Slabs of various geometric shapes, probably in part, at least, from the facing of the tomb, are currently stored in the Magazzino della Dogana of the Soprintendenza ai Beni Artistici e Storici, Venice.

The original appearance of the tomb is preserved in a detailed engraving of 1692 by Suor Isabella Piccini.[1] An engraving of ca. 1710 by Vincenzo Coronelli is more summary.[2] On a much smaller scale, the tomb was reproduced from the reverse of a medal supposedly struck or cast under Agostino Barbarigo, in a book of 1732 on medals commemorating the Barbarigo family.[3]

These engravings, supplemented by documents that relate to the adornment of the Barbarigo Altar, permit a reconstruction of the

tomb. It encompassed three contiguous, shallow, barrel-vaulted bays, the central one of which was illumined by an oculus and two arched windows. The central bay contained an altar with an image of the Madonna flanked by the kneeling figures of Marco on the left and Agostino on the right. In the second story, between the windows, was the *Resurrection*. The epitaph of Doge Marco Barbarigo, surmounted by a console-borne sarcophagus, bier, and reclining effigy, occupied the left-hand bay. The arrangement was repeated in the right bay dedicated to Doge Agostino. The sculptural decoration was completed by four free-standing statues installed in the niches of the four piers between the bays; from left to right the statues represented *St. Mark*, the *Annunciate Angel*, the *Annunciate Virgin*, and *St. Augustine*.

The kneeling *Doge* and *Resurrection* are made of white marble and limestone, respectively. There are traces of dark paint in the eyeballs of the *Doge*. The tomb was faced with veined marble and inlaid slabs of porphyry, *verde antico*, and red-veined marble. The Barbarigo arms were evidently polychromed. Sansovino described the gilding of the epitaphs.[4]

The carving of the *Doge* is essentially complete: only the decoration of the left side of the ducal bonnet was omitted. A crack and chip at the juncture of the figure's neck and shoulders indicate that the *Doge*'s head was once dislodged. Where the *Doge*'s mantle covers the figure's left wrist, the mantle is badly cracked and chipped. The nose of the statue is severely chipped and his thumbs are missing. Minor chips are visible in the figure's right eyebrow, the tips of his fingers, and in the *Doge*'s mantle. Otherwise the surface of the statue is in good condition.

The *Resurrection*, by contrast, is poorly preserved. The right corner of the relief, most of the raised arm and hand of the rearmost soldier, the top of Christ's banner, and half of Christ's left foot are missing. Chips are visible in the right corner of the sarcophagus, the foot of the central soldier, Christ's right foot, and the end of the banner. The entire surface is scarred, pitted, and abraded. Several fissures are evident in the lower part of the relief.

Munman estimated that the entire tomb measured ca. 12 m. x 19 m.[5] *Doge*: 120 cm. high; *Resurrection*: 190 cm. high; the molding below it: 72.8 cm. wide.

MARCI BARBADICI PRINCIPIS OSSA HIC SUNT. EIUS- DEM RECTE FACTO- / RUM INTER HOMINES NUN- QUAM INTERITURA LAUS. QUEM CUM / DIU IN PRINCIPATU ADMIRARI NON POTUISSENT EUMDEM PENE / VIVENTEM PATRIAE ITERUM RESTITUENTES AUGUSTINUM FRATREM / EI SUFFECERUNT. DEBI- TUM VIRTUTI TESTIMONIUM QUOD ANTEA / INAUDITUM POSTEROS AD GLORIAM SEMPER EX- CITABIT. PRAEFUIT / MENSES IX, VIX. ANN. LXXII, MCCCCLXXXVI.

AUGUSTINUS BARBADICUS FRATRI DUCI OPTIMO INCREDIBILI TOTIUS / CIVITATIS CONSENSU SUF- FECTUS RHETICO BELLO CONFECTO CYPRO / RECEPTA PIRATIS TOTO MARI SUBLATIS REBUS ITALIAE POST / FUSOS AD TARUM GALLOS FER- DINANDUMQUE IUNIOREM IN RE- / GNUM RESTITU- TUM COMPOSITIS MARITIMIS APULIAE OPPIDIS IM- / PERIO ADIUNCTIS HETRUSCO TUMULTU SEDATO CREMONA ABDUA- / NAQUE GLAREA RECEPTIS CE- PHALONIA DE TURCIS CAPTA FLO- / RENTISS. REIP. STATU VIVENS M. H. P. VIXIT ANN. LXXXII / PRAEFUIT XV D. XXIII OBIIT MDI.[6]

Sanudo, (1493) 1980, p. 50; Sanudo, *RIs*, xxii, (1490-1530) 1733, col. 1239; Sanudo, *Diarii*, iv, 1880, col. 113; Egnazio, 1554, pp. 189v; Sans., 1581, pp. 80r, 95vf.; Henninges, 1598, p. 1158; Megiser, 1610, pp. 95f.; Martinelli, [1]1684, pp. 399f.; Pacifico, 1697, p. 460; Coronelli, n.d. [ca. 1710] n.p.; Barbarigo, 1732, pp. 75, 91f.; Cor- ner, *Eccl. Ven.*, 1749, v, p. 173; [Giampiccoli], 1779, p. 89; Maier, pt. 1, [2]1795, p. 459; Cico- gnara, ii, 1816, pp. 149f., pl. 38; [Moschini], *Ragguaglio*, 1819, p. 31; Venice, Mus. Cor., MS Cicogna 2008, Cicogna, *Inscrizioni veneziane*, no. 10, "S. Maria della Carità," pp. 1f.; E. Pa- oletti, iii, 1840, p. 136, n. 1; Moschini, 1842, p. 89; Selvatico, 1847, pp. 225, 503; Sagredo in *Venezia e le sue lagune*, 1847, i, pt. 2, p. 406; Selvatico/Lazari, 1852, pp. 207f., 261; Ven., Gall. dell'Accademia. Catalogue, 1854, p. 4; Zanotto, *Nuovissima guida*, 1856, pp. 509, 568; Mothes, ii, 1860, pp. 35f.; Dall'Acqua Giusti, Ven., Accademia. *Atti*, 1873, pp. 49f.; Tassini, *Arch. ven.*, 1876, pp. 364ff.; Urbani de Ghel- tof, 1877, p. 10; Fulin/Molmenti, 1881, p. 336; Venice, Bibl. Marc., Cod. it., Cl. VII, 2289 (= 9125), Fapanni, "Marmi sparsi," *Monumenti veneziani*, ii, 1870-88, p. 4, "Marmi di sog- getto vario," p. 5; ibid., Fapanni, "Oggetti d'arte," *Monumenti veneziani*, ii, 1870-88 [Aug. 28, 1886], no. 9; Venice, Bibl. Marc., Cod. it., Cl. VII, 2511 (= 12216), Fapanni, *Vicende e mutazioni*, pp. 150ff.; Semrau, 1890, p. 84; Baldoria, *Arch. stor. dell'arte*, 1891, p. 185; Pa- oletti, 1893, ii, pp. 142, 161, 184f., 266, 269f.; Venturi, *Le gallerie nazionali italiane*, 1896, pp. 54ff.; Burckhardt/Bode/Fabriczy, [7]1898, ii, pt. 1, pp. 128f; Schlosser, 1901, pp. 13f., pl. xxi, 1; Berlin, Königl. Mus. Catalogue by Knapp, [2]1904, pp. 28f., nos. 434, 437; Bode, i, 1907, pp. 38f.; Venturi, *Storia*, vi, 1908, p. 1072, n. 1, pp. 1088, 1096; Vienna, Ksthis. Mus. Cata- logue by Schlosser, 1910, p. 2; Breck, *Art in America*, 1913, pp. 126f.; Planiscig, 1921, pp. 209ff., 254f.; Berlin, Staatl. Mus. Catalogue by Bange, [3]1922, pp. 4f., nos. 23-25; Ven., Gall. dell'Accademia. Catalogue, 1924, p. 7; Fogo- lari, *Arch. ven.*, 1924, pp. 90f.; Vienna, Ksthis. Mus. Catalogue by Planiscig, 1924, p. 80; Lo- renzetti, [1]1926, pp. 503, 573, 638; Ven., Ca' d'Oro, *Guida-catalogo*, by Fogolari *et al.*, 1929, p. 148; Piva, 1930, p. 133; Berlin, Staatl. Mus., Kaiser-Friedrich-Mus. Catalogue by Bode, [4]1930, pp. 24f., no. 112; Lorenzetti, *Enc. ital.*, x, 1931, p. 693; Venturi, *Storia*, x, pt. 1, 1935, p. 394; Da Mosto, 1939, pp. 139ff.; Angelini, 1945, pp. 71ff., 132; Mariacher, *Arte ven.*, 1948, pp. 80f.; Fogolari, [2]1950, p. 16; Pope-Hen- nessy, [1]1958, p. 349; G. Scarpa in Tramontin *et al.*, 1958, p. 50; Muraro in *Essays . . . Panof- sky*, 1960, i, pp. 357, 361; Florence, Pal. Strozzi. *Bronzetti italiani*, by Pope-Hennessy,

1962, nos. 80, 84; Sinding–Larsen, *Acta ad archaeologiam*, 1962, p. 164; Lorenzetti, [3]1963, pp. 436, 534, 602; Romanini, *Arte lom.*, Jan.–June 1964, pp. 91, 98; Hubala in Egg *et al.*, [1]1965, pp. 825, 911, 989; Vienna, Ksthis. Mus. Catalogue by Mahl *et al.*, 1966, p. 21, no. 215; Mariacher, 1966, n.p. [p. 5]; Munman, 1968, pp. 237, 258-273, 324f.; Deiseroth, 1970, p. 269, n. 551; Ven., Procuratie Nuove. *Arte a Ven.*, by Mariacher, 1971, pp. 139, 156, nos. 75-77: Pohlandt, *BJ*, 1971, pp. 204ff.; Mariacher, 1971, pp. 16f., 34, nos. 110-111; Niero, 1971, n.p.; Sheard, 1971, pp. 26, 80f., 236ff.; A. Zorzi, 1972, ii, pp. 522ff.; Munman, *AB*, lv, 1973, p. 85, n. 11; Malsburg, 1976, p. 188, n. 185; Munman, *Arte lom.*, 1977, pp. 89-98; Puppi/Puppi, 1977, pp. 110, 226f.; Sheard, *Yale Ital. Studies*, 1977, pp. 258f., n. 7; Ruggeri in Ven., Gall. dell'Accademia. *Giorgione a Ven.*, by Ruggeri *et al.*, 1978, pp. 206-209; McAndrew, 1980, pp. 76ff.; Schulz in *Studies . . . Janson*, 1981, pp. 171-192.

The double tomb was dedicated to the brothers Marco and Agostino Barbarigo, seventy-third and seventy-fourth doges, respectively. Marco ruled from 1485 to 1486; Agostino ruled from 1486 to 1501. The Barbarigo Tomb no longer exists. Originally it occupied three bays of the right aisle wall to the west of the *barco* in the church of S. Maria della Carità. When in 1807 the church, school, and convent of the Carità were chosen as the new seat of the Accademia di Belle Arti, the tomb was demolished: only fragments of it survive today.

In an article published in 1981 I reviewed the historical evidence concerning the construction of the tomb.[7] This evidence allowed the following conclusions. The Tomb of Marco Barbarigo was begun sometime after the doge's death on August 14, 1486. In its original form the monument seems to have been finished by 1493. Apparently there were some later alterations, for on April 3, 1499, work still remained to be done on it. We do not know when that work was accomplished. Perhaps the two campaigns of work on Marco's tomb are to be explained by an intervening decision on Agostino's part to unite his own tomb with that of his brother: such an expansion of Marco's original single tomb might have necessitated fundamental changes in design. Agostino's tomb, we know, was not yet built in 1493. By July 17, 1501—two months before the doge's death on September 20, 1501—both his tomb and the

altar between the two sarcophagi were finished. In 1515 Vincenzo Grimani had a gilded, copper grille, with many bronze figures, made for the Barbarigo Altar. From this commission come the three reliefs in the Ca' d'Oro. Grimani's grille stood in front of an image of the Madonna which rested on the altar; only much later were portions of the grille incorporated into the altarpiece itself, as Piccini shows it. The Barbarigo Altar was finally consecrated on October 18, 1544.

Concerning the attribution of the architecture and sculpture of the tomb opinion is divided. The architecture of the tomb has been assigned to Mauro Codussi by Paoletti,[8] Fogolari,[9] and Angelini,[10] among others;[11] to Antonio Rizzo by Muraro,[12] Munman,[13] and McAndrew;[14] to Tullio Lombardo by Venturi.[15] The attribution of the kneeling *Doge*, in part or in entirety, to Antonio Rizzo or to a close follower of his, is most often met with in the literature.[16] But the attribution has been vigorously contested by Venturi,[17] Planiscig,[18] Fogolari,[19] and Pohlandt.[20] On the rare occasions when the *Resurrection* has been thought worthy of remark, it has been given to an incompetent sculptor,[21] sometimes identified as a follower of Rizzo's.[22]

In a recent article I sought to prove the attribution of both the architecture and sculpture of the Barbarigo Tomb to Pietro Lombardo.[23] With its architecture—diametrically opposed in style to that of Rizzo—the articulation and proportions of the facade of S. Maria dei Miracoli, the marble facing of its interior, and the disposition of windows at its east end, were compared. The generalization of the portrait of *Doge Barbarigo* was contrasted with the particularity of *Doge Tron*'s physiognomy; similarities of facial type were found in Pietro's *St. Mark* from the Giustiniani Chapel in S. Francesco della Vigna. The technique, perspective, drapery style, and facial types of the *Resurrection* were shown to have numerous parallels in Pietro's sculpture.

[1] Venice, Mus. Cor., Raccolta Gherro, iii, no. 435.
[2] Coronelli, n.d. [ca. 1710], n.p.
[3] Barbarigo, 1732, p. 91, no. xxxxvi.
[4] Sans., 1581, p. 95v.
[5] Munman, 1968, p. 266.
[6] From Tassini, *Arch. ven.*, 1876, p. 364, no. 3, p. 365, no. 4.
[7] Schulz in *Studies . . . Janson*, 1981, pp. 173f.
[8] Paoletti, 1893, ii, pp. 184, 185.

[9] Fogolari, *Arch. ven.*, 1924, p. 90.

[10] Angelini, 1945, pp. 72, 132.

[11] Lorenzetti, *Enc. ital.*, x, 1931, p. 693; Malsburg, 1976, p. 188, n. 185. The attribution was accepted with reservations by: Planiscig, 1921, p. 209; Mariacher, *Arte ven.*, 1948, p. 80, n. 1; Mariacher, 1966, n.p. [p. 5]; and Ruggeri in Ven., Gall. dell'Accademia. *Giorgione a Ven.*, by Ruggeri *et al.*, 1978, p. 208.

[12] Muraro in *Essays . . . Panofsky*, 1960, i, p. 357.

[13] Munman, 1968, pp. 267ff.; Munman, *AB*, 1973, p. 85, n. 11; Munman, *Arte lom.*, 1977, pp. 93ff.; Deiseroth, 1970, p. 269, n. 551. The attribution was accepted with reservations by Sheard, 1971, pp. 80f.

[14] McAndrew, 1980, pp. 76ff.

[15] Venturi, *Le gallerie nazionali italiane*, 1896, p. 56. Puppi/Puppi, 1977, p. 110, could come to no decision concerning the attribution of the architecture of the Barbarigo Tomb.

[16] Paoletti, 1893, ii, pp. 142, 185; Lorenzetti, ¹1926, p. 503; Mariacher, *Arte ven.*, 1948, pp. 80f.; Pope-Hennessy, ¹1958, p. 349; Muraro in *Essays . . . Panofsky*, 1960, i, p. 361; Romanini, *Arte lom.*, Jan.– June 1964, pp. 91, 98; Munman, 1968, pp. 262, 267; Niero, 1971, n.p.; Munman, *AB*, 1973, p. 85, n. 11; Ven., Procuratie Nuove. *Arte a Ven.*, by Mariacher, 1971, p. 139; Munman, *Arte lom.*, 1977, p. 91; McAndrew, 1980, p. 79. Accepted with reservations by Angelini, 1945, p. 71.

[17] Venturi, *Storia*, vi, 1908, p. 1072, n. 1.

[18] Planiscig, 1921, p. 209.

[19] Fogolari, *Arch. ven.*, 1924, pp. 90f.

[20] Pohlandt, *BJ*, 1971, p. 207. The attribution to Rizzo does not figure in Planiscig, T-B, xxviii, 1934, pp. 408-410, or in Hubala's description of the church of the Salute in Egg *et al.*, ¹1965, p. 911.

[21] Paoletti, 1893, ii, pp. 184, 185. Calling it mediocre or modest, Planiscig, 1921, p. 209, and Pohlandt, *BJ*, 1971, p. 205, n. 83, refrained from assigning it any author.

[22] Lorenzetti, ¹1926, p. 573; Munman, 1968, p. 261; Munman, *Arte lom.*, 1977, p. 91; McAndrew, 1980, p. 79. Fogolari, *Arch. ven.*, 1924, pp. 90f., thought that the relief, like the effigy of Barbarigo, had hardly been begun when Rizzo was forced to flee Venice.

[23] Schulz in *Studies . . . Janson*, 1981, pp. 176ff.

Bibliography

Manuscripts

In footnotes the following abbreviations
have been employed:

ASV	Venice, Archivio di Stato
Venice, Bibl. Marc.	Venice, Biblioteca Marciana
Venice, Mus. Cor.	Venice, Museo Correr
Vicenza, Mus. Civ.	Vicenza, Museo Civico

Udine, Arcivescovado, Biblioteca Arcivescovile, Sala Bartolini, MS Vale 522

Udine, Seminario Arcivescovile, Archivio Capitolare, *Acta Capituli Aquileiensis*, iii

Venice, Archivio di Stato, Archivio Notarile, *Testamenti*, Busta 1214 (not. Antonio Marsilio)

Venice, Archivio di Stato, Fondi ecclesiastici, S. Maria Gloriosa dei Frari, Chiesa e Conventi, *Processi, etc., T-Z*

Venice, Archivio di Stato, *Libro di cerimoniale*, i.

Venice, Archivio di Stato, Mani morte, Convento di S. Maria dei Servi in Venezia, Busta 9

Venice, Biblioteca Marciana, Cod. it., Cl. VII, 56 (= 8636), attributed to Marcantonio Erizzo, *Cronaca veneta* (with events up to 1495), 16th century

Venice, Biblioteca Marciana, Cod. it., Cl. VII, 323 (= 8646), *Cronaca veneta* (with events up to 1528)

Venice, Biblioteca Marciana, Cod. it., Cl. VII, 791 (= 7589), *Cronaca Veniera* (with events up to 1580)

Venice, Biblioteca Marciana, Cod. it., Cl. VII, 1676 (= 9037), *Cose spettanti al Monastero di S. Elena*, 18th century

Venice, Biblioteca Marciana, Cod. it., Cl. VII, 2283 (= 9121), Francesco Fapanni, *Chiese claustrali e monasteri di Venezia*

Venice, Biblioteca Marciana, Cod. it., Cl. VII, 2288 (= 9124), Francesco Fapanni, *Monumenti veneziani*, i

Venice, Biblioteca Marciana, Cod. it., Cl. VII, 2289 (= 9125), Francesco Fapanni, *Monumenti veneziani*, ii

Venice, Biblioteca Marciana, Cod. it., Cl. VII, 2511 (= 12216), Francesco Fapanni, *Vicende e mutazioni avvenute in questo secolo xix intorno i monumenti d'ogni sorta in Venezia*

Venice, Biblioteca Marciana, Cod. it., Cl. VII, 2512 (= 12217), Francesco Fapanni, *Inscrizioni sparse per sei sestieri di Venezia*

Venice, Biblioteca Marciana, Cod. lat., Cl. VIII, 2 (= 2796), Averulinus (Filarete), *Architecturae*, 1484

Venice, Museo Correr, Cassettiere, Giovanni De Pellegrini, *Stemmario* (collection of 1214 annotated cards with the arms of nonpatrician Venetian families), 1890

Venice, Museo Correr, MS Cicogna 1536, Giuseppe Giacinto Bergantini, "Memorie della famiglia Emo P. V. esistenti nel Monastero de' Servi di S. Maria di Venezia," *Memorie spettanti alla città e dominio di Venezia*, pp. 281-313

Venice, Museo Correr, MS Cicogna 2008, Emmanuele Antonio Cicogna, *Inscrizioni veneziane nelle chiese e luoghi pubblici*

Venice, Museo Correr, MS Cicogna 2017, Emmanuele Antonio Cicogna, *Inscrizioni varie sparse per la città*, i

Venice, Museo Correr, MS Cicogna 3533, Stefano Magno, *Annali veneti* (with events up to 1497 in the original hand), v

Venice, Museo Correr, MS Cicogna Cons. XI-E 2, Marco Barbaro, *Discendenze patrizie*, vii

Venice, Museo Correr, MS Gradenigo 49, Johannes Grevembroch, *Gli abiti de veneziani di quasi ogni età con diligenza raccolti e dipinti nel secolo xviii*, i

Venice, Museo Correr, MS Gradenigo 219, Johannes Grevembroch, *Varie venete curiosità sacre e profane*; i, 1755; ii, 1760; iii, 1764

Venice, Museo Correr, MS Gradenigo 228, Johannes Grevembroch, *Monumenta Veneta ex antiquis ruderibus*; i, 1754; ii, 1754; iii, 1759

Venice, Museo Correr, MS P. D. 2d, Antonio Vucetich, *Pietre e frammenti storici e artistici della citta di Venezia*, end of the 19th century

Venice, Museo Correr, MS P.D. C307, no. xvi, Pietro Pasini, *Cenni indirizzati al Chiar. Signore Giovanni Casoni Imp. R. Ingegnere Idraulico intorno al Palazzo Ducale, ed alla Scala dei Giganti*, December 30, 1843

Vicenza, Museo Civico, Eraclio Minozzi, *Inventario generale delle pitture e sculture esistenti nel Civico Museo di Vicenza*, 1902

Vicenza, Museo Civico, *Inventario del Museo Civico di Vicenza E-II*, 1950, "Statuaria e pezzi vari"

Books

Das Adamsspiel, 1928	*Das Adamsspiel, anglonormannisches Mysterium des XII. Jahrhunderts*, ed. Karl Grass, Halle an der Saale, 1928
"Additions," N.Y., Met. Mus. of Art. *Bull.*, Oct. 1956	"Additions to the Collections," New York, Metropolitan Museum of Art. *Bulletin*, xv, no. 2, Oct. 1956, p. 46
Adelmann/Weise, 1954	G. S. Adelmann and G. Weise, *Das Fortleben gotischer Ausdrucks- und Bewegungsmotive in der Kunst des Manierismus* (Tübinger Forschungen zur Kunstgeschichte, ed. G. Weise, 9), Tübingen, 1954
"Alberto Maffiolo," *Rass. d'arte*, 1902	"Alberto Maffiolo da Carrara è veramente l'autore del lavabo nella Certosa di Pavia?" *Rassegna d'arte antica e moderna*, ii, 1902, pp. 13-15
[Albrizzi], 1740	[Giovambatista Albrizzi], *Forestiere illuminato intorno le cose più rare, e curiose, antiche, e moderne della città di Venezia, e dell'isole circonvicine*, Venice, 1740
Amsterdam, Muller and Co. Collections . . . Castiglioni, Nov. 1925	Amsterdam, Frederik Muller and Co. *Collections Camillo Castiglioni de Vienne*, i, *Catalogue des tableaux, sculptures, meubles, etc.*, Nov. 17-20, 1925, n.p., n.d.

Angelini, 1945 — Luigi Angelini, *Le opere in Venezia di Mauro Codussi*, Milan, 1945

Armstrong, 1976 — Lilian Armstrong, *The Paintings and Drawings of Marco Zoppo*, Garland Series of Outstanding Dissertations in the Fine Arts, New York, 1976

Arnaldi, 1767 — Enea Arnaldi, *Delle basiliche antiche e specialmente di quella di Vicenza*, Vicenza, 1767

Arslan, *GBA*, Sept. 1953 — Edoardo Arslan, "Oeuvres de jeunesse d'Antonio Rizzo," *Gazette des beaux-arts*, series 6, xlii, Sept. 1953, pp. 105-114

Arslan in *Storia di Milano*, vii, 1956 — Edoardo Arslan, "Parte VI. La scultura nella seconda metà del Quattrocento," *Storia di Milano*, Milan, vii, 1956, pp. 691-746

Arslan, 1970 — Edoardo Arslan, *Venezia gotica: l'architettura civile gotica veneziana*, Venice, 1970

Baldoria, *Arch. stor. dell'arte*, 1891 — N. Baldoria, "Andrea Briosco ed Alessandro Leopardi architetti," *Archivio storico dell'arte*, iv, 1891, pp. 180-194

Barbarigo, 1732 — Giovanni Francesco Barbarigo, *Numismata virorum illustrium ex Barbadica gente*, Padua, 1732

Bartoli, 1793 — Francesco Bartoli, *Le pitture sculture ed architetture della città di Rovigo*, Venice, 1793

Bascapè, 1972 — Giacomo C. Bascapè, *Gli ordini cavallereschi in Italia: storia e diritto*, Milan, 1972

Bassi/Trincanato, 1960 — Elena Bassi and Egle Renata Trincanato, *Il Palazzo Ducale nella storia e nell'arte di Venezia*, Milan, 1960

Bassi, 1962 — Elena Bassi, *Architettura del sei e settecento a Venezia*, Naples, 1962

Bassi, *Critica d'arte*, May–June 1962 — Elena Bassi, "Appunti per la storia del Palazzo Ducale di Venezia, I," *Critica d'arte*, ix, no. 51, May–June 1962, pp. 25-38

Bassi, Vicenza, Cen. internaz. . . . Andrea Palladio. *Boll.*, 1964, pt. 2 — Elena Bassi, "Il Palazzo Ducale nel '400," Vicenza, Centro internazionale di studi di architettura Andrea Palladio. *Bollettino*, vi, pt. 2, 1964, pp. 181-187

Bassi/Trincanato, 1964 — Elena Bassi and Egle Renata Trincanato, *Guida alla visita del Palazzo Ducale di Venezia*, Milan, 1964

Bassi in Zorzi *et al.*, 1971 — Elena Bassi in Alvise Zorzi, Bassi, Terisio Pignatti, Camillo Semenzato, *Il Palazzo Ducale di Venezia*, Turin, 1971

Bassi, 1976 — Elena Bassi, *Palazzi di Venezia*, Venice, 1976

Bauch, 1976 — Kurt Bauch, *Das mittelalterliche Grabbild: figürliche Grabmäler des 11. bis 15. Jahrhunderts in Europa*, Berlin/New York, 1976

Belotti, ²1933 — Bortolo Belotti, *La vita di Bartolomeo Colleoni*, Bergamo, ²1933

Beltrami, *Arch. stor. dell'arte*, 1894 — Luca Beltrami, "Antonello da Messina chiamato alla corte di Galeazzo Maria Sforza," *Archivio storico dell'arte*, vii, 1894, pp. 56-57

Belvedere, 1960 — Ettore Belvedere, *Il Palazzo Ducale di Venezia*, Milan, 1960

Berefelt, 1968 — Gunnar Berefelt, *A Study on the Winged Angel. The Origin of a Motif*, trans. Patrick Hort, Stockholm, 1968

Berlin, Ball and Graupe. *Die Sammlung Castiglioni*, by Falke, 1930 — Berlin, Hermann Ball and Paul Graupe. *Die Sammlung C. Castiglioni, Wien: Gemälde—Skulpturen, Möbel, Keramik, Textilien*, Nov. 28-29, 1930, catalogue by Otto von Falke, Berlin, 1930

Berlin, Königl. Mus. Catalogue by Bode/Tschudi, 1888 — Berlin, Königliche Museen. *Beschreibung der Bildwerke der christlichen Epochen*, catalogue by Wilhelm Bode and Hugo von Tschudi, Berlin, 1888

Berlin, Königl. Mus. Catalogue by Knapp, ²1904 — Berlin, Königliche Museen. *Beschreibung der Bildwerke der christlichen Epochen*, ii, *Die italienischen Bronzen*, catalogue by Fritz Knapp, Berlin, ²1904

Berlin, Königl. Mus. Catalogue by Schottmüller, ¹1913 — Berlin, Königliche Museen. *Die italienischen und spanischen Bildwerke der Renaissance und des Barocks in Marmor, Ton, Holz und Stuck*, catalogue by Frida Schottmüller, Berlin, ¹1913

Berlin, Staatl. Mus. Catalogue by Bange, ³1922 — Berlin, Staatliche Museen. *Beschreibung der Bildwerke der christlichen Epochen*, ii, *Die italienischen Bronzen der Renaissance und des Barock*, pt. 2, *Reliefs und Plaketten*, catalogue by E. F. Bange, Berlin/Leipzig, ³1922

Berlin, Staatl. Mus., Kaiser-Friedrich-Mus. Catalogue by Bode, ⁴1930 — Berlin, Staatliche Museen, Kaiser-Friedrich-Museum. *Die italienischen Bildwerke der Renaissance und des Barock*, ii, *Bronzestatuetten, Büsten und Gebrauchsgegenstände*, catalogue by Wilhelm von Bode, Berlin/Leipzig, ⁴1930

Berlin, Staatl. Mus., Kaiser-Friedrich-Mus. Catalogue by Schottmüller, ²1933 — Berlin, Staatliche Museen, Kaiser-Friedrich-Museum. *Die italienischen und spanischen Bildwerke der Renaissance und des Barock*, i, *Die Bildwerke in Stein, Holz, Ton und Wachs*, catalogue by Frida Schottmüller, Berlin/Leipzig, ²1933

Berlin-Dahlem, Stift. Preuss. Kulturbesitz, Staatl. Mus. Catalogue ed. Metz, 1966 — Berlin-Dahlem, Stiftung Preussischer Kulturbesitz, Staatlichen Museen. *Bildwerke der christlichen Epochen von der Spätantike bis zum Klassizismus*, catalogue ed. Peter Metz, Munich, 1966

Bernasconi, 1859 — Cesare Bernasconi, *Intorno la vita e le opere di Antonio Rizzo, architetto e scultore veronese del secolo xv: cenni*, Verona, 1859

Bernasconi, 1863 — Cesare Bernasconi, *Appendice ai cenni intorno la vita e le opere di Antonio Rizzo architetto e scultore veronese del secolo xv e memorie d'altri architetti suoi concittadini del medesimo secolo*, Verona, 1863

Bernstein, 1972 — JoAnne Gitlin Bernstein, "The Architectural Sculpture of the Cloisters of the Certosa di Pavia," Ph.D. Dissertation, New York University, New York, 1972

Berti, n.d. [1916] — Giuseppe Berti, *L'architettura e la scultura a Venezia attraverso i secoli. Il rinascimento*, Turin, n.d. [1916]

[Bianchini], 1892 — [Giuseppe Bianchini], *Il Convento e la Chiesa di S. Maria de' Servi in Venezia*, Venice, 1892

Bibb, *The American Architect*, July 15, 1899; Nov. 4, 1899 — A. B. Bibb, "Santa Maria dei Miracoli and the Lombardi," *The American Architect and Building News*, lxv, no. 1229, July 15, 1899, pp. 19-21; lxvi, no. 1245, Nov. 4, 1899, pp. 35-36

Bieber, 1977 — Margarete Bieber, *Ancient Copies: Contributions to the History of Greek and Roman Art*, New York, 1977

Bigaglia, 1937 — Giuseppe Bigaglia, *La Chiesa della Madonna dell'Orto in Venezia*, Venice, 1937

Biscaro, 1897 — Gerolamo Biscaro, *Note e documenti per servire alla storia delle arti trivigiane*, Treviso, 1897

Bode, text, 1892-1905; iv, 1895-96 — Wilhelm Bode, *Denkmäler der Renaissance-Sculptur Toscanas*, Munich, text, 1892-1905; iv, 1895-96

Bode, i, 1907 — Wilhelm Bode, *Die italienischen Bronzestatuetten der Renaissance*, Berlin, i, 1907

Bode, [6]1922

Wilhelm Bode, *Die italienische Plastik. Handbücher der Staatlichen Museen zu Berlin*, Berlin/Leipzig, [6]1922

Bode, *Der Kunstwanderer*, May 15-31, 1922

Wilhelm Bode, review of Leo Planiscig, *Venezianische Bildhauer der Renaissance*, in *Der Kunstwanderer*, iv, May 15-31, 1922, pp. 425-427

Boito, 1884

Camillo Boito, *Gite di un artista*, Milan, 1884

Boni, *Arch. ven.*, xxxiii, 1887

Giacomo Boni, "Santa Maria dei Miracoli in Venezia," *Archivio veneto*, xxxiii, 1887, pp. 237-274

Bortolan/Rumor, 1919

Domenico Bortolan and Sebastiano Rumor, *Guida di Vicenza*, Vicenza, 1919

Bossaglia in Albertini Ottolenghi *et al.*, 1968

Rossana Bossaglia, "La scultura," in Maria Grazia Albertini Ottolenghi, Bossaglia, and Franco Renzo Pesenti, *La Certosa di Pavia*, Milan, 1968, pp. 41-80

Bouchaud, 1913

Pierre de Bouchaud, *La sculpture vénitienne*, Paris, 1913

Brand, 1977

Hans Gerhard Brand, *Die Grabmonumente Pietro Lombardos. Studien zum Venezianischen Wandgrabmal des späten Quattrocento*, Dissertation, Friedrich-Alexander-Universität, Erlangen-Nuremberg, 1977

Brasca, (1480) 1966

Santo Brasca, *Viaggio in Terrasanta di Santo Brasca 1480 con l'Itinerario di Gabriele Capodilista 1458*, ed. Anna Momigliano Lepschy (*I cento viaggi*, ed. F. Marenco, 4), Milan, 1966

E. W. Braun, *Belvedere*, 1922

E. W. Braun, "Eine Sammlung italienischer Skulpturen in Wien," *Belvedere*, i, 1922, pp. 41-47

J. Braun, 1924

Joseph Braun, *Der christliche Altar in seiner geschichtlichen Entwicklung*, Munich, 1924, 2 vols.

Breck, *Art in America*, 1913

Joseph Breck, "A Bronze Relief by Alessandro Leopardi," *Art in America*, i, 1913, pp. 126-129

Bregenz, Künstlerhaus, Palais Thurn und Taxis. *Meisterwerke der Plastik*, ed. Sandner, 1967

Bregenz, Künstlerhaus, Palais Thurn und Taxis. *Meisterwerke der Plastik aus Privatsammlungen im Bodenseegebiet*, July 1–Sept. 30, 1967, catalogue ed. Oscar Sandner, Bregenz, 1967

Brenzoni, Ist. ven. SLA. *Atti* (Cl. di scienze morali), 1957-58

Raffaello Brenzoni, "La Loggia del Consiglio veronese nel suo quadro documentario," Venice, Istituto veneto di scienze, lettere ed arti. *Atti* (Classe di scienze morali e lettere), cxvi, 1957-58, pp. 265-307

Brenzoni in *Arte e artisti*, 1959, i

Raffaello Brenzoni, "Architetti e scultori dei laghi lombardi a Verona," Società archeologica comense. Convegno sugli artisti del Laria e del Ceresio, 2nd, Varenna, 1957. *Arte e artisti dei laghi lombardi*, ed. Edoardo Arslan, Como, 1959, i, pp. 89-130

Brenzoni, 1972

Raffaello Brenzoni, *Dizionario di artisti veneti: pittori, scultori, architetti, etc. dal xiii al xviii secolo*, Florence, 1972

Brooklyn, N.Y., Institute of Arts and Sciences, Museum. *European Art 1450-1500*, 1936

Brooklyn, N.Y., Institute of Arts and Sciences, Museum. *An Exhibition of European Art 1450-1500 presented by the Rockefeller Foundation Internes of the Brooklyn Museum*, May 8–June 8, 1936, catalogue, n.p., n.d.

Brunetti in Atti, *Jacopo della Quercia*, 1977

Giulia Brunetti, "Sull'attività di Nanni di Bartolo nell' Italia settentrionale," Siena, Facoltà di lettere e filosofia. Convegno di studi, 1975, Atti, *Jacopo della Quercia fra gotico e rinascimento*, ed. Giulietta Chelazzi Dini, Florence, 1977, pp. 189-200

Brusin, ⁴1961   Giovanni Brusin, *Aquileia, guida breve*, Padua, ⁴1961

Budapest, Szépművészeti Mú-   Budapest, Szépművészeti Múzeum. *Katalog der ausländischen*
zeum. Catalogue by Balogh,   *Bildwerke des Museums der Bildenden Künste in Budapest, iv.-xviii.*
1975   *Jahrhundert*, by Jolán Balogh, Budapest, 1975, 2 vols.

Burckhardt, ¹1855   Jacob Burckhardt, *Der Cicerone*, Basel, ¹1855

Burckhardt/Zahn, ³1874   Jacob Burckhardt, *Der Cicerone*, with A. von Zahn, Leipzig,
                                       ³1874

Burckhardt/Bode, ⁴1879   Jacob Burckhardt, *Der Cicerone*, with Wilhelm Bode, Leipzig,
                                       ⁴1879

Burckhardt/Bode, ⁵1884   Jacob Burckhardt, *Der Cicerone*, with Wilhelm Bode, Leipzig,
                                       ⁵1884

Burckhardt/Bode/Fabriczy,   Jacob Burckhardt, *Der Cicerone*, with W. Bode and C. von Fa-
⁷1898   briczy, Leipzig, ⁷1898

Burckhardt/Bode/Fabriczy,   Jacob Burckhardt, *Der Cicerone*, with W. Bode and C. von Fa-
⁸1901   briczy, Leipzig/Berlin, ⁸1901

Burckhardt/Bode/Fabriczy,   Jacob Burckhardt, *Der Cicerone*, with W. Bode and C. von Fa-
¹⁰1910   briczy, Leipzig, ¹⁰1910

Cadorin, 1837   Giuseppe Cadorin, *Notizie storiche della fabbrica del Palazzo Du-*
                                       cale, Venice, 1837

Cadorin, 1838   Giuseppe Cadorin, *Pareri di xv architetti e notizie storiche intorno*
                                       al Palazzo Ducale di Venezia, Venice, 1838

Cadorin, *Il vaglio*, Sept. 30,   Giuseppe Cadorin, "Cose patrie. Polemica. Articolo II. Se An-
1843; Oct. 28, 1843   tonio Bregno od Antonio Riccio sia l'architetto del Palazzo Du-
                                       cale dal 1485 al 1498," *Il vaglio* (Venice), viii, no. 39, Sept. 30,
                                       1843, pp. 506-508; Cadorin, "Articolo III," ibid., viii, no. 43,
                                       Oct. 28, 1843, Supplement, pp. 1-15

Caffi, *Arte e storia*, June 5,   Michele Caffi, "Venezia, il Tempietto del Miracoli," *Arte e sto-*
1887   *ria* (Florence), vi, no. 15, June 5, 1887, pp. 105-107

Callegari, *Dedalo*, ix, 1928-29   Adolfo Callegari, "Pietro Lombardo e il lombardismo nel basso
                                       Padovano," *Dedalo*, ix, 1928-29, pp. 357-385

Cappelleti, iii, 1853   Giuseppe Cappelletti, *Storia della chiesa di Venezia dalla sua fon-*
                                       dazione sino ai nostri giorni, Venice, iii, 1853

Cappelletti, 1854   Giuseppe Cappelletti, *La Basilica di San Marco*, Venice, 1854

Carlyle/Carlyle, ³1930   R. W. Carlyle and A. J. Carlyle, *A History of Mediaeval Political*
                                      Theory in the West, Edinburgh/London, ³1930, i

Carrer, Ven., Aten. ven. *Es-*   Luigi Carrer, "Relazione degli studii nelle scienze morali, nelle
ercitazioni, 1847   lettere e nelle arti dell'Ateneo di Venezia durante gli anni acca-
                                      demici 1843-1844 e 1844-1845 letta il 14 giugno 1846," Venice,
                                      Ateneo veneto. *Esercitazioni scientifiche e letterarie*, vi, 1847, pp.
                                      39-50

Casola, (1494) 1855   Pietro Casola, *Viaggio di Pietro Casola a Gerusalemme, tratto*
                                      dall'autografo esistente nella Biblioteca Trivulzio, Milan, 1855

Casola, (1494) 1907   Pietro Casola, *Canon Pietro Casola's Pilgrimage to Jerusalem in the*
                                      Year 1494, trans. M. Margaret Newett, Manchester, 1907

Caspary, 1964   Hans Caspary, *Das Sakramentstabernakel in Italien bis zum Konzil*
                                      von Trient: Gestalt, Ikonographie und Symbolik, kultische Funktion,
                                      Dissertation, Ludwig-Maximilians-Universität, Munich, 1964

Cecchetti in Ongania, ed., *Basilica*, vii, 1886

Bartolomeo Cecchetti, *Documenti per la storia dell'augusta ducale Basilica di San Marco* in Ferdinando Ongania, ed., *La Basilica di San Marco in Venezia illustrata nei riguardi dell'arte e della storia da scrittori veneziani*, Venice, vii, 1886

Cecchetti, *Arch. ven.*, xxxiii, 1887

Bartolomeo Cecchetti, "Nomi di pittori e lapicidi antichi," *Archivio veneto*, xxxiii, 1887, pp. 43-65

Cecchetti, *Arch. ven.*, xxxiii, 1887; xxxiv, 1887

Bartolomeo Cecchetti, "Saggio di cognomi ed autografi di artisti in Venezia, secoli xiv-xvi," *Archivio veneto*, xxxiii, 1887, pp. 397-424; xxxiv, 1887, pp. 203-214

Cessi, *Medioevo e umanesimo*, 1979, ii

Francesco Cessi, "Una proposta per Antonio Rizzo scultore," *Medioevo e umanesimo*, xxxv, *Medioevo e rinascimento veneto con altri studi in onore di Lino Lazzarini*, Padua, 1979, ii, pp. 11-13

Cevc, *Likovni svet*, 1951

Emilijan Cevc, "Kipar Janez Lipec," *Likovni svet* (Ljubljana), 1951, pp. 202-216

Chiminelli, *Aten. ven.*, 1912, pt. 1

Caterina Chiminelli, "Le scale scoperte nei palazzi veneziani," *Ateneo veneto*, xxxv, pt. 1, 1912, pp. 209-253

Cicogna, *Giornale*, 1822

Emmanuele Antonio Cicogna, "*Le chiese di Venezia . . . da Gio. Battista Soravia. Lettera a Pier-Alessandro Paravia,*" *Giornale sulle scienze e lettere delle provincie venete* (Treviso), iii, no. 18, Dec. 1822, pp. 301-311

Cicogna, i, 1824, etc.

Emmanuele Antonio Cicogna, *Delle inscrizioni veneziane*, Venice: i, 1824; ii, 1827; iii, 1830; iv, 1834; v, 1842; vi, 1853

Cicognara et al., i, ¹1815; ii, ¹1820

Leopoldo Cicognara, Antonio Diedo, Giannantonio Selva, *Le fabbriche più cospicue di Venezia*, Venice; i, ¹1815; ii, ¹1820

Cicognara, ii, 1816

Leopoldo Cicognara, *Storia della scultura dal suo risorgimento in Italia sino al secolo xix*, Venice, ii, 1816

Cicognara et al., i, ²1838; ii, ²1840

Leopoldo Cicognara, Antonio Diedo, Giannantonio Selva, *Le fabbriche e i monumenti cospicui di Venezia*, Venice; i, ²1838; ii, ²1840

Cipolla, *L'arte*, 1914, 1915

Carlo Cipolla, "Ricerche storiche intorno alla Chiesa di Santa Anastasia in Verona," *L'arte*; xvii, 1914, pp. 91-106, pp. 181-197, pp. 396-414; xviii, 1915, pp. 157-171, pp. 296-304, pp. 459-467; xix, 1916, pp. 115-124, pp. 234-240

Clark, 1956

Kenneth Clark, *The Nude: A Study of Ideal Art*, London, 1956

Clarke/Rylands, eds., 1977

Ashley Clarke and Philip Rylands, eds., *The Church of the Madonna dell'Orto*, London, 1977

Colatius, (1475) 1486

Matthaeus Colatius, *De fine et genere rhetoricae*, Venice, 1486

Collezione de' migliori ornamenti, 1831

Collezione de' migliori ornamenti antichi sparsi nella città di Venezia, Venice, 1831

Comune di Ven., 1905

Comune di Venezia, *Elenco degli edifici monumentali e dei frammenti storici ed artistici della città di Venezia*, Venice, 1905

Connell, 1976

Susan Mary Connell, "The Employment of Sculptors and Stonemasons in Venice in the Fifteenth Century," Ph.D. Dissertation, University of London, Warburg Institute, London, 1976

Contarini, n.d. [ca. 1542]

Pietro Contarini, *Argo vulgar*, Venice, n.d. [ca. 1542]

Corner, *Eccl. Ven.*, 1749

Flaminio Corner, *Ecclesiae Venetae antiquis monumentis*, Venice, 1749, ii, v, x, xiii

Corner, *Supplementa*, 1749   Flaminio Corner, *Supplementa ad Ecclesias Venetas et Torcellanas antiquis documentis*, Venice, 1749

Corner, 1758   Flaminio Corner, *Notizie storiche delle chiese e monasteri di Venezia, e di Torcello*, Padua, 1758

Coronelli, pt. 1, 1696   Vincenzo Coronelli, *Isolario dell'Atlante veneto*, Venice, pt. 1, 1696

Coronelli, n.d. [ca. 1710]   Vincenzo Coronelli, *Singolarità di Venezia*, Venice, n.d. [ca. 1710]

Corp. inscr. lat., v, pt. 1, 1872   *Corpus inscriptionum latinarum*, ed. Theodor Mommsen, Berlin, v, pt. 1, 1872

Corsini, 1912   Andrea Corsini, *Il costume del medico nelle pitture fiorentine del rinascimento*, Florence, 1912

Corwegh, 1909   Robert Corwegh, *Donatellos Sängerkanzel im Dom zu Florenz*, Berlin, 1909

Coryate, 1611   Thomas Coryate, *Coryat's Crudities*, London, 1611

Costantini, n.d. [1916]   Celso Costantini, *Aquileia e Grado*, Milan, n.d. [1916]

Covi, *AB*, 1966   Dario A. Covi, "Four New Documents concerning Andrea del Verrocchio," *Art Bulletin*, xlviii, 1966, pp. 97-103

"Critica," *Il gondoliere*, Oct. 28, 1843   "Critica, Cose patrie" (review of G. Cadorin, *Pareri di xv architetti e notizie storiche intorno al Palazzo Ducale di Venezia*), *Il gondoliere* (Venice), xi, no. 86, Oct. 28, 1843, pp. 341-343

Cuppini in *Verona e il suo territorio*, iii, pt. 2, 1969   Maria Teresa Cuppini, "L'arte gotica a Verona dei secoli xiv-xv," *Verona e il suo territorio*, Verona, iii, pt. 2, 1969, pp. 211-366

Da Mosto, 1939   Andrea Da Mosto, *I dogi di Venezia con particolare riguardo alle loro tombe*, Venice, 1939

Da Mosto, 1966   Andrea Da Mosto, *I dogi di Venezia nella vita pubblica e privata*, Milan, 1966

Dall'Acqua Giusti, 1864   Antonio Dall'Acqua Giusti, *Il Palazzo Ducale di Venezia*, Venice, 1864

Dall'Acqua Giusti, Ven., Accademia. *Atti*, 1873   A. Dall'Acqua Giusti, "Relazione 1.a: L'Accademia," in "L'Accademia e la Galleria di Venezia. Due relazioni storiche per l'esposizione di Vienna del 1873," Venice, Accademia (Reale) di Belle Arti. *Atti*, 1873, pp. 5-34

Degenhart/Schmitt, 1968   Bernhard Degenhart and Annegrit Schmitt, *Corpus der italienischen Zeichnungen 1300-1450*, pt. 1, *Süd- und Mittelitalien*, Berlin, 1968, i

Degli Agostini, i, 1752   Giovanni Degli Agostini, *Notizie istorico-critiche intorno la vita, e le opere degli scrittori viniziani*, Venice, i, 1752; ii, 1754

Deiseroth, 1970   Wolf Deiseroth, *Der Triumphbogen als grosse Form in der Renaissancebaukunst Italiens*, Dissertation, Ludgwig-Maximilians-Universität, Munich, 1970

Dell'Acqua, *Proporzioni*, 1950   Gian Alberto Dell'Acqua, "Problemi di scultura lombarda: Mantegazza e Amadeo," *Proporzioni*, iii, 1950, pp. 123-140

Della Rovere, n.d. [ca. 1880]   Antonio Della Rovere, *Il Palazzo Ducale in Venezia*, Mestre, n.d. [ca. 1880]

Demus, 1960

Otto Demus, *The Church of San Marco in Venice: History, Architecture, Sculpture* (Dumbarton Oaks Studies, 6), Washington, D.C., 1960

Detroit, Inst. of Arts. *Italian Sculptures*, 1938, by Valentiner

Detroit, Institute of Arts. *Italian Gothic and Early Renaissance Sculptures*, Jan. 7–Feb. 20, 1938, catalogue by W. R. Valentiner, n.p. [Detroit], n.d. [1938]

Diario patrio per Venezia, 1806

Diario patrio per Venezia nell'anno MDCCCVI, Venice, 1806

Diedo/Zanotto, 1839

Antonio Diedo and Francesco Zanotto, *I monumenti sepolcrali di Venezia*, Milan, 1839

Dodgson, 1923

Campbell Dodgson, *A Book of Drawings Formerly Ascribed to Mantegna Presented to the British Museum in 1920 by the Earl of Rosebery*, London, 1923

Doglioni, 1662

Nicolò Doglioni, *Le cose notabili, et maravigliose della città di Venetia*, enlarged by Zuanne Zittio, Venice, 1662

Donati, 1961

Ugo Donati, *Artisti ticinesi a Venezia dal xv al xviii secolo*, Lugano, 1961

Dunkelman, *AB*, 1980

Martha Levine Dunkelman, "Donatello's Influence on Mantegna's Early Narrative Scenes," *Art Bulletin*, lxii, 1980, pp. 226-235

Egnazio, 1554

Giovanni Battista Egnazio, *De exemplis illustrium virorum Venetae civitatis, atque aliarum gentium*, Venice, 1554

El Paso, Texas, Museum of Art. *Kress Collection*, by Shapley, 1961

El Paso, Texas, Museum of Art. *The Samuel H. Kress Collection*, catalogue by Fern Rusk Shapley, El Paso, Texas, 1961

Elenco . . . di Vicenza, 1881

Elenco dei principali monumenti ed oggetti d'arte esistenti nella provincia di Vicenza . . . , pitture, sculture, oreficerie, incisioni, Vicenza, 1881

Erizzo, *Gazz. di Ven.*, (Aug. 10, 1843) Aug. 16, 1843

Nicolò Erizzo, "Polemica. La Scala de' Giganti—Il Doge Marin Faliero" (letter of August 10, 1843), *Gazzetta privilegiata di Venezia*, no. 185, Aug. 16, 1843, pp. 739, 740

Erizzo, *Gazz. di Ven.*, (Sept. 20, 1843) Sept. 22, 1843

Nicolò Erizzo, "Polemica. Sulla chiacchierata inserita nel giornale *Il gondoliere* ai N. 70 e 71" (letter of September 20, 1843), *Gazzetta privilegiata di Venezia*, no. 216, Sept. 22, 1843, p. 866

Erizzo, [2]1866

Nicolò Erizzo, *Relazione storico-artistica della Torre dell'Orologio di S. Marco in Venezia*, Venice, [2]1866

Esche, 1957

Sigrid Esche, *Adam und Eva: Sündenfall und Erlösung* (Lukas-Bücherei zur christlichen Ikonographie, 8), Düsseldorf, 1957

F., *Gazz. di Ven.*, Oct. 2, 1834

F. "Appendice di letteratura, teatri e varietà, Belle Arti, De' pubblici capiteli.—Altarini delle vie," *Gazzetta privilegiata di Venezia*, no. 223, Oct. 2, 1834, pp. 1-2

Faber, i, (1483-84) 1843

Felix Faber, *Evagatorium in Terrae Sanctae, Arabiae et Egypti peregrinationem*, ed. C. Hassler, Stuttgart; i, 1843; ii, 1843; iii, 1849

Fabriczy, *Rep. f. Kstw.*, 1894

Cornelius von Fabriczy, "Der Votivaltar Tarchetta im Dom zu Mailand," *Repertorium für Kunstwissenschaft*, xvii, 1894, pp. 249-251

Fainelli, *L'arte*, 1910

Vittorio Fainelli. "Per la storia dell'arte a Verona." *L'arte*, xiii, 1910, pp. 219-222

Fantelli, *Padova e la sua provincia*, Nov.–Dec. 1977 — Pier Luigi Fantelli, "Luigi Lanzi a Tommaso degli Obizzi," *Padova e la sua provincia*, xxiii, nos. 11-12, Nov.–Dec. 1977, pp. 12-16

Fasolo, 1940 — Giulio Fasolo, *Guida del Museo Civico di Vicenza*, Vicenza, 1940

Federici, i, 1818 — Luigi Federici, *Elogi istorici de' più illustri ecclesiastici veronesi*, Verona, i, 1818

Felletti Maj, *Archeologia classica*, 1951 — Bianca Maria Felletti Maj," 'Afrodite Pudica': saggio d'arte ellenistica," *Archeologia classica*, iii, 1951, pp. 33-65

Ferrante, 1852 — Gaetano Ferrante, *Piani e memorie dell'antica Basilica di Aquileja con i capolavori d'arte che in essa si trovano*, Trieste, 1852

Fiocco, T-B, xiv, 1921 — Giuseppe Fiocco, "Giolfino," *Allgemeines Lexikon der bildenden Künstler*, ed. U. Thieme and F. Becker. Leipzig, xiv, 1921, pp. 70-72

Fiocco, *Dedalo*, viii, 1927-28 — Giuseppe Fiocco, "I Lamberti a Venezia—III, Imitatori e seguaci," *Dedalo*, viii, 1927-28, pp. 432-458

Fiocco, *R. di Ven.*, 1930 — Giuseppe Fiocco, "Agostino di Duccio a Venezia," *Rivista di Venezia*, ix, 1930, pp. 261-276

Fiocco, *R. d'arte*, 1930 — Giuseppe Fiocco, "Ancora di Agostino di Duccio a Venezia," *Rivista d'arte*, xii, 1930, pp. 457-484

Fiocco, *Dedalo*, xii, 1932 — Giuseppe Fiocco, "Michele da Firenze," *Dedalo*, xii, 1932, pp. 542-563

Fiocco, *Enc. ital.*, xxix, 1936 — Giuseppe Fiocco, "Rizzo, Antonio," *Enciclopedia italiana di scienze, lettere ed arti*, Milan, xxix, 1936, pp. 502-503

Florence, Pal. Strozzi. *Bronzetti italiani*, by Pope-Hennessy, 1962 — Florence, Palazzo Strozzi. *Bronzetti italiani del rinascimento*, Feb.–Mar. 1962, catalogue by John Pope-Hennessy, Florence, 1962

Fogolari, *Arch. ven.*, 1924 — Gino Fogolari, "La Chiesa di Santa Maria della Carità di Venezia," *Archivio veneto*, series 4, v, 1924, pp. 57-119

Fogolari, n.d. [ca. 1927] — Gino Fogolari, *Il Palazzo Ducale di Venezia*, Milan, n.d. [ca. 1927]

Fogolari, 1931 — Gino Fogolari, *Chiese veneziane. I Frari e i SS. Giovanni e Paolo*, Milan, 1931

Fogolari, *Dedalo*, xii, 1932 — Gino Fogolari, "Disegni per gioco e incunabili pittorici del Giambellino," *Dedalo*, xii, 1932, pp. 360-390

Fogolari, ²1950 — Gino Fogolari, *The Giorgio Franchetti Gallery in the Cà d'Oro in Venice* (Guide Books to the Museums and Monuments of Italy, 56), Rome, ²1950

Folnesics/Planiscig, 1916 — Hans Folnesics and Leo Planiscig, *Bau- und Kunstdenkmale des Küstenlandes*, Vienna, 1916

Fontana, 1836 — Gian Jacopo Fontana, *Illustrazione storico-critica della Chiesa di S. Sofia*, Venice, 1836

Fontana, *Il vaglio*, Oct. 23, 1841 — Gian Jacopo Fontana, "Cose patrie. La piazzetta di San Marco," *Il vaglio*, vi, no. 43, Oct. 23, 1841, p. 343

Fontana, *Il vaglio*, May 21, 1842 — Gian Jacopo Fontana, "Cose patrie. La Porta della Carta e la Scala dei Giganti del Palazzo Ducale," *Il vaglio*, vii, no. 21, May 21, 1842, pp. 162, 164

[Fontana], *Il gondoliere*, Sept. 2, 1843; Sept. 6, 1843; Sept. 30, 1843; Oct. 4, 1843

[Gian Jacopo Fontana], "Cose patrie. Sul vero architetto della Scala dei Giganti del Palazzo Ducale. Diaologo primo," *Il gondoliere*, xi, no. 70, Sept. 2, 1843, pp. 277, 279; [Fontana], "Dialogo secondo," ibid., xi, no. 71, Sept. 6, 1843, pp. 281, 283; [Fontana], "Diaologo terzo," ibid., xi, no. 78, Sept. 30, 1843, pp. 309, 311; [Fontana], "Dialogo terzo (fine)," ibid., xi, no. 79, Oct. 4, 1843, pp. 313, 314

[Fontana], *Il gondoliere*, Nov. 4, 1843

[Gian Jacopo Fontana], "Cose patrie. Conclusione sulle conclusioni dell'Ab. Giuseppe Cadorin intorno la quistione sull'architetto della Scala dei Giganti. Ultimo dialogo," *Il gondoliere*, xi, no. 88, Nov. 4, 1843, pp. 349-350

Fossi Todorow, 1966

Maria Fossi Todorow, *I disegni del Pisanello e della sua cerchia*, Florence, 1966

Francovich, *Boll. d'arte*, 1928-29

Géza de Francovich, "Un gruppo di sculture in legno umbro-marchigiane," *Bolletino d'arte*, series 2, viii, 1928-29, pp. 481-512

Franzoi, Ven., Mus. Civ. ven. *Boll.*, 1965, no. 4

Umberto Franzoi, "La Scala dei Giganti," Venice, Musei Civici veneziani. *Bollettino*, x, no. 4, 1965, pp. 8-34

Franzoi, 1973

Umberto Franzoi, *Il Palazzo Ducale di Venezia*, Venice, 1973

Franzoi/Di Stefano, 1975

Umberto Franzoi and Dina Di Stefano, *Le chiese di Venezia*, Venice, 1975

Franzoi, Ven., Mus. Civ. ven. *Boll.*, 1977

Umberto Franzoi, "Le trasformazioni architettoniche dell'Arco Foscari attraverso i secoli," Venice, Musei Civici veneziani. *Bollettino*, xxii, 1977, pp. 9-26

Fulin/Molmenti, 1881

R. Fulin and P. G. Molmenti, *Guida artistica e storica di Venezia e delle isole circonvicine*, Venice, 1881

Gagé, *Reallexikon für Antike und Christentum*, vii, 1969

Jean Gagé, "Fackel (Kerze)," *Reallexikon für Antike und Christentum*, ed. Theodor Klauser, Stuttgart, vii, 1969, coll. 154-217

Gallo, *R. di Ven.*, 1926

Rodolfo Gallo, "La Chiesa di Sant'Elena," *Rivista di Venezia*, v, 1926, pp. 423-520

Gallo, *R. di Ven.*, 1933

Rodolfo Gallo, "Il Portico della Carta del Palazzo Ducale," *Rivista di Venezia*, xii, 1933, pp. 283-296

Gallo, Ist. ven. SLA. *Atti* (Cl. di scienze morali), 1961-62

Rodolfo Gallo, "L'architettura di transizione dal gotico al rinascimento e Bartolomeo Bon," Venice, istituto veneto di scienze, lettere ed arti. *Atti* (Classe di scienze morali e lettere), cxx, 1961-62, pp. 187-204

Garzoni, [1]1585

Tomaso Garzoni, *La piazza universale di tutte le professioni del mondo, e nobili et ignobili*, Venice, [1]1585

Gauricus, (1504) 1969

Pomponius Gauricus, *De Sculptura (1504)*, ed. and trans. André Chastel and Robert Klein (Centre de recherches d'histoire et de philologie de la ive section de l'Ecole pratique des Hautes Etudes, V, Hautes études médiévales et modernes, 5), Geneva/Paris, 1969

Gautier, 1881

Théophile Gautier, *Voyage en Italie*, Paris, 1881

Ghiberti/Schlosser, 1912

Lorenzo Ghiberti, *Lorenzo Ghibertis Denkwürdigkeiten (I commentarii)*, ed. Julius von Schlosser, Berlin, 1912, 2 vols.

[Giampiccoli], 1779

[Marco Sebastiano Giampiccoli], *Notizie interessanti, che servono a far conoscere in tutti i suoi sestieri l'inclita città di Venezia*, Belluno, 1779

Giovio, 1784

Giovanni Battista Giovio, *Gli uomini della comasca diocesi antichi, e moderni nelle arti, e nelle lettere illustri*, Modena, 1784

Giustiniani, 1560

Pietro Giustiniani, *Rerum Venetarum ab urbe condita historia*, Venice, 1560

Givin, *La fenice*, n.d. [mid-Sept. 1843]

Francesco Givin, "Sul vero architetto della Scalea dei Giganti," *La fenice, enciclopedia contemporanea di scienze, lettere ed arti* (Venice), n.d. [mid-Sept. 1843], pp. 94, 95

Goffen, *AB*, 1979

Rona Goffen, "*Nostra Conversatio in Caelis Est*: Observations on the *Sacra Conversazione* in the Trecento," *Art Bulletin*, lxi, 1979, pp. 198-222

Goloubew, i, 1912; ii, 1908

Victor Goloubew, *Les dessins de Jacopo Bellini au Louvre et au British Museum*, Brussels; i, 1912; ii, 1908

Gottschewski, *ZbK*, 1908

Adolf Gottschewski, "Eine Holzstatue des Antonio Rizzo," *Zeitschrift für bildende Kunst*, xix, 1908, pp. 131-132

Gradenigo, (1748-74) 1942

Pietro Gradenigo, *Notizie d'arte tratte dai notatori e dagli annali del N. H. Pietro Gradenigo*, ed. Lina Livan (Venice. Reale deputazione veneta di storia patria. *Miscellanea di studi e memorie*, 5), Venice, 1942

Grevembroch, *Gli abiti*
Grevembroch, *Mon. Ven.*
Grevembroch, *Varie venete curiosità*

See under "Manuscripts," Venice, Museo Correr, MS Gradenigo 49, 228, 219

Grigioni, *L'arte*, 1910

Carlo Grigioni, "Un'opera ignota di Lorenzo Bregno," *L'arte*, xiii, 1910, pp. 42-48

Guerzoni, Ven., Accademia. *Atti*, 1878

Giuseppe Guerzoni, "San Marco nell'arte e nella storia," Venice, Accademia (Reale) di Belle Arti. *Atti*, 1878, pp. 5-42

Guggenheim, 1898

Michelangelo Guggenheim, *Due capolavori di Antonio Rizzo nel Palazzo Ducale di Venezia*, Venice, 1898

Guisconi [Sans.], 1556

Anselmo Giusconi [Francesco Sansovino], *Tutte le cose notabili e belle che sono in Venetia*, Venice, 1556

Guyer, 1928

S. Guyer, *Venice, Buildings and Sculptures*, trans. L. B. Ellis (Mirabilia Mundi, 1), Augsburg, 1928

Harff, (1496-99) 1860

Arnold von Harff, *Die Pilgerfahrt des Ritters Arnold von Harff von Cöln durch Italien, Syrien, Aegypten, Arabien, Aethiopien, Nubien, Palästina, die Türkei, Frankreich und Spanien, wie er sie in den Jahren 1496 bis 1499 vollendet*, ed. E. von Groote, Cologne, 1860

Harff, (1496-99) 1946

Arnold von Harff, *The Pilgrimage of Arnold von Harff Knight*, ed. and trans. Malcolm Letts (The Hakluyt Society. *Works*, series 2, 94), London, 1946

Henninges, 1598

Hieronymus Henninges, *Theatrum genealogicum, ostentans omnes omnium aetatum familias*, Magdeburg, 1598, "Appendix primi regni quartae monarchias Italiae, Venetiarum ducum catalogus et familiae generosae," pp. 1133-1168

Hermann in Egger/Hermann, *ZbK*, 1906

Hermann Julius Hermann in Otto Egger and Hermann, "Aus den Kunstsammlungen des Hauses Este in Wien," *Zeitschrift für bildende Kunst*, xvii, 1906, pp. 84-105

Heynold-v. Graefe, *Weltkunst*, July 15, 1971

Blida Heynold-v. Graefe, "Kunstnotizen aus Italien. Kunst in Venedig," *Weltkunst*, xli, no. 14, July 15, 1971, pp. 892-893

Hill, 1930

George Francis Hill, *A Corpus of Italian Medals of the Renaissance before Cellini*, London, 1930, 2 vols.

Hind, pt. 1, i, 1938

Arthur M. Hind, *Early Italian Engraving: A Critical Catalogue with Complete Reproduction of All the Prints Described*, London, pt. 1, i, 1938

Howard, 1980

Deborah Howard, *The Architectural History of Venice*, London, 1980

Hubala in Egg et al., ¹1965

Erich Hubala in Erich Egg, Hubala, Peter Tigler, Wladimir Timofiewitsch, Manfred Wundram, *Oberitalien Ost* (Reclams Kunstführer, ed. Wundram, *Italien*, ii), Stuttgart, ¹1965

Humfrey, 1977

Peter Humfrey, "The Altarpieces of Cima da Conegliano," Ph.D. Dissertation, University of London, London, 1977

Humfrey, *AB*, 1980

Peter Humfrey, "Cima da Conegliano, Sebastiano Mariani, and Alvise Vivarini at the East End of S. Giovanni in Bragora in Venice," *Art Bulletin*, lxii, 1980, pp. 350-363

Jacob, 1954

Henriette s'Jacob, *Idealism and Realism; a Study of Sepulchral Symbolism*, Leiden, 1954

Janson in *Propyläen Kstge.*, vii, 1972

Horst W. Janson, "Plastik, Zentral-, Süd-, und Nordeuropa," *Propyläen Kunstgeschichte*, vii, *Spätmittelalter und beginnende Neuzeit*, ed. Jan Białostocki, Berlin, 1972, pp. 261-267, pp. 270-311

Joppi, *Archeografo triestino*, 1895

Vincenzo Joppi, "La Basilica di Aquileia, note storico-artistiche con documenti," *Archeografo triestino*, n.s., xx, 1895, pp. 209-276

Keydel, 1969

Julia Helen Keydel, "A Group of Altarpieces by Giovanni Bellini Considered in Relation to the Context for which They Were Made," Ph.D. Dissertation, Harvard University, Cambridge, Mass., 1969

Kirchner, 1903

Josef Kirchner, *Die Darstellung des ersten Menschenpaares in der bildenden Kunst von der ältesten Zeit bis auf unsere Tage*, Stuttgart, 1903

[Labus] in *Chiese principali*, 1824

[Giovanni Labus], "Descrizione della I. R. Basilica di S. Marco," in *Chiese principali d'Europa dedicate a Sua Santità Leone XII. Pon. Mas.*, Milan, 1824–

Lazzarini, *Bull. di arti*, Sept. 1894

Vittorio Lazzarini, "Per le 'Pietre' di Venezia," *Bullettino di arti e curiosità veneziane*, iv, no. 1, Sept. 1894, pp. 1-3

Lengherand, (1485-86) 1861

Georges Lengherand, *Voyage de Georges Lengherand, Mayeur de Mons en Haynaut, à Venise, Rome, Jérusalem, Mont Sinai & Le Kayre, 1485-86*, ed. Marquis de Godefroy Ménilglaise, Mons, 1861

Levi, ³1895

Cesare Augusto Levi, *Notizie storiche di alcune antiche scuole d'arti e mestieri scomparse o esistenti ancora in Venezia*, Venice, ³1895

Levi, 1900

Cesare Augusto Levi, *Le collezioni veneziane d'arte e d'antichità dal secolo xiv. ai nostri giorni*, Venice, 1900, i

Ljubljana, Narodna galerija. *Gotska plastika*, by Cevc, 1973 — Ljubljana, Narodna galerija. *Gotska plastika na Slovenskem*, Oct. 9–Dec. 30, 1973, catalogue by Emilijan Cevc, Ljubljana, 1973

London, BM, Catalogue by Popham/Pouncey, 1950 — London, British Museum. *Italian Drawings in the Department of Prints and Drawings in the British Museum. The Fourteenth and Fifteenth Centuries*, catalogue by A. E. Popham and Philip Pouncey, London, 1950

Lorenzetti, [1]1926, [3]1963 — Giulio Lorenzetti, *Venezia e il suo estuario*, Venice et al., [1]1926, [3]1963

Lorenzetti, *Enc. Ital.*, x, 1931 — G. Lorenzetti, "Coducci, Mauro," *Enciclopedia italiana di scienze, lettere ed arti*, Milan, x, 1931, pp. 693-694

Lorenzi, 1868 — Giambattista Lorenzi, *Monumenti per servire alla storia del Palazzo Ducale di Venezia*, Venice, 1868, i

Ludwig, 1911 — Gustav Ludwig, *Archivalische Beiträge zur Geschichte der venezianischen Kunst aus dem Nachlass Gustav Ludwigs*, ed. Wilhelm Bode, Georg Gronau, Detlev v. Hadeln (Florence, Kunsthistorisches Institut. *Italienische Forschungen*, 4), Berlin, 1911

R. Ludwig, 1939 — Rudolf Martin Ludwig, *Die Treppe in der Baukunst der Renaissance*, Kassel, 1939

Lübke, 1872, ii — Wilhelm Lübke, *History of Sculpture, from the Earliest Ages to the Present Time*, trans. F. E. Bunnètt, London, 1872, ii

Luzio/Renier — Alessandro Luzio and Rodolfo Renier, *Delle relazioni di Isabella d'Este Gonzaga con Ludovico e Beatrice Sforza*, Milan, 1890

MacCurdy, ed., 1955 — *The Notebooks of Leonardo da Vinci*, ed. and trans. Edward MacCurdy, New York, 1955

Maffei, iii, 1732 — Scipione Maffei, *Verona illustrata*, Verona, iii, 1732

Magenta, 1897 — Carlo Magenta, *La Certosa di Pavia*, Milan, 1897

Magrini, 1855 — Antonio Magrini, *Il Museo Civico di Vicenza, solennemente inaugurato il 18 agosto 1855*, Vicenza, 1855

Maier, i, [1]1787; pt. 1, [2]1795 — Johann Christoph Maier, *Beschreibung von Venedig*, Frankfurt/Leipzig; i, [1]1787; ii, [1]1789; iii, n.d. Ibid., Leipzig; pt. 1, [2]1795; pt. 2, [2]1795; pt. 3, [2]1796; pt. 4, [2]1796

Maimeri, *Vita veronese*, 1960, nos. 1-2 — Mario Maimeri, "Artisti veronesi in Roma nei sec. xv-xvi-xvii," *Vita veronese*, 1960, nos. 1-2, pp. 16-25

Malaguzzi Valeri, 1904 — Francesco Malaguzzi Valeri, *Gio. Antonio Amadeo, scultore e architetto lombardo*, Bergamo, 1904

Malipiero, *Arch. stor. ital.*, 1844, pt. 2 — Domenico Malipiero, "Annali venete dall'anno 1457 al 1500," ed. Francesco Longo and Agostino Sagredo, *Archivio storico italiano*; vii, pt. i, 1843; vii, pt. 2, 1844

Malsburg, 1976 — Raban von der Malsburg, "Die Architektur der Scuola Grande di San Rocco in Venedig," Dissertation, Ruprecht-Karl-Universität, Heidelberg, 1976

Mandelli, *Critica d'arte*, 1972, no. 124 — Claudia Mandelli, "I primordi di Benedetto Briosco, i," *Critica d'arte*, xix, no. 124, 1972, pp. 41-56

Marangoni, n.d. [1910] — L. Marangoni, *La Basilica di S. Marco in Venezia*, Milan, n.d. [1910]

Marchini in Atti, *Jacopo della Quercia*, 1977 — Giuseppe Marchini, "Su Michele da Firenze," Siena, Facoltà di lettere e filosofia. Convegno di studi, 1975, Atti, *Jacopo della Quercia fra gotico e rinascimento*, ed. Giulietta Chelazzi Dini, Florence, 1977, pp. 201-202

Mariacher, Ist. ven. SLA. *Atti* (Cl. di scienze morali), 1937-38, pt. 2 — Giovanni Mariacher, "Premesse storiche alla venuta dei Lombardi a Venezia nel '400," Venice, Istituto veneto di scienze, lettere ed arti. *Atti* (Classe di scienze morali e lettere), xcvii, pt. 2, 1937-38, pp. 577-586

Mariacher, *Aten. ven.*, 1940 — Giovanni Mariacher, "Di alcune sculture della 'Madonna dell'Orto'," *Ateneo veneto*, cxxxi, 1940, pp. 155-159

Mariacher, *Le arti*, 1940-41 — Giovanni Mariacher, "Note su Antonio da Righeggio e Antonio Rizzo," *Le arti*, iii, 1940-41, pp. 193-198

Mariacher, *Aten. ven.*, 1942 — Giovanni Mariacher, "Scultori veneziani in Lombardia nei secoli xiv-xvi," *Ateneo veneto*, cxxxiii, 1942, pp. 237-243

Mariacher, *Arte ven.*, 1948 — Giovanni Mariacher, "Profilo di Antonio Rizzo," *Arte veneta*, ii, 1948, pp. 67-84

Mariacher, *Arte ven.*, 1950 — Giovanni Mariacher, "Problemi di scultura veneziana (II)," *Arte veneta*, iv, 1950, pp. 105-109

Mariacher, *Pal. Duc.*, 1950 — Giovanni Mariacher, *Il Palazzo Ducale di Venezia*, Florence, 1950

Mariacher, *BM*, 1950 — Giovanni Mariacher, "New Light on Antonio Bregno," *Burlington Magazine*, xcii, 1950, pp. 123-128

Mariacher/Pignatti, 1950 — Giovanni Mariacher and Terisio Pignatti, *La Basilica di San Marco a Venezia*, Florence, 1950

Mariacher, *R. d'arte*, 1951-52 — Giovanni Mariacher, "Due inedite sculture di Antonio Rizzo," *Rivista d'arte*, xxvii, 1951-52, pp. 185-189

Mariacher, *Arte ven.*, 1955 — Giovanni Mariacher, "Pietro Lombardo a Venezia," *Arte veneta*, ix, 1955, pp. 36-52

Mariacher in *Arte e artisti*, 1959, i — Giovanni Mariacher, "Contributi sull'attività di scultori caronesi e comaschi a Venezia nei sec. xv-xvi," Società archeologica comense. Convegno sugli artisti del Laria e del Ceresio, 2nd, Varenna, 1957. *Arte e artisti dei laghi lombardi*, ed. Edoardo Arslan, Como, 1959, i, pp. 191-206

Mariacher, 1966 — Giovanni Mariacher, *Antonio Rizzo* (I maestri della scultura, 35), Milan, 1966

Mariacher, *Le muse*, x, 1968 — Giovanni Mariacher, "Antonio Rizzo," *Le muse, enciclopedia di tutte le arti*, Novara, x, 1968, pp. 145-146

Mariacher, 1971 — Giovanni Mariacher, *Bronzetti veneti del rinascimento*, Vicenza, 1971

Mariacher, *Apollo*, Sept. 1975 — Giovanni Mariacher, "Unfamiliar Masterpieces of North Italian Sculpture," *Apollo*, cii, Sept. 1975, pp. 174-189

Mariacher, *Aten. ven.*, 1976 — Giovanni Mariacher, "La mostra della scultura gotica in Slovenia, a Lubiana," *Ateneo veneto*, n.s. xiv, 1976, pp. 71-73

Marini, 1905 — Ernesto Marini, *Venezia antica e moderna*, Venice, 1905

Marquand, *Art in America*, 1917-18 — Allan Marquand, "Two Works of Venetian Sculpture," *Art in America*, vi, 1917-18, pp. 53-60

Marquet de Vasselot, *Les arts,* July 1903 — J.-J. Marquet de Vasselot, "La collection de Madame la Marquise Arconati-Visconti," *Les arts,* ii, no. 19, July 1903, pp. 17-32

Martinelli, ¹1684 — Domenico Martinelli, *Il ritratto di Venezia,* Venice, ¹1684

Mattingly, iii, 1930 — Harold Mattingly, *The Roman Imperial Coinage,* iii, *Antoninus Pius to Commodus,* London, 1930

Matz, iv, pt. 1, 1968; iv, pt. 2, 1968; iv, pt. 3, 1969 — Friedrich Matz, ed., *Die antiken Sarkophagreliefs,* iv, Matz, *Die dionysischen Sarkophage,* Berlin; pt. 1, 1968; pt. 2, 1968; pt. 3, 1969

Mazzi, *Madonna Verona,* 1913 — Attilio Mazzi, "Gli estimi e le anagrafi inedite dei lapicidi veronesi del secolo xv," *Madonna Verona. Bollettino del Museo Civico di Verona,* vi, 1912, pp. 221-228; vii, 1913, pp. 25-38

McAndrew, *AB,* 1969 — John McAndrew, "Sant'Andrea della Certosa," *Art Bulletin,* li, 1969, pp. 15-28

McAndrew, 1980 — John McAndrew, *Venetian Architecture of the Early Renaissance,* Cambridge, Mass./London, 1980

Megiser, 1610 — Hieronymus Megiser, *Paradisus deliciarum; das ist, eigentliche und warhafftige Beschreibung der wunderbaren, mechtigen und in aller Welt hochberühmten Stadt Venedig,* Leipzig, 1610

Meller in *Ren. and Man.,* 1963 — Peter Meller, "Physiognomical Theory in Renaissance Heroic Portraits," *The Renaissance and Mannerism. Studies in Western Art.* Acts of the Twentieth International Congress of the History of Art, Princeton, 1963, ii, pp. 53-69

Mercati, 1939, ii — G. Mercati, *Ultimi contributi alla storia degli umanisti,* Vatican City, 1939, ii

Merzario, 1893 — Giuseppe Merzario, *I maestri comacini,* Milan, 1893, 2 vols.

Meschinello, ii, 1753; iii, 1754 — Giovanni Meschinello, *La Chiesa ducale di S. Marco,* Venice; i, 1753; ii, 1753; iii, pt. 1, 1754; iii, pt. 2, 1754

Meyer, *JpK,* 1889 — Alfred Gotthold Meyer, "Das Venezianische Grabdenkmal der Frührenaissance," *Jahrbuch der preussischen Kunstsammlungen,* x, 1889, pp. 79-102, pp. 187-208

Meyer, ii, 1900 — Alfred Gotthold Meyer, *Oberitalienische Frührenaissance, Bauten und Bildwerke der Lombardei,* Berlin, i, 1897; ii, 1900

Michel, iv, pt. 1, 1909 — André Michel, *Histoire de l'art depuis les premiers temps chrétiens jusqu'à nos jours,* Paris, iv, pt. 1, 1909

Michel in Paris, Louvre. Catalogue by Leprieur *et al.,* 1917 — André Michel in Paris, Louvre. *Catalogue de la collection Arconati Visconti,* by Paul Leprieur, Michel, Gaston Migeon, J.-J. Marquet de Vasselot, Paris, 1917

[Michiel]/Morelli, 1800 — [Marcantonio Michiel], *Notizia d'opere di disegno,* ed. Jacopo Morelli, Bassano, 1800

Michiel/Frimmel, 1896 — Marcantonio Michiel, *Der Anonimo Morelliano (Marcanton Michiel's Notizia d'opere del disegno),* ed. and trans. Theodor Frimmel, Vienna, 1896

Middeldorf, *Pantheon,* July-Dec. 1938 — Ulrich Middeldorf, "Die Ausstellung italienischer Renaissanceskulptur in Detroit," *Pantheon,* xxii, July-Dec. 1938, pp. 315-318

Middeldorf, 1976   Ulrich Middeldorf, *Sculptures from the Samuel H. Kress Collection. European Schools xiv-xix Century*, London, 1976

Middeldorf, *Apollo*, Apr. 1978   Ulrich Middeldorf, "On the Dilettante Sculptor," *Apollo*, cvii, Apr. 1978, pp. 310-322

Migeon, *Les arts*, March 1905   Gaston Migeon, "La collection Chabrière-Arlès," *Les arts*, no. 39, March 1905, pp. 8-18

Milan, Castello Sforzesco. *Guida sommaria*, 1900   Milan, Castello Sforzesco. *Guida sommaria del museo archeologico ed artistico nel Castello Sforzesco di Milano*, Milan, 1900

Modigliani, *L'arte*, 1900   Ettore Modigliani, Review of D. Sant'Ambrogio, "Nel Museo di Porta Giovia: il Maestro di San Trovaso," *L'arte*, iii, 1900, p. 396

Molmenti/Mantovani, ²1925   Pompeo Molmenti and D. Mantovani, *Le isole della laguna veneta*, Bergamo, ²1925

Molmenti, i, ⁷1927; ii, ⁷1928   Pompeo G. Molmenti, *La storia di Venezia nella vita privata dalle origini alla caduta della repubblica*, Bergamo; i, ⁷1927; ii, ⁷1928

[Mongeri], ¹1881   [Mongeri], *Notizie sul Museo patrio archeologico in Milano*, Milan, ¹1881

Morassi in *La Basilica di Aquileia*, 1933   Antonio Morassi, "La pittura e la scultura nella basilica," in *La Basilica di Aquileia*, Bologna, 1933, pp. 301-344

Moreni, i, 1816   Domenico Moreni, *Continuazione delle memorie istoriche dell'ambrosiana imperial Basilica di S. Lorenzo di Firenze*, Florence, i, 1816

Moretti, *Paragone*, 1958, no. 99   Lino Moretti, "Di Leonardo Bellini, pittore e miniatore," *Paragone*, Mar. 1958, no. 99, pp. 58-66

Morini, *Rass. d'arte*, 1911   Adolfo Morini, "Alcuni lavori della bottega di Antonio Rizzo a Cascia," *Rassegna d'arte*, xi, 1911, pp. 70-72

[Moro], 1835   [Gaspare Moro], *Parole agli artisti*, Venice, 1835

Moryson, i, (1594) 1907   Fynes Moryson, *An Itinerary containing his Ten Yeeres Travell through the Twelve Dominions of Germany, Bohmerland, Sweitzerland, Netherland, Denmarke, Poland, Italy, Turky, France, England, Scotland & Ireland*, Glasgow, i, 1907

Moschetti, Padua, Mus. Civ. *Boll.*, 1914   Andrea Moschetti, "Un quadriennio di Pietro Lombardo a Padova (1464-1467) con una appendice sulla data di nascita e di morte di Bartolommeo Bellano," Padua, Museo Civico. *Bollettino*; xvi, 1913, pp. 1-99; xvii, 1914, pp. 1-43

Moschetti, Ist. ven. SLA. *Atti*, 1927-28, pt. 2   Andrea Moschetti, "Pietro e altri lapicidi lombardi a Belluno," Venice, Istituto veneto di scienze, lettere ed arti. *Atti*, lxxxvii, pt. 2, 1927-28, pp. 1481-1515

Moschetti, T-B, xxiii, 1929   Andrea Moschetti, "Lombardo, Pietro," *Allgemeines Lexikon der bildenden Künstler*, ed. U. Thieme and F. Becker, Leipzig, xxiii, 1929, pp. 343-344

Moschini, 1815   Giannantonio Moschini, *Guida per la città di Venezia*, Venice, 1815, 2 vols.

Moschini, 1819   Giannantonio Moschini, *Itinéraire de la ville de Venise et des îles circonvoisines*, Venice, 1819

[Moschini], *Ragguaglio*, 1819   [Giannantonio Moschini], *Ragguaglio delle cose notabili nella Chiesa e nel Seminario Patriarcale di Santa Maria della Salute in Venezia*, Venice, 1819

Moschini, ii, 1826   Giannantonio Moschini, *Le belle arti in Venezia*, ii, *Istoria della scultura in Venezia*, Venice, 1826

Moschini, 1842   Giannantonio Moschini, *La Chiesa e il Seminario di Santa Maria della Salute in Venezia*, Venice, 1842

Mothes, i, 1859; ii, 1860   Oscar Mothes, *Geschichte der Baukunst und Bildhauerei Venedigs*, Leipzig; i, 1859; ii, 1860

Munman, 1968   Robert Munman, "Venetian Renaissance Tomb Monuments," Ph.D. Dissertation, Harvard University, Cambridge, Mass., 1968

Munman, *BM*, 1971   Robert Munman, "The Monument to Vittore Cappello of Antonio Rizzo," *Burlington Magazine,* cxiii, 1971, pp. 138-145

Munman, *AB*, 1973   Robert Munman, "Antonio Rizzo's Sarcophagus for Nicolò Tron: A Closer Look," *Art Bulletin*, lv, 1973, pp. 77-85

Munman, *Arte ven.*, 1976   Robert Munman, "Giovanni Buora: the 'Missing' Sculpture," *Arte veneta*, xxx, 1976, pp. 41-61

Munman, *Arte lom.*, 1977   Robert Munman, "The Last Work of Antonio Rizzo," *Arte lombarda*, xvii, 1977, pp. 89-98

Munman, *AB*, 1979   Robert Munman, review of Debra Pincus, *The Arco Foscari: The Building of a Triumphal Gateway in Fifteenth Century Venice*, in *Art Bulletin*, lxi, 1979, pp. 637-642

Munman, *Arte ven.*, 1979   Robert Munman, "The Sculpture of Giovanni Buora: A Supplement," *Arte veneta*, xxxiii, 1979, pp. 19-28

Muñoz in Pollak/Muñoz, ii, 1911   Antonio Muñoz in Ludwig Pollak and Muñoz, *Pièces de choix de la collection du Comte Grégoire Stroganoff*, ii, *Moyen-âge, renaissance, époque moderne*, Rome, 1911

Muraro, 1953   Michelangelo Muraro, *Nuova guida di Venezia e delle sue isole*, Florence, 1953

Muraro, *Scuola e vita*, Sept. 15, 1953   Michelangelo Muraro, "La mostra di Lorenzo Lotto," *Scuola e vita*, i, no. 12, Sept. 15, 1953, pp. 4-5

Muraro in *Essays . . . Panofsky*, 1960, i   Michelangelo Muraro, "La Scala senza Giganti," *De artibus opuscula XL. Essays in Honor of Erwin Panofsky*, ed. Millard Meiss, Zurich, 1960, i, pp. 350-370

Musatti, *Arch. ven.*, 1912   Cesare Musatti, "Antonio Bregno e Antonio Rizzo in un sonetto di Emanuele Cicogna," *Archivio veneto*, series 3, xxiii, 1912, pp. 203-204

Musolino, 1955   Giovanni Musolino, *La Basilica di San Marco in Venezia*, Venice, 1955

Musolino in Tramontin *et al.*, 1965   G. Musolino in S. Tramontin, A. Niero, Musolino, C. Candiani, *Culto dei santi a Venezia*, Venice, 1965

Mutinelli, 1842   Fabio Mutinelli, *Guida del forestiero per Venezia antica*, Venice, 1842

N.Y., A. S. Drey Galleries. *Sculpture*, 1935   New York, A. S. Drey Galleries. *Sculpture of the Italian Renaissance*, March 1935, catalogue, n.p., n.d.

N.Y., Met. Mus. of Art. Catalogue by Breck, 1913
New York, Metropolitan Museum of Art. *Catalogue of Romanesque, Gothic and Renaissance Sculpture*, by Joseph Breck, New York, 1913

Niemann in Lanckoroński, 1906
George Niemann in Karl Lanckoroński, *Der Dom von Aquileia, sein Bau und seine Geschichte*, with Niemann and Heinrich Swoboda, Vienna, 1906

Niero, 1971
Antonio Niero, *Chiesa di S. Maria della Salute*, Venice, 1971

Niero in Niero *et al.*, 1972
Antonio Niero in Niero, G. Musolino, S. Tramontin, *Santità a Venezia*, Venice, 1972

Niero, 1972
Antonio Niero, *La Chiesa di Santa Sofia in Venezia, storia ed arte*, Venice, 1972

Nuova cronaca veneta compilata del 1795, 1813
Nuova cronaca veneta compilata del 1795, Venice, 1813

Ongania, ed., 1889
F. Ongania, ed., *Raccolta delle vere da pozzo (marmi puteali) in Venezia*, Venice, 1889, 2 vols.

Ongaro, Vicenza, Mus. Civ. *Boll.*, Jan.–Mar. 1910
Luigi Ongaro, "Il riordinamento del Museo Civico," Vicenza, Museo Civico. *Bollettino*, Jan.–Mar. 1910, no. 1, pp. 7-10

M. Ongaro, n.d. [ca. 1913]
Max Ongaro, *Venezia, il Palazzo Ducale* (Il piccolo cicerone moderno, 6), Milan, n.d. [ca. 1913]

Onofri, [1]1663, [2]1682
Fedele Onofri, *Cronologia veneta*, Venice, [1]1663, [2]1682

Paccagnini, *Boll. d'arte*, 1961
Giovanni Paccagnini, "Il Mantegna e la plastica dell'Italia settentrionale," *Bollettino d'arte*, xlvi, 1961, pp. 65-100

Pacifico, 1697
Pietro Antonio Pacifico, *Cronica veneta, overo succinto racconto di tutte le cose più cospicue, & antiche della città di Venetia*, Venice, 1697

Pacioli, 1494
Luca Pacioli, *Summa de arithmetica, geometria, proportioni et proportionalita*, Venice, 1494

Pal. Duc., 1912
Il Palazzo Ducale, guida illustrata, Venice, 1912

E. Paoletti, i, 1837; ii, 1839; iii, 1840
Ermolao Paoletti, *Il fiore di Venezia*, Venice; i, 1837; ii, 1839; iii, 1840; iv, 1840

Paoletti, 1893
Pietro Paoletti, *L'architettura e la scultura del rinascimento in Venezia*, Venice, 1893, 3 vols.

Paoletti, fasc. 1, 1894
Pietro Paoletti, *Raccolta di documenti inediti per servire alla storia della pittura veneziana nei secoli xv e xvi.* Padua, fasc. 1, 1894

Paoletti, *L'arte*, 1902
Pietro Paoletti, "Notizie di Venezia," *L'arte*, v, 1902, pp. 125-126

Paoletti, "Bono," T-B, iv, 1910
Pietro Paoletti, "Bono, Bartolomeo di Giovanni," *Allgemeines Lexikon der bildenden Künstler*, ed. U. Thieme and F. Becker, Leipzig, iv, 1910, pp. 315-316

Paoletti, "Bregno, Antonio," T-B, iv, 1910
Pietro Paoletti, "Bregno, Antonio di Pietro," *Allgemeines Lexikon der bildenden Künstler*, ed. U. Thieme and F. Becker, Leipzig, iv, 1910, pp. 568-569

Paoletti, 1929
Pietro Paoletti, *La Scuola Grande di San Marco*, Venice, 1929

Papadopoli, ii, 1907
Nicolò Papadopoli, *Le monete di Venezia*, Venice; i, 1893; ii, 1907; iii, 1919

Paris, Jacquemart-André. Catalogue by Gavoty, 1975

Paris, Institut de France, Musée Jacquemart-André. *Sculpture italienne*, catalogue by Françoise de la Moureyre-Gavoty (Inventaire des collections publiques françaises, 19), Paris, 1975

Paris, Louvre. Catalogue, i, 1922

Paris, Musée National du Louvre. *Catalogue des sculptures du moyen âge, de la renaissance et des temps modernes*, i, *Moyen âge et renaissance*, Paris, 1922

Paris, Petit Palais. *Exposition de l'art italien*, cat., 1935

Paris, Petit Palais. *Exposition de l'art italien de Cimabue à Tiepolo*, May–July 1935, catalogue, Argenteuil, 1935

Pasini, 1888

Antonio Pasini, *Guide de la Basilique St. Marc à Venise*, Schio, 1888

Passavant, 1959

Günter Passavant, *Andrea del Verrocchio als Maler*, Düsseldorf, 1959

Paul, 1963

Jürgen Paul, *Die mittelalterlichen Kommunalpaläste in Italien*, Dissertation, Albert-Ludwigs-Universität, Freiburg im Breisgau, 1963

Pauli, ²1900

Gustav Pauli, *Venedig*, Leipzig/Berlin, ²1900

Pellegrini, *Studi storici veronesi*, 1949-50

Ottavio Pellegrini, "Su di un particolare delle terrecotte di S. Anastasia in Verona," *Studi storici veronesi*, ii, 1949-50, pp. 209-214

Perkins, 1883

Charles C. Perkins, *Historical Handbook of Italian Sculpture*, New York, 1883

Perosa in Ongania, ed., *Basilica*, vi, 1888, pt. 2 [1890]

Leonardo Perosa, "Modificazioni, abbellimenti e restauri fatti alla Basilica di San Marco dal secolo xii al xviii. Supplemento cronologico," in Ferdinando Ongania, ed., *La Basilica di San Marco in Venezia illustrata nei riguardi dell'arte e della storia da scrittori veneziani*, Venice, vi, 1888, pt. 2, [1890], pp. 201-216

Phillips, N.Y., Met. Mus. of Art. *Bull.*, Feb. 1957

John Goldsmith Phillips, "Recent Accessions of European Sculpture," New York, Metropolitan Museum of Art. *Bulletin*, xv, no. 6, February 1957, pp. 150-154

Piamonte, [1966]

Giannina Piamonte, *Venezia vista dall'acqua. Guida dei rii di Venezia e delle isole*, Venice, n.d. [1966]

Piazza, 1835

Giuseppe Piazza, *La R. Basilica di S. Marco esposta in sei tavole*, Venice, 1835

Pignatti, 1956

Terisio Pignatti, *Piazza San Marco*, Novara, 1956

Pignatti, 1964

Terisio Pignatti, *Palazzo Ducale, Venezia*, Novara, 1964

Pincus, *AB*, 1969

Debra Pincus, "A Hand by Antonio Rizzo and the Double Caritas Scheme of the Tron Tomb," *Art Bulletin*, li, 1969, pp. 247-256

Pincus, 1974

Debra Pincus, *The Arco Foscari: The Building of a Triumphal Gateway in Fifteenth-Century Venice*, Garland Series of Outstanding Dissertations in the Fine Arts, New York, 1976

Pincus, *Arte ven.*, 1979

Debra Pincus, "Tullio Lombardo as a Restorer of Antiquities: An Aspect of Fifteenth Century Venetian Antiquarianism," *Arte veneta*, xxxiii, 1979, pp. 29-42

Pincus in *Studies . . . Janson*, 1981

Debra Pincus, "The Tomb of Doge Nicolò Tron and Venetian Renaissance Ruler Imagery," in *Art the Ape of Nature. Studies in*

	Honor of H. W. Janson, ed. M. Barash, L. F. Sandler, P. Egan, New York, 1981, pp. 127-150
Piva, 1930	Vittorio Piva, *Il Tempio della Salute eretto per voto de la Repubblica veneta*, Venice, 1930
Planiscig, *Forum Iulii*, 1910	Leo Planiscig, "Il rinascimento nella Basilica d'Aquileia," *Forum Iulii* (Gorizia), i, 1910, pp. 53-56
Planiscig, *Emporium*, 1911	Leo Planiscig, "La Basilica d'Aquileja," *Emporium*, xxxiii, 1911, pp. 274-293
Planiscig, *Kunst und Kunst-handwerk*, 1916	Leo Planiscig, "Uber eine Figur Tullio Lombardis und andere Holzskulpturen des frühen Venezianischen Cinquecento," *Kunst und Kunsthandwerk*, xix, 1916, pp. 372-386
Planiscig, 1921	Leo Planiscig, *Venezianische Bildhauer der Renaissance*, Vienna, 1921
Planiscig, *ZbK*, 1921	Leo Planiscig, "Ein Relief des Agostino di Duccio in der Markuskirche zu Venedig," *Zeitschrift für bildende Kunst*, xxxii, 1921, pp. 143-146
Planiscig, *VJ*, 1926	Leo Planiscig, "Das Grabdenkmal des Orsato Giustiniani. Ein Beitrag zur Geschichte der Venezianischen Skulptur im Quattrocento," *Jahrbuch der kunsthistorischen Sammlungen in Wien*, n.s., i, 1926, pp. 93-102
Planiscig, 1927	Leo Planiscig, *Andrea Riccio*, Vienna, 1927
Planiscig, *Pantheon*, Jan.–June 1929	Leo Planiscig, "Italienische Renaissanceplastiken aus der Sammlung E. Foulc, Paris," *Pantheon*, iii, Jan.–June 1929, pp. 215-220
Planiscig, *Dedalo*, x, 1929-30	Leo Planiscig, "Pietro Lombardi ed alcuni bassirilievi veneziani del '400," *Dedalo*, x, 1929-30, pp. 460-481
Planiscig, *Dedalo*, xi, 1930-31	Leo Planiscig, "Lettera al Professor Adolfo Venturi," *Dedalo*, xi, 1930-31, pp. 24-34
Planiscig, *T-B*, xxvii, 1933	Leo Planiscig, "Pyrgoteles," *Allgemeines Lexikon der bildenden Künstler*, ed. U. Thieme and F. Becker, Leipzig, xxvii, 1933, pp. 480-481
Planiscig, *T-B*, xxviii, 1934	Leo Planiscig, "Rizzo, Antonio," *Allgemeines Lexikon der bildenden Künstler*, ed. U. Thieme and F. Becker, Leipzig, xxviii, 1934, pp. 408-410
Planiscig, *VJ*, 1937	Leo Planiscig, "Pietro, Tullio und Antonio Lombardo. (Neue Beiträge zu ihrem Werk)," *Jahrbuch der kunsthistorischen Sammlungen in Wien*, n.s., xi, 1937, pp. 87-115
Pohlandt, *BJ*, 1971	Wiebke Pohlandt, "Antonio Rizzo," *Jahrbuch der Berliner Museen*, n.s., xiii, 1971, pp. 162-207
Pope-Hennessy, [1]1958	John Pope-Hennessy, *Italian Renaissance Sculpture*, London, [1]1958
Pope-Hennessy, 1964	John Pope-Hennessy, *Catalogue of Italian Sculpture in the Victoria and Albert Museum*, London, 1964, 3 vols.
Pope-Hennessy, 1965	John Pope-Hennessy, *Renaissance Bronzes from the Samuel H. Kress Collection*, London, 1965
Pope-Hennessy, *Apollo*, Mar. 1976	John Pope-Hennessy, "The Madonna Reliefs of Donatello," *Apollo*, ciii, Mar. 1976, pp. 172-191

Pozzi/Ciapponi, *Lettere italiane*, 1962

Giovanni Pozzi and Lucia A. Ciapponi, "La cultura figurativa di Francesco Colonna e l'arte veneta," *Lettere italiane*, xiv, 1962, pp. 151-169

Pozzi, *Revue numismatique*, 1914

S. Pozzi, "Un portrait du Général Vittore Cappello, plaquette inédite d'Ant. Rizzo," *Revue numismatique*, series 4, xviii, 1914, pp. 201-206

Precerutti Garberi, 1974

Mercedes Precerutti Garberi, *Il Castello Sforzesco. Le raccolte artistiche: pittura e scultura*, Milan, 1974

Puppi, 1972

Lionello Puppi, *Il trittico di Andrea Mantegna per la Basilica di San Zeno Maggiore in Verona*, Verona, 1972

Puppi/Puppi, 1977

Loredana Olivato Puppi and Lionello Puppi, *Mauro Codussi*, Milan, 1977

Quadri, 1831

Antonio Quadri, *La Piazza di San Marco in Venezia*, Venice, 1831

Quadri, 1835

Antonio Quadri, *I due Templi de' SS. Giovanni e Paolo e di Santa Maria Gloriosa detta de' Frari in Venezia*, Venice, 1835

Ragghianti, *Critica d'arte*, 1938

Carlo Ragghianti, "La mostra di scultura italiana antica a Detroit (U.S.A.)," *Critica d'arte*, iii, 1938, pp. 170-183

Rambaldi da Imola, 1887

Benvenuto Rambaldi da Imola, *Comentum super Dantis Aldigherij Comoediam*, ed. Jacopo Filippo Lacaita, Florence, 1887, iii

Rambaldi, *Aten. ven.*, 1910, pt. 2

P. L. Rambaldi, "La Scala dei Giganti nel Palazzo Ducale di Venezia," *Ateneo veneto*, xxxiii, pt. 2, pp. 87-121, pp. 193-239

Reinach, i, 1897; ii, pt. 1, 1897

Salomon Reinach, *Répertoire de la statuaire grecque et romaine*, Paris; i, 1897; ii, pt. 1, 1897; ii, pt. 2, 1898; iii, 1904

Reinach, i, 1909; iii, 1912

Salomon Reinach, *Répertoire de reliefs grecs et romains*, Paris; i, 1909; ii, 1912; iii, 1912

Ricci, *Arte e storia*, Feb. 20, 1897

Corrado Ricci, "Un sonetto artistico del sec. xv," *Arte e storia*, xvi, no. 4, February 20, 1897, pp. 27-28

Ricci, *Ausonia*, (1910) 1909

Corrado Ricci, "Marmi ravennati erratici," *Ausonia*, iv, no. 2 (1910) 1909, pp. 247-289

Rizzi, Ist. ven. SLA. *Atti* (Cl. di scienze morali), 1972-73

Alberto Rizzi, "Scultura erratica veneziana: sestier de S. Crose," Venice, Istituto veneto di scienze, lettere ed arti. *Atti* (Classe di scienze morali, lettere ed arti), cxxxi, 1972-73, pp. 255-303

Robert, ii, 1890

Carl Robert, *Die antiken Sarkophag-Reliefs*, Berlin, ii, 1890

Robertson, *WJ*, 1960

Giles Robertson, "The Earlier Work of Giovanni Bellini," *Journal of the Warburg and Courtauld Institutes*, xxiii, 1960, pp. 45-59

Robertson, 1968

Giles Robertson, *Giovanni Bellini*, Oxford, 1968

Rogissart/Havard, 1706

Rogissart, sieur de and abbé Havard, *Les delices de l'Italie*, Leiden, 1706, 3 vols.

Romanin, ³1973, iv

S. Romanin, *Storia documentata di Venezia*, Venice, ³1973, iv

Romanini, *Arte lom.*, Jan.–June 1964

Angiola Maria Romanini, "L'incontro tra Cristoforo Mantegazza e il Rizzo nel settimo decennio del Quattrocento," *Arte lombarda*, ix, Jan.–June 1964 (*Studi in onore di Giusta Nicco Fasola*, i), pp. 91-102

Ruhmer, 1959

Eberhard Ruhmer, *Francesco del Cossa*, Munich, 1959

Ruhmer, *Arte ven.*, 1974 — Eberhard, Ruhmer, "Antonio Lombardo: Versuch einer Charakteristik," *Arte veneta*, xxviii, 1974, pp. 39-74

Rumor/Ongaro, Vicenza, Mus. Civ. *Boll.*, Jan.–Mar. 1910 — Sebastiano Rumor, "Giovanni Emo, il suo monumento nella distrutta Chiesa dei Servi a Venezia," with a postscript by Luigi Ongaro, Vicenza, Museo Civico. *Bollettino*, Jan.–Mar. 1910, no. 1, pp. 20-25

Rumor, n.d. [1910?] — Sebastiano Rumor, *Storia breve degli Emo*, Vicenza, n.d. [1910?]

Ruskin, iii, 1853 — John Ruskin, *The Stones of Venice*, London; i, 1851; ii, 1853; iii, 1853

Sabellico, 1487 — Marc'Antonio Sabellico, *Rerum Venetarum ab urbe condita ad sua usque tempora libri xxxiii*, Venice, May 21, 1487

Sabellico, (1491-92) n.d. — Marc'Antonio Sabellico, *De situ urbis Venetae libri tres*, n.p., (1491-92) n.d.

F. Saccardo in Ongania, ed., *Basilica*, vi, 1888, pt. 3, [1893] — Francesco Saccardo, "Sculture diverse," in Ferdinando Ongania, ed., *La Basilica di San Marco in Venezia illustrata nei riguardi dell'arte e della storia da scrittori veneziani*, Venice, vi, 1888, pt. 3, [1893], pp. 269-275

G. Saccardo, *La difesa*, June 2-3, 1886 — G. Saccardo, "Appendice. Il 'Capitello' della Maddalena," *La difesa* (Venice), xx, no. 126, June 2-3, 1886, n.p. [p. 2]

P. Saccardo, *Arch. ven.*, xxxi, 1886 — Pietro Saccardo, "Relazione intorno ai principali lavori che furono eseguiti nella Basilica di S. Marco in Venezia durante l'anno 1885 e proposte per quelli da farsi nell' anno 1886," *Archivio veneto*, xxxi, 1886, pp. 499-514

P. Saccardo, 1890 — Pietro Saccardo, *I restauri della Basilica di San Marco nell'ultimo decennio*, Venice, 1890

Sagredo. *Annali universali*, July–Sept. 1843 — A. Sagredo, "Note sugli ammiglioramenti di Venezia," *Annali universali di statistica, di economia pubblica, ecc.* (Milan), lxxvii, July–Sept. 1843, pp. 187-201

Sagredo in *Venezia e le sue lagune*, 1847, i, pt. 2 — A. Sagredo, "Pittura, architettura, scultura e calcografia," in *Venezia e le sue lagune*, Venice, 1847, i, pt. 2, pp. 285-413

Sagredo, 1856 — Agostino Sagredo, *Sulle consorterie delle arti edificative in Venezia*, Venice, 1856

Salmi in *Umanesimo europeo*, 1963 — Mario Salmi, "Arte toscana e arte veneta: contrasti e concordanze," *Umanesimo europeo e umanesimo veneziano*, ed. Vittore Branca (Civiltà europea e civiltà veneziana; aspetti e problemi, 2), Florence, 1963, pp. 373-393

Sans., 1581 — Francesco Sansovino, *Venetia citta nobilissima et singolare, descritta in xiiii. libri*, Venice, 1581

Sans./Stringa, 1604 — Francesco Sansovino, *Venetia città nobilissima, et singolare*, enlarged by Giovanni Stringa, Venice, 1604

Sant'Ambrogio, *Arch. stor. lom.*, 1892 — Diego Sant'Ambrogio, "Notizie preliminari ed induzioni per uno studio di ricomposizione dell'Edicola Tarchetta nel Duomo di Milano," *Archivio storico lombardo*, xix, 1892, pp. 141-160

Sant'Ambrogio, *Lega lom.*, June 22-23, 1900 — Diego Sant'Ambrogio, "Nel Museo di Porta Giovia: 'Il Maestro di San Trovaso'," *Lega lombarda*, xv, no. 166, June 22-23, 1900, pp. 1-2

Sanudo, (1493) 1880
Marin Sanudo, *Cronachetta*, ed. Rinaldo Fulin (per nozze Papadopoli-Hellenbach), Venice, 1880

Sanudo, (1493) 1980
Marin Sanudo, *De origine, situ et magistratibus urbis Venetae ovvero la città di Venetia (1493-1530)*, ed. Angela Caracciolo Aricò, Milan, 1980

Sanudo, *RIs*, xxii, (1490-1530) 1733
Marin Sanudo, "Vite de' duchi di Venezia," in Lodovico Antonio Muratori, *Rerum Italicarum scriptores*, Milan, xxii, 1733

Sanudo, *Diarii*
Marin Sanudo, *I diarii*, Venice; i, 1879; ii, 1879; iii, 1880; iv, 1880; vii, 1882; xxx, 1891; xxxv, 1892; xl, 1894

Scardeone, 1560
Bernardino Scardeone, *De antiquitate urbis Patavii*, Basil, 1560

A. Scarpa, 1935
Angelo Scarpa, *La storia della Chiesa e dell'Isola di S. Elena in Venezia*, Venice, 1935

G. Scarpa in Tramontin *et al.*, 1958
G. Scarpa, "L'Isola nell'arte," in S. Tramontin, Scarpa, A. Niero, *L'Isola de la Salute*, Venice, 1958, pp. 35-67

Scattolin, 1961
Giorgia Scattolin, *Contributo allo studio dell'architettura civile veneziana dal ix al xiii secolo. Le case-fondaco sul Canal Grande*, Venice, 1961

Schiller, ii, 1972
Gertrud Schiller, *Iconography of Christian Art*, trans. Janet Seligman, Greenwich, Conn., ii, 1972

Schlosser, 1901
Julius von Schlosser, *Album ausgewählter Gegenstände der Kunstindustriellen Sammlung des allerhöchsten Kaiserhauses*, Vienna, 1901

Schmitt in Degenhart/Schmitt, *MJ*, 1960
Annegrit Schmitt in Bernhard Degenhart and Schmitt, "Gentile da Fabriano in Rom und die Anfänge des Antikenstudiums," *Münchner Jahrbuch der bildenden Kunst*, xi, 1960, pp. 59-151

Schottmüller, *Kunstchronik und Kunstmarkt*, Feb. 3, 1922
Frida Schottmüller, review of Leo Planiscig, *Venezianische Bildhauer der Renaissance*, in *Kunstchronik und Kunstmarkt*, n.s., xxxiii, Feb. 3, 1922, pp. 321-324

Schottmüller, *Rep. f. Kstw.*, 1924
Frida Schottmüller, review of Leo Planiscig, *Die Estensische Kunstsammlung*, in *Repertorium für Kunstwissenschaft*, xliv, 1924, pp. 134-136

Schubring, 1919
Paul Schubring, *Die italienische Plastik des Quattrocento* (Handbuch der Kunstwissenschaft), Berlin, 1919

Schulz in *Von Simson Festschrift*, 1977
Anne Markham Schulz, "A New Venetian Project by Verrocchio: The Altar of the Virgin in SS. Giovanni e Paolo," in *Festschrift für Otto von Simson zum 65. Geburtstag*, ed. L. Grisebach and K. Renger, Berlin, 1977, pp. 197-208

Schulz, *Antichità viva*, Mar.-Apr. 1977
Anne Markham Schulz, "The Giustiniani Chapel and the Art of the Lombardo," *Antichità viva*, Mar.-Apr. 1977, no. 2, pp. 27-44

Schulz, TAPS, 1978, pt. 3
Anne Markham Schulz, "The Sculpture of Giovanni and Bartolomeo Bon and Their Workshop," *Transactions of the American Philosophical Society*, lxviii, pt. 3, June 1978, pp. 1-81

Schulz, *NdiGF*, 1978
Anne Markham Schulz, *Niccolò di Giovanni Fiorentino and Venetian Sculpture of the Early Renaissance* (Monographs on Archaeology and Fine Arts sponsored by the Archaeological Institute of America and the College Art Association of America, 33), New York, 1978

Schulz, *BJ*, 1980   Anne Markham Schulz, "Giambattista Bregno," *Jahrbuch der Berliner Museen*, n.s. xxii, 1980, pp. 173-202

Schulz, Washington, D.C., Anne Markham Schulz, "A Portrait of Giovanni Emo in the
Nat. Gall. of Art. *Studies*, National Gallery of Art," Washington, D.C., National Gallery
1980   of Art. *Studies in the History of Art*, ix, 1980, pp. 7-11

Schulz in *Studies . . . Janson*, Anne Markham Schulz, "Pietro Lombardo's Barbarigo Tomb
1981   in the Venetian Church of S. Maria della Carità," in *Art the Ape of Nature. Studies in Honor of H.W. Janson*, ed. M. Barash, L. F. Sandler, P. Egan, New York, 1981, pp. 171-192

Sciolla, 1970   Gianni Carlo Sciolla, *La scultura di Mino da Fiesole*, Università di Torino, Facoltà di lettere e filosofia. Archeologia e storia dell'arte, 3, Turin, 1970

Scolari, *Venezia*, 1920 Aldo Scolari, "La Chiesa di Santa Maria Gloriosa dei Frari ed il suo recente restauro," Venice, Museo Civico Correr. *Venezia, studi di arte e storia*, i, 1920, pp. 148-171

Scrinari, 1958   Valnea Scrinari, *Guida di Aquileia*, Milan, 1958

Selvatico, 1847   Pietro Selvatico, *Sulla architettura e sulla scultura in Venezia dal medio evo sino ai nostri giorni*, Venice, 1847

Selvatico/Lazari, 1852 Pietro Selvatico and V. Lazari, *Guida artistica e storica di Venezia e delle isole circonvicine*, Venice et al., 1852

Semenzato in Zorzi et al., Camillo Semenzato in Alvise Zorzi, Elena Bassi, Terisio Pi-
1971   gnatti, Semenzato, *Il Palazzo Ducale di Venezia*, Turin, 1971

Semrau, 1890   Max Semrau, *Venedig*, Stuttgart et al., 1890

Serra, 1933   Luigi Serra, *Il Palazzo Ducale di Venezia* (Itinerari dei musei e monumenti d'Italia, 23), Rome, 1933

Serra, *Boll. d'arte*, 1935-36 Luigi Serra, "La mostra dell'antica arte italiana a Parigi, la scultura e le arti industriali," *Bollettino d'arte*, xxix, 1935-36, pp. 89-104

Seymour, 1966   Charles Seymour, Jr., *Sculpture in Italy 1400 to 1500*, Harmondsworth, 1966

Sheard, 1971   Wendy Stedman Sheard, "The Tomb of Doge Andrea Vendramin in Venice by Tullio Lombardo," Ph.D. Dissertation, Yale University, New Haven, Conn., 1971

Sheard, *Yale Ital. Studies*, Wendy Stedman Sheard, "Sanudo's List of Notable Things in
1977   Venetian Churches and the Date of the Vendramin Tomb," *Yale Italian Studies*, i, 1977, pp. 219-268

Sheard, *BJ*, 1978   Wendy Stedman Sheard, " 'Asa adorna': The Prehistory of the Vendramin Tomb," *Jahrbuch der Berliner Museen*, n.s., xx, 1978, pp. 117-156

Shelton in N.Y., Met. Mus. Kathleen J. Shelton in New York, Metropolitan Museum of
of Art. *Age of Spirituality*, ed. Art. *Age of Spirituality: Late Antique and Early Christian Art, Third
Weitzmann, 1979 to Seventh Century*, Nov. 19, 1977–February 12, 1978, catalogue ed. Kurt Weitzmann, New York, 1979

Simeoni, 1909   Luigi Simeoni, *Verona, guida storico-artistica della città e provincia*, Verona, [1]1909

Simon in Helbig, ii, [4]1966 Erika Simon in Wolfgang Helbig, *Führer durch die öffentlichen Sammlungen klassischer Altertümer in Rom*, ed. Hermine Speier, ii, *Die städtischen Sammlungen*, Tübingen, ii, [4]1966

Sinding-Larsen, *Acta ad archaeologiam*, 1962

Staale Sinding-Larsen, "Titian's Madonna di Ca' Pesaro and its Historical Significance," *Acta ad archaeologiam et artium historiam pertinentia*, i, 1962, pp. 139-169

Sinding-Larsen, *Acta ad archaeologiam*, 1974

Staale Sinding-Larsen, "Christ in the Council Hall. Studies in the Religious Iconography of the Venetian Republic," with a contribution by A. Kuhn, *Acta ad archaeologiam et artium historiam pertinentia*, v, 1974

Siti storici, 1838

Siti storici e monumentali di Venezia, drawings by Giovanni Pividor, notes by Pietro Chevalier, Venice, 1838

Sohm, 1978

Philip Lindsay Sohm, "The Scuola Grande di San Marco, 1437-1550: The Architecture of a Venetian Lay Confraternity," Ph.D. Dissertation, The Johns Hopkins University, Baltimore, 1978

Someda in *Arte e artisti*, 1959, i

Carlo Someda de Marco, "Architetti e lapicidi lombardi in Friuli nei secoli xv e xvi," Società archeologica comense. Convegno sugli artisti del Laria e del Ceresio, 2nd, Varenna, 1957. *Arte e artisti dei laghi lombardi*, ed. Edoardo Arslan, Como, 1959, i, pp. 309-342

Soràvia, i, 1822; ii, 1823

Giambattista Soràvia, *Le chiese di Venezia*, Venice; i, 1822; ii, 1823; iii, 1824

Stefanutti, 1961

Ugo Stefanutti, *Documentazioni cronologiche per la storia della medicina chirurgia e farmacia in Venezia dal 1258 al 1332*, Venice, 1961

Stringa, *La Chiesa di S. Marco*, 1610

Giovanni Stringa, *La Chiesa di S. Marco*, Venice, 1610

Stringa, *Vita di S. Marco*, 1610

Giovanni Stringa, *Vita di S. Marco Evangelista, . . . con una breve descrittione di detta chiesa, & delle cose più notabili, che vi si contengono, posta in fine, & separatamente*, Venice, 1610

Superbi, 1629, ii

Agostino Superbi, *Trionfo glorioso d'heroi illustri, et eminenti dell'inclita, & maravigliosa città di Venetia*, Venice, 1629, ii

Swoboda in Lanckoroński, 1906

Heinrich Swoboda in Karl Lanckoroński, *Der Dom von Aquileia, sein Bau und seine Geschichte*, with George Niemann and Swoboda, Vienna, 1906

Tassini, ¹1863, ⁸1970

Giuseppe Tassini, *Curiosità veneziane*, Venice, ¹1863, ⁸1970

Tassini, *Arch. ven.*, 1876

Giuseppe Tassini, "Iscrizioni dell'ex Chiesa, Convento e Confraternita di S. Maria della Carità in Venezia," *Archivio veneto*, vi, 1876, pp. 357-392

Tassini, 1885

Giuseppe Tassini, *Edifici di Venezia distrutti o vôlti ad uso diverso*, Venice, 1885

Temanza, (1738-78) 1963

Tommaso Temanza, *Zibaldon*, ed. Nicola Ivanoff (Civiltà veneziana, Fonti e testi, vi, series 1, 3), Venice/Rome, 1963

Temanza, 1778

Tommaso Temanza, *Vite dei più celebri architetti, e scultori veneziani*, Venice, 1778

Tervarent, i, 1958; ii, 1959

Guy de Tervarent, *Attributs et symboles dans l'art profane, 1450-1600*, Geneva; i, 1958; ii, 1959

Ticozzi, i, 1830

Stefano Ticozzi, *Dizionario degli architetti, scultori, pittori*, Milan; i, 1830; ii, 1831; iii, 1832; iv, 1833

Tietze, *Vie d'Italia*, 1931

Hans Tietze, "L'arte italiana nel mondo. L'arte italiana nei musei di Vienna, 2. Le collezioni minori," *Le vie d'Italia*, xxxvii, no. 6, June 1931, pp. 401-413

Tietze/Tietze-Conrat, 1944 — Hans Tietze and E. Tietze-Conrat, *The Drawings of the Venetian Painters in the 15th and 16th Centuries*, New York, 1944

Tigler in Egg *et al.*, [1]1965 — Peter Tigler in Erich Egg, Erich Hubala, Tigler, Wladimir Timofiewitsch, Manfred Wundram, *Oberitalien Ost* (Reclams Kunstführer, ed. Wundram, *Italien*, ii), Stuttgart, [1]1965

Tigler in Egg *et al.*, [2]1972 — Peter Tigler in Erich Egg, Erich Hubala, Tigler, Wladimir Timofiewitsch, Manfred Wundram, *Südtirol, Trentino, Venezia Giulia, Friaul, Veneto* (Reclams Kunstführer, ed. Wundram, *Italien*, ii, pt. 2), Stuttgart, [2]1972

Tiraboschi, xvi, [2]1823; xviii, [2]1824 — Girolamo Tiraboschi, *Storia della letteratura italiana*, Venice; xvi, [2]1823; xviii, [2]1824

Toffoli, 1883 — Francesco Toffoli, *Guida artistica al Palazzo Ducale di Venezia*, Venice, 1883

TCI, *Ven.*, 1951 — Touring Club Italiano, *Guida d'Italia. Venezia e dintorni*, Milan, 1951

TCI, *Friúli*, 1963 — Touring Club Italiano, *Guida d'Italia. Friúli—Venezia Giulia*, Milan, 1963

TCI, *Veneto*, 1969 — Touring Club Italiano, *Guida d'Italia. Veneto*, Milan, 1969

Tramontin in Tramontin *et al.*, 1965 — S. Tramontin in Tramontin, A. Niero, G. Musolino, C. Candiani, *Culto dei santi a Venezia*, Venice, 1965

Trevisani in Treviso, S. Nicolò *et al.*, *Lotto a Treviso*, 1980, ed. Dillon — Filippo Trevisani, "Il monumento funebre per Agostino Onigo," Treviso, S. Nicolò; Quinto, S. Cristina; Asolo, Duomo. *Lorenzo Lotto a Treviso: ricerche e restauri*, Sept.–Nov. 1980, catalogue ed. Gianvittorio Dillon, Treviso, n.d. [1980], pp. 67-100

Trincanato/Mariacher, 1966 — Egle Renata Trincanato and Giovanni Mariacher, *Il Palazzo Ducale di Venezia* (*I tesori*, 18), Florence, 1966

Trincanato, 1969 — Egle Renata Trincanato, *Palazzo Ducale, Venezia* (*I documentari*, 23), Novara, 1969

Ubertalli, 1910 — P. Ubertalli, *Il Palazzo Ducale di Venezia*, Milan, 1910

Urbani de Gheltof, 1877 — G.M. Urbani de Gheltof, *Saggio di iconografia veneziana*, Venice, 1877

Vale in *La Basilica di Aquileia*, 1933 — Giuseppe Vale, "Storia della basilica dopo il secolo ix," in *La Basilica di Aquileia*, Bologna, 1933, pp. 49-105

[Valentiner], N.Y., Met. Mus. of Art. *Bull.*, Dec. 1908 — [W. R. Valentiner], "Principal Accessions," New York, Metropolitan Museum of Art. *Bulletin*, iii, December 1908, pp. 228-231

Valentiner, *Art in America*, 1925 — W. R. Valentiner, "The Clarence H. Mackay Collection of Italian Renaissance Sculptures, pt. 2," *Art in America*, xiii, 1925, pp. 315-331

[Valussi], 1876 — [E. C. Valussi], *Cenni storici della Basilica patriarcale d'Aquileia in occasione della seconda sua consecrazione il xiii luglio MDCCCLXXVI*, Gorizia, 1876

Vas./Ricci, (1550) 1927 — Giorgio Vasari, *Le vite de piu eccellenti architetti, pittori, et scultori italiani*, ed. Corrado Ricci, Milan/Rome, 1927, 4 vols.

Vas./Mil., ii, iii, (1568) 1878 — Giorgio Vasari, *Le vite de' più eccellenti pittori scultori ed architettori*, ed. Gaetano Milanesi, Florence, ii, iii, (1568) 1878

Vecellio, [1]1590

Cesare Vecellio, *De gli habiti antichi, et moderni di diverse parti del mondo libri due*, Venice, [1]1590

Ven., Ca' d'Oro. *Guida-catalogo*, by Fogolari *et al.*, 1929

Venice, Ca' d'Oro. *La R. Galleria Giorgio Franchetti alla Ca' d'Oro. Guida-catalogo*, by Fogolari, Nebbia, Moschini, Venice, 1929

Ven., Gall. dell'Accademia. Catalogue, 1854

Venice, Gallerie dell'Accademia. *Catalogo delle opere d'arte contenute nella Sala delle Sedute dell'I. R. Accademia di Venezia*, Venice, 1854

Ven., Gall. dell'Accademia. Catalogue, 1924

Venice, Gallerie dell'Accademia. *Le Regie Gallerie della Accademia di Venezia. Catalogo*, Bologna, 1924

Ven., Gall. dell'Accademia. Catalogue by Moschini Marconi, 1955

Venice, Gallerie dell'Accademia. *Opere d'arte dei secoli xiv e xv*, catalogue by Sandra Moschini Marconi (Ministero della pubblica istruzione. Cataloghi dei musei e gallerie d'Italia), Rome, 1955

Ven., Gall. dell'Accademia. *Giorgione a Ven.*, by Ruggeri *et al.*, 1978

Venice, Gallerie dell'Accademia. *Giorgione a Venezia*, Sept.–Nov. 1978, catalogue by A. Ruggeri, P. L. Fantelli, E. Merkel, S. Moschini Marconi, A. Rizzi, G. Scirè Nepi, S. Sponza, F. Valcanover, Milan, 1978

Ven., Procuratie Nuove. *Arte a Ven.*, by Mariacher, 1971

Venice, Procuratie Nuove. *Arte a Venezia dal medioevo al settecento*, June 26–Oct. 31, 1971, catalogue by Giovanni Mariacher, Venice, 1971

Venturi, *Arch. stor. dell'arte*, 1894

Adolfo Venturi, "Nuovi documenti," *Archivio storico dell'arte*, vii, 1894, pp. 52-55

Venturi, *Le gallerie nazionali italiane*, 1896

Adolfo Venturi, "IV. Museo del Palazzo Ducale in Venezia. i. Raccolta medioevale e del rinascimento," *Le gallerie nazionali italiane*, ii, 1896, pp. 47-61

Venturi, *Storia*

Adolfo Venturi, *Storia dell'arte italiano*, Milan; vi, 1908; viii, pt. 2, 1924; x, pt. i, 1935; x, pt. 3, 1937

Venturi, *L'arte*, 1930

Adolfo Venturi, "Pietro Lombardi e alcuni bassorilievi veneziani del '400," *L'arte*, 1930, xxxiii, pp. 191-205

L. Venturi, *L'arte*, 1916

Lionello Venturi, "Opere di scultura nelle Marche," *L'arte*, xix, 1916, pp. 25-50

Vermeule, *Berytus*, 1959

Cornelius C. Vermeule III, "Hellenistic and Roman Cuirassed Statues. The Evidence of Paintings and Reliefs in the Chronological Development of Cuirass Types," *Berytus*, xiii, 1959, pp. 1-82

Vermeule, *Berytus*, 1964

Cornelius C. Vermeule III, "Hellenistic and Roman Cuirassed Statues: a Supplement," *Berytus*, xv, 1964, pp. 95-110

Vicentini, *Cinque secoli*, 1920

Antonio M. Vicentini, *Cinque secoli di storia*, Treviglio, 1920

Vicentini, *Ideale risurrezione*, 1920

Antonio M. Vicentini, *Ideale risurrezione d'un tempio*, Treviglio, 1920

Vicentini, *S. Maria de' Servi*, 1920

Antonio M. Vicentini, *S. Maria de' Servi in Venezia*, Treviglio, 1920

Vicenza, Mus. Civ. Catalogue by Barbieri, 1962

Vicenza, Museo Civico. *Il Museo Civico di Vicenza. Dipinti e sculture dal xiv al xv secolo*, catalogue by Franco Barbieri, Venice, 1962

Vienna, Ksthis. Mus. Catalogue by Schlosser, 1910 — Vienna, Kunsthistorisches Museum. *Werke der Kleinplastik in der Skulpturensammlung des A. H. Kaiserhauses*, i, *Bildwerke in Bronze, Stein und Ton*, catalogue by Julius von Schlosser, Vienna, 1910

Vienna, Ksthis. Mus. Catalogue by Planiscig, 1919 — Vienna, Kunsthistorisches Museum. *Die Estensische Kunstsammlung*, i, *Skulpturen und Plastiken des Mittelalters und der Renaissance*, catalogue by Leo Planiscig, Vienna, 1919

Vienna, Ksthis. Mus. Catalogue by Planiscig, 1924 — Vienna, Kunsthistorisches Museum. *Publikationem aus den Sammlungen für Plastik und Kunstgewerbe*, ed. Julius von Schlosser, iv, *Die Bronzeplastiken, Statuetten, Reliefs, Geräte und Plaketten*, catalogue by Leo Planiscig, Vienna, 1924

Vienna, Ksthis. Mus. Catalogue by Planiscig/Kris, 1935 — Vienna, Kunsthistorisches Museum. *Katalog der Sammlungen für Plastik und Kunstgewerbe*, by L. Planiscig and E. Kris (Führer durch die Kunsthistorischen Sammlungen in Wien, 27), Vienna, 1935

Vienna, Ksthis. Mus. Catalogue by Mahl et al., 1966 — Vienna, Kunsthistorisches Museum. *Katalog der Sammlung für Plastik und Kunstgewerbe*, ii, *Renaissance*, by Elisabeth Mahl, Erwin Neumann, Ernst Schuselka, Vienna, 1966

Vienna, Secession, Vereins der Museumsfreunde. *Meisterwerke*, 1924 — Vienna, Secession, Vereins der Museumsfreunde in Wien. *Meisterwerke italienischer Renaissancekunst aus Privatbesitz*, 1924, catalogue, n.p., n.d.

Vigezzi, 1928 — Silvio Vigezzi, *La scultura lombarda*, i, *Dall'Antelami all'Amadeo (sec. xiii-xv)*, Milan, 1928

Vigezzi, 1934 — Silvio Vigezzi, *La scultura in Milano*, Milan, 1934

[Visentini], 1761 — [Antonio Visentini], *L'augusta ducale Basilica dell'Evangelista San Marco nell'inclita dominante di Venezia*, Venice, 1761

[Visinoni], *Bull. di arti*, Aug. 1877 — [L.A. Visinoni], "Intorno ad alcune statue del Monumento di Giovanni Emo," *Bullettino di arti, industrie e curiosità veneziane*, i, no. 4, Aug. 1877, pp. 34-37

Vucetich, n.d. — See under "Manuscripts," Venice, Museo Correr, MS P. D. 2d

Washington, Nat. Gall. of Art. *Early Italian Engravings*, 1973 — Washington, D.C., National Gallery of Art. *Early Italian Engravings from the National Gallery of Art*, catalogue by Jay A. Levenson, Konrad Oberhuber, Jacquelyn L. Sheehan, Washington, D.C., 1973

Waźbiński, 1967 — Zygmunt Waźbiński, *Renesansowy akt Wenecki*, Warsaw, 1967

Weisbach, 1919 — Werner Weisbach, *Trionfi*, Berlin, 1919

Wilk, 1977 — Sarah Wilk, "Iconological Problems in the Sculpture of Tullio Lombardo," Ph.D. Dissertation, New York University, New York, 1977

Wolters, Florence, Ksthis. Inst. *Mitt.*, 1965-66 — Wolfgang Wolters, "Der Programmentwurf zur Dekoration des Dogenpalastes nach dem Brand vom 20. Dezember 1577," Florence, Kunsthistorisches Institut. *Mitteilungen*, xii, 1965-66, pp. 271-318

Wolters, *Pantheon*, 1974 — Wolfgang Wolters, "Eine Antikenergänzung aus dem Kreis des Donatello in Venedig," *Pantheon*, xxxii, 1974, pp. 130-133

Wolters, 1976 — Wolfgang Wolters, *La scultura veneziana gotica 1300-1460*, Venice, 1976, 2 vols.

[Wynne], 1787 — [Justine Wynne, Countess of Rosenberg-Orsini], *Alticchiero*, Padua, 1787

Zagata/Biancolini, pt. 2, ii, 1749 — Pier Zagata, *Supplementi alla cronica della città di Verona*, Verona, enlarged by Giambattista Biancolini, pt. 2, ii, 1749

A. Zanetti, *Enc. ital.*, iv, 1841 — Alessandro Zanetti, "Buono Bartolomeo," *Enciclopedia italiana, o dizionario della conversazione*, Venice, iv, 1841, pp. 1338-1339

V. Zanetti, 1870 — Vincenzo Zanetti, *La Chiesa della Madonna dell'Orto in Venezia*, Venice, 1870

Zangirolami, 1962 — Cesare Zangirolami, *Storia delle chiese, dei monasteri, delle scuole di Venezia rapinate e distrutte da Napoleone Bonaparte*, Venice, 1962

Zani, v, pt. 1, 1820; xvi, pt. 1, 1823 — Pietro Zani, *Enciclopedia metodica critico-ragionata delle belle arti*, Parma, v, pt. 1, 1820, pp. 165ff; xvi, pt. 1, 1823, p. 103

Zannandreis, 1891 — Diego Sannandreis, *Le vite dei pittori scultori e architetti veronesi*, ed. Giuseppe Biadego, Verona, 1891, pp. 56-58

Zanotto, i, 1842-53 — Francesco Zanottò, *Il Palazzo Ducale di Venezia*, Venice, i, 1842-53

Zanotto in *Venezia e le sue lagune*, 1847, ii, pt. 2 — Francesco Zanotto, "Descrizione della città," *Venezia e le sue lagune*, Venice, 1847, ii, pt. 2, pp. 1-482

Zanotto, *Nuovissima guida*, 1856 — Francesco Zanotto, *Nuovissima guida di Venezia e delle isole della sua laguna*, Venice, 1856

Zanotto, *Venezia prospettica*, 1856 — Francesco Zanotto, *Venezia prospettica, monumentale, storica ed artistica*, with lithographs by Marco Moro and Giuseppe Rebellato, Venice, 1856

Zanotto in Cicognara *et al.*, i, [3]1858 — Francesco Zanotto in Leopoldo Cicognara, Antonio Diedo, Giannantonio Selva, *Le fabbriche e i monumenti cospicui di Venezia*, i, [3]1858, "Aggiunta al Palazzo Ducale"

Zava Boccazzi, 1965 — Franca Zava Boccazzi, *La Basilica dei Santi Giovanni e Paolo in Venezia*, Padua, 1965

Zenier, 1825 — Vincenzo Zenier, *Guida per la Chiesa di S. Maria Gloriosa dei Frari*, Venice, 1825

Ziliotto, 1950 — Baccio Ziliotto, *Raffaele Zovenzoni, la vita, i carmi* (Comune di Trieste. Celebrazioni degli istriani illustri, 3), Trieste, 1950

A. P. Zorzi, *L'art*, 1883, pt. 4 — A.P. Zorzi, "Sant'Elena et Santa Marta a Venise," *L'art*, xxxv (ix, pt. 4), 1883, pp. 212-220

A. Zorzi, 1972 — Alvise Zorzi, *Venezia scomparsa*, Milan, 1972, 2 vols.

Zorzi, iii, 1937 — Giangiorgio Zorzi, *Contributo alla storia dell'arte vicentina nei secoli xv e xvi*, iii, *Il preclassicismo e i prepalladiani* (Venice, Reale deputazione veneta di storia patria. *Miscellanea di studi e memorie*, 3), Venice, 1937

Zorzi, *Arte ven.*, 1953 — Giangiorgio Zorzi, "Nuove rivelazioni sulla ricostruzione delle sale al piano nobile del Palazzo Ducale di Venezia dopo l'incendio dell'11 maggio 1574," *Arte veneta*, vii, 1953, pp. 123-151

Zorzi, Ist. ven. SLA. *Atti* (Cl. di scienze morali), 1960-61, — Giangiorgio Zorzi, "Notizie di arte e di artisti nei diarii di Marino Sanudo," Venice, Istituto veneto di scienze, lettere ed arti. *Atti* (Classe di scienze morali e lettere), cxix, 1960-61, pp. 471-604

Zucchini, ii, 1784 — Tommas'Arcangelo Zucchini, *Nuova cronaca veneta, ossia descrizione di tutte le pubbliche architetture, sculture e pitture della città di Venezia ed isole circovicine*, Venice; i, 1785; ii, 1784

Index

Pyrgoteles (*cont.*)
ani, *Christ Carrying the Cross,*
9; S. Maria dei Miracoli, *Ma-*
donna and Child, 9

Quintin, Master, 94, 130
Quirini, Alvise, 125
Quirini, Angelo, 142

Rambaldi da Imola, Benvenuto:
Comentum, 34, 34 n. 11
Ranieri del Porrina: *Effigy* (attrib.
Gano da Siena), Casole d'Elsa,
Collegiata, 47
Ravenna: Palazzo Arcivescovile,
"*Throne of Ceres,*" 11, 49, 61,
Fig. 219; Tomb of Dante, 77
Regio, Rafaello, 12
Riccio, Andrea, 13, 16, 156
Ricio, Master, 7, 124
Rizzo, Antonio: birth, 3, 123;
embezzlement and flight from
Venice, 16, 17, 87, 113, 118,
121, 138; in Florence, 7-8, 11,
22, 36, 121; marriage, 9, 123;
military service against the
Turks, 11, 43, 64, 65, 84, 125;
in Padua, 7, 22; in Venice, 7-
16 *passim,* 118, 126, 135-136
Work and Technique: assistants and workshop, 63, 86, 94,
94 n. 59, 119, 119 n. 29, 129;
costume, treatment of, 22, 29,
31, 39, 42, 52, 57, 59, 67, 75
n. 28, 75-76, 76 n. 30, 78, 80
n. 36, 81, 104; decorative detail, 5-6, 18, 19, 21, 22, 23,
40, 51, 61-63, 77, 93-94, 102-
105, 119, 120; drapery, treatment of, 6-7, 20-21, 24, 25,
26, 28, 38-39, 42, 54, 57, 59,
60, 63, 66, 68, 71, 72, 73, 79,
81, 95, 96, 97, 110-112, 120,
121; foreshortening, 23, 25,
39, 61, 69, 95, 96-97, 112, 119;
human figure, treatment of,
20-26 *passim,* 28-36 *passim,* 38,
39, 42-43, 52-61 *passim,* 63,
66, 68-73 *passim,* 78, 79, 80,
95, 96, 97, 107-113 *passim,*
121; influence of, 15-16, 57;
influence on, of Antonello da
Messina, 14, 14 n. 82, 56, 57,
58, 63, 64, 80, 81, 121; influence on, of classical art, 11,
34, 49, 56, 59, 60, 61, 72, 75,
78, 81, 103, 109, 110; influence
on, of Donatello, 6, 7, 8, 10,
21, 29, 120; influence on, of

Tullio Lombardo, 13, 14, 57,
63, 64, 77-78, 81, 121; influence on, of Mantegna, 6, 7,
10, 23, 28-29, 75: influence on,
of Antonio Pollaiuolo, 11, 14,
35-36, 97, 121; influence on, of
Verrocchio, 14-15, 78 n. 35;
landscape and background,
treatment of, 22, 23, 38, 67-
68, 97-98; light and shadow,
treatment of, 15, 108, 113;
member of Scuola di S.
Marco, 10, 44, 116, 126, 135;
patent for mills, 10, 135; perspective, aerial, 15, 23, 38,
113; perspective, linear, 67, 70,
119, 120; portraiture, 30, 53,
54, 78-79; possible self-portrait
in "*Mars,*" 30; proportion and
scale, 22, 23, 36, 67, 68, 70,
79, 80, 93, 97, 121; *schiacciato*
relief, use of, 22-23, 38, 57,
60, 97, 102, 111; space, treatment of, 23, 25, 37, 38, 61,
62, 67, 68, 70, 95, 105, 112-
113; training, 5, 22, 120
Works: Amsterdam, private
collection, formerly, *Madonna*
and Child (cat. no. 1), 26, 28,
95, 117, 121, 139, Fig. 29;
Aquileia, Basilica, Altar of the
Sacrament, *Man of Sorrows*
(cat. no. 2), 11, 37-42 *passim,*
54, 63, 70, 73, 118, 119, 139-
141, Figs. 53-59; Berlin, Kaiser-Friedrich-Museum, formerly, *Victories* (cat. no. 3),
12, 71-72, 81, 112, 117, 142,
145, Figs. 130, 131; East Berlin, Staatliche Museen, *St. John*
the Evangelist (cat. no. 4), 12,
80-81, 117, 121, 142-143, Fig.
135; Paris, Louvre, Tomb of
Giovanni Emo, *Pages* (formerly, Venice, S. Maria dei
Servi; cat. no. 17), 12, 74, 75,
75 n. 28, 76, 79-80, 81, 95,
117, 177, 178, 179, Figs. 138,
141, 142, 145, 146; Vaduz,
Collection of the Prince of
Liechtenstein, *Madonna and*
Child (cat. no. 5), 15, 95, 96,
117, 121, 143-144, Fig. 160
Works: Venice, Ducal Palace:
9, 10, 12, 15, 16, 65, 114-115,
119, 156; Androne Foscari,
Angel, 12, 73, 154-155, 158,
Fig. 134; appointment as *proto-*
maestro, 9, 10, 15, 27, 43, 84-

85, 115, 116, 120, 121, 127-
135 *passim,* 147, 156; Arco
Foscari (cat. no. 9), 10, 27, 50,
50 n. 37, 65, 84, 101, 114,
115, 119-120, 126-127, 152-
159, Figs. 30-51, 136, 137,
147, 148; *Adam,* 11, 15, 16, 30,
32-38 *passim,* 33 nn. 4, 6, 7, 34
n. 8, 42, 56, 57, 58-59, 61, 69,
70, 73, 79, 81, 107, 108, 115,
119, 121, 152-153, 156, 157,
Figs. 38-43, 45; *Angels,* 11, 28,
30, 108, 112, 115, 120, 154-
155, 158, Figs. 32, 33; *Doge*
Pietro or Giovanni Mocenigo
Kneeling before the Lion of St.
Mark (destroyed), 28, 155;
Eve, 11, 12, 15, 16-17, 30, 32-
38 *passim,* 33 n. 7, 34 n. 8, 44,
54, 55-56, 58-59, 73, 79, 81,
96, 107, 108, 115, 119, 121,
152-153, 156, 157, Figs. 46-51;
"*Mars,*" 6, 7, 10, 28-31, 36,
58, 79, 115, 119, 154, 157,
Figs. 34-37, 44; *Mocenigo War-*
rior, 12, 80, 80 n. 36, 120, 154,
157-158, Fig. 147; *Personifica-*
tions, 12, 73, 80, 120, 155, 158,
Figs. 136, 137, 148; Camera
degli Scarlatti, *Madonna and*
Child (cat. no. 6), 15, 96-97,
112, 115, 144-145, Fig. 161;
east wing, 10, 15, 16, 76, 84-
90 *passim,* 115, 132; courtyard
facade, 76, 77, 83, 85, 92, 93-
94, 103, Figs. 156-159; *rio* facade, 92, 93, Figs. 151-154; *rio*
facade, *Putti with Arms of the*
Barbarigo Family (cat. no. 7),
15, 85, 94-95, 96, 109, 115,
142, 145, Fig. 155; Sala degli
Scuderi, *Battle Scene,* 97, Fig.
162; Sala delle Mappe, *Battle*
Scene, 97, Fig. 163; Scala dei
Giganti (cat. no. 8), 15, 63,
81, 88-89, 90, 94, 98-106 *pas-*
sim, 108-113 *passim,* 115, 119,
121, 145-152, Figs. 164-184,
190-192, 195-202; *Bust of a*
Girl, 15, 111, Fig. 177; *Justice,*
15, 103, Fig. 173; *Putto Playing*
a Pipe, 15, Fig. 175; *Victories,*
15, 109-113, 119, 121, 142,
184, Figs. 190, 195-202; *Youth*
with Fantastic Helmet, 15, 104,
Fig. 178
Works: Venice, Galleria
Giorgio Franchetti alla Ca'
d'Oro, *Angel with Attributes of*

Illustrations

1. Antonio Rizzo, Altar of St. James, S. Marco, Venice

2. Antonio Rizzo, Altar of St. Paul, S. Marco, Venice

3. Antonio Rizzo, *St. James*, Altar of St. James, S. Marco, Venice

4. Antonio Rizzo, detail, *St. James*, Altar of St. James, S. Marco, Venice

5. Antonio Rizzo, detail, *St. Paul*, Altar of St. Paul, S. Marco, Venice

6. Antonio Rizzo, *St. Paul*, Altar of St. Paul, S. Marco, Venice

7. Antonio Rizzo, lunette, Altar of St. James, S. Marco, Venice

8. Antonio Rizzo, lunette, Altar of St. Paul, S. Marco, Venice

9. Antonio Rizzo, pilaster, Altar of St. James, S. Marco, Venice

10. Altar of St. Clement, S. Marco, Venice

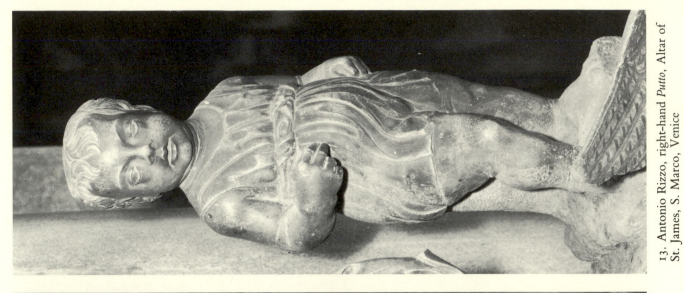

13. Antonio Rizzo, right-hand *Putto*, Altar of St. James, S. Marco, Venice

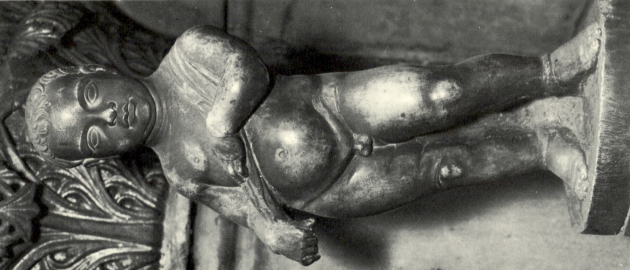

12. Antonio Rizzo, central *Putto*, Altar of St. James, S. Marco, Venice

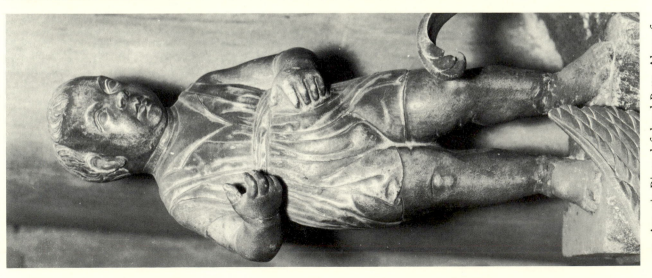

11. Antonio Rizzo, left-hand *Putto*, Altar of St. James, S. Marco, Venice

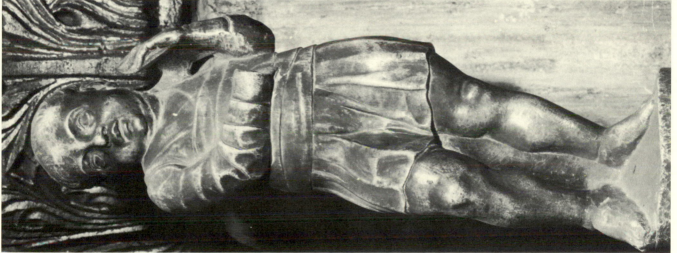

16. Antonio Rizzo, right-hand *Putto*, Altar of St. Paul, S. Marco, Venice

15. Antonio Rizzo, central *Putto*, Altar of St. Paul, S. Marco, Venice

14. Antonio Rizzo, left-hand *Putto*, Altar of St. Paul, S. Marco, Venice

17. Antonio Rizzo, *Conversion of St. Paul*, Altar of St. Paul, S. Marco, Venice

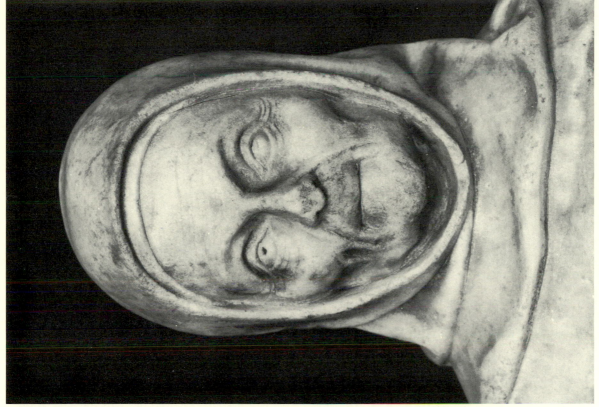

19. Antonio Rizzo, detail, *St. Bernardino*, Altar of St. Clement, S. Marco, Venice

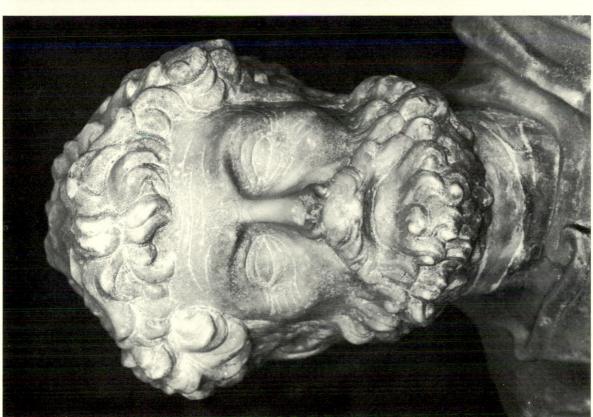

18. Antonio Rizzo, detail, *St. Mark*, Altar of St. Clement, S. Marco, Venice

20. Antonio Rizzo, *St. Mark*, Altar of St. Clement, S. Marco, Venice

21. Antonio Rizzo, *St. Bernardino*, Altar of St. Clement, S. Marco, Venice

22. Antonio Rizzo, *Madonna and Child*, Altar of St. Clement, S. Marco, Venice

23. Antonio Rizzo, left-hand *Angel*, Altar of St. James, S. Marco, Venice

24. Antonio Rizzo, right-hand *Angel*, Altar of St. James, S. Marco, Venice

25. Antonio Rizzo, left-hand *Angel*, Altar of St. James, S. Marco, Venice

26. Antonio Rizzo, right-hand *Angel*, Altar of St. James, S. Marco, Venice

27. Antonio Rizzo, right-hand *Angel*, Altar of St. James, S. Marco, Venice

28. Antonio Rizzo, left-hand *Angel*, Altar of St. James, S. Marco, Venice

29. Antonio Rizzo, *Madonna and Child*, formerly, private collection, Amsterdam

31. South face of the Arco Foscari, courtyard, Ducal Palace, Venice

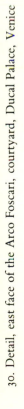

30. Detail, east face of the Arco Foscari, courtyard, Ducal Palace, Venice

32. Antonio Rizzo, *Angel*, east face of the
Arco Foscari, courtyard, Ducal Palace,
Venice

33. Antonio Rizzo, *Angel*, south face of the
Arco Foscari, courtyard, Ducal Palace,
Venice

34. Antonio Rizzo, "*Mars*," Ducal Palace, Venice   35. Antonio Rizzo, "*Mars*," Ducal Palace, Venice

36. Antonio Rizzo, "*Mars*," Ducal Palace, Venice

37. Antonio Rizzo, detail, *"Mars,"* Ducal Palace, Venice

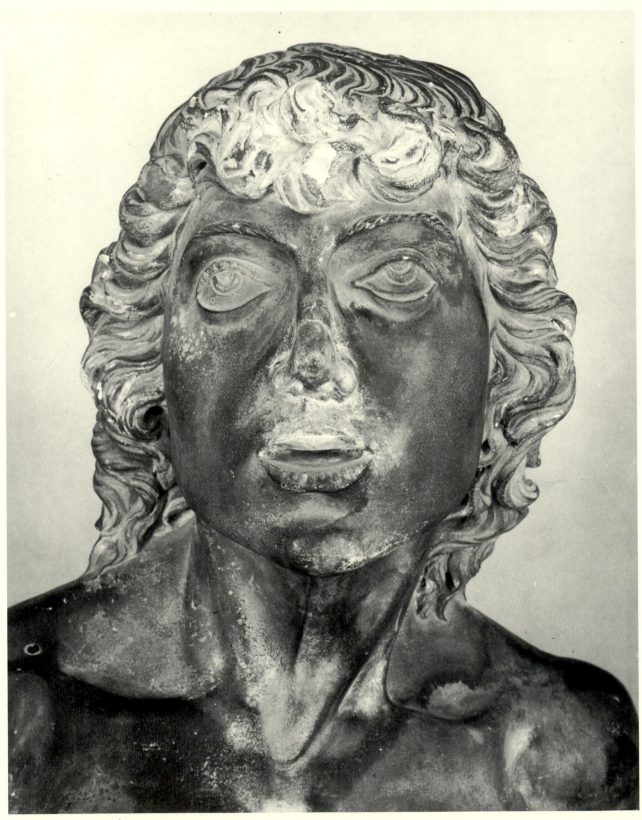

38. Antonio Rizzo, detail, *Adam*, Ducal Palace, Venice

39. Antonio Rizzo, *Adam*, Ducal Palace, Venice

40. Antonio Rizzo, *Adam*, Ducal Palace, Venice

41. Antonio Rizzo, *Adam*, Ducal Palace, Venice

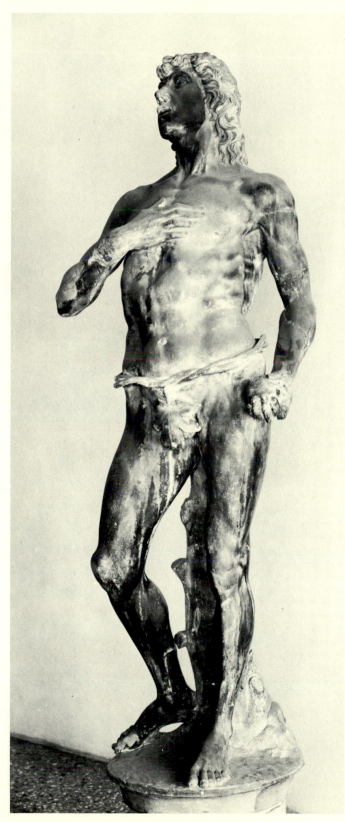

42. Antonio Rizzo, *Adam*, Ducal Palace, Venice   43. Antonio Rizzo, *Adam*, Ducal Palace, Venice

45. Antonio Rizzo, detail, *Adam*, Ducal Palace, Venice

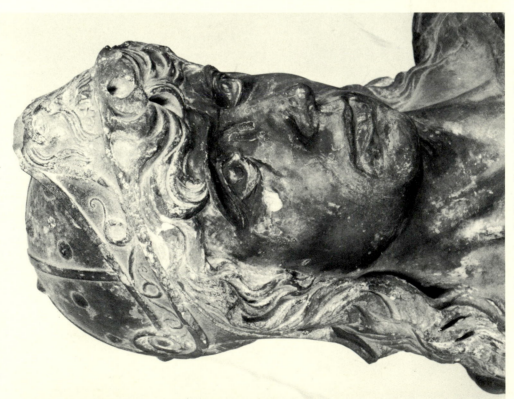

44. Antonio Rizzo, detail, "*Mars*," Ducal Palace, Venice

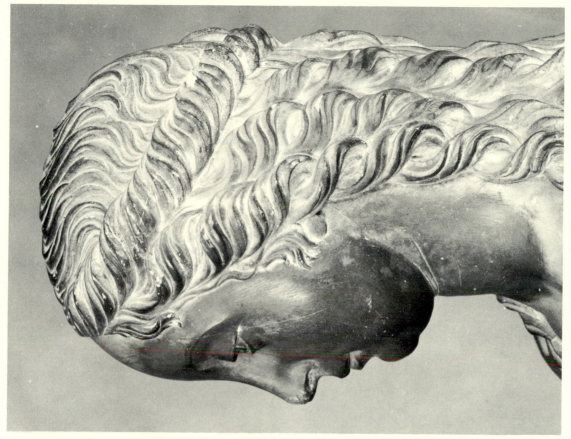

47. Antonio Rizzo, detail, *Eve*, Ducal Palace, Venice

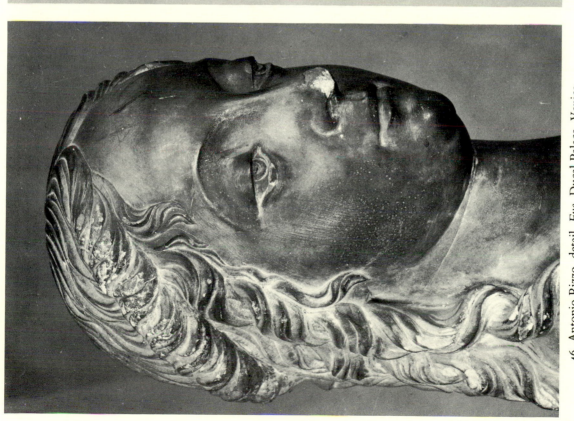

46. Antonio Rizzo, detail, *Eve*, Ducal Palace, Venice

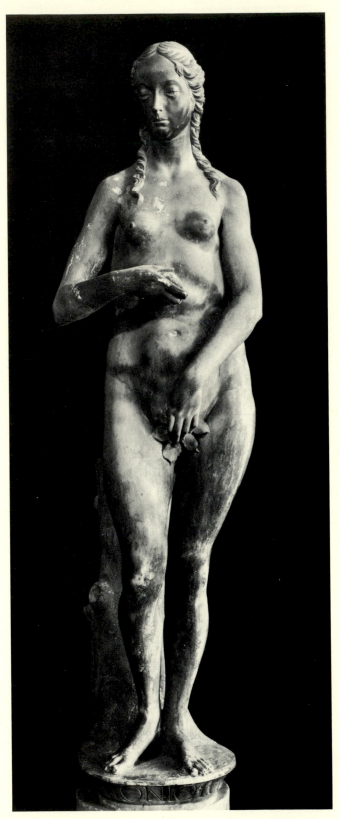

48. Antonio Rizzo, *Eve*, Ducal Palace, Venice

49. Antonio Rizzo, *Eve*, Ducal
Palace, Venice

50. Antonio Rizzo, detail, *Eve*, Ducal Palace, Venice

51. Antonio Rizzo, detail, *Eve*, Ducal Palace, Venice

52. Antonio Rizzo, *Angel with Simbeni Arms*, Rio Terrà Barba Fruttarol, Venice

53. Antonio Rizzo, detail, *Man of Sorrows*, Altar of the Sacrament, Basilica, Aquileia

54. Assistant of Antonio Rizzo, detail, *Man of Sorrows*, Altar of the Sacrament, Basilica, Aquileia

55. Antonio Rizzo, detail, *Man of Sorrows*, Altar of the Sacrament, Basilica, Aquileia

56. Antonio Rizzo, detail, *Man of Sorrows*, Altar of the Sacrament, Basilica, Aquileia

58. Altar of the Sacrament, Basilica, Aquileia

57. Retable, Altar of the Sacrament, Basilica, Aquileia

59. Antonio Rizzo and assistant, *Man of Sorrows*, Altar of the Sacrament, Basilica, Aquileia

60. Assistant of Antonio Rizzo, *St. Luke*, S. Sofia, Venice   61. Assistant of Antonio Rizzo, *St. Andrew*, S. Sofia, Venice

62. Assistant of Antonio Rizzo, *St. Damian*, S. Sofia, Venice   63. Assistant of Antonio Rizzo, *St. Cosmas*, S. Sofia, Venice

64. Antonio Rizzo and assistants, Tomb of Doge Niccolò Tron, S. Maria dei Frari, Venice

65. Antonio Rizzo, detail, *Pedestrian Effigy of Tron*, Tomb of Doge Niccolò Tron, S. Maria dei Frari, Venice

66. Antonio Rizzo, *Pedestrian Effigy of Tron*, Tomb of Doge Niccolò Tron, S. Maria dei Frari, Venice

67. Antonio Rizzo, *Recumbent Effigy of Tron*, Tomb of Doge
Niccolò Tron, S. Maria dei Frari, Venice

68. Antonio Rizzo, detail, *Pedestrian Effigy of Tron*, Tomb of Doge Niccolò Tron, S. Maria dei Frari, Venice

69. Antonio Rizzo, detail, *Pedestrian Effigy of Tron*, Tomb of Doge Niccolò Tron, S. Maria dei Frari, Venice

71. Antonio Rizzo, detail, *Recumbent Effigy of Tron*, Tomb of Doge Niccolò Tron, S. Maria dei Frari, Venice

70. Antonio Rizzo, detail, *Recumbent Effigy of Tron*, Tomb of Doge Niccolò Tron, S. Maria dei Frari, Venice

72. Antonio Rizzo, detail, *Recumbent Effigy of Tron*, Tomb of Doge Niccolò Tron, S. Maria dei Frari, Venice

73. Antonio Rizzo and assistants, detail, Tomb of Doge Niccolò Tron, S. Maria dei Frari, Venice

74. Antonio Rizzo, detail, *Recumbent Effigy of Tron*, Tomb of Doge Niccolò Tron, S. Maria dei Frari, Venice

75. Antonio Rizzo, detail, *Charity–Amor Dei*, Tomb of Doge Niccolò Tron, S. Maria dei Frari, Venice

76. Antonio Rizzo and assistant, *Prudence*, Tomb of Doge Niccolò Tron, S. Maria dei Frari, Venice

77. Antonio Rizzo and assistant, *Prudence*, Tomb of Doge Niccolò Tron, S. Maria dei Frari, Venice

78. Antonio Rizzo and assistant, *Prudence*, Tomb of Doge Niccolò Tron, S. Maria dei Frari, Venice

79. Antonio Rizzo and assistant, *Prudence*, Tomb of
Doge Niccolò Tron, S. Maria dei Frari, Venice

80. Antonio Rizzo and assistant, *Prudence*, Tomb of
Doge Niccolò Tron, S. Maria dei Frari, Venice

81. Antonio Rizzo, detail, *Prudence*, Tomb of Doge Niccolò Tron, S. Maria dei Frari, Venice

82. Antonio Rizzo, detail, *Charity–Amor Dei*, Tomb of Doge Niccolò Tron, S. Maria dei Frari, Venice

84. Antonio Rizzo, detail, *Charity–Amor Dei*, Tomb of Doge Niccolò Tron, S. Maria dei Frari, Venice

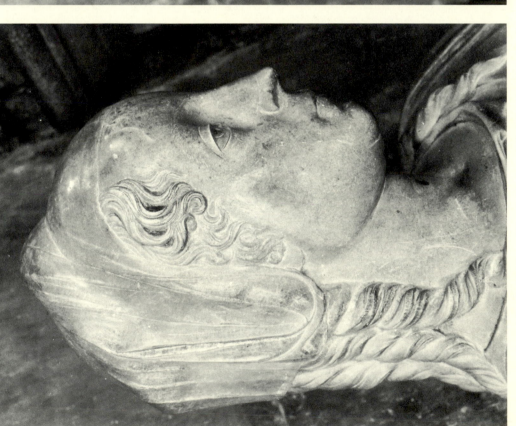

83. Antonio Rizzo, detail, *Prudence*, Tomb of Doge Niccolò Tron, S. Maria dei Frari, Venice

86. Antonio Rizzo, detail, left-hand *Warrior*, Tomb of Doge Niccolò Tron, S. Maria dei Frari, Venice

85. Antonio Rizzo, detail, *Prudence*, Tomb of Doge Niccolò Tron, S. Maria dei Frari, Venice

87. Antonio Rizzo, *Charity–Amor Dei*, Tomb of
Doge Niccolò Tron, S. Maria dei Frari, Venice

88. Antonio Rizzo, *Charity–Amor Dei*, Tomb of
Doge Niccolò Tron, S. Maria dei Frari, Venice

89. Antonio Rizzo, *Charity–Amor Dei*, Tomb of Doge Niccolò Tron, S. Maria dei Frari, Venice

90. Antonio Rizzo, *Charity–Amor Dei*, Tomb of Doge Niccolò Tron, S. Maria dei Frari, Venice

91. Antonio Rizzo, left-hand *Warrior*, Tomb of Doge
Niccolò Tron, S. Maria dei Frari, Venice

92. Assistant of Antonio Rizzo, right-hand *Warrior*, Tomb
of Doge Niccolò Tron, S. Maria dei Frari, Venice

93. Antonio Rizzo, *Security*, Tomb of Doge Niccolò Tron, S. Maria dei
Frari, Venice

94. Assistant of Antonio Rizzo, *Abundance/Concord*, Tomb of Doge Niccolò Tron, S. Maria dei Frari, Venice

95. Antonio Rizzo, *Peace*, Tomb of Doge Niccolò Tron, S. Maria dei Frari, Venice

96. Antonio Rizzo and assistant, *Arithmetic/Grammar*, Tomb of Doge Niccolò Tron, S. Maria dei Frari, Venice

97. Antonio Rizzo and assistant, *Music*, Tomb of Doge Niccolò Tron, S. Maria dei Frari, Venice

98. Antonio Rizzo and assistant, *Fortitude*, Tomb of Doge Niccolò Tron, S. Maria dei Frari, Venice

99. Antonio Rizzo and assistant, *Personification*, Tomb of Doge Niccolò Tron, S. Maria dei Frari, Venice

100. Antonio Rizzo and assistant, *Charity*, Tomb of
Doge Niccolò Tron, S. Maria dei Frari, Venice

101. Antonio Rizzo and assistant, *Hope*, Tomb of
Doge Niccolò Tron, S. Maria dei Frari, Venice

102. Antonio Rizzo and assistant, *Personification*, Tomb of Doge Niccolò Tron, S. Maria dei Frari, Venice

103. Antonio Rizzo and assistant, *Charity–Amor proximi*, Tomb of Doge Niccolò Tron, S. Maria dei Frari, Venice

104. Assistant of Antonio Rizzo, *Personification*, Tomb of Doge Niccolò Tron, S. Maria dei Frari, Venice

105. Antonio Rizzo and assistant, *Risen Christ*, Tomb of Doge Niccolò Tron, S. Maria dei Frari, Venice

106. Antonio Rizzo and assistant, *Annunciate Angel*, Tomb of Doge Niccolò Tron, S. Maria dei Frari, Venice

107. Antonio Rizzo and assistant, *Annunciate Virgin*, Tomb of Doge Niccolò Tron, S. Maria dei Frari, Venice

108. Antonio Rizzo and assistant, detail, *Music*, Tomb of Doge Niccolò Tron, S. Maria dei Frari, Venice

109. Antonio Rizzo and assistant, detail, *Hope*, Tomb of Doge Niccolò Tron, S. Maria dei Frari, Venice

110. Antonio Rizzo and assistant, detail, *Fortitude*, Tomb of Doge Niccolò Tron, S. Maria dei Frari, Venice

111. Assistant of Antonio Rizzo, detail, right-hand *Warrior*, Tomb of Doge Niccolò Tron, S. Maria dei Frari, Venice

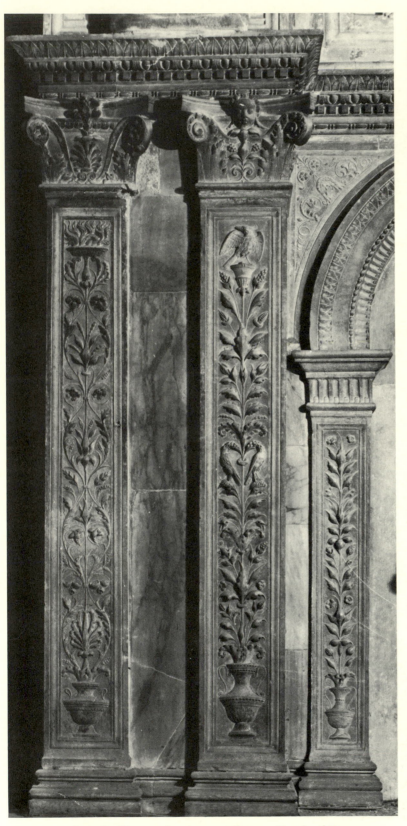

112. Antonio Rizzo and assistants, pilasters, Tomb of Doge Niccolò Tron, S. Maria dei Frari, Venice

113. Assistant of Antonio Rizzo, pilasters, Tomb of Do Niccolò Tron, S. Maria dei Frari, Venice

115. Antonio Rizzo, spandrel, Tomb of Doge Niccolò Tron, S. Maria dei Frari, Venice

114. Assistant of Antonio Rizzo, pilaster, Tomb of Doge Niccolò Tron, S. Maria dei Frari, Venice

116. Assistant of Antonio Rizzo, spandrel, Tomb of Doge Niccolò Tron, S. Maria dei Frari, Venice

117. Antonio Rizzo, left-hand relief with *putti*, Tomb of Doge Niccolò Tron, S. Maria dei Frari, Venice

118. Antonio Rizzo and assistant, right-hand relief with *putti*, Tomb of Doge Niccolò Tron, S. Maria dei Frari, Venice

119. Antonio Rizzo, detail, *Annunciate Angel*, Madonna dell'Orto, Venice

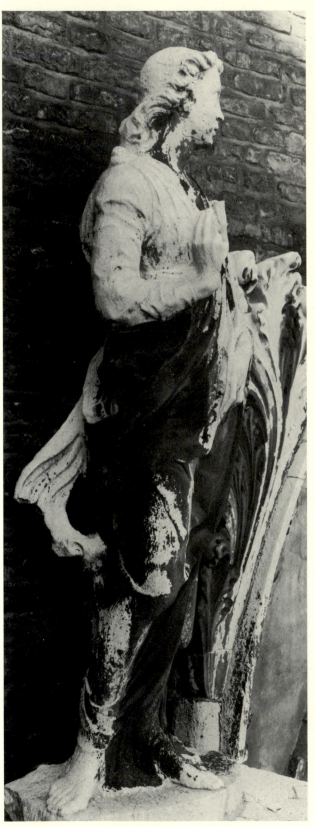

120. Antonio Rizzo, *Annunciate Angel*, Madonna
dell'Orto, Venice

121. Antonio Rizzo, *Annunciate Angel*,
Madonna dell'Orto, Venice

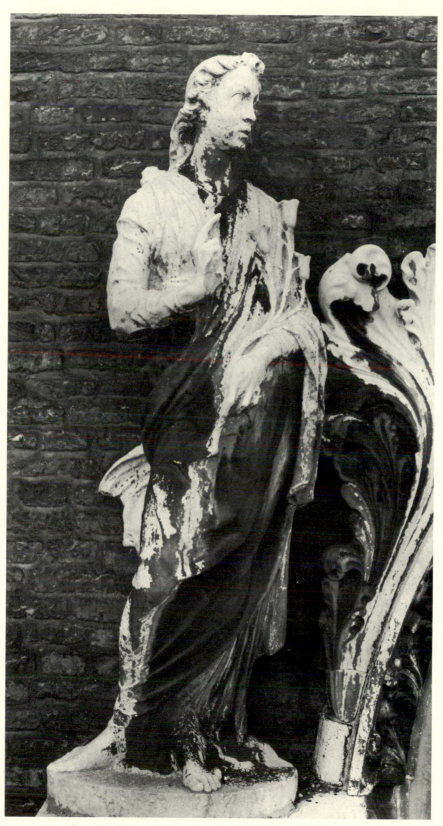

122. Antonio Rizzo, *Annunciate Angel*, Madonna dell'Orto, Venice

123. Antonio Rizzo, detail, *The Miraculous Cure of St. Anianus*, Scuola dei Calegheri, Venice

124. Antonio Rizzo and assistant, *The Miraculous Cure of St. Anianus*, Scuola dei Calegheri, Venice

125. Antonio Rizzo, detail, *The Miraculous Cure of St. Anianus*, Scuola dei Calegheri, Venice

126. Antonio Rizzo, lunette, Altar of the Traghetto della Maddalena, Museo Correr, Venice

127. Johannes Grevembroch, drawing of the Altar of the Traghetto della Maddalena, *Monumenta Veneta ex antiquis ruderibus*, ii, 1754, p. 24 (Venice, Museo Correr, MS Gradenigo 228)

128. Antonio Rizzo, detail, Altar of the Traghetto della Maddalena, Museo Correr, Venice

129. Antonio Rizzo, detail, Altar of the Traghetto della Maddalena, Museo Correr, Venice

130. Antonio Rizzo, left-hand *Victory*, formerly, Kaiser-Friedrich-Museum, Berlin

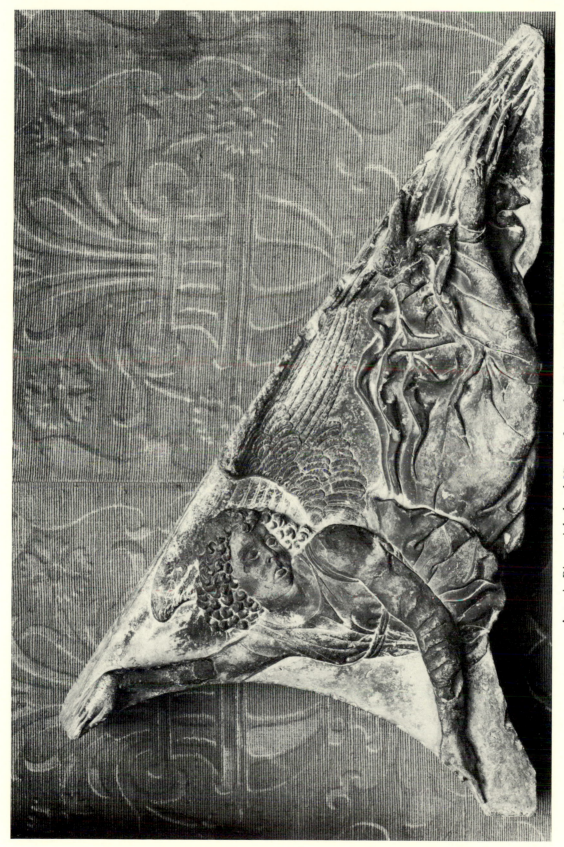

131. Antonio Rizzo, right-hand *Victory*, formerly, Kaiser-Friedrich-Museum, Berlin

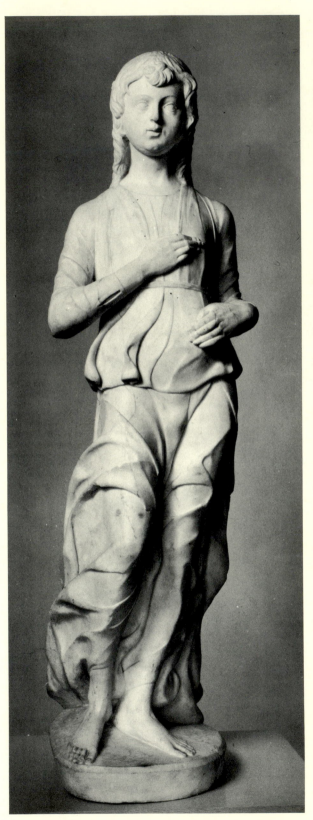

132. Antonio Rizzo, *Angel*, Kunsthistorisches
Museum, Vienna

133. Antonio Rizzo, *Angel*, Kunsthistorisches
Museum, Vienna

134. Assistant of Antonio Rizzo,
Angel, Androne Foscari, courtyard,
Ducal Palace, Venice

135. Antonio Rizzo, *St. John the Evangelist*,
Staatliche Museen, East Berlin

136. Assistant of Antonio Rizzo,
Personification, rear of the Arco Foscari,
courtyard, Ducal Palace, Venice

137. Assistant of Antonio Rizzo,
Personification, south face of the Arco
Foscari, courtyard, Ducal Palace, Venice

138. Johannes Grevembroch, drawing of the Tomb of Giovanni Emo, *Monumenta Veneta ex antiquis ruderibus*, iii, 1759, p. 27 (Venice, Museo Correr, MS Gradenigo 228)

139. Antonio Rizzo and assistant, *Pedestrian Effigy of Giovanni Emo*, Tomb of Giovanni Emo, Museo Civico, Vicenza

140. Antonio Rizzo and assistant, *Pedestrian Effigy of Giovanni Emo*, Tomb of Giovanni Emo, Museo Civico, Vicenza

141. Assistant of Antonio Rizzo, left-hand *Page*, Tomb of Giovanni Emo, Louvre, Paris

142. Antonio Rizzo, right-hand *Page*, Tomb of Giovanni Emo, Louvre, Paris

144. Antonio Rizzo, detail, *Pedestrian Effigy of Giovanni Emo*, Tomb of Giovanni Emo, Vicenza, Museo Civico

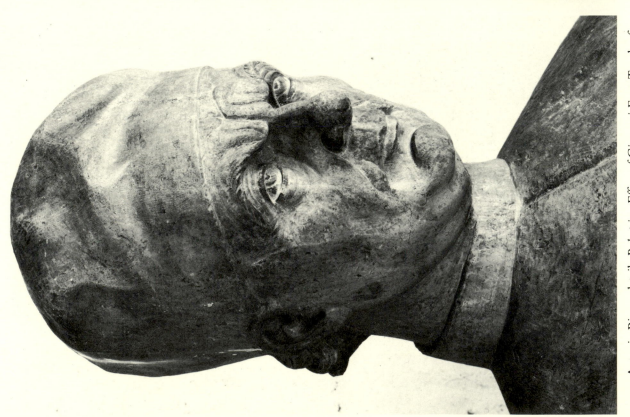

143. Antonio Rizzo, detail, *Pedestrian Effigy of Giovanni Emo*, Tomb of Giovanni Emo, Vicenza, Museo Civico

146. Assistant of Antonio Rizzo, detail, left-hand *Page*, Tomb of Giovanni Emo, Louvre, Paris

145. Antonio Rizzo, detail, right-hand *Page*, Tomb of Giovanni Emo, Louvre, Paris

147. Assistant of Antonio Rizzo, *Mocenigo
Warrior*, south face of the Arco Foscari,
courtyard, Ducal Palace, Venice

148. Assistant of Antonio Rizzo, *Personification*,
south face of the Arco Foscari, courtyard,
Ducal Palace, Venice

Rio del Palazzo

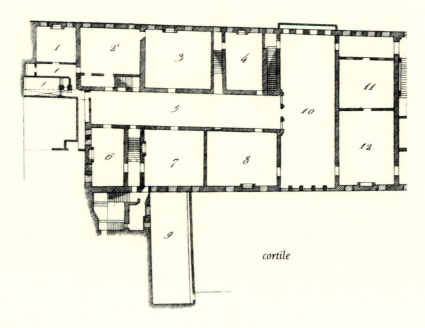

149. Plan of Appartamenti dei Dogi, east wing, Ducal Palace, Venice

Rio del Palazzo

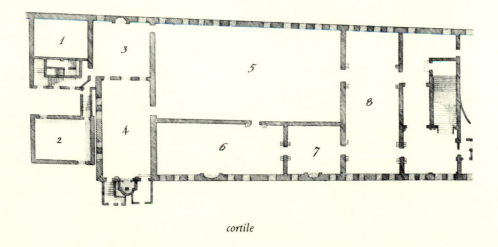

cortile

150. Plan of fourth floor, northern part of east wing, Ducal Palace, Venice

151. Detail, *rio* facade, east wing, Ducal Palace, Venice

152. *Rio* facade, east wing, Ducal Palace, Venice

154. Detail, *rio* facade, east wing, Ducal Palace, Venice

153. Detail, *rio* facade, east wing, Ducal Palace, Venice

155. Antonio Rizzo, *Putti with Arms of the Barbarigo Family*, rio facade, east wing, Ducal Palace, Venice

157. Detail, courtyard facade, east wing, Ducal Palace, Venice

156. Courtyard facade, east wing, Ducal Palace, Venice

159. Detail, courtyard facade, east wing, Ducal Palace, Venice

158. Detail, courtyard facade, east wing, Ducal Palace, Venice

160. Antonio Rizzo, *Madonna and Child*, Collection of the Prince of Liechtenstein, Vaduz

161. Antonio Rizzo, *Madonna and Child*, Camera degli Scarlatti, Ducal Palace, Venice

162. Antonio Rizzo, *Battle Scene*, Sala degli Scuderi, Ducal Palace, Venice

163. Antonio Rizzo, *Battle Scene*, Sala delle Mappe, Ducal Palace, Venice

164. Antonio Rizzo, detail, Scala dei Giganti, courtyard, Ducal Palace, Venice

165. Antonio Rizzo, Scala dei Giganti, courtyard, Ducal Palace, Venice

166. Antonio Rizzo, Scala dei Giganti, courtyard, Ducal Palace, Venice

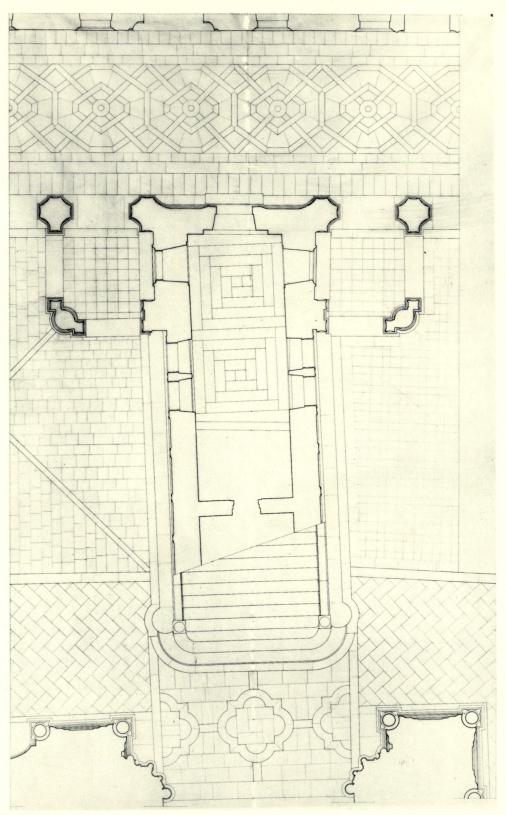

167. Plan at the level of the *pianterreno*, Scala dei Giganti, courtyard, Ducal Palace, Venice (measured and drawn by Silvano Boldrin)

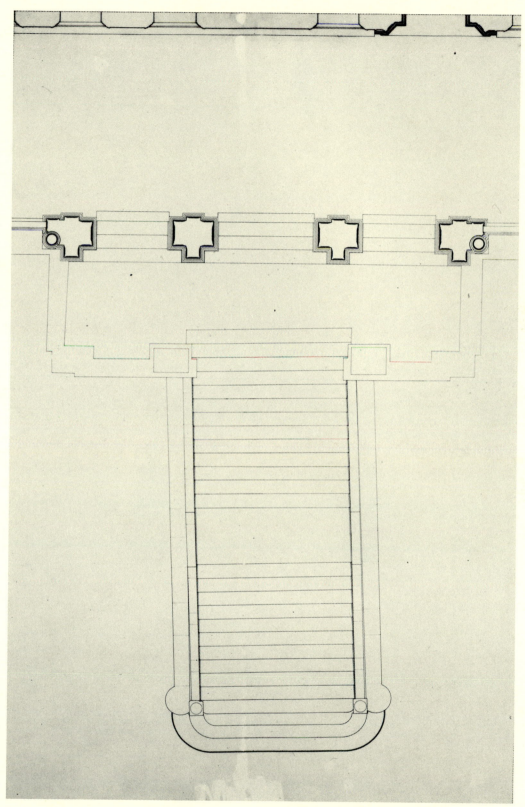

168. Plan at the level of the *piano nobile*, Scala dei Giganti, courtyard, Ducal Palace, Venice (measured and drawn by Silvano Boldrin)

169. Longitudinal elevation, Scala dei Giganti, courtyard, Ducal Palace, Venice (measured and drawn by Silvano Boldrin)

170. Transverse elevation, Scala dei Giganti, courtyard, Ducal Palace, Venice (measured and drawn by Silvano Boldrin)

171. Longitudinal section, Scala dei Giganti, courtyard, Ducal Palace, Venice (measured and drawn by Silvano Boldrin)

172. Transverse section, Scala dei Giganti, courtyard, Ducal Palace, Venice (measured and drawn by Silvano Boldrin)

173. Antonio Rizzo, *Justice*, detail of a lesene, Scala dei Giganti, courtyard, Ducal Palace, Venice

174. Antonio Rizzo, detail of a lesene, Scala dei Giganti, courtyard, Ducal Palace, Venice

175. Antonio Rizzo, *Putto Playing a Pipe*, detail of a lesene, Scala dei Giganti, courtyard, Ducal Palace, Venice

176. Antonio Rizzo, detail of a lesene, Scala dei Giganti, courtyard, Ducal Palace, Venice

177. Antonio Rizzo, *Bust of a Girl*, detail of a lesene, Scala dei Giganti, courtyard, Ducal Palace, Venice

178. Antonio Rizzo, *Youth with Fantastic Helmet*, detail of a lesene, Scala dei Giganti, courtyard, Ducal Palace, Venice

179. Antonio Rizzo, lesene,
Scala dei Giganti, courtyard,
Ducal Palace, Venice

180. Antonio Rizzo, lesene,
Scala dei Giganti, courtyard,
Ducal Palace, Venice

181. Antonio Rizzo, lesene,
Scala dei Giganti, courtyard,
Ducal Palace, Venice

182. Antonio Rizzo, lesene, Scala
dei Giganti, courtyard, Ducal
Palace, Venice

183. Antonio Rizzo, lesene, Scala
dei Giganti, courtyard, Ducal
Palace, Venice

184. Antonio Rizzo, lesene, Scala
dei Giganti, courtyard, Ducal
Palace, Venice

185. Antonio Rizzo, *Angel with Attributes of Christ*, Ca' d'Oro, Venice

186. Antonio Rizzo, *Angel with Attributes of Christ*, Ca' d'Oro, Venice

187. Antonio Rizzo, *Angel with Attributes of Christ*, Ca' d'Oro, Venice

188. Antonio Rizzo, *Angel with Attributes of Christ*, Ca' d'Oro, Venice

189. Antonio Rizzo, detail, *Angel with Attributes of Christ*, Ca' d'Oro, Venice

190. Antonio Rizzo, detail, *Victory*, Scala dei Giganti, courtyard, Ducal Palace, Venice

191. Antonio Rizzo, detail, Scala dei Giganti, courtyard, Ducal Palace, Venice

192. Antonio Rizzo, detail, Scala dei Giganti, courtyard, Ducal Palace, Venice

193. Detail, capital of first
pier of the *pianterreno*,
courtyard facade, east wing,
Ducal Palace, Venice

194. Antonio Rizzo, *vera da pozzo*, courtyard, Palazzo Decazes, Venice

195. Assistant of Antonio Rizzo, *Victory*, Scala dei Giganti, courtyard, Ducal Palace, Venice

196. Assistant of Antonio Rizzo, *Victory*, Scala dei Giganti, courtyard, Ducal Palace, Venice

197. Antonio Rizzo, *Victory*, Scala dei Giganti, courtyard, Ducal Palace, Venice

198. Antonio Rizzo, *Victory*, Scala dei Giganti, courtyard, Ducal Palace, Venice

199. Assistant of Antonio Rizzo, *Victory*, Scala dei Giganti, courtyard, Ducal Palace, Venice

200. Antonio Rizzo, *Victory*, Scala dei Giganti, courtyard, Ducal Palace, Venice

201. Antonio Rizzo, *Victory*, Scala dei Giganti, courtyard, Ducal Palace, Venice

202. Antonio Rizzo and assistant, *Victory*, Scala dei Giganti, courtyard, Ducal Palace, Venice

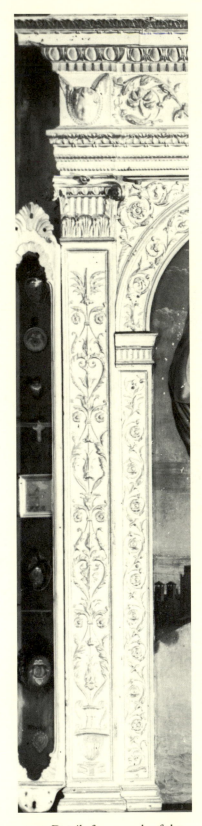

204. Marco Zoppo, *Sketchbook*, fol. 4r, British Museum, London

205. Andrea Mantegna, *St. Peter*, Ovetari Chapel, Eremitani, Padua

203. Detail, framework of the Altar of St. Vincent Ferrer, SS. Giovanni e Paolo, Venice

206. Niccolò Pizzolo, detail, *St. Gregory*, Ovetari Chapel, Eremitani, Padua

207. Goro di Neroccio, *Fortitude*, Baptismal Font, Baptistry, Siena

208. Donatello, *St. Justina*, High Altar, S. Antonio, Padua

209. Andrea Mantegna, detail, S. Zeno Altarpiece, S. Zeno, Verona

210. Donatello, *Crucified Christ*, S. Antonio, Padua

211. Antonio Pollaiuolo, *Battle of the Ten Nudes*, first state, Cleveland Museum of Art, Cleveland, Ohio

212. Andrea Mantegna, detail, *St. James Led to Execution*, Ovetari Chapel, Eremihtani, Padua

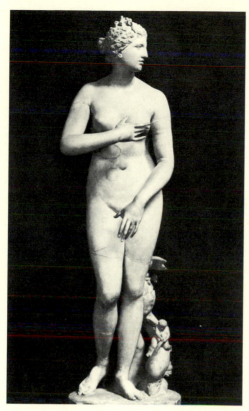

213. Roman, *Medici Venus*, Galleria degli
Uffizi, Florence

214. Antonio Pollaiuolo, *Eve*, Galleria degli
Uffizi, Florence

215. Antonio Pollaiuolo, *Hercules and Anteus*,
Museo Nazionale, Florence

216. Antonio Pollaiuolo, *Dancing Nudes*, Villa
Gallina, Arcetri

217. Assistant of Pietro Lombardo, detail, *Warrior*, Tomb of Doge Pietro Mocenigo, SS. Giovanni e Paolo, Venice

219. Roman, relief from the "*Throne of Ceres*," Palazzo Arciveccovile, Ravenna

218. Assistant of Pietro Lombardo, detail, *Charity*, Tomb of Doge Pasquale Malipiero, SS. Giovanni e Paolo, Venice

220. Shop of Donatello, *Madonna and Child*, Kress Collection, National Gallery of Art, Washington, D. C.

221. Pietro Lombardo and assistants, Tomb of Doge Pasquale Malipiero,
SS. Giovanni e Paolo, Venice

222. Shop of Pietro Lombardo,
pilaster, choir, S. Giobbe, Venice

223. Tullio Lombardo, *Virtue*, Tomb of Doge Andrea Vendramin, SS. Giovanni e Paolo, Venice

224. Tullio Lombardo, *Justice*, Tomb of Doge Andrea Vendramin, SS. Giovanni e Paolo, Venice

225. Antonello da Messina, detail, S. Cassiano Altarpiece, Kunsthistorisches Museum, Vienna

226. Andrea del Verrocchio, detail, Equestrian Monument of Bartolommeo Colleoni, Campo SS. Giovanni e Paolo, Venice

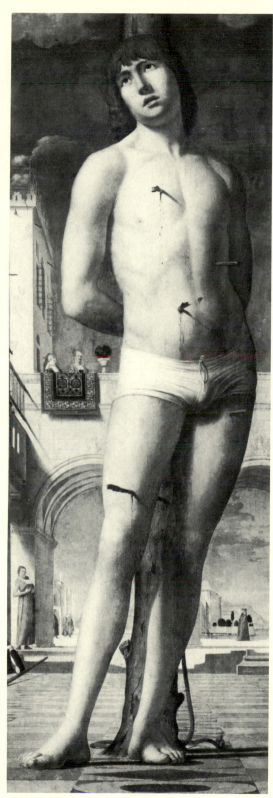

227. Antonello da Messina, *St. Sebastian*, Gemäldegalerie, Dresden

228. Venetian, fifteenth century, sarcophagus, Museo Civico, Vicenza

229. Mino da Fiesole, Tomb of Cardinal Niccolò Forteguerri, S. Cecilia in Trastevere, Rome

230. Tullio Lombardo, entablature of the base, Tomb of Doge Andrea Vendramin, SS. Giovanni e Paolo, Venice

231. Tullio Lombardo, Tomb of Doge Andrea Vendramin, SS. Giovanni e Paolo, Venice

233. Marco Zoppo, *Sketchbook*, fol. 20v, British Museum, London

234. Marco Zoppo, *Sketchbook*, fol. 24v, British Museum, London

232. Jacopo Bellini, *Sketchbook*, fol. 57r, British Museum, London

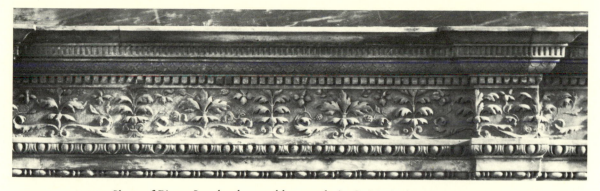

235. Shop of Pietro Lombardo, entablature, choir, S. Maria dei Miracoli, Venice

236. School of Avignon, fifteenth century, *Angel with Symbols of the Passion*, Museum of Art, Rhode Island School of Design, Providence, R.I.

237. Niccolò di Giovanni Fiorentino, detail, *Annunciate Virgin*, Madonna dell'Orto, Venice

238. Niccolò di Giovanni Fiorentino and assistant, *Annunciate Virgin*, Madonna dell'Orto, Venice

239. Niccolò di Giovanni Fiorentino and assistant, *Annunciate Virgin*, Madonna dell'Orto, Venice

OPERA DEL MAESTRO
DI S. TROVASO
ANTICA RACCOLTA DI G. BOSSI
SECONDA METÀ DEL XV° S°
1191

240. Italian, nineteenth century, Tabernacle, Castello Sforzesco, Milan

DAT